DATE DUE

The Grandees of Government

THE
Grandees of Government

⸎

THE
ORIGINS AND
PERSISTENCE OF
UNDEMOCRATIC
POLITICS
IN VIRGINIA

Brent Tarter

University of Virginia Press

CHARLOTTESVILLE AND LONDON

University of Virginia Press
© 2013 by the Rector and Visitors of the University of Virginia
All rights reserved
Printed in the United States of America on acid-free paper

First published 2013

1 3 5 7 9 8 6 4 2

Library of Congress Cataloging-in-Publication Data
Tarter, Brent, 1948–
The grandees of government : the origins and persistence of
undemocratic politics in Virginia / Brent Tarter.
pages   cm
Includes bibliographical references and index.
ISBN 978-0-8139-3431-0 (cloth : alk. paper) — ISBN 978-0-8139-3432-7 (e-book)
1. Virginia—Politics and government—To 1775. 2. Virginia—
Politics and government—1775–1865. 3. Virginia—Politics and
government—1865–1950. 4. Political culture—Virginia—History. 5. Constitutional
history—Virginia. 6. African Americans—Legal status, laws, etc.—Virginia—History.
I. Title.
JK3916.T37 2013
320.9755—dc23
2012049863

CONTENTS

ACKNOWLEDGMENTS

I have lived in Virginia and studied aspects of its history and culture for more than forty years, for approximately one-tenth of its English-language history. During that time I have read all of the leading monographs and biographies of prominent people and discussed Virginia's history with scores of researchers who generously shared their insights with me. That pointed me toward some of the episodes and sources on which these essays are based, but my own research in the primary sources of all decades of Virginia's English-language history led me to the other events and sources and shaped my own perspective on Virginia's political past. During the composition of these essays, I reread most of the major books on Virginia's political history and culture, some of them for the severalth time. Even though in many instances I depart from the interpretations in the existing historical literature, I readily acknowledge the importance of the many valuable insights and even of the occasional false leads that I found there. Because none embraces the whole, none truly inspired or guided this inquiry, and I went back to the primary sources to free my mind, insofar as possible, from the perceptions and interpretations of other people (many of them good friends who produced excellent scholarship) so that I might reevaluate the evidence afresh.

I particularly want to thank the late Professor Edward E. Younger, of the University of Virginia, who introduced me to Virginia's history in 1971; Penelope Kaiserlian, director, Richard Holway, acquisitions editor, Martha Farlow, design and production manager, and Mark Mones, project editor, of the University of Virginia Press; and Susan Lee Foard, editor. Without in any way implicating any of them individually I also thank my many current and former colleagues and friends at the Library of Virginia from whom I learned much during a tenure there of almost forty years and with whom I discussed many aspects of Virginia's history and on whom I inflicted some of the raw ideas that developed into the parts of this whole. One of them, John G. Deal, read the first version of the manuscript and offered many valuable critical comments. So did my friends John d'Entremont and Warren M. Billings who read the manuscript for the press and offered many helpful suggestions. The illness and the death in February 2012 of my longtime friend and colleague Sara B. Bearss deprived me and the readers of her keen insights and the benefits of her deft editorial pencil during the period of final revision.

Some of the essays have appeared in other guises and also benefited from comments and advice of other people.

The prologue benefited from the comments of Ryan K. Smith, Philip J. Schwarz, Marion Nelson, Robin Lind, Jon Kukla, Terri Halperin, Joshua Eckhardt, and Mathias Bergmann, members of the informal Richmond group known as Fall Line Early Americanists.

Another version of "True Religion and a Civil Course of Life" was the opening oral presentation at the symposium "From Jamestown to Jefferson: The Evolution of Religious Authority in Colonial Virginia" at Virginia Wesleyan College, Norfolk, on 6 September 2007. It was subsequently published as "Evidence of Religion in Seventeenth-Century Virginia," in Paul Rasor and Rich Bond, eds., *From Jamestown to Jefferson: Religious Authority in Colonial Virginia* (Charlottesville, 2011), 17–42, and appears here with permission of the publisher in expanded form but without some historiographical commentary. Both versions owe much to many years of conversations on this and related topics with Jon Kukla, Thomas E. Buckley, SJ, Edward L. Bond, and Warren M. Billings; and it also received constructive criticism from Doug Winiarski, Mark Valeri, Marion Nelson, Mark McGarvie, Isabelle Richman, and Woody Holton, members of the Fall Line Early Americanists.

Portions of "The Grievances of the People" appeared in a different form in a historiographical essay entitled "Bacon's Rebellion, the Grievances of the People, and the Political Culture of Seventeenth-Century Virginia," *Virginia Magazine of History and Biography* 119 (2011): 3–41, and appears here with permission of the editor but without some historiographical commentary. Both versions owe much to many years of conversations with Jon Kukla and Warren M. Billings and received constructive criticism from Wil M. Verhoeven, Doug Winiarski, Marion Nelson, and Sarah Meacham, members of the Fall Line Early Americanists.

"The Grandees of Government" profited from the critical commentary of Mark Valeri, Doug Winiarski, Ryan K. Smith, John Pagan, Marion Nelson, Sarah Meacham, Woody Holton, Teri Halperin, and Mathias Bergmann, members of the Fall Line Early Americanists.

"All Men Are Not Created Equal" bears resemblances to the scholarship of Mike McDonnell and Woody Holton, and I readily acknowledge the value of their work and of many conversations with them as they refined their thinking and, as a consequence, mine.

"On Domestic Slavery" does not strictly follow in the footsteps of Melvin Patrick Ely, but my many long lunchtime conversations with him as he researched and wrote *Israel on the Appomattox* provided me with much rich food for thought when I came to draft that essay, for which he deserves many thanks and no blame.

"Constitutions Construed" grew out of an oral presentation at the fifth annual Virginia Forum, at Christopher Newport University, Newport News, on 17 April 2010.

A longer draft of "House Divided" served as a working paper in the initial planning for the Library of Virginia's 2010–11 exhibition "Union or Secession: Virginians Decide" and the accompanying educational Web site of the same title. Portions of it formed the heart of an oral presentation, "Union Conventions in Virginia, 1861," at the sixth annual Virginia Forum at Virginia Military Institute and Washington and Lee University, Lexington, on 26 March 2011. It benefited from conversations with William W. Freehling about his scholarship on the politics of secession, with Walter Kyle Planitzer about his research on slavery and taxation, and with John E. Stealey III and Sara B. Bearss about their research on the constitutional consequences of secession and the Civil War in Virginia. The first version also had the benefit of the careful scrutiny and suggestions of members of the exhibition working group, Jennifer R. Loux, Gregg D. Kimball, Tameka Hobbs, Trenton E. Hizer, John G. Deal, Sara B. Bearss, Barbara C. Batson, and especially Marianne E. Julienne.

Portions of "An Anglo-Saxon Electorate" formed the basis for an oral presentation with the title "Carry Me Back as Far as Possible: The Virginia Constitutional Convention of 1901–1902" in the Library of Virginia's Mining the Treasure House Lecture Series on 18 June 2002.

"The Byrdocracy" is a greatly expanded elaboration of "History and Harry Byrd," an oral presentation at the fourth annual Virginia Forum, at Longwood University, Farmville, on 25 April 2009. It owes much to many years of conversations on this and related topics with James R. Sweeney, James H. Hershman Jr., and Ronald L. Heinemann, all of whom read and commented on the first draft.

"Public Good and Private Interest" opens with a vignette at the 1978 Democratic Party state convention. I was a delegate and for part of the time sat across the aisle from Pat Robertson. When I later contemplated the causes and consequences of the late twentieth-century reversal of positions of the state's Democratic and Republican Parties and discussed that phenomenon with James R. Sweeney and James H. Hershman Jr. (who was also a delegate to that convention), I was struck by how many aspects of that convention and of that year's campaign for a seat in the United States Senate embodied those changes and the enduring ideological continuities of Virginia's political culture.

I am also glad to acknowledge the importance to my scholarly career of the Greater Richmond Transit Corporation. I read thousands of books and journal articles during decades of riding the city bus to and from the Library of Virginia where I worked and studied Virginia's long, fascinating, and often frustrating history.

PROLOGUE

The cartouche from the 1755 edition of the map of Virginia that Joshua Fry and Peter Jefferson prepared in 1751 (courtesy of the Library of Virginia) depicts Virginia as its most influential residents and people in Great Britain thought of it. Dressed in the latest English fashions and wearing three-cornered hats, three white gentlemen planters smoke, drink, and do business with a merchant wearing a smock and cloth cap. Three African Americans, minimally dressed and presumably enslaved, prepare casks of tobacco for loading aboard a ship for transportation and sale in England. A fourth African American serves a glass of wine to one of the gentlemen. Excluding any depiction of agricultural or domestic life in the colony, this cartouche focuses on the central importance of tobacco cultivation and the men who were most important in that enterprise, the planters and slaves. The political economy of tobacco production and slavery shaped the political institutions and practices of colonial Virginia.

En route to the new colony of Maryland in the summer of 1634, Thomas Yong stopped in Virginia to repair his storm-damaged ship. Before resuming his voyage he inquired about affairs in Maryland and learned that the government there was engaged in a dispute with William Claiborne, a member of the governor's Council of State in Virginia. Claiborne claimed ownership of Kent Island, in Chesapeake Bay, where he had established a profitable fur-trading post. Under the terms of the charter that King Charles I issued to Lord Baltimore that created the colony of Maryland, Kent Island was in Maryland and subject to its government and no longer in Virginia as defined in the charters that King James I had issued to the Virginia Company. Yong learned that Claiborne and other influential merchant-planters on the Virginia Council were obstructing the efforts of the governor, Sir John Harvey, to settle the dispute peacefully, which would be to Claiborne's disadvantage.

Writing to his patrons back in England, Yong complained that Claiborne and the others had "exasperated & incensed all the English Collony of Virginia" to such an extent "as here it is accounted a crime almost as heynous as treason to favour nay allmost to speak well" of Maryland at all. Yong continued, "I have observed myself a palpable kind of strangeness & distance between those of the best sort in the Country who have formerly been very familiar & loving one to another & onely because the one hath bene suspected but to have bene a wellwisher to the Plantation of Maryland." The captain wrote that the governor had been "a great reformer in the abuses in the Government especially in the point of Justice, wch at his first entrance was full of corruption & partiality the richest & most powerfull opposing & swallowing upp the poorer," but that "he is somtimes overborn by the strength & power of some factious & turbulent spiritts of his Council. For here in this place all things are carried by the most voyces of the Council, & they are for the most part united in a kind of faction against the Govern^{or}, in so much as they make their publick consultations give strength and authority to their faction." Consequently, Yong wrote, "it is hard for the Govern^{or} to determine or order any thing here contrary to their dictations, for they come all hither pre-occupied & resolved to follow & concur wth the votes of their leaders." The council members "dislike any propositions of his," Yong concluded, "how beneficiall soever to the Country, so choosing rather to deprive themselves of the good that might arise to themselves thereby than that he should be the Author of such a benefitt to the country."[1]

Harvey was a former ship captain who was accustomed to issuing orders bluntly and without consultation and having them carried out promptly and without question. Both his behavior and his policies alienated the ambitious men like Claiborne whom he found in office when he arrived in 1630. In May 1635, the year following Yong's brief stop in Virginia, those bold and powerful members of the council arrested Harvey, expelled him from the colony, and installed one of their own as governor. The king immediately sent Harvey back to Virginia to show the Virginians who had the exclusive right to dismiss royal governors. Harvey's second administration accomplished little more than that, though, because the king's demonstration of authority did not break or even reduce the power of Virginia's resident politicians.[2]

With Harvey when he returned to Virginia early in 1637 was George Donne, whom the king made muster-master general and a member of Harvey's council. Donne soon went back to England and prepared a long report for the king. His "Virginia Reviewed" was blatantly partisan, as might have been expected, and it was full of pretentious literary tropes and classical allusions, as might also have been expected from the less-talented son of the clergyman and poet John Donne. Echoing Thomas Yong, George Donne concluded that "without Excepcion it must bee graunted that till of very late daies every mans owne particular profitt hath bene more earnestly pursued" in Virginia than the good "of the Country it selfe."[3]

Yong tarried but a few weeks in Virginia, and Donne lived there for only a few months—the bell tolled for him early in 1639 on his way back to Virginia. Other men who visited Virginia or resided there later in the seventeenth century also described how its emerging social and political cultures functioned, and some of them discussed the important subject that Yong and Donne had raised: was the colony going wrong about the proper relationship between the almost-unchecked pursuit of personal profit and the cultivation of a properly regulated version of English civilization on the western shore of the Atlantic Ocean?

Lionel Gatford was one. The namesake son of a prominent English clergyman, he made a tour of the colonies in the 1640s or early 1650s on his way to Virginia, where he ministered to a church for a few years before returning to England. In 1657 he published a pamphlet addressed to Lord Protector Oliver Cromwell in which he enumerated "the Epidemical distempers and maladies, under which the poor Plantation of *Virginea* grones and labours." Gatford meant social and political, not medical, disorders and criticized the government's policy of allowing, even encouraging, Virginians to establish their plantations and farms at scattered sites up and down the colony's rivers. In such places the planters could be of no help to one another if attacked, and they could not form communities of mutual benefit because other than the little capital of Jamestown they had no towns, not to mention cities, in which to gather. That is, they lacked proper centers of civilized society.

Gatford also complained that the planters regularly "abused & cousened" English traders and dominated the government and its courts to such an extent that the traders could not obtain judicial relief because "most commonly the parties guilty are the judges." Moreover, he continued, the planters on their separate and separated private plantations where no higher authority could control them treated their servants badly, "causing many of them either to ly all the time of their servitude in ash heaps, or otherwise to kennel up and down like dogs, where they can find room; scarce feeding them so well as our scornfull servants here in England feed our dogs." Those scattered households also made more difficult the work of the colony's clergymen, who were in any event not yet numerous enough to form the dispersed population into a more civilized Christian society. Gatford significantly entitled his pamphlet full of recommendations for reform *Publick Good Without Private Interest.*[4]

Gatford no doubt exaggerated, but he was not entirely wrong. Another seventeenth-century clergyman published a similar commentary a few years later. Morgan Godwyn resided in Virginia for several years late in the 1660s and early in the 1670s and thereafter in the Caribbean. His long book, printed in 1680, consisted chiefly of a scathing denunciation on religious grounds of slavery in England's island colonies, but he also denounced the practices and consequences of slavery in the emerging plantation economy of Virginia. With italic type that draws the eye to it much as a loud voice in a quiet room attracts attention, Godwyn angrily concluded one passage on enslaved residents of Virginia with an exclamation of wonder *"That God should Damn so great a number of Men, for the abominable Lucre of a few greedy Epicures and Mammonists."*[5]

The plantations of the most successful Virginia planters had evolved by then into separate little principalities where the owners ruled their households and field hands as petty potentates. The plantations even looked the part. In the 1680s a French visitor arrived at one such planter's residence with its numerous outbuildings and cabins where slaves and servants resided. "When I reached his place," the traveler wrote, "I thought I was entering a rather large village, but later on was told that all of it belonged to him."[6] The ability of a favored few families during several successive generations to become much more wealthy than everybody else led those families to view themselves during the eighteenth century as a miniature English aristocracy. Even though the greatest of the Virginia plantation mansions (and also those in South Carolina) did not approach in size and magnificence any of the great country houses of England, they were much larger and more luxurious than any other private residences anywhere else in the Southern colonies. People who never saw anything grander could not escape noticing how much wealthier those planter families were than everybody else and therefore how great a social distance existed between those few families and all of the white husbandmen and artisans, to say nothing of the enslaved African and American Indian laborers. On the eve of the American Revolution, a visitor from New Jersey observed that the wealthiest of Virginia's planter families had held sway as they pleased on their plantations for so long that it "blows up the owners to an imagination, which is visible in all, but in various degrees according to their respective virtue, that they are exalted as much above other Men in worth & precedency, as blind stupid fortune has made a difference in their property."[7]

It was not blind stupid fortune but generations of ambitious self-aggrandizement that made the great differences among men's property holdings and therefore their social status, which in turn fixed their places in the body politic. Regularly during the seventeen decades of the colony's history visitors and other commentators noted the ability of men with political power to shape government policies for the benefit of their private or collective interests. They did the same during and after the American Revolution, too. The richest white men—the grandees of government, as one man referred to them in the 1750s—who ran the plantations and governed Virginia pursued their personal ambitions and acquisition of wealth and individual freedom in ways that led them to deprive other people of their freedom. Indeed, one twenty-first-century student of the development of Virginia's political economy based on slavery entitled his book *Foul Means*.[8]

The Grandees of Government explores how the first founders and the plantation economy initially shaped Virginia's political institutions and culture. That beginning profoundly influenced practical politics and institutions of government later, indeed, right into the twenty-first century. From the beginning each of the colonies had—and each of the states still has—a unique legal and political culture that evolved in its own way and that directly and indirectly shaped many aspects of the lives of the people who lived there. In 1656, a mere two decades after the founding of Maryland, John Hammond published a pamphlet describing the differences between it and Virginia. His *Leah and Rachel: Or, The Two Fruitfull Sisters Virginia and Mary-land: Their Present Condition, Impartially Stated and Related* was no more impartial than the writings of Yong and Donne, but it pointed out a number of differences between the two polities that were already discernible and that originated in the purposes for which the colonies were founded and the ways they were initially governed.[9] Much as the lives of the biblical sisters Leah and Rachel, who both married Jacob, took radically different turns, the subsequent histories of the two neighboring colonies and their political traditions and cultures also increasingly diverged.

The political and legal institutions and the practices that evolved in Virginia changed slowly and episodically. Political practices, legal doctrines, and government institutions with constitutional sanction constrained the workings of representative, or republican, government. The limited representative government that the colony's leaders created in the seventeenth century did not become democratic government in the nineteenth or twentieth century any more than the hierarchical culture originally based on indentured servitude and slavery became fully democratic or egalitarian. In spite of their durability, some of those practices and institutions and the formidable obstructions that they placed in the path of democratic change became so commonplace that they ceased to be noticed and appeared to be part of the natural order of things. Legal and constitutional historians by and large have not given them much consideration, and authors of biographies and political historians who wrote about important episodes or epochs have also ignored them or missed their importance. Much of the modern popular literature on Virginia and the textbooks that several generations of schoolchildren have read also dismissed or evaded those critical aspects of the state's political culture in favor of shallow praise for ideals that those institutions and practices made it difficult or impossible to achieve. In the long view, though, much as an Impressionist painting looks different from a distance than up close, what stands out is the continuity, not the change. The obstacles in the way of men and women who tried to introduce genuine representative government and democratic politics command the center of attention.

The political institutions and processes did not arise by spontaneous generation or persist and operate mindlessly like plate tectonics. Powerful political leaders created and preserved those institutions and practices, even if they were not always aware of all of the short- or long-term consequences of their actions when they made important decisions. Other people defended or tried to change them and in the process explained their motivations and beliefs. This account of Virginia's political history and culture consequently includes words and actions of men who dominated Virginia's politics and government during a span of four centuries and also words and actions of men and women who challenged the dominant political leaders at various times. Quotations from their writings and orations are frequently extended because how those people explained themselves was sometimes as important or revealing as what they said or wrote.

Men with access to political office and influence shaped laws and public policies for their own benefit, but ideas also shaped the political culture and the laws and practices of Virginia. People's religious beliefs, their ideas about society and culture, about race and class, about economic change, and the relationship of individual men and women with their governments were all influential and important and created competing interests within the political culture. People's actions were occasionally inconsistent with their words.

Their actions sometimes spoke louder or more clearly about their core beliefs than their words did. Their ideas, sometimes expressed in direct language and sometimes in their actions, are of the utmost importance.

The Grandees of Government is neither formal intellectual history nor popular intellectual history, and it is certainly not a history of formal political theory, but the ideas of the men who created and of the men and women who defended and challenged the political institutions and practices of Virginia are at the heart of this extended inquiry. Because the book treats 400 years of history, I have purposely avoided any use of the modern words *conservative* and *liberal*. Neither has ever had a very clear or consistent definition, and for much of Virginia's history either would be anachronistic or, worse, misleading. Political party names, too, can suggest false continuities, obscure real continuities, or misrepresent the nature of change. Thomas Jefferson's Republicans of 1800 were not the same as Abraham Lincoln's Republicans of 1860, and neither was the same as Billy Mahone's Republicans of the 1880s or other Virginia Republicans of the 1920s, 1950s, or the early years of the twenty-first century. Andrew Jackson's Democrats of the 1830s were not the same as Harry Byrd's Democrats of the 1930s or Barack Obama's Democrats of 2008.

This is also not a complete political history of Virginia. It is a sequential and cumulative examination of several events and subjects that illuminate one another and trace some important political and institutional changes within a context of continuity. The book is about the grandees of government, about political leaders and leadership in Virginia, about the people who imposed, preserved, and profited from the institutions and practices. Consequently it is to a large extent about white men. Government and politics were exclusively a white male preserve during most of Virginia's history and overwhelmingly white and male during the remainder. Indians, African Americans, women of all races and classes, and many other white men nevertheless influenced what political leaders did even during the many decades when they were all excluded from participation in the government. From the formation in Virginia of the first institutions of representative government and the creation of slavery early in the seventeenth century through the American Revolution, the American Civil War, the civil rights movement, and into the twenty-first century, the political history of Virginia, which is peculiarly Virginian, is also a set of Virginia variations on some of the most important themes in American history.

1

FOR THE GLORY OF GOD AND THE GOOD OF THE PLANTATION

This late nineteenth-century etching by Margaret M. Taylor (courtesy of the Library of Virginia) for Historic Churches of America: Their Romance and Their History *(Philadelphia, ca. 1891–94) depicts the ruin of the church at Jamestown. In a smaller church that once stood near the site of the 1640 tower, the first General Assembly of Virginia met from 30 July through 4 August 1619. Nearly two centuries after Jamestown ceased to be the capital of Virginia, portions of the town site reverted to a state not unlike what the first settlers encountered in 1607. The lasting importance of what took place in Jamestown during the seventeenth century made the island a popular tourist destination and, as the title of the illustrated volumes for which the image was produced suggests, generated romanticized interpretations of the past, to which this image in turn contributed. The reality of what the members of the first assembly did is fundamentally important for understanding Virginia's history and political culture.*

THE CHURCH AND THE STOREHOUSE
in Jamestown were the most substantial buildings that the English settlers erected during their first years in Virginia. From the beginning they served both God and Mammon. On Friday, 30 July 1619, something new and important happened in the church. The governor, the members of his advisory council, the treasurer, the secretary of the colony, and twenty-two other men gathered there to make some regulations for the better management of the colony. They acted under an authorization of the Virginia Company of London, which had just received from the king the new Charter of 1618, soon to be known as the Great Charter, in part because of what began in the church that day. It was the little colony's second change of administration. The dysfunctional council of 1607, of which Captain John Smith had once been president, gave way in 1610 to a military government that imposed order on the English outpost. By the time King James I granted the Great Charter, the English-speaking residents of Virginia had made themselves more or less self-sufficient. They had imported cattle and swine, planted grain, and made good use of the fruits and the game and fish that the land and water provided in abundance after fresh rains resumed and ended a long and severe drought midway through the military regime. In 1619 they began again.[1]

That the colony had survived the first dreadful years was almost miraculous. Virtually everything that could have gone wrong in the beginning had gone wrong. Drought had reduced the Indians' harvest on which the first settlers planned to rely, and the men of 1607, following the company's instructions, carefully selected a particularly poor site for settlement in a time of drought, although they did not know that one of the worst dry spells in all of Virginia's history had just begun. By drinking water from the river or from the well that they dug a few paces from the riverbank, they may have contracted an enervating low-grade salt poisoning. Jamestown was also adjacent to a marsh that exhaled a foul-smelling breath, but it was not the marsh gases, it was the malaria that the marsh's mosquitoes carried that made people sick or die. The resident Indians were sometimes helpful, sometimes harmful. Until Captain John Smith took charge in 1608, the colony's leaders had squabbled among themselves and the enterprise looked doomed, but he took command and ordered that men who did not work would not eat. After Smith left in 1609, the people hid themselves in the little fort at Jamestown and during the following winter, which soon was called the starving time, died miserably of disease and hunger, reduced to eating rats and snakes, even the corpses of other men and women.

During the first years of military government, the acting governor, Sir Thomas Dale, made Captain John Smith look like a softie. Dale enforced to the letter the brutal Laws Divine, Moral, and Martial. He executed men who blasphemed, shirked their responsibilities, or refused to obey. When a man stole food from the common stock, Dale had him tied to a tree and left him there to starve to death in plain sight, for the encouragement of the others, as the French would later say. But Dale made the colony succeed. He ordered men to plant grain, raided Indian towns for food, destroyed other Indian towns, erected palisades to protect the little settlements, and created a new town upriver on a high, easily defended bluff. He called it Henricus after the king's son. Dale also allowed men to farm small tracts of land for themselves rather than work communally on company land. By the time he returned to England in the spring of 1616, having been in charge for more than half of the colony's short history, the future prospects for Virginia had begun to look bright. He took with him one of the first large crops of Virginia tobacco and also its grower, John Rolfe, and also Rolfe's wife, Rebecca, or Pocahontas, or Matoaka.

On the same ship with Dale, the Rolfes, and the tobacco was an Indian man, Uttamatomakkin, or Tomocomo. He was a principal adviser of Wahunsenacawh, also known as Powhatan, the paramount chief who thirty or forty years earlier had assembled an affiliation of Indian tribes into the most impressive alliance on the mid-Atlantic coast. His chiefdom, called Tsenacomoco, covered the same part of the earth as the English company's colony, called Virginia, and he was worried. During his long life he had seen Spaniards and Englishmen come into the great bay of Chesapeake in their ships and then leave. Some tarried a few days or weeks, but they all soon left except one group of Spanish Jesuits who in 1570 established a mission on the banks of the York River, but the Indians wiped it out a few months later. The English who arrived in 1607 showed signs of staying, but they did a poor job of surviving until after the drought broke and Dale brought over cattle, hogs, and heavily armed soldiers in 1611. By 1616 they had remained far longer than any other Europeans, and Wahunsenacawh sent Uttamatomakkin to England and directed him to count the men and the trees there in order to learn how many more Englishmen might come and whether they merely came for trees to build more of their ships. It is not certain whether Wahunsenacawh, who died in 1618, ever received a report of Uttamatomakkin's observations. In fact, so numerous were the men and trees in England that he gave up trying to count them; the stick on which he notched his tally was too short. If Wahunsenacawh did not learn, he probably suspected that the population of England and its technological resources were so superior to those of his people that the future prospects for Tsenacomoco no longer looked bright.

By the summer of 1619 the English settlers numbered several hundred and lived in four little towns and worked on several company-owned farms, called particular plantations or hundreds, along the James River. They had erected a large church building in Jamestown, probably the only European-style building in the colony large enough that all of the members of the assembly could meet in one room without having to shift casks of tobacco, supplies, and trade goods out of the way. The settlement on the island had been "reduced into a hansome forme, and hath in it two faire rowes of howses, all of framed Timber, two stories, and an upper Garret, or Corne loft high, besides three large, and substantial Storehowses, joined togeather in length some hundred and twenty foot, and in breadth forty." Adjacent to the original town site were "some very pleasant, and beutiful howses," two blockhouses, "and certain other farme howses."[2]

Governor Sir George Yeardley, the council members, Treasurer Edwin Sandys, Secretary John Pory, and the other men who assembled in the church in Jamestown on that 30 July 1619 had all, so far as can be determined, arrived in Virginia after the starving time winter of 1609–10. The colony that the Virginia Company had planted in the New World was a mere twelve years old, but it was already by far the longest-lasting English settlement in the Western Hemisphere.

Beginning that Friday in July 1619, those men completed the formation of a new local government. They still operated under the general superintendence of the governing council—the board of directors, as it were—of the Virginia Company back in London, and they still functioned within limits that the king's charter imposed on them; but the new charter empowered a governor and a Council of State to govern the colony, and the governor's instructions authorized him to summon a second council, called the General Assembly, to make the laws. What they did and how they did it influenced the whole future of Virginia's history and the history of the United States. The political history and culture of both began with what the company's officers and employees did that day in the church in Jamestown.

When the men met in the church that morning, it was probably not the first time that day that they had been to the church. From the very first landing of English-speaking people in Virginia, the company's instructions had required all of the settlers to attend the morning and evening services of the Church of England and the two services and sermons on Sundays. It is likely that many or most of the men summoned to meet as a General Assembly had probably attended the morning service that day and watched and listened as Richard Bucke, the minister, read from his copies of the Bible and the Book of Common Prayer. Precisely which words he read and the men and women assembled in the church heard is unclear. The Latin, Greek, and Hebrew texts had been translated by then into several English-language editions of the Bible, each with subtle and sometimes significant differences in tone and meaning. Bucke probably had a copy of what was called the Geneva Bible, which was likely the English version most widely used at the beginning of the seventeenth century and the edition that the church's reformers, known as Puritans, preferred. The Virginia Company's shareholders and officers included many Puritans, and several of the colony's early clergymen, including Bucke, were sympathetic to the Puritans. Bucke might possibly have had a copy of the new translation of the Bible, the one that King James had commissioned not long before he issued the first charter to the Virginia Company in 1606 and that was published in 1611, not long after Bucke first stepped ashore in Virginia and walked among the starving men in Jamestown.

Directions printed in Bucke's copy of the Book of Common Prayer required that he read the service and the words of Scripture distinctly and with a loud voice that the people might hear, that none by virtue of being unlettered remain ignorant of the word of God. The words that he read would have been familiar to the people in the church. The services of the church were so arranged that the same significant texts were read aloud once each year and the psalms once in every month, "that the people (by daily hearing of holy scripture read in the Churche)," according to the explanatory preface in the 1559 Elizabethan Book of Common Prayer, "shoulde continually profite more and more in the knowledge of God, & be the more enflamed with the love of his true religion."[3]

If Bucke conducted the full morning service for the thirtieth of July, the first of the three psalms for the day was Psalm 144, which began, in the words of the Geneva Bible, "Blessed *be* the Lord my strength, w^c teacheth mine hands to fight, & my fingers to battel. *He is* my goodness & my fortres, my tower & my deliverer, my shield, and in him I trust, which subdueth my people under me."[4] Those words may have carried a special significance that morning to the men who gathered in the church in that little town on the bank of a great river on the edge of a vast continent that contained no more than a few hundred Protestant Christians. They needed all the earthly help and divine aid that they could get. The psalm concluded with the prayer "That our corners *may* be ful, and abunding with divers sortes, *and* that our shepe may bring forthe thousands, and tens thousands in our stretes: That our oxen may be strong to labour: that their be none invasion, nor going out, nor no crying in our stretes. Blessed *are* the people, that be so, *yea,* blessed *are* the people, whose God is the Lord."

Those words of the psalmist must have resonated in the souls of the men in the church that day. They needed moral and spiritual support to make a reality of their dreams of peace, full storehouses, and plentiful flocks. One wonders what Richard Bucke thought about those words. He had been ship-wrecked en route to Virginia in 1609 (in the storm that suggested to William Shakespeare the plot for the *Tempest*) and had been in the first ship to reach Jamestown in May 1610 at the end of the starving winter. His wife died. It is possible that he married a second time and that his second wife died, also. He named his children Mara (meaning bitter), Gershon (expulsion), Peleg (divi-sion), and Benoni (sorrow), and Benoni was feeble-minded.[5] Bucke's life in Virginia was hard, but that was one of his bonds with every other man and woman who entered the church then or any other day.

Bucke then read the two passages from Scripture prescribed for that day. From chapter 8 of the book of Jeremiah, he read about how the kings and people of Judah had sinned and ignored God's warnings and how as a conse-quence their bones were taken out of their tombs and spread "as dung upon the earth." In the third verse were the words of warning that would have made any one who recalled or knew about the starving time in Virginia shudder: "And death shalbe desired rather then life of all the residue that remaineth of this wicked familie, which remaine in all the places where I have scatred them, saith the Lord of hostes." Bucke then read from chapter 18 of the book of John about the arrest of Jesus in the garden, how Peter thrice denied him, how Jesus denied that he was a mere earthly king, and how Pilate prepared to hand Jesus over to the Jews for trial and execution.

The lessons that day, for both the lettered and the unlettered, reminded men and women of their duty to obey God and to avoid sin, to recognize Jesus as a greater king than an earthly king, and that even earthly kings were subject to the word of God through the words of Jesus. To the people in the church in Jamestown that day, the words in the psalm about subduing "my people under me" meant not only the unchristianized and possibly dangerous Indians, they also meant all of the men and women, all of the people who were free and those who were bonded by indenture to labor for other people or for the com-pany. Except the king, every soul was under some other person's temporal and spiritual authority.

Later that morning Bucke met in the church with the governor, council-ors, company officers, and other men when they assembled as the first General Assembly of Virginia. The report of the meeting records that "forasmuche as mens affaires doe little prosper where Gods service is neglected," Bucke of-fered a prayer "that it would please God to guide & sanctifie all our proceed-ings, to his owne glory, and the good of this plantation."[6] The assembly mem-bers conducted their secular business as if with God's eyes watching over their shoulders.

The eyes of the king and the officers of the Virginia Company were also looking over their shoulders. Perhaps, too, residents of the town peered in at the church windows or stood inside or sat on the benches in the church to watch and listen. The official report of the proceedings of that and the succeeding four days does not mention Jamestown's residents. The eyes of God, king, and company were doubtless of much more concern to the members of the assembly than the eyes and ears of the people. If the men and women who lived in Jamestown were watching and listening and not busy working in their tobacco or corn fields, tending their cattle, fishing in the river, cooking, or looking after children and supervising servants, they would have seen and heard that the men in the church acted in the combined contexts of obedience to God and to the king: proper service and obedience to either was proper service and obedience to the other.

The assembly first met sometime in the morning of Friday, 30 July 1619. The members resumed their work later in the day after dinner, and they met again all day on Saturday. The members did not meet on Sunday. They no doubt attended the morning and evening church services, but on that day one of the members, Walter Shelley, from Smith's Hundred, died,[7] and the weather probably being hot, they may have buried him that same day. On Monday and Tuesday the members again met for most of the day, but the weather was so very hot on Wednesday that they hastened to conclude their business that afternoon rather than continue one or more additional days as originally planned.

In several very important ways, but not in all, their proceedings resembled meetings of Parliament, even though the participants were not officers of a government in the modern sense but merely members and employees of the Virginia Company of London meeting to regulate the company's local business. The governor's instructions for convening the assembly are lost, but when the company appointed Sir Francis Wyatt governor in 1621, officials probably copied Yeardley's instructions for Wyatt's use as they did on several later occasions. Wyatt's required him to convene the assembly annually but no oftener unless an emergency arose. The company specified that burgesses from the principal settlements be "Chosen by the inhabitants" and their decisions in the assembly be made "by the greater part of the voyces then present, Reserveing alwaies to the Governor a negative voyce," or veto. The governor named Secretary John Pory to be Speaker and appointed a clerk to assist him. He also named a sergeant at arms, and Bucke acted as chaplain. The assembly's officers had the same titles as the officers of the House of Commons. The company's instructions to the governor required that the assembly's laws be consistent with England's laws, and the company reserved the right to disapprove them; but the instructions also required the assembly to approve new company policies before they went into effect in the colony.[8] Neither king nor Parliament had any role in the creation or enforcement of what the company's assembly called laws.

The similarities between the assembly's procedures and Parliament's were important, but so were the differences. In its structure the assembly more nearly resembled a royal court or a very early version of Parliament, with the monarch—in this instance, the governor—attended by his assistants and functionaries. All of the members met in unicameral consultation, including the governor, council members, and burgesses, and they not only considered laws and regulations for the colony, they also received and passed along or ruled on complaints, petitions, and charges of misbehavior, more like a medieval princely court than like a modern legislature. Pory had the title of Speaker, but the governor presided. Pory acted as secretary, organized the business of the five days, and prepared the copies of the "reporte of the manner of proceeding in the General assembly" for each of the jurisdictions represented in the assembly and for the officers of the Virginia Company of London.[9] The copy that he prepared for the company is the only one that survives and the only account of the proceedings.

Pory was a remarkable linguist and translator, a graduate and former tutor in Greek at Cambridge, and he was the only member of the assembly who had once been a member of the House of Commons. It is possible that he more than any other one person was responsible for the resemblances between the assembly's proceedings and those of Parliament.[10] Before the assembly members met, the governor, perhaps with the advice of the council members, Treasurer Sandys, and Secretary Pory, prepared an agenda, which Pory presented after Bucke said his prayer and the members were sworn and took their seats.

The preliminaries were important and deserve some attention. Pory's report did not indicate how the twenty-two burgesses from the towns, hundreds, and particular plantations were elected and who elected them. The governor's instructions stated that they were to be especially "Chosen by the inhabitants" but not how. Pory's report indicates only that the governor "having sente his summons all over the Country" for "the election of Burgesses," two men from each of the eleven settlements appeared in Jamestown.[11] The words *election* and *chosen* meant and mean essentially the same thing and did not imply the method of selection or indicate whether all inhabitants of each settlement participated in the selection or only adult men who were not in any way dependent on, or subservient to, anyone else. The idea that women or servants might participate in the selection of representatives probably would have been regarded in Virginia in 1619 as absurd, and in England only men who owned certain classes of property were permitted to vote for members of the House of Commons. The scant surviving documents do not indicate who chose the first Virginia burgesses. The assembly's own records and the regulations that it adopted routinely distinguished between commanders and masters and free men on the one hand and servants on the other, and the two were not equal in the eyes of the assemblymen. The word *burgess* back in England signified a free man entitled to exercise certain civic responsibilities in a city or borough; in Virginia the word may have been employed to signify a free man thought to be correspondingly respectable enough in his community for this new role in the management of the company's colony. Those twenty-two men were certainly responsible men in their towns or plantations, and the commanders no doubt approved their selection. Two of the men, Christopher Lawne and John Warde, were actually the commanders of their plantations.

After Bucke's prayer, Pory called the names of the twenty-two burgesses and administered to them the oath of supremacy, which required them to swear that the king was supreme over the pope. That should have exposed and disqualified any Catholics. Pory noted with satisfaction in his report, "(none staggering at it)."[12] When he reached the name of Captain John Warde, Pory stopped and explained that Warde had settled on Captain John Martin's portion of the company land without the company's permission and might therefore be regarded not as his own man representing his own plantation but as a mere "limb or member" of Martin's settlement. Pory put the question whether Warde and his fellow burgess, John Gibbes, as men in some ways dependent on Martin and in the same ways independent of the company, should be allowed to participate in the company's assembly. The two men withdrew. "After muche debate" and Warde's agreeing to seek the company's approbation for his plantation, the members voted to admit Warde and Gibbes, explaining that Warde had expended a great deal of his own money to establish his plantation and that he had imported a valuable cargo of fish. Moreover, as the commander of a plantation, Warde had received a summons from the governor, and therefore he and Gibbes were entitled to seats in the assembly.[13]

Governor Yeardley then interrupted and produced and read from a copy of the company's commission to John Martin, which allowed his plantation, Martin's Brandon, a unique exemption from obedience to the decisions of the assembly. The members voted to summon Martin and ask him to forgo that portion of his commission and on behalf of his settlement submit in advance to the regulations that the assembly adopted before they seated the two burgesses from Martin's Brandon. Otherwise, Pory wrote in his account of the decision about Martin's burgesses, "they wer utterly to be excluded, as being spies, rather than loyal Burgesses; because they had offered themselves to be assisting at the making of lawes, wch both themselves, and those whom they represented might chuse whether they would obey or not."[14] Martin appeared on Monday and refused to relinquish that privilege in his commission. The members of the assembly then refused to allow his two burgesses to take their seats,[15] so Martin's Brandon and its inhabitants were not represented in the first General Assembly of Virginia and did not participate in making its laws and were therefore not bound to obey them.

After voting on that first morning to ask Martin to relinquish that one privilege in his commission, the members of the assembly also heard a complaint about the behavior of some of the men of Martin's Brandon, which perhaps influenced the decision that they made on Monday about the burgesses. Some of Martin's employees (including Thomas Davis, one of the men selected as a burgess) had risked the fragile peace with the Indians by seizing a canoe and its corn after the Indians refused to sell the corn. Opechancanough (Wahunsenacawh's brother and successor as paramount chief) complained to the governor. Keeping the peace with the Indians was a matter of such importance to the whole colony that the governor presented the issue to the assembly. When, on Monday, Martin appeared before the assembly, he agreed that for the future he would pledge that when he sent his men into the bay to trade, he would guarantee the "good behaviour of his people towardes the Indians."[16]

Even before making any laws for the better management of the colony, the assembly members had made a rule and established a precedent, rooted in parliamentary law and practice, asserting their own exclusive right to judge who was qualified to take part in the assembly and requiring that those who took part and the people at the settlements they represented adhere to the decisions of its members. Regardless of whether commanders of towns and plantations allowed democratic means to select the members, the assembly in effect treated the individual burgesses as representatives in a modern sense, with the understanding that the commanders and residents of the towns and plantations would obey what their representatives agreed to as members of the assembly. That was the essence of, and the beginning of, representative government in Virginia.

The qualified members being sworn in, Pory read the company's commission and instructions for holding the assembly and then informed the members about the agenda, which he—or perhaps the governor—had divided into business of four kinds. The first was to examine the charter, laws, and privileges of the colony to ascertain whether the assembly should request the company's board to make modifications of provisions "not perfectly squaring wth the state of this Colony, or any lawe wch did presse or binde too harde . . . especially because this great charter is to binde us and our heyers for ever." The second was to inquire into which provisions of the company's instructions to the governors since 1610 should be enacted into law in the colony. The third was to consist of all private matters that members might bring before the assembly, and the fourth was to determine what petitions on behalf of the colony the assembly should send to the company in England.[17]

Pory appointed two eight-member committees of burgesses to look into the first of the "bookes" of business and report back to the full assembly. Then after dinner the governor, councilors, and "Non Committies" took up consideration of the second of the four subjects and discussed it for three hours, until the two committees reported. It being late in the day by then, the assembly adjourned until the next morning.[18] The appointment of committees to investigate or consult and then report to the whole assembly was in imitation of recent innovations in the procedures of the House of Commons, another of Pory's important contributions to American parliamentary practice. Moreover, most of the recommendations from committees or from the floor were read out loud to the members for their assent at least twice, normally three times, also in imitation of parliamentary practice.

The orders that the assembly began adopting on Saturday contain much useful evidence for evaluating the condition of affairs in the colony; and just as important, they also indicate what subjects were most important to the men in charge.

The two committees brought in six requests, which the whole membership considered and adopted. The first subject in the sequence and perhaps the first in importance involved landownership. During the military regime the governors beginning with Dale had granted portions of land to men who had been in the colony since the early days—later records refer to them as ancient planters—but the assembly members were uncertain whether the company had fully authorized the governors to make those grants. The assembly requested the company to explain the land-granting authority with which it had invested the military governors. The members wanted assurances that the land "might not nowe, after so muche labour and coste, and so many yeares habitation be taken from them."[19] Private landownership had only recently been introduced into Virginia, but it remained for centuries the single most important concern and after 1670 also the basis for participation in public affairs.

The second request to the company was in two parts, the first that it send out more men to work the land at the "fower Incorporations"—James City, Charles City, Kicoughtan, and Henricus—to provide better for the maintenance of members of the new Council of State, "who are nowe to their extream hinderance often drawen far from their private busines" to attend council meetings. The second part was that the company also send men to the four settlements as tenants for the ministers to cultivate "theire gleab to the intente that the allowance they have allotted them of 200£ a yeare may the more easily be raised."[20] The ministers' glebes were tracts of land with a house that the company provided for their residence and support. With proper tenants working the glebe lands, the ministers' salaries could be raised on the property set aside for that purpose. Glebes provided at public expense and taxes that parish vestries later levied on the inhabitants supported the ministers of the Church of England in Virginia, who were vitally important members of the community in many ways, for 157 more years. All of the expenses of the

government and the church—each was a part of the other—were paid by the people whose lives were to be governed and whose souls were to be saved.

The assembly's third request of the company was that all men who had settled in Virginia "upon their owne chardges" since the departure of Dale in 1616—men like John Warde, presumably—should have equal shares of land with the men the company had sent out and supported. The assembly also requested that the company "alowe to the male children of them and of all others begotten in Virginia, being the onely hope of a Posterity, a single share a piece, and shares for their wives as for themselves; because that in a newe plantation it is not knowen, whether man or woman be the more necessary."[21] That recommendation indicates that the assembly members clearly intended that the settlement become a permanent colony, that it should be populated with families rather than with male soldiers and explorers, and that private landownership and the ability to acquire and bequeath land to descendants would be, as in England, the foundation of the society.

Company officers in London were beginning at that very time to consider measures to increase the number of women who could be enticed to settle in Virginia and convert the commercial and military outpost into an agricultural society. The company's officers stated part of the problem two years later: too many men in Virginia were "enflamed wth a desire to returne for England only through the wants of the Comforts of Marriage without wch God saw that Man could not live contentedlie noe not in Paradize." The men in the colony, "uppon esteeminge Virginia, not as a place of habitation butt only of a short sojourninge: have applied themselves and their labours wholly to the raysinge of present profitt, and utterly neglected not onlie the Staple Commodities, but even the verie necessities of Mans liffe."[22]

The fourth petition was that the company send out a subtreasurer with authority to receive rent in the colony rather than in London and in kind rather than "to exacte mony of us (wherof we have none at all, as we have no minte) but the true value of the rente in comodity."[23] Among themselves in their private transactions, the settlers probably engaged in day-to-day exchanges of goods and foodstuffs by barter because money—coins—was in very short supply. At an early stage some of the merchants and other men in the colony began using account books that allowed them to make a permanent written record of who owed how much to whom and when and how it was paid so that honest business could be done when there was no money to change hands, rather as modern credit card accounts and electronic funds transfers allow business transactions without any actual money changing hands. In practice it was to be the merchants, commanders, planters, and ship captains who kept the account books, not the ordinary farmers and laborers; and until the mid-1640s account book entries were evidently treated in court as conclusive evidence of a debt, giving the keepers of account books a distinct advantage over all other people.[24]

It is also very likely that from the early days those accounts expressed the value of goods and services not only in English pounds or even Spanish coins, which circulated in the American colonies, but in pounds of tobacco. Tobacco, or notes promising payment in tobacco, or book accounts expressed in pounds of tobacco, became the currency of the Virginia economy and remained so for nearly two hundred years. That fact indicates how thoroughly the production of tobacco influenced the society throughout the colonial period. The colony's surviving archival records show that the colonial government, too, used pounds of tobacco to express the value of many things, to assess taxes, to set rates of payment, and to specify the value of land, slaves, ships, and other goods. In fact, one of the last things the first assembly did, on Wednesday, 4 August 1619, was to assess every person in the colony one pound of tobacco to compensate the Speaker, clerk, and sergeant at arms for their time and services.[25]

The fifth recommendation from the committees was that the company build the college that had been proposed for the colony and send over "workmen of all sortes fitt for that purpose."[26] The college intended for the inland settlement at Henricus was to provide education for both English and Indian children in the rudiments of Protestant Christianity and in reading, writing, and arithmetic, so that they could read their Bibles and perhaps even keep their own accounts. It remained a plan only, because the community at that place was almost completely wiped out in the spring of 1622 when Opechancanough launched coordinated raids on several of the outlying English settlements. That the company and its colonial residents planned an institution of the kind was another indication that they expected the colony to be permanent and to resemble England and also that they hoped to convert Indians to the Christianity of the Church of England. Colonists and English men and women largely abandoned that latter objective following the king's revocation of the company's charter in 1624, which left no organization with the authority or the ability to command and marshal resources for the conversion of the Indians of Virginia.

"The sixte and laste" of the committee recommendations that the assembly approved that Saturday was to request that the company "wilbe pleased to change the savage name of Kicowtan and to give that Incorporation a newe name."[27] That may not seem like nearly so important a recommendation to the company's English directors as the first five, but it is interesting and instructive, nonetheless. In the first place, it probably came from the elected burgesses, perhaps from one or both of the members from that town, William Capps and William Tucker. From the day back in the spring of 1607 when Captain Christopher Newport first entered Chesapeake Bay with three little ships, 104 men and boys, and plans to explore and settle North America, English-speaking men had been imposing English names on the landscape of Tsenacomoco—beginning by giving Cape Henry, Cape Charles, James City, and James River the names of the king and of his two sons—taking possession of the land in that subtle but significant manner. What the Indians thought about that act, if they knew about it or understood it, is not clear; but to English settlers far from home, giving English names to their new places in their new colony was no doubt a matter of importance. The council in England agreed to this request and later named Kicoughtan after the king's daughter, Elizabeth City. Within a few years maps of Virginia sported dozens of English names: York River, Elizabeth River, and Warwick River (and later a Warwick County) and counties named for English places including Northampton, Southampton, Isle of Wight, Norfolk, and many more.

Before concluding its business on Saturday, the assembly members adopted one of the orders that the governor and council members and the burgesses who were not on committee duty had prepared on Friday afternoon. It had its origin in the company's instructions to the governor. With the consent of Abraham Peirsey, the cape merchant who was in charge of the colony's stores and its trade, the assembly ordered that all tobacco planters sell their crops to the cape merchant for transportation to the company in England, the best quality of tobacco at a rate of three shillings per pound and inferior tobacco at half that rate, one shilling six pence.[28] All of the other items that the assembly had discussed on Friday afternoon were then referred to the two committees, which reported back on Monday.[29]

On Sunday the members of the assembly attended the morning and afternoon services in the church and perhaps attended the funeral of Walter Shelley, who had been a member of the first of the two committees. The seven surviving members of the first committee and the eight members of the second probably worked that day to present on Monday a draft of "lawes drawen out of the Instructions" to the colony's governors since 1610.[30]

"By this present generall Assembly be it enacted," Pory wrote in his report about Monday's work, "that no injury, or oppression be wrought by the Englishe against the Indians, wherby the present peace might be disturbed and antient quarrells might be revived."[31] Another law adopted later in the day specified how Indians working for colonists in "places well peopled" were to be treated, protected, housed, and guarded, "for generally (though some amongst many may proove good)," Pory explained in the official report, "they are a most trecherous people, and quickly gone when they have done a villany."[32] A law "for laying a surer foundation of the conversion of the Indians to Christian Religion" required each town and settlement to admit "a certaine number of the natives children" for education "in true religion and a civile course of life." A few of the most promising boys were to be taught "the firste

Elements of litterature so to be fitted for the Colledge intended for them; that from thence they may be sente to that worke of conversion."[33]

In "detestation of Idlenes" the assembly directed that the commanders of towns and plantations have power to appoint a master for any person, even a free man, "founde to live as an Idler or runagate," the idler to work "til he shewe apparant signes of amendment" in his behavior.[34] It required people convicted of "gaming at dice & Cardes" to forfeit their winnings and fined all winners and losers ten shillings. Perhaps to encourage vigilance against the vice of gambling, but also in keeping with English laws at the time, the person who disclosed the gambling was entitled to receive ten shillings by way of reward.[35]

The law "Against drunkenes" discriminated according to the rank of the person. It empowered the minister quietly to reprove a "private person" for the first offense and publicly for a second offense, but for a third offense the person was to be sentenced to lie in irons for twelve hours in custody of the provost marshal and pay the fee that the provost marshal imposed, "and if he still continue in that vice, to undergo suche severe punishment, as the Governoʳ and Counsell of Estate shall thinke fitt to be inflicted on him." A company officer, however, if convicted of drunkenness, would be reproved by the governor for a first offense, openly by the minister in church for a second offense, and for a third would be stripped of his office, although the governor retained the right to restore a man to office.[36]

Men who violated standards of proper apparel for their stations in life—standards that the assembly's law did not specify—were to be assessed a penalty in support of the church according to his station or "if he be married, according to his owne and his wives, or either of their apparell."[37] That simple but vague law, together with the gradations of punishment in the law against drunkenness, suggest two important things about the culture of Virginia in 1619 and the values of the men who made the laws. All men were not equal, and they were not to appear dressed in such a manner as to give a false appearance about their rank in the society. Everyone had a place in the society and a specific role to play, and as with modern military insignia, each person's rank and role should always be visible for the maintenance of order and discipline and for the preservation of the social structure. It is not clear how many visible gradations of social status there were between the governor at the top and the lowest serving girl or Indian laborer at the bottom, but the vague wording of the law indicates that there were several and that they were so well recognized that the assembly members did not think they needed to enumerate them.

The laws included several regulations designed to guard against food shortages and to promote agricultural diversification. One law required that every household have on hand for every inhabitant one spare barrel of corn.[38] (In seventeenth-century English the word *corn* meant any small grain such as wheat or oats or barley; when Virginians of that time meant what twenty-first-century Americans call corn, they specified maize or Indian corn.) The law required every household to plant or purchase more grain than the head of the household anticipated needing for the current year, much as Joseph had advised the Egyptians to store extra grain after his dream of famine. Another law required that every man who worked his own land plant and tend at least six mulberry trees each year for seven consecutive years, cultivate "silke-flaxe" and hemp, and plant and tend ten grapevines each year.[39] Repeatedly throughout the seventeenth century the company's officers and royal officials tried to stimulate production of silk, cloth, cordage, and wine in Virginia, at which some of the planters were fairly successful during the middle decades of the century.

The assembly decreed that "necessary tradesmen"—smiths, coopers, cobblers, and other craftsmen—should be paid "according to the quality of his trade and worke, to be estimated, if he shall not be contented, by the Governoͬ and officers of the place where he worketh."[40] The terms of all contracts made in England between employers and servants, between the company and its employees, were to be enforced, and the assembly ordered that no person employ any "crafty" or "advantagious meanes" to entice away another person's servants or laborers.[41] Management of laborers and control of the behavior of laborers were of fundamental importance to the members of the first General Assembly and became increasingly so later, as the surviving records of the colony's courts and future General Assemblies demonstrate.

The assembly endorsed a company order allowing the cape merchant, as manager of the colony's principal storehouse, called the magazine, to keep as his allowance 25 percent of the value of the merchandise and the tobacco, sassafras, and other crops that passed through it or were grown for sale in England. The law repeated the requirement that all planters sell their tobacco to the cape merchant, but it allowed managers of particular plantations established with the company's approval to trade on their own account, and if any private ships arrived in Virginia with goods that colonists wished to purchase, they could ship tobacco to England on those ships rather than through the magazine.[42] The assembly's final regulation about tobacco specified that leaf tobacco in such bad condition that it could not be sold even at one shilling six pence was to be "burnt before the owners face,"[43] a measure intended to keep the worst leaf from depressing the price that the planters and the company hoped to receive for the better and the best.

On Tuesday morning the assembly referred to the committees the subjects that individual members submitted for consideration and again read and again approved the acts that it had approved on Monday.[44] While the committees worked, the governor, council members, and other burgesses received and considered a complaint from Captain William Powell, a burgess for James City. Powell charged that one of his employees neglected his work, engaged in lewd behavior with Powell's widowed servant, and also made false charges to the governor that Powell was guilty of drunkenness and theft, which charges might cost Powell his captaincy. The assembly ordered that the servant stand four consecutive days with his ears nailed to the pillory and be whipped each day.

The records of the first decades of the colony are replete with instances of courts routinely ordering severe corporal and even capital punishment for both major and minor misdeeds. As the records of the first General Assembly indicate, misdeeds of servants were often punished differently than those of gentlemen or freemen. The lower classes were more often the object of physical punishment, the upper classes of degradation from their military or social ranks. The latter was probably regarded as a severe disgrace among the commanders and planters, who relied on their social standing and official positions for their leadership roles. Physical punishment of a man of status was the most degrading punishment of all. For both masters and servants, shaming, such as forcing an offender to stand in the stocks or cutting his ears off, was a punishment, but the threat of it might have been regarded as a deterrent, and the experience of it might have been perceived as an occasion for a miscreant to repent of misdeeds and resolve to do better in future. The assembly members allowed the governor and council to determine "what satisfaction" Powell's servant was to be required to make to his master for neglecting his work.[45] The power of masters over servants was expansive, as long as the master did not grossly violate the explicit contractual provisions of the indenture that bound the laborer to him.

During Tuesday afternoon the committees reported and the assembly spent most of the remainder of the day discussing "the third sorte of lawes," but John Rolfe also submitted a petition against John Martin. He alleged that Martin had criticized Rolfe and also the "present government," probably meaning Sir George Yeardley's administration.[46] Pory's report indicates that the assembly referred Rolfe's complaint to the governor's council, but the text leaves it unclear whether it was Rolfe's opinion, Pory's opinion, or the collective opinion of the assembly members that the "present government" was "the most temperate and juste that ever was in this country, too milde indeed for many of this Colony, whom unwoonted liberty hath made insolente, and not to knowe themselves."[47] The men in charge clearly believed that they needed a strong controlling hand to maintain social order, economic prosperity, and their own superior status.

Wednesday, 4 August, began hot, and the members agreed to conclude their business. Even though the Speaker had been ill, he read, "as he was required by the Assembly," all the laws and orders that had already passed, "to give the same yett one reviewe more and to see, whether there were any thing to be amended, or that might be excepted against."[48] The members then adopted the laws.

The assembly allowed all men, "servants onely excepted," to trade with the Indians but prohibited selling Indians "any Englishe dog of quality." It ordered that no person sell firearms, shot, or powder to Indians "upon paine of being helde a Traytour to the Colony, and of being hanged, so soon as the facte is prooved, w^{th}out all Redemption" or any opportunity for pardon or reprieve. Men had to obtain permission to visit an Indian town or to go more than twenty miles from their dwelling places.[49] Later in the day the assembly also required that any person traveling by water either from above or below James-town was to stop there and register with the governor, and it required people trading in sailing vessels in the bay to obtain a license from the governor.[50]

Another act required the commander of every settlement to provide the secretary of the colony with a correct list of all people residing there, the de-tails of their commissions and land grants, and the terms of service remaining for each of the servants.[51] And another law required the ministers to provide the secretary annually with lists of all the people they had christened, married, and buried. In settlements without ministers, the law required commanders to send in these lists.[52]

The assembly also forbade the killing of "any Neatt-cattle whatsoever."[53] Draft animals were more valued for their work cultivating fields and perhaps producing milk, butter, and cheese than for their meat. The assembly specified penalties for stealing boats, oars, and canoes. Stealing from English-speaking owners would be proceeded against as a felony; stealing from Indians was to be punished by making restitution and a fine of £5 if committed by a free man or a fine of £2 and a whipping if by a servant.[54]

At different times during that final day the assembly adopted several laws concerning religion, all evidently at the suggestion of the members of the assembly. One required ministers to "read divine service, and exercise their Ministerial function, according to the Ecclesiasticall lawes and orders of the churche of England, and every Sunday in the afternoon shall Catechize suche as are not yet ripe" to take Communion.[55] Another required the min-isters and churchwardens to present to the court evidence of "all ungodly disorders" and "skandalous offenses, as suspicions of whordomes, dishonest Company-keeping with woemen, and suche like."[56] Yet another specified pun-ishments, including excommunication from the church, if "any person, after two warnings doe not amende his or her life, in point of evident suspicion of Incontinency"—sexual misbehavior generally—"or of the commission of any other enormous sinnes."[57] A law "For reformation of swearing" levied a fine of five shillings on every free man guilty of swearing and decreed that servants who swore would be whipped and their owners would be fined five shillings.[58]

The first of the final two laws concerning religion directed that "All persons whatsoever upon the Sabaoth daye shall frequente divine service and sermons both forenoon and afternoon; and all suche as beare armes, shall bring their pieces, swordes, poulder, and shotte."[59] That some people were entitled to bear arms indicates that others were not, and those others probably included not only women and children but some or all of the colony's indentured servants. The other law directed that "No maide or woman servant" marry without the consent of her parents or of her master or mistress "or of the Magistrat and Minister of the place both together."[60] The law imposed no corresponding restriction on male servants, which suggests that masters and mistresses were determined to keep serving women from the childbearing that would interfere with the performance of their work, or even might well kill them. Fornication and begetting or giving birth to an illegitimate child were already illegal under English law, and both men and women were subjected to specific punishments for those offenses; forbidding serving women from marrying in Virginia might have been regarded as an attempt to reduce the loss of work that masters and mistresses might expect to get out of their female servants.

Before writing "Here ende the lawes," Pory entered the final act of the assembly, directing that any person who contracted to work for a man in Virginia but stealthily remained in England and sold his services to another man had to serve the full terms of both contracts consecutively.[61]

Completing the adoption of the laws did not conclude the assembly's business that hot Wednesday. Captain Henry Spellman, one of the young men who early in the colony's history had been sent to live with the Indians to learn the language and act as an interpreter, was "called to the Barre" and examined on charges that he had defamed the government "in Opochancanos courte" and as a consequence put "the whole Colony in danger of their slippery designes." Spellman admitted some details in the charge against him, but when the assembly moved to strip him of his title of captain and sentence him to seven years of service to the company, Pory wrote that "hee as one that had in him more of the Savage then of the Christian, muttered certain wordes to himselfe, neither shewing any remorse for his offences, nor yet any thankfulness to the Assembly for their so favourable censure."[62] Pory may have believed that Spellman should have been grateful for not being hanged. More likely, Spellman was not destitute of notions of civilization; he did not fail to grasp the seriousness of being reduced in rank from a valued interpreter with the rank of captain to a mere servant facing seven years of service to the company.

The residents of nearby Paspeheigh (also called Argall's Town and Martin's Hundred) then petitioned to be relieved of paying bonds that they had once posted for the acquisition of land there. The assembly requested that the company cancel the bonds because the company had since set aside that land as a plantation to provide income to support the governor of the colony.[63]

"The last acte of the Generall assembly was a Contribution to gratifie their officers," which required every person older than sixteen to contribute one pound of the best quality tobacco to be delivered to Speaker John Pory, who would divide it among himself, the clerk, and the sergeant at arms "according to their degrees and rankes."[64]

The assembly adopted resolves apologizing to the company for adjourning the proceedings so soon, as a consequence of the heat, and authorizing Pory to make and authenticate copies of the proceedings for all of the settlements represented in the assembly and for the company's council in England.[65] The assembly begged the company not to reject the whole body of laws if it adjudged any part defective but to allow "these lawes wch we have nowe brought to light, do passe currant & be of force" pending the company's final determination. "Otherwise," Pory wrote, "this people (who nowe at lengthe have gotte the raines for former servitude into their owne swindge) would in shorte time growe so insolent, as they would shake off all government, and there would be no living among them."[66] Pory's condescension toward and apprehensions about his social inferiors were typical for an English gentleman of his standing, and Virginia's planters and public officials exhibited the same attitudes for many decades thereafter.

The assembly repeated its plea that the company allow it to pass on the propriety of rules that the company proposed just as the king "hath given them power to allowe or to reject our lawes," and the governor then adjourned the assembly until the first day of March.[67]

That was the beginning of representative government in Virginia. It was also to a large extent the beginning of the political culture that nourished the ideas and beliefs that informed Virginia's subsequent political history. What the assembly members did and how they did it were both important, and the nature and details of the laws that they adopted indicate what was most important to them. The men who met in Jamestown and adopted those laws made certain that they sustained their authority, defended their people against sins and enemies, regulated the economy in what they believed was their best interest, imposed regulations on servants and laborers, and more or less formally established the Church of England as the official church of the colony investing it with important responsibilities in keeping good order, peace, and civility in the colony. All governments then and all governments before and after them shared or share most of those same concerns. All governments at that time also were intimately involved in prescribing and proscribing religious beliefs and practices. From that beginning in Jamestown, the church and the state were part of each other, and neither, from the perspectives of the governors or the governed, was likely to be perceived as possible without the other. The symbolism of the company's officers doing secular business in a sacred place may not have been something that the people in Jamestown that week needed to have pointed out to them.

Perhaps the members of the assembly who resided in Jamestown or nearby remained in town that hot Wednesday afternoon for the evening service at the church. When Richard Bucke read the prayers and passages of Scripture, the second of the two psalms for the day was the twenty-third. Appropriately enough, it offered a kind of benediction on the secular business that the governor and the other company officers and the burgesses had done in that sacred place. Listen to it in the accents of the Geneva Bible:

> The Lord *is* my shepherd, I shal not want.
> He maketh me to rest in grene pasture, & leadeth me by the stil waters.
> He restoreth my soule, & leadeth me in the paths of righteousnes for his
>   Names sake.
> Yea, thogh I shulde walke through the valley of the shadow of death, I wil
>   feare no evil: for thou art with me: thy rod and thy staffe, they comfort
>   me.
> Thou doest prepare a table before me in the sight of mine adversaries: thou
>   doest anoint mine head with oyle, *and* my cup runneth over.
> Doubtles kindenes, & mercie shal follow me all the dayes of my life, and I
>   shal remaine a long season in the house of the Lord.

Those blessings intended for the deserving godly were in sharp contrast to the punishments intended for the undeserving ungodly. The first lesson from Scripture that day was chapter 19 of the book of Jeremiah, from which Bucke read the dire warning that the prophet pronounced to the wicked people of Tophet, concluding with the fifteenth and final verse: "Thus saith the Lord of hostes, the God of Israél, Beholde, I wil bring upon this citie, and upon all her townes, all the plagues that I have pronounced against it, because they have hardened their neckes, and wolde not heare my wordes." And from chapter 7 of Paul's letter to the Hebrews, Bucke read how Jesus offered people who believed in him a better covenant with the Lord, in the words of the twenty-fifth verse: "Wherefore, he is able also perfitely to save them that come unto God by him, seing he ever liveth, to make intercession for them."

About three weeks later, long before Pory's report could have reached London, probably even before he had an opportunity to put it on board a ship to send back to his employers in the capital of the emerging English empire, a ship that belonged to the company arrived at Point Comfort, near Ki-coughtan, which still had its "savage" name. On board, in the words of John Rolfe, were "20. and odd Negroes, wch the Governo' and Cape Marchant bought."[68] Those recent captives from the west coast of Africa may or may not have been the first Africans to arrive in Virginia. It is possible that a few had arrived earlier, and more certainly arrived not long afterward.[69] The men who made the first laws and established representative government in Virginia also took the first steps toward creating a system of slavery. Unlike the inden-tured servants and employees of the company about whom the laws of 1619 had much to say, the Africans came without indentures, without any legal protections or status at all, falling through the cracks in English statute and common law and adding to the small population of the colony a new group of laborers who by the middle of the century were degraded far below the most contemptible servant or Indian.

To purchase the labor or bodies of a few captive Africans was a small step for the men in Jamestown who had already purchased the labor of indentured servants and written laws to control them, but it was a step with large conse-quences, much as with the first legislative steps that they also took. It added one new lower level to the social ranks, and it ultimately augmented the au-thority of heads of households, who ruled their African laborers free of some of the restraints of law and contracts that governed how they ruled their in-dentured servants. Later General Assembly members had to create a whole new body of law that permitted masters to rule their new laboring force more violently than their indentured servants, not a contractual law of master and servant but a brutal law of master and slave.

In Jamestown in 1619 a small number of influential men took the first steps in creating two antithetical social systems, republican government and slavery. In 1624 King James I revoked the company's charter, and in 1625 King Charles I made Virginia the English Crown's first royal colony. During the subsequent decades the institutions and practices that the first General Assembly created and the political economy based on slavery that had its beginnings at the same time and place developed along lines that the planters and government offi-cials of Virginia directed without much royal or any parliamentary interfer-ence. Republican government and slavery dwelled together in the colony and commonwealth of Virginia for nearly two hundred and fifty more years.

Representative government got off to a promising beginning in 1619. Slav-ery got off to an ominous beginning. Less than five years after the first assem-bly met, William Capps, a prominent company officer and a burgess, asked for "3 or 4 score slaves to work about a ffort or for servile work." He was well aware of the troubles that owners or masters could have with involuntary workers, but he knew exactly what to do if they tried to run away. He also knew that he need not worry about other owners or company officials interfering with him when he disciplined or terrorized his workmen into obedience. And he knew that nothing in English law as it was being administered in Virginia would hinder him in doing what he believed he needed to do to control his workers. "I will make them sing new Toes, old Toes, no Toes at all," Capps wrote, "because they shall not outrun me."[70]

2

TRUE RELIGION AND A CIVIL COURSE OF LIFE

St. Peter's Episcopal Church, New Kent County (Virginia Department of Historic Re-sources), was begun about 1701 and is one of the oldest surviving church buildings in Virginia. The tower was added in 1739–41. The substantial brick structure exhibits care in its construction and is typical of the simple design of early colonial churches. This and its fellow churches, most of which no longer survive, stood as testimony to the importance of the Church of England in Virginia. During the seventeenth century the colonists' religious beliefs and practices influenced the political practices and institutions that they developed, and those practices and institutions had influences that persisted for centuries.

PROTESTANT CHRISTIANITY GOT OFF
to an inauspicious start in Virginia. Late in life Captain John Smith set down
a short recollection of how in 1607 "we beganne to preach the Gospell in Virginia." He wrote, "wee did hang an awning (which is an old saile) to three or foure trees to shadow us from the Sunne, our walls were rales of wood, our seats unhewed trees, till we cut plankes, our Pulpit a bar of wood nailed to two neighbouring trees, in foule weather we shifted into an old rotten tent . . . this was our Church, till wee built a homely thing like a barne . . . yet wee had daily Common Prayer morning and evening, every Sunday two Sermons, and every three moneths the holy Communion, till our Minister died, but our Prayers daily, with an Homily on Sundaies; we continued two or three yeares after till more Preachers came."[1]

The Protestant Christianity of the Church of England provided the center of gravity for the spiritual and intellectual lives of most of the English-speaking residents of Virginia for a century and a half after the arrival of the first settlers. The people who moved to Virginia brought with them an Elizabethan version of English civilization of which the English Reformation was an essential component. By the time that the first few English men and boys set foot in Virginia in 1607, three generations of English men and women had experienced tumultuous religious changes that rocked their native land to its political foundations and severed the relationship of a vast majority of the English people with the Christian Church headquartered in Rome. It had exposed many residents of sixteenth-century England to requirements of belief and practice that they did not share and that could damn them eternally to hell. That was not just a figure of speech. For Catholics in England the Reformation exposed them to the risk of excommunication or the damnation of their souls if they went along with it or to many forms of physical and mental abuse or even death if they did not. For English Protestants, at least during the reign of the first Queen Mary, they, too, were equally at risk of spiritual and physical death. The English Reformation and its consequences affected every person in England.

The English men and women who colonized Virginia and their descendants who lived there, freed from Roman Catholicism, believed themselves to be a chosen people in an almost biblical sense. They did not doubt that their Protestant nation, their church, their faith was the one true Christian nation, church, faith. The English Reformation and its implications were as fundamentally a part of their lives as their language, dress, and legal culture.[2] The linkage in their minds between true religion and civilization can be seen in documents from the very earliest days of the colony when they recorded facts about those few English men who left the settlement and took up more or less permanent residence with the Indians. Scarcely any event was more difficult for them to comprehend. The language that they used to describe the abandonment of civilization for savagery, as well as the language that they used to discuss differences between themselves and their Indian neighbors, was heavily freighted with religious meaning. They wrote about Christians and heathens and also about Englishmen and heathens. They wrote about Christians and Indians and also about Englishmen and Indians. They wrote about Christians and savages and about Englishmen and savages. The words *English*, *Christian*, and variations on *civilization* identified one set of people and their culture. The words *savage*, *heathen*, and *uncivilized* identified another. The religiously based language, which they also used in discussions involving persons of African origin or descent, indicates that English-speaking Virginians viewed themselves and their world from a thoroughly religious perspective.[3]

For them, religion and civilization were one and inseparable. During the winter of 1609–10 when the garrison at Jamestown was dwindling away from disease and starvation, the suffering and hardship drove men to do dreadful deeds that were unchristian and uncivilized. One man killed his pregnant wife, disposed of the fetus, butchered her body, and fed on her corpse until he was discovered. If people lost their religion, they behaved as uncivilized; if they behaved as uncivilized, it was because they had lost their religion. The fate of another man during that same winter clearly revealed the inextricable linkage of religion with civilization and of irreligion with savagery. The account of the event that George Percy composed is rich with religious overtones. He recalled later that "one thinge hapned wch was very Remarkable wherein god sheowd his juste Judgmt For one Hughe Pryse beinge pinched wth extreme famin, In a furious distracted moode did come openly into the markett place Blaspheaminge exclameinge and Cryeing outt thatt there was noe god, alledgeing thatt if there were a god he wode nott suffer his creatures whome he had made and framed to indure those miseries and to perish for wante of foode and Sustenance Butt itt appeared the same day thatt the Almighty was displease wth him for goinge thatt afternoene wth a Butcher a corpulennt fatt man, into the Woode to seke for some reliefe, bothe of them weare slaine by the salvages, and after beinge fownde gods Indignacyon was sheowed upon Pryses corpes wch was Rente in pieces wth wolves or other wylde Beastes and his Bowles Torne outt of his boddy, being a leane spare man. And the fatt Butchers nott lyeing above six yards from him was found altogether untouched onely by the salvages Arrowes whereby he recieved his deathe."[4] Pryse denied God and behaved and therefore suffered accordingly.

The regulations and the language of the famous—or infamous—Laws

Divine, Moral, and Martial of 1610 and 1611 indicate how inextricably intertwined governance itself was with religious beliefs and practices and how much the governors believed that English Protestantism was essential to the well-being of the colony and the colonists. Governor De La Warr opened the code with this tangled preamble: "Whereas his Majestie like himselfe a most zealous Prince hath in his owne Realmes a principall care of true Religion, and reverence to God, and hath alwaies strictly commaunded his Generals and Governours, with all his forces wheresoever, to let their waies be like his ends, for the glorie of God."[5]

The laws required that English men and women in Virginia "have a care that the Almightie God bee duly and daily served"; that "no man speake impiously or maliciously, against the holy and blessed Trinitie"; that "no man blaspheme Gods holy name upon paine of death, or use unlawfull oathes"; that no man "shall speake any word, or do any act, which may tend to the derision, or despight of Gods holy word upon paine of death"; that all colonists attend religious services twice daily; and that all clergymen "within this our Colonie, or Colonies, shall in the Forts, where they are resident, after divine Service, duly preach every Sabbath day in the forenoone, and Catechise in the afternoone, and weekly say the divine service, twice every day, and preach every Wednesday."[6] Those religious regulations accompanied the strict rules governing personal behavior and prescribing severe punishment for violations. The following year the military commander added as an appendix a seven-page prayer that he ordered to be "duly said Morning and Evening upon the Court of Guard, either by the Captaine of the watch himselfe, or by some one of his principall officers."[7] Each twice-daily recitation of that prayer required a quarter to half an hour.

Protestant Christianity was of fundamental importance to the rulers, and they expected it to be of fundamental importance to those whom they ruled. That is why the General Assembly of 1619 ordered that each settlement admit a small number of Indian children to be educated "in true religion and a civile course of life."[8] This rich phrase concisely blends the essential objectives that the church and the Virginia Company shared and that the church and the state later shared. The order suggests that the assembly hoped to incorporate at least some Indians—perhaps the next generation—into English Virginia society, for which religious and civic instruction were both and equally essential. Most seventeenth-century English Protestants believed that true religion was not possible without a civil course of life, nor was a civil course of life possible without true religion. They almost certainly could not have imagined a religious life and a civic life that were not entwined. Each was part of the other, and both were under the protection of the Crown and in Virginia after 1625 of the Crown's personal deputy, the royal governor. Except during the Commonwealth years in the 1650s, the king was the head of the church and of the state. James I believed and stated that he ruled by divine right. He was the king because he was God's man on earth, and he was God's man on earth because he was the king. Through the combined and mutually reinforcing powers of the word and the sword, the king led and protected his people in true religion and a civil course of life.

The language of the laws of 1610 and 1619 and the language of the times are replete with religious references, and the daily lives of the colonists were punctuated with the rhythms of religious rituals. During the 1610s and 1620s, as during John Smith's time, the colonists lived their lives constantly, not just on Sundays, in a cultural environment that repeatedly emphasized religious beliefs and practices. That death was a constant companion no doubt made that religious basis for their lives the more important and those repetitions more comforting. They understood that a wholesome, well-ordered English civilization required the people to share those same fundamental beliefs and join in the same common religious observances that inculcated and reinforced their shared fundamental beliefs.

The Church of England treated the colony during the first decades of the seventeenth century as a place of missionary work. Ministers were missionaries to the Indians and also missionaries to the colonists.[9] Formal creation of parish structures and modes of church governance proceeded haphazardly. As early as 1619 the assembly ordered churchwardens to police the moral behavior of the people in their settlements, and it enacted several laws to regulate religious behavior; in effect it established the Church of England as the official church of the colony. As early as 1619 a rudimentary form of local church governance was in place in Virginia, resembling, as would be expected, the forms of local church governance in England. Few records and references survive to document the development of local or colonial church organization during the first half of the seventeenth century, but it is likely that ministers and congregations devised practices consistent with expectations that they brought with them from England in the same kit with their religious beliefs.

As the English-speaking population increased and spread over a larger portion of the countryside during the 1630s, the original, compact settlements where regular religious ceremonies and a community of religious interest could easily be maintained gave way to more numerous scattered and smaller communities. Some were very small, only a small farm and its resident family or a larger plantation under the management of one owner who took responsibility for its residents. As a consequence, the nature of religious life in the still small colony began to change. It ceased to resemble the church- and town-based culture familiar to residents of old England and to the new residents of New England.

In 1643 the General Assembly enacted the first surviving comprehensive law since 1619 to regulate religious affairs "for the advancement of God's glo-

rie and the weale publique." The law required the colonists to attend church
and specified the duties of ministers and churchwardens. It also directed that
"there be a vestrie held in each parish, for the makeing of the leavies and assessments for such uses as are requisite & necessary for the repairing of the
churches, &c."[10] The wording suggests that for some or many or most of the
churches in the colony, but perhaps not yet for all, a select number of lay members had begun taking responsibility for the parish.

That same statute also empowered vestries to select parish ministers.[11] A
departure from English custom, this was undoubtedly a concession to local
circumstances because there was no bishop or anybody else in the colony to exercise that essential work on behalf of the church. The governor as well as the
commanders of hundreds and particular plantations had formerly appointed
some ministers, but by, or beginning in, the 1640s lay vestries in Virginia took
on the responsibility. An act of 1652 went further and explicitly empowered
parish vestries to act by "theire owne orderinge and dispossall from time to
time, as they shall thinke ffitt" in all matters concerning the minister, the
church, the churchwardens, the poor, and the behavior of their parishioners.[12]
Local control of the colonial church and of its congregations coincidentally
became complete after Virginia surrendered to the Puritan Commonwealth
in 1652. There was virtually no church hierarchy then or thereafter in Virginia,
and the congregations were largely self-governing until after the American
Revolution.[13] The organization of the Church of England in Virginia during
the seventeenth century resembled the organization of the Church of England in England only superficially, even at the local level.[14] In fact, it more
nearly resembled the Puritan and Congregational churches in New England
or the Church of Scotland.

Parishes as local units of governance were important in many ways. Lay
vestries assumed responsibility for the orphans, the poor, and the roads. Ministers in the seventeenth century may also have conducted schools as many
of them did in the eighteenth century. Literacy may be taken as prima facie
evidence of a religious education. Churches also had important responsibilities in maintaining public order and morality. It is likely that until the middle
of the seventeenth century the churches in Virginia, as in old England and in
New England, allowed people suspected of serious moral lapses, such as fornication or adultery, to purge themselves of sin and to cleanse the community
of immorality by confessing in church in a ritual ceremony called compurga-
tion.[15] For an undetermined number of years in the middle of the seventeenth
century some parishes even sent representatives to the General Assembly just
as counties did.[16] That suggests just how important churches and parishes
were to the people, who had to pay the expenses of their parochial burgesses,
and how important parishes were to the General Assembly, which admitted
their burgesses on equal terms with the county representatives.

In 1656 the assembly required that the counties that had not already established boundaries for the parishes within their jurisdictions or created parishes for the local churches forthwith do so.[17] That statute was, in effect, a directive to complete the formal organization of the colonial church into a system of uniformly managed parishes. The wording of the law suggests that the development of local church government had proceeded at different paces and perhaps in different ways in the different localities. Some parishes already had settled boundaries and boards of superintending vestrymen, but perhaps some did not.

The preamble of the 1656 law stated that "there are many places destitute of ministers, and like still to continue soe, the people content not payinge their accustomed dues, which makes them negligent to procure those which should teach and instruct them."[18] That did not necessarily mean that seventeenth-century Virginia was a place with a chronic shortage of ministers because religion was not of enough importance that colonists were willing to pay ministers a salary. Members of the Church of England, as Captain John Smith recalled, could and did conduct their own religious services without an ordained minister, but the 1650s was no ordinary decade in Virginia or in England. During that decade Oliver Cromwell's Puritan Commonwealth attempted to suppress the performance of the church's liturgical worship service and the use of its Book of Common Prayer in England. Puritans were in powerful political offices in Virginia, too, including the governorship, so what were vestrymen to do? What were prayer book ministers to do? It may have been that clergymen were in short supply or unwilling to take parishes in the colony at the rates parishioners could afford to pay or that vestrymen were of divided opinion or reluctant to chose a minister whose religious persuasion differed from their own.

It is by no means clear whether or how Cromwell's government or the local Puritan regime altered the religious landscape in Virginia, nor is the language of the preamble to the 1656 law, even though repeated almost verbatim two years later, clear evidence that there was always a chronic shortage of clergymen in the colony throughout the century. Ministers were, indeed, in short supply in some places and at some times, but court records and other government documents contain as many passing references to clergymen in their parishes as comments on a shortage of ministers of the Gospel. If clergymen were in short supply, it may have been the supply side, not the demand side, that was responsible. In fact, in 1656 the General Assembly offered a bounty of £20 to every clergyman who would move to Virginia and take charge of a vacant parish, and as a further encouragement it exempted all clergymen and six of their servants from paying local taxes.[19]

Dispersion of the population allowed some diversity of religious opinion to exist within the Protestant community without disrupting the colony's culture. Between the middle of the sixteenth century and the middle of the seventeenth, when Virginia was first being settled, there was a wide continuum of beliefs about how much reform of the English church was the right amount to complete and preserve the English Reformation. Many English churchmen revered the solemn liturgical service of the ancient church, which they had codified early in the years of the English Reformation in the Book of Common Prayer. The reforming impulse led other English Protestants to greater or lesser degrees of dissatisfaction with the formalities of the liturgical service. At the opposite end of the continuum were English Protestants who insisted on purifying the church by ridding it of most or all vestiges of its Catholic past; they rejected the liturgical service and the Book of Common Prayer entirely. Most English Protestants were somewhere between the extremes, and within that middle ground differences of opinion were often times not so great as to disrupt congregations or communities.

The liturgical services of the Church of England, the language of the Book of Common Prayer, and the emphasis on godly living and salvation may have given most Virginia Protestants in that middle ground few occasions to engage in theological disputes on fine points of doctrine or interpretation of Scripture. In the words of the preface to the Book of Common Prayer, "Christ's Gospel is not a Ceremonial Law, (as much of Moses' Law was,) but it is a Religion to serve God, not in bondage of the figure or shadow, but in the freedom of the Spirit; being content only with those Ceremonies which do serve to a decent Order and godly Discipline, and such as be apt to stir up the dull mind of man to the remembrance of his duty to God, by some notable and special signification, whereby he might be edified." Every soul in Virginia belonged to the Church of England, unlike in New England where church membership (as opposed to church attendance) was strictly limited to a sanctified few. In Virginia men and women did not have to debate degrees of sanctification and worthiness, the theological or scriptural bases for making distinctions, or decide who was competent to make the definitions. Many of the aspects of the Protestant community that provoked contention in New England were absent from Virginia, where the residents consequently had few or no reasons to argue about those questions.

Through its services and the ministering of its clergy, the church sought to persuade parishioners in Virginia to seek in their own ways the salvation that God offered to them. Even the Book of Common Prayer, which prescribed set biblical texts and prayers for each of the scores of devotional occasions throughout the year, left it in the discretion of individual clergymen (and perhaps of their more-or-less superintending congregations in Virginia) whether to deviate from the prescribed forms of worship by omitting or substituting texts. The theological tenets of the church were short on Calvinism and appeared to some people to be too short on strict theology, but they were long on and stressed the importance of faith and good conduct.

Some, perhaps most, white Virginians were comfortable with the Book of Common Prayer and the liturgical service, even though their worship services may have been simpler than the formalities that the Book of Common Prayer prescribed. John Clayton, for instance, who was rector of James City Parish from 1684 to 1686, stated that he believed that he was the first clergyman in the colony to use the full evening service of the Book of Common Prayer and "the first that wore a Surplice there."[20] The comparative informality would have pleased the Puritans who resided in the colony during the early years. It is entirely possible that in the first half of the seventeenth century there may have been as many Puritans in Virginia as in New England, middle-ground Puritans of the reforming sort rather than doctrinaire Puritans of the separatist sort. In seventeenth-century Virginia both prayer book churchmen and moderate Puritans occupied that broad middle ground and coexisted most of the time in comparative harmony.[21] The small band of separatists who resided in the Low Countries for several years before settling at Plymouth in December 1620 had intended to settle farther south in the northern part of Virginia, where they had reason to believe that they would be welcomed rather than ostracized. During the 1630s Virginians sold corn, livestock, and other supplies to what one visitor to the southern colony described as "their zealous neighbours of New England."[22]

In 1641 and 1642 in Upper Norfolk County in the southeastern corner of Virginia, the people had become numerous enough to create three parishes, requiring them to recruit three ministers, but they did not send to England for new ministers. In the spring of 1642, they wrote a letter to Puritans in New England and asked the church worthies there to select three pastors to take over care of the souls in the three new parishes. The first signature on that letter is Richard Bennett's. He was to be the Puritan governor of Virginia from 1652 to 1655, elected by the General Assembly. As it turns out, the three ministers returned to New England fairly soon, their zealous beliefs making them incompatible with some Virginians,[23] but the important point about that episode and the lesson to be learned from the public career of Richard Bennett[24] is that members of the Church of England in Virginia, with or without Puritan ideas, got along reasonably well most of the time.

Every individual person sought salvation as he or she could, and so long as their public behavior posed no danger to public order, their strict adherence to a prescribed set of religious beliefs did not much matter. Protestants could reinforce their faith weekly, for those who attended church that regularly, or daily, for those who had a copy of the Book of Common Prayer and were inclined to observe its daily offices in their homes. Moreover, parish clerks could perform many of the ceremonial functions of the church in the absence of a clergyman. A considerable variety of individual belief systems could dwell together peaceably enough on the colony's scattered plantations and in its independent congregations. It was not that Protestant clergymen and lay leaders did not care about or believe in anything, it was that they did not always insist that everybody else care about and believe in precisely the same things and for exactly the same reasons. It is probably within that context that white seventeenth-century Virginians managed not to be at each others' throats very often about matters of religious belief and practice. Their differences of opinion on religious matters did not often approach the intolerant extremes.

The English Civil Wars of the 1640s pitted the extremes against each other in what can be thought of as a belated and bloody chapter of the English Reformation. The violence did not, by and large, spill over into Virginia, even though the colonial government remained loyal to the Crown long after Charles I lost his head. Virginia's political leaders, however, did not lose their heads, for they ultimately surrendered peacefully to the authority of Parliament when they had no other choice.[25] Some government officials in the colony persecuted some Puritans, and a significant portion of Virginia's Puritans eventually moved to Maryland or dispersed into the Northern Neck. That took place during the 1640s, when England was engaged in a bloody civil war, and it is entirely possible or even probable that avoidance of like violence in Virginia seemed as important as, or more important than, imposing rigorous religious uniformity.[26]

It is not clear to what extent after the colony surrendered to Parliament in 1652 that officials in Virginia attempted to enforce the discontinuance of the use of the Book of Common Prayer either in private or in the churches, nor is it clear whether Puritan officials imposed hardships on the royalists. In 1652 the General Assembly elected Puritan Richard Bennett governor. Edward Digges, who was the son of a prominent Puritan merchant in England and who got along well with both Cromwell and with Charles II, succeeded him in 1655, and Samuel Mathews, the namesake son of a Puritan merchant and powerful political officeholder in Virginia from before the Civil Wars, succeeded Digges in 1656.[27] The striking thing is how comparatively nonviolent Virginia was during most of the decades that produced profound upheavals in old England.

Virginia was a colony of churches as well as of tobacco farms in the seventeenth century and of more churches than courthouses, which are usually perceived as the centers of social and political life in the colony. A considerable body of surviving written evidence confirms the existence of church buildings throughout the settled Virginia landscape and from fairly early dates. An even greater amount of evidence would be available if it were not for the propensity of courthouses to burn down just like frame churches did, and if wars and floods had not also destroyed the contents of many of those courthouses. The surviving county records, including court order books, deed books, and will books, have references to churches scattered all through them. People sometimes identified their places of residence or the locations of their property by the name of the parish or by a direction or distance from a church in the same way that they casually mentioned the courthouse or a watercourse or a neighbor's property line. Churches were probably as familiar and unremarkable a part of the settled landscape as dwelling houses and sheds and barns and bad roads, none of which elicited comment unless something out of the ordinary happened to or near them. The surviving parish records from the second half of the colonial period not only contain information about parish churches, they also contain references to smaller chapels of ease that parishes provided for parishioners who lived too far from the main church to attend it regularly or conveniently.

The parish was the most local unit of government in the colony. Throughout the seventeenth century almost every county included several parishes. These parishes were much larger than parishes in England but in nearly every instance smaller than any county. The vestrymen, churchwardens, parish clerks, and clergymen would have been personally known to most or all of the residents of the parish. The same probably could not have been said about all of the officers of the larger counties, of the justices of the peace, sheriffs, and surveyors. Many of the most important events of people's lives took place at the parish, or neighborhood, level. That is where they married, baptized their babies, educated their children in the ways of God, buried their dead; where they closely scrutinized the quality of their neighbors' tobacco crops and bartered chickens, grain, cloth, or seed corn with their near neighbors, the same people with whom they attended church. The parish under the management of the vestrymen and the churchwardens may have been the counterpart for colonial Virginians of the New England town.[28]

Seventeenth- and eighteenth-century Virginians fully appreciated the fundamental importance of the parish both for its religious role in the community and for the community of interest that it represented in secular affairs. In the spring of 1662 the General Assembly passed a law intended to reduce the number of locally divisive disputes about property lines by introducing an ancient English practice into Virginia law. Land grants, deeds, and records of surveys should have amply defined the boundaries of every landowner's property, but many of the boundary lines were marked by trees with slashes cut in them or by other physical features of the landscape that could change or disappear or be hard to identify. Slashes healed, and trees toppled over or burned or were cut. The assembly therefore ordered that the churchwardens of every parish assemble the people and that in procession they perambulate the boundaries of all the landowners. The participants jointly pointed out to everybody the landmarks of their property boundaries, and they renewed the slashes on the boundary trees. This common endeavor provided everybody the same information and should have reduced the temptation or ability of any one of them to complain about the result or to encroach on a neighbor's property. If a difference of opinion arose during the process, the churchwardens brought up documents and called in two disinterested men to make a final determination. The law required that the churchwardens conduct these processions every fourth year to refresh the marks and the memories and also to incorporate new owners into the collective community memory as they came of age or moved into the parish or inherited property from owners who had died.[29]

The General Assembly entrusted the responsibility for this important act of keeping the peace and this essential means of protecting people's rights to their property to the vestries and their churchwardens, not to the county surveyor, sheriff, or justices of the peace. The legislators elaborated on and renewed the law in 1691, 1705, 1710, 1744, and 1748.[30] The collective community memory was of such importance that the 1705 codification of the statutes directed the churchwardens to record the results of their processioning in a permanent book of record. After a boundary line had been thus publicly marked three consecutive times without objection, the landmarks could not be questioned in a court of law.[31] That the vox populi of the parish was to be of equal validity with written words on land grants, deeds, and survey records is powerful testimony to the importance of the parish as a focus of community life.

The few surviving parish records and the county records do not disclose whether the churchwardens observed the letter of the law during the final third of the seventeenth century, but they amply indicate that the processioning of the land, or beating the bounds, as it was also called, was probably undertaken every fourth year, probably nearly everywhere, through the end of the colonial period and in many places well into the nineteenth century.[32]

For English-speaking residents of Virginia the church and Protestant Christianity were of equal importance with the government and its laws. That was inescapable to any seventeenth-century Virginian with eyes to read or ears to hear. Laws required them to attend church services regularly, although it is impossible to know how many did so. Necessity or curiosity also must have impelled many of them to frequent the regularly scheduled meetings of the county courts, which by the time that the church's local governance was finally established were also firmly fixed as centrally important organs of civil government. At both places Virginians would have heard sacred and secular texts read out loud, the mingling of sacred and secular language reinforcing the fact that church and state were one, that true religion and civilization were one. They might very well have regarded that phrase from the 1619 assembly, "true religion and a civil course of life," as a singular rather than a plural phrase. Neither was possible without the other. The two were one, and the one was both, in parallel to their understanding of the Trinity.

Even at church, clerks or ministers read secular texts from the pulpits, just as county clerks or sheriffs read them to the public at meetings of the county courts. After each session of the assembly, scribes made copies of all of the new laws in order that the county clerks or sheriffs could read them to the residents. That is how they were published, made public. Proclamations concerning high matters of state, such as the death of a sovereign and the succession of a new royal governor, and minor matters of police, such as the apprehension of thieves or runaway servants, were all read aloud at the courthouse, and parish clerks may have also read them at the church. People were accustomed to receiving information aurally.[33] They had to listen. What they heard, regardless of the subject matter of the text, was clothed in language that mixed the sacred and the secular. Indictments charged that accused criminals acted at the instigation of the Devil and without the fear of God in them. Public documents were dated in the such-and-such year of Our Lord and Savior and also in the such-and-such year of the reign of Our Sovereign Lord the King. Some public events were officially scheduled for a saint's day or for one of the days of the church calendar rather than on a specific day of a specific month. The 1662 law for processioning property lines, for example, ordered that it be done between Easter and Whitsunday.[34] Such means of reckoning the rhythms of life not only testified to the importance that religious observances had in the society at large but also presupposed a certain common knowledge about when those named days would come around or an expectation that people would learn of the approach of such days through their regular attendance at church.

The combination of secular and sacred language and imagery abounds in the public records of the colony. For example, the tax that county courts imposed for erecting courthouses and jails or arming the militia and the tax that vestries imposed for erecting churches and paying the minister or caring for orphans and the poor were charged at a rate of so many pounds of tobacco per able-bodied laborer. They were poll taxes, or head taxes, on people who by their own labor or by the labor of their able-bodied servants, slaves, and children contributed to the colonial economy. English and Virginia laws and the record books in the courthouses and parish offices identified a taxable person as a "tithable," a term that originated in the church, not in the exchequer. Until 1781 in Virginia that adjective-made-noun identified every person who was required to pay all local taxes to the county sheriffs, who collected both the county and the parish taxes.

The language of the Book of Common Prayer also combined the sacred and the secular. Every day when the minister or parish clerk or head of a household read the lessons and prayers, he (or perhaps, in the household, she) also read the prayers for the preservation of the king and royal family. And whenever it was in the seventeenth century that Virginians began buying or their ministers began reading from the pulpit the new English translation of the Bible, it reinforced their awareness of the dual role of their sovereign. The title page of the Bible bore the name of its sponsor, King James. The pages of the new Bible were also clean of the Calvinistic asides and criticisms of monarchy that had filled the margins of the so-called Geneva Bible most widely used during the first decades of the colony. The change may have subtly led to an increase in the variety of ways that individual Protestants in Virginia interpreted and understood the Scriptures and in turn allowed for a largely uncontested range of religious diversity within the larger church.

When men and women wrote their wills or dictated the terms of their wills to a clergyman or some other person who could write, the opening words were almost always, "In the name of God." Wills nearly always required a decent Christian burial of the body and commended the soul to God before proceeding to provide for the payment of earthly debts and to dispose of earthly property. Those phrases and forms were the standard language of wills, but they were read aloud to the family and perhaps also in court when it came time to settle a dead person's estate, and those words in a context of death may have worked as subtle reminders for the men and women who heard them in the courthouse or at the dead person's house.

On other occasions in courthouses or at the statehouse in Jamestown, men and women witnessed rituals that blended religious obligations with secular responsibilities, such as taking an oath before testifying in a court case or before entering into the duties of a public office. By the end of the century, following the so-called Glorious Revolution, all men before taking a public office had to swear three interlocking oaths: one of allegiance to the king, one affirming that the king was of superior temporal and religious authority to the pope, and one disavowing belief in the Catholic doctrine of transubstantiation. In effect, one oath to the king, one oath to the church, and one oath to the Reformation.

Religious beliefs permeated the society and informed people's understandings of events in their daily lives. An instructive example occurred on the Eastern Shore in the spring of 1680. A young, unmarried woman gave birth to a child, and the child died. The county court investigated the crime of fornication that produced the pregnancy and also investigated allegations that the child had been killed. The court questioned the midwife about how, at the time of the woman's most extreme difficulty in labor, she had demanded that the mother identify the father and withheld her assistance until the woman complied. That was a standard test for ascertaining paternity because people believed, and the courts acknowledged, that a person in imminent danger of dying could not lie and face the prospect of going directly to hell. The court also had the body of the child dug up and handed around so that people who were suspected of having a part in its death could fondle it. That was another standard test because people believed, and the courts acknowledged, that a murdered corpse would bleed or its wounds would change color if the murderer touched it. It was called trial by touch. Both of those tests assumed and required a shared firm foundation in religious belief, both in hell and in God's miracles. When the mother's stepfather handled the infant's corpse and witnesses saw the bruised places grow "fresh & red so that blud was redy to come through the skin," they knew that they had identified the culprit. The stepfather went pale on the spot, and the court charged him with murder and getting a bastard child on the body of his stepdaughter. He fled and drowned while trying to escape.[35] Perhaps his neighbors drew the same lesson from his death that the witnesses of the blasphemer Hughe Pryse drew from his disemboweled corpse seventy years earlier.

The trial by water of persons accused of witchcraft rested on the same basis of shared religious belief. The best known of the Virginia witchcraft accusations occurred in Princess Anne County in 1706, and the county court records preserve the account of Grace Sherwood's trial by water. The court ordered that her hands and feet be tied and that she be lowered into consecrated water. That was a standard test to ascertain whether somebody was a witch because people believed, and the courts acknowledged, that consecrated water would not accept a witch, an agent of the Devil. If the person sank, he or she was innocent of the charge and would be hauled out (if lucky) before drowning. If the person floated, he or she was adjudged a witch.[36]

Bystanders who watched the proceedings and people who heard them reported orally to the court could not miss the point. They knew what it all meant. God was a living and active presence in their lives. They knew that God took part in identifying murderers and witches, just as the law and the courts presumed. Most or all of the white people in seventeenth-century Virginia believed that God and the Devil worked their wills in the daily lives of the people. The Devil sometimes worked through the agency of witches, and in Virginia as well as in New England. The ordeals of trial by touch and trial by water were deeply rooted in widespread beliefs in the agency of God and the compatibility of Protestant Christianity and the occult.[37]

Even without ministers of the Gospel resident in all of the colony's parishes all of the time, Protestant Christianity remained a fundamentally important ingredient of colonial culture. The scattered remnants of private letters of those Virginians contain religious and biblical references in abundance, which like the language of wills should be viewed not as meaningless literary tropes but as expressions of religious opinions or religious orientation. Governor Sir William Berkeley, whose writings survive in greater abundance than those of any other seventeenth-century Virginian, filled his public and private papers with religious references that clearly demonstrate that he believed in divine intervention in human affairs and that God punished sinful people and rewarded righteous people in this life as well as in the next.

Berkeley was a committed churchman and accounted for most of the calamities of his time as God's punishment of Englishmen generally because some Englishmen had killed King Charles I. In an address to the House of Burgesses in 1660 when Berkeley resumed the governorship about the time that Charles II assumed the throne, he alluded to the ill consequences that the execution of the king and the advent of the Parliamentarians had for Virginians back then "When God's wrath lay heavie on us for the sins of our nation."[38] In explaining the great London fire of 1666, Berkeley wrote, "I am most confident if more than an accident was the cause of this judgment twas the anger of god for the murther of the late blessed master," Charles I.[39] He similarly described some of the causes and probable consequences of Indian attacks in New England, called King Philip's War, in 1675, "which in al reasonable conclusions wil end in their utter ruine and but al men feare and tremble at the justice of God on the Kings and his most Blessed fathers Ennimies and learne from them that God can make or find every where Instruments enoughe to destroy the Kings Ennimies. I say this because the New England men might as soone & as well have expected to have been envaded by the Persian or Mogul as from their Indians and yet what cannot God doe when he is provoked by Rebellion and undoubtedly the New England men weare as guilty of the late Blessed Kings Murther by Councells Emissaries and wishes as any that most aggresively acted in it."[40]

To Berkeley the wrath of God for the king's death even caused the sudden outbreak of Bacon's Rebellion in the royalist colony of Virginia in 1676. He wrote, "I then thought this Country would have beene the last that would have Expected Gods Anger for that wicked act."[41] In the aftermath of the rebellion, he expressed uncomprehending surprise at being held responsible for the rebellion. "I am as Innocent as anyone in the Extremities of the world, yet I cannot but thinke God was angry with me when this Dire misfortune happened for I alwaies thought that if I Carelessly threw a stone over a howse and kild a friends Child I was att that time out of the favour of God."[42] Berkeley's sense of the agency of God in men's lives was not a personal oddity. His letters indicate that he believed he and his contemporaries, including the men and women to whom he wrote, were people for whom religious beliefs were powerfully important.

Most white English-speaking residents of seventeenth-century Virginia were members of the Church of England, doubtless some more and some less committed, some more and some less inclined toward Puritanism; but white English-speaking Virginians were not the only Virginians. African and Indian residents of Virginia had a much more varied collection of religious and cultural heritages than white English-speaking Virginians, and not all white

Virginians were members of the Church of England, or even native speakers of English, either. In the very first years of the colony, the Virginia Company sent artisans and craftsmen from other European countries to Jamestown, among them some Poles and Germans and also the Italian glassmakers, who are the best known. Archaeological excavations of the original fort site have recovered religious artifacts that suggest the presence at a very early date of at least one Catholic.[43] It is not known whether the artifacts belonged to a Continental Catholic or to an English Catholic. Neither is it known whether any English Catholics who might have been present kept their religious identities a secret, or whether, if they disclosed their faith, it made any difference in how they fitted in to the largely Protestant English community.

Another thing that is not clear is how Catholics from other countries were treated in the early years of the colony as a consequence of being Catholic. Perhaps, as in the case of the Italian glassmakers, usefulness outweighed the unsettling dangers of difference. English Protestant merchants and manufacturers certainly had no scruples about doing business with Continental Catholics, some of whom resided in England, even as some Protestant Englishmen resided for extended times in Catholic countries. The mercantile Bland family, for instance, that furnished Virginia during the seventeenth century with one of its most important explorers, a collector of the royal customs, and a Speaker of the House of Burgesses also had a branch of the family that resided for decades in Catholic Portugal and another that resided for a time in Spain and its colonies.[44] A few Catholics in the colony probably were not regarded as so dangerous as the presence of even one priest would have been.

For a few years early in the history of the neighboring colony of Maryland, Catholics predominated. By the middle of the seventeenth century, some Maryland Catholics moved to and resided unmolested on the south bank of the Potomac River at the northern edge of settled Virginia. They and their children and grandchildren became prosperous and respected planters, but they were never very numerous and posed no real threat to the colony's Protestant institutions and culture, and there were no priests there, so far as is known. This is not to say that English Virginians harbored no prejudices against Catholics, only that a prejudice against a church and a fear of its influence did not always extend with equal power to a few of its quiet and peaceable members. The English laws against Catholics taking part in public affairs were sometimes ignored in Virginia, and some Catholics served as high-ranking militia officers, practiced law, and sat on the county courts. Catholic George Brent was a major in the Stafford County militia, acting attorney general of the colony from the autumn of 1686 until the spring of 1688 (late in the reign of Catholic King James II), and a member of the House of Burgesses in the latter year.[45]

One group of white English-speaking Virginians did not initially fit in well and certainly were not welcomed when they first arrived. The Friends, or Quakers, arrived in the 1650s when memories of the violence of the English Civil Wars were still fresh. The beliefs of the Friends directly connected each individual believer with God, and that immediate connection with God and the equality of all believers meant that Quakers perceived no need for ministers and engaged in no uniform formal worship service. It is possible that their religious beliefs alone would have made Quakers appear a threat to the stability and propriety, to the true religion and civil course of life, that the Church of England promoted. Their outward behavior certainly did. Quakers refused to abide by the legal requirement that they attend the services of the Church of England. They eschewed virtually all of the outward manifestations of properly churched civilized Englishmen and engaged in a number of potentially disruptive practices. Not only did they have no minister or formal worship service, they let anyone speak at meetings at any time, even women. They appeared, from the perspective of the Church of England, to be dangerous and subversive of good order.[46]

At the spring 1660 assembly session that restored Governor Sir William Berkeley to office after the collapse of the Puritan Commonwealth in England, the legislators passed An Act for the Supressing the Quakers. It described them as "an unreasonable and turbulent sort of people" who taught "lies, miracles, false visions, prophecies and doctrines" that threatened "to destroy religion, laws, comunities and all bonds of civil societie." The legislators prohibited ship captains from landing Quakers in the colony, forbade colonists from entertaining or hosting them, and ordered "that no person do presume on their peril to dispose or publish their bookes, pamphlets or libells."[47] Within a few years, though, the behavior of the Quakers in Virginia convinced most churchmen that they were no threat, and the larger society tolerated them or absorbed them as it did most of the Puritans and Catholics. Stability and order were prime objectives and key components of the version of English society that evolved in seventeenth-century Virginia, and acceptance of peaceful nonconformists served that purpose better than attempts to enforce uniformity.

The institutions and practices as well as the beliefs and habits of the Church of England were very well matched to the colony's social and political orders. Indeed, the nature of the church itself and its practices and teachings undoubtedly contributed importantly to the nature of the colonial culture. There was no ecclesiastical hierarchy in Virginia comparable to the political and social hierarchies evident in the structure of colonial government (in the conspicuous distinctions between militia officers, justices of the peace, sheriffs, burgesses, councilors, royal appointees, and governors) and in the society (between slaves, indentured servants, small farmers and artisans, and the great planter families). But within each neighborhood parish there was a miniature hierarchy of parishioners, churchwardens, vestrymen, and clergy that almost perfectly replicated the county's political and social hierarchies and reinforced them. Without the Church of England in colonial Virginia, the colony would not have been what it was.[48]

Even without a formal governing hierarchy and even with inconvenient vacancies in parish pulpits, the church was an essential and reasonably strong institution during the seventeenth century. In 1684 the bishop of London appointed a young clergyman, John Clayton, then rector of James City Parish, as his commissary, or personal representative, in the colony. The bishop may have believed that the loosely organized colonial church needed a firm controlling hand and proper management as the population continued to grow and spread out, although he provided his commissary with few tools to impose discipline or order on the local clergymen or their congregations or to curb the powers of the parish vestries. On the other hand, the bishop may have hoped that in a colony with a rapidly growing population and with more and more ministers, parishes, and parishioners all the time, a resident representative could assist the loosely organized believers in the colony to continue effectively taking care of their religious needs in their neighborhood parishes.[49] Whatever the bishop's intention, the latter more nearly represented what people in Virginia believed. During the long tenure, from 1690 to 1743, of the second commissary, James Blair, the colony's church structure remained decentralized, and neither he nor any of his successors was able to dictate to the colony's clergymen, who remained beholden to their parish vestries rather than to the bishop or his commissary.[50] A decentralized church, every bit as much as a hierarchical church, was compatible with the persistence and importance of active religious faith, and from the 1690s to the American Revolution, the bishop's commissary almost always had a seat on the powerful governor's council.

The literate white men who filled most or all of the public offices in seventeenth-century Virginia and guided the colony's public life were predisposed by virtue of their religious faith and their membership in the Church of England to perceive the world in which they lived as a place in flux, a place to which they had to adapt themselves but also one that they could to some extent shape. They were not doctrinaire, for the most part. That led them in the political part of their public lives, as they did in their religious lives, to seek accommodation of minor differences rather than attempt to impose strict uniformity of belief and practice. An Aristotelian temperament, as it has been called, allowed them to view the imperfect world with a certain realism and to recognize their own limitations as well as to take advantage of the possibilities that the world offered to them.[51] Because well into the eighteenth century they continued to live on their scattered small farms or plantations where each of them was the head of a small principality, they may have had relatively few temptations to engage in disputes with one another on religious subjects and also a collective disposition to leave one another alone, to allow their neighbors to mind their own personal and family and plantation affairs as they pleased. Insofar as their political culture was concerned, their religious beliefs and their political interests made them practical statesmen, even though their increasing reliance at the end of the seventeenth century on slavery also made them domestic tyrants.

It all fitted together, their political institutions and culture, their religious faith and church, and their plantation society. The natural world in which they lived and the civil world that they created appeared to them to be internally cohesive, just as a well-ordered English civilization should be. It appeared to be to the advantage of those free white men to manage the public affairs of their colony in such a way as to incorporate as many other white people as possible into its functioning, to emphasize their shared religious beliefs, their shared need for public safety, and their shared opportunities for personal profit in the international tobacco economy. Those mutually reinforcing objectives and the institutions that supported them thrived on and protected true religion and a civil course of life.[52]

Early in the eighteenth century after Hugh Jones had spent five years ministering to two parishes in Virginia, he returned to England and wrote a book about the colony. In one revealing passage he commented on the importance of English Protestantism to the colony's culture and also noted how, as a consequence of its religious culture, Virginia was in some ways different from the other colonies. Writing as if painting with broad strokes that covered the subtleties but highlighted the distinctions, Jones postulated that "If *New England* be called a Receptacle of Dissenters, and an *Amsterdam* of Religion, *Pensylvania* the Nursery of Quakers, *Maryland* the Retirement of *Roman* Catholicks, *North Carolina* the Refuge of Run-aways, and *South Carolina* the Delight of Buccaneers and Pyrates, *Virginia* may be justly esteemed the happy Retreat of *true Britons* and *true Churchmen* for the most Part; neither soaring too high nor drooping too low, consequently should merit the greater Esteem and Encouragement."[53]

"And I will make of thee a great nation," God said unto Abraham, "and I will bless thee, and make thy name great; and thou shalt bee a blessing. And I will bless them that bless thee, and curse him, that curseth thee: and in thee shall all families of the earth be blessed." Protestant Christians in the colony of Virginia would have read these words of verses 2 and 3 of chapter 12 of the book of Genesis or heard them read from their church pulpits and doubted not that God was speaking directly to and about them, also.

3

THE
GRIEVANCES
OF THE
PEOPLE

Sir William Berkeley (1602–1677) (Trustees of the Berkeley Will Trust) was governor of Virginia from 1642 to 1652 and again from 1660 until 1677. He was undoubtedly the most important white man in seventeenth-century Virginia. His administration and attempts to diversify the colonial economy shaped the evolution of Virginia during the century. His separation of the burgesses and council members into a bicameral legislature in 1643 allowed the political institutions and culture of Virginia to develop strong traditions and strong leaders that guided its history for decades. Local political institutions functioned during his second administration in a way that led to Bacon's Rebellion of 1676. Berkeley was not personally responsible for the conditions that led to the rebellion, but his response to it permanently damaged his reputation.

THE FIRST OF THE WARSHIPS BEARING the thousand or more soldiers that King Charles II sent to Virginia to suppress Bacon's Rebellion and the three commissioners he sent to ascertain its causes arrived at the end of January 1677—January 1676 by the old calendar. By then the rebellion had collapsed, and Nathaniel Bacon, its leader, was dead of dysentery and other loathsome afflictions. Governor Sir William Berkeley and men loyal to his administration had rounded up most of the remaining leaders, and Berkeley had tried them before courts martial and hanged them. He had put down the largest and most violent uprising of white people that took place in any of England's North American colonies before the one that began exactly a century later. He was old, tired, angry, partially deaf, and very perplexed at how such a bloody rebellion could have broken out in the colony that he had governed with success for twenty-six of the previous thirty-four years, almost 40 percent of its entire history. Berkeley was a bitter man when he climbed aboard the flagship of the fleet to greet the commissioners and commanders of the force that arrived too late to help.

He knew one of the commissioners, Francis Moryson, who had lived in Virginia in the 1640s during Berkeley's first administration as governor. Moryson was Speaker of the House of Burgesses in 1656, compiled one of the first printed digests of the colonial laws, sat on the governor's council early in the 1660s during Berkeley's second administration, and was acting governor of the colony from the spring of 1661 to the autumn of 1662. By 1677, though, Moryson had been out of the colony for more than a decade and was the king's agent and no longer the governor's ally. The other two commissioners were strangers to Berkeley and had no personal knowledge of Virginia. Sir John Berry was a career naval officer and commander of the fleet that the king sent to Virginia, and Colonel Herbert Jeffreys was a career army officer and commander of the regiment that the king sent to Virginia.

Berkeley and the commissioners got on badly from the beginning. The commissioners brought the king's order summoning the governor back to London to report to him in person and empowering Jeffreys to supplant him as lieutenant governor. The old governor may have interpreted that as a royal rebuke or statement of no confidence. Berkeley did not leave for three months, until well after his relationship with the commissioners had deteriorated to exchanging insults, some veiled, some not. He was frustrated and angry about everything that had happened since the previous spring, and he soon grew frustrated and angry about the officious behavior of the commissioners, who undermined his authority and issued orders as well as asked questions. Berkeley's deafness made his initial discussions with the commissioners difficult. They had to shout at him to be heard, and like many hearing-impaired people he probably shouted at them, too, unaware of how he sounded to them. They were yelling at each other even before they were angry with each other.[1]

When Berkeley met with the commissioners aboard the king's warship on the first day of February, he read through the papers and royal instructions that they brought, and on the next day he wrote a long, detailed account of his handling of the rebellion for the information of his king and his king's ministers.[2] On the third day of the month, the governor addressed a letter to each of the twenty county sheriffs, sending them the commissioners' request that they "make enquiry after the aggreivances of his Majesties Subjects in Virginia to rectify the said abuses, administring equity to every man without respect of persons, and to report the same to His Majestie."[3]

In the decades between the meeting of the first General Assembly in 1619 and the outbreak of Bacon's Rebellion in 1676, Virginia changed remarkably. It became the English king's first royal colony in 1625. Its population increased several times over and spread through much of the land on both sides of Chesapeake Bay and along the rivers as far west and north as the tides flowed. Two deadly Powhatan attacks in 1622 and 1644 temporarily retarded but did not halt that expansion, and after the second attack the colonial government so overwhelmed the Indians that English-speaking Virginians usually cultivated their tobacco in peace. The governors and the assembly delegated authority over many day-to-day matters to local military and civil officers, creating the first of the counties to which Berkeley sent the commissioners' request for information. In each county, parish vestries oversaw the religious and moral welfare of the people, and a county court, presided over by justices of the peace whom the governor appointed, settled local disputes and maintained order. County sheriffs served writs, arrested miscreants, and collected the taxes; clerks recorded deeds and wills and kept the county's public records; and surveyors marked property boundaries and drew plats, guaranteeing to the tobacco planters their titles to their valuable land. Those parish vestries and county courts and the comparatively prosperous men who sat on them created twenty local polities and sets of leaders from whom the county's voters elected the county's members of the General Assembly.

After Berkeley's decision in 1643 to have the burgesses sit apart from the governor and council members in a bicameral legislature, the landowning tobacco planters in the House of Burgesses, supported by their neighbors and relatives at home and on the county courts, became the representatives of their class and their interests. They and Berkeley fashioned public policies that promoted landownership, attempted to regulate the behavior of indentured and enslaved laborers, and sought high prices for the leaf tobacco that was the principal source of income for them all. After the assembly in 1662 instituted in Virginia the old English practice of requiring the parish church-wardens to assemble all of the landowners every fourth year to perambulate their property lines,[4] the owners of land, who were nearly all white and for the most part male, avoided disputes among themselves as much as possible, creating a political system that reflected the social and economic systems and giving a measure of security and stability.

As if to fortify the relationship between tobacco planters and the govern-ment, in 1670 the General Assembly adopted a law that restricted the suffrage to those "ffreeholders and housekeepers who only are answerable to the pub-lique for the levies." That is, the assembly redefined the social contract and declared that only men who owned taxable land were sufficiently invested in the welfare of the country to be allowed to take part in its governance. The new law adduced English practice as precedent, reciting that English laws "grant a voyce in such election only to such as by their estates real or personall have interest enough to tye them to the endevour of the publique good." The explanatory preface to the new law revealed the thinking of the men who en-acted it and was in no way complimentary to the men they disfranchised as unworthy. The "usuall way of chuseing burgesses" in which all free men had formerly taken part, the statute began, had provided men without property an opportunity to "make tumults at the election to the disturbance of his maj-esties peace" rather than to elect "persons fitly qualifyed."[5] The assemblymen who wrote this statute echoed the low opinion of the common men of Vir-ginia that John Pory had written at the end of the assembly session of 1619, that if those men were not under proper control, "there would be no living among them."[6]

Until the rebellion broke out in 1676, it had all seemed to work. The in-stitutions of government served the planters well even as they competed with one another for land, labor, and commercial advantage. They differed among themselves chiefly about whether to allow the tobacco trade with the Neth-erlands to remain open or to confine the trade to English ports. Berkeley and a significant number of Virginia planters opposed schemes to revive the Vir-ginia Company or otherwise confine the trade to English mercantile houses. Influential merchant-planters like Samuel Mathews, a prominent Puritan and longtime member of the governor's council, and William Claiborne, also a veteran member of the council, favored restricting the trade to England. They had been company men before Virginia became a royal colony and had close commercial connections with the increasingly powerful class of colonial trad-ers like Maurice Thomson and his numerous allies and partners in London. The competition between the two factions did not seriously disrupt politics in Virginia before the English Civil Wars, during which Thomson's commer-cial and Puritan associates pushed through the House of Commons the first of a series of navigation acts that made colonial trade with the Netherlands illegal.[7]

The colony escaped most of the convulsions that plagued England during its civil wars, but white Virginians experienced occasional episodes of violence on the frontiers, persistent and annoying local problems with laborers of the kind that everyone had, and some frictions between churchmen and Puritans or Quakers. Tobacco planters were also at the mercy of unpredictable weather, which destroyed or reduced their cash crop, and of overproduction, which reduced the prices they received when the crop was good. But on the whole the political, economic, and social arrangements seemed to work. At the middle of the century, some of the wealthier planters, mercantile families, and occupants of high government office began acquiring a larger proportion of their labor force from ships engaged in the African slave trade, allowing some trading and planting families to prosper disproportionately. But so long as most or all of the tobacco planters shared the same objectives and hazards, Berkeley's policy of regulating the Indian trade so as to reduce chances of frontier violence and his participation with them in the tobacco economy created what appeared to them to be practical and generally profitable political and economic systems.[8]

The rebellion that Nathaniel Bacon led broke out early in 1676 and was a complete surprise, not only that it happened at all but that it swept up in it a great many people in eastern Virginia—including indentured servants and enslaved laborers and even women—who did not appear to be immediately threatened by its most evident cause, which was fear of renewed Indian attacks on the margins of the western and northern areas of English settlement. Some people looked back and saw obvious warning signs. "About the year 1675," Thomas Mathew later wrote, "appear'd three prodigies in that country, which, from th' attending Disasters, were Look'd upon as ominous presages." The comet that was not yet named for Edmund Halley showed itself in the sky every evening for a week, and everybody knew that comets were warnings of trouble. Another ill omen was an enormous flight of passenger pigeons, which seldom occurred in Virginia. "This Sight put the old planters under the more portentous Apprehensions," Mathew recalled, "because the like was Seen (as they said) in the year 1640 When th' Indians Committed the last Massacre"—the attack took place in 1644—"but not after, untill that present year 1675." And then a swarm of thirteen- or seventeen-year locusts stripped trees of their leaves.[9]

Nathaniel Bacon, the leader of the rebellion and the man for whom it was named, was a recent arrival in Virginia. After a party of militiamen in northern Virginia attacked members of the Doeg tribe in 1675 and drove them across the Potomac River into Maryland and killed several of them, a party of Indians killed Bacon's plantation overseer near the falls of the James River.

Bacon and several of his drinking companions plotted a retaliation that Bacon alone then organized and commanded. Among the drinking buddies who withdrew from the enterprise at an early date was the first William Byrd, who was then building his fortune by marrying into a wealthy family and by engaging in the lucrative Indian trade. That trade very likely involved purchasing enslaved Indians from distant tribes or through Indian intermediaries at frontier trading posts. If Bacon meant to fight Byrd's trading partners or disrupt trading relations, that could explain why Byrd soon backed out.[10]

Receipt in Virginia early in 1676 of news of King Philip's War between Indians and English colonists in New England in 1675 naturally alarmed English-speaking Virginians. Eastern Woodland tribes were certainly capable of launching an organized, large-scale assault on English settlements, but they did not. Violence escalated during the winter of 1675–76, though, in the form of increasingly bloody attacks and retaliations that began with the conflict between the militiamen and the Doegs. The estimates of white Virginians who died during the warfare ranged as high as three hundred. These clashes confirmed fears of many white Virginians about a concerted plan to overrun all the settlements.[11]

Members of tribes resident in or near Virginia may have had more to fear than the English residents did. The Westo Indians, soon to be known for violently seizing control of the trade in enslaved Indians on the South Atlantic and eastern Gulf coasts, were in Virginia in the 1670s and probably were already engaged in capturing and selling enslaved Indians to English planters and members of other tribes.[12]

In fact, Bacon himself posed the greatest danger to frontier peace. The series of attacks that he led late in 1675 and into the summer of 1676 were all against towns of tribes with peaceful trading and treaty relationships with English-speaking Virginians. He had no strategic plan and never attacked any tribe that exhibited outward hostility toward the colony's government or its residents.[13] Bacon acted on occasion like an angry person who was out of control and indiscriminately racing about slamming doors and smashing furniture. In May 1676 he told the governor that he was willing to "goe in the defense of the Country against all Indians in generall for that they were all enemies."[14] Bacon then attacked and killed people at an Occaneechi town near a trading post on the southwestern perimeter. Late in the summer, at the height of the rebellion, he attacked the Pamunkey town deep inside the English settlements and drove its warriors and head woman into the Dragon Swamp.

Berkeley acted indecisively in the face of the fear of a war with Indians that he shared with everybody else and in reacting to Bacon's inconsistent behavior. The governor vacillated between protecting the frontier settlers and not disturbing the generally peaceful trading relationships he had fashioned with the Indians. In March 1676 Berkeley summoned the General Assembly back into session. It created a mobile army of 500 men and authorized the creation of a few posts on the frontier to warn of approaching danger,[15] but the people did not seem able to support anything more. A drought had ruined the tobacco crop, plunging people into debt, and taxes were already high in the colony for two reasons: the governor had proposed to buy out the proprietors of the Northern Neck (the land between the Potomac and Rappahannock Rivers) that the king had granted to a set of court favorites, and the governor and assembly had incurred huge expenses during two recent wars with the Dutch when the king and his ministers commanded that a large fort be built at Point Comfort at the mouth of the James River, even though the breadth of the river and the shallowness of the near-shore water made the fort useless.

Widespread dissatisfaction with the expense of building western posts and raising an army led Berkeley to call for the election of a new assembly to meet in June. There, late in the session, he confronted Bacon in a dramatic scene. The governor literally bared his chest and invited the rebel leader to shoot him. This assembly created a new thousand-man army, one-fifth of which was to be cavalry, and specified how many men each county's militia commanders were to recruit or impress into service. Bacon threatened the assembly members and extorted from them a commission as the general of the new army.[16] The law so named him, and the governor, against his better judgment, reluctantly acquiesced in the appointment. "How miserable that man is," Berkeley grumbled a few days after the assembly adjourned, "that Governes a People wher six parts of seaven at least are Poore Endebted Discontented and Armed and to take away their Armes now the Indians are at our Throats were to rayse an Universall mutiny."[17]

In the end, Bacon's impetuous leadership and thousands of frightened men overwhelmed Berkeley's irresolute prudence and plunged the colony into a full-scale civil war that resulted in scores or perhaps hundreds of people being killed; an uncounted number of farms plundered, including Berkeley's own mansion at Green Spring; and Jamestown, the capital itself, burned to the ground. Most surprisingly of all, once the rebellion began to gather force, men and women who lived close in, far from the outlying settlements where Indian raids were a greater possibility, also took sides with Bacon against Berkeley's government. It appeared that the widespread support of the rebellion involved more than rumors of war. But what? Did all of those people respond to Bacon's appeals as a consequence of some incompatibility between reality and the principles by which Berkeley's long and apparently successful administration had functioned? How seriously were they (and are we) to take the implications of Bacon's public pronouncements against the governor to which he signed himself "General, by the consent of the people"?[18] Bacon was too young to remember the execution of King Charles I in 1649, but most of the responsible government officials in England and in Virginia remembered it. Was Bacon's Rebellion something similar?

Virginia politicians and imperial administrators then and historians ever since have debated these questions. The lists of grievances that men in all but one of the counties submitted in response to the request of the governor and the royal commissioners during February and March 1677 consequently invite attention as a prime source of the colonists' opinions on those and related questions and for understanding their beliefs about their political and social institutions.[19] A very lean summary of what are called the county grievances forms a significant portion of the official report of the commissioners. It is known as Samuel Wiseman's Book of Record, named for the commissioners' secretary whose manuscript copy survives.[20]

The commissioners casually dismissed the complaints contained in the county grievances as "soe few and Triviall" that they could not have set off the rebellion. Instead, they complained, "if the Governour and his Party would leave off their depredations, and Answer to those matters hee by his Majestie is Instructed and by us desired to doe, Wee can see noe urgent occasion to stay a fortnight longer upon the Place."[21] That conclusion, which the commissioners reached after being in the colony for two months and coming to loggerheads in their dealings with Berkeley, indicates that by then they were inclined to blame Berkeley and his adherents for the colony's problems both before and after the rebellion rather than to blame the leaders of the rebellion for beginning it. What the commissioners reported to the king for the most part were complaints about the heavy-handed way in which Berkeley had treated the rebels and confiscated the property of the rebellion's participants afterward. The complaints that a good many colonists individually submitted to the commissioners emphasized Berkeley's violent suppression of the rebellion, which may have diverted the commissioners' attention away from the causes of the rebellion. The summary almost certainly has diverted the attention of many historians away from the county grievances, which were so inadequately summarized in the commissioners' report that their significance and value got missed. Chroniclers and interpreters of Bacon's Rebellion largely ignored them and what they reveal. And the commissioners, too, either suppressed— or more likely missed entirely—the import of much of what the county grievances and individual complaints contained.

One thing that the commissioners did not report, from reading either the county grievances or the numerous personal complaints of colonists, was widespread dissatisfaction with royal government per se. Their report mentioned only one person, Anthony Arnold, who expressed what might be called antimonarchical or republican sentiments. His "Crimes," the commissioners wrote, "were more horrid and heinous, saying that (twas well knowne) hee had noe kindnesse for Kings, and that they had noe Right but what they gott by Conquest and the Sword." Arnold had declared "that if the King should deny him right (or what in himselfe hee thought such)," he would think no more of thrusting his sword into the king's "Heart or Bowells" than of doing the same to "his owne mortall Enemyes." For which treasonous utterances the commissioners ordered as an example to the people that Arnold be hanged from the county's gallows and that he be left there to die and his body to rot.[22]

The first complaint that the commissioners heard on their arrival and the only complaint in the county grievances that they seriously regarded afterward was that the governor had summoned the General Assembly annually, which they said was unnecessary and too often. County taxpayers were consequently overburdened by paying what they characterized as the exorbitant rates of compensation that the assembly members voted themselves for their attendance at the meetings.[23] The second part of that complaint was a grievance that the taxpayers had against their own elected representatives, though, and not actually against the governor or the government. Nobody declared it a cause of the rebellion. The commissioners merely recommended that the General Assembly pass a law specifying that it meet every other year and no oftener and that burgesses' expense allowances be reduced.[24]

The commissioners did not comment on Berkeley's neglecting to call for new elections of members of the General Assembly at any time since 1660, shortly after he was restored to the governorship and Charles II was restored to the throne. Whenever a member of the House of Burgesses died, resigned, got promoted to the council, or moved out of his county, the governor called a special election to fill that seat, so from time to time the qualified men of every county selected a new burgess; but there was no general election for sixteen years. It is unclear whether landowning Virginians or the men who were disfranchised in 1670 believed that frequent elections or frequent meetings of the assembly were important or essential features of their representative government. By the year of the rebellion, though, Berkeley acknowledged that some people felt aggrieved by the long continuance of the assembly—known in the literature of Virginia's history as the Long Assembly, as if it were a counterpart to the Long Parliament of Charles I—and in May when he ordered a general election he stated as much in his writ that the secretary of the colony sent to each of the county sheriffs who conducted the election.[25]

Had the commissioners looked beyond the surface of the county grievances and the personal complaints, or had they listened carefully to the words and paid more attention to the recent history of the colony, they might have come closer to discovering the causes of the rebellion or developed a more sensitive appreciation of the reasons other than fear that drew people into it. But it is entirely possible that the three commissioners were as deaf to the nuances of the language of the common men of Virginia as the old governor was to the voices of everybody. The commissioners' language and that of the political leaders of Virginia reveal that they had a different set of beliefs than some of the people whose voices they did not listen to attentively. The commissioners missed some of what Thomas Mathew called "ominous presages."

The full texts of the largely neglected county grievances, a majority of which have never been published,[26] contain revealing language and descriptions that are as important for understanding the political culture of the colony as for ascertaining the cause or causes of the rebellion. When considered in the larger context of life in Virginia during the 1670s, the documents disclose a number of very important, though not very surprising, things.

The commissioners' report took no notice that the county grievances exhibited interesting similarities and differences that revealed some important information about the complaints and the men who complained. There were standard forms for presenting grievances to county courts, the assembly, the governor and council, or the king in his Privy Council, and for the most part the county statements followed the proper form. Most began in the standard language of petitions, with submissive prayers to the commissioners to hear and grant redress of grievances, but however numerous or serious the grievances, none was in the form of a bold assertion of rights or demand for reform. The men of York County prefaced their grievances to the commissioners with just such a submissive trope: "That being invited by a declaration from the hon^ble his Mat^ies Commisso^ns w^thout favour or favours to make knowne the Greivances wch were the Occasion of the late distractions among the people of this Countrey and astonished at the wonderfull grace mercy good will & favour of his most sacred Matie to his most unworthy Subjects of this Countrey . . ."[27] To the modern reader this phrasing appears groveling, overripe with protestations of love for the king and reverence for the commissioners and the government, but the form itself was and is meaningful. It indicates that people in the kingdom believed that when addressing high government officials, they had to act and speak submissively, as if they had such rights only as the government allowed and that the law and the might of the Crown protected.

Some of the county grievances were signed, some were not. The James City County statement, the first that the commissioners considered and the one with which they compared all of the others when severely condensing their substance into the final report, bore the signatures of twenty men and the marks of eighteen men, suggesting that it may have represented a fairly broad spectrum of white men's sentiments in the county. The document from New Kent County bore twenty-eight signatures and fifty-two marks, twenty-one men signed the statement from Elizabeth City County, and ten men signed the grievances from Gloucester County. Two very similar documents from Stafford County contained the same seven signatures and two marks. The document from Northampton County had eight signatures and two marks. The grievances from Henrico County, Rappahannock County, and

York County each had five signatures. The document from Warwick County bore two signatures and one mark, and the document from Westmoreland County bore three signatures. Two sets of documents from Surry County had no names set to them at all.

On the other hand, the commissioners received from Lower Norfolk County a document formed as a petition to the governor and House of Burgesses. The paper that sixteen men signed and fourteen men made their marks on from Lancaster County was headed "Instructions to our Burgesses Coll William Ball and Major Edward Dale to bee by them presented to the Assembly for redress,"[28] but they or the burgesses delivered it to the commissioners. One document from Isle of Wight County contained one mark and six signatures (next to the signature of Richard Jordan is a notation in another handwriting, "one of Bacons Representatives"[29]) and was also cast as instructions to the county's two burgesses; but in the upper parish of the county thirty-six men signed and thirty-seven men made their marks on a counterdocument addressed to the commissioners, and other sheets evidently once attached to that document contained twenty-nine more signatures and fifty marks. From Nansemond County the commissioners received at least three, perhaps four, sets of grievances. The commissioners' report characterized the substance of that county's grievances differently than it appeared in the transcription that Samuel Wiseman authenticated of an unlocated manuscript and also differently than in the two extant originals, one bearing forty-one signatures and seventy-two marks and the other from "his Majtie Poor butt Loyall Subjects of Nansemond" that had thirty-four signatures and twelve marks.[30] There obviously was a wide diversity of opinion in Nansemond County reflecting divisions within the population, or at least among the white men.

The submission from Accomack County, on the Eastern Shore, bore ten signatures and made an unusual request. Its authors declared that "Whereas wee are Sensible of the vast Charge this Unhappy Warr and Rebellion hath put the Country to: and it must be Expected to be defrayed out of the Country wee desire wee may bee Excluded from all and Every parte of the same (Wee being no way the Cause of it.)"[31] The commissioners received or preserved no record of grievances from Middlesex County, residence of Robert Beverley, one of Berkeley's most active allies in suppressing the rebellion, and they received nothing from Charles City County until the middle of May, after they had already completed the bulk of their report.

Much is not clear from and about the county grievances. Extant records do not disclose who composed and who agreed to the unsigned documents or describe any of the meetings at which the texts were adopted. Nor is it known how many people in some of the counties, or how many altogether in the colony, took part in their preparation. The documents with a few signatures may be texts that some respectable local men composed or authenticated by appending their names, but it is quite possible that the documents with numerous signatures and/or marks of unlettered men represented a wider consensus of opinion than documents signed by only a few men. The presence of the sheriff or his responsibility to circulate the governor's request and to transmit the reports may have influenced what got mentioned and what did not, but considering how many sharp criticisms of local officials the grievances contained, that seems unlikely. The statements of grievance may be fairly understood as embodying the opinions of a substantial number of Virginia men who were not part of the governing circles.

The men who compiled or endorsed the county grievances referred to themselves as English or Christian, never as Virginian. They referred to the Indians they feared as heathens, savages, or barbarians. One of the two Isle of Wight County documents declared the unambiguous "desire that ther may be a continuall warr with the Indians that wee may have once have done with them."[32] No women signed or made their marks on the documents, nor is it clear that any indentured servants or enslaved laborers signed or made their marks. Women, servants, and slaves were undoubtedly not even asked or permitted to take part.

The similarities among the documents impressed the royal commissioners and are certainly conspicuous. Most of the documents complained that the governor called the assembly into session too often and that the burgesses voted themselves large per diem allowances and tavern bills that the county's taxpayers had to pay. Most of the county documents also charged that other unenumerated taxes were too high. The assembly had long placed an export tax on tobacco at the rate of two shillings per hogshead (a cask that held several hundred pounds of compressed leaf tobacco) to defray the ordinary expenses of the colony's government. The colony also provided a large plantation for the governor and a smaller one for the secretary of the colony, the assembly had long since exempted members of the governor's Council of State from paying taxes, and county courts and parish vestries also routinely exempted from taxation elderly and infirm people. Men from nearly all of the counties complained about the high taxes assessed for constructing the obviously useless and ruinous fort at Point Comfort and another that was never even completed at Jamestown; and some of them mentioned other taxes levied for purposes that they claimed not to know, probably for erecting public buildings in the capital and for attempting to buy out the proprietors of the Northern Neck. No set of grievances complained about the land tax, called a quitrent, that all property owners paid to the king or about any of the customs charges and duties that acts of Parliament required be collected at the colony's port of entry. A few men complained that the defenseless state of the colony could be attributed in part to the failure of royal customs officers to collect what were called castle duties, gunpowder and shot that captains of ships were to supply when clearing through port.

High taxes that the General Assembly levied were a common complaint, but the commissioners ignored the almost universal complaints about local taxes. The men of most counties complained about high county taxes and the manner in which the county courts levied them. All of the local taxes were levied at a rate of so many pounds of tobacco per poll, or person: that is, every head of a household and every laboring man was assessed the same amount, and every paid, indentured, or enslaved laborer, whether white or black, male or female, was also assessed the same amount, the employer or owner being responsible for payment. These taxes paid for the construction and maintenance of courthouses and jails, and parish taxes paid the expenses of churches, ministers' salaries, and provision for the poor and orphans. Throughout the complaints about local taxation ran two themes: one was about how high the taxes were without benefiting the people at large; the other was that the manner of taxation appeared to benefit the people with property, the tobacco planters, at the expense of people who owned little or no land or raised little or no tobacco but were required to pay high taxes in tobacco anyway.

Most of the county grievances, particularly the ones with large numbers of signatures and marks, singled out that poll tax as the most serious complaint about taxation and recommended that all taxes instead be assessed on the land that people owned as a more nearly fair method of raising taxes. "We humbly propose," the James City County grievances (and several others) suggested, "the raisinge of our taxes & Cuntry dues, to be by a Land tax, & according to the estate & abillity of the Inhabitants of this Collony."[33] One of the Isle of Wight County documents, perhaps the least literate of them all, also complained about how poor people were at the mercy of wealthy and well-connected people. "Whereas ther are some great persons," their scribe wrote, "both in honor, rich in estat and have severall ways of gaines and profitts are exempted from paying Leavies and the poorest inhabitant being compelld to pay the great taxes which wee are burdened with having a hogshead or two of tobacco to pay for rent" and nearly two hundred pounds of tobacco annually for taxes, and "having a wife and two or three children to maintain whether our taxes are not the greater by such favour and priviledges granted them which wee desire to be safe of by their paying of Leavies as well as wee they having noe necessitie from being soe exempted."[34] The poorest, unsurprisingly, resented being taxed or overtaxed when the wealthiest appeared to be untaxed or undertaxed.

The men from Henrico County, where Nathaniel Bacon resided, also complained that local magistrates acted against the interest of the people and in their own interest. "It is a very great Greevance," they informed the commissioners, "that wee have these many years laine under heavy & unsupportable taxes officially Sixty pounds of tobacco for each tithable for 2 years following. . . . Wee are much Greeved that the major part of the Commissioners of our County Court are men of a Consanguinity, and wee farther Request that noe County or Parish taxes bee levyed without at least six of the Comonalty such as the County or parish shall make Choyse of to sit with the Comissioners when the same is levied."[35] That at least some of the justices of the peace—who were sometimes called commissioners of the peace—were "men of a Consanguinity"—that is, closely related to each other—made their actions appear even more devious and self-serving.

Some Surry County residents likewise requested "that for the future the Collectors of the Leavy (who Instead of Satisfaction were wont to give Churlish Answers) may be obliged to render Account In writing what the leavy is for to any that Shall desire it."[36] Other residents of the same county reported "That itt has been the custome of the County Courts att the Laying of the Levy to withdraw into A privat Roome by means the poore people not knowing for what they paid the levy" and why "theire taxes, should be so high."[37] From Northampton County came a pair of recommendations on that subject: "That no person may be sett tax free" unless by a public vote of a full bench of justices of the peace, and "That our County Records may be free open for Every man to Search and Require Copies as there ocasions from time to time shall and may Require . . . paying the Clerk his Just fees."[38]

In these complaints the language of class consciousness is clearly evident.[39] What was wrong, they complained, was not just that taxes were too high and the assembly met too often, which is what the commissioners heard, but that the class of landed men who made the laws and ran the parish and county governments were unfairly taxing the poor and the landless, who since passage of the 1670 act limiting who could vote were without a voice in selecting the men who levied the colony's taxes. Moreover, because the governor filled vacant seats on the county courts following recommendations from the justices of the peace, no other taxpayers had a voice in who made local government decisions and set local tax rates, either.

These were not new complaints, nor were the differences in perspective between landed and landless colonists new or surprising. The surviving records of almost every county for almost every decade in the colony's history contain evidences of resentment at what some people regarded as high-handed actions by local officeholders and wealthy men who appeared to act as if they believed that they were entitled to govern and to govern as they pleased. The language in which people expressed their resentment and the manner in which the county courts attempted to regulate or suppress the complaints exhibit the values and perspectives of both groups. A few examples may suggest the nature of the differences and also how conspicuous and important the differences were.

In Lancaster County in July 1659, Henry Corbyn, a member of the county court and later a member of the governor's council, hauled John Jones into court and accused him of stating that "he was a[s] good a man as the sd Mr Corbyn." For that insubordination and no other cause, the court fined Jones 400 pounds of tobacco.[40] The following year in Surry County the court took action against Bartholomew Owen "for his Scandalous & Mallitious" statements about Captain George Jordan, "Calling him Raskell & Rogue & short Arsed Raskell & severall other such base tearmes." *Short-arsed* meant low or contemptible, and "Calling him shortarsed & publickly in Company" was degrading to the dignity of a gentleman—a gentleman with the title of captain—and consequently slanderous. When the court rebuked him for insubordination, "the said Owen Replyed Swearing many oaths Saying God Damn him."[41]

In April 1671 in Lancaster County the court prosecuted Richard Price after he drunkenly entered the church in the parish of St. Mary's White Chapel and did "in a rude irreligious & uncivill manner intrude himself into the seats purposely designed & made use off by his Ma^ts Justices of the peace," forcing himself into the seat of the sheriff, "to the dishon^r of God Almighty in contempt of his Ma^tis Magistrates." (The sheriff then was the same Edward Dale who as a burgess in 1677 received the county's grievances.) Local leaders, as was the case with the governor and council in Jamestown, had preferred seats in the church to set them apart, both literally and figuratively, from the remainder of the population. That reminded everyone of who was most important and of who governed whom in the king's name. The "scandall" of a man pushing himself into his betters' pew in church was serious enough that the case went to the General Court in Jamestown for final settlement.[42]

And early in the rebellion year of 1676 in Surry County the resentment of William Spring boiled over when Colonel Thomas Swann sent a messenger to summon him to a meeting. As the messenger related the ensuing conversation to the court, Spring "very hastily, unadvisedly by his looks very malitiously returned ... these words, I Have waited upon his Arss often Enough, I will meete him ... & shall not be afraid to Speake to him for he is but a man."[43] That incident suggests that the county's elite regarded it as dangerous and subversive for a mere farmer to assert that he was the equal of a colonel, that the colonel could as easily await his convenience as he the colonel's, or that the colonel was "but a man," too.

The limits on seventeenth-century speech, and by implication on thought and belief, were very different from twenty-first-century presumptions that words expressing opinions are allowed if they do not incite illegal action. In seventeenth-century Virginia if anybody in authority deemed the words subversively disrespectful, the speech itself and the ideas that it embodied were treated as unlawful. There were degrees of dignity among free men, just as there were differences in degree between men and women and between free men and their servants and enslaved laborers. Suggesting that a man had risen above his natural level or degrading a man below it were both serious offenses because they undermined the social hierarchy that the structure and processes of government reflected and protected.

In the summer of 1668 the Westmoreland County justices of the peace took depositions from several people who heard Richard Cole, a foul-mouthed man who slandered a number of his male and female neighbors, to ascertain precisely what he had said about the honor of the governor, who was a knight of the realm and the king's personal deputy. The court's incomplete records do not disclose what, if any, punishment the court imposed on Cole, who did in the "most Grosse, scurrilous, & obseane Languadge, abuse several persons of Qualitie & amongst the Rest the Right Honor^ble S^ir William Berke-ley saying that S^ir William Berkeley Durst not shew his face in England, And that if he the said Cole were in England, he had better Creditt there than his Hono^r." Several witnesses quoted Cole as declaring that his pimp was a better man than Sir William Berkeley. "I know said hee," a deponent quoted Cole, "the Governo^r Loves a Prettie Wooman, therefore, send Downe my wife, And my Businesse will Goe well Enou^gh, or words to this Effect." Another man swore that "Mr. Richd Cole Did Rayle against the Right Hono^rable S^ir Wil-liam Berkeley in most obsceane and filthy Languadge, saying he was a Loggar-head & a Puppie to call him a ffoole, & that he had fucked him out of twenty five pounds sterling & that he would neither be Kicked nor fucked out of his money by never a Governo^r of Christendome, And since God Damn him he would tell him soe, & many other unhandsome Expressions." Cole's indigna-tion at the governor and council members was also mixed with resentment and perhaps with envy at how they appeared to profit from their honored places, and he "said that he would be a Counsellor, not that he Cared a Turd for it but that he might Act Knavery by Authoritie."[44]

Government officials, wealthy planters, less wealthy farmers and landown-ers, and householders who owned little or no land all had their own percep-tions of their importance to and places in the community, but the disfran-chisement in 1670 of the men who owned no taxable land placed that group at a distinct disadvantage in maintaining that they, too, were responsible heads of households with families and personal interests in the peace and prosperity of the colony. When rumors of war appeared in the mid-1670s, those disfranchised men and overtaxed small farmers complained that the most wealthy and most politically powerful of their neighbors were overbear-ing, exploitive, and abusive and that by their selfish actions they also endan-gered the safety of everybody.

Much evidence for that set of class-conscious beliefs is in the county grievances and in other documents generated during and as a consequence of the
rebellion. White men of all but the very highest and very lowest classes endorsed or wrote documents expressed in a peculiar late medieval English vo-
cabulary. They called themselves the commons of Virginia or the "commonalty" to distinguish themselves from their more prosperous, more powerful,
or more privileged neighbors. Earlier Englishmen and some men as late as
Cromwell's time had used the word *commonalty* to identify people who were
not of the landed gentry or the nobility. The word had begun to disappear
from use in England by the 1670s, but it was in wide use in Virginia because it
was exactly the right word that the lower orders of white residents needed to
distinguish themselves and to define their interests.[45] These distinctive words
and phrases appeared in five sets of county grievances, including in the Henrico County recommendation that "at least six of the Comonalty" be permitted to join the justices of the peace in setting the county levy. Variants on them
or their essence appeared in many other documents, including Bacon's own
declarations that he signed as "General, by the consent of the people."[46]

Evidences for that self-perception can be glimpsed in some prerebellion
events that the contents of the county grievances reveal were in fact antecedents of the rebellion and not merely more instances of unruly behavior
among the lower classes. In Surry County early in January 1674, the county's
magistrates arrested and interrogated fourteen men who had met twice in
December, first in the church of Lawne's Creek Parish and later in a place
called the Devil's Field. The men who attended the meetings readily admitted
that they had gathered to discuss and condemn the method that the county
court had used to assess the taxes they were supposed to pay.[47] That the justices of the peace had them all arrested and interrogated indicates that the
magistrates, who for the most part belonged to the wealthier, landowning
part of the community, believed that it was seditious for lesser men to question or even to discuss their actions.

The two justices of the peace who conducted the interrogations wrote a
preface for the collected documents in the case when they were copied into
the county's record books. Justices of the Peace Lawrence Baker and Robert
Spencer wrote, "Of how Dangerous consequence unlawfull Assemblyes and
meetings have bin, is Evident by the Chronicles of our Native Country wch are
occationed by the Giddy headed Multitude, & unless repressed may prove the
ruin of a Country." The two justices described the fourteen men as "a Company of Seditious & rude people" who by "theire Contemptuous behaviour &
Carriage, not respecting Authority," deserved to be arrested and prosecuted
under the English Riot Act.[48]

The fourteen men (a rather small multitude) discussed how the county's
taxes were levied, and therefore the justices of the peace fined them and

bound them over to appear before the next session of the General Court in Jamestown, at which time, in April 1674, the court fined Mathew Swann, "the ringleader of them," 2,000 pounds of tobacco and required all of the men to pay court costs. The following September the governor remitted Swann's fine "and alsoe the fines of the other poore men," provided that they "acknowledge there fault in the said County Court, and pay the Court Charges."[49] The governor did not so much pardon their actions as mitigate their punishment for the sake of preventing further disorder, and he appointed Justice of the Peace Robert Spencer to the office of county sheriff the following November.[50] That was how Berkeley had governed, keeping order but incorporating as many of the colony's white men as possible into his political orbit and system through obligation or conspicuous shared interest.[51] Not so, the Surry County justices of the peace. That even discussion of the propriety of their actions appeared to them to warrant prosecution reveals a good deal about their values and their belief that they were to be respected. The county's records also do not disclose that any of the men acknowledged fault or paid court costs, which reveals what the other poor men thought about their local government.

This episode sometimes has been exaggeratedly referred to as the Lawne's Creek uprising. It is moderately well documented, but it was not the only event of its kind. In 1674 some taxpayers in New Kent County also threatened to resist collection of the local taxes, and in 1675 Berkeley "appeas'd two mutinies . . . raysed by some secret villaines that wisphered amongst the people."[52] The governor and county officials obviously worried that small farmers and tradesmen might rebel, just as they worried about unrest among indentured servants and enslaved laborers, and also about real criminals. In 1671 the governor's council issued orders against and disciplined ship captains who landed convicted prisoners in the colony,[53] a socially disruptive consequence of English public policy that allowed some criminals to serve their time in colonial servitude instead of in English prisons and that continued with some interruptions until the mid-1770s. The men who governed the colony and its counties made little obvious distinction between the dangers posed by complaining poor men or convicted criminals.

One of the three extant sets of 1677 grievances from Nansemond County, the one that exists only in transcription, included a vivid narrative that brought all of the complaints about taxes and favoritism and the language of class into focus. "Yoʳ Honʳˢ are sensible," they informed the commissioners, "there was a rising in This part of the Country in May last," yet another of what at the time were called mutinies, "occasion'd by the grevious taxations & burthens wee lay under for many years before & to increase our pressures the militia would have Houses built intitul'd Forts under the pretence of destroying the Heathen." The authors of the grievances charged that the militia commanders had directed that the forts "be erected upon their owne lands which wee well perceived would have beene the utter ruine of us the poore Comonalty & only self interest to themselves wee see & knowing the Heathen must be destroy'd by a moving force, and the charge of these forts would have gone beyond our ability either to maintaine or build." The militia command-ers ordered the complaining militiamen "to assemble together," but at that muster the men "roared them down by a generall roar of Commonalty." Com-mon militiamen shouting down commissioned officers! That must have been astonishing and frightening, a humiliating and potentially very dangerous ex-hibition of insubordination. The soldiers must have been very angry, indeed, to be so bold. This episode, which was described in only the one unpublished document, was much more serious than the so-called Lawne's Creek uprising.

"Yet," the men of Nansemond County continued their narration, "our Mi-litia order'd all manner of necessaryes as Axes, hoos, Halborrds, provisions & the like fitt for the worke & seeing ourselves in this sad condition the Heathen hourely expected to come upon us the excessive tax likewise that wee did read-ily account needlesse, and unnecessary," they asked permission to take their case to the governor. The commanding officer prudently "caused us to assem-ble ourselves together and every man to make his complaint personally." The militia commander, either frightened or perhaps cautious, may have emulated Berkeley in giving the angry men an opportunity to state their complaints, as if understanding the principle of the safety valve long before the invention of the steam engine. "And that it might be thought noe tumult," the men's narra-tion continued, "(as God knowes wee were with noe tumultuous intensions) wee chose five men to goe to his Honr." When the men arrived in Jamestown, they learned that Berkeley was away on one of several trips into the interior of the colony to ascertain what Nathaniel Bacon and his men were doing. The men who filed their grievances in 1677 related how the governor's wife "writ to his Honr on our behalfes, and sent a Coppie of the letter downe to us, which was such a Satisfaction to us, that wee every man return'd to his owne home, for his Honr had appointed an Assembly to be on the fifth of May"—it was summoned for the fifth of June 1676—"& issued out Warrants for the chusing Burgesses & every free borne mans voat was hear'd in Election. Against which Assembly wee drew up our Grievances & sent by our Burgesses who gave us great Satisfaction at their returne most of our grievances being satisfied."[54]

The list of complaints that the men of Nansemond County "drew up" in 1676 and that the assembly then "satisfied" is extant. That document is one of several unusual things about the June 1676 meeting of the General Assembly that deserve mention because they have been overlooked or misinterpreted. The discontent mentioned in 1676 and again in 1677 was as important a reason for the governor's calling the assembly into session as the necessity to prepare for an anticipated war. The two causes converged, as the Nansemond County narrative and other events indicate, by an accident of timing.

When Berkeley, who was out west in Henrico County, issued his call for the election of a new assembly in 1676, "for the better security of the Country from our Barbarous Enemies the Indians and better settling and quieting our domestick disorders and discontents," he also requested that "at the Election of the said Burgesses all and every person or persons there present have liberty to present freely to their said Burgesses all just Complaints as they or any of them have against mee as Governor." He promised that he would "most gladly joine with them in a Petition to his Sacred Majestie to appoint a new Governor of Virginia and thereby to ease and discharge mee from the great care and trouble thereof in my old age." Berkeley specifically asked that the men elected to the House of Burgesses "discharge that duty of their owne personall charge for the ease of the Country" and not require the county taxpayers to pay their expenses.[55] As the men from Nansemond County and elsewhere understood the writ for election, they not only had the right to submit all of their grievances to the assembly, they also believed that the governor was allowing all free men to vote, ignoring the law of 1670. He had, in fact, intended just that, and in some counties men disfranchised in 1670 voted in 1676.[56]

The undated document (internal evidence clearly indicates that it was drafted in the spring of 1676) to which the 1677 list of grievances from Nansemond County referred, and which in parts closely resembled that list, was entitled "Considerations upon the present troubles in Virginia with the means by which they may be settled to the great benefitt of the Crowne & the good of that Collonie." It began, "The great oppression the people complaine of is the great taxes Levied on them Every yeer and the Unequall way of taxing them by the poles, for that a poor man that hath nothing to maintain himself wife & child[r] pays as much for his levie as he that hath 20000 acres of Land." The men of Nansemond County, either as petitioners addressing the General Assembly or as electors instructing their burgesses, requested that county sheriffs (who kept part of the tobacco they collected to compensate them for their work) not be permitted to serve more than one year at the time (as in England, and they cited English law on that point). They also complained that the annual meetings of the assembly cost every free person in the county more tobacco than most could afford, not only to pay the expenses of the burgesses but also the 400 pounds of tobacco that the secretary of the colony charged each county for sending out the writ of election. Because of these "burdens the people began to Mutinie in the year 1674," shortly after the Lawne's Creek disturbances and at about the same time that the taxpayers in New Kent County threatened to withhold their tobacco. The authors of the "Considerations" therefore recommended that burgesses and other officials not be paid large salaries, that local officers do their jobs without pay to keep down costs, and that such taxes as remained necessary "be levied by a land tax, which seems to be the most Equall Imposition, and will generally take of the complaints of the people, although perhapps some of the worst sorte wil not like it who hould greater proportions of land then they can make use of."[57]

Another unrelated document, entitled "The Virginian plan for opposing the Indians without the Governor's order" and also evidently composed in the spring of 1676, asserted that the inability or unwillingness of the government to protect the people from anticipated Indian attacks required common people to take collective steps to protect themselves and wage full-scale war against all Indians, even to their extermination.[58] The "Considerations" of 1676 and many of the grievances of 1677, in spite of the submissive form and tone in which they were phrased, bristled with resentment against haughty local magistrates, sheriffs, militia officers, burgesses, and tax-exempt elites. The commissioners' formal report contained not one syllable about any of those dramatic events or serious complaints or any hints that the commissioners recognized their significance.

The incomplete nature of the list of burgesses who attended the June 1676 assembly makes it difficult to know what proportion of the members won election as advocates for local reform, how many as supporters of making war on the Indians, and how many opposed or supported both. Berkeley estimated that only eight of the maximum number of forty burgesses were not part of Bacon's "faction and at his direction."[59] As the 1677 narrative of the men from Nansemond County stated, the reformers elected to the June 1676 assembly passed laws to solve several of the serious problems. The assembly required annual rotation in the office of sheriff; it forbade the holding of more than one local office at a time; it regulated fees and practices in county clerks' offices and the office of the secretary of the colony; it authorized representatives of the people to be selected to meet with justices of the peace when the county taxes were laid; it required that vestrymen in each parish be elected every third year; it rescinded the tax exemption for members of the governor's council; it quashed all legal proceedings instituted against participants in the "many unlawfull tumults routs and riotts in divers parts of this country"; it repealed the 1670 law that limited the vote to freeholders and housekeepers; and it permanently disqualified two wealthy men from Charles City County, Edward Hill and John Stith, from all public offices as a consequence of their bullying behavior and "stirring up the late differences and misunderstandings that have happened between the honourable governor and his majesties good and loyal subjects."[60]

By passing these measures, the June 1676 assembly dealt with much more than fear of war; it fully redressed many of the people's grievances that had fueled the spirit of rebellion. Yet if the laws of that assembly may be taken as evidence that the political system over which Sir William Berkeley presided could respond effectively or even justly to pressure for redress of grievances, that does not explain why those grievances grew to such a height that riots or mutinies took place in more than one-fourth of the counties before they could be redressed, or why, if they were redressed in June, Nathaniel Bacon was able to enlist a great many Virginians in his revolt against Berkeley's government in August.

What happened between 28 June when the assembly adjourned and 31 July when Bacon began issuing proclamations against Berkeley? The events of July 1676, while Bacon and the county militia officers were recruiting the new army, were poorly recounted in the contemporary narratives of events. It is quite likely that the reforms of the June assembly were imperfectly known before the end of July. There being no printing press in Virginia, laws were published by being read out loud to the people, first on the statehouse steps on the day that the assembly adjourned[61] and later at each courthouse when the monthly meeting of the county court took place.[62] If full handwritten sets of the laws of June 1676 were available for every county as early as their respective July court days, which is possible but by no means certain, only those people who were present and sober and paying close attention throughout the long readings of tedious text would have learned precisely what the laws contained. Other people may have learned little or nothing or heard about them only vaguely or piecemeal and therefore continued to nurture their grievances. That would account in part for the appeal that Bacon's declarations carried.

At the end of July, Bacon issued "The Declaration of the People against Sir William Berkeley," the first of his proclamations challenging the right of the governor to govern. The first in its long list of complaints was that the governor "having upon specious pretences of publick works, raised unjust taxes upon the Commonalty for advancing of private Favourites and other sinister ends," and the second was that he had "abused & rendered compemptible his Maties Justices by advancing to places of Judicature Scandalous & ignorant favourites."[63] Those and other specifications, which epitomized the numerous individual complaints contained in the county grievances of 1677, blamed them all on Berkeley in 1676. Without, so far as is known, ever previously complaining much about taxes or local government, Bacon in effect attempted to supersede Berkeley as governor of the colony in August 1676 by appealing to men and women, in addition to the thousand-man army that he legally commanded, by repeating their complaints about local officials' misconduct and stating that it was Berkeley's maladministration that had introduced corruption and favoritism everywhere and also left the colony defenseless.

That is exactly what parts of the belated Charles City County grievances that the commissioners received in May 1677 appeared to state. They recited a number of Bacon's charges against Berkeley and indicated that those charges appealed to "a handfull of poore ignorant and unlearned people, whose unskillfullness in the law, may Easilye lay us open to divers failings." The men of Charles City County, repeating something that the men of Gloucester

County had also asserted,[64] claimed that they were "seduced into beliefe" that
Berkeley aspired to tyrannical government and that he appointed unqualified
sycophants to office, raised taxes to support them, and perverted the courts
and the course of justice. The Charles City County protest also included a
long list of specific complaints about the abusive behavior of Edward Hill,
whom a June 1676 law had barred from public office for those very acts. Berkeley nevertheless had appointed Hill to the command of the county during the
rebellion, and it is entirely possible that Hill obstructed or delayed the compi-
lation of the county's grievances in the spring of 1677.[65]

After it was clear that Berkeley was leaving Virginia and therefore taking
with him whatever protection the governor could supply to Hill, an unknown
number of angry residents of Charles City County compiled and submitted
their list of grievances, which was much the longest of any of the county documents. It was easy for the commissioners and for later readers of the belated
Charles City County grievances, which were unlike any of the others and are
also among the few to have been published, to be seduced also into believing
that Berkeley's misrule was the cause of the rebellion and that he and men like
Hill had obstructed reform.

In the autumn of 1676 when the king issued his instructions to the three
royal commissioners, he required that all of the laws of the June 1676 session
be annulled when the assembly next met, which it did while the commissioners and the governor were getting at each others' throats in February 1677.[66]
Bacon's extortion of a general's commission from the assembly evidently led
the king and his ministers to believe that the entire budget of laws was of Bacon's doing, and the king invalidated them all; but in truth, although Bacon
was elected to that assembly from Henrico County, he did not attend it except to threaten it late in the session. If Bacon had a reforming agenda in June
1676, he never presented it. The laws of June 1676 were not something he or
the rebels imposed on the colony but were instead a redress of grievances in
a legitimate parliamentary manner and with the consent of the governor. In
fact, the burgesses who passed the reform laws and also elected Bacon a general refused to endorse Berkeley's request that they join him in petitioning the
king to replace him with a younger and more vigorous governor.[67]

The 1677 county grievances contained complaints about conditions that
the laws of June 1676 remedied, but these were repealed by an ill-informed
royal edict.[68] Residents of Virginia knew that, even if the king and his royal
commissioners did not. The Gloucester County grievances of 1677 specifically requested "That whereas Their were severall Grievances presented to
the Assembly in June last, in order to prevent many exorbitant fees, & other
Disorders in Governmᵗ upon which, many good lawes were consented to, &
agreed upon by that grand Assembly; before the Rebell Bacon came to in-
terrupt the said Assembly: We beg that those good & wholesom Lawes, may

be confirmed."[69] A similar request in one of the documents from Nansemond County to reinstate the work of their "Burgesses who gave us great Satisfaction"[70] brought from the commissioners a tart response. They denounced it as "Impudent and mutinous to aske seeinge his Majestie has by his instructions and proclamations declared all that assemblys Laws null and void, because of Bacons force att the time upon the Assembly then sittinge."[71]

Englishmen in England and Englishmen in England's colonies shared a long tradition of rioting under stressful conditions. The unrest in the counties in the 1670s and the simultaneous fear of an eruption of warfare in 1675 and 1676 created some of the most stressful conditions during the lifetimes of any of the English-speaking Virginians. The documentary records of the events of the 1670s disclose that in Virginia, as in England, the society and the economy were conspicuously hierarchical, and that it was the haughty and self-serving behavior of county officials against whom county residents had no legal mode of redress that created much of the anger and resentment that gave Bacon's declarations their appeal in the summer of 1676. People at or near the bottom often believed that they had reason to resent people at or near the top, and people at or near the top often believed that they had reason to distrust or fear people from below.

The attitudes of the men near the bottom are readily apparent in the language of the county grievances. The attitudes of the men nearer the top are equally evident in their words. Throughout the seventeenth century gentlemen of high standing regularly behaved and expressed themselves contemptuously toward their social inferiors. Bacon's Rebellion gave them additional opportunities. Listen to William Sherwood, who already was or soon would be attorney general of Virginia. At the beginning of June 1676, he called Bacon's first volunteers "indigent & disaffected persons" and "rabble." Following the appearance of Bacon at the head of several hundred armed men later that month to wrest a general's commission from the General Assembly, Sherwood once again labeled Bacon's men "rabble" and called them "the scum of the Country."[72]

At the beginning of August 1676, Nicholas Spencer, an influential merchant-planter, also described Bacon's followers as "Rabble, of which sort this country chiefly consists, wee serving as but A sinke to drayen Engld of her filth." Spencer wrote that "Bacon in the first place is A knowne and declared Atheist" and that another man was "sd to be A padder"—footpad, highwayman, or robber—"in Engld." He dismissed another as merely "A carpenter who some yeares since run out of Maryld with another mans wife." About Captain Giles Brent, who had led one of the parties in 1675 that attacked and killed Doeg Indians in Maryland and then became one of Bacon's principal lieutenants, Spencer wrote that he was "borne in Virginia his mothers an Indian woman, and he himselfe wholly of theire brutish nature and principles,

who about ten dayes since froliking with his souldiers"—itself a serious criticism of Brent, inasmuch as a good officer then would never have socialized
freely with his subordinates—drank a toast to the Devil "and fired a pistol
upon it to give the devill a gun."[73]

About the time that his friend Berkeley left Virginia, Edward Hill composed a long and indignant response to the Charles City County grievances,
filling both sides of fourteen large sheets of paper. Hill was utterly contemptuous of the men of his county who accused him of misbehavior, and he did
not spare his words even when criticizing women. "Sarah Weeks," he wrote,
was "an Idle infamous slutt to the highest degrees, of robing, thieving, &
whoreing, &c." To be accused by those people was the worst possible insult.
"I cannot but with trouble & sorrow consider," Hill began his response to the
county complaints, objecting "that to be called to a barr, & to be Charged w[th]
Severall crimes & misdemeanors, & clamour'd against by a route of people,
how base, mallicious, envious, & Ignorant soever, it is still a lessening of reputation & darkening of good fame let ones Loyalty, inocency, Justice, & integrity be never so great." Hill also wrote that Sir William Berkeley "by the Judg-
m[ts] of the moste wise of this Country . . . hath been thought to have governed
this thirty odd years wth the moste Candour, Justice, wisdome, & integrity,
that was possible for man to governe, and more especially considering whome
he had to governe."[74]

Berkeley's wealthy close friend Philip Ludwell also described the members of Bacon's army as "the scume of the countrey." He characterized them
as "men, whose fortunes & Inclinations being equally Desperate, were ffitt for
the purpose there being not 20 in the whole Route, but what were Idle & will
not worke, or such whose Debaucherie or Ill Husbandry has brought in Debt
beyond hopes or thought of payment these are the men that were sett up ffor
the Good of the Countrey, who for the ease of the poore will have noe taxes
paied, though for the most part of them, they pay none themselves, would
have all magistracie & Governm[nt] taken away & sett up one themselves, & to
make their Good Intentions more manifest stick not to talk openly of share-
ing mens Estates among them selves." Ludwell also took pains to point out
that not only did Bacon acknowledge no "Law of God or man," he frequently
uttered many "new Coyned oaths of w[ch] (as If he thought God was delighted
wth his Ingenuite in that kind) he was very liberall."[75]

Other contemporaries also commented on Bacon's swearing, a serious affront to the society and the social order then. The governor was a devoted churchman and was especially disgusted at Bacon's swearing. "His
usual oath," Berkeley wrote, "which he swore at least a Thousand times a
day was God damme my Blood"—language that several other witnesses also
reported[76]—"and god so infected his blood that it bred lice in incredible
numbers so that for twenty dayes he never washt his shirts but burned them.

To this God added the Bloody flux and an honest minister wrote this Epitaph on him

Bacon is Dead I am sorry at my hart
that Lice and flux should take the hangmans part."[77]

Berkeley, too, on occasion referred to Bacon's followers as rabble,[78] but for a man who put down the rebellion brutally and was charged with abusing his powers as governor, he was surprisingly and generally tolerant of the people he governed, and to his regret he yielded too often during 1676 to the opinions of councilors and members of the House of Burgesses who represented the colony's people rather than relying on his own best judgment.

Before he returned to England and died, the governor expressed his anger at the commissioners in a conspicuously class-conscious and theatrical way. Berkeley was a playwright and a wordsmith of great ability, and in spite of protests that he and his wife later composed, he or she or they may have staged a small but significant theatrical event. A few days before the governor departed for England, the commissioners went out to his Green Spring plantation for yet another argument. As they left, Berkeley's politically astute wife, Frances Culpeper Stephens, Lady Berkeley, arranged for the governor's carriage and horses to be brought around so that the commissioners could ride and not have to walk down to the river landing to get aboard their ship and return to their lodgings. The colony's common hangman suddenly appeared, ordered the postilion down, and mounted up in his stead. The commissioners were appalled. When they looked back at the governor's mansion in astonishment, they saw the governor's wife peering out an upper window at them. Aghast at being publicly insulted, and by a woman at that—they called it a "trick (wch looks more like a Woman's than a Man's malice)"—they angrily forsook the carriage and walked all the way to the dock in high dudgeon.[79]

That event brought to a close the political career of an extraordinary man who lived and governed too long for his reputation, which the rebellion and his conduct during its aftermath permanently sullied. Berkeley returned to England but died before he was able to explain himself in person to his king. His widow remained in Virginia and made their Green Spring plantation the rallying point for the Virginia planters and politicians who strove to preserve the political and economic institutions and practices that were Berkeley's legacy.

Even though the February 1677 General Assembly reenacted many of the laws of the June 1676 session, it did not reinstate the most significant reforms included in the king's wholesale repeal: restoration of white adult manhood suffrage, authority for the commonalty to participate in levying local taxes, and triennial election of vestrymen;[80] and in spite of all the sharp public criticism of the poll tax, the landowning men in the General Assembly did not replace it with a tax on land. They did not increase taxes on themselves, even though during subsequent decades the men who owned increasingly large numbers of enslaved laborers did have to pay more taxes on that part of their property. The county elites lost or yielded nothing to the commonalty.

During the final years of the seventeenth century, the tobacco planters ruled their households and their colony just as the commonalty of Virginia in the 1670s charged that the justices of the peace dominated the counties. In their households and in their tobacco fields, those men ruled as if they believed that they were entitled to rule, and they governed the colony as if they believed that they were entitled to govern it.[81] The laws that their representatives in the General Assembly enacted exempted them and their prized enslaved laborers from most of the legal and contractual restraints that governed indentured servitude. In the planters' patriarchy that emerged into full flower in the decades following Bacon's Rebellion, whether as a consequence of it or merely as a chronological coincidence, authority of all kinds was conspicuously concentrated in the hands of the heads of households, in the hands of plantation patriarchs, in the hands of the self-perpetuating groups of men who sat on the parish vestries and county courts, in the hands of the influential men who held public office as clerks, surveyors, and customs officers, men who collected large fees and often served for life, and in the hands of the members of the governor's council who received their lifetime appointments from the Crown. There may be a chicken-and-egg problem in attempting to sort out whether the political and economic cultures of Berkeley's Virginia made the creation of the slave economy possible or whether the slave economy shored it up and allowed it to flourish. Either way, that was the origin of the Old South.[82]

The political institutions and practices of Berkeley's time may be regarded as his legacy, for good or ill; but most of them were firmly in place and fully functioning when he arrived in Virginia in 1642, long before the rebellion challenged them. Berkeley undoubtedly strengthened and therefore helped to preserve the central institution of representative government in the colony, the General Assembly that had been formed in 1619, and therefore his legacy contained within it the essence of representative government. There was no representative government at all in the counties and parishes, though, where the justices of the peace and vestrymen ruled as oligarchs. During Berkeley's years in Virginia, those political institutions and practices became a government of the tobacco planters, by the tobacco planters, and for the tobacco planters. Not all men were entitled to take part in the government, not even all white men, and even among those who were, not all were equal; but tobacco planters as a group were more nearly equal to each other than to any other people and were therefore more equal, as George Orwell's pigs later stated, than all the others.

4

THE
GRANDEES OF
GOVERNMENT

John Robinson Jr. (1705–1766) (courtesy of the Library of Virginia) was Speaker of the House of Burgesses and treasurer of Virginia from 1738 until his death and was one of the most talented and formidable political leaders in colonial Virginia. Wealthy and influential, he was also at the center of the largest financial scandal in the history of the colonial government. As such, he personified the political culture of the colony that blended and reinforced personal, family, and class interests with public service. It was he who in 1756 was first referred to as one of the "Grandees of Government."

RICHARD BLAND BEGAN AN ARGU-
ment in a case before the General Court in the Capitol in Williamsburg one
day in April 1772 by saying that "societies of men could not subsist unless
there were a subordination of one to another, and that from the highest to
the lowest degree. That this was conformable with the general scheme of the
Creator, observable in other parts of his great work, where no chasm was to be
discovered, but the several links run imperceptibly into one another. That in
this subordination the department of slaves must be filled by some, or there
would be a defect in the scale of order." That was how attorney Thomas Jefferson recorded Bland's remarks that day when some of the colony's finest legal
minds were arguing about which one of their laws applied in a suit that several
people filed claiming illegal enslavement of their female Indian ancestor and
consequently illegal enslavement of themselves.[1]

Bland was the oldest and most senior member of the elite corps of Virginia men qualified to practice law in the General Court, the highest court
in the colony. He was also one of the longest-serving members of the House
of Burgesses and one of its guiding members, second only, but just barely,
to Speaker Peyton Randolph in respect and influence. Bland was the most
learned student of the colony's history and its laws. He collected and studied
ancient documents, reading and rereading them through his thick eyeglasses.
Known for his studiousness and his spectacles, Bland, according to one of his
neighbors, had "something of the look of musty old Parchen^ts wch he handleth
& studieth much."[2]

The political culture that Bland studied was the one that had survived Bacon's Rebellion of 1676 and flourished in its aftermath. During the century
between that rebellion and the one that began in 1776, the differences between
the governing elites and all of the people whom they governed grew more conspicuous. The great tobacco planters imported thousands of enslaved men,
women, and children from Africa to work their plantations. They built stately
mansions where they and their privileged families lived in comparative opu-
lence. They built new and larger churches where the justices of the peace and
other local notables continued to have their own seats or private pews. They
built handsome brick courthouses where on court day the justices of the peace
ascended to a bench and literally looked down upon the people whose local
affairs they regulated and policed. They built a brick capitol in the new city of
Williamsburg and a stately residence (significantly, they called it a palace) for
the royal governor or his deputy, the lieutenant governor. The wealthiest of

them rode to church, to court, or to the capital of the colony in fine carriages that they imported from England. They raced their finest horses against each other and bet large sums of money as if, or in order to show that, they could afford to lose any amount. They danced formal minuets or lively reels and jigs at country-house parties and at the governor's palace in Williamsburg.

Exactly halfway between the two rebellions, William Byrd II wrote in 1726 what many another privileged Virginia gentleman could have written at almost any time during the previous or the following half century had any of them had his gift of language. He boasted about the benefits that Virginia provided to members of families who thrived and reached the top and to which many others near the top aspired. "We abound in all kinds of provisions, without expence (I mean we who have plantations)," Byrd informed an English earl who never saw the small-scale aristocracy of the colony in its natural setting. Byrd clearly recognized in his parenthetical reference to elites who had plantations that they, not everybody, could thereby enjoy the good life as defined in the colony. "I have a large family of my own," he wrote, "and my doors are open to every body, yet I have no bills to pay, and half-a-crown will rest undisturbed in my pocket for many moons together. Like one of the patriarchs, I have my flocks and my herds, my bond-men, and bond-women, and every soart of trade amongst my own servants, so that I live in a kind of independance on every one, but Providence." Believing that men like himself were beholden to none in their midst and therefore as independent as it was possible for a man to be so long as he had enslaved laborers to do his work, Byrd concluded his biblical trope by writing luxuriously, "we sit securely under our vines, and our fig-trees without any danger to our property."[3]

In fact, Byrd was utterly dependent on his bondmen and bondwomen for his economic security and his social eminence. Without enslaved laborers there would have been no liberty or independence as he defined and enjoyed them. What he meant by being independent of the world was being largely independent of, or not under the control or influence of, men or institutions superior to him in influence or eminence. The ideal, which he described in almost Panglossian language, was of a gentleman planter in complete control of his plantation and financial security, at the head of his household and family, able to indulge his love of learning and the arts, free to move about the countryside as he pleased, and able to enjoy the respect and envy of his neighbors and the obedience of his servants and slaves. He also knew that in spite of his human failings and personal sins, he was a member of an Anglican community that would enable him to save his soul. In the pursuit of earthly and eternal happiness, William Byrd believed that he had succeeded in obtaining that blessing in all its richness in eighteenth-century Virginia.

He was not alone in that happy state, but he and men like him were a select and privileged few. As the population of the colony spread farther west during the eighteenth century, the colonial government tripled the number of counties where men who aspired to Byrd's independent happiness replicated many essential features of local politics that had come up for discussion in 1676 and 1677. The number of prominent men who took part in running the colony, its counties, and the parishes in the 1770s was three or four times the number who had taken part in the 1670s, but the proportion of the whole population who governed was almost certainly smaller. Almost all of the counties created between Bacon's Rebellion and the American Revolution were more populous than the ones that existed in 1676, but in each county the number of justices of the peace remained at most two dozen, often fewer, and of the whole number only a few routinely attended the monthly meetings of the court. Parishes of the Church of England also increased in number, and each had a board of vestrymen to manage the secular and ecclesiastical affairs of the parish. That number was never large, and comparison of lists of justices of the peace and of parish vestrymen discloses that many prominent men held seats on both of the only two institutions of local government in Virginia. From the fairly small population of responsible public officeholders and members of great planter families in each county the voters usually selected the two men who from time to time represented their county in the House of Burgesses. These men were the only elected officials in the colony.

A small number of elite families furnished a disproportionately large number of important county and provincial leaders, and an even smaller number of families was represented on the Council of State. The colonial governor's executive advisory board also functioned as the upper house of the colonial legislature and as the General Court. It was the highest court in the colony, the only court of appeal, and the court in which all serious criminal cases against white people and all of the most important civil cases were tried. The six or eight of the dozen or so members of the council who attended each meeting helped make the colony's laws, served as its highest judges, and guided the course of administration. They used their influence with the governor or the secretary of the colony to have family members appointed to lucrative offices such as county surveyor and customs collector and also to guide through the bureaucracy applications for grants of potentially valuable tracts of western land. As in the seventeenth century, political power, wealth, and access to and control of land and labor remained inextricably intertwined.

The importance of the council was such that a seat on that board was the most desirable and prestigious public office to which a Virginia tobacco planter could ordinarily aspire. The king himself (or the queen, during the reign of Anne) made appointments to the council, usually following recommendations of the royal governor or lieutenant governor but also hearing and from time to time taking the advice of powerful British mercantile houses or powerful Virginia political families. The families of council members were intermarried extensively, and some families had one or more members on the council for several decades. Brothers-in-law, uncles, cousins, nephews, sons-in-law, and fathers-in-law sat on the council together. Twice during the second and third quarters of the eighteenth century the dozen members of the council included a father and son combination and for part of the third quarter a wealthy pair of Yorktown merchants who were brothers.[4]

In the spring of 1714, Lieutenant Governor Alexander Spotswood complained to the queen's ministers about their hasty filling of several council vacancies. In particular he objected to recent appointments of William Bassett and Edmund Berkeley, wealthy and well-connected planters who in all respects were entirely qualified for seats on the council but whom he had not recommended. "I beg your Lordships will do me the justice to believe," Spotswood wrote to the Board of Trade, "that I have not been hasty in filling up the Council out of any dislike to Mr Berkeley, or upon the account of his being put in without my recommendation, but rather to construe it a seasonable precaution to supply the Generall Court, (which now draws near,) with a sufficient number of Judges not allyed to one particular family for . . . the greater part of the present Council are related to the Family of the Burwells. And as there are sundry other Gentlemen of the same Family whose qualifications may entitle them to be of the Council, if they also should be admitted upon the said private Recommendation as Mr Berkeley hath been, the whole Council would in a short time be of one Kindred. As it is now, if Mr Bassett and Mr Berkeley should take their places, there will be no less than seven so near related that they will go off the Bench whenever a cause of the Burwells come to be tryed; whereby there must in all such cases be a failure of Justice, unless the Council (who are by law constituted the sole Judges of the Generall Court) be composed of a competent number of other persons not liable to the same exception."[5]

Spotswood then attempted to appoint men who were not council members to the semiannual courts of oyer and terminer that met midway between the semiannual sessions of the General Court to dispose of some classes of cases that came up in the interims. The General Assembly adamantly refused to allow him to circumvent their law that designated council members as the only appellate judges. Such was the influence of the most wealthy and politically powerful families in Virginia that both royal governors and their resident deputies could be obstructed or outmaneuvered and rendered ineffective or possibly dismissed from office.

A majority of the council members united early in the eighteenth century to petition for the removal from office of Governor Francis Nicholson. He had presided over the colony as lieutenant governor from 1690 to 1692 and returned as governor late in 1698. Nicholson was a talented man who had helped found the College of William and Mary and designed the new capital,

Williamsburg. He was also short-tempered and imperious, and during his second administration he alienated so many influential Virginia political leaders that they were partly responsible, and probably believed that they were entirely responsible, for his recall in 1705. A decade later council members again united and tried to force Spotswood from office. When Spotswood was finally replaced in 1722, it was probably more a consequence of his having lost support from patrons in England, but in both instances the leading men of Virginia believed that they were capable of breaking a royal governor. One of them, James Blair, a longtime council member and also president of the College of William and Mary, was later thought to be able to turn the trick himself, so that when he boarded a ship for England, the resident governor had might as well begin packing his trunks.[6]

Royal governors of Virginia, or their lieutenants who usually governed in their stead, had surprisingly little actual political power except the power of persuasion and the authority that they had by virtue of royal commissions to veto bills that the General Assembly passed. Even though in law the governor, in the Crown's name, appointed the justices of the peace and the county sheriffs who ran the counties, in fact he appointed to vacancies on the county courts the men whom the sitting justices recommended, and he appointed sheriffs in the same way. The General Assembly circumscribed his ability to use appointment of a man to the lucrative office of sheriff as a way of currying favor with members of the House of Burgesses because the assembly required that any burgess appointed sheriff had to resign. He could run for reelection, but the governor could not be certain that a man would be beholden to him or that the county's voters would return the new sheriff to the assembly. So, too, with official inspectors at the tobacco warehouses. Governors and their deputies also complained that the choicest and most profitable patronage positions remained in the gift of the secretary of the colony, who held his office by royal patent and who appointed all of the county clerks and as their patron received a percentage of their fee income. County surveyors, who often became wealthy landowners while holding office, received their licenses from the College of William and Mary, not from the governor.

The British practice of awarding lucrative royal appointments (including the governorship) to men who chose to reside in Great Britain, drawing large salaries and collecting fees while deputies did the work, also operated to the disadvantage of public administration in the colony. Powerful members of the council disapproved of the practice, too, because it undercut their political positions. In 1741 council member William Byrd II, who was as wealthy and as well connected by marriages as almost any man in Virginia, issued a warning to a friend of the absentee royal governor, the earl of Albemarle. So powerful were the Virginia politicians, himself included, Byrd wrote, that the resident lieutenant governor "will not have the least influence with our assemblys, if he cant make friends by the skillfull distribution of the few places that have always been in his gift. All other arts of perswasion are empty and vain, and my Lord may as well send over his picture as a lieutenant governour, who has it not in his power to gain over men of figure and interest in the country."[7]

It was in the House of Burgesses during the eighteenth century that the Virginia politicians most conspicuously exhibited their talents and independence. None was more talented and powerful than John Robinson Jr., who was Speaker of the House from 1738 until his death in 1766. He was from a wealthy family of tobacco planters and was related through his three marriages and by the marriages of his near relatives to most of the other leading political families, and his father was a member of the governor's council until he died in 1749. By force of personality, talent, and knowledge of parliamentary procedure, Robinson became the dominant figure in the House of Burgesses and in the colony. He presided over the House with commanding dignity and named allies to influential leadership positions on the most important committees. He also on occasion had an ally move that the members resolve themselves into a committee of the whole house. Then, the ally would preside as chair of the committee, and Robinson would descend to the floor and sit among the other burgesses where he directed the debate and proceedings, sometimes instructing members about making motions or replying to questions, sometimes taking part in the debates himself, shouting objections, or even prodding members with his cane to play their assigned supporting roles.[8]

During most of his tenure as Speaker of the House of Burgesses, Robinson was also treasurer of the colony. Royal appointees collected the customs and quitrents and other revenue of the Crown, but the General Assembly created the office of colonial treasurer to manage the funds that it raised through taxation or appropriated by law. Each session of the assembly passed a law to appoint the Speaker to the office of treasurer. To support the dignity of the office of Speaker of the House and in lieu of a salary, the laws permitted the treasurer to retain a stated percentage of all the money that passed through the treasurer's office. The wealthy and influential Robinson consequently became more wealthy and more influential. He and all of the other public officials who handled public money (sheriffs, county clerks, surveyors, tobacco inspectors, and the like) received fees regulated by law or a percentage of the tobacco notes or money that they handled while doing their work. They kept all of the money and used it as their own until required to pay it to a superior authority. There was no authority superior to Speaker Treasurer John Robinson Jr. except the committees of burgesses who from time to time made perfunctory examinations of the office accounts and always reported that they were in perfect order.

During the decades when the offices of Speaker and treasurer were thus united, the Crown repeatedly instructed its governors and lieutenant governors in Virginia to separate the two offices to lessen the possibility of corruption and to prevent any man not holding an office in the gift of the Crown from accumulating too much political influence. But so popular and powerful was Robinson that not one of them, not even the most popular and able, Sir William Gooch and Francis Fauquier, even tried.[9] The example of Robinson's political power and his staying power was a conspicuous and enduring symbol of the political culture of colonial Virginia at its prime.

It was therefore the Williamsburg town house of John Robinson Jr., not the governor's palace, where John Kirkpatrick first went when he rode down to the capital in August 1756 to pick up the payroll and expense money for George Washington's frontier regiment that was attempting to guard the people of northwestern Virginia from their French and Indian enemies. The General Assembly, not entirely trusting Lieutenant Governor Robert Dinwiddie with managing the money that it raised for paying and equipping the army, had created a committee of burgesses to oversee the fund. Robinson was the chair of the committee, and without him and a quorum of committee members, Kirkpatrick could not receive the money that Washington had sent him to collect; but when Kirkpatrick arrived in Williamsburg, Robinson was not there. "The Speaker was from home when we call'd," Kirkpatrick explained the delay to Washington, "its Said on Courtship of Miss Chiswell—and only came to town last night—today he proposes a Committee, but the uncertainty of Collecting a Sufficient Number is so great that I fancy, this day Will Stand a Blank in Business—& then we can expect, he says, no Committee before Tuesday—However we must assume patience, and waite the Conveniency of the Grandees of Government."[10]

Kirkpatrick's frustration would not have surprised the men who back in 1677 complained about how sheriffs and justices of the peace ran the county governments. That was how the government operated at all levels at all times, and the local grandees also stood to profit from it. It was far from a perfect system, and the journals of the House of Burgesses contain numerous references to sheriffs who were in arrears in their accounts or who failed to pay what they owed to the treasurer. Unlike the receiver general and the auditor general of the royal revenues, whom the governor and the treasury and customs officials back in England oversaw, only the General Assembly and the treasurer oversaw the sheriffs and other local officers, and the burgesses did not adequately oversee their own treasurer.

After Robinson died in 1766, an examination of his accounts disclosed that he was in arrears to the colony in the stupendous sum of more than £100,000 sterling. When financing the war during which Kirkpatrick had his difficulties, the General Assembly not only created the committee that Robinson chaired; it also emitted a large sum of paper money that government officers paid to provisioning agents, soldiers, and others. The law specified that the paper money could be used to pay taxes that were levied to support the war and that after the paper bills entered the office of the treasurer, he would burn them to retire the currency from circulation and extinguish the colony's obligations. Instead, Robinson intermingled the paper money with all of his other public and private funds and quietly lent large sums of that money to friends and political supporters. He lent some very large sums, indeed, and also lent money to some political adversaries, so that he stood to earn interest and influence even as he frustrated the anti-inflationary intention of the law that required destruction of the bills.[11]

The discovery of the scandal proved that the Crown had been right in urging that the offices of Speaker and treasurer be separated. It was the largest financial scandal in the history of the colony. The committees of burgesses who approved Robinson's faulty accounts were implicated in protecting one of their own and also of protecting themselves because most of them were beneficiaries of Robinson's largesse and were also his political allies and supporters. The webs of political life for the men of Virginia were a tangle of family, financial, and personal connections that reinforced one other.

Down at the county and parish levels, the justices of the peace and vestrymen created corresponding polities and tangled webs. Except on rare occasions when necessity required a board of vestrymen to be replaced, and then a local election took place, the vestrymen and the justices of the peace in effect named their own successors. The only occasion on which any men had a voice in government was when they petitioned the county court, the General Assembly, or the governor for some special favor, such as moving the county seat or authorizing a toll ferry, or when from time to time they met to elect each county's two members of the House of Burgesses.

Free white men who owned a certain minimum amount of land, or in the towns of Norfolk and Williamsburg owned a town lot of a certain size, and some who held long-term leases on land remained the only Virginians permitted to vote. That right to take some part in government continued to be tied directly to landownership. Even the almost depopulated old capital on Jamestown Island was still entitled to send one member to the House of Burgesses even though no more than a small handful of white men lived or voted there. The president and professors of the College of William and Mary, being in possession of a royal charter that created a corporation, another kind of valuable property, were also allowed to elect one burgess. They did not elect one of their own, however, but preferred to chose a member of the board of visitors or on several occasions the colony's attorney general. Otherwise, it was still the tobacco planters who voted, and by the middle of the century, their representatives in the General Assembly had modified the election laws to permit any man who owned property in more than one county to vote in either or both or all of the counties in which he owned property and to be eligible to serve in the assembly as a representative of a county where he owned land but did not reside. Ownership of land was the most important qualification for office, not residence among the people whom the burgesses represented. George Washington's first service in the House of Burgesses was as a representative of Frederick County where he owned land, not of Fairfax County where he lived.

Calculations from tax and voting records suggest that during the middle decades of the eighteenth century about two-thirds to three-quarters of the adult white males in Virginia may have owned enough land to qualify to vote and that at any given election half to three-quarters of the qualified men may have actually voted.[12] Evidence also suggests that during those decades the proportion of adult white men who owned enough land to qualify slowly but steadily declined. Moreover, during the same decades other records disclose a slow and steady decline in the number of candidates for the House of Burgesses, the number of close elections, the number of contested results, and the number of incumbents defeated, with a corresponding rise in the length of legislative service of burgesses who chose to stand for reelection.[13] Whether participants were aware of those trends is unclear. It is also unclear whether, if they were, they might have viewed the trends with satisfaction as suggesting that men qualified to vote were well-enough pleased with the functioning of the colony's government not to agitate for change even as the number of men who took part in its governance declined.

The eligible voters who appeared at the courthouse on election day voted viva voce, that is, each announced his vote out loud in the presence of everyone. The election was entirely public in that the candidates and the voters were all there, and everybody knew who everybody else voted for. Personal, family, and financial ties no doubt weighed with the voters in the decisions that they made, but on most occasions matters of public policy did not. It was improper for candidates to promise to vote for or against any particular measure if elected (a few members-elect got expelled for doing so), so a man's chances of being elected depended largely on his personal reputation and connections within the community. Politics was therefore a very personal matter, and local standing in the community was a matter of great significance. By law, candidates were not allowed to try to influence voters in any way, certainly not by bribery or offering favors, but they easily got around that part of their own law by putting out bowls of rum punch for everybody who showed up on election day without regard to whether they could vote or who they voted for.[14] Election day, far from being a solemn event, was often much like a fair, insomuch that in 1765 somebody described one of the candidates as "swilling the planters with bumbo."[15]

Those political and governmental institutions and practices evolved during the seventeenth century and were firmly in place for the most part by 1705 when the General Assembly completed its first major overhaul of the colony's statutes in decades. The revisal of 1705 is also notable because it collapsed all of the earlier laws relating to slavery and servitude into the colony's first slave code, an entirely new body of law unlike anything in English statute or common law. It was, in fact, a legal dispute about the meaning of one clause in that act that brought on the 1772 court case in which Richard Bland described the natural hierarchical character of civilized society. At the time of the revisal, the planters and merchants of the colony were entering the busiest epoch of the Virginia slave trade, importing thousands of men, women, and children from Africa to labor in the fields of Virginia under the new slave code. Three decades after Bacon's Rebellion and seven decades before the American Revolution, all of the legal, political, economic, and social institutions of colonial Virginia were fully developed and in operation. Thereafter they changed very little. That was the political culture that Richard Bland knew, and no other.

It was purely coincidental that 1705 was the year that the assembly completed the important revisal of the laws, that the grandees rejoiced in Nicholson's recall, that John Robinson Jr. was born, and that Robert Beverley (son and namesake of the man who had helped Governor Sir William Berkeley suppress Bacon's rebels) published the first book-length history of the colony, the first history of Virginia by a native. In it he described himself, curiously, as an Indian.[16] That is, he and his contemporaries did not think of themselves, as the men of his father's generation had done, primarily as Englishmen residing in Virginia or as Christians residing among the heathen. Beverley's choice of the word *Indian* seems strange, but it signified that he was not an English man in Virginia but a Virginian.

Subsequent generations of white men, like Bland, and the other men who thought of themselves as Virginians, not as Indians or as English men in Virginia, had to defend their political institutions and practices beginning in the 1750s. In defending them, they also explained them. As Bland stated in the 1772 court case, the society was hierarchical, in keeping with the natural laws of God. The political institutions were also imbued with constitutional legitimacy in keeping with the constitutional and common law of England. At each stage of his explanations, and to greater or lesser degrees in the explanations of other defenders of Virginia's political culture, he adduced political, parliamentary, and legal precedents for the Virginia rights and practices that he defended. Once established, the practices and precedents became permanent parts of the colony's constitution, a constitution that precisely like the celebrated English constitution was to be found in written charters, laws, judicial precedents, and long-agreed-upon practices. The practices and institutions all had origins back in the seventeenth century and evolved without the participation of Parliament, when the king and his ministers had allowed Englishmen in Virginia to develop such institutions and practices as they required, so long as they were generally consistent with English institutions and practices. That long continuance with the silent or express approval of the Crown created, so far as attorneys and politicians in Virginia were concerned, a constitutional law of the colony in the English common-law tradition, exactly in the same way that the common law of England had arisen. Necessary measures and institutions, if just and enduring, gained legitimacy by being obeyed and relied on.

Virginians were not unusual among English-speaking colonists in North America in their understandings about the independent constitution of their colony. Those beliefs were widely shared along the east coast of North America.[17] To use a maxim of English common law that was already hundreds of years old by the eighteenth century, the political institutions and practices of Virginia and the other colonies were legitimate and constitutional because all lawful authorities had allowed them to remain the same for so long that "the memory of man runneth not to the contrary."

The challenges to Virginia's political institutions and practices that required men like Richard Bland to defend and explain them came from different sources: from the king's lieutenant governor, from members of the clergy in the colony, and from Parliament.

It began in 1752 not long after the adjournment of a session of the General Assembly. Lieutenant Governor Robert Dinwiddie announced that he was instituting a new fee, a charge of one pistole (a Spanish coin then worth £1 2s. 6d. in the colonies) for affixing his signature and the seal of the colony to land grants. The governor of Virginia was one of only a few royal governors in North America who did not collect such a fee, so before Dinwiddie assumed office he sought an amendment to his royal instructions to allow him, with the consent of the council, to impose the fee for the benefit of himself and the royal treasury. The members of the council had seen the royal instructions and approved the lieutenant governor's imposition of the fee.

Members of the House of Burgesses had not seen the instructions and did not approve, but they could do nothing about it until the lieutenant governor summoned them back into session on other business eighteen months later. Then they complained, demanded an explanation, and refused to accept Dinwiddie's assertion that his instructions and the royal prerogative authorized him to institute a new fee for performing one of his duties. If Dinwiddie had a reasonable need for revenue, the burgesses replied, he could have asked the General Assembly to provide money or to authorize the new fee by statute. No governor or lieutenant governor or any other official, royal appointee or not, had attempted to impose a new fee or charge on the people of Virginia since Governor Francis Howard, Baron Howard of Effingham, in the 1680s. For reasons entirely unrelated to legal or constitutional considerations in the colony, the Crown had quashed that fee. The burgesses therefore asserted in the 1750s that the members of the General Assembly as the sole representatives of the planters and taxpayers of Virginia were the only people constitutionally empowered to impose a fee or tax on the people of the colony.

The House of Burgesses directed the colony's treasurer, John Robinson Jr., to pay out of the colony's revenue all of the expenses of sending the attorney general, Peyton Randolph, to London to engage counsel there and attempt to persuade the king and his Privy Council to disallow the pistole fee on the grounds of the precedent established by the disallowance of Effingham's fee. Bland drafted a statement of the case that may have been published in an issue of the Williamsburg *Virginia Gazette* that does not survive. A copy of his draft survives among the papers of Thomas Jefferson in the Library of Congress. When it was printed in 1891, it acquired the title *A Fragment on the Pistole Fee, Claimed by the Governor of Virginia, 1753.*

"The Rights of the Subject are so secured by Law," Bland wrote, "that they cannot be deprived of the least part of their property without their own consent Upon this Principle of Law, the Liberty & Property of every Person who has the felicity to live under a British Government is founded the Question then ought not to be about the Smallness of the demand but the Lawfulness of it For if it is against Law the same Power which imposes one Pistole may impose an Hundred and this not in the one instance only but in every Case in which this Leviathan of Power shall think fit to exercise its authority."

Bland sought for and found a useful simile. "Liberty & Property," he wrote, "are like those precious Vessels whose soundness is destroyed by the least flaw and whose use is lost by the smallest hole. Impositions destroy their Beauty nor are they to be Soldered by patch-work which will always discover and frequently widen the original Flaw.

"This shews the Iniquity of every measure which has the least tendency to break through the legal Forms of Government and the expediency nay the necessity of opposing in a legal way every attempt of this sort which like a small spark if not extinguished in the beginning will soon gain ground and at last blaze out into an irresistable Flame."[18]

The members of the House of Burgesses, Bland's fragment, and the arguments of the attorney general and the legal counsel he hired in London all made the same point, that the Crown had established a precedent when disallowing the fee that Effingham had tried to establish and that therefore only the General Assembly had legal and constitutional authority to tax the residents of Virginia or to create new fees. The legal counsel that Dinwiddie and the council hired relied instead on the preservation of the royal prerogative and the king's instructions to the governor and ridiculed the very idea that the House of Burgesses could even dispute the lieutenant governor's action. "The King," one of them (the king's own attorney general) argued, "has an absolute Right to all the Lands in this Colony, & may dispose of them as he pleases;

without the Controul of any Power whatsoever; without the leave of *this little Assembly,* who, because they now enjoy the Happiness of a mild Government, have presumed to demand *that as a matter of Right,* which was heretofore indulged them only as a favour." The governor's other counsel was equally condescending and ridiculed the assembly itself. "This little Assembly," he sniffed, "this puny House of Burgesses have boldly dared to do, what the House of Commons in England never presumed to Attempt."[19]

The Privy Council issued a compromise decision that sustained the right of Dinwiddie to charge the fee but refused to allow him to receive the fee for land grants that were already made out but remained unsigned at the time that he instituted the fee. It also restored Peyton Randolph to the office of attorney general, which the lieutenant governor's counsel insisted he had forfeited by leaving Virginia without Dinwiddie's consent and by opposing the lieutenant governor's exercise of a delegated portion of the royal prerogative, by the effrontery of objecting to the lieutenant governor's exercise of the king's power.

The men who lived in England and the men who lived in Virginia had dramatically different and equally strong opinions about the nature of the House of Burgesses and the authority of the Virginia General Assembly, reminiscent of the differences of opinion between the men who governed and the men who were governed in the colony back in the 1670s. In the 1750s the grandees of government and many other Virginians expressed their opinions with what was probably the first political slogan in the colony, one that concisely summarized their understanding of the origins and nature of their rights. The president of the College of William and Mary, William Stith, coined it in a very public toast that deeply offended Dinwiddie. Stith raised his glass and proposed, "Liberty and Property and no Pistole."[20]

The second challenge came from a small number of Virginia clergymen. In 1755 and 1758 when drought severely reduced tobacco harvests, the General Assembly passed temporary laws allowing financial obligations owed in tobacco to be paid in money at a rate approximating two pence per pound of tobacco. The colony's clergymen objected to the so-called Two-Penny Acts because their salaries were legally set at 16,000 pounds of tobacco and cask per year, and at a rate of two pence per pound rather than at the temporarily high market price of tobacco, they stood to lose considerably in the amount that their annual salary payments were worth. Following passage of the 1758 law, some of the clergymen appealed to the Privy Council to have the king invalidate it, arguing that the act effectively amended the salary law that had already received royal approval and did not contain the mandatory clause suspending its operation until the king could review it. The king declared it invalid from the date of its passage.

Royal disallowance of bills that the General Assembly had passed often frustrated colonial legislators, and legislative leaders argued that the assembly had and should have constitutional authority to legislate for the good of the whole colony if an emergency did not allow time for the king to be consulted. During the five years in which the appeal to the Privy Council and the associated public debates slowly poisoned the political atmosphere in Virginia, Richard Bland and Landon Carter, another prominent member of the House of Burgesses, engaged in a spirited pamphlet debate with John Camm, the clergyman who organized opposition to the second Two-Penny Act. The bitter personal animosity that filled the pages of their printed texts might have diverted attention from the constitutional issues, but both of Bland's two extended publications contained full historical and legal accounts of the operations of the Church of England in Virginia and justifications for the necessity and legitimacy of the assembly's Two-Penny Acts.

The first of Bland's tracts was a pamphlet printed in Williamsburg in 1760, *A Letter to the Clergy of Virginia, in Which the Conduct of the General-Assembly is Vindicated, Against the Reflexions Contained in a Letter to the Lords of Trade and Plantations, From the Lord-Bishop of London.* The bishop had accused the assembly of allowing lay vestries to exercise excessive ecclesiastical power in the colony, and he had written that the assembly had illegally and improperly reduced the income of the clergymen.

"By an Act of Assembly, made so long ago as the Year 1642," Bland began his account of the history of the church in the colony, "which was revised and re-enacted in the Year 1662," the church had prospered under the care of the General Assembly and the responsible supervision of parish vestries, all without the assistance of Parliament or the bishop.[21] Lay government of the church in Virginia worked very satisfactorily, so far as the grandees of government were concerned. Bland also argued that the Two-Penny Acts were not intended specifically to harm the clergymen because they applied to all Virginians alike. Moreover, if a short-term emergency arose, such as the ones that brought about the Two-Penny Acts, and the assembly could not act for the benefit of the whole colony without waiting for the king's approval, which could not be obtained before the emergency had done its damage, then that interpretation of the king's right to pass on acts that modified existing laws rendered the government in the colony impotent in the protection of its residents. For that reason, Bland continued, the king's governor or lieutenant governor should have an unquestioned right to approve emergency laws, as the lieutenant governors had done in the cases of both Two-Penny Acts in spite of clear royal instructions that they not assent to any bill modifying a law that the Crown had already approved if it had no suspending clause.

"Royal Instructions ought certainly to be obeyed," Bland wrote, "and nothing but the most pressing Necessity can justify any Person for infringing them; but, as *salus populi est suprema lex,* where this Necessity prevails, every

Consideration must give Place to it, and even these Instructions may be deviated from with Impunity: This is so evident to Reason, and so clear and fundamental a Rule of the *English* Constitution, that it would be losing of Time to produce Instances of it."[22]

Salus populi est suprema lex. The good of the people is the supreme law. That was what it all boiled down to, and who but the people themselves, through their elected representatives in the General Assembly, were to understand and provide for the good of the people of Virginia in emergency situations when there was not time for the king personally to be consulted?

In his second pamphlet, published in 1764, Bland expanded on this theme. His second pamphlet was one of the strangest literary productions of the colonial period. Camm had published a fairly scurrilous attack on Carter and Bland for defending the Two-Penny Acts, to which Bland responded with a somewhat clumsy satiric piece in which he pretended to defend Camm against himself and in the process inadvertently exposed Camm's arguments as indecent and indefensible and presented his own and Carter's as sensible and persuasive. The short title of one of Carter's attacks on Camm was *The Rector Detected,* and the title of Bland's second publication was therefore *Colonel Dismounted: or the Rector Vindicated. In a Letter Addressed to His Reverence: Containing A Dissertation upon the Constitution of the Colony. By Common Sense.* None doubted the real name of the author.

"I do not suppose, Sir," Bland wrote, "that you look upon the present Inhabitants of *Virginia* as a People conquered by the *British* Arms. If indeed we are to be considered only as the savage ABORIGINES of this Part of *America,* we cannot pretend to the Rights of *English* Subjects; but if we are Descendents of *Englishmen,* who by their own Consent, and at the Expense of their own Blood and Treasure, undertook to settle this new Region for the Benefit and Aggrandisement of the parent Kingdom, the native Privileges our Progenitors enjoyed must be derived to us from them, as they could not be forfeited by their Migration to *America.*"[23]

"Under an *English* Government," Bland went on, "all Men are born free, are only subject to Laws made with their own Consent, and cannot be deprived of the Benefit of these Laws without a Transgression of them. To assert this is sufficient, to demonstrate it to an *Englishman* is useless: He not only KNOWS, but, if I may use the Expression, FEELS it as a vital Principle in the Constitution, which places him in a Situation without the Reach of the highest EXECUTIVE Power in the State, if he lives in an Obedience to its Laws.

"If then the People of this Colony are free born," he continued, "and have a Right to the Liberties and Privileges of *English* Subjects, they must necessarily have a legal Constitution, that is, a Legislature, composed, in Part, of the Representatives of the People, who may enact Laws for the INTERNAL Government of the Colony, and suitable to its various Circumstances and Occasions;

and without such a Representative, I am bold enough to say, no Law can be made."[24]

"From these Principles, which I take to be incontrovertible," Bland concluded, "as they are deduced from the Nature of the *English* Constitution, it is evident that the Legislature of the Colony have a Right to enact ANY Law they shall think necessary for their INTERNAL Government."[25] Bland also cited an analogy. "The King frequently gives his Assent to Acts of Parliament by Commission to Persons appointed for that Purpose," as Kings George I and George II occasionally had done when visiting their principalities in Europe. The king "does the same Thing by his Commission to the Governour, who thereby becomes the King's Representative in his legislative Character: So that the Governour's Assent, to Laws here, is, in Effect, the King's Assent. But as the King cannot be informed of the Nature of the Laws passed by his Commissioner, while under the Consideration of the General Assembly, he reserves to himself a Power of abrogating them, notwithstanding his Commissioner's Assent; and FROM THE TIME of such Abrogation, and NOT BEFORE."[26]

In the last sentence Bland attacked the propriety, indeed the justice, of the king's disallowance of the Two-Penny Act from the date of its passage and not from the date of the king's action. "The King's Instructions then being only intended as Guides and Directions to Governours," Bland continued, "and not being obligatory upon the People ... it is evident that the General Assembly may pass an Act which alters or repeals an Act that has received the royal Approbation, without destroying the *old Constitution,* or *attempting to bind the King's Hands;* and if such Act is passed, it must have the Force and Obligation of a Law until the King declares his royal Disallowance of it."[27]

That was bold, indeed, for a member of a colonial assembly to lecture the Crown on limits that the colonial constitutions imposed on the king himself. Patrick Henry made Bland's argument into law in Virginia. After the Privy Council disallowed the 1758 Two-Penny Act, a clergyman sued in the Hanover County Court to recover the difference between what he had received under the act and what he would have received at the market price of tobacco. Henry, representing the vestrymen (and therefore the government and constitution of the colony), denounced the clergyman in 1763 as rapacious and the king as tyrannical for disallowing a legitimate act that the representatives of Virginians had every constitutional right to enact for the good of the colony. He persuaded the jury to award the minister one penny in damages. That effectively overturned the king's disallowance of the law because it denied the clergyman all but one penny of what he and the king's ruling stated was his due and allowed him only what the second Two-Penny Act entitled him to, plus the one penny more.

Henry employed the same line of reasoning in May 1765 during the third challenge to the colonial constitutions as the colonists understood them. He introduced into the House of Burgesses and a slim majority in a thin House passed resolutions denouncing the Stamp Act. Members accused him of uttering treasonous remarks when he compared the king to a tyrant for approving an act of Parliament to tax colonists who were not represented in either the House of Commons or the House of Lords. In the autumn of that year, the justices of the peace of three Virginia counties resigned en masse rather than perform their duties under the Stamp Act. The following February the justices of the peace in Northampton County "unanimously declared it to be their opinion that the said act did not bind, affect, or concern the inhabitants of this colony, inasmuch as they conceive the same to be unconstitutional." Bland's arguments about the nature of the Virginia constitution and who could rightfully and constitutionally tax Virginians were by then the common currency of political discourse among most of the colony's political leaders and thinkers; indeed, those ideas were widely shared throughout the English colonies.[28]

The Stamp Act Crisis began a decade of conflict between Parliament and the colonies that provided the occasion for Bland's most important summary of the Virginia constitution and the relationship between the colony and the Crown and Parliament. He published *An Inquiry into the Rights of the British Colonies* in 1766, about the time that Parliament repealed the Stamp Act and passed the Declaratory Act, which stated that Parliament had the full right and power to legislate for the colonies in all matters whatever. With that, Bland could not possibly have agreed. Going back over the ground he had covered in defending the right of the General Assembly to legislate for the good of the people of the colony, he also went back over the ground he had covered in the history of the colonial church to demonstrate that the inhabitants of Virginia had freely immigrated to Virginia and taken with them all of their rights as Englishmen, including the right and responsibility to govern themselves under the supervision of a royal governor but without the intervention or superintendence or even assistance of Parliament.

"It is in vain to search into the civil Constitution of *England*," Bland wrote, "for Directions in fixing the proper Connexion between the Colonies and the Mother Kingdom; I mean what their reciprocal Duties to each other are, and what Obedience is due from the Children to the Parent."[29] He therefore looked to the history of the colony and at the royal charters under which governments of the colonies functioned. Among other instances he adduced (copying an inexact passage from Robert Beverley's 1705 *History and Present State of Virginia*) was the action of the General Assembly in March 1660 (March 1659 by the old calendar), which, on receiving news that exiled Charles II would soon return to England, proclaimed "*Charles* the 2d King of

England, Scotland, France, Ireland, and *Virginia;* so that he was King in *Virginia* some Time before he had any certain Assurance of being restored to his Throne in *England.*"[30]

In short, the colony's tie to the mother country was through the Crown only. The colonies were subject to the king's administration but in most cases not to the laws of Parliament. Because no representatives of the colonies sat in either house of Parliament, Bland denounced the British doctrine of virtual representation—that all subjects of the Crown were virtually represented in Parliament even if they did not vote for members of the House of Commons—as illogical and a violation of the rights of Englishmen that the English men who settled in Virginia brought over with them. He concluded that "there is really no such Representation known in the *British* Constitution and consequently that the Colonies are not subject to an *internal* Taxation by Authority of Parliament."[31]

Thomas Jefferson, who acquired Bland's library and manuscripts after his death, later wrote that Bland's writings, particularly the *Inquiry* of 1766, were the best and most accurate analyses of the historic relationship between Virginia and England. Jefferson himself went back over much of the same ground in his 1774 *Summary View of the Rights of British America,* wherein he refined and expanded on Bland's interpretation of the relationship between the colonies and the Crown.[32] The *Summary View* was a logical extension of the *Inquiry.* Both explicitly denied the constitutional or natural right of Parliament to legislate about the internal affairs of the colonies or to tax the colonists. They asserted that the General Assembly and the House of Burgesses were the equivalents in Virginia of Parliament and the House of Commons in England. By then, though, most people in Great Britain believed that as a result of the Glorious Revolution of 1689, Parliament had become supreme, even over the king, throughout the realm, which left no room for them to sympathize with the position that colonial thinkers advanced about multiple equal legislatures.

In the same year of 1766 in which Bland published his *Inquiry,* George Wythe published a public letter that made a corresponding assertion about the colony's highest court. One of the most distinguished attorneys in the colony, who twice served as acting attorney general, Wythe wrote during a public controversy that erupted after the General Court allowed out on bail a man accused of murder. After somebody pointed out that Virginia law did not permit bail under that circumstance, Wythe wrote, "The Court of King's Bench in England have power to admit all offenders whatsoever to bail, even those accused of high treason and murder. The origin of this power, which cannot be traced at this day, must be referred to the common law." Because the General Court in Virginia was the colony's counterpart to the Court of King's Bench in England, Wythe concluded, "The General Court are, equally with the King's Bench, judges of all high offences. . . . In short, it hath been agreed, and was never contested, as far as I have heard"—the memory of man runneth not to the contrary—"that the powers of those Courts are the same within their respective jurisdictions."[33]

When in 1815 Thomas Jefferson, who had been one of Wythe's law students, wrote about his intellectual debt to Richard Bland and the importance of Bland's writings, he knew that defending Virginian rights against parliamentary assertions of authority had led to independence. Jefferson declared that Bland "was the most learned & logical man of those who took prominent lead in public affairs, profound in Constitutional lore." He praised the *Inquiry* as "the first pamphlet on the nature of the connection with Gr. Britain, which had any pretension to accuracy of view on that subject; but it was a singular one." Jefferson wrote that Bland "would set out on sound principles, pursue them logically till he found them leading to the precipice which we had to leap, start back alarmed, then resume his ground, go over it in another direction, be led again by the correctness of his reasoning to the same place, and again back about, and try other processes to reconcile right and wrong, but finally left his reader & himself bewildered between the steady index of the compass in their hand and the phantasm to which it seemed to point."[34]

Jefferson was not entirely fair to Bland, nor was his depiction of the *Inquiry* accurate. Bland concisely explained the nature of the constitutional relationship of Virginia to Great Britain and the understandings that Virginia's political establishment generally shared in the 1750s and 1760s about the relationship of the colony to the king and of the colony's substantial independence of Parliament. Bland was not a revolutionary, and when he wrote he was not envisioning independence. He was engaged in an act of preservation. Bland did not perceive in 1766, as Jefferson might have begun to glimpse when he wrote the *Summary View* in 1774, that a complete breach might become an unavoidable consequence of the actions they took and the beliefs that they adduced in support of their actions. During the recurring crises and debates between 1765 and 1776, though, Bland almost certainly did "start back," as he had not done in the *Inquiry,* at the alarming possibility that persistent defense of Virginia's constitution placed him and his fellow political leaders on a course that could lead to direct conflict between what he had described as the children and the parent.

Midway between the publication of Bland's and Jefferson's pamphlets, though, the second to the last royal governor, Norborne Berkeley, baron de Botetourt, clearly saw what Bland and the Virginians did not. (In 1768 and again in 1771 the Crown sent over noblemen as full-fledged governors general, no more lieutenant governors as deputies to absentee placeholders.) Botetourt had sat in both Houses of Parliament and looked at the empire from the point of view of the center and not as an advocate of any one colony's interests or constitutional traditions. He understood all about parliamentary supremacy

and fully recognized the implications of the powers to which the colonial legislators believed that they were entitled. "My Duty to the King," he wrote in
a 1769 "Secret and Confidential" note to the colonial secretary in London,
"obliges me to inform Your Lordship, that Opinions of the Independancy of
the Legislature of the Colonies are grown to such a Height in this Country,
that it becomes Great Britain, if ever she intends it, immediately to assert her
Supremacy in a manner which may be felt, and to loose no more time in Declarations which irritate but do not decide."[35]

Before the final crisis in the empire that led the colonists up to the brink
of the precipice again, Bland once more explained another part of the colonial constitution. An episode arose early in the 1770s that produced an appeal to the royal governor to discipline a clergyman of the Church of England.
Had there been a bishop in the colony or for the colonies or had there been
ecclesiastical courts, the case would properly have gone to the bishop or to
the court for resolution. Bland remembered a comparable episode from the
1740s when the lieutenant governor had turned the case over to the bishop
of London's commissary for disposition, but the minister resigned before the
commissary could take action. By the 1770s a succession of bishops had neglected to provide commissions to their commissaries in Virginia, who without commissions could not act. Several clergymen therefore asked Bland, the
keenest student of the colony's laws and history, to advise them whether the
governor could act.

In his letter *To the Clergy of Virginia,* published sometime in 1773–74,[36]
Bland explained that the king's commissions to the governor did not grant the
governor authority to act, and that the absence of a bishop's commission to
the commissary meant that the commissary could not act. Who could? Bland
recommended that the General Assembly do one of two things. It could pass a
law to remedy that "defect in the constitution to the disadvantage of religion"
because it was the duty of the legislature "to remove all defects in the constitution; especially those which affect the established religion. This defect may be
easily remedied either by a law for that purpose, or by a proper representation
to the king, who, it cannot be doubted, would, upon such application, delegate his visitatorial prerogative to some proper person constantly residing the
colony. But if the legislature, or that part of it who call themselves the guard-
ians of the rights and liberties of the people"—clearly meaning the House of
Burgesses—"will neglect this essential part of their duty, we must submit to
the evil, and make the best of it we can."[37]

Bland's suggestion that the General Assembly of Virginia could create an
institution of ecclesiastic discipline and that he suggested it before suggesting
that the assembly make an application to the king to name a proper church
officer was very remarkable. In effect, he assigned the General Assembly a role
for church government in Virginia comparable to the role that the king had

in Great Britain, where he was the sole head of the church. If the assembly of the colony had passed such a law, the king almost certainly would have disallowed it as a breach of the royal prerogative. Such an event would have added another argument in support of a recent proposal to create a bishop for the colonies, and that was not a proposal that Bland approved. "I profess my self a sincere Son of the Established Church," he wrote in a private letter in 1771 when the proposal for a bishop was first being discussed, "but I can embrace her Doctrines, without approving of her Hierarchy, which I know to be a Relick of the Papal Incroachments upon the Common Law."[38] As always, he referred back to the common law and the benefits that its application and meaning had for Virginia's responsible government officials.

Without royal intervention or a colonial tribunal to discipline ministers, the colonial church was left without any recourse when those very uncommon events took place. But they were, indeed, very uncommon events, and otherwise the organization and operation of the Church of England in Virginia needed no amendment, as Bland had gone to considerable length to point out in the 1760s in his first *Letter to the Clergy of Virginia* and in *Colonel Dismounted.* The local parish vestries governed their churches, managed the property of the attached glebes, and took care of the parishes' people precisely as the grandees who served on the vestries wanted, and without a bishop and his ecclesiastical courts. As during the seventeenth century, the Church of England and its parishes in Virginia remained vitally important, central elements of the society's culture, and they furnished its members with a religious outlook on the world that informed their sense of self. So important was the church to the colony that in order to support the church and its ministers properly and to attend to the needs of the parishioners, the parish vestrymen often taxed the residents of their parishes more than the justices of the peace taxed the people to run their counties or than the General Assembly taxed the colonists to run the colony.[39]

Bland's suggestion that the General Assembly might remedy the defective constitution by providing a means of disciplining the clergy is the only suggestion in the corpus of his surviving writings that something might need to be changed in the colony's common-law constitution. That is an indication of how much he believed that the church required proper support, how much he believed in the efficacy of the General Assembly to govern the colony and its residents, and of how he believed it should be governed. That it is his only suggestion for reform indicates how thoroughly satisfied he was with the colonial constitution and its functioning. In sum, for Richard Bland and very likely for most of his peers—the property-owning white adult men who sat on county courts and on parish vestries, voted for members of the House of Burgesses or sat as members of the House—the constitution of Virginia was exactly to their liking. It invested them with ample authority to manage their households, plantations, parishes, counties, and colony exactly as they pleased. They extolled the benefits of liberty and representative government but hoarded them jealously and held them tightly to their chests, not yielding them to kings or bishops or majorities in Parliament, but neither sharing them with any other people in Virginia.

Virginians like Richard Bland moved haltingly and reluctantly toward independence, which was not their objective. Their objective was to preserve their political, legal, and social cultures from threats and challenges that came from the outside, from a Parliament in which they were not represented or from a king who conspired with that Parliament; and from within in the form of Indians on the frontier where settlers moved in violation of treaty rights and British proclamations, and also in the form of potentially rebellious slaves to whom the last of the royal governors offered freedom in November 1775 if they would fight for the king and against their former owners. And finally, in 1775 when the king declared the colonies to be in a state of rebellion and outside of his protection, they had to protect their constitution from their king himself.[40]

In August 1774 the first of five conventions that met in Virginia, consisting for the most part of members of the House of Burgesses, elected Bland one of the colony's delegates to the first Continental Congress that met in Philadelphia. At age sixty-four, he was one of the oldest members, and he told John Adams of Massachusetts that to protect American and Virginian liberties he would if necessary have gone all the way to Jericho.[41] Richard Bland, playing Joshua to save the chosen people!

When declaring independence from Great Britain became an unavoidable necessity to a large majority of adult white Virginia men in the spring of 1776, they suddenly had to face the implications of being thrown back into a state of nature, or anarchy, of living in a state without a king, a thing completely foreign to their own experience. It was also a thing with frightening implications for men who studied the history of republics, which had almost all been short-lived and often deteriorated into tyranny. Following discussions about that topic in Philadelphia early in 1776 between John Adams and some of the Virginia delegates to Congress, Adams wrote and published a pamphlet entitled *Thoughts on Government* to assist Virginians scheduled to meet in convention in Williamsburg in May to create a new government. His ideas came from his political experiences in New England which had, especially in its smaller localities, a much less highly stratified social structure and a more egalitarian political culture than existed in Virginia. Adams recommended the New England model that he believed would foster a sense of public virtue, or community patriotism, that would lead men to put the good of the society ahead of their private and personal desires. He even advocated adopting sumptuary laws to prohibit excessive ostentation, looking toward a respectful egalitarianism among the citizens.[42]

Carter Braxton was a Virginia delegate to Congress who had not been a party to the discussions that led Adams to publish the *Thoughts*. Braxton was alarmed that Adams recommended that Virginians make changes in their ways that might undermine what he believed was an entirely wholesome inequality of wealth and also desirable inequalities of political rights. Braxton then published his own pamphlet, *An Address to the Convention of the Colony and Ancient Dominion of Virginia*, in rebuttal to Adams.

"The happiness and dignity of man I admit," Braxton wrote, "consists in the practice of *private* virtues, and to this he is stimulated by the rewards promised to such conduct. In this he acts for himself, and with a view of promoting his own particular welfare." If all men had equal shares in the government, though, men with lesser amounts of property, who would therefore have a lesser share of *"public* virtue," would seek to bring men with greater amounts of property down to their own levels. "Schemes like these," Braxton warned, "may be practicable in countries so steril by nature as to afford a scanty supply of the necessaries and none of the conveniences of life: But they can never meet with a favourable reception from people who inhabit a country to which providence has been more bountiful. They will always claim a right of using and enjoying the fruits of their honest industry"—in Virginia the planters enjoyed the fruits of the coerced industry of their enslaved laborers—"unrestrained by any ideal principles of government, and will gather estates for themselves and children without regarding the whimsical impropriety of being richer than their neighbors. These are rights which freemen will never consent to relinquish, and after fighting for deliverance from one species of tyranny, it would be unreasonable to expect they should tamely acquiesce under another."[43]

In May 1776 the fifth and last of the revolutionary conventions to which Adams and Braxton had addressed their pamphlets, and of which Bland was a member, voted for independence but without an intention of letting loose a revolution. The convention enlarged the army that it had created the previous year, created a navy, and joined with the other colonies to defend their inherited rights. Early in June the convention adopted a Declaration of Rights that itemized the rights of Englishmen in the colony that English men in England had endangered and that required the declaration of independence. They declared that trial by jury be protected, that accused people be allowed to go free on bail pending their trials, that cruel and unusual punishments not be inflicted, that general warrants authorizing broad searches of people's papers and property be forbidden, that freedom of the press not be infringed, and that all men should enjoy the free exercise of religion. The declaration also enumerated some of the animating principles of good government as they un-derstood it: "That all power is vested in and consequently derived from the People that Magistrates are their Trustees and Servants and at all times amien-able to them"; that the people had the right of revolution; that no men were entitled to inherit public office; that no officer had the power of suspending the operation of the laws; and that the legislative and executive branches of government should be separate and distinct from the judicial branch.[44]

Late in June the convention adopted a new constitution for Virginia, for the commonwealth, they called it, to signify a government with no royalty. The new constitution of Virginia placed sovereignty in the body politic and its representatives in the General Assembly where Bland had already located it. The convention cast out of the old common-law constitution the one old element of it, the Crown, that in the end proved the greatest threat to the constitution that Bland had tried to protect. The new constitution radically reduced the authority of the executive and authorized the General Assembly to elect a governor for a maximum of three one-year terms. The constitution also redistributed the combined powers of the colonial governor's council. The convention lodged the judicial power in a separate court system, the exec-utive advisory function in a new Council of State that met with the governor as a plural executive, and the legislative function in a new state senate elected by the same voters who elected members of the lower house of the assembly, which came to be called the House of Delegates. The new constitution gave explicit legitimacy to the colonial practice of the governor appointing justices of the peace only on the recommendation of members of the county courts, insulating the local political elites from supervision, interference, or change. Otherwise, except for depriving the almost depopulated island of Jamestown of its burgess and the loyalist faculty of the College of William and Mary of theirs, the Constitution of 1776 changed very little in the structure and oper-ations of Virginia's political institutions. It left the undemocratic and unrep-resentative county and parish government structures exactly as they had been. The Constitution of 1776 simply and for the most part silently reauthorized nearly all of the other political institutions and practices that had existed in Virginia since long before Richard Bland had been born, during which none of their memories ran to the contrary.

The members of the convention left the franchise exactly as it had been, too. The sixth article of the Declaration of Rights paraphrased the English law that the General Assembly of 1670 had cited when disfranchising men who owned no substantial amount of real estate and then unknowingly para-phrased Speaker John Pory's report on the exclusion from the 1619 assembly of burgesses from Martin's Brandon who reserved a right not to abide by the laws adopted at that first assembly. The article stated in part "that all Men hav-ing sufficient evidence of permanent common Interest with and attachment to the Community have the right of Suffrage and cannot be taxed or deprived of their Property for Publick Uses without their own Consent or that of their Representatives so Elected nor bound by any Law to which they have not in like manner assented for the public good."[45] The new constitution declared, "The right of Suffrage in the Election of members for both Houses shall remain as exercised at present."[46]

Edmund Randolph, who was a member of the convention, later wrote, "That the qualification of electors to the General Assembly should be restricted to freeholds was the natural effect of Virginia having been habituated to it for very many years, more than a century. The members of the Convention were themselves freeholders and from this circumstance felt a proud attachment to the country in which the ownership of the soil was a certain source of comfort." He then continued, "It is not recollected that a hint was uttered in contravention of this principle. There can be no doubt that if it had been, it would have soon perished under a discussion."[47]

The Constitution of 1776 changed very little in Virginia's political culture and its practices, and therefore it probably pleased suspicious and apprehensive men like Carter Braxton. For the time being it also pleased most of the other Virginia Revolutionary leaders. Richard Henry Lee wrote on the day that the convention adopted the new constitution, " 'Tis very much of the democratic kind," even though it was not very democratic. What he evidently meant was that the constitution contained guarantees against what Lee called "the Monster Tyranny,"[48] chiefly in the form of protections against the acts of a king, which the state no longer had. Perhaps he also had in mind the requirement that voters elect members of the House of Delegates annually, as John Adams had insisted, which terminated the royal prerogative of allowing the governor to determine whether and when to hold elections.

The few surviving documents that describe the convention's proceedings do not indicate that any significant number of delegates even thought about whether, or if so what or how, to change the political culture and institutions of Virginia. Patrick Henry told John Adams that *Thoughts on Government* expressed his own thoughts perfectly well,[49] but he did not succeed, if he tried to introduce any of Adams's suggestions into the new constitution. Thomas Jefferson almost alone desired to make some serious changes in Virginia's old constitution and did take action, but it failed in its purpose.

Jefferson was serving in the Continental Congress when the men in Williamsburg were writing the constitution, but he was thinking about change in Virginia at the very same time that he was being asked to draft the Declaration of Independence. He sent a long draft constitution to Williamsburg that if adopted would have made some important changes in the body politic. It would have replaced the two-members-per-county apportionment of the House of Delegates with a number that varied from county to county depend-

ing on the county's population. It would have given voters the right to elect
county sheriffs. And it stated that every man "of full age" who did not own as
much as fifty acres of land was "entitled to an appropriation" of so much land
as was necessary to endow him with fifty acres, the minimum necessary to be
qualified to vote. At that time Jefferson continued to believe, as did other Virginia politicians, that landownership should be the basis for participation in
the government, but his proposal would have made every adult white male in
the colony a freeholder and voter, which would have enlarged the body politic
and made elective politics in Virginia more nearly democratic and certainly
more representative than it had been since 1670.[50]

George Wythe showed Jefferson's draft to a few members of the convention, but they differed in opinion about its provisions and were impatient to
adjourn, so his proposals at that time came to nothing.[51] As adopted the Constitution of 1776 restricted participation in government to the men who had
always exercised that right, to the gentlemen freeholders whose conception of
government allowed no place for any women or for any men who did not own
land. Nor did their conception of liberty and justice lead them into a temptation to abolish or undermine the institution of slavery on which their economic and social lives depended. Neither Jefferson's draft nor the new state
constitution contained a single word about slaves or slavery. In 1776 the meaning of the social contract and the definition of the political nation remained
unchanged. It was still a political nation of, by, and for the tobacco planters,
the same old grandees of government.

Richard Bland lived into the first months of the new era. In the spring of
1776 he leaped from the precipice from which he had repeatedly started back
and as a member of the fifth and final convention voted to instruct the Virginia delegates to the Second Continental Congress to move a resolution of
independence. When he died in Williamsburg in October 1776, Bland was a
member of the first House of Delegates of the independent Commonwealth
of Virginia. He did not live to see that declaring independence would help set
loose forces and ideas that threatened to undermine the political culture that
he better than anybody else had defended and that he as fervently as anybody
else had hoped to preserve unchanged.

5

ALL MEN
ARE NOT
CREATED
EQUAL

Thomas Jefferson (1743–1826) (courtesy of the Library of Virginia) drafted the Declaration of Independence that in 1776 stated that all men are created equal and endowed with the right to life, liberty, and the pursuit of happiness. It is unlikely that he anticipated the consequences of the language he wrote, and it is also doubtful that he actually believed that all men, women, and enslaved people were inherently equal. Yet the words he wrote when he was a young man contain a promise of inclusion in the political nation that animated much of American history and shaped the course of Virginia's history for more than two centuries. A large and influential group of the state's political leaders, though, had not adopted Jefferson's stated beliefs even by the time of his death.

WHEN GEORGE MASON SAT DOWN IN a room in Williamsburg during the third week of May 1776 to begin work on the first draft of the Virginia Declaration of Rights, and when Thomas Jefferson sat down in a room in Philadelphia a few weeks later to begin work on the first draft of the Declaration of Independence, each of them could have begun with extremely memorable words. They could have inked their quills and written, "Four score and seven years ago our forefathers . . ." They did not, but they could have. Four score and seven years later when Abraham Lincoln wrote those words, he referred back to 1776 in order to place in context what he was going to say about rededicating the nation to its historic purpose of creating a government (using Lincoln's economical words) "of the people, by the people, and for the people." Lincoln was a genius that way, in using a few choice words to conjure up rich volumes of meaning. With those words he invoked the history and meaning of the American Revolution and the American nation to set the stage for his plea for a fulfillment of the promise of the Declaration of Independence, that all men were created equal.

Fourscore and seven years was not so long a time. When Lincoln and the men of his generation were young, they had known people who had lived through the years of the American Revolution. Many of their grandfathers had fought in that war, and the father of General Robert E. Lee had been one of its authentic heroes. Lincoln was speaking to people whose extended family memories included the experience of the American Revolution. Through his words they understood all that they knew and all that they needed to know about the ideas on which the nation had been founded. It would have been odd, in fact, had Lincoln begun his rededication of the nation without a clear reference to what many people of his generation believed were the cardinal tenets of its founders.

Fourscore and seven years was not so long a time when George Mason and Thomas Jefferson wrote in 1776, and they could have begun with the very same words and for the same reason, to invoke the essential legacy of the Glorious Revolution of 1688 and the adoption in 1689 of the English Bill of Rights to explain the steps that they were taking to preserve English liberty in Virginia and the other American colonies. When Mason and Jefferson and the men of their generation were young, they had known people who had lived through the years of that earlier revolution, when Parliament expelled a king from the country and invited William and Mary onto the throne. Parliament and the new king and queen adopted the Bill of Rights, a landmark statement of the liberties of freeborn Englishmen. By opening with the words "Four score and seven years ago," Mason and Jefferson could have reminded their readers of all that they knew and all that they needed to know about their shared heritage of English liberty; and in Virginia they would have thereby reminded everyone of the political culture that had evolved there during the previous one and two-thirds centuries and that the colony's leading men had been defending and explaining for a quarter of a century.

Instead, Mason and Jefferson began with very different language that became equally memorable but had consequences that neither of them, nor any of the other men who voted to adopt the language that they wrote, ever imagined. The first sentence of Mason's first draft for the Virginia Declaration of Rights read, "That all Men are born equally free and independant, and have certain inherent natural Rights, of which they can not by any Compact, deprive or divest their Posterity; among which are the Enjoyment of Life and Liberty, with the Means of acquiring and possessing Property, and pursueing and obtaining Happiness and Safety."[1] The second sentence of Jefferson's Declaration of Independence as adopted began, "We hold these truths to be self-evident, that all men are created equal, that they are endowed by their Creator with certain inalienable Rights, that among these are Life, Liberty, and the pursuit of Happiness . . ."[2] The drafts that Mason and Jefferson prepared were similar in other important ways, and because Jefferson almost certainly saw a copy of Mason's original language, Mason's words may have helped Jefferson shape his.

The decision of the delegates at the last of the five conventions that met in Virginia between August 1774 and July 1776 to compile and adopt a declaration of rights prior to adopting a new constitution was probably in deliberate imitation of the actions of the Convention Parliament of 1688 in first declaring the rights of Englishmen that the new monarchs must protect before offering the throne to William and Mary.[3] The delegates in Williamsburg borrowed from English precedent in other ways, too, such as paraphrasing or copying language from the English Bill of Rights into the Virginia Declaration of Rights and choosing the word *commonwealth*, a government without royalty or nobility, one dedicated to the common weal, or common good, as the style for their new independent government.

The convention made several important changes to Mason's draft declaration before unanimously adopting it on 12 June 1776. The unanimity masked some strong differences of opinion among the convention members, who had been elected in April and shared the emerging majority opinion among the colony's gentlemen freeholders that preservation of their liberties required that the colonies all become independent of the king of Great Britain. At least two of the changes provoked serious controversy, including alterations to Mason's opening language, leaving the members of the convention, in the evocative words of Delegate Thomas Ludwell Lee, "stumbling at the threshold."[4]

If all men were, indeed, born equally free and independent, would the convention by adopting that language declare itself in opposition to slavery or open the door to a moral or legal mandate to abolish slavery? The debates, about which only a little is recorded, suggest that few or no delegates favored the outright abolition of slavery, and the events of the American Revolution in Virginia leave no room to believe that in the phrase "all men" Mason or any other important leaders intended to include any enslaved laborers of African origin or descent, any Indians, or any women (even white women). But what of the free white farm laborers, smiths, shipwrights, and carters, the hewers of wood and drawers of water who, like the men in the counties in 1676 and 1677 had families to care for and believed that they were equally essential to and equally interested in the well-being of the society? Lee hinted that some members of the convention feared that those men might claim more than they deserved, and he wrote that "a certain set of Aristocrates, for we have such monsters here, finding that their execrable system cannot be reared on such foundations, have to this time kept us at bay on the first line which declares all men to be born equally free and independant."[5]

That a Lee could make such a statement and betray no evident sense of incongruity or sense of irony suggests something about the gradations of rank and the personal differences that may have existed among the grandees of Virginia in the 1770s. The Lee family was wealthy and as privileged and as deeply intermarried into the political cousinhood as any other. His father had been a member of the governor's council and acting governor of the colony. His own generation included a number of remarkably influential public men. His eldest brother had also been a member of the council before dying young; two of his brothers were serving in the Continental Congress when the delegates were stumbling in Williamsburg, and both of them signed the Declaration of Independence; two other brothers, one recently an alderman of London, emerged as some of the new nation's first foreign diplomats; and he was, himself, one of the leading men in the Virginia Convention of 1776. That Thomas Ludwell Lee could grumble about Virginia aristocrats suggests that he had no sense of humor and no appreciation for irony and also that the members of the convention included men strenuously opposed to an enlargement of the political nation or to letting independence usher in revolution.

It was the maintenance of slavery that led the delegates to amend Mason's language.[6] They voted to delete his word "born" and after "which" inserted a short phrase, "when they enter into a state of Society." Free men had natural rights that they could not surrender when they entered into a state of society; that is what the Virginia Declaration of Rights as adopted clearly stated. What it also clearly meant was that enslaved men, because they had been born unfree and because they had not voluntarily entered or been admitted into society, had no natural right to life, liberty, property, happiness, or safety. The members of the Virginia convention kept enslaved African Americans locked out of the political nation. The phrase "all men" did not mean all men.

The men in Philadelphia who adopted Jefferson's language that appeared to be equally clear and was even more economically and powerfully phrased did not stumble. They amended portions of his draft and deleted some of his favorite words condemning the Crown for supporting the international slave trade, but they did not stop to question, as had the men in Williamsburg, whether, in fact, all men were created equal and endowed with inalienable rights to life, liberty, and the pursuit of happiness. To them, the most important thing was to appeal for the support of their constituents to seek independence as a consequence of a long list of specific infringements of their rights that filled most of the text of the declaration. More so than the Virginia Declaration of Rights, the Declaration of Independence was a powerful political propaganda statement intended to convince Americans to support independence and to justify that action to what Jefferson described as a candid world. It was a statement by the leaders of a new political nation to the members of that political nation and on behalf of their political nation. In the context of the Declaration of Independence, the phrase "all men are created equal" was a rejection of the subordinate status of Englishmen in America to Englishmen in England, of gentlemen to titled nobility, of free men to royalty. To most Americans who read the Declaration of Independence in 1776 the word *men* meant the free adult white males who in most of the new states were required to own a certain minimum amount of land or to exhibit some strong attachment to the welfare of the society in order to take any part at all in its governance. The men in Philadelphia probably did not believe or intend to state what Lincoln certainly believed that they had undoubtedly meant.

The ideas that the second sentence of the Declaration of Independence carried—all men are created equal; life, liberty, and the pursuit of happiness— gave those words a power of their own that reached far beyond anything the author or the men who voted for it ever imagined. For much of the remainder of the history of the United States and of Virginia, people who wished to read the word *men* to mean "people" read Jefferson's words and understood that they implied a promise of freedom and inclusion in the political nation. Their long quests animated much of the history of the country and state, as Lincoln and the men of his generation understood fourscore and seven years later. Those words and that promise drove the fight for universal white manhood suffrage during the nineteenth century; the struggle for the abolition of slavery; the attempts of freed people after the Civil War to secure and preserve their rights to vote, to obtain an education, and to live as free people in a free land; the campaign for woman suffrage; and the civil rights and woman's movements of the twentieth century.

The second of the amendments to George Mason's draft Declaration of Rights that provoked discussion and disagreement changed the wording and the meaning of the final clause. Mason concluded his draft with a long sentence that contained a brief paraphrase of the essence of the English Act of Toleration, "that all men shou'd enjoy the fullest Toleration in the Exercise of Religion."[7] The amendment came from either James Madison, who had been revolted at the persecution of Baptist ministers and was then serving his first term in any deliberative assembly, or from Patrick Henry, who had defended Baptists during that persecution and refused payment for his legal services. One of them moved to replace the concept of toleration for dissent with a declaration of full religious liberty, by amending the article on religion to read, "all men are equally entitled to the full and free exercise of it accordg. to the dictates of Conscience; and therefore that no man or class of men ought on account of religion to be invested with peculiar emoluments or privileges; nor subjected to any penalties or disabilities."[8] Some devoted churchmen among the delegates perceived a threat to the privileged position of the established Church of England and objected, so Madison offered a substitute amendment which, when adopted and inserted into the middle of Mason's original language, gave the Declaration of Rights a powerful conclusion: "That Religion or the Duty which we owe to our Creator and the manner of discharging it can be directed only by reason and Conviction not by force or Violence and therefore all Men are equally intitled to the free exercise of Religion according to the Dictates of Conscience And that it is the mutual Duty of all to practice Christian Forbearance Love and Charity towards each other."[9]

Together the amended texts of the Virginia Declaration of Rights and the Declaration of Independence well served the people in Virginia who during the Revolutionary War challenged some of the institutions and practices of the grandees of government. What those people wrote and said and did reveals their beliefs and perspectives. In a rapidly changing, indeed revolutionary, setting, the language of liberty and equality provided powerful leverage for them to challenge some of the institutions and practices of the old grandees. The unamended text of the Declaration of Rights did, too, because it was published throughout the colonies while the convention was still stumbling, and Mason's initial words about all men being born free were better known during the Revolution than the text as adopted.[10]

It is unlikely that the convention delegates intended to produce or even to allow change or revolution when they chose independence from the Crown and Parliament of Great Britain, but once the ball of independence began to roll downhill, the British could not stop it, and even the skillful political leaders of Virginia could not always direct its path. In order "to prevent Disorders in each Colony," John Page wrote late in April 1776, "a Constitution should be formed as nearly resembling the old one as Circumstances, and the Merit of that Constitution will admit of."[11] Page, a college classmate of Jefferson, was a member of the royal governor's council that had not met for more than a year and also a leading member of the Virginia Committee of Safety that governed the colony between the summer of 1775 and the summer of 1776. Page was at the center of the action during those years and played a major leadership role. The Virginia convention did precisely what he advised. The constitution that the fifth convention adopted at the end of June 1776 made almost no changes to the structure or operations of the government other than to strip the secretary of the colony under his new style secretary of the commonwealth of the politically influential and very profitable appointment of county clerks, to reduce the powerful office of governor to a feeble one, and to lodge almost all the powers of government in the General Assembly, where the men who had always dominated government at the parish, county, and provincial levels could continue their domination and protect their interests.

Immediately following the unanimous adoption of the new constitution on 29 June 1776, the delegates elected the first governor of the independent Commonwealth of Virginia. Of the 106 men who voted, 60 voted for Patrick Henry, who was the acknowledged leader of the bolder members, and 45 for Thomas Nelson, the wealthy Yorktown merchant who was the senior member of the defunct royal governor's council. One man voted for John Page,[12] who as vice president of the colony's Committee of Safety had pushed hard for independence during the spring months. That 45 out of 106 men voted for the most senior royal appointee in the old government and that 46 men voted against Patrick Henry indicate that as of that time caution and continuity continued to exercise a strong appeal to a large proportion of the representatives of the political nation. For weeks after the delegates instructed their members of Congress to move a resolution of independence, the men in Williamsburg continued to refer to Virginia as a colony, even in the titles of the acts that they passed. Habits of thought and action changed more slowly than the course of human events.

Even in the matter of religious liberty the delegates who voted for Madison's amendment to Mason's draft Declaration of Rights did not intend to jeopardize the Church of England's privileged position. Indeed, one of their final acts on the final day of the final convention was to reenact for Virginia the liturgical service of the Church of England's Book of Common Prayer, but they replaced the prayers for the king and members of the royal family in the texts of the morning and evening services with prayers for the magistrates of the Commonwealth of Virginia.[13] Insofar as a majority of the convention delegates were concerned, the Church of England was, and they expected it to remain, a part of Virginia's government and vice versa.

They were wrong. A successful revolution against that part of the old constitution began twenty years before the war against the king and for independence, and it cast out the church. Beginning in the middle of the eighteenth century, New Light Presbyterians moved into the colony in large numbers, and then Baptists began drawing off parishioners of the Church of England. The Great Awakening, as it was called, added an enlarged measure of Calvinism to the religious culture of Virginia, and the Baptists introduced a different form of worship and a more egalitarian form of church governance. Baptists entirely discarded the liturgical service and the church hierarchy, regarding each congregation as a separate and self-governing body that chose its minister and regulated the behavior of its members according to their shared beliefs. In some instances Anglican churchmen retaliated with violence and imprisoned Baptist ministers, intensifying the resentment that Baptists felt toward the establishment, for which they had many reasons. The laws required that every person who paid local taxes also had to pay for the support of the Church of England's ministers and churches. They also required that every person who married had to be married by a minister of the established church.

Dissenters of all denominations objected more or less strenuously to the taxes and the restrictions on their clergymen and forms of worship, and in some western counties Presbyterians were so numerous and Anglicans so scarce that the parish vestries of the Church of England included more Presbyterians than Anglicans. In some of the eastern parishes, the long continuation in office of vestries that selected replacements for members who died led to disputes and dysfunctional vestries. By the end of the 1760s, the colony's leaders faced two related and serious problems. The House of Burgesses for the first time created a Committee of Religion to deal with the problems of church governance and also to formulate a new act of toleration for Virginia that would preserve the Church of England intact and permit dissenting Protestants a measure of religious liberty that dissenters almost certainly regarded as insufficient.[14]

The obstacles that Baptists faced were formidable. When, during the winter of 1771-72, Baptists in Caroline County protested that the county court had oppressed them by imprisoning their ministers, a person learned in the law (probably the county clerk or a member of the county court)[15] lectured them in a letter printed in one of the colony's two *Virginia Gazette*s about the colony's brand of representative government. He wrote that "every Member of a Community is obliged to submit to such Laws as are made for the Good of the Whole, however contrary to his Inclination or Interest, which he must give up to the Opinion or Interest of a Majority." The writer acknowledged that the personal religious opinions of individual members of society "are not the Objects of Law or Government; while they keep those to themselves, they may enjoy them without Interruption from the civil Magistrates. But if they go about publickly preaching and inculcating their Errours, raising Factions tending to disturb the publick Peace, or utter Doctrines which in their Nature are subversive of all Religion or Morality, they become obnoxious" and liable to "civil Punishment."[16] The majority of the adult white male property owners who voted placed limits on ideas and behavior not consistent with their own ideas and behavior, which they wished to preserve unchanged; and their unelected judges determined what ideas and what behaviors were in error, subversive, or obnoxious.

Baptist dissenters seized every opportunity to liberate themselves from the legal restrictions that the government and the established church imposed on them. In the summer of 1775, the third Virginia convention created an army in which clergymen of the Church of England served as paid chaplains. Baptist leaders shrewdly injected themselves and their campaign for respectful recognition of their ministers into the politics of the Revolution. On 14 August 1775 delegates from several Baptist churches petitioned the convention and directly linked their religious objectives with the convention's political objectives. The Baptists acknowledged that they were "distinguished from the Body of our Countrymen, by Appellatives and Sentiments of a religious Nature," but "nevertheless look upon ourselves as Members of the Same Common-Wealth, and therefore with respect to Matters of a civil Nature, embarked in the same common Cause." The Baptist leaders had decided that the times justified Baptists and other Virginians going to war, "And as some have inlisted, and many more" were "likely so to do, who will have earnest Desires for their Ministers to preach to them during the Campaign," they requested that Baptists ministers "may have free Liberty to preach to the Troops at convenient Times without Molestation or abuse."[17] The hint of quid pro quo could not have escaped notice.

The convention received the petition two days later and immediately adopted a resolution that Patrick Henry drafted instructing the commanding officers of the colony's new army "to permit dissenting Clergymen to celebrate divine Worship and to preach to the Soldiers or exhort from Time to Time as the various operations of the Military Service may admit for the Ease of such scrupulous Consciences, as may not chuse to attend divine Worship as celebrated by the Chaplain."[18] They made no provision, though, for paying Baptist ministers.

In May 1776 almost fifty Baptists in Prince William County petitioned the fifth convention and requested in such firm language that it almost amounted to a demand that all Baptists and their clergymen be allowed the same rights and privileges as all members and clergymen of the Church of England. The tattered remnant of their petition argued, "That whereas this colony with others, is now contending for [the civil rights &] liberties of mankind against the enslaving Scheme of a power[ful Enemy.] We being convinced, that the strictest unanimity among oursel[ves i]s very [necess]ary in this most critical conjuncture of public affairs; And that [ever]y remainin[g c]ause of animosity and division may if possible be removed, have t[hou]ght it our d[u]ty as peaceable Christians, to petition for several religious pri[vil]eges which as[s]et[s] we have not been indulged with in this part of the World. Vi[z.] 1. That we be [a]lowed to worship God in our own way, without interruption. [2.] That we be per[mite]d to maintain our own Ministers &c. and no other. 3. That [we a]nd our friends who desire it, may be married, buried and the like, without paying th[e] Parsons of any [other] denomination. These things granted, we will gladly unite with our Brethren of other denominations, and to the utmost of our ability, promote the common cause of Freedom, always praying for your welfare & success."[19] Quid pro quo, sine qua non, ergo e pluribus unum.

The amended language of the final clause of the Declaration of Rights pushed the linkage between the religious revolution and the political revolution to the forefront and led during the next nine and a half years to the adoption of Thomas Jefferson's Act for Establishing Religious Freedom in Virginia. Baptists in all parts of the state where they had formed congregations petitioned the General Assembly repeatedly beginning in the autumn of 1776 and organized an unprecedented and successful campaign that disestablished the Church of England.

One of the first and also one of the most eloquent and explicit of the petitions came from 160 Baptists in Prince Edward County who in September 1776 informed the House of Delegates, successor to the House of Burgesses and the recent convention, that "we heartily approve and Chearfully submit ourselves to the form of Government adopted at your last Session: hoping that our united American States will long continue free and Independent. The last Article of the Bill of Rights we also esteem as the rising Sun of religious Liberty, to releave us from a long Night of ecclesiastic Bondage: And we do most earnestly request and expect that you would go on to complete what is so nobly begun; raise religious as well as civil Liberty to the Zenith of Glory, and make Virginia an Asylum for free enquiry, knowlege, and the virtuous of every Denomination. Justice to ourselves and Posterity, as well as a regard to the honour of the Common Wealth, makes it our indispensable Duty, in particular to intreat, That without Delay, You would pull down all Church E[s]tablishments; Abolish every Tax upon Conscience and private Judgment; and leave each Individual to rise or sink according to his Merit, and the general Laws of the Land. The whole amount of what we desire, is, That Our Honourable Legislature would blot out every Vestige of British Tyranny and

Bondage, and define accurately between civil and ecclesiastic Authority; then leave our Lord Jesus Christ the Honour of being the Sole Lawgiver and Governor in his Church; and every one in the Things of Religion to stand or fall to Him; he being, in this respect the only rightful Master."[20]

The Baptist petitioning campaign was unlike anything any Virginians had ever done before. Baptists organized their members to persuade and pressure the General Assembly to change a fundamentally important public policy. Before that time individual residents of Virginia or groups often petitioned the General Assembly for private relief or for enactment of bills of local interest;[21] but never before had a matter of public policy that affected everybody been the subject of an organized and widespread petitioning campaign. Their use of the revolutionary language of liberty and their development of a new technique of political action created a new and unprecedented democratic element of Virginia's political culture. Nowhere else was the power of an idea and a new political technique more conspicuous or successful. During the American Revolution in Virginia, the Baptists were the most democratic and democratizing of all Virginians. They were true revolutionaries.

Baptists grew rapidly in number and political importance during the Revolutionary years, but they required assistance from Presbyterians and other dissenters in the face of determined opposition from leaders of the established church. One of the counterproposals, which Patrick Henry energetically supported and George Washington quietly endorsed, was to tax everybody in Virginia equally and to distribute the revenue to the different denominations according to the wishes of the people taxed. James Madison assisted the Baptists and the cause of full religious freedom in two critical ways. As a member of the General Assembly, he arranged in 1785 for Patrick Henry to be elected governor, getting him out of the assembly and diluting his political influence, and that same year he anonymously circulated a broadside in the form of a long petition to the assembly criticizing the religious assessment, as the tax plan was called, and providing additional arguments why disentangling the church and the state in Virginia was good for each and fully in keeping with the spirit of the American Revolution.[22]

The Act Establishing Religious Freedom that the General Assembly adopted in January 1786 is one of the most important bills that it ever enacted, and it might be regarded as the most important and revolutionary accomplishment of the American Revolution in Virginia.[23] The statute opened with an eloquent assertion of the importance of religious and intellectual freedom. It transformed religious beliefs and institutions in Virginia into purely private and personal matters. It also knocked the legal props out from under the established church with these words, "That no man shall be compelled to frequent or support any religious worship, place, or Ministry whatsoever, nor shall be enforced, restrained, molested, or burthened in his body or goods, nor shall otherwise suffer on account of his religious opinions or belief; but that all men shall be free to profess, and by argument to maintain, their opinion in matters of religion, and that the same shall in no wise diminish, enlarge, or affect their civil capacities."[24]

The Baptists and other dissenters from the Church of England won, and after January 1786 the Church of England was no longer a part of the government of Virginia. The increasing religious diversity of the population had led to that important constitutional change; and that change in turn led to even greater religious diversity in a new legal climate of full religious liberty.

Other men and women were also keenly aware of the implications of the language of political rights that circulated widely during the years and months before the Revolution began. It appeared in a petition that more than a hundred men filed early in the summer of 1775. The colonel of the Berkeley County militia called for the election of the county's two delegates to the third of the Revolutionary conventions to be held on a day when, according to the petitioners, many of the eligible voters were unable to attend. The men complained to the convention that it was "a most daring and violent attack upon their Liberty of Suffrage at a time when the public Voice in all matters referred to them ought to be collected in the most free open and unbiassed manner." Their complaint unseated one of the victorious candidates, the colonel himself.[25]

One wealthy white Virginia widow wanted women to profit from the principles of the Revolution equally with men in the new Virginia. During the war Hannah Lee Corbin (or Hannah Lee Corbin Hall) asked her brother Richard Henry Lee to use his influence to grant the vote to widows like herself who owned land and paid taxes but had no voice in how their taxes were raised or how the money was spent;[26] but she failed to persuade her brother to act on her proposal, and she and the other women who owned property continued to be taxed without representation. Landownership remained the basis on which men claimed a right to take responsible roles in public life, but being a man and not a woman was an even more fundamentally important prerequisite.

It is not surprising that the bold Hannah Corbin (or Hall) made that suggestion. She was the sister of the Lee brothers who played such a large role in the Revolution in Virginia and the United States. She was also a convert from the Church of England to the Baptist Church. Sometime after her husband died, she had a religious conversion experience and then fell in love with Richard Lingan Hall, also a Baptist. They lived together as if married until he died a decade later, not long before the Revolution began. The terms of her first husband's will allowed her to control and profit from his property until such time as she remarried, so in order to retain management of several profitable plantations for the benefit of her children, she and Hall did not marry. At least, they did not marry in the Church of England. It is possible that they may have engaged a Baptist clergyman to marry them because a marriage that a Baptist minister performed would have had no legal standing that invoked the terms of her first husband's will. She and Hall could have been married in the eyes of God, themselves, and their families even if not in the eyes of the law.[27]

Another widow, Ann Makemie Holden, of Accomack County, may have gone further in 1787 when she deeded land to four male relatives who did not then own real estate and consequently could not vote. Having given them enough land to enfranchise them, she required that they "Vote at the Annual Elections for the most Wise and Discreet men who have proved themselves real friends to the American Independance to represent the County of Acco-mack."[28] Holden died not long thereafter, and it is not clear from her words (as it might have become from her actions) whether she merely enfranchised four relatives or hoped through them to have four proxy votes in elections for members of the General Assembly.

Inspired by the language of liberty and equality, Hannah Corbin (or Hall) and Ann Holden and many other Virginia men and women ingeniously did as much as they could to obtain its promise for themselves. Just as Bacon's Rebellion in 1676 had exposed resentments and frustrations that lay just be-neath the surface of what appeared to be a comfortably stable social order, the events of the 1770s demonstrated that large and small planters and less prosperous white men shared many attitudes and values in good times, but the men near the top and those near the bottom of the economic and political ladders often had very different, conflicting perceptions that appeared during troublous times.

The differences in perception and intent appeared at the very beginning. The first Continental Congress that met in Philadelphia in the autumn of 1774 directed the men of each county and town to form a committee to en-force the terms of the trade embargo that it put into effect in hopes of put-ting enough economic pressure on British merchants that they would in turn pressure Parliament to repeal the obnoxious taxes and Coercive Acts. The men who assembled in mass meetings in most or all of the counties of Vir-ginia during the winter of 1774–75 and elected committee members took part for the very first time in choosing men to manage a local political in-stitution. Their first taste of participation in local politics had unforeseen consequences. Even though they often elected burgesses, justices of the peace, and prominent local planters to their county committees, placing the tradi-tional local leaders in leadership positions, in some instances they chose large committees that included men who had never before held such responsibility. The zeal with which some of the committees badgered merchants or hounded neighbors with suspected loyalist sympathies may have been behind John

Page's April 1776 suggestion that new governments as nearly as possible like the existing ones be speedily created. But even before that, in the summer of 1775, the third of the Virginia Revolutionary conventions had already reined in the local committees, requiring that they be elected annually and by qualified voters only and that every committee consist of twenty-one members, about the same number normally entitled to sit on the county courts. The reason, the convention stated, was that "many inconveniencies have arisen by the supernumerary committee-men elected in some counties."[29]

During the winter of 1774–75, after the colony's militia law had expired, leaving it defenseless against frontier Indians, potentially rebellious slaves, and the British, several men recruited military companies that styled themselves gentlemen volunteers. George Mason later boasted that when one of his sons joined one of these companies, it "consisted entirely of Gentlemen."[30] That he made that remark indicates that these companies soon thereafter also included lesser young men than proper gentlemen and their sons, and that in Mason's view that changed things and perhaps not for the better. Indeed, these companies acted in ways that frightened many members of the native governing elite as much as they frightened the royal governor and his loyalist adherents. During the night of 20–21 April 1775, John Murray, fourth earl of Dunmore, the last royal governor of Virginia, ordered that the colony's supply of gunpowder be secretly conveyed from the public powder magazine in the center of Williamsburg to a royal warship in the York River. News of the fighting between British troops and volunteers at Lexington and Concord, in Massachusetts, begun by a corresponding action of the royal military governor there, had not yet reached Virginia, but the actions of the volunteers in Virginia were very like those of the Massachusetts minutemen. Some of the volunteers were assembled in Fredericksburg when they received news of the governor's action, and they sent a rider to Alexandria to request advice from their commander, Colonel George Washington, and another to Williamsburg to ascertain whether they should ready themselves to march to the defense of the capital. Speaker Peyton Randolph assured them that city officials had matters under control and that they should remain at home.[31]

In Hanover County, closer to Williamsburg, Patrick Henry addressed the volunteers who assembled there and then led them off in arms on a march toward the capital. To prevent a violent clash between Henry's gentlemen volunteers and the governor's marines, several high-ranking officials intervened and contrived a financial ruse by which the royal revenue in Virginia was made to appear to pay for the powder that Dunmore had removed. The Fredericksburg assembly and Henry's march provided the royal governor with material for a long letter of complaint to the king's ministers in London about colonial rebellion, and they provided the leaders of the resistance with food for thoughts of their own. It was a frightening event all around, and the old political leaders just barely reclaimed control of their followers. Afterward, another small group of gentlemen volunteers camped just outside of Williamsburg, reminding the royal governor and the colony's political leaders just how essentially unstable, unpredictable, and potentially uncontrollable the circumstances had become.[32]

The same convention in the summer of 1775 that regulated committee membership back into line also regulated the volunteers out of existence. The convention adopted an innovative method to recruit and select officers for the soldiers, minutemen, and militia that it ordained into being. The convention authorized each county committee to re-create the county militia under its own authority, and it provided for a corps of minutemen who could be ready to take the field at a minute's notice and who would train more often than the militia, which customarily assembled for one day every few months. The convention directed representatives of committees from adjacent counties to meet and select field- and company-grade officers for the minutemen and also captains and subalterns for the companies being recruited for the two regular army regiments that it created.[33] But that expedient, too, unnerved some influential members of the Committee of Safety that the convention created to manage the army and be the de facto government of Virginia. The conventions and the Committee of Safety gradually restricted the influence and incipient democracy of the county committees. Those restrictions and the terms of the recruitment acts provoked reactions that demonstrated how much the poor and the middling classes of Virginians resented being excluded from making decisions about public affairs that directly affected them and then being expected to bear what they believed to be more than their share of the burdens.

The first recruitment acts and ordinances for governing the new Virginia army resembled earlier Virginia and British laws that set rates of pay according to the rank of the soldier or officer. High-ranking officers who were likely to be from families that were more prominent and prosperous than average were paid much more than enlisted soldiers. Colonels received 25 shillings a day and lieutenant colonels half that; majors received 10 shillings, captains 6, and lieutenants 4; but private soldiers received a mere 1 shilling and 4 pence,[34] or a little more than 5 percent of what a colonel received and 22 percent of what a lieutenant received. The dramatic differences provoked dissent. Early in 1776 James Cleveland organized tenant farmers in Loudoun County, in the northern part of Virginia, who threatened to withhold their rents until the convention met their demand that all soldiers and officers be paid exactly the same amount. Cleveland announced that "there is no inducement for a poor Man to Fight, for he has nothing to defend."[35] A man without his own property believed that he therefore had no real liberty, and men with property believed the same thing, which is why the men with property allowed the men without property no vote.

The colony's first recruitment acts provoked resentment. Like the recruitment acts passed in the 1740s and during the French and Indian War in the 1750s and 1760s that had targeted for conscription unmarried white men who owned no property, they exempted holders of certain essential civilian occupations, such as mill operators and plantation overseers, from service and permitted any man who could afford it to hire a substitute to serve in his place. In the spring of 1776 in Lunenburg County, in the southern part of Virginia, more than two hundred men complained to the last of the Virginia conventions about inequities in the recent recruitment act, particularly the exemption from militia service that it allowed to men who were serving as overseers of four or more laborers. The unpolished language of the petition from Lunenburg County, not unlike the county grievances compiled ninety-nine years earlier, contained ample evidence of what poor white farming men in Virginia thought about how their leaders were leading and about the ill consequences for themselves and their families. "The Petition of the freeholders & Sundry of the Inhabitants" who expressed themselves as "being deeply Empress'd with a tender Sense & feeling for the distresses of his Majestys good Subjects in this & the rest of the Colonies & Provinces on the Continent" explained that they "must Observe (tho' its with Sorrow & reluctance)" that the exemption of overseers from militia service and from compulsory service in time of emergency was a mistake in public policy. "From this Indulgence," they complained, "many persons are become Overseers that Otherways wou'd not, on purpose to Secure themselves from Fighting in defence of their Country as well as their own property. Many of your Petitioners are poor men with Families that are Incapable of Supporti[ng th]emselves without Our labour & Assistance and we look up[on] it to be extremly hard . . . that we Should be Obliged to leave our Farms" while the overseers remained at home and "that if ever we Shou'd return again Wou'd find our Wives & Children disper'd up & down the Country abeging, or at home aSlaving, and at the same time quite unable to help them to the Necessaries of life while the Overseers are aliving in ease & Affluence at the Expense of their Employers."[36]

The language and forms of petitions during the eighteenth century were less obsequious when addressed to local or colonial officials than during the seventeenth when addressed to royal officers. By the end of the Revolution, when twenty-eight men in western Virginia petitioned the General Assembly for permission to create a new state, they explained but did not apologize for the bluntness of their request by writing, "In this Address we have discarded the complimentary Stile of adulation & insincerity—it becomes Freemen when speaking to Fr[eemen], to imploy the plain, man[ly], unadorned Lan[gu]age of Independance."[37] Petitioners asserted their rights as well as requested redress of their grievances. Indeed, petitions to the Revolutionary conventions and to the General Assembly during and after the American

Revolution contain by far the most abundant expressions of the varying viewpoints of the people in Virginia and how they explained their actions and beliefs. Throughout the war and from every part of Virginia, men complained about inequities and iniquities and often with the revolutionary language of liberty and equality that George Mason and Thomas Jefferson had inadvertently let out of Pandora's box.

Recruitment of soldiers and service in the field produced the most intense frustration to be found in the petitions. From the formation of the new army in 1775 through the end of the war, the state found it increasingly difficult to recruit full regiments, to keep full regiments in the field, and to rely on the militia when it was necessary that they march far from home. In every year of the war somewhere in Virginia men refused to march off to defend other people and leave their own counties defenseless or their own families without laborers. In every year of the war somewhere in Virginia men refused increasingly large bounties offered to tempt them to enlist in the Continental Army. In several instances throughout the war and in different regions of Virginia men obstructed recruitment officers and prevented them from raising conscripts or even volunteers. Riots and bloodshed took place on several occasions and were not the result of residual loyalism alone. The longer the war lasted, the more it appeared that James Cleveland had been correct, that poor men believed that they had little to fight for and resented that they were required to do most of the fighting and to pay more than their share of the war's cost.[38]

Late in 1780 the General Assembly, as it had once or twice every year since 1775, debated yet another recruitment act. The earlier acts had offered progressively larger cash bounties or grants of fresh land in the west for men who enlisted, but the number of men who joined the army remained inadequate. That autumn the House of Delegates went so far as to give preliminary approval to a bill that would have required owners of large numbers of slaves to turn over one in every twenty to the state to be awarded in turn to each man who enlisted in the army for the duration of the war. The bill promised that the slaves' owners would be compensated later. The proposal came from members of the General Assembly who complained that wealthy planters were not bearing their part of the burden. The assembly did not pass the measure, which if enacted would have spread ownership of slaves to an enlarged number of Virginia farmers, but that the legislators even considered such a radical measure was an indication of the difficulty that recruitment posed as the war dragged on and on without evident progress toward conclusion.[39]

That same 1780 session of the assembly received a petition from sixty-one men in Berkeley County who proclaimed themselves "Grievously oppressed By the present mode of Raising Continental Troops." They denounced the public policy that allowed "A Mercinary Soldier who embarks in a Cause for money only As all or nearly all our volunteers now are Will look at our Laws, to enable him to make the best market of himself," which "put it in Their power and points out the way for them to Fleece from the virtuous and good part of our Citizens Whatever their avaricious inclinations may prompt Them to exact." From "the frequent fluctuating of The standing army, The militia are Haras'd in such a manner as Causes great uneasiness and Disgust in the Country, indeed we are much allarm'd at the Confusion and Disorder . . . a Cloud we apprehend to be Gathering, which if not Dispel'd, by a proper and Vigorous attention, to procuring a standing army we fear will prove highly Injurious to the Cause of america."[40]

One of the most poignant of the petitions, and one that contains very explicit criticism of local leaders, came to the same session of the assembly from twenty-one militiamen of Amherst County. They had been called into the field in the summer of 1780 and marched against their will to South Carolina. At the Battle of Camden, in their first exposure to combat, they ran away and then returned home, as they later said, to obtain clothing and supplies that their commanders could not provide. They blamed their incompetent and amateurish gentlemen militia officers for the men's "being wholly unacquainted with Military Discipline, which we had not time to learn; Greatly Exhausted by Fatigue at that hot Season, which we had not been inured to; Dispirited for want of Rest & Diet; and Panick-struck by the Noise and Terror of a Battle which was entirely New to most of us." They complained "That had our inferior Militia Officers been experienc'd in Military Discipline or Capable of encouraging us by their Example as well as Orders and particularly had we not been drawn up in such Close Order but had more space to Act; And Lastly been Permitted to Fire on the Enemy before we receiv'd their Fire, or before we came so near We verily believe the Event had been Otherwise." The militiamen requested (in vain, as it turned out) time to refresh themselves and to care for their families and also that experienced, regular army officers be appointed to command them before they returned to the field, which they promised to do, "That we shall by our future Conduct not only retrieve our own Reputation as Citizens of a Free State But also the losses & Dishonour which our Country has Sustain'd by our former Pusillanimity."[41]

Following the end of the war and the generally unsatisfactory performance of the county militia, the General Assembly, prodded by former governor Patrick Henry, enacted a new militia law that revised the rules governing the militia and gave the governor greater authority to appoint and displace officers for the good of the service. Henry was elected governor again soon after adoption of the law, but local courts and militia officers, still exercising as much power as the local grandees had done before the war, obstructed his implementation of the law by what can accurately be described as a mass act of passive-aggressive noncompliance.[42]

During the 1770s and 1780s, as during the 1670s, taxes prompted men to complain in revealing ways. In the summer of 1775 the convention levied taxes to pay for the two regiments of regular soldiers it voted into existence. As it had for a brief time back during the French and Indian War, the delegates at last taxed land, in 1775 at a rate of four shillings for every hundred acres. The convention also taxed certain legal writs and marriage and tavern licenses, and it imposed new taxes on some of the property of the wealthier colonists including "an annual tax or duty of forty shillings upon every coach, chariot, or four-wheel carriage, except common waggons, and twenty shillings for every chair or two-wheel chaise, to be paid by the proprietor thereof."[43] In the beginning the political leaders sought to lead by setting an example, even though it was not a very expensive example for most of them.

In the autumn of 1777, eighty-six men in Orange County submitted two virtually identical petitions that read as if they had employed the county grievances of a century earlier as a starting place for a more egalitarian proposal. "Whereas our Just defence against the cruel Enemies of our Country" made emissions of paper money necessary and taxes to retire it from circulation inevitable, "we beg leave to address you," they wrote to the General Assembly, "more particularly as to the mode of Taxation. First then we cannot but determine that a Tax on Land by the acre Unequal in the general, and in many Cases to a degree of more than a hundred to one; therefore exceedingly unjust, we consider Land as a proper subject of Taxation, but the Tax ought to be in proportion to the value thereof." They also requested that "all Taxes may be by assessment on all visible property, in proportion to the Value, which mode we believe the most Just."[44] Sixty-nine men in neighboring Culpeper County almost simultaneously submitted a petition to the same effect, requesting that in order to pay the expenses of the war, the assembly replace the law "for Levying on Land and Poll Tax" with "an Act on more equitable Principles; which we conceive would be by Taxing each man in proportion to the Value of the Real and Personal Estate he possesses."[45]

In the spring of 1780 a petition from 143 men in Charlotte County coupled a plea for elimination of the poll tax with reforms in military service. First, they pointed out that "in the personal services expected from the Citizens of this Commonwealth, the poor among us who scarce obtain a precarious subsistance by the Sweat of their brow, are call'd upon as often and bound to perform equal Military duty in defence of their little as the great & oppulent in defence of their abundance; that the latter of these who contribute very little personal labour in support of their families, often find means to secure themselves altogether from those military services which the poor and indigent are on all occasions taken from their homes to perform in person." Second, they complained that the laws imposed hardship "by laying a poll tax indiscriminately on all and thereby compelling the poor who bear the heat and burthen of Military duty to pay nearly an equal proportion of Taxes with him who labours only to support the extravagance of a Voluptuous master."[46]

The General Assembly raised taxes frequently during the war to pay for additional regiments and to compensate for rampant inflation. The landowners in the assembly resisted as long as possible taxing land according to its market value rather than by the acre or placing more reliance on the land tax and less on the poll tax that had been a grievance of small farmers and artisans for more than a century. Local governments continued to collect all of their revenue from the poll tax, which required every person to pay the same amount, a proportionately heavier burden on people with moderate incomes and small farms than on people with large incomes and extended plantations.[47] But when in 1781 the legislators passed the first law containing in its title the significant words "and for Establishing a Permanent Revenue," they instituted a permanent poll tax of 10 shillings per person, but they also taxed all land at the rate of £1 for every hundred acres and five shillings per hundred acres on all newly patented and unimproved land in excess of 1,400 acres. They refused to tax land on its market value, but they taxed certain imports and exports, all slaves of working age, livestock, and "all coaches, chariots, phaetons, four-wheeled chaises, stage waggons for riding carriages, chairs and two-wheeled chaises" of the prosperous planters, and they taxed billiard tables at a rate of £50 per year.[48]

After years of argument, in 1782 the assembly passed An Act for Equalizing the Land Tax. It created no equality but instead created four zones in the state and taxed the land in them at different rates. Residents of the eastern counties where the largest planters lived paid more taxes per acre than did the residents of the Piedmont where large plantations were comparatively less common. Residents of the Piedmont in turn paid more than residents of counties along the North Carolina border and in the valleys of the west where large plantations were even less common. They in turn paid more than the residents of the mountains and far west where small farms were overwhelmingly the rule.[49]

The commonalty of Virginia, to reprise the language of the 1670s, was not able to seize control, but they were able in some measure to prevent the men who governed from governing entirely as they pleased. As the grandees and legislators often did, they accommodated the commonalty but only so much as was absolutely necessary. They did not always voluntarily adapt their policies to the needs of their constituents or to the egalitarian implications of their own declarations. As George Mason admitted as early as October 1778, "nothing has been done without the Approbation of the People, who have indeed out run their Leaders; so that no capital Measure hath been adopted, until they called loudly for it."[50]

In some ways the minority of the whole population who voted reduced the influence of the smaller minority of larger landowners and men who participated in government. At the first session of the General Assembly in the autumn of 1776, when the lower house of the assembly was first designated the House of Delegates instead of the House of Burgesses, an observer noted that on the whole the members were "not quite so well dressed—nor so politely Educated—nor so highly born" as the members of the House of Burgesses had "formerly been."[51] The members of the House of Delegates then were the men who were elected in April 1776 to the fifth and last of the conventions. Almost 40 percent of the seats changed hands in that election, the largest percentage since the general election of 1758, which ushered in almost two decades of unusual stability in the membership of the House of Burgesses. The new members in 1776 were not all new to politics because several of them had sat in previous conventions or in the colonial assembly, but beginning in 1776 turnover in membership of the assembly increased, allowing more men from each of the counties a chance to serve in the legislature and perhaps leading in incremental ways to a moderate increase in the influence of men who had not theretofore been influential in government and politics.[52]

It may be, too, that the complaints about taxation and military recruitment that poured into the House of Delegates at every session during the war changed the dynamics of legislative and electoral politics in other ways. The petitions addressed issues of widespread importance as those of the Baptists had done in pursuit of religious liberty. The opinions of the men who stood for election probably became of increasing interest to the freeholders on election day, and that slowly and subtly transformed the relationship between legislators and constituents. The men who complained about taxes, militia service, or recruitment altered the politics of their communities. One clear evidence of that can be seen in the practice that began in the House of Delegates in 1779[53] and increased in frequency during the 1790s of recording for publication in the legislative journals the results of roll-call votes on important matters of public policy. That had never been done in the House of Burgesses, but the slow adoption late in the eighteenth century of that method of making legislators more accountable to constituents (to employ language that became popular late in the twentieth century) indicates that the American Revolution produced some important modifications in the political culture of Virginia.

Men like Patrick Henry had already begun speaking out on issues of importance and speaking in ways that identified themselves as representatives of the interests and opinions of their constituents, not merely as locally respectable gentlemen sent to the legislature to exercise their best judgment for the good of everybody. Candidates and voters gradually came to see themselves in different ways, and after the American Revolution candidates made speeches to voters and talked about issues of importance to them, something that almost never took place before. The political nation (and everybody else who attended the festivities on election day) became more acutely aware of the relationship between the actions of their representatives and their own opinions and interests. Republican government gained a firmer purchase during those years, and democracy made some very important but small steps.

The domestic revolution remained limited. The undemocratic features of the new state constitution remained in effect in spite of some attempts to amend them. Within a few months of the adoption of the constitution in the summer of 1776, a large number of men in Albemarle County adopted two sets of instructions to their members of the House of Delegates, Thomas Jefferson and Charles Lewis. They asked for amendments to the constitution to make it possible "to call to account" magistrates who abused their authority; to place limits on how many terms members of the General Assembly could serve; to forbid men from voting in more than one county at election time; to apportion seats in the legislature according "to the number of Electors" rather than allow two members per county; to give electors the right to pass on the propriety of bills the assembly enacted; to abolish the new state senate as unnecessary; to require all eligible electors to vote; to provide for full freedom of the press and religion; to abolish primogeniture and entail and require that in the absence of a will all property belonging to a deceased person be equally distributed to his or her lawful heirs; that regular "Grandjury courts should be holden more frequently" at which citizens could air their grievances; and that electors elect "Civil Magistrates," meaning the county justices of the peace and perhaps county sheriffs.[54]

Nothing immediately came of their instructions, but from the budget of revised laws that Jefferson and the other members of the committee of revisors prepared during the ensuing two years, the General Assembly eventually adopted the Act for Establishing Religious Freedom. It also passed laws abolishing primogeniture and entail that reformed the laws of inheritance. Abolition of primogeniture meant that when a person died without a will, the land and slave property would be divided among the heirs, not conveyed intact to the eldest male heir. Abolition of entail ended the practice of allowing people to specify in their wills and deeds that parcels of property not be divided or sold. Those reforms placed severe restrictions on the ability of the great landed families to guarantee that their large estates would remain large and in the hands of the eldest male heirs and their eldest male descendants. Primogeniture and entail had enabled the creation of the class of great landed families, and without them those great landed families as a class slowly began to dwindle in number and proportion and also in prominence and influence. That had long-term implications for creating a less hierarchical social structure and a more democratic political culture.[55]

Jefferson prepared a new draft constitution early in the 1780s but was unable to obtain agreement from the assembly to consider it or to call a convention to revise the Constitution of 1776. Jefferson's draft was revolutionary in several ways. It required a special election for a convention to be called for the sole purpose of revising the social contract. It also contained more specific details about the separation of powers and limitations on the powers of the governor and the assembly. In what might be regarded as a reversal of democratic reform, Jefferson's draft provided for election of members of the House of Delegates for three-year terms instead of one-year terms and of state senators for six-year terms instead of four-year terms. His draft also proposed that the General Assembly elect the governor for one five-year term with no eligibility for reelection. Jefferson's constitution would have granted the vote to "all free male citizens of full age and sane mind, who for one year before shall have been resident in the county" or possessed a freehold in land. Among the other substantial changes that Jefferson proposed but that went undebated was a truly revolutionary one to forbid "the introduction of any more slaves to reside in this state, or the continuance of slavery beyond the generation which shall be living on the 31st. day of December 1800; all persons born after that day being hereby declared free."[56]

The robust language of liberty and individual rights that circulated from the eve of the Revolution right through to its conclusion continued to drive the state's politics during the debates about the ratification of the Constitution of the United States at the end of the 1780s. That language worked both ways in the matter of slavery. The members of the Convention of 1776 collectively shared the same lack of sense of irony that Thomas Ludwell Lee exhibited when they adopted a device that George Wythe designed for a new seal of the independent Commonwealth of Virginia. The seal depicted "Virtus the genius of the commonwealth dressed like an Amazon resting on a Spear with one hand and holding a Sword in the other and treading on Tyranny represented by a man prostrate a Crown fallen from his Head a broken chain in his left Hand and a Scourge in his right." The seal also carried the new motto of the new commonwealth: *Sic semper tyrannis,* thus always to tyrants.[57] The white male property-owning body politic of the commonwealth rejected tyranny in the form of a monarch; it did not reject tyranny in the form of a slave-owning planter.

No wonder that as early as 1775 the celebrated British scholar and lexicographer, Dr. Samuel Johnson, threw the apparently contradictory practices and principles of the American revolutionaries right back at them when he demanded to know "how is it that we hear the loudest yelps for liberty among the drivers of negroes?" What Johnson failed to see or chose to ignore in order to undermine the legitimacy of the yelps—and what twenty-first-century readers may fail to see or find difficult to comprehend—is that it was the social inequality generally, and the ownership of slaves specifically, that gave the planter-patriots of Virginia their social status and enabled them to exercise political leadership and thereby made their own personal liberty possible.[58]

The Convention of 1776 had excluded enslaved Virginians from the body politic, but the autumn 1778 session of the General Assembly prohibited the importation of additional slaves into Virginia,[59] and the spring session of 1782 passed a law allowing private manumissions.[60] During the following two decades, several hundred or several thousand owners of enslaved Virginians freed some or all of their slaves. But at the same time, as Edmund Randolph acknowledged in a history of Virginia that he drafted not long thereafter, "The system of slavery, howsoever baneful to virtue, begat a pride which nourished a quick and acute sense of the rights of freemen,"[61] and one of the rights of freemen enumerated in George Mason's Declaration of Rights was the right "of acquiring and possessing Property."

For many of those freemen that meant property in human form. During the General Assembly sessions of 1784 and 1785, several hundred residents of five central and southern Virginia counties submitted petitions complaining about proposals for emancipation of slaves or abolition of slavery; rumors were circulating either of Jefferson's new proposed draft constitution or that Methodists, not yet formally separated from the Church of England, were about to petition for the abolition of slavery. The petitions are extraordinary in several respects, notably in their early use of citations from the Bible and assertions of the inherent inferiority of Africans to justify slavery and to justify ownership of slaves.[62] The petitioners also employed the Revolution's language of liberty to defend their ownership of slaves. In the autumn of 1785, for instance, 260 men in Halifax County began with a reference to the Revolution. "When the British Parliament usurped a Right to dispose of our Property without our Consent," they explained, "we dissolved the Union with our Parent Country, & established a Constitution and Form of Government of our own, that our Property might be secure in Future. In Order to effect this, we risked our Lives & Fortunes, and waded through Seas of Blood. Divine Providence smiled on our Enterprize, and crowned it with Success. And our Rights of Liberty and Property are now as well secured to us, as they can be by any human Constitution & Form of Government.

"But notwithstanding this, we understand, a very subtle and daring Attempt is on Foot to deprive us of a very important Part of our Property. An Attempt carried on by the Enemies of our Country, Tools of the British Administration, and supported by a Number of deluded Men among us, to wrest from us our Slaves by an Act of the Legislature for a general Emancipation of them."[63]

Enslaved men and women of African birth or ancestry had never had any part in governing anything in Virginia, not even all aspects of their own personal and family lives, and the Revolution did not change that. A great many thousands of them, how many cannot be accurately estimated, ran away from their owners, beginning as early as 1775, even before the last of the royal governors, the earl of Dunmore, issued a proclamation in November of that year offering freedom to the slaves of disloyal Virginians who agreed to fight for the king. At the end of that year he formed a black regiment, Lord Dunmore's Ethiopian Corps. In 1775 and 1776 a large number of black men and women ran away and took refuge with Dunmore, and later during the war when British ships entered the Chesapeake and again near the end when the British army arrived, thousands more fled to the British.[64]

Some black Virginia men served in the Continental Army during the war, although neither the Virginia government nor the Continental Congress allowed them to enlist until the war was well advanced. In 1783 the General Assembly granted freedom to these black soldiers,[65] and it passed several special acts freeing individual men who performed extraordinary services for the state during the war. Not all of the black Continental soldiers from Virginia volunteered. Some of them entered the army as involuntary stand-ins for their owners who took advantage of the recruitment acts and provided a substitute to avoid having to serve. They made their slaves serve, instead.[66]

More black Virginians probably gained their freedom by fighting for the king of England than by fighting for American independence, and many more died than succeeded in making the attempt. When Benjamin Henry Latrobe visited Norfolk in 1796, he observed a gruesome sight that exhibited the fate of a majority of the black men, women, and children who escaped from slavery to join Dunmore in 1775 and 1776, who tried to reach the British fleet later, or who tried to join Lord Cornwallis in 1781. In all three episodes people who reached the protection of the British died in appalling numbers aboard the royal warships and transports. Each night naval commanders dropped into the bay the dead bodies of these men, women, and children who had sought freedom, just as the captains of slave ships carrying human cargo to lifetime servitude in the Americas had tossed bodies into the shark-infested oceans. On the banks of the Elizabeth River near Norfolk, Latrobe saw where "Many Waggon loads of the bones of Men women and Children, stripped of the flesh by Vultures and Hawks which abound here, covered the sand for a most considerable length.... The hopes of getting on board the English fleet collected them at the mouth of the Chesapeak bay, they were left behind in thousands and perished. Children died sucking the breasts of their dead mothers, and Women feeding upon the corpses of their starved children. The remnants of decaying rags still point to the skeletons of many of these miserable victims."[67]

6

ON
DOMESTIC
SLAVERY

This portrait of Martha Haines Butt (1833–1871) (courtesy of the Library of Virginia) appeared in Frank Leslie's Illustrated Weekly *on 14 January 1860 at the time of the publication of her second book,* The Leisure Moments of Martha Haines Butt, A.M. *Born in Norfolk after nearly all of the Virginians who lived through the American Revolution were dead, she imbibed ideas about slavery that became widespread during the decades before the American Civil War. She published her first book in 1853, a novel entitled* Antifanaticism: A Tale of the South, *to counter the influence of Harriet Beecher Stowe's antislavery novel,* Uncle Tom's Cabin. *Unlike Virginians of earlier generations, Butt and a large proportion of white Virginians of her generation believed that slavery was an institution beneficial to enslaved laborers as well as to their owners.*

"DEATH OR LIBERTY." ENSLAVED VIRginians planned to raise a flag with those words over the Capitol of Virginia in Richmond at the end of August 1800 when they began the war against slavery. During the trials of the men who planned to wage the war or to employ the threat of war to negotiate for the end of slavery, one of the conspirators described the flag, which contained in inverted order the critical memorable words of Patrick Henry's March 1775 speech. The men may have intended the flag to express their determination to gain freedom, or it may have been a threat to the city's white population.[1] A few years later a plausible but possibly apocryphal story circulated that one of the conspirators had stated "in a manly tone of voice" at his trial, "I have nothing more to offer than what General Washington would have had to offer, had he been taken by the British and put to trial by them. I have adventured my life in endeavouring to obtain the liberty of my countrymen, and am a willing sacrifice in their cause: and I beg, as a favour, that I may be immediately led to execution. I know that you have pre-determined to shed my blood, why then all this mockery of a trial?"[2]

The actions and words of the Revolutionary generation were very familiar to Virginians, both white and black. The ideas that the words conveyed across the years resonated powerfully among the enslaved black men who planned to fight for their liberty in Virginia and to be freed from slavery just as the patriots of the American Revolution had fought for their liberty and to be freed from the king. Twenty-five years after Patrick Henry made his speech and more than fifteen years before the first account of his speech was printed, enslaved Virginians knew all about the meaning and the inspiring words of the Revolution: about liberty or death, about all men being created equal and endowed with rights to life, liberty, and the pursuit of happiness. Gabriel and his numerous conspirators, foiled by informants who disclosed their plan and by a flash flood that prevented them from assembling to put their plan into execution, drew on pure Virginia precedents and principles to fight against an impure Virginia creation, slavery.

In the decades after the American Revolution, white Virginians and other Americans expressed a wide variety of conflicting ideas about slavery in their republic founded on the ideas of liberty and equality. Some of them believed that slavery was a mere fact of life; others that it was an unavoidable inheritance or a necessary evil; that it was incompatible with Christianity; that it was incompatible with republican government; that it was morally unjustifiable but impossible to change; or later that it was even a positive good for the owners and for the enslaved people.[3]

Prior to the Revolution, as Richard Bland had indicated in his courtroom argument in 1772, white Virginians generally perceived slavery as a naturally occurring institution, a form of master and servant relationship with some distinctly unpleasant characteristics and consequences. Quakers in the colonies, including Quakers in Virginia, were among the first Americans to argue that the institution was immoral and a violation of Christian principles. Later, as evangelical Christianity worked its way into the sensibilities of the age and the considerations of the body politic, more and more Virginians came to share that view. By the end of the Revolutionary decade, many other Americans also came to a determination that slavery was incompatible with the principles on which they had founded their new nation. In all of the states north of Maryland and Delaware, constitutions and legislatures provided for the gradual abolition of slavery, either by declaring that all persons born after a certain date were to be free or that after a certain date enslaved persons on reaching a given age were to receive their freedom. Congress also forbade the introduction of slavery into the territory (obtained from Virginia) north of the Ohio River and by implication into any new states to be created in that territory.

During the American Revolution the Virginia General Assembly prohibited the forced importation of Africans and allowed men and women to free their enslaved laborers. Several thousand Virginians gained their freedom during the twenty-five years between the outbreak of the American Revolution and Gabriel's conspiracy. The men and women who emancipated individual people or whole families or communities adduced both Christian and republican sentiments to explain their actions. Richard Randolph, for example, wrote his will in February 1796, "in the twentieth year of american Independance," and provided for the emancipation of the enslaved men and women he had inherited and deeded them a portion of land where they could live as free men, women, and children in Virginia.

"In the first place," Randolph began, to make restitution "as far as I am able, to an unfortunate race of bondmen, over whom my ancestors have usurped and exercised the most lawless and monstrous tyranny, and in whom my countrymen (by their iniquitous Laws, in contradiction of their own declaration of rights, and in violation of every sacred Law of nature; of the inherent, unalienable & impriscriptible rights of man; and of every principle of moral & political honesty;) have vested me with absolute property:

"To express my abhorance of the Theory, as well as infamous practice of usurping the rights of our fellow creatures, equally intituled with ourselves to the enjoyment of Liberty and happiness:

"To exculpate myself, to those who may perchance to think or hear of me after death from the black crime, which might otherwise be imputed to me, of voluntarily holding the above mentioned miserable beings in the same state of abject slavery in which I found them on receiving my patrimony, at Lawful age; To impress my children with just horror at a crime so enormous & indelible, to enjure them in the last words of a fond father never to participate in it, in any the remotest degree, however sanctioned by Laws (framed by the tyrants themselves who oppress them,) or supported by false reasoning, used always and to soil the sordid views of avarice, and the lust of power."[4]

The urgent language of the preamble to Randolph's will was unusually powerful, but the beliefs it expressed were not unusual, and even though his provision of land for the people he freed was unusual, it was not unique. A former member of the royal governor's council, Robert Carter, experienced a profound religious conversion and freed a much larger number of slaves and made even more elaborate plans for their independent freedom, and George Washington also provided in his will for freeing his slaves as a public example to nurture free republican government and left instructions and resources for establishing them in economic and civil freedom. George Mason, the author of the Virginia Declaration of Rights, and Thomas Jefferson, the author of the Declaration of Independence, did not free any or many of their slaves.

Jefferson's lifelong personal and political involvement with slavery was particularly important, revealing, and influential. His very first recollection, according to family members who provided the morsel to Jefferson's first biographer, was of being handed up when quite young to the care of an enslaved person who carried him on a pillow on horseback.[5] The memory and mental image are richly suggestive inasmuch as throughout Jefferson's entire life all of his accomplishments were possible because of the labor of people he and his family owned. Slaves and slavery provided the income to support his education, his lavish lifestyle, his mania for collecting books and works of art, and his ability for long periods of time to devote himself to reading and writing and public service, none of which he could have done had they not done his work. In a very real, as well as in a metaphorical, sense slaves and slavery carried Jefferson on a pillow of support throughout his life, as they carried Virginia and many other Virginians, too.

Jefferson's ideas about slavery and enslaved people ranged far across the field of opinions that other people held and were also at war with one another and effectively scuttled his statement that "all men are created equal." During the 1780s Jefferson wrote eloquently about abolishing slavery, but he could not imagine a peaceful or just method. "I tremble for my country," he wrote in his celebrated book, *Notes on the State of Virginia,* "when I reflect that God is just: that his justice cannot sleep for ever." If the grievances of the enslaved led them to rise up in revolt against the enslavers, God "has no attribute which can take side with us in such a contest."[6]

"The whole commerce between master and slave," Jefferson wrote in another passage in that book, "is a perpetual exercise of the most boisterous passions, the most unremitting despotism on the one part, and degrading submissions on the other." It is perhaps revealing that Jefferson's comments on the dehumanizing aspects of American slavery appeared in a short chapter entitled "Manners" and that it dealt with the manners and behavior of white Virginians, not with the manners of black Virginians, and only mentioned somewhat incidentally the effects of slavery on black Virginians. "Our children see this," Jefferson continued, "and learn to imitate it; for man is an imitative animal. This quality is the germ of all education in him. From his cradle to his grave he is learning to do what he sees others do. If a parent could find no motive either in his philanthropy or in his self-love, for restraining the intemperance of passion towards his slave, it should always be a sufficient one that his child is present. But generally it is not sufficient. The parent storms, the child looks on, catches the lineaments of wrath, puts on the same airs in the circle of smaller slaves, gives a loose to his worst of passions, and thus nursed, educated, and daily exercised in tyranny, cannot but be stamped by it with odious peculiarities. The man must be a prodigy who can retain his manners and morals undepraved by such circumstances."[7]

Jefferson's commentary was less compelling on what black people may have thought and learned from the effects of white people's treatment of their slaves. Whether his commentary was purely theoretical or partly autobiographical is not possible to state. Evidence does not exist from Jefferson's childhood or early adulthood to demonstrate whether the causes and consequences of the domestic tyranny of master over slave that he described derived from his personal experiences or merely his observations or his deductions from the commonplace behaviors of white owners of black slaves.

Jefferson was certainly a witness to, and participant in, some of the physical violence that maintaining slavery required. In a private exchange of letters with Governor James Monroe in September 1800, when Jefferson was vice president of the United States and a candidate for president, and when Monroe was reviewing trial records and approving of the hanging of some of Gabriel's coconspirators, Jefferson cautioned against excessively repressive punishment of the conspirators in order not to undermine public support for the strong measures that remained necessary to preserve slavery and to prevent other enslaved people from attempting more insurrections. "Where to stay the hand of the executioner is an important question," he wrote, weighing the necessity to punish the conspirators (who had not killed anybody) in the interest of public order but recognizing that "where a familiarity with slavery, and a possibility of danger from that quarter prepare the general mind for some severities, there is a strong sentiment that there has been hanging enough." The choices that faced Monroe in particular, the state government as a whole, and the class of slave owners, including Jefferson himself, generally, was "indeed a difficult one."[8] In the end Monroe decided to allow the execution of the conspirators.

That Jefferson disapproved of slavery and hoped to ameliorate its consequences or abolish it entirely is quite clear. The emancipation provision in the draft constitution that he tried to promote early in the 1780s[9] evidently incited opposition. It also avoided all mention of the status of the people to be freed. However, the committee that the assembly appointed in 1776 to revise the laws of the state, a committee of which he was a leading member, proposed that all children of enslaved Virginians "should continue with their parents to a certain age, then be brought up, at the public expence, to tillage, arts or sciences, according to their geniusses, till the females should be eighteen, and the males twenty-one years of age, when they should be colonized to such place as the circumstances of the time should render most proper, sending them out with arms, implements of houshold and of the handicraft arts, seeds, pairs of the useful domestic animals, &c."[10] That proposal went nowhere, either, perhaps because of the expensive requirement that the state raise the young slaves to adulthood.

What to do about freed people and how to compensate their owners became the most difficult problems for opponents of slavery during the first half of the nineteenth century. Slavery being in a very real sense a national as well as a personal and sectional problem, Jefferson even considered enlisting the federal government and its potentially great power to tax as a means of raising enough money to compensate owners and pay for deportation, but common-sense practicality and repugnance to so powerful an exercise of federal power quickly dissuaded him.[11] Many people who disliked slavery, as Jefferson did, despaired of ever finding a way for white Southerners to live in comfortable freedom without enslaved black people or to live in comfortable safety with free black people.

Jefferson was ahead of many other Americans in his ideas about freedom and democracy, he was ahead of them in his ideas about slavery, too, and he also was ahead of them in being one of the first Americans to suggest that biological differences—innate, permanent differences—between people of European origin or descent and people of African origin or descent would dictate the perpetual superiority of the one over the other and the ultimate incompatibility of the two in a state of equality. That is to say, he was ahead of them in thinking and writing about race, too.

Jefferson wrote all that and more during the 1780s in his *Notes on the State of Virginia*. "It will probably be asked," he replied to anticipated objections to the cohabitation of white and black people in the United States, "Why not retain and incorporate the blacks into the state, and thus save the expence of supplying, by importation of white settlers, the vacancies they will leave?" He answered his own question: "Deep rooted prejudices entertained by the whites; ten thousand recollections, by the blacks, of the injuries they have sustained; new provocations; the real distinctions which nature has made; and many other circumstances, will divide us into parties, and produce convulsions which will probably never end but in the extermination of the one or the other race."[12]

"To these objections," Jefferson continued, "which are political, may be added others, which are physical and moral," opening for future generations a line of reasoning that allowed white people to identify themselves as of a superior order of creation—not merely as more technologically advanced or culturally refined—and therefore entitled to maintain white supremacy on the degraded status of other people. "The first difference which strikes us is that of colour," Jefferson wrote, a difference that was "fixed in nature, and is as real as if its seat and cause were better known to us. And is this difference of no importance?" Jefferson then advanced his line of argument another step further with a pair of rhetorical questions reflecting his belief in the natural or cultural superiority of the one race over the other and answered in part by an allusion to supposedly documented (natural?) sexual attractions of inferior beings to superior beings. "Is it not the foundation of a greater or less share of beauty in the two races?" he inquired. "Are not the fine mixtures of red and white, the expressions of every passion by greater or less suffusions of colour in the one, preferable to that eternal monotony, which reigns in the countenances, that immoveable veil of black which covers all the emotions of the other race? Add to these, flowing hair, a more elegant symmetry of form, their own judgment in favour of the whites, declared by their preference of them, as uniformly as is the preference of the Oron-ootan for the black women over those of his own species."[13]

Without breaking his line of argument so much as even to begin a new paragraph, Jefferson continued in the same vein. "The circumstance of superior beauty, is thought worthy attention in the propagation of our horses, dogs, and other domestic animals; why not in that of man?" He slipped the word *other* in the next sentence to link horses, dogs, farm animals, and man: black enslaved farm laborers. "Besides those of colour, figure, and hair," he wrote, "there are other physical distinctions proving a difference of race. They have less hair on the face and body." That is, black people had less hair than white people, white people being the standard of beauty, intellect, and talent in all of these passages. "They secrete less by the kidnies, and more by the glands of the skin, which gives them a very strong and disagreeable odour. This greater degree of transpiration renders them more tolerant of heat, and less so of cold, than the whites."[14]

Jefferson adduced other supposed physical differences between white and black people and then described what he believed were behavioral and intellectual differences, all innate and permanent and all to the disadvantage of

Africans. "They seem to require less sleep," he wrote. "A black, after hard labour through the day, will be induced by the slightest amusements to sit up till midnight, or later, though knowing he must be out with the first dawn of the morning. They are at least as brave, and more adventuresome. But this may perhaps proceed from a want of fore-thought, which prevents their seeing a danger till it be present. When present, they do not go through it with more coolness or steadiness than the whites. They are more ardent after their female: but love seems with them to be more an eager desire, than a tender delicate mixture of sentiment and sensation." Men, in this sentence, were the standard by which he measured both black and white people, and he completely ignored women's passions and intellects. "Their griefs," he continued, "are transient. Those numberless afflictions, which render it doubtful whether heaven has given life to us in mercy or in wrath, are less felt, and sooner forgotten with them. In general, their existence appears to participate more of sensation than reflection. To this must be ascribed their disposition to sleep when abstracted from their diversions, and unemployed in labour."[15] Jefferson contradicted there what he had written a few lines above where he stated that blacks needed less sleep than whites. That self-contradiction, which he failed to explain or perhaps even to detect, disclosed that he believed that black people were inherently indolent and therefore less socially valuable and individually responsible than white people.

"Comparing them by their faculties of memory, reason, and imagination," Jefferson resumed, "it appears to me, that in memory they are equal to the whites; in reason much inferior, as I think one could scarcely be found capable of tracing and comprehending the investigations of Euclid; and that in imagination they are dull, tasteless, and anomalous."[16] He then admitted the possibility that free people in Africa might exhibit different behaviors and talents than enslaved people in America and that it was not possible to discover if the hard work and living conditions of slavery debased their natural talents or whether their inability to learn more from their superiors indicated the outermost boundaries of their natural abilities.[17]

Jefferson inclined toward the latter conclusion and wrote that black people "might have availed themselves of the conversation of their masters; many have been brought up to the handicraft arts, and from that circumstance have always been associated with the whites. Some have been liberally educated, and all have lived in countries where the arts and sciences are cultivated to a considerable degree, and have had before their eyes samples of the best works from abroad." Then he made a stark comparison. "The Indians," he wrote, "with no advantages of this kind, will often carve figures on their pipes not destitute of design and merit. They will crayon out an animal, a plant, or a country, so as to prove the existence of a germ in their minds which only wants cultivation. They astonish you with strokes of the most sublime oratory; such as prove their reason and sentiment strong, their imagination glowing and elevated. But never yet could I find that a black had uttered a thought above the level of plain narration; never see even an elementary trait of painting or sculpture." In music, he admitted, "they are more generally gifted than the whites with accurate ears for tune and time." Jefferson closed his enumeration of incapacities by writing: "Misery is often the parent of the most affecting touches in poetry.—Among the blacks is misery enough, God knows, but no poetry. Love is the peculiar œstrum of the poet. Their love is ardent, but it kindles the senses only, not the imagination."[18]

Jefferson's language was not the language of his early seventeenth-century predecessors in Virginia who had contrasted English and savage behavior, compared Christian and heathen people, and distinguished between civilized and barbaric populations. Jefferson compared the physical and moral attributes and the behaviors of the cultured beneficiaries of Anglo-American civilization with people under the control of animalistic urges. His long catalog of evidences of innate and irrevocable inferiority of people of African origin or descent, when compared with people of European origin or descent and of American Indian origin or descent, either led him, or derived from his predisposition, to accept slavery as an unavoidable evil and blunted his willingness to challenge his contemporaries by aggressively pursuing his own early antislavery beliefs.

Whether or how much Jefferson's opinions about people of African origin or descent changed after the 1780s is not clear. If, as seems likely, he engaged during the following decades in a long and perhaps affectionate sexual relationship with his enslaved woman Sally Hemings, and if, as also seems likely, they had several children, for whom he uniquely provided opportunities for freedom, then it might be that Jefferson's ideas about the innate inferiority of Africans or of people of African origin or descent may have softened or changed into less dogmatic or more sensitive or subtle ideas.[19]

But perhaps not. Jefferson wrote more than once during his life about how interbreeding between white and black people degraded the white race. He also wrote in 1815, in response to a question about racial classifications in Virginia, that by repeated matings of descendants of a black person with white people, the descendants of a black person could become white. Anticipating the genetic theories of Gregor Mendel, Jefferson demonstrated, based on his reading, on his management of his plantation animals, and with several long algebraic formulae, that "it is understood in Natural history that a 4th cross of one race of animals with another gives an issue equivalent for all sensible purposes to the original blood." The law of Virginia "considers 2. crosses with the pure white, and a 3d with any degree of mixture, however small, as clearing the issue of the negro blood." The word *clearing* suggested cleansing an impurity. He then observed, "that this does not reestablish freedom, which depends" as it had since the 1660s "on the condition of the mother."[20] Sally Hemings's children, white by Jefferson's mathematical calculations and the language of Virginia's laws, remained enslaved by the requirements of those laws until he allowed some of them, in spite of those laws, to enjoy freedom, but only by denying their pasts and their families.

Jefferson became politically paralyzed on the subject of slavery even before the end of the American Revolution. Early in his career in the House of Burgesses, about 1769, he persuaded Richard Bland "to move for certain moderate extensions of the protection of the laws" to enslaved people. Jefferson recalled in 1814 that he seconded Bland's motion "and, as a younger member, was more spared in the debate: but he was denounced as an enemy to his country, & was treated with the grossest indecorum."[21] The journals of the House of Burgesses do not disclose the precise nature of Bland's motion, but it is possible that Jefferson referred to an amendment proposed by a member not identified in the journal and adopted in 1769 to the 1748 Act Directing the Trial of Slaves Committing Capital Crimes; and for the More Effectual Punishing Conspiracies and Insurrections of Them; and for the Better Government of Negroes, Mulattoes, and Indians, Bond or Free. The amendment of 1769 repealed an authorization to the county courts to permit the castration of repeat runaways.[22] Castration was, of course, a severe punishment, but it was probably also regarded as a deterrent not only by its threat but in the same way that gelding a colt produced a horse more docile than a stallion.

In the 1780s Jefferson's *post nati* proposals for the gradual abolition of slavery and deportation of freed people died. After those few failed attempts to change the laws of Virginia, he resigned himself to a reluctant acceptance of a reality that he could not devise a means to change. He even refused to assist other people who tried to change things in their own ways. In 1814 Jefferson wrote a revealing letter to a young Virginian of his acquaintance, Edward Coles, who having grown disgusted with slavery proposed to take his enslaved people north of the Ohio River and give them their freedom. Coles did so, anyway, in spite of a frosty response that he received from Jefferson after asking for the old man's blessing on the project.

"I had always hoped," Jefferson wrote to Coles, "that the younger generation, receiving their early impressions after the flame of liberty had been kindled in every breast, and had become as it were the vital spirit of every American, that the generous temperament of youth, analogous to the motion of their blood, and above the suggestions of avarice, would have sympathised" with victims of oppression "wherever found, and proved their love of liberty beyond their own share of it." That was something that Jefferson and a large majority of white Virginia men of his own generation did not do, significantly extend the empire of liberty beyond their own share of it. Coles's "solitary but welcome voice is the first which has brought this sound to my ear," Jefferson went on, throwing the first dash of cold water on the proposal because "I have considered the general silence which prevails on this subject as indicating an apathy unfavorable to every hope."

Jefferson had done little to combat that apathy, and in 1814 when repeating his own hope that the abolition of slavery would eventually take place, he nevertheless expressed deep skepticism about Coles's proposal, founded in large part on his own want of confidence in the capacities of African Americans to live on their own and also on their owners' pervasive omission of preparing them for freedom. He was one of those negligent owners, himself. For "men, probably of any colour, but of this color we know," Jefferson cautioned revealingly, "brought up from their infancy without necessity for thought or forecast, are by their habits rendered as incapable as children of taking care of themselves, and are extinguished promptly wherever industry is necessary for raising the young. in the mean time they are pests in society by their idleness, and the depredations to which this leads them. their amalgamation with the other colour produces a degradation to which no lover of his country, no lover of excellence in the human character can innocently consent."

Jefferson excused himself in his old age from taking even a small part in promoting the dream of his youth. Declining to endorse Coles's plan, he explained that "this enterprise is for the young, for those who can follow it up, and bear it through to it's consummation. it shall have all my prayers, and these are the only weapons of an old man." Jefferson then retreated another step and wrote, "but in the mean time are you right in abandoning this property, and your country with it? I think not. my opinion has ever been that, until more can be done for them, we should endeavor, with those whom fortune has thrown on our hands, to feed & clothe them well, protect them from ill usage, require such reasonable labor only as is performed voluntarily by freemen, and be led by no repugnancies to abdicate them, and our duties to them. the laws do not permit us to turn them loose, if that were for their good: and to commute them for other property"—that is, to sell the enslaved men, women, and children, who were a very valuable property that naturally increased in value as it increased in number—"is to commit them to those whose usage of them we cannot controul."[23]

A large gap yawns open in Jefferson's cautious words "until more can be done for them." Who? What? When? Jefferson lived more than eighty years, most of them in Virginia, and during that time he and most of his contemporaries did very little toward preparing enslaved Virginians for freedom and responsible independent living. Jefferson wrote some of the most eloquent antislavery language of any Revolutionary Virginian, but his political paralysis in the face of slavery and its supporters together with his deep skepticism about the capacity of black people for independence and freedom starkly exposed the limits of his and other white people's antislavery opinions. Had there been then a Martin Luther King Jr., he would have been fully justified in interrupting at that point in Thomas Jefferson's letter to Edward Coles and asking, as he asked almost 150 years later in his letter from the Birmingham jail, How long?

The white men who controlled public life and the law of Virginia during Jefferson's lifetime answered with their actions, Never.

During the decades that Thomas Jefferson lived and wrote about slavery, the religious considerations and the Revolutionary rhetoric that had prompted changes in the law late in the eighteenth century and led to numerous manumissions lost much of their purchase. Six years after Gabriel's conspiracy, the General Assembly required that any person freed from slavery leave the state within a year or be reenslaved. The assembly allowed freed people to petition the General Assembly or county and municipal courts for special permission to remain, but the law signaled that political opinion in Virginia had begun to harden against emancipation of slaves and also against an enlargement of the population in Virginia of what the laws and public records of the time distinguished as "free persons of color"—not free persons, but free persons of color—white men's laws always distinguished between free white people and other free people, whether black or Indian, indicating that the law and the lawmakers viewed them as essentially, not superficially, different from white people.[24]

Moral, religious, political, and also economic considerations figured in public discussions of slavery. Although the institution was primarily a system of agricultural labor in Virginia, men and women who lived in towns and cities also participated in the slave economy if they owned or leased enslaved people to perform domestic tasks such as cleaning, cooking, washing, or caring for children. The iron and transportation industries and many other enterprises in Virginia also employed slave labor, both owning and leasing laborers. The whole economy, in fact, relied on the work of enslaved laborers. The entire culture, in fact, relied on slavery.

The profitability of slavery was nevertheless a frequent topic of discussion. Planters with more enslaved laborers than they could profitably use on their plantations or rent out to other people complained that for them slavery could be unprofitable. The birthrate exceeded the death rate, and the natural increase of their enslaved population necessitated maintenance costs that the labor and rent they derived from ownerships of slaves did not always fully cover. Hence, a very large and profitable business of buying and shipping surplus enslaved laborers for sale in labor-hungry markets to the southwest developed. It is very likely that selling and transporting surplus slaves out of Virginia became the largest business enterprise in the state during the half century before the American Civil War. During that time Virginians exported perhaps as many as eight or ten thousand human beings out of Virginia annually, a larger number of men, women, and children than their ancestors had imported into Virginia from Africa during the century and a half before the American Revolution.[25]

That movement of enslaved laborers suggested to some public men who debated the profitability or the propriety of maintaining slavery that if settlers in the western and southwestern states and territories continued to purchase laborers from the eastern, and particularly northeastern, slave states such as Virginia, the institution of slavery might eventually become extinct in those states by the simple operation of the laws of supply and demand. Some of those men also argued that the diffusion of slavery over a wider territory would reduce its economic significance in all of the places where it existed and therefore put it on the slow road to eventual extinction. Expounders of both of those theories, however, conveniently ignored or underestimated the natural increase of the enslaved population and also the capital investment that people who purchased slaves incurred. They were as unlikely to cast aside that valuable property as owners of enslaved people in Virginia were to free their own slaves without compensation merely to be rid of the distasteful institution. At bottom, white men may have advanced the diffusion argument to make Virginia a whiter and freer state than it had been, not to extinguish slavery.[26]

Then, in August 1831, as in August 1800, another group of enslaved Virginians planned to begin the war against slavery. Thirty-one years after Gabriel's aborted conspiracy, five years after Thomas Jefferson's death, and a year and a half after a constitutional convention that had reinforced the political power of the class of men who owned the most slaves, the war against slavery began in Southampton County. It lasted two days. Nat Turner and several other enslaved men led small parties armed with guns and swords on a race through the rural countryside, killing nearly sixty white men, women, and children before the county militia dispersed and apprehended them. In retaliation the militia and other groups of white people in the county killed perhaps as many as two hundred black people, most of whom had no part in or prior knowledge of the rebellion. It was the bloodiest uprising against slavery in Virginia's history and also the bloodiest pogrom that white Virginians ever perpetrated.[27] All of the rebellion's leaders perished on the gallows, including its namesake, Nat Turner.

The trials of Turner and his confederates, precisely like the trials of Gabriel and his fellow conspirators, took place before a select number of the county's justices of the peace assembled in what had been known since the latter years of the seventeenth century as a court of oyer and terminer, literally, a court that could hear and determine a case. As in most trials of enslaved people in Virginia, the court allowed the accused men advice of counsel, but the court did not afford them the full budget of rights to which white people were entitled, including the procedural protections of the common law, a jury to decide guilt or innocence, or an ability to appeal a verdict or a procedural error to a higher court. Justices of the peace, who were also owners of slaves and for the most part not trained in the law, decided guilt or innocence and decreed punishment. Slavery had led Virginia's otherwise punctilious legal establishment to create a separate and unequal judicial system for trying enslaved people accused of serious crimes that their owners did not or were not permitted to punish privately.[28] The trials of 1800 and of 1831 were not the same legal processes that white Virginians faced when accused of crimes and about which white attorneys, judges, law professors, and nineteenth-century historians boasted.

Nat Turner's Rebellion prompted the General Assembly to pass several new laws in support of slavery and to place additional limitations on free blacks. The process was already in the works. A few months before the rebellion the assembly made it a criminal offense for any person to receive a salary for instructing enslaved people how to read and write, and it also made it a criminal offense for "any white person or persons" to "assemble with free negroes or mulattoes, at any school-house, church, meeting-house, or other place for the purpose of instructing such free negroes or mulattoes to read or write."[29] (The state's laws did not, as popularly believed, make it illegal for people to teach their own property to read and write.) In 1832 the assembly amended the state's criminal code to require prosecution of all criminal charges against free blacks, as well as against slaves, in the courts of oyer and terminer and under disadvantageous rules of procedure that they never imposed on any white people and that the courts and kings of England had never imposed on any white Virginians, either.[30] The assembly also restricted the freedom of religious worship that enslaved black and free white and free black Virginians had all theoretically enjoyed. A new law of 1832 forbade slaves to preach, and it required that black congregations, which existed in a number of communities in Virginia, have white clergymen to superintend their worship services.[31] That in spite of the state's celebrated Declaration of Rights of 1776 and its equally celebrated Act for Establishing Religious Freedom, passed in 1786 and engrafted in part into the Constitution of 1830, that appeared to guarantee the free exercise of religion for all Virginians.

In 1833 the General Assembly passed An Act Making Appropriations for the Removal of Free Persons of Colour.[32] It was underfunded, unpopular with the state's free black population, and did not work, but its ineffectiveness did not stop white Virginians from writing and talking about means to expel what they increasingly appear to have regarded as a dangerous population. By then Virginia members of the American Colonization Society were promoting colonization as a means of ridding the state of free black people, not as a technique for ending slavery, which many of the society's founders and Northern members desired.[33]

One of the remarkable things about the rebellion of Nat Turner is that shortly after his capture and shortly before his execution, he made a long statement to an attorney who published it (with how much alteration is not possible to say) as a pamphlet, *The Confessions of Nat Turner, The Leader of the Late Insurrection in Southampton, Va.* In it Turner described himself as acting in the tradition of the Old Testament prophets. The *Confessions* quoted him as stating that divine revelation endowed him with a postmessianic mission when "on the 12th of May, 1828, I heard a loud noise in the heavens, and the Spirit instantly appeared to me and said the Serpent was loosened, and Christ had laid down the yoke he had borne for the sins of men, and that I should take it on and fight against the Serpent, for the time was fast approaching when the first should be last and the last should be first."[34] Another heavenly sign instructed him when to act.

Most white Virginians and an appreciable number of free and enslaved black Virginians shared essential elements of the same evangelical Protestant beliefs during the first decades of the nineteenth century. They would have recognized Turner's paraphrase of chapter 10, verse 31 of the book of Mark. That made Nat Turner's published confessions a singularly influential document; but as Turner's amanuensis presented the text, Turner appeared as an impractical and immoral fanatic, not as a religiously motivated or principled opponent of oppression. That may have made it easier for legislators and white church officials to impose restrictions on the religious practices of free and enslaved black people without worrying that they were violating the letter or spirit of their own law against state involvement in religious and church affairs. It is likely that they did not worry about that very much, anyway, as they routinely denied black Virginians, both free and enslaved, other civil and human rights that they never tried to deny to white Virginians. The *Confessions* as published also allowed them to indulge in some comfortable self-delusion and to dismiss Nat Turner and his rebellion as a freakish event, the consequence of a fanatic on a rampage, and not as evidence that evangelical Protestant Christianity contained antislavery principles or that other enslaved people, if proficient in religious understanding, would also rebel.[35]

Five months after the rebellion, in January 1832, members of the House of Delegates engaged in a two-week debate about slavery. The Richmond *Enquirer* and the Richmond *Constitutional Whig* covered the debates in detail, and ten delegates printed full texts of their elaborate speeches in pamphlet form for wider distribution and influence. The debates revealed that although many of the leading public men in the state continued to regard slavery as an evil or immoral institution, as had their predecessors, they could not devise or agree to a means of abolishing or reducing it. Too many other influential public men firmly opposed ending slavery. They would not or could not force themselves to abolish slavery without compensating owners for the value of the lost property. That cost was too high, and for the same reason they could not or would not force themselves to pay for the transportation of freed people out of Virginia, which they regarded as an absolutely essential component of emancipation.[36]

Living with slavery in a land of freedom involved white Virginians in many contradictions, some of which they may not have even perceived, like Jefferson's comments on black people and sleep. Early in 1838, for example, 106 men in Lancaster County sent a petition to the General Assembly asking that a new means be devised to export free blacks from Virginia. They wrote, in part, "The degraded condition of this unhappy class of persons must necessarily produce the lowest state of morals amongst them; and it is notorious that a very large proportion of the whole class subsists, either by their own predatory habits, or by acting as factors for the reception and disposal of the goods stolen by slaves.—This consideration alone, to say nothing of the malign influences which their residence amongst them exerts upon the slave population, conclusively proves, we think, that as a mere question of economy, their colonization in Africa would prove a great blessing to the community. Indeed, it is confidently believed, that in a very large majority of cases, the actual cost of their removal to Africa would bear but a small proportion to the loss sustained by the community from their dishonest habits." But the petitioners also wrote, directly contradicting their description of the bad character and influence of free blacks in Virginia, that the deportation of the state's free black population to Africa would be an act of "philanthropy in carrying the lights of civilization and christianity to the dark shores of benighted Africa, and of thus rendering to that unhappy land a rich remuneration for all the injuries and cruelties inflicted upon her."[37]

How immoral men and women if deported from Virginia to Africa were to introduce improved morality there not only remained an unanswered question; the authors of the petition probably did not even perceive that they had contradicted themselves. Neither did public men in the city of Richmond ever betray any sense of irony or shame that when they needed a very large hall in which to gather and celebrate Independence Day or to pass resolutions against the dangers of abolitionists or to extol state's rights and defend slavery, they often rented the city's First African Baptist Church, which was the largest room in the city. They celebrated their liberty in a church that their social and legal inferiors owned and that included a large percentage of enslaved men and women among its members.[38]

Just as Nat Turner's Rebellion led to the important debate about slavery in the General Assembly in January 1832, that debate led to the publication of an important book, Thomas R. Dew's *Review of the Debate in the Virginia Legislature of 1831 and 1832.*[39] It was not so much a review of the debate as an extended historical reflection on slavery and its importance in Southern economics and society. Dew advanced his own explanations of how and why emancipation without deportation was unsafe and impractical, which echoed what the legislators had said; about the absolute necessity to protect the rights of property that owners of slaves enjoyed, which in turn echoed what the members of the recent Constitutional Convention of 1829–30 had said; and that any discussion at all of general emancipation was inherently dangerous in a society of slaves, even though he believed that enslaved people individually or in small groups were incapable, because of their dispersed condition and lack of education, of making an effective revolution.

Dew wrote that slavery in one form or another had always been a natural and accepted part of human society, which detached everything else that he wrote on the subject from questions of morality and republican political theory. As part of God's creation, slavery was natural and therefore good. Dew then went on to write at length about the inferiority of black people to white people, echoing Thomas Jefferson in some respects, and adding that the skin color of enslaved people in the Southern states would forever set them apart from free white people. In the United States, in short, Dew wrote, slavery was the natural and proper status for people of African descent. John C. Calhoun soon took the small next step and as if building on what Dew wrote stated flatly that slavery was a positive good for the whole society.

The nature of discourse about slavery in Virginia changed slowly at first and then more rapidly during the decades between the American Revolution and the American Civil War, during the decades that included Gabriel's conspiracy of 1800, Nat Turner's Rebellion of 1831, and John Brown's raid on Harpers Ferry in 1859.[40] The generations of Virginians who came of age during the middle decades of the nineteenth century were less likely to view slavery as a problem of civic or religious morality than the men and women who had discussed it during the first decades after the American Revolution. When Northern critics of slavery attacked the institution at midcentury as immoral, un-Christian, or unwholesome for the republic, white Virginians became less likely to agree and more likely to respond indignantly, as if insulted. After Harriet Beecher Stowe published *Uncle Tom's Cabin* in 1852 and created a sensation by condemning the immorality of slavery and slave owners, a young Norfolk writer, Martha Haines Butt, published a novel in response, *Antifanaticism: A Tale of the South,* in which she described owners of slaves as admirable Christian stewards of an unfortunate people who learned civilization and Christianity from them. Another Virginia native, Mary Henderson Eastman, published another novel, *Aunt Phillis's Cabin, or, Southern Life as*

It Is, that carried the same political message and interpretation of slavery as a wholesome institution.[41]

Along with Thomas R. Dew, perhaps the most famous nineteenth-century Virginia writer on the subject of slavery was George Fitzhugh. His two books, *Cannibals All: Or, Slaves without Masters,* published in 1854, and *Sociology for the South,* published in 1857,[42] compared Southern agricultural slavery with labor systems in industrial England and in the Northern states. Fitzhugh declared that Southern slave owners treated their enslaved laborers better than Northern or European capitalists treated their wage laborers. Fitzhugh carried the theory of slave labor to its logical extreme, which appeared to many people to be an illogical extreme. Slavery might very well be the best labor management system for all workers regardless of race because owners of enslaved laborers had a capital investment in their workers, and the owners' self-interest would lead them to treat their enslaved property more humanely than the heartless entrepreneurs could afford or would provide to their exploited wage laborers.

For most writers on slavery it was impossible to separate labor management from race as Fitzhugh appeared to do; and for many men and women of faith during the nineteenth century, like Butt and Eastman, slavery could be reconciled to Christian morality. The proslavery theology that developed in the Southern states during the second third of the nineteenth century did not teach that slavery was un-Christian; it taught Christian masters and mistresses to be benevolent protectors of the lesser beings that history had thrown into their protection. The Bible contained no explicit condemnations of slavery as it existed in the ancient world, but it did contain admonitions to servants to obey their masters and to masters to treat their servants kindly. Men of the cloth who made their theological peace with slavery ignored or dismissed the many differences between slavery as it was practiced in biblical or in Greek or Roman times and slavery as it had developed by the nineteenth century in the Southern states of North America. They adopted an interpretation of the story of Ham in the book of Genesis to justify slavery, even though nothing in that story explicitly linked Africans with Ham, who was cursed along with all of his descendants to perpetual servitude; but that was an easy omission to step across for people who sought and were eager to find differences between themselves and their dark-skinned lifetime servants. By the 1850s some Virginia clergymen and clergymen elsewhere in the states where slavery existed took a second and larger step and suggested that the people of Africa were not the same as the people of the Bible (and themselves), that Africans were the result of a separate creation, not of the biblical creation of man and woman in Eden where God gave his favored creatures dominion over all of his other creatures.[43]

Most Southern writers placed race at the center of their discussions, leading them along a parallel interpretive path. Jefferson's long catalog of evidences of innate inferiority of people of African origin or descent that he published in *Notes on the State of Virginia* in the 1780s was one of the first compilations of its kind in a long train of such commentaries that led by the beginning of the twentieth century to a respectable science of racial distinctions within the human population that very closely resembled Jefferson's and Richard Bland's own understandings of the natural order of human society. For a man of the Enlightenment like Jefferson and for men of science later, distinguishing gradations of quality in the great chain of being emphasized the differences and made it easier for them to vary their attitudes and their treatment of different groups of people according to a sliding scale of value. They easily deduced that people of western European origin or descent were so different from and superior to people of African origin or descent as to be a separate and superior species. Jefferson's *Notes on the State of Virginia* pointed directly to that conclusion, to the social and legal segregation of the Jim Crow era in the twentieth century.[44]

The political economy of slavery in Virginia rested on imported ancient English property rights, on personal vested interests and fears, and on evolving attitudes about race and culture. Building on the ideas that Thomas Jefferson and Thomas R. Dew expounded, Abel Parker Upshur sketched out the interrelated set of beliefs that gained the common ground of white political discourse in Virginia during the second quarter of the nineteenth century. A talented attorney who lived on the Eastern Shore of Virginia, Upshur was the first delegate to speak during the Constitutional Convention of 1829–30, and the man who spoke at the greatest length, in opposition to the Revolutionary beliefs that all men were created equal and that they had inherent natural rights. He declared that the structure of the society in which people lived dictated the nature of their rights and the distribution of all rights.[45] In 1839, nearly a decade after the convention, two years before he became secretary of the navy, and four years before he became secretary of state, Upshur published a long essay entitled "On Domestic Slavery" in the popular and influential Richmond magazine, the *Southern Literary Messenger.*

Upshur dismissed the notion that the people then held in slavery in the United States had ever had a natural right to liberty or freedom, and he argued that the institution of slavery in the agrarian South conferred many advantages on the society, that is, on the society of white people. "Here the slave is black, and the white man never is a slave," he wrote. "The distinction addresses itself to the eye, and is proclaimed wherever the two classes appear. It is certainly well calculated to inspire the humblest white man with a high sense of his own comparative dignity and importance, to see a whole class below him in the scale of society. However poor, or ignorant or miserable he

may be, he has yet the consoling consciousness that there is a still lower condition to which he can never be reduced. He sees continually around him,
men whose inferiority to himself is acknowledged, whose rights and privileges
are less than his own, and between whom and himself there is an impassable
barrier, which every white man, however proud of his condition, is interested
in preserving unbroken. . . . In our slave-holding communities, the white man,
whatever be his condition, is accustomed to exercise absolute authority over
the negro, and to receive from him continual proofs of deference and respect."
Upshur concluded that part of his article, "The best foundation of political
liberty for white men is personal independence and self-respect; and these
feelings are necessarily inspired in a high degree by the very nature of the relation between master and slave."[46]

"Most men in such circumstances," Upshur wrote, referring to the enslaved
population, "would be apt to charge their misfortunes to errors in the systems
around them; to the laws which recognize and maintain differences of condition among men, odious to them, because they feel them to be oppressive in
their own persons. Not so with the slave. He is born to his condition; he grows
up with the conviction that it is unchangeable; he submits to his destiny with
resignation, because he has no hope that he can ever make it materially better.
Even freedom is scarcely a blessing to him, for the external brand is upon his
face—his caste is irrevocably fixed—and although he may cease to acknowledge a master, he can never cease to belong to the lowest class of mankind. It
is the deep conviction of this truth which so often induces the slaves of kind
masters to refuse freedom, when it is offered to them. Freedom is no boon to
them, since it brings with it all the cares and difficulties of self-dependence,
without any of the usual advantages of independence in thought and action.
The African slave is contented from necessity. He has no motive to quarrel
with a lot which he knows that he cannot change, and the burthens of which
are best relieved by a cheerful discharge of the duties which attend them. The
history of slavery in the United States, attests the truth of this reasoning. In
no part of the world has the laboring class been more distinguished for con-
tentment, cheerfulness, and even gaiety; and such the negro slave will always
be, if he be not taught to feel or to imagine other evils than those which his
condition itself imposes on him."[47]

"Our safety," Upshur concluded, referring to the white people, "is in the
color of the slave; in an eternal, ineffaceable distinction of nature. . . . His caste
is everlasting, and whether bond or free, he is the negro still. This he knows
and feels continually. It gives him a habit of obedience and submission, not
easy to be broken, and it teaches him not to put his own safety to hazard for
objects which Nature herself has placed forever beyond his reach."[48]

Upshur had gone beyond Thomas Jefferson's musings on racial distinctions to declare that racial inferiority was, itself, the foundation stone in the

permanent enslavement of African Americans, which was therefore their natural condition. For Upshur, slavery was not a necessary evil, an inheritance to be despised, or an immoral, un-Christian, or unrepublican institution. It was the right thing. He pretended, as many other white Southerners did then and later, to understand what African Americans thought and believed, whether they were enslaved or free, but his own thoughts and beliefs blinded him so much that he omitted to mention the obvious flights of enslaved people from the slave states to the free states, their numerous individual and collective acts of disobedience or obstruction, the occasional threatened or overt revolts like Gabriel's conspiracy of 1800 and Nat Turner's Rebellion of 1831, and the behavior of free black men that the white men of Essex County complained about to the legislature one year before Upshur published his essay.

Upshur's firm belief in the rightness of American slavery and in the contentedness of American slaves may have blinded him to another thing. If American slavery was so conspicuously right and just and good, why did he think it necessary to write and add yet another long essay to an already large and rapidly increasing body of literature explaining and defending the interests of Southern slave owners? In the nineteenth-century slave South, as elsewhere and in other times and places, white people could and did firmly believe mutually incompatible things or ignore facts that contradicted their beliefs.

Upshur proposed a theory of social equality for all white men within a regime of white supremacy that in some Southern states led to universal white manhood suffrage, something that he when a member of the Constitutional Convention of 1829–30 had successfully opposed but which eventually came to pass in Virginia in 1851 after he was dead. "There is not, it is true," Upshur remarked tellingly about the white Virginians for whom he presumed to speak, "much of that rude and levelling democracy, which seeks to establish a *perfect* equality, forbidden by the very nature of man."[49]

It would not be correct to give Thomas Jefferson or Thomas R. Dew or George Fitzhugh or Abel P. Upshur too much individual credit for shaping proslavery thought in the old South. They said and wrote what many other people said and wrote. Each was influential, but many more people made the same or similar arguments. The weight of white Southern public opinion slowly shifted away from the ideas expressed during and immediately after the American Revolution when Southern antislavery thought was at its height but still failed to extinguish slavery anywhere below the Mason-Dixon Line. At first slowly and then more speedily after the generations that had lived through the American Revolution or had grown up in its afterglow gradually died out, public opinion shifted toward the assumptions and beliefs that Upshur bluntly expressed in 1839.

In spite of what Upshur wrote about the contented enslaved population, the social and economic importance of slavery required strict control over the lives of enslaved Virginians and also over the lives of free black Virginians, and it required controls over the lives of many white Virginians. About half of the General Assembly's 1848 revised law Of Offences Against Public Policy, which regulated gambling and sharp financial practices, concerned slaves and slavery. The law made it illegal for any "free person" to speak, write, or maintain "that owners have not right of property in their slaves" or to "write, print, or cause to be written or printed, any book, pamphlet, or other writing" that promoted insurrection or that denied "the rights of masters to property in their slaves." It also made it illegal for any federal postmaster to allow such printed materials to pass through the mail in the state, and it made it illegal for owners of slaves to allow enslaved men or women to fend for themselves and live as if free.[50]

In practice, magistrates often ignored the state's restrictive laws for the protection of slavery and the regulation of both free and enslaved black Virginians or enforced them only when the safety of white people appeared to require enforcement. Within the slave regime many individual personal relationships of trust and respect could flourish, but by its laws the state government, expressing the values of the white male residents, established boundaries around the behavior of both white people and black people that benefited only white people and most benefited the white people who owned slaves or who feared that free or enslaved black people posed dangers to their public peace.[51]

The maintenance of slavery also overrode some important political beliefs, including state's rights. For example, James Murray Mason was a grandson of George Mason, who drafted the Virginia Declaration of Rights in 1776 and opposed ratification of the United States Constitution in 1788 because he feared a too-strong federal government; but as a member of the United States Senate, James Murray Mason was a principal author of the Fugitive Slave Act that Congress passed in 1850 as part of the great compromise of that year. Mason and nearly all of the other members of Congress from the states where slavery was legal supported passage of the law to require that states where slavery was not legal return to their owners all people who had escaped from slavery. The Supreme Court of the United States had ruled that states had a right to decline to empower their officers and courts to return fugitives from slavery, and the federal government had no agency that could act independently of the states when owners of slaves sought to seize men and women who they claimed had escaped. The new law of 1850 allowed slave owners to pursue runaways into free states and to seize and return them to slave states without interference from state authorities. When acting to protect slave owners' rights to their enslaved property and the institution of slavery, Southern slave owners required strong congressional action to limit Northern states' rights to pass and enforce what were called personal liberty laws that assisted people escaping from slavery. Those same Southern politicians objected that Congress had no constitutional authority to prohibit slavery in the western territories but demanded that Congress exercise its authority to protect the property rights of slaveholders who moved into the territories and took their slave property with them. Protection of slavery became a major preoccupation of Southern politics and Southern politicians.

Upshur's understanding of the political economy of slavery in Virginia in 1839 was on the road to becoming the norm. It became the thinking of the men from the South who voted for the Fugitive Slave Act of 1850. It was the thinking of the men of the Virginia Constitutional Convention of 1850–51 who inserted the words *slave* and *slavery* for the first time into the state's constitution when they placed severe restrictions on manumissions in order to protect slavery.[52] It was the thinking of the members of Congress and of political writers in Virginia who during the 1850s denounced proposals to restrict the ability of people from moving into the western territories and taking their enslaved laborers with them, taking their slave codes with them, and setting up new slave states there.

White men and women who came of age in Virginia during the 1840s and 1850s shared a different set of beliefs than their parents and grandparents. "I can recollect," forty-one-year-old John Brown Baldwin, of Staunton, stated in the spring of 1861, "and I am not a very old man—I can remember myself when slavery, and the evil and the sin of slavery rested upon the minds and conscience of the South like an incubus. I can recollect, sir, when it was only spoken of by Northern men to denounce it, and by Southern men to offer up a feeble apology for its existence. That was the condition of the public opinion of the South upon this question when I first recollect it. What is it now? Sir, since the day when the Reformation of the Church was proclaimed by the Reformers, there never has occurred so wonderful, so thorough a revolution in public opinion in any country on any subject as has occurred in the opinion of the people of the South on the subject of slavery. Instead of its being looked upon now as a curse or a crime it is not only defended, but justified, aye, and approved by the South as a system of servitude between an inferior and a superior race, conferring benefits and blessings upon them both. Sir, the conscience of the South is easy. The South stands self-acquitted on this subject of our greatest institution and our greatest blessing."[53]

By the end of the 1850s, candidates for public office in Virginia felt compelled to affirm their belief in the South's peculiar institution. Democratic congressman John Letcher, who had once questioned the propriety of slavery, had to reassert his rightful place among the politically worthy in 1858 when he was advancing himself as a candidate for governor. He published a letter boasting that he was "the owner of slave property, by purchase, and not by inheritance," stating categorically that he fully approved of slavery and deliberately chose to own slaves.[54] Three years later one of western Virginia's most outspoken proslavery opponents of secession, John Snyder Carlile, asserted precisely the same thing and in almost the same words when he denounced secession as a danger to slavery. "I have been a slaveholder, not by inheritance, but by purchase," he stated, "and believe that slavery is a social, political and religious blessing."[55] Upshur's thinking and the proslavery doctrines of John C. Calhoun and other lower South defenders of slavery had become the thinking of the men who met in convention in Richmond during the dramatic early months of 1861 and debated whether the institution of slavery could best be preserved within the old Union or by leaving it and joining the new Confederacy.

7

CONSTITUTIONS CONSTRUED

View from Gamble's Hill, *by Edward Beyer (courtesy of the Library of Virginia),*
depicts part of the city of Richmond in the mid-1850s. The scene is filled with industry,
including railroads, a section of the James River and Kanawha Canal, and very large
factories and mills on the banks of the James River. The political rhetoric of antebellum
Virginia emphasized limited, representative government and grew out of opposition to
the federal government's early attempts to stimulate manufacturing and transporta-
tion. At the same time, Virginians employed the almost unlimited power of the state
government to form joint-stock companies for constructing turnpikes, canals, and rail-
roads to carry agricultural products to market. They also erected large mills and manu-
facturing establishments and created banks and other institutions of nineteenth-century
capitalism that made this scene possible. The political rhetoric ignored the commercial
and industrial realities of Virginia as well as the undemocratic political institutions
and practices that persisted from the colonial period through the age of Jacksonian
Democracy.

REPRESENTATIVE JAMES MADISON
was engaged during the winter months of 1791–92 composing newspaper
essays to explain the opposition that he and other members of Congress were
mounting to the policies that Secretary of the Treasury Alexander Hamilton proposed and that President George Washington endorsed. Madison and
his friend and political ally Secretary of State Thomas Jefferson feared that
Hamilton's policies would place Virginia farmers and other Southerners at
political and economic disadvantages in the new nation and also enlarge the
powers of the national government too much and at the expense of the state
governments.

As Madison often did prior to composing essays on public affairs, he made
notes from his wide-ranging reading in history and political economy. One
day or night when he was making notes, Madison wrote, "In proportion as
slavery prevails in a State, the Government, however democratic in name,
must be aristocratic in fact. The power lies in a part instead of the whole; in
the hands of property, not numbers. All the antient popular governments,
were for this reason aristocracies. The majority were slaves," and here he cited
the authority of Aristotle. "The Southern States of America, are on the same
principle aristocracies. In Virginia the aristocratic character is increased by
the rule of suffrage, which requiring a freehold in land excludes nearly half
the free inhabitants, and must exclude a greater proportion, as the population
increases. At present the slaves and non-freeholders amount to nearly ¾ of the
State. The power is therefore in about ¼. Were the slaves freed and the right of
suffrage extended to all, the operation of the Government might be very different. The slavery of the Southern States, throws the power much more into
the hands of property, than in the Northern States."[1]

Madison did not employ his note about slavery and aristocracy when composing his articles in opposition to Hamilton's political proposals. He laid it
aside because the discussion of slavery and aristocracy in the South (and by
implication the more fertile soil for the growth of democracy in the North)
would not have advanced Madison's cause an inch. He was not concealing a
secret. A few years later a young attorney named William Wirt moved to Virginia from neighboring Maryland, and as he traversed the Northern Neck en
route to his new home, he could see on the face of the landscape precisely
what Madison had written about. In the first of his 1803 essays published
anonymously in a Richmond newspaper and then collected into a small book
entitled *The Letters of the British Spy,* Wirt wrote about how different the Vir-

ginia counties on the south side of the Potomac River were from the Maryland counties on the north side. "I am in Virginia," he wrote, "that state, which, of all the rest, plumes herself most highly on the democratic spirit of her principles. Her political principles are, indeed, democratic enough in all conscience. Rights and privileges, as regulated by the constitution of the state, belong in equal degree to all the citizens." But, "however, they may vaunt of 'equal liberty in church and state,' they have but little to boast on the subject of equal property. Indeed there is no country, I believe, where property is more unequally distributed than in Virginia. This inequality struck me with peculiar force in riding through the lower counties on the Potomack. Here and there a stately aristocratic palace, with all its appurtenances, strikes the view: while all around, for many miles, no other buildings are to be seen but the little smoky huts and log cabins of the poor, laborious, ignorant tenants. And, what is very ridiculous, these tenants, while they approach *the great house,* cap in hand, with all the fearful, trembling submission of the lowest feudal vassals, boast in their court yards, with obstreperous exultation, that they live in a land of freemen, a land of equal liberty and equal rights."[2]

By the time Madison was making notes early in the 1790s, he had emerged as the first great national legislative leader in the United States. Service in the Virginia House of Delegates and in the Continental Congress during and after the Revolutionary War had taught him the art and mystery of legislating, at which he excelled in part because of his extraordinary natural talents, the high quality of his systematic and original mind, and the examples of many skilled Virginia politicians from whom he learned how to move ideas through the political tangles of parliamentary procedure and into effective laws. He had helped to pass Jefferson's Act for Establishing Religious Freedom in 1786 with a shrewd combination of political maneuvering and public pressure rooted in sound ideas persuasively presented. So, too, at the Constitutional Convention in Philadelphia in 1787 and in the ratification convention in Richmond the following year, and in between he composed some of the most original and insightful numbers of the celebrated *Federalist Papers* that defined the nature of the new national government. When Madison undertook early in the 1790s to form a national constituency for his political agenda, he merely extended into another and an enlarged realm the political practices that he had learned in Virginia.

Madison's concerns early in the 1790s were unlike his concerns in the 1780s when he helped bring the United States Constitution into being. The struggle for ratification, especially in his home state of Virginia, had convinced him that many influential men would remain unreconciled to the significantly strengthened national government that the new Constitution created unless some of their apprehensions were relieved. He proposed and saw through to passage in the First Congress several amendments to the Constitution to shield some individual rights of citizens from congressional encroachment. Among them were freedoms of speech, press, and assembly, the right to petition for redress of grievances, freedom of religion, the right to jury trials in civil and criminal cases: the whole budget of the Bill of Rights that was finally ratified in December 1791. Madison did not, however, propose, and Congress did not submit to the states any amendments to weaken any of the branches of the new national government or to reinforce or untangle the checks and balances and separation of powers that he and other advocates of the new Constitution had originally asserted would protect the rights of the citizens. The Ninth and Tenth Amendments in the Bill of Rights stated that all governmental powers not specifically granted to the branches of the national government remained with the people and the states and that the enumeration of specific rights in the Constitution was not self-limiting and was to be construed as meaning that other rights, not enumerated, also remained with the people and the states.

Nevertheless, as government under the new Constitution began to take shape, Madison faced new issues that aroused in his mind some doubts about its operations that resembled some of the fears that leading opponents of ratification had voiced in June 1788 during the Virginia ratification convention, where Patrick Henry, George Mason, and William Grayson had criticized the new Constitution as potentially dangerous to the sovereignty of the states and to the liberties of the people.

The Constitution of the United States granted Congress authority to exercise several specific powers and denied Congress authority to act on another list of specific topics. During the ratification debates supporters of the Constitution, Madison among the most important of them, argued that the new national government that the Constitution envisioned could not become too powerful or tyrannical because it was a government of strictly limited authority. Opponents of ratification were not persuaded because the Constitution also included a clause making laws and treaties of the United States supreme over the laws of the states and because vagueness in the wording of the Constitution appeared to allow too much flexibility in stretching limited, specific grants of authority into unlimited grants. They pointed to the words in the preamble about establishing justice, ensuring domestic tranquillity, providing for the common defense, and promoting the general welfare as providing potential excuses for enlarging the scope of the specific grants and to the clause in Article I, Section 8 that permitted Congress to pass any laws that a majority of its members believed were "necessary and proper" for carrying out the limited specific grants of power. The only safe and also accurate method of interpreting the new Constitution therefore would be literally and strictly according to its precise wording, keeping in mind the preexisting nature of the states, which retained their own independent measure of sovereignty.

Madison resisted those arguments late in the 1780s, but even before Washington completed his first four-year term as president early in the 1790s, the country's politicians were dividing into opposing factions, and Madison and other Virginia political leaders began arguing that Hamilton's proposed innovations in political economy were likely to be injurious to Virginia and were a threat to the states because they were based on an improper interpretation of the powers of Congress. Early in the 1790s Madison drafted a veto message for Washington to use when the president was uncertain whether to sign a bill that Congress passed to charter a national bank. Madison believed that the bill was unconstitutional because the Constitution did not specifically grant Congress power to issue charters of incorporation. He tried to persuade the president that Hamilton, who proposed the measure, was wrong in believing that the bank would be a necessary and proper and therefore constitutionally permissible agent to enable the government to fund the national debt, but he failed to convince Washington, who signed the bill.

During the Adams administration late in the 1790s, Congress passed the Alien and Sedition Acts to make certain criticisms of government policy and of government officeholders a criminal offense and to allow the president to order the deportation of any foreigners he deemed dangerous or undesirable. The Sedition Act more than any other measure alarmed men like Madison and Jefferson and their allies in Virginia and elsewhere, and by the end of the 1790s they formed the first national political organization and enunciated a political philosophy and a mode of constitutional interpretation in support of it.

They sought to mobilize public opinion by having state legislatures pronounce the acts dangerous and unconstitutional. In the Virginia and Kentucky Resolutions of 1798 that Madison and Jefferson, respectively, drafted, they declared that the states, not the federal government, were the seats of the sovereignty of the people; that the states came first and that the states, not the people, ratified the Constitution; that therefore the Constitution was a compact among the states and not a compact between the nation's people and its national government; that every clause of the Constitution should be construed strictly and literally and that no power not expressly granted to the federal government or to one of its branches was constitutionally permissible; and that all other governmental powers, as the Ninth and Tenth Amendments specifically stated, remained with the states and with the people. They went further and suggested that when an act of the federal government violated the Constitution, it was the responsibility of the state governments to intervene to protect the people in the states from the states' creature in the national capital. Jefferson went even further than Madison in the resolutions that he drafted and that the legislature of Kentucky adopted and suggested that state legislatures had the right and power to prevent the operation of unconstitutional federal laws.

Jefferson and Madison laid the intellectual groundwork for Southern participation in national politics during the decades between the ratification of the Constitution in 1788 and the outbreak of the American Civil War in 1861. Their Spirit of 1798, as it was called—strict interpretation of the Constitution and the primacy of the state governments—was the lodestone for other men who drew on and amplified the two principal themes during debates about protective tariffs, national banks, federal financing for harbor improvements, roads, canals, and railroads, and whether Congress when creating temporary governments for western territories or when deciding to admit new states had legitimate authority to forbid or restrict the introduction and legal protection of slavery in those territories and states. The logic and power of the strict-construction, state's-rights perspective was very broadly appealing. The circumstances under which the Constitution was written and ratified appeared to confirm the correctness of interpreting the Constitution in that manner.

The logic and power of the alternative interpretation of the Constitution was also broadly appealing. Alexander Hamilton first employed it, Henry Clay relied on it for his American System of economic development, and a Virginian, Chief Justice John Marshall, most thoroughly developed and expounded it. Marshall's boldest assertion of national superiority over the states and his boldest assertion of congressional power to legislate both appeared in his 1819 opinion in the case *McCulloch v. Maryland,* which tested the constitutionality of the congressional act that chartered the Second Bank of the United States. President James Madison had signed the bill, experience having changed his mind about the necessity and propriety and therefore the constitutionality of a congressionally chartered national bank.

Marshall dismissed the argument that the states, not the people, ratified the Constitution and grounded American constitutional law on the premise that the Constitution was a compact between the people—"We the people," in the opening words of the Constitution's preamble—and their national government. The government that the Constitution created, Marshall wrote, was "intended to endure for ages to come, and, consequently, to be adapted to the various *crises* of human affairs." The prohibitions on congressional action were specific, but the specific grants of authority were not therefore all self-limiting. "We must admit," Marshall stated for the other members of the Supreme Court in the most controversial passage in his forty-page opinion, "as all must admit, that the powers of the government are limited, and that its limits are not to be transcended. But we think the sound construction of the constitution must allow to the national legislature that discretion, with respect to the means by which the powers it confers are to be carried into execution, which will enable that body to perform the high duties assigned to it, in the manner most beneficial to the people. Let the end be legitimate, let it be within the scope of the constitution, and all means which are appropriate, which are plainly adapted to that end, which are not prohibited, but consistent with the letter and spirit of the constitution, are constitutional."[3] The "necessary and proper" clause never received a more elastic and powerful explication.

Among the strongest critics of Marshall and the strongest disciples of Jefferson and Madison, few were as respected or as influential as John Taylor, known as John Taylor of Caroline because he lived in Caroline County, which distinguished him from other men of the same name who lived elsewhere in Virginia. Taylor served from time to time in the House of Delegates, where he introduced Madison's draft resolutions of 1798 and attempted to add to them Jefferson's nullification clause, and in the House of Representatives and in the United States Senate. A man of wide and deep reading, a planter and serious student of agriculture, Taylor wrote voluminously and published essays in newspapers and several famously long and repetitive books that were popular and influential among the Southerners who agreed with his political opinions. His popular essays on agriculture, *Arator*, first published in 1813 and in several subsequent and enlarged editions, contained sections on the political economy of Southern agriculture that provided a distinct Virginia context for his political tracts. His major books, some of them evocatively titled, included *An Enquiry into the Principles and Tendency of Certain Public Measures* (1794), *A Defence of the Measures of the Administration of Thomas Jefferson* (1804), *An Inquiry into the Principles and Policy of the Government of the United States* (1814), *Construction Construed, and Constitutions Vindicated* (1820), *Tyranny Unmasked* (1822), and *New Views of the Constitution of the United States* (1823).

Southern law professors, newspaper editors, politicians, and jurists in great numbers adopted the logic and power of Taylor's strict-construction, state's-rights interpretation of the Constitution. Whatever measures Taylor and the men who agreed with him regarded as unnecessary and improper they consequently also regarded as unconstitutional, which lured much of Southern public discourse about national policies away from discussions of utility or desirability and into discussions of constitutionality. Such discussions particularly engaged men who had been trained in the law. Virginia's leading attorneys and legal educators, most notably Nathaniel Beverley Tucker, of the College of William and Mary, and judges, chiefly Spencer Roane, of the Virginia Court of Appeals, set much of the context for public policy discussions in Virginia and kept them focused on questions of constitutional interpretation. Marshall on the one side and Roane and a host of other writers on the other side wrote brilliant and powerful prose that was irresistibly persuasive to people who were disposed to agree with them but was stubbornly intractable to people who disagreed and tried to refute them. Just as neither side persuaded the other, the body politic mustered itself into opposing camps or parties of equally firm conviction.

Very much as Richard Bland two generations earlier, Taylor wrote to defend the political economy of his Virginia from an outside threat, and also like Bland, Taylor wrote rather little about the political economy or the constitution of Virginia that he defended. He evidently took it for granted that the Virginia Constitution of 1776 and the institutions and practices of the old colonial common-law constitution that it legitimated and extended into the nineteenth century offered the best model for representative government. It guaranteed to the planters of nineteenth-century Virginia all the rights and liberties that the grandees of government enjoyed before the American Revolution and that were theirs and his by right, by natural right or by right of long occupation. Taylor wrote glowingly of republican political institutions even though he lived all of his life among free white men who owned too little land to vote. When he wrote about republican and representative government, state's rights, and political freedom, he wrote about himself and other prosperous Virginia tobacco planters and their relationship to the federal government. The sovereignty of the people, which lay at the heart of his political theory, was in reality the sovereignty of the adult white male owners of land. Taylor's political economy was easily extensible to planters of rice, cotton, and sugar elsewhere in the South, but he evidently did not regard it as extensible even within Virginia to the artisans, urban workingmen, or small farmers who owned only a few acres of land or rented the fields that they tilled.

Men and women who read some or all of Taylor's often-repetitious books could easily forget, because he so seldom alluded to them at all, the poor farmers and workingmen William Writ saw and wrote about who had few or no political rights. They are so completely absent from Taylor's writings that the general language in which he composed his essays makes their absence invisible. It is remarkable how little he had to say about any other group of people than planters like himself, whom he appeared to regard as the only legitimate members of the body politic. When he wrote about the people, that is who he meant. Republican government in the Virginia formulations most widely publicized was theirs, and theirs alone.

Taylor's perspective was also an almost entirely pastoral one as viewed by a comparatively wealthy planter. It was a somewhat romanticized view of rural, agricultural life that he shared with Thomas Jefferson and perhaps a few other privileged planters and to some extent with the eccentric throwback and walking anachronism, John Randolph of Roanoke. That is to say, Taylor wrote from a perspective that very few other Virginians, even among the white male planters, fully shared. He and his perspective were in the minority and were also out of step with his own times and culture.

One thing that readers of Taylor's tracts could not miss was the nature of the danger that he perceived to his pastoral planters' republic. His writings overflow with criticisms of banks and other institutions of finance capitalism. He characterized them as the tools of burglars and thieves whenever he contemplated tariffs, the public debt, national banks, or public policies that he believed would enrich one portion of the country at the expense of another, by which he always meant enrich Northern and Eastern financiers and speculators at the expense of honest Southern planters. Throughout his essays and books Taylor grounded his objections to loose interpretations of the Constitution in a fear that if loosely interpreted as John Marshall interpreted it, the Constitution would permit avaricious Northerners to consume the wealth and with it the rights of virtuous Southerners as in Joseph's dream of the lean and fat cattle. Taylor condemned both the means and the object, and he also condemned the means because of the object.

A majority of Virginia's political leaders during the first decades of the nineteenth century evidently shared Taylor's ideas about limited national government and strict interpretation of the national Constitution. Almost all of the state's Democrats more or less firmly embraced Taylor's ideas. So, too, from the 1830s to the 1850s, did a large number of the state's Whigs. The Whig Party comprised a large minority in Virginia most of the time and regularly won seats in the House of Representatives. Whigs captured majorities in the General Assembly several times and elected some Whigs to the United States Senate. Unlike the Democrats, though, the Whigs in Virginia were not united. Many of them endorsed the political ideas that Henry Clay pursued and that John Marshall's interpretation of the Constitution could make possible, but many of them adhered as firmly as Democrats to state's-rights principles.

Even though Taylor's writings on national politics reflected or influenced the opinions of a majority of the state's political leaders, his pastoral perspective did not. The General Assembly chartered banks and joint-stock companies to construct toll roads, canals, and later railroads, and in 1816 it created the Board of Public Works to provide financing for those public works projects. Through the board the state government purchased stock in the corporations it created and selected some members of their boards of directors. The innovative public-private partnership employed tax money to stimulate economic development by private companies, and when tax money became inadequate, the state borrowed money and created a public debt in order to continue supplying money to new private companies.[4] Both state's-rights Democrats and state's-rights Whigs were shareholders and officers in and promoters of those banks and corporations. Some of the leading members of what in the 1820s was referred to as the Richmond Junto, a group of state's-rights Democrats who might have been seen as Taylor's own handpicked tertium quids—third things, neither Federalists nor Jeffersonian Republicans, neither Whigs nor

Democrats—were principal officers of some of the state-chartered banks.[5] They were not philosophically opposed to banks and finance capitalism but to a strong national government that might create competition for or restrict their abilities to manage their enterprises and govern them and their state as they wished.

Some of their Virginia enterprises were less successful than similar enterprises in other states such as New York and Pennsylvania, but that was not because there were too many disapproving influential Virginians. It was because the supplies of coal and iron ore in Virginia were inferior in quality and quantity, and the men in Virginia were not as good as the men of those other states at shaping public policies that allowed for adequate capital accumulation and more robust economic development. The large population of enslaved people in Virginia, unlike the large population of free farmers and artisans in other states, furnished no market for the state's manufacturers, which retarded industrial and commercial growth. And in spite of providing much of the capital, the General Assembly created no overall plan to exploit the natural resources of the state or to make the new transportation networks effective. Virginia enterprise and economic development set a good pace, but similar enterprises elsewhere raced faster and further ahead.[6]

The capital, Richmond, was the state's transportation and industrial leader. Early in the 1820s a traveler spent a few days in the city, which he described as "populous with slaves, and mules." He admired the "many beautifully picturesque seats in its environs, and along the river, which is winding and broken, but romantic in summer, when the midway rocks are covered with anglers." The scene was a spoiled one, though, and he complained that Richmond's air was thick with "the dense murky effluvia of coal-smoke, which begrimes the pores of the skin, and affects respiration." The coal, he explained, "is brought down a canal in barges, and landed from a broad basin in the city."[7]

The coalfields near Richmond had been under commercial exploitation for nearly a century by then and were some of the largest being worked in the United States. From deep pits and shallow mines men dug the soft, sulfurous coal for use in household heating and cooking and also in the local iron industry that made Richmond the most industrially significant Southern city during the first half of the nineteenth century. The canal was the first portion of and near the eastern end of a projected continuous transportation link between the Chesapeake Bay and the Ohio River. The elaborate plan for the project had been completed nearly a decade before the visitor breathed Richmond's unwholesome air, more than a decade before the last of John Taylor's pastoral rants against finance capitalism and the federal government. The assembly named a distinguished commission to design the system, with Chief Justice John Marshall as senior member. As explained in Marshall's report to the General Assembly endorsing the project, locks and improvements to the navigation of the James River in the east and to the Kanawha River in the west with a connecting road over the mountains promised to make Richmond, and Norfolk farther downstream, the new west's primary commercial connection with the Atlantic Ocean and the markets of the rest of the country and the world. In boldness of conception, length, and engineering difficulty, the James River and Kanawha Canal dwarfed the similarly conceived Erie Canal in New York.

The Virginia entrepreneurs who supported it with a large infusion of state tax money required decades to push the project through the first range of mountains near Lynchburg, and by the time the first portion was complete, steam locomotives on the railroads outraced the canal boats. George Washington's favorite project, a similar canal around the falls and the shoal sections of the Potomac River to draw western commerce and wealth to Alexandria from as far away as the headwaters of the Ohio River, had a very similar history. The Baltimore and Ohio Railroad made it to Harpers Ferry first. The Erie Canal, on the other hand, was completed in 1825, before any steam railroad carrying passengers or freight ran along any American track.

The canal in Richmond and the smoke from the coal that it transported into the city offered a vivid contrast to the plantation economy about which John Taylor of Caroline wrote. Had the visitor of the 1820s been able, like one of the weightless particles of soot, to rise up with the smoke from the chimneys and mills of Richmond and float high above the state, he would have perceived numerous smaller plumes rising from other population centers such as Norfolk near the coast in the southeast, Fredericksburg and Petersburg along the fall line north and south of Richmond, towns in the Valley of Virginia west of the Blue Ridge, new industrial sites in the Kanawha Valley in the west, and Wheeling on the Ohio River in the northern panhandle, a city on nearly the same latitude with Pittsburgh but farther west.

Wheeling, like Richmond, later relied on coal for its industrial development, too, but most of the smoke rising from the hearths and mills was from wood or charcoal, which in the mountains and western valleys supplied iron furnaces where coal was not then readily available. Those plumes of smoke marked centers of population and commercial and industrial enterprise during the decades between the American Revolution and the American Civil War, rather like the pillars of smoke and fire that guided the Israelites through the barren wilderness toward the promised land. That comparison might have appealed to Virginia's hopeful entrepreneurs. In the decades after the visitor complained about Richmond's vile atmosphere, those smoke signals also indicated where Henry Clay's Whigs were likely to be more numerous than Democrats and state's-rights Whigs.[8]

The manner in which politicians in Virginia practiced republican government did not closely resemble the well-known archetype that John Taylor of

Caroline and other influential writers wrote about when they advocated limitations on the national government and discussed the relationship between it and the states. They expounded a theory of federalism, not a theory of representative government, even though many of their readers and disciples, as well as some historians, regarded what they wrote as defining representative government. At home, their representative government was a combination of the slave-owning aristocrats that Madison noted and energetic entrepreneurs in republican clothing. They extolled a strictly limited federal government under the control of representatives of the voters, but in Virginia there were virtually no limitations on the state government, and men who could vote remained a minority of the people who were governed. The policies that the state legislature adopted make it evident that the political leaders of Virginia did not employ the same rationale for evaluating the purposes and powers of the national and state governments and that they did not, in fact, possess and act from one consistent set of political beliefs.

The contrasts between the constitutions of the United States and Virginia were striking. The Virginia Constitution of 1776 included very few specific grants of power to the General Assembly—chiefly listing which officers of government it was empowered to elect—and almost no restrictions other than the few admonitions about freedom of the press and trial by jury in the Declaration of Rights. In effect and without any specific constitutional authorization or restriction, Virginia's legislators interpreted and applied the Constitution of 1776 as vesting in the General Assembly all of the powers of sovereignty that it or the Crown had exercised under the colonial constitution. The General Assembly decided whether people could incorporate a bank or an orphanage, whether a county had a right to offer a bounty to encourage the destruction of crows or wolves, whether a town might prohibit swine from running free in its streets, whether a person might operate a toll ferry over a river, or whether the widow of a Revolutionary soldier could receive a pension. The Constitution of 1776 left unchanged and firmly in place the undemocratic, self-perpetuating county courts that exercised legislative, executive, and judicial powers. The laws and practices of the old colonial common-law constitution continued fully in force without any implicit or explicit sanction or restriction in the constitution of the Commonwealth of Virginia written in 1776.

It is an overlooked irony that the latitudinarian interpretation of the United States Constitution that John Marshall employed to invest Congress with energy is an almost exact counterpart to the unrestrained interpretation of the meaning of the Virginia Constitution of 1776 that many of Marshall's critics employed to invest the General Assembly with its great powers. The state's constitution allowed and effectively endowed the legislature with unlimited power to extend into the nineteenth century the undemocratic political institutions and practices of Virginia as they existed when the American Revolution began even as it also allowed the state government to pursue economic development policies within the state that closely resembled the economic development policies that John Taylor of Caroline denounced when Congress attempted to implement them throughout the nation.

During much of Taylor's adulthood and afterward, the state's politics was rent not so much with debates about whether economic and industrial development employing the new implements of finance capitalism was good or bad or whether it should take place in Virginia but about who could get cuts of the pie and whether the old constitution of the grandees stood in the way of progress and genuine liberty, especially in the western portion of the state.

Demographic, economic, and social changes in Virginia after the American Revolution produced demands for changes in the old constitution. The population of the western counties grew, in some instances very rapidly, during the decades after the Revolution, but the population of most of the eastern counties, particularly the ones in the southeastern portion of the state, remained fairly stable or, in some instances, declined. The movement of people into the western portions was for the most part a movement of free white people whose families owned fewer slaves than in the older portions of Virginia. The movement of people out of the eastern portion was an emigration of both white and black, free and enslaved, as families with too many sons or too few acres of land migrated to the newly opened southwestern frontiers. The movement of peoples led to an increasing disproportion of white and black residents in the various regions of Virginia. In some counties in south-central Virginia and along the North Carolina border, white people became a minority, and among them the large planters an even smaller minority. To the immediate west, in the Blue Ridge and the Valley of Virginia, large plantations and slaves were relatively less common, and in the Allegheny Mountains and the Ohio River valley, large plantations and significant numbers of slaves were almost nonexistent.

A combination of grievances about taxation and other public policies and the American Revolution's language of personal equality and equal political rights generated repeated and repeatedly strong demands for revision of the Constitution of 1776 to reflect the new realities in Virginia. Many of the western farmers possessed too little land to qualify for the suffrage under the colonial laws that the constitution had retained intact. The apportionment of seats in the House of Delegates, also carried over from the colonial period, allocated two members to each county regardless of the size of its whole population or its white population alone. As a result the small eastern counties with smaller populations (and even smaller populations of landowning white male voters) than in the counties in the west enjoyed a lopsided influence in the House of Delegates. The lines for the twenty-four districts in the Senate of Virginia, hastily drawn in 1776, produced a corresponding disparity.

The disproportion between the representation of the smaller eastern counties and that of the larger and more populous western counties was a subject of complaint at least as early the 1780s, when Thomas Jefferson in *Notes on the State of Virginia* published calculations derived from militia returns (before the first reliable enumeration or census had been compiled) to dramatize how disproportionate the representation was, even then. He wrote that Warwick County, the smallest and least populous county, "with only one hundred fighting men, has an equal representation with the county of Loudon, which has 1746. So that every man in Warwick has as much influence in the government as 17 men in Loudon." Jefferson went on to calculate that "nineteen thousand men, living below the falls of the rivers, possess half the senate, and want four members only of possessing a majority of the house of delegates; a want more than supplied by the vicinity of their situation to the seat of government, and of course the greater degree of convenience and punctuality with which their members may and will attend the legislature. These nineteen thousand, therefore, living in one part of the country, give law to upwards of thirty thousand, living in another, and appoint all their chief officers executive and judiciary."[9]

The Revolutionary language of equal liberty figured prominently in the campaigns of western Virginians for a convention to revise the Constitution of 1776, which contained no provision for amendment, as if the men who wrote and adopted it never considered that it might require change. The old constitution worked so well in support of the financial, political, and philosophical interests of political leaders in the east that they resisted all proposals for change. The undemocratic county courts and the juries that they impaneled from the county's landowners, for instance, allowed the descendants of the grandees to continue running their counties and communities as they wished and afforded them valuable protection from external challenges. Following the Revolutionary War county court juries in effect nullified a provision of the Treaty of 1783 that concluded the war and that, among other things, required payment of debts that planters owed to British mercantile houses before the war. During the war the state had allowed planters to pay their debts in depreciated paper currency into a state fund to reimburse the British merchants, but the merchants refused to accept the depreciated payments. British firms then sued Virginia planters and their heirs in Virginia county courts to recover the old debts, but in many instances, in spite of the wording of the treaty and the evidence presented in court, juries ruled in favor of local debtors, their own neighbors, and the state's appellate courts did not reverse the judgments of the juries.[10]

Local nullification of laws and court rulings was nothing new in Virginia.

Patrick Henry's argument and the judgment of the Hanover County jury in the Parson's Cause in 1763 effectively nullified the king's disallowance of the second Two-Penny Act, county courts and public opinion virtually nullified the Stamp Act of 1765 before Parliament repealed it, and county courts and militia officers obstructed Henry's enforcement of the militia reform law that he helped enact after the American Revolution, effectively nullifying that state law. The powers of county political leaders and their base of power, the county courts, led them to oppose reform because the Constitution of 1776 and the political influence it gave them worked extremely well for them.[11]

Early in the summer of 1816, twenty-two men from eleven northern counties that sprawled across the state from the northwestern panhandle to Fairfax and Fauquier Counties in the northeast issued a call for a convention to press for a new state constitution. "There is no political maxim whose truth is more forcibly illustrated by experience," their announcement began, "than one contained in the declaration of rights of Virginia, 'That no free government, or the blessing of liberty, can be preserved to any people, but by a frequent recurrence to fundamental principles.'" They abridged the actual language but got the substance exactly right. "The entire neglect of this invaluable maxim has produced a crisis in the internal affairs of Virginia, whose novelty and importance demand the earnest attention and consideration of every citizen of the state." They declared that political institutions and practices under the Constitution of 1776 had produced "an absolute mockery of the principles of free government."

The two-delegates-per-county rule exaggerated the political inequality that Jefferson had described three decades earlier. "If representation were equalized," they calculated, "and Warwick county were taken as the standard by which the number of representatives from all the other counties should be regulated, the counties of Loudoun and Frederick would be entitled to forty-five delegates each!" Voters residing west of the Blue Ridge, where the majority of the white population of the state lived, elected a minority of members of the House of Delegates; voters in the western region elected but four instead of nine members of the Senate of Virginia that they would have been entitled to if representation were based on population, and voters in the eastern region elected thirteen instead of seven.

"If it be asked," the twenty-two men demanded, "why so gross and flagrant an inequality of representation in the senate has been suffered to exist for so long—why a law has not been passed for new modeling the senatorial districts—the answer is an obvious one. The representatives of a minority of the people have the whole powers of government in their hands, and they will consent to no measure which has a tendency to transfer that power to its rightful owners, the majority. We say the rightful owners; for we presume it will not, and cannot, be denied, that it is a fundamental principle of our government, that the will of the majority should govern." But so long as the inequality of representation remained unchanged and eastern politicians had no incentive to redress the complaints of the westerners, *"From this quarter it is idle to hope for aid."*[12]

In August of that year about seventy men purporting to represent nearly forty counties, none of them in the east, met in Staunton and petitioned the General Assembly to pass an enabling law to hold a state convention to revise the old constitution. "No doctrine has received a more universal assent," they declared, "than that in a republican government, the will of the majority should be the law of the land. And yet in a state, boasting of the pure republican character of its institutions, this first and fundamental principle of republicanism, does not exist."[13] The General Assembly refused the request, and the disproportion between the east and the west continued to increase. In 1825 another convention, more numerously attended by delegates from a larger number of mountain and western counties, met in Staunton and renewed the plea for a convention to revise the constitution.[14] The assembly again refused to act.

Hard as the able representatives of the privileged eastern counties fought against it, eventually the increasing numbers of westerners wielding the powerful language of liberty and equality from the American Revolution forced a bill through the General Assembly, and from 5 October 1829 to 15 January 1830 a constitutional convention met in Richmond to debate the critical issues of who should be allowed to vote and who should be represented in the General Assembly. The dominant easterners in the assembly, though, were able to require that representation at the convention be by senatorial district, four members for each of twenty-four districts, guaranteeing that the western reformers would be at a severe proportional disadvantage.

The Convention of 1829–30 was one of the most distinguished assemblages of Virginia men anywhere, anytime. Ninety-six men were elected to it, but 103 took part. One delegate-elect died and another resigned before the convention met, and seven delegates resigned during the convention, but their successors all attended. Among the 103 men, scores had been justices of the peace or members of the General Assembly, and many of them had held or later held several important positions. Several of them were sitting or former or future members of the state's Court of Appeals; thirty-one men were, had been, or would be members of the House of Representatives; eight were, had been, or would be members of the United States Senate; and the governor was a member, as were four former or future governors; two attorneys general of Virginia; the chief justice of the United States and a future associate justice; three secretaries of state, two secretaries of the navy, one secretary of war, and two former presidents and one future president of the United States. The first president of the convention, James Monroe, had been president of the United

States, a member of Congress, governor twice, United States senator once, secretary of war, secretary of state, a diplomat, member of the ratification convention of 1788, and colonel in the Revolutionary War.[15]

The published text of the three and a half months of formal and learned (and as the days wore on, angry and bitter) debates fill nearly nine hundred pages of small type. Although the delegates spent many hours on fine points of wording and interpretation, they began by debating the large issues at length. As future appeals court judge Briscoe G. Baldwin, of Augusta County, remarked early in the proceedings, they were debating changes to create a form of government that would be "emphatically a Government of principles: principles established by the wisdom, and consecrated by the blood of our fathers. . . . Without, therefore, indulging in abstract theories, or referring to the systems of other nations, let us resort to those fundamental truths which constitute the basis of our own system. We shall find them all-sufficient for every useful purpose; they will serve as 'a lamp to our feet, and a light to our path,' upon this or any other subject of our duties."[16] The all-sufficient principles that Baldwin invoked were the Revolutionary ideas of political liberty and equality. (It was his son, John Brown Baldwin, who thirty-one years later proclaimed that slavery was the South's greatest institution and blessing.)

By the 1830s the Revolutionary ideals had evolved into what came to be called Jacksonian Democracy. Briefly stated, the principles to which Baldwin alluded implied the substantial political equality of all white men, the right of all adult white men to vote, and the ability of ordinary men to hold responsible public offices. Elsewhere in the United States by then, most state constitutions allowed voters to elect governors, judges, and most local officials. Elsewhere in the Southern states at the same time, legislatures and conventions introduced universal white manhood suffrage, based on the racial theories and the doctrine of white supremacy that Abel P. Upshur, who was an influential member of the Virginia Convention of 1829–30, wrote about in his 1839 essay "On Domestic Slavery."

The delegates focused primarily on two interrelated questions and revealed that, as in the past, public men in Virginia did not all share the same fundamental principles or agree about fundamental truths. The questions were: should adult white men who owned little or no property be allowed to vote, and should the areas of the state with less valuable taxable property (i.e., fewer slaves) be allotted representation in the General Assembly in proportion to their whole population or their free white population or by the old colonial apportionment of two delegates per county? For the most part the debaters acknowledged that the state was divided on those questions largely on geographical lines, between the counties to the east of the Blue Ridge or the Valley of Virginia and the counties to the west.

Except for suffrage and representation and the related issue of taxation, few other political or social reforms were proposed or debated during the convention. There was one significant exception. Alexander Campbell, of Brooke County in the northern panhandle, the only clergyman in the convention, the founder of what came to be known as the Church of Christ, introduced a major reform resolution on 26 December. "Whereas republican institutions and the blessings of free Government," it began, "originate in, and must always depend upon, the intelligence, virtue and patriotism of the community; and whereas, neither intelligence nor virtue can be maintained or promoted in any community without education, it shall always be the duty of the Legislature of this Commonwealth to patronize and encourage such a system of education, or such common schools and seminaries of learning, as will in their wisdom be deemed to be most conducive to secure to the youth of this Commonwealth, such an education as may most promote the public good." The other delegates refused even to consider, much less debate, Campbell's resolution[17] and thereby rejected a Jeffersonian vision of an educated, enlightened, free people equipped with the intellectual and moral tools to be self-governing.

The General Assembly had created the state Literary Fund two decades earlier and authorized it to allocate the meager proceeds it raised to counties that created local schools, but as a system of public schooling it amounted to almost nothing. As a number of residents of Halifax County later explained to the assembly about that system's successor, "the school system of Virginia, from its commencement down to the present time, has been a failure. It has failed to enlist public confidence, because it has failed to confer public benefits. No school houses have arisen under its fostering care—ignorant children have become ignorant men, and the rising generation now, like the rising generation one hundred years ago, has no lamp of learning to guide its infant steps, and will be without its light and its comfort in ripe manhood and declining age." Because of the manner in which the few schools were conducted, the petitioners continued, "Our system of education, if system it can be called, is a system of charity. The parent must be degraded, before the child can be instructed. The man must prove himself a pauper, before his offspring can be admitted to the school room. In a country like ours, where labour is so abundantly rewarded, and where the evils of extreme poverty are generally so easily escaped, by industry and care, pauperism is oftener the badge of idleness and vice, than of misfortune, and no citizen of decent pride will wear this badge of degredation, so long as he can conceal it from the eyes of his acquaintances. The poor parent, too often ignorant of the blessings of learning, erects a barrier of pride against the progress of his child. He refuses as a gift, what he would gladly use as a right."[18]

Even what little the white men of affairs in Virginia did early in the nineteenth century in pursuit of public education and an educated democracy failed. By their actions and by their inactions the freeholders of Virginia who attended the Constitutional Convention of 1829–30 demonstrated what was important to them and what was not. The people who needed education in order to govern already had access to education. The people who did not take part in governing did not have access to education and, in the perspective of the political leaders, probably did not need it or deserve it.

The competing interests in the convention were not so starkly geographical in origin as the arguments of the delegates appeared to indicate. On the second day of the second week of the convention, the delegates received a long petition from *"the Non-Freeholders of the City of Richmond"* in eastern Virginia. It quoted from the Virginia Declaration of Rights, relied on writings of Thomas Jefferson, and cited the petitioners' services in the militia in the defense of the state to buttress their request that the convention remove the distinctions "between the privileged and the proscribed classes" in Virginia. The Richmond men stated that they needed and deserved the right to vote. "Experience has but too clearly evinced," their long plea began, "what, indeed, reason had always foretold, by how frail a tenure they hold every other right, who are denied this, the highest prerogative of freemen. . . . Comprising a very large part, probably a majority of male citizens of mature age, they have been passed by, like aliens or slaves, as if destitute of interest, or unworthy of a voice, in measures involving their future political destiny: whilst the freeholders, sole possessors, under the existing Constitution, of the elective franchise, have, upon the strength of that possession alone, asserted and maintained in themselves the exclusive power of new-modelling the fundamental laws of the State: in other words, have seized upon the sovereign authority."[19]

The convention received similar petitions from residents of Fairfax County, in northeastern Virginia, and from Shenandoah and Rockingham Counties, in the Shenandoah Valley.[20] One of the delegates from the Eastern Shore announced that he favored extension of the franchise beyond the ranks of freeholders in part because the limited amount of land and the increasing number of men in the two counties between the bay and the ocean made it virtually impossible for men there to become freeholders.[21] The delegates from the district in the southeastern corner of the state received resolutions from a meeting of men in Norfolk instructing them to oppose an extension of the suffrage to men who were not freeholders, which led Robert B. Taylor, who lived in Norfolk and was a seasoned legislator and a general of the militia during the War of 1812, to resign rather than disobey his constituents or vote against enlargement of the franchise.[22] He was one of the few eastern men who favored that democratic reform.

Those discussions filled column after column of the state's newspapers, allowing men and women who were unable to crowd into the gallery to follow the debates. One of them, writing as VIRGINIA FREEWOMAN, published a radical proposal in the *Richmond Enquirer* of 20 October 1829. VIRGINIA

FREEWOMAN demanded that the convention consider granting the vote to white women, or if not to all white women, at least to the white women who owned property and therefore paid taxes. Probably knowing nothing at all about the similar proposal that Hannah Lee Corbin (or Hannah Lee Corbin Hall) had made privately during the American Revolution, VIRGINIA FREE-WOMAN described the convention delegates as arrogant men who acted as if they were "the Lords of the Creation." She demanded an answer to her question, why was it that "*one half of the Society* is to be cut off, at one blow, from all share in the administration of the government? Are *we* not as free as the Lords of the Creation? Are *we* not as much affected by the laws which are passed as the Lords of the Creation themselves? What just reason can be given for this unjust exclusion?"

During the debates that VIRGINIA FREEWOMAN had been following, no delegate proposed to allow women to vote, and none condescended to mention or reply to her newspaper article. In fact, many delegates when defending the denial of suffrage to free white men who owned no real estate thought that they should enumerate other classes of Virginians who could claim no right to vote because they lived in a dependent status or had inferior moral and intellectual abilities. Delegates listed common laborers, slaves, children, people of unsound mind, and women. Some of the convention's leading men made that argument at length to justify denying the vote to a considerable number of free adult white men.[23]

"You say," VIRGINIA FREEWOMAN wrote, summarizing some of the arguments that delegates had made in the convention, "we have not intellect enough to vote, and assist in the government. Where are the proofs of your superiority? You keep us in ignorance—and then you boast of your superior attainments. You make us embroider for you; thrum upon the guitar or piano; draw sketches of your lordly faces; convert us into spinsters and seamstresses, to make your garments; but you exclude us from your best schools. You prevent us from cultivating sciences, studying politics, improving our understandings; and then you insist upon our ignorance as the evidence of our mental Incapacity." (Many white men in Virginia and almost all black people in the state would have been justified in making the very same argument.)

In her public letter VIRGINIA FREEWOMAN showed herself well informed on public affairs, noting correctly that the attorney general of the state had drafted the long and eloquent appeal for suffrage from the nonfreeholders of Richmond. She also knew her history, and she showed that she knew her Shakespeare when she asked, "Why are we proscribed? Why are we denied the privilege of voting? Why are we eternally to be kept in the bondage of a despotic government? 'Have *we* not eyes? have *we* not hands, organs, dimensions, senses, affections, passions? fed with the same food, hurt with the same weapons,—subject to the same diseases, healed by the same means, warmed and cooled by the same winter and summer, as a *man* is? if you prick us, do we not bleed? if you tickle us, do we not laugh? if you poison us, do we not die? and if you wrong us,' shall we, (no, not revenge!) but assert our rights, and expose your gross injustice?"

The convention delegates ignored the women and debated their differences of opinion about white manhood suffrage, representation, and taxation openly and honestly. They acknowledged that the principal differences between the advocates of reform and the opponents of reform derived from the uneven distribution of slavery in the state. They did not debate whether slavery was good or bad or should be retained or restricted or abolished.

The men who advocated change relied on and cited or quoted the Virginia Declaration of Rights, "That all Men are by nature equally free and Independent and have certain inherent Rights of which when they enter into a state of Society they cannot by any compact deprive or divest their Posterity namely the enjoyment of Life and liberty with the means of acquiring and possessing property and pursuing and obtaining happiness and Safety."[24] They argued that the rights to vote and to take part in government equally with other free men were theirs as a legacy of the American Revolution, an inheritance that the Constitution of 1776 and the requirement of the freehold franchise denied them.

The men who argued against changing the freehold requirement and allowing more representation to the western counties had not embraced the concepts of Jacksonian Democracy and had even rejected its Jeffersonian foundations. They denied that any man had a natural right to take part in politics or that there was a natural law that governed civil society and its members. They argued that political rights derived entirely from the structure of the society in which they lived. Abel P. Upshur, from the Eastern Shore, spoke bluntly and at great length to deny that the natural rights that the Revolutionary generation relied on even existed or should be discussed in the convention.[25] Benjamin Watkins Leigh, of Chesterfield County, succinctly summarized that argument in the baldest possible language. "We are employed," he proclaimed loftily, "in forming a Government for civilized men, not for a horde of savages just emerging from an imaginary state of nature."[26] Because of the essential importance of private property and because property was one of the most important objects of taxation and legislation, only men who owned property, they rounded off their political syllogism, possessed any legitimate right to take part in the politics that affected property, either by voting or by holding office.[27]

Some of the men who opposed reform also praised the Virginia Declaration of Rights, but none of them relied on it or on the natural rights doctrines of the American Revolution when arguing that ownership of land was the only safe prerequisite for participation in the political nation. Some of those delegates predicted that if the reformers succeeded, catastrophe would follow and Virginia would fall victim to the class violence that the French Revolution unleashed. The convention's president, James Monroe, also mentioned the violence of the French Revolution, to some of which he had been an eyewitness when serving as a diplomat in France. He urged compromise, that the convention meet at least some of the reformers' demands. He warned that if opponents of reform resisted the reformers' pleas, a division of the state into eastern and western portions was a possibility, and eastern opponents of reform would draw recriminations or violence on themselves, just as the violence of the French Revolution had been the inevitable result of the resistance of French aristocrats to reform and the resentment that their resistance naturally generated. "I will carry the right of suffrage as far as any reasonable men can desire," Monroe stated one day, siding with the reformers. "Then the rights of all the citizens will stand upon the same ground: the poor man and the rich, will stand on the same level."[28] Monroe vacillated and waffled back and forth, but before he resigned from the convention as a consequence of his feeble health, he somewhat reluctantly accepted the logic and language of the reformers, who in turn relied heavily on Monroe's old friend and mentor Thomas Jefferson, who was by then three and a half years dead.

Monroe and Jefferson's presidential colleague, James Madison, was also a member of the convention, but he, also somewhat reluctantly, did not support the reformers. Madison had always been more skeptical about democracy than Jefferson and more concerned that if the rights of owners of property were not adequately secured, representative government had no future, and the rights of minorities and majorities would both be in jeopardy. He had written at length about his differences with Jefferson on those points in the 1780s when Jefferson proposed democratic reform of the state constitution,[29] and he wrote about them again in the 1790s when preparing to challenge the political economy of Alexander Hamilton. At the time of the 1829–30 constitutional convention in Virginia, Madison made still more notes on the suffrage, reminding himself of all the good reasons why protection of the rights of owners of all kinds of property was among the most essential objects of good government and that, therefore, participation in government, either by voting or holding office, had to be restricted to owners of real estate.[30] Madison spoke several times and voted that way consistently in the convention, with the opponents of reform. Madison voted with the men who openly denounced democracy and denied that all men, even all white men, were created equal or were equally entitled to participate in the government that governed them, a government that, in violation of one of the rallying cries of the Revolutionary generation, still taxed them without representation.[31]

The new constitution that the convention submitted to the old electorate for ratification—and that the white male freeholders in the eastern counties overwhelmingly approved and the smaller number of white male freeholders in the western counties overwhelmingly rejected[32]—changed very little. The article on the General Assembly contained the convention's apportionment scheme. It discarded the two-delegates-per-county apportionment and created four legislative regions, roughly comparable to the tax districts created after the American Revolution. The voters of twenty-six counties west of the Allegheny Mountains were to elect thirty-one delegates; in fourteen counties between the Allegheny Mountains and the Blue Ridge, twenty-five delegates; in twenty-nine counties between the Blue Ridge and Tidewater, forty-two delegates; and in thirty-six counties and the incorporated cities and boroughs facing the ocean, Chesapeake Bay, or along the rivers where the tide rose and fell, thirty-six delegates. The advantage clearly remained with the white male landowning residents east of the mountains where a minority of the state's white men and a very large majority of enslaved black Virginians resided.[33]

In the Senate of Virginia, which the convention enlarged from twenty-four to thirty-two members, the same disproportion persisted. The new constitution created thirteen single-member electoral districts for the forty counties west of the Blue Ridge and nineteen single-member electoral districts for the sixty-five counties and corporations east of the Blue Ridge and in the Tidewater.[34] The constitution required the General Assembly to reapportion the districts within each region every tenth year but did not permit it to change the regional boundaries or numbers of delegates and senators allotted to each.[35] That guaranteed to perpetuate the dominance in both houses of the legislature of representatives of the eastern counties where slaves were numerous and where adult white men were a declining population in proportion to the adult white male population in the western regions of the state.

The new Article III on the suffrage slightly modified the old English and colonial rule that only white men age twenty-one or older who were owners of land were sufficiently invested in the well-being of the society to be allowed to vote. Following a suggestion by Benjamin Watkins Leigh, the most brilliant and belligerent defender of the status quo in the convention, it extended the definition of property beyond owners of land in freehold to some urban householders and to men who through leases and rights of inheritance and joint ownership had a long-term interest in land worth at least $25. That provision enlarged the electorate somewhat, although by precisely how many members is not certainly known. The change signaled a subtle and perhaps not very well understood shift from an agricultural, land-based conception of property to a more commercial, value-based conception. It did not extend the definition of property very far or for purposes of the franchise so far as to incorporate into the electorate any men whose property consisted entirely or largely of shares of stock in banks, railroads, ownership of shops or other businesses or industries, or even of enslaved laborers.[36]

The convention added the 1776 Declaration of Rights to the constitution,[37] and it included a provision, derived in part from the 1786 Act for Establishing Religious Freedom, that guaranteed Virginians the free exercise of religion, barred incorporation of religious denominations and societies, forbade taxation to support religious denominations or congregations, and prohibited the assembly from requiring any religious test for public office holding.[38] Like the amended Constitution of the United States, the new Constitution of Virginia also prohibited suspension of the writ of habeas corpus, enactment of bills of attainder and ex post facto laws, taking of private property without just compensation, and abridgement of the freedoms of speech and of the press.[39] The new constitution placed no additional restrictions on the powers of the General Assembly and made no new specific grants of power, leaving the legislature in full possession of the otherwise almost unlimited authority that the Constitution of 1776 permitted and that had originated in the old colonial common-law constitution. The new constitution also retained the prohibition contained in the Constitution of 1776 on the introduction of original bills in the Senate of Virginia, leaving the lion's share of legislative, and therefore political, power in the House of Delegates, where the eastern freeholders retained their comfortable numerical advantage.[40]

The executive power remained imprecisely defined in the new constitution, and the office of governor remained weak. Even though some delegates advocated abolishing the governor's advisory Council of State, the constitution merely reduced it from eight members to three. The constitution increased the governor's term of office from one year to three with no eligibility for reelection and continued to require the governor to have the approval of the Council of State for all discretionary actions. The governor gained no role in the legislative process and no authority to veto bills. And even though all delegates agreed that the governor was almost politically impotent, they defeated as dangerous a proposal to allow the voters to elect the governor or any public officials other than members of the legislature and the municipal councils of a few of the larger towns.[41]

The article on the judiciary was somewhat more specific about the organization of the courts but left election of judges in the hands of the General Assembly and allowed the assembly to modify the arrangement and jurisdiction of courts.[42] In spite of complaints during the convention about the undemocratic and amateurish county courts, the only references to the powerful county governments in the article on the judiciary allowed the General Assembly to specify how the first justices of the peace were to be selected when it created new counties and reauthorized the regal colonial practice that the governor appoint men to vacancies in the office of justice of the peace "on the recommendation of the respective County Courts," making it impossible for any future majority in the assembly to alter the ancient practice.[43]

The delegates who in the end controlled what the new constitution included spoke eloquently and often about the necessity for the government and the constitution to protect men's rights to their property. But even as all adult white men were not, in their judgment, equal, all property was not equal, either. It was not men's right to own land that any of them ever stated was at risk. Ownership of slaves, though, might be if men who owned few or no slaves were permitted to take part in taxing men who owned more than a few and converted slavery into an unprofitable and therefore unsustainable institution. The opponents of reform required ownership of land as a prerequisite for participation in public affairs in order to protect ownership of enslaved laborers.

On all the major points, the reformers in the Convention of 1829–30 lost, very likely because the apportionment of seats in the convention allowed opponents of change a dominant majority. All adult white men were still not politically equal in Virginia, and the constitution, laws, and institutions of the state continued to make it extremely difficult for them to change that. Two weeks after the adjournment of the convention, James Madison reflected in a private letter on what was at stake and what the convention did and did not do. "Besides the ordinary conflicts of opinions concerning the structure of Gov:," he wrote, "the peculiarity of local interests real or supposed, and above all the case of our coloured population which happens to be confined to a geographical half of the State, and to have been a disproportionate object of taxation, were sources of a jealousy & collisions, which infected the proceedings throughout, & were finally overcome by a small majority only." The new constitution, he continued, was in a way a sop to "the ultramontane part of the State, the part which had called loudest for & contributed most to the experiment for amending the Constitution. But on the other hand it alleviates greatly where it does not remove the objections which had been urged & justly urged by that part; whilst the other part of the State, which was most opposed to any changes will regard the result as an obstacle to another Convention, which might bring about greater & more obnoxious innovations."[44]

Madison was wrong on all counts. The new constitution did not alleviate grievances or guard against renewal of pleas for change. The western freeholders overwhelmingly voted against the new constitution, but the more numerous eastern freeholders overwhelming ratified the new constitution. Westerners and other reformers had been blocked in their attempt to change the politics of Virginia, and the new constitution, like the old constitution, contained no provision by which the people might amend it. Late in the deliberations the delegates considered and rejected a proposal to insert into the new constitution a provision to allow for later amendments. The men who opposed revision of the old constitution tried to make the new one permanent, too. During that debate John Randolph of Roanoke, the equal of Benja-

min Watkins Leigh in hatred of democracy and of changing the constitution
or laws of old Virginia, predicted that the new constitution would not last
more than twenty years.[45]

Randolph was correct right down to the year. The pressure built up again,
and reformers succeeded in forcing a vote in the General Assembly to hold
another constitutional convention. During the winter and spring of 1850–51,
hard on the heels of the congressional debates that produced the Compromise
of 1850 and preserved the United States from possible dissolution, another
convention met in the Capitol in Richmond and adopted nearly all of the reformers' proposals.[46]

That was because much changed in Virginia during the two decades. The
men of the Revolutionary generation and their sons were nearly all gone from
public life by 1850, as were most of the men who perceived themselves as the
heirs of the grandees. Only three or four men who attended the Convention
of 1829–30 won election to the Convention of 1850–51. Nearly two-thirds of
the delegates to the second convention were practicing attorneys or had once
practiced law. The delegates also included five medical doctors, three clergymen, two merchants, and one each hotelier, newspaper editor, tobacco manu-
facturer, and millwright. Fewer than two dozen of the 135 members were substantial planters, and few of them qualified as major slave owners. Professional
men, not wealthy slave-owning planters or even small farmers, dominated the
convention's membership and its proceedings.[47] The membership of the Convention of 1850–51 was different than that of either of the previous two Virginia constitutional conventions but probably not significantly different than
the membership of a convention elected at that time in any one of the free
states would have been.

At midcentury the state's Democrats remained committed to state's rights
and were even more firmly committed to the institution of slavery. Most
Democrats even in the eastern section by then were inclined to accept than
to reject, as a majority of members of the Convention of 1829–30 had done,
the Revolutionary ideals of the equality of all white men and the essence of
Jacksonian Democracy. Many of the state's Whigs, especially in the western
counties, also accepted the essential political equality of white men, but some
in the east did not. A Petersburg physician overstated and misrepresented,
but there was a kernel of truth in the hyperbole that he later wrote about the
state's Whigs. He believed that at midcentury they "undoubtedly represented
the conservative element in Virginia. It was the party that had always represented the culture and the wealth of the State. It was the party of the cities
and of the older eastern sections of the State, the party of the low grounds
on the big rivers, and the party of the owners of the old colonial mansions. It
had become an old saw that 'Whigs knew each other by the instincts of gentlemen.'"[48] Nevertheless, the political equality of white men that slavery made

possible, as Abel P. Upshur admitted without saying so in his 1839 article "On Domestic Slavery," allowed a majority of the members of the Convention of 1850–51 to accept universal white manhood suffrage and to discard the property qualification for voting.[49] The convention delegates accepted in Virginia in 1851 what most other states had embraced a generation earlier.[50]

The delegates abolished the useless old executive advisory council and allowed Virginia voters for the first time to elect the governor, lieutenant governor, attorney general, and members of the Board of Public Works.[51] In that year, when white men for the first time voted for governor, both candidates for governor were from the western mountains. Before that year the eastern men who had controlled the General Assembly never considered any man from the western mountains as a potential governor.

The convention delegates went much further and also allowed the popular election of all local and appellate judges in the state and also the justices of the peace and almost all local officials.[52] The new constitution allowed members of the Senate of Virginia for the first time to introduce bills and enlarged it to fifty members who served four-year terms, half to be elected every second year.[53] It restricted the assembly to holding one session every other year and retained the prohibitions, inspired by the Constitution of the United States and the Bill of Rights, that were added to the Constitution of 1830. It also retained the 1830 provision that placed the essence of the 1786 Act for Establishing Religious Freedom in the section imposing limitations on the authority of the assembly.[54]

The significant democratic changes passed in spite of the fact that the General Assembly of 1850, in which eastern members retained a majority in both houses, once again discriminated against the west in apportioning representation in the convention. Much as the enabling act for the Convention of 1829–30 had allocated more seats in the convention to the eastern region than to the western, the assembly in 1850 created districts by region and then allocated seats within those regions using a formula based on estimates (derived from personal property tax returns) of the number of white people in each county and city plus the number of dollars that the residents of each jurisdiction paid in personal property taxes. Each delegate represented an average of 13,151 white people and $7,000.24 in taxes paid on personal property. In effect, delegates from east of the mountains represented fewer white people and more property (i.e., represented the slave property) than delegates from the west.[55]

If one eccentric man could be said to exemplify what by the 1850s had become the new norm for Virginia's politicians, that man was Henry A. Wise, the grandson of two prominent Eastern Shore Federalists. He was a walking and talking set of contradictions and inconsistencies that, in fact, made him emblematic in some essential ways of the mid-nineteenth-century Southern Democrat. Wise was a domineering personality and powerful public speaker and courtroom advocate as well as a brilliant and often sarcastic debater. One of his speeches in the convention in the spring of 1851 required five days to deliver. Wise entered politics early in the 1830s as a supporter of President Andrew Jackson but soon became an anti-Jackson Whig. He was a John Tyler Whig during the 1840s and became a John Tyler Democrat after the Whigs in Congress in effect read Tyler out of their party. Wise welcomed white urban workingmen into politics and campaigned for their votes. He spoke eloquently during the convention for establishing a statewide system of free public schools for all white Virginians. Later, as governor from 1856 to 1860, Wise fought for economic diversification and industrialization as good for the state and for its white workingmen, as well as to free it from reliance on slavery. But Wise, who himself owned slaves and often appeared sympathetic toward the enslaved people he owned, also defended with as much energy and ingenuity as he could the rights that owners of slaves had to their human property. Henry A. Wise and men like him accepted universal white manhood suffrage and the election of most public officials in 1851. They no longer feared or despised working-class white men as much as Upshur and Leigh had in 1830. In 1851 Wise and a majority of white Virginians understood that slavery had made possible political democracy for white men and that white men of all classes appeared to accept slavery as an essential component of their shared society and their economic future.[56]

The Virginia Constitution of 1851 was very like state constitutions elsewhere in the United States, but slavery made all Southern state constitutions distinctive. In Virginia the General Assembly allowed slavery to dictate how convention delegates were selected, and the delegates for the first time put the words *slave* and *slavery* into the state's constitution. Section 19 of Article IV, which was derived from an 1806 act of assembly, required every emancipated slave to leave Virginia within one year or be reenslaved; Section 20 authorized the General Assembly to place restrictions on private emancipations and to rid the state of "the free negro population, by removal or otherwise"; and Section 21 positively prohibited the assembly from emancipating any slaves at all.[57]

Slavery directly affected taxation and produced inequities in taxation in Virginia as in the other slave states.[58] Section 23 of Article IV placed a cap of $300 on the valuation of individual slaves for taxation purposes. All owners of valuable items of personal property, such as horses, cattle, silver plate, gold watches, and the like, paid a tax on the value of the items. Enslaved people were also personal property for purposes of taxation, and in fact, the official tax returns itemized slave property right along with horses, cattle, and swine. Much as men had complained in the 1670s and again during the American

Revolution, the planters and other men and women who owned significant numbers of enslaved laborers paid a relatively lower tax on the whole value of their personal property than men and women whose personal property did not consist to any appreciable degree of human beings. Western delegates opposed the limitation on the taxable value of slaves, but the advantage that the eastern portion of the state enjoyed in the convention enabled eastern delegates to get their way. The rapid rise in the market value of enslaved laborers during the 1850s made that provision increasingly irksome to people who owned few or no slaves.

After long and bitter debate, the convention contrived a set of interrelated compromises on the important question of whether the valuable property of slave owners would continue to dictate apportionment of representation in the General Assembly. It assigned a majority of seats in the House of Delegates to the western region and a majority of seats in the Senate of Virginia to the eastern region[59] with a proviso that in 1865 the General Assembly would reapportion representation in both houses. If the assembly members could not agree then on the method of apportionment, the voters would decide by referendum from among four options that the new constitution specified: 1. Allot seats in both houses according to the number of voters in each city and county. 2. Allot seats in both houses on a mixed basis counting the number of white inhabitants and the amount of taxes paid. 3. Allot seats in the House of Delegates based on the number of white inhabitants and seats in the Senate on the amount of all state taxes paid. 4. Allot seats in the House of Delegates on the basis of the number of voters and seats in the Senate on the mixed basis of the number of white inhabitants and the amount of taxes paid.[60] If demographic trends that had been working in Virginia during the nineteenth century continued, by 1865 the General Assembly might very well be able to reapportion legislative representation on something approximating a one-white-man, one-vote basis.

By the middle of the nineteenth century, the old class of large planters was but a small fraction of the population in the eastern counties and almost nonexistent elsewhere in Virginia. Even though James Madison had linked slavery and undemocratic politics in the 1790s, slavery did not have to be abolished to take a large measure of political power out of the hands of a minority of men who owned land and slaves and lodge it in the more numerous hands of free white men. By a vote of 63 to 43, the Convention of 1850–51 allowed the men who were to be enfranchised by it to vote in the ratification referendum and did not restrict voting to owners of land, who had been the only voters since 1670.[61] As a consequence, the new constitution won overwhelming approval by a popular vote of 75,748 to 11,063, almost a seven-to-one margin.[62] White men who owned slaves and who lived in the region where enslaved people were most numerous could still exercise a greater electoral influence in the

General Assembly than other white men, but the political culture of Virginia's colonial and Revolutionary past had changed so much that an approximation of democratic government by white men in Virginia finally began in 1851, seventy-five years after George Mason and Thomas Jefferson had declared that all men were created equal.

8

HOUSE
DIVIDED

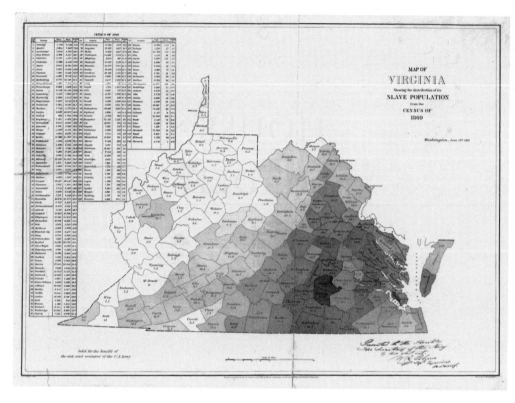

Map of Virginia Showing the Distribution of Its Slave Population from the Census of 1860 *(courtesy of the Library of Virginia) was printed in Philadelphia in 1861. Between the presidential election in November 1860 and the outbreak of the Civil War in the spring of 1861, advocates of secession were most numerous in the counties east of the Blue Ridge and south of the Rappahannock River where slavery was of the greatest importance. Virginia's voting men remained loyal to the United States by a margin of two or three to one until April 1861 when the war began. Men who opposed secession argued that slavery in Virginia would be safer if Virginia remained in the United States than if it left and became one of the Confederate States.*

THE CONVENTION THAT MET IN RICH-
mond from 14 February through 1 May 1861 is known in the literature of Virginia's history as the Secession Convention because on 17 April the delegates voted 88 to 55 to secede from the United States,[1] but for its first two months it was a Union convention.

The Virginia convention differed in several important ways from the other Southern state conventions that assembled following the election of Abraham Lincoln as president of the United States early in November 1860. Most of the other conventions met and almost immediately voted to secede, but the Virginia convention met for two and a half months and until mid-April refused to secede. Moreover, the secession crisis that saw seven slave states secede between 20 December 1860 and 1 February 1861 and four more in the following April, May, and June also led to the secession from Virginia of nearly fifty of its western counties, creating the new state of West Virginia in 1863 and putting Virginia in a unique position. It had two state governments from 1861 to 1865, one that was part of the Confederate States of America and another that was part of the United States of America. The two secession crises, one interstate and the other intrastate, revealed what was most important to the white people who lived in the different regions of Virginia. The war that followed also allowed the nearly half a million black Virginians who lived in slavery to disclose by their actions what they believed and what was most important to them. Many of them freed themselves by running away from their owners even before the outcome of the Civil War freed them all.

Following the statewide election of convention delegates on a snowy 4 February 1861, the editor of an Abingdon newspaper in southwestern Virginia announced that to his surprise "the *immediate* secession candidates have been badly whipped—in fact, have been almost annihilated,—and the gentlemen representing the *'wait-a-bit'* ticket triumphantly elected."[2] That was a very apt characterization of a large majority of the men elected that day. Another western Virginia journalist of the time later wrote that only about one-fourth of the delegates initially favored secession, another fourth opposed secession no matter what, and fully half strongly opposed secession under the circumstances that then existed and believed that they could settle the sectional crisis and reunite the country.[3]

When the delegates first assembled in Richmond in mid-February, they spent two days adopting rules, electing a clerk, a sergeant at arms, and doorkeepers, and arranging for their debates to be printed in full and distributed throughout the state. The wait-a-bit men settled in for an extended session, not merely to vote down the small minority that wanted Virginia to secede at once but also to await the outcome of a national peace conference that the General Assembly of the state had called into being and that was even then meeting in Washington, D.C. That conference tried without success to find a means of reconciling the differences between the political leaders in the states without slavery and those in the states with slavery that had already voted to secede. The delegates in Richmond tried repeatedly during the first two months to find a means for the political leaders in Virginia and the other states with slavery that remained in the United States to broker a deal that would achieve the same result. The wait-a-bit delegates needed time. As the secessionists in the convention grew increasingly frustrated and fussed and shouted at the Unionists, the wait-a-bits worked hard but without success to reunite the country.[4]

The presidential election early in November 1860 that precipitated the secession crisis was conducted under radically different conditions than the election of convention delegates early in February 1861. The presidential election came at the end of a decade that had witnessed an escalation of sectional tension in the country, including bloody conflicts between advocates and opponents of slavery in Kansas, John Brown's October 1859 raid on Harpers Ferry in Virginia, and the breaking apart in the spring of 1860 of the Democratic Party, the last political organization in the country that was still truly national. Those episodes convinced many Southern leaders that Northern extremists posed an increasingly dangerous threat to the South and to slavery.

One of the main issues that split the Democrats was instrumental in splitting the country. The Kansas-Nebraska Act of 1854 repealed the Missouri Compromise that had prohibited the introduction of slavery into western territories north of 36°30' north latitude. In 1857 the Supreme Court in *Dred Scott v. Sandford* invalidated the repealed compromise law in a decision that prohibited Congress from interfering with the introduction of slavery into any of the western territories and that could be interpreted to require congressional legislation to protect slavery there. The Kansas-Nebraska Act authorized what its sponsors called popular sovereignty, allowing immigrants to the west to decide for themselves whether to permit slavery. Many Northern leaders became convinced that Southern extremists intent on spreading slavery into the western territories posed a danger to the preservation of representative government and to the free-labor economy of the whole United States.

Unlike the election of convention delegates, the presidential election was not strictly about union or disunion; it was about whether a Northern Republican, a border-state Whig, or one of two Democrats would win the presidency, which, to be sure, had serious implications for whether the nation could survive unchanged. The election was unusual in that four men ran for president of the United States and all received votes in the Electoral College. The Republican Party nominated Abraham Lincoln, of Illinois, and Hannibal Hamlin, of Maine. A convention of Democrats nominated John C. Breckinridge, of Kentucky, and Joseph Lane, of Oregon; these two were sometimes, in spite of the place of residence of the candidate for vice president, called the nominees of Southern Democrats. Another convention of Democrats nominated Stephen A. Douglas, of Illinois, and Herschel Johnson, of Georgia; these men were sometimes, in spite of the place of residence of the candidate for vice president, called the nominees of Northern Democrats. The new Constitutional Union Party nominated two former Whigs, John Bell, of Tennessee, and Edward Everett, of Massachusetts. Lincoln won a plurality of the nation's popular vote and a majority of the Electoral College votes.

The presidential election of 1860 was the closest ever in Virginia. Several published vote totals for the state, all characterized as official, reported the margin of victory for Bell over Breckinridge in Virginia as ranging from a mere 124 votes to a mere 358 votes.[5] Between the published numbers and the incomplete file of official county and city returns,[6] there are some unexplained differences.[7] What is probably the most reliable count was printed in the *Daily Richmond Enquirer* on 24 December 1860:

John Bell	74,701
John C. Breckinridge	74,379
Stephan A. Douglas	16,292
Abraham Lincoln	1,929

It was no surprise that Abraham Lincoln received only a small number of votes in Virginia, most of them in the northwestern cities and towns. A few men in the Shenandoah Valley and northeastern Virginia and 4 men in Portsmouth voted for Lincoln, as did 55 men in the Aquia Creek region of Prince William County.[8] It is quite possible that more than 1,929 Virginians wanted to vote for Lincoln but were afraid to. Voting then remained viva voce, as it had been in Virginia since the early years of the seventeenth century. Even though voters in presidential elections (only) could hand in tickets, or ballots, bearing the names of the candidates for presidential elector, they had to announce out loud the names of the electors or presidential candidates for whom they voted,[9] exposing all voters to hostile reactions from men who deplored their choices.

Dislike of Lincoln and Republicans was intense and widespread in much of Virginia because they opposed allowing slavery into western territories, and the party included many openly antislavery leaders and some abolitionists. In July 1860 some Republicans in the northeastern county of Prince William raised a flagpole and hoisted a Lincoln and Hamlin banner. Threats of violence caused them to appeal to the adjutant general and the governor for protection. The governor ordered out the county militia, which marched to the site and protected men who chopped the pole down and then chopped it up into souvenirs.[10]

In September a man in mountainous Giles County sent a letter to the governor. "As the Presidential election is approaching," he wrote, "I would like to Know from you what is to prevent me from Voting for Lincoln. as he is the man I prefer. the reason of this letter is that there is a great deal of threatning on the part of Slave holders in regard to poor men exerciseing the elective franchise and as I am a law abideing citizen and has paid my taxes to the commonwealth of Virginia every year and performed all the duties and complied with all the obligations imposed on me I think it hard if I should be prevented from exerciseing the wright of suffrage that other men do in selecting any one of the four candidates before the people for the office of President of the United states as my choice."[11] There is no surviving officially certified election return from Giles County, but none of the published election results indicates that anybody in that county voted for Lincoln or that if anybody did, that vote was properly recorded.

That Stephen A. Douglas received so few votes might have been a surprise to a good many lifelong Democrats, but his advocacy of popular sovereignty cost him the votes of most Southern Democrats because popular sovereignty could produce antislavery territorial laws and more free states. Douglas fared better in the state's cities and in some counties where Whigs had traditionally been strong and where the white population was more diverse than in many rural areas of Virginia. The state's Democrats, especially rural Democrats, overwhelmingly preferred John C. Breckinridge, the one presidential candidate who unreservedly supported the unrestrained right of owners of enslaved laborers to move with their slave property into the western territories, to legislate legal protection for slavery in those territories, and to draft constitutions that legalized slavery when petitioning Congress for admission as new states.

Bell's platform included no statements on any of the outstanding political issues of the time and merely advocated preservation of the Union. He relied solely on his prominence as a former Whig and his opposition to disunion. His strongholds in Virginia were the eastern cities, the populous and prosperous counties of the Shenandoah Valley, and other areas of the state where Whigs had traditionally been strong.

The state's attorney general required that some official returns with misspelled names of candidates for presidential elector be tabulated as counted for other men than the candidates, which reduced the number of legal votes for several candidates. Because of the closeness of the vote, the governor then certified the election of nine Bell electors and six Breckinridge electors.[12] Neither Virginia's election laws nor the Constitution of the United States required that all of the state's electoral votes be cast for the candidate whose presidential electors received the largest number of votes, but the Breckinridge electors bowed to the seventy-two-year-old winner-take-all tradition and resigned. The nine Bell electors met in the state Capitol on 5 December and selected six replacement electors, four of whom had been Bell candidates for presidential elector in November. The fifteen men then cast all of the state's electoral votes for John Bell and Edward Everett.[13]

The national outcome of the election did not change as a consequence of the close and confused Virginia vote, and the closeness and confusion were soon forgotten. At the time newspaper editors and politicians in Virginia did not interpret the election as a contest between union and disunion or even so much as a defeat for the Democrats, who had run strongly nearly everywhere in the state where they had traditionally been strong. What stood out was the resurgence of the state's Whigs, a formidable segment of the electorate who had been without a national party for more than five years. Some of them had flirted with the American (or Know-Nothing) Party during the mid-1850s, then most of them reunited as the Opposition against the Democratic Party in the 1859 gubernatorial election. The former Whig John Bell outpolled Democrat John C. Breckinridge by less than 0.2 percent in Virginia, and the state's Democrats consoled themselves by pointing out that the combined Breckinridge and Douglas vote was larger than Bell's vote and larger even than the combined vote of Bell and Lincoln, who was also a former Whig.[14]

Even though some Virginians talked about secession following each of the dramatic events of the 1850s, fear of disunion was resilient in Virginia and in the other slave states. The word *union* embraced the American Revolution's national heritage of personal liberty, representative government, and national greatness. Disunion threatened that legacy.[15] Outside the state Capitol in Richmond where the convention delegates first met was a two-year-old greater-than-life-sized bronze equestrian statue of George Washington, the great founding hero of the United States. Not far away on the grounds was a one-year-old life-sized marble statue of Henry Clay, the Virginia native and Whig leader who earned the honorable nickname of the Great Compromiser for helping engineer the Missouri Compromise of 1820 and the Compromise of 1850 that were widely believed to have saved the country from disunion. The dedication ceremonies for both statues had emphasized Virginia's role in the founding and preservation of the nation and the state's continuing devotion to the Union in a time of increasing sectional tension.[16]

Breckinridge was not a secessionist candidate for president, nor did most Virginia men who voted for him favor immediate secession before or after Lincoln won the election. Nevertheless, some Virginians believed that Lincoln's election alone justified secession. White men in some Virginia counties and cities held public meetings in November and December 1860 and adopted resolutions in favor of secession, but the election of the first antislavery president, the first who received no electoral votes in any slave state, did not immediately propel a majority of the state's political leaders, even of its Democrats, into the secessionist camp. Wait-a-bit also appeared to be the attitude of many of the disappointed Democrats.

The outpouring of secessionist resolutions at postelection city and county meetings held in many parts of Virginia indicated, though, that some Virginians perceived that the preservation of slavery in Virginia and in the South would be impossible in a nation that had a Republican president. Aggressive men of like mind in South Carolina assembled a state convention and on 20 December 1860 dissolved that state's legal connection to the United States. Secessionists did the same thing in Mississippi on 9 January 1861, in Florida on 10 January, in Alabama on 11 January, in Georgia on 19 January, in Louisiana on 29 January, and in Texas on 1 February. It was in that very different political climate, in the midst of a great national crisis in which the choice was union or disunion—not a traditional partisan choice between political party candidates—that Virginia's voters went through the snow and cold rain to their polling places on 4 February to elect members of a convention that would determine whether Virginia remained one of the United States.

Virginia men also voted that day whether to require the convention, if it decided that Virginia should secede, to submit its decision to a ratification referendum before secession could become effective. A few of the counties did not report results, but in the large majority that did, about two-thirds of the voters favored requiring a referendum.[17] In most of the counties where a majority of the voters insisted on a referendum, they elected delegates who opposed secession. That included in many counties that Breckinridge had carried, some by wide margins and some by narrow margins, in November 1860. Breckinridge ran strongly in the traditionally Democratic counties of western Virginia—indeed, Breckinridge received more votes in the counties that later became West Virginia than Bell received, even as Bell received more than Breckinridge in the counties that remained Virginia—but western Virginia voters elected many more opponents than advocates of secession to the convention in February 1861 and strongly endorsed the referendum requirement. In the counties where a majority of the voters opposed the referendum, a majority of the delegates that they elected voted for secession at the first chance they got, on 4 April 1861, and some of them spoke in favor of disunion long before that. The strongest opposition to the referendum came from voters in the southern and southeastern counties that had the state's largest population of slaves. Voters there elected men who favored secession and were anxious not to delay lest the crisis pass and the slower democracy of the referendum process defeat their ends. On 4 February the wait-a-bit candidates defeated impatient secessionists by a statewide margin of two or three to one.[18]

The assembly's enabling act provided that the voters in each of the state's

House of Delegates districts elect members of the convention. Some districts included more than one county, and some populous counties and cities elected more than one delegate. The districts were not all of equal population, but because nearly all adult white men were eligible to vote and because the allocation of seats in the convention was not heavily weighted to favor any region, the election on 4 February 1861 was the first statewide election of a constituent assembly in which the members might have reasonably well represented the opinions of the whole white male population of Virginia.

The 152 men elected to the Virginia convention included one railroad executive, one newspaperman, one banker, one Methodist minister, and four medical doctors; fifteen men engaged in manufacturing or mercantile pursuits; and fewer than two dozen men who were primarily farmers or planters. Of great planters owning many scores of slaves, James Coles Bruce, of Halifax County, was the only one elected. More than two-thirds of the delegates, 105 of them, were or had been practicing attorneys (and one of them was a professor of law at the University of Virginia), although many of the attorneys also owned farms or plantations or had substantial investments in banks or other businesses.[19] As in the Constitutional Convention of 1850–51, the planter elite that had dominated Virginia's politics during its first two and a half centuries was only a small minority.

During the debates the delegates exhibited many examples of brilliance, eloquence, wit, and passion and some remarkable examples of endurance. Several of the convention's leading men spoke for several hours at a time or even for several hours on each of several successive days. They demonstrated their oratorical abilities in many ways, but evasion and subtlety were not among them. The men spoke honestly and openly about their interests, hopes, and fears. What they spoke about, how they spoke about it, and what they did not speak about clearly revealed what they thought, hoped, and feared.

The Virginia whose future the delegates debated was a very diverse state. The composition of the convention and the variety of viewpoints that the delegates brought to it illuminated that diversity. Virginia had the largest populations of owners of slaves and of enslaved people in the country and except for neighboring Maryland the largest population of free black people. Of the slave states Virginia was the most economically and socially diverse, lower Louisiana possibly excepted. Only Missouri (by a small margin) and Texas (only seminomadic Indians populated much of Texas then) were larger. Missouri was more populous but also by a very small margin, and slavery was a much less important bulwark of the economy there than in Virginia. Fully aware of the importance of their state and their responsibilities, the delegates and apprehensive observers throughout what had once been the United States recognized that what Virginians did could determine whether the states could be reunited or would remain disunited.

In spite of the many natural affinities that white residents of the slave state of Virginia had with white residents of the other Southern slave states, white Virginians' identification with residents of the other slave states was not in every way strong and varied with the regional diversity in the state. Virginians of the time usually distinguished the differences between the sections by referring to the Blue Ridge or Allegheny Mountains as forming the principal division between eastern and western Virginia, but the most illuminating way to view the diversity in the middle of the nineteenth century is to consider the watercourses.[20]

The Ohio River formed the northwestern boundary of Virginia, but the river was a boundary only for legal and political purposes in that it separated the slave state of Virginia from the free state of Ohio. In fact, Virginia was an important Ohio Valley state in the same way that other parts of Virginia made it a Southern state and also a mid-Atlantic state. A busy network of steamboats that navigated the Ohio River together with the National Road and the Baltimore and Ohio Railroad and its connecting line between Grafton and Parkersburg reinforced the linkage of the Ohio Valley region of Virginia with free states during the 1850s. A supporter of secession in the northwestern town of Clarksburg pointedly informed the governor in the spring of 1861 that "it must be recollected that our intercourse is almost entirely with the West and the North, we have none with The Central and eastern portions of Virginia. We are not slaveholders, many of us are of Northern birth. We read almost exclusively Northern newspapers and books, and listen to Northern preachers."[21]

Two tiers of western Virginia counties were Ohio Valley counties, and in those counties and in the watershed of the Monongahela River that flowed northward into southwestern Pennsylvania, the residents probably shared more socially and economically with residents of Pennsylvania and Ohio on the other side of the river and to the north and west than with residents of the remainder of Virginia on the other side of the mountains to the east and south. Slavery was relatively uncommon in the Ohio Valley counties of Virginia and plantation slavery almost unknown. As a consequence and on the whole, Virginians in the Ohio River valley looked to the north, northeast, and northwest, and even though Breckinridge easily won the largest number of votes in that region in November 1860, the voting men there in February 1861 elected almost none but firm opponents of secession to the Virginia convention.

It was a very different Virginia on the western slopes of the Allegheny Mountains east and south of the Ohio River counties. The mountains were the most sparsely populated region of Virginia, and slavery was of minimal social and economic importance. In nearly every county of that region, the voting-age men shared very few economic interests with the slave-owning planters of the other Southern states, but they may have shared little with Northern and mid-western farmers, too. Those men voted their traditional partisan allegiances in November 1860 and carried most of the region's counties for Breckenridge, but the delegates that they elected to the convention in February 1861 almost all opposed secession at that time.

The counties in the upper watershed of the Tennessee River where rivers and streams flowed southward out of Virginia into Tennessee were part of a larger economic and cultural region that underwent swift and dramatic change during the decade prior to the secession crisis. At the midpoint of the nineteenth century, the construction of the Virginia and Tennessee Railroad from Lynchburg southwest to the Tennessee border at the little town that was later renamed Bristol opened up commercial and communications networks that stimulated rapid economic change in the Virginia counties through which it ran and in the neighboring counties east and west of the railroad. The white and black populations of the region rose rapidly during the 1850s, and the proportion of the region's population that lived in slavery increased by more than 15 percent during the decade,[22] linking that region for the first time economically and culturally and more strongly in a political sense to the counties of more distant eastern Virginia than to the nearby mountain counties of western Virginia. By 1861 the people in southwestern Virginia looked more to the northeast into central Virginia than they ever had before, but the regional identification of voters there remained strong. Voting men there gave Breckinridge more votes than any other presidential candidate in November 1860, but in February 1861 they elected to the convention fewer advocates of secession and more wait-a-bit opponents than the editor of the *Abingdon Democrat* had anticipated.

In eastern Virginia the landscape took its shape and character from the great bay of Chesapeake and its tributaries. Two Eastern Shore counties between the bay and the ocean were physically detached from the rest of Virginia and by the middle of the nineteenth century were more nearly commercial and cultural appendages of Maryland than integral parts of old Virginia. Indeed, later in 1861 some men there contemplated holding a referendum in March 1862 to decide whether Accomack and Northampton Counties should become counties in the state of Maryland rather than counties in the state of Virginia.[23] The Virginia counties along the Potomac River and on the western shore of the bay were also closely linked commercially and otherwise with Baltimore and other mid-Atlantic cities. The density of the enslaved population was greater throughout the region than farther west, and white men's commitment to the institution was virtually unshakable by 1860. The cities of eastern Virginia had been strongholds of the Whig Party, and Bell as well as Douglas did well in them. The voters in the cities elected more opponents of secession than supporters in 1861.

The rural counties of eastern and southern Virginia more nearly resembled the lower South. East of the Blue Ridge and south of the Rappahannock River, nearly every county had more than 40 percent of its population living in slavery. In eighteen of the fifty-six counties, more than 50 percent of the population was enslaved, in another twelve more than 60 percent, and in two others more than 70 percent.[24] The farmers and planters in the vast rural parts of the region with the large slave population in their midst often identified their interests with those of the cotton planters in the Carolinas and Georgia. Breckinridge won victories in most of the counties in November 1860, and in February 1861 voters in those counties elected more supporters than opponents of secession. It was the only region of Virginia where more supporters than opponents of secession won election to the convention.

Between the eastward-flowing rivers and the westward-flowing rivers was the northward-flowing Shenandoah River that squeezed itself between the Blue Ridge Mountains to the east and the Allegheny Mountains to the west. The North and South Branches of the Potomac River drained the eastern slope of the Allegheny Mountains immediately to the west of the Valley counties. The Valley and the counties in the upper reaches of the Potomac River watershed lay between the portion of Virginia where slavery was an essential and integral part of life that influenced how everybody lived and the portion of the state where slavery was a relatively inconspicuous and inconsequential part of the lives of most people. In some counties in the Shenandoah Valley, slaves were numerous, but Quakers, Mennonites, and some members of other religious denominations in the old German Reformed tradition and their descendants disapproved of slavery. In Shenandoah County thirteen men voted for Lincoln in 1860. The Valley's historic commercial connections with Baltimore and Philadelphia, not with Richmond or Norfolk, gave it a social and political orientation that more nearly resembled the outlook of people to the west than that of people to the east. Douglas received stronger support in the valleys than in most other regions of Virginia, and Bell ran very well there, too. Voters there returned more firm opponents of disunion to the convention of 1861 than anywhere else east of the mountains. The Whig Party had been a thriving and powerful political force there, and among the delegates that the white men of the Valley counties elected in February 1861 were several very able and experienced men who had been Whigs.

Former Whigs who opposed secession dominated the convention.[25] They initially placed their hopes on the national peace conference that the General Assembly of Virginia had called for early in 1861. The proposals that the conference made to Congress late in February were unacceptable to a great many of the political leaders of the free states because they appeared to concede too much to the slave states, and they were unacceptable to many of the political leaders of the slave states because they appeared to concede too much to the free states. The conference's presiding officer, former president John Tyler, of Virginia, disavowed the proposals of the conference because they offered too few inducements for the seceded states to return.[26] Even after the failure of the peace conference, the opponents of secession in the Virginia convention persisted in seeking a compromise. They were reluctant to admit that the differences between the extremes might have become uncompromisable by then. They succeeded in keeping Virginia in the United States, but they failed to find a solution to the national crisis.

Throughout the long and often tedious speeches that filled the afternoon and evening sessions during the first two months of the convention, not one delegate uttered a single word critical of slavery. Delegates who believed in immediate secession frequently referred to the first lower South states to secede as fellow slave states, but they and the other delegates more often differentiated Virginia's interests from the interests of those states by referring to them as cotton states or as Gulf states, almost as if they were alien regions. They all agreed, though, that a Republican president and Congress were potentially threatening to slavery in Virginia and in the South and positively dangerous to slavery in the nation by restricting or prohibiting its spread into the western territories. Delegates from all parts of Virginia and from all political backgrounds said much the same thing as they debated whether slavery would be safer if Virginia remained in the United States or became part of the Confederate States.

Many of the delegates included within their long speeches detailed accounts of American political history, but when discussing the crisis of 1861, they ignored some divisive issues that had once been of great consequence, among them federal tariff policy. Only five delegates even mentioned the tariff, once a contentious issue between Northern and Southern politicians. Virginia politicians had always been divided on the subject. A significant number of Virginia industrialists, bankers, and businessmen had supported a protective tariff as good public policy or as good for their own personal interests, even though it resulted in higher prices that Southern people, especially Southern farmers and planters, had to pay for manufactured goods imported from abroad or from Northern states. John Brown Baldwin, of Staunton, one of the most able former Whigs who opposed secession, suggested that residents of the Confederate States would be at a tariff disadvantage in commercial dealings with residents of the United States and that insofar as tariffs were concerned, Virginians were better off remaining in the Union than leaving it.[27] Secessionist George Wythe Randolph, of Richmond, countered that within the Confederate States a proper tariff policy would make Virginia the New York—and Richmond the New York City—of the new nation.[28]

For all of the oratory and ink that had been devoted since the days of Thomas Jefferson, James Madison, and John Taylor of Caroline to the subject of state's rights, the delegates in Richmond during the final weeks of winter and the first weeks of spring 1861 said almost nothing about state's rights. Six—only six—of the delegates—and two of them Whig Unionists—identified themselves as lifelong state's-rights Southerners, but for the most part they did not explain what that meant in practical political terms. Delegate Jubal Early during one of his several speeches attacking secession asked twice what those men meant by the phrase "state's rights" and did not get a satisfactory answer.[29]

Delegate and former governor Henry A. Wise described Virginia as the "mother of State rights" and later stated what he believed the other delegates should understand the phrase to mean when he impatiently repeated that he was at the convention to "defend Southern rights and," raising his voice and shouting, "Southern slavery!"[30] As Wise's comment indicated, it was not state's rights but slavery that was at stake. George W. Richardson, of Hanover County, summarized the case for joining the Confederacy by explaining, "The Constitution of the Confederate States will be administered by a Southern Congress, a Southern President, with a Southern Cabinet, and construed by Southern Judges, all looking to the interest of Southern slaveholders; and not by a Northern free soil executive and abolition Congress, and a Supreme Court to be abolitionized as rapidly as death shall remove the remainder of the venerable States rights Judges who now grace its bench."[31]

The only right of any state that any delegates discussed, and it was in doubt, was whether states had individual rights as South Carolina had done to withdraw or to repeal its ratification of the Constitution of the United States. The debates in the Virginia Convention of 1861 were not about state's rights or the tariff or even about slavery itself; they were about how to bring the parts of the severed nation back together and whether slavery in Virginia and Virginia as a slave state would be safer in the United States or in the Confederate States.

The majority of delegates, who opposed secession, argued that slavery in Virginia and in the South was well protected under the terms of the United States Constitution and the laws that Congress had enacted, including the Fugitive Slave Act of 1850, as the Supreme Court of the United States had interpreted them. If Virginia seceded, they argued, owners of slaves would be permanently banned from taking their slave property into the western territories of the United States, a restriction that a four-year Republican administration in the 1860s could not make permanent. Secession would destroy what secessionists stated was essential for the preservation of slavery. Moreover, if residents of the upper South slave states seceded, owners of slaves would lose the valuable legal authority and potent political power of the United States Constitution and government to enable them to recover runaway slaves. Several of them pointedly forecast that the effect of Virginia's seceding would be to bring the Canadian border several hundred miles south and offer more havens for men and women escaping from Virginia servitude. Worse, if secession provoked war, as George William Brent, of Alexandria, predicted, that would be "the doom of slavery in the border States."[32]

For two months the men in the convention who opposed secession tried repeatedly and without success to find a means of reconciling freedom and slavery in the United States. For nearly two months the men who favored speedy secession recognized their minority status and were reluctant to force the issue, but on 4 April, Lewis E. Harvie sprang a secession resolution on the delegates. Harvie represented the counties of Amelia and Powhatan, the two counties in the state where more than 70 percent of the population lived in slavery. His resolution failed spectacularly, by a two-to-one margin, 90 to 45 (not 88 to 45 as appears in most reference works).[33] Some convention members reported that five other delegates were known to favor the resolution and that six opposed it. Five months after Abraham Lincoln won the presidency, Virginia and the other upper South slave states Tennessee, North Carolina, Missouri, Maryland, Kentucky, Delaware, and Arkansas remained part of the United States. During the first three and a half months of 1861, the decision that each state's political leaders had to make was whether secession was wise or prudent or in their state's interest. There was no irresistible rush to disunion except in the lower South cotton states where, as opponents of secession in Virginia believed (and they were probably correct), disunionists may have been a minority but such a vigorous and loud minority that they successfully outmaneuvered and overpowered Unionist majorities.[34]

Secessionists were a vigorous and loud minority in Virginia but not a successful one. Lincoln's 4 March inaugural address in which he promised to hold federal property in the seceded states and to enforce the laws and collect the taxes there was widely unpopular in Virginia. Many men who vigorously opposed secession denounced it as a threat of unacceptable coercion. It did not, however, reduce their majority in the convention. Appeals from the new Confederate government to the delegates to join the lower South states in defense of slavery failed.[35] Even a clause in the provisional constitution of the Confederacy that prevented the importation of slaves from a foreign country, which would have made it illegal for Virginians to continue the profitable business of selling slaves in southwestern markets, did not persuade opponents of disunion to change their minds for purely selfish gain.

Advocates of secession consequently organized more meetings in many of the state's cities and counties and adopted stern resolutions insisting on Virginia's immediate secession, giving the appearance that the white people of the state were overwhelmingly becoming disunionists. But even as the November 1860 meetings that called for immediate secession did not lead to or produce a secessionist victory in the February 1861 election of convention delegates, it is unclear that the many public meetings that called for immediate secession in the spring of 1861 indicated that as a whole the white people of Virginia had changed their minds in proportion to the number of published public declarations. With very few exceptions opponents of secession, especially east of the mountains, did not assemble in public meetings and adopt resolutions in favor of remaining in the United States. Most of the state's newspaper editors who opposed secession during the winter remained opposed to secession as spring began.

The active advocates of secession were the squeaky wheels of Virginia politics late in 1860 and early in 1861 and seized the initiative, but they did not move the convention delegates along the path that they desired. Their carefully choreographed assembling in Richmond in mid-April of what they called a spontaneous Southern rights convention merely confirmed their adversaries' apprehensions about the conspiratorial and undemocratic tactics and purposes of the secessionists. Some opponents of secession feared that the Southern rights convention might actually attempt to overthrow the government, disband the legitimately elected convention, and take the state out of the Union by force.

In spite of the best that the advocates of secession could do, the opponents of disunion maintained their control of the convention until the middle of April and continued to debate one proposal after another to enlist the other upper South slave states to find a compromise. The wait-a-bits in the convention succeeded in keeping Virginia in the Union, and the secessionists failed to take it out.

Secession nevertheless occurred in Virginia on 17 April 1861 when it was certain that war was going to break out. After Abraham Lincoln attempted to resupply Fort Sumter in Charleston harbor, men in South Carolina opened fire on the fort and forced it to surrender. At almost the same time former governor Wise on his own personal authority secretly arranged for Virginia militiamen to seize the United States arsenal at Harpers Ferry and the navy yard at Norfolk.[36] Lincoln then called for 75,000 militiamen, specifically including 2,340 officers and men from Virginia[37] and hundreds more from the other Southern slave states, to put down the rebellion. Two weeks later after watching the consequences unfold, the editor of the *Lynchburg Daily Virginian* wrote that "the President's infamous Proclamation, indicating a purpose to subjugate the Southern States . . . did the business in Virginia, not the attack on Fort Sumter. It was this that swept away the last refuge of the Union men of Virginia. They could not maintain their ground in the face of this Proclamation breathing nothing but vengeance, subjugation and war."[38]

Almost forty delegates who had voted against secession on 4 April changed their minds, and on 17 April the convention voted 88 to 55 to submit an ordinance of secession to the voters for ratification in May. Even then, the

delegates voted to secede by a margin of only eight to five. The majority of
the delegates agreed on secession only when the question before the convention was no longer whether secession was wise or desirable or whether slavery
in Virginia was safer in the Union or out of it. Secession passed the Virginia
convention only after it was clear that there was going to be a war, and because
the war would obviously be fought at least in part in Virginia, delegates had to
decide who they would fight with and who they would shoot at.[39]

It was obvious that the United States Army and Navy would try to re-
take the arsenal at Harpers Ferry and the navy yard near Norfolk as well as
to reinforce Fort Monroe at the mouth of the James River. Some of the delegates explained their votes as necessary to defend Virginia, and others talked
of joining Virginia with the other Southern slave states to defend the South or
slavery. They did not all act from the same motives or with the same reasoning.
It is not at all clear what proportion of the delegates who changed their minds
and voted for secession did so with an intention of fighting in partnership
with the Southern slave states against the United States rather than fighting
to defend Virginia from an immediate invasion. In the aftermath of the vote
to secede, though, most of the delegates and white Virginians who initially
opposed secession decided that violent conflict had become inevitable, and
their state no longer had any choice but to leave the Union, and that in turn
left Virginia no other viable choice than to join the Southern Confederacy.

Several men who voted against secession on 17 April later changed their
votes, and about half of them remained in the convention to prepare for the
war that they all believed had broken out as a result of arguments about the
future of slavery in the United States. The thousands of men who then rushed
to volunteer to fight in the war in defense of Virginia or perhaps on behalf
of the South certainly did not all enlist in order to defend slavery. Indeed, a
majority of men from Virginia and from the other Southern states who fought
in the Southern armies during the Civil War did not own slaves. They enlisted
for a wide variety of personal and political motives, but the most common was
an intense need to protect their families and their society that was based on
slavery from armed men from distant and different places who had radically
different purposes.[40]

State loyalties and regional loyalties within states were strong in 1861 when
the country began to break apart and controlled how it broke apart. Many
of the convention delegates said when explaining their votes of 17 April or
their willingness to remain in the convention even though they had opposed
secession that they were Virginians, meaning that they identified themselves
more as Virginians in that crisis than as Southerners or even as Americans.
When their state went to war, they went with their state. The president of the
convention, who voted against secession both times and spoke against it on 17
April, told his constituents in May when he voted to ratify the ordinance of

secession, "The destiny of Virginia is my destiny, and with her I shall sink or swim."[41]

The man the convention chose to lead the defense of Virginia, Robert E. Lee, explained in the same way his decision to resign his colonel's commission in the United States Army, to which President Abraham Lincoln had promoted him one month earlier, and to accept command of the army being assembled to defend Virginia. In his private letters and conversations, Lee repeatedly stated that he had no desire ever again to draw his sword save in defense of his native country, by which he meant Virginia, not the United States or the Confederate States. The convention's president used that language, too, when presenting Lee with his commission. Both men and the assembled convention delegates and audience in the gallery knew that the language about drawing the sword was the language with which George Washington had bequeathed his battle swords to his nephews.[42] They also knew that Lee was closely related to the Washington family by marriage. In April 1861 one of the most important decisions that Virginians ever made was to come to the immediate aid of Virginia first. It was not until after the war reached a crescendo that allegiance to the South or to the Confederacy became as widespread as disenchantment with and hostility toward the United States had become.

Advocates of disunion resided in the west just as opponents of disunion resided in the east, but the convention's vote on 17 April and the subsequent war fever swiftly altered political opinions throughout most of Virginia. Between the 17 April convention vote and the 23 May referendum, secession fever swept across Virginia from the eastern coast to the western slope of the Allegheny Mountains. In some counties the vote was unanimous for secession. In the city of Richmond the vote was 3,139 for secession and 3 against, and in Shenandoah County, where 13 men voted for Abraham Lincoln in November 1860, only 5 voted against secession in May 1861.[43] Reliable reports from several counties indicate that in some places secessionists used intimidation or physical violence against men who wanted to vote against secession in the ratification referendum.[44]

The failure of some counties to send reports to Richmond makes a close analysis of the vote impossible, but unofficial reports and anecdotal evidence clearly indicate that only in the Ohio River counties, those bordering southwestern Pennsylvania, and one or two other northern Potomac River counties did a majority of white voting men still oppose disunion.[45] The official totals that the governor certified were 125,950 for secession, 20,373 against. From unofficial information not identified in the official records, he estimated that another 2,934 men, mostly in eastern or mountain counties, voted for secession, and 11,761 men, mostly in western and northwestern counties, voted against secession.[46]

Many of the men who supported secession in the Ohio River counties and cities belonged to families with histories of long residence in the region, who had family, commercial, and political ties to eastern Virginia or personal involvement in politics and government that gave them a strong interest in preserving the political status quo in the state and in their localities, whatever their opinions about slavery or former partisan allegiances.[47] The larger number of men in that area who had family, personal, and commercial ties to other parts of the country were more likely to remain committed to the United States. In Wheeling, which with surrounding Ohio County provided 771 votes for Abraham Lincoln (21.4 percent of the local vote), the Republican editor of the *Daily Intelligencer* (Archibald W. Campbell, a native of Ohio)[48] printed a broadside titled *Traitors in Wheeling* that listed by name all of the men who voted for secession.[49] Opponents of disunion, if so inclined, learned whom they could threaten with intimidation or physical violence much as advocates of disunion had treated opponents on election day.

Just as important differences separated residents of free states from residents of slave states, the existence and extremely uneven distribution of the enslaved population of Virginia created differences among the regions of the state. The sectional crisis within the United States unleashed a sectional crisis within Virginia. The sectional divisions within Virginia, like the sectional divisions in the nation, had been alternately building and subsiding for decades but also building higher each time and subsiding less. The evolving differences were evident long before the secession crisis. Shortly after the end of the legislative debates about slavery in Virginia early in 1832, a member of the House of Delegates from the southern county of Mecklenburg remarked that "the Eastern and Western people were not at all the same people, that they were essentially a different people, that they did not think alike, feel alike, and had no interests in common, that a separation of the State must ensue."[50]

The differences increased during the middle decades of the nineteenth century.[51] Eastern Virginians overwhelmingly adopted a proslavery ideology, and western Virginia men and women often adopted that ideology, too, and the ideas of racial superiority that were part of that ideology. During the Convention of 1861 westerners often went out of their way to emphasize their support for slavery and the general absence of antislavery sentiment in the west, but their immediate investment in the slave economy was not so great as in the east, and the political culture of the west developed differently and had a more egalitarian character than in the east.

The easterners' persistent insistence on special protection for their slave property generated hostility and resentment in the west. As in the other slave states, slavery shaped public policies in many ways that did not always appear at first glance to involve slavery. Tax policy, though, certainly did.[52] The editor of *Cooper's Clarksburg Register,* in western Virginia, complained in 1858 about how often issues relating to slavery took over conversations about public policy and taxation and that laws to protect the interests of men who owned slaves anywhere often injured the interests of men everywhere who did not. Editor William Pope Cooper unleashed an angry torrent against the people of "Eastern Virginia, where it is nigger first, nigger last, and nigger all the time. They don't seem to have a single idea above or beyond a nigger. But in this section of the State, where we take *all* questions of political economy into consideration, we claim that there should be some protection to *white men* as well as *niggers*. We are more sound here on the 'nigger question' than they are. We are for the protection of *all* property recognized by the Constitution, *upon principle,* while they are actuated by *self interest,* which is very apt to lead a person astray in their own favor. We, the people of Western Virginia, desire to protect every man in his property, be it negroes or any thing else, but we have no desire or disposition to give one kind of property especial privileges or advantages over another.... *Our* 'live stock' is as much entitled to exemption from taxation as that of Eastern Virginia, and it is as right that our *cattle* should be subject to a *'separate protection'* as their *slaves,* and we defy the world to prove to the contrary."[53]

Moreover, for more than half a century the General Assembly of Virginia, under the domination for the most part of delegates and senators from east of the Allegheny Mountains, had issued charters of incorporation for banks and other businesses and also to create canal and turnpike companies and railroads. The assembly had appropriated tax money to purchase stock in those firms to stimulate construction and economic development. Few major canals or railroads operated in western Virginia except the Baltimore and Ohio and its spur line from Grafton to Parkersburg, and it served only the northwestern tier of counties and cities and a few other Ohio Valley counties and towns. Westerners complained that they had to pay for easterners' canals and railroads and got little or nothing in return.

The other principal problem that had agitated state politics for more than a decade and that occupied more time during the debates in the Convention of 1861 than any subjects other than disunion and the protection of slavery was the $300 limit that the Constitution of 1851 placed on the taxable value of slaves. That was what set off editor Cooper in 1858. In the spring of 1861, western members of the Virginia convention brought their complaints into the debates about the future of Virginia and the nation. Western delegates spoke repeatedly, at length, and with much passion in favor of taxing slaves on their full market value, called ad valorem taxation. They pointed out that the large population of eastern white men and women who owned few or no slaves were also proportionally overtaxed along with the even larger population of western men and women who owned few or no slaves. Their demands offended the impatient secessionists almost as much as their repeated attempts to find a Union-saving compromise. Eastern delegates tried without success to stifle the movement for ad valorem taxation on the grounds that the convention had not been called for that or any like purpose and because ad valorem taxation would cost owners of slaves more money than they could afford. Because of a brisk demand for laborers in the lower Mississippi Valley, prices of slaves in Virginia had doubled or tripled since 1851. Westerners' pleas for a change in how slave property was taxed no doubt reinforced some easterners' suspicions that loyalty to the United States among the western delegates masked a secret opposition to slavery even though the western Unionists repeatedly denounced abolitionists and antislavery agitation and ideas.

Eastern members of the convention missed an opportunity in 1861, probably through ignorance of the proceedings of the 1860 state convention of the Republican Party of Virginia, to condemn the ad valorem tax proposal as a secret Republican plan to destroy slavery. In May 1860 the party's convention meeting in Wheeling adopted resolutions that conformed in most respects to Republican Party beliefs in the free states, but they contained no explicit condemnation of slavery or even any implicit antislavery language. The longest resolution by far, though, repeated the complaints about the personal property tax on slaves. The Republicans declared that it was unjust that the majority of all white Virginians who owned no slaves paid a proportionally larger tax on their personal property than did the minority who owned slaves. "The Republican Party," the resolution declared in part, "is an organization established for the protection of the personal rights of our citizens, as well as the rights of property, and we hold that one of the chief objects of our laws and Constitution is to prevent the one from encroaching upon the rights of the other. Nevertheless, here in Virginia, as in other parts of the United States, we have suffered under the steady, yearly increasing encroachments of the Slave capital upon the personal rights of the laboring white man. The non-Slaveholding farmers, mechanics, and workingmen of Western Virginia are oppressed and weighed down with taxations for the benefit of Eastern Virginia Slave capitalists, merely because they have the political power and choose to exercise its tyrannies without mercy."[54]

The western delegates in the Convention of 1861 ultimately prevailed on taxation of slave property. Secessionist George Wythe Randolph, of Richmond, announced on the day after the convention voted for secession, "For one, I am prepared to say that, after what has been done in this house by Western members" who voted for secession, "I am prepared to face the consequences and give them a satisfactory adjustment of that question."[55] A week later one of the western Unionists, George W. Berlin, of Upshur County, asked for leave to change his vote, to have his vote recorded in favor of the ordinance of secession. To his short speech he added, "I had hoped that the Convention would see the importance of removing this source of difficulty, and doing that which would lead to conciliation and harmony among our people at this time. If they would pass this tax ordinance we could go home to our constituents and say we had done our duty, and having been defeated in our efforts at peace by the machinations of the powers at Washington, we changed our policy and went in for secession. Our Eastern brethren found it their duty to pursue this line of policy, and we aided them in it. But they have done you justice by adopting the *ad valorem* principle of taxation in reference to the negro property and we have no cause now for any misunderstanding. They would hail joyfully this change, and unite heartily with the East."[56]

A few days later the convention voted to submit to the voters on the third Thursday in May, on the day that the voters were to decide whether to ratify the ordinance of secession, an amendment to the state constitution that all personal property, including slaves, be taxed according to its market value.[57] It was the first constitutional amendment ever submitted to Virginia voters for ratification. The Constitution of 1851 contained no provision for amendment, but the delegates in April 1861 convinced themselves that as the state's constituent assembly, they were competent to submit an amendment for ratification or rejection.

The voters ratified the amendment by a similar margin to that by which they confirmed secession. The official returns from the 126 of the 154 counties and cities that reported yielded a total of 111,854 votes for the amendment and 16,745 votes against,[58] but the distribution of the votes on secession and on taxation were not the same. Voting men in the Ohio Valley counties and in the counties bordering Pennsylvania overwhelmingly opposed secession and overwhelmingly ratified the amendment. Voting men everywhere else overwhelmingly ratified secession and in most places also ratified the amendment, but in many of the eastern counties the voters cast an appreciable number of votes against the amendment. Perhaps the western delegates' appeal to the men in the east who owned no slaves was successful with enough voters that the amendment passed in most eastern jurisdictions. Perhaps the reasoning of George Wythe Randolph and George W. Berlin was persuasive, but in the areas of Virginia where owners of slaves were most numerous, the voters cast thousands of votes against the proposed constitutional amendment that would raise their taxes to appease men who owned few or no slaves.

The sectional crisis within Virginia grew worse during the weeks and months of the convention debates that brought out and reinforced opposing perspectives and objectives. Western resentment against eastern interests intensified, perhaps even more than eastern suspicion of western motives. Within two or three days after the 17 April vote on secession, many of the delegates from the west fled Richmond, fearing for their personal safety, and returned home. The subsequent reluctant decision of some eastern delegates to agree to a revision of the method of taxing slaves did not mollify the angriest westerners. John Snyder Carlile, of Harrison County, one of the most outspoken proslavery opponents of secession in the convention, organized the second Virginia convention of the year. Men loyal to the United States met for the first time in Wheeling in mid-May, two weeks after the convention in Richmond adjourned.

Some of the actions of the Richmond convention in the immediate aftermath of the vote on secession and some of the actions of the first two sessions of the Wheeling convention were remarkably similar and revolutionary.

In the convention in Richmond during the evening session after the vote for secession, Henry A. Wise engaged in a sharp debate with John Brown Baldwin, who stated that because the ordinance of secession could not legally take effect unless ratified in the required referendum on 23 May 1861, the convention therefore should wait until the ultimate authority, the voters, ratified secession before taking any additional steps, such as raising an army or affiliating Virginia with the Southern Confederacy. Wise sharply attacked Baldwin and intimidated or convinced the other doubters by pointing out how dangerous the situation was late in April. By rescinding the state's ratification of the Constitution of the United States, he argued, the convention had become the sole agent of the people of Virginia in an emergency that required immediate action.

Wise pointed out that the convention's vote set in motion a train of events that made secession a fact as of 17 April. "What are we to do in the meantime?" he demanded. "Are we to stand still—we, the conservators of the people—and do nothing between now and May? I put the question, and will answer. I take it on either horn of this dilemma. If the invaders come down upon us, you are certain to have no election. If the invading army is to cross the line, West, North, and East, by sea and by land, where and how is the election to be held? Invasion can and will suspend the constitutional power, in the elective power of the State from doing anything.

"Take the other horn of the dilemma. Let the people say, we have seceded; our Convention has advised us to secede. In order to defend ourselves, in case we elect to secede, we will take the arms necessary to defend ourselves—we will take the forts that now threaten our lives and liberties; we will take the Navy-yard, that holds all the ship timber, the best in the United States." Wise denounced as "a mere stickling upon a point between tweedledum and tweedledee" the continued debate about the legality of the convention's acting to defend Virginia from military action that the president of the United States was certain to take.[59]

Without any serious consideration of calling the state's legislature back into session, the delegates began preparing the state for war. They appointed field officers for the state's new army and retroactively approved Wise's personal directives to the officers who had seized the arsenal at Harpers Ferry and the navy yard at Norfolk. For the time being the delegates in Richmond acted as if the state had been thrown back into a state of nature and they were the only representatives of the white male people. The convention effectively became the government of Virginia, and the governor acted as its obedient executive officer.

In Wheeling several score of western men and men from two or three Potomac River counties met in the second Virginia Convention of 1861. A great many men from Wheeling and Ohio County showed up, and from the other counties smaller delegations attended, most of them selected in public mass meetings that served as their authorization to represent their neighbors. They concluded that the actions of the convention in Richmond had in effect thrown them back into a state of nature, too, and required them to act with similar boldness for all of the loyal men of Virginia, as if the government of Virginia had been dissolved and they were the only legitimate representatives of the loyal white male people. Carlile announced on the first day of the convention that the men in Wheeling "were accredited representatives of the loyal people of Virginia . . . to put our feet upon the usurpations of power that have been exercised in the last two weeks" and to act on behalf of the whole people of Virginia.[60]

Carlile drafted and a committee of which he was a member circulated two long public addresses. The first, published on 21 May, contained an urgent plea that the men in northwestern Virginia vote against secession in the referendum to be conducted two days later. The committee asked, "Why should the people of North Western Virginia allow themselves to be dragged into the rebellion inaugurated by ambitious and heartless men, who have banded themselves together to destroy a government formed for you by your patriot fathers, and which has secured to you all the liberties consistent with the nature of man, and has, for near three-fourths of a century, sheltered you in sunshine and in storm, made you the admiration of the civilized world, and conferred upon you a title more honored, respected and revered, than that of King or Potentate—the title of an American citizen. Will you passively surrender it, and submit to be used by the conspirators engaged in this effort to enslave you, as their instruments by which your enslavement is to be effected? . . . We will maintain, protect and defend that Constitution and the Union with all our strength, and with all our powers, ever remembering"—and here the committee of which Carlile was the draftsman quoted Thomas Jefferson's adopted personal motto—"that 'Resistance to tyrants is obedience to God.'"[61]

The committee's second address, dated 22 May when ratification of secession in the following day's referendum was easily predictable, appeared on 27 May 1861. Carlile and the other committee members laid out the next steps that they had to take. "Whilst we have a Constitution and code of laws for our State government, and local officers to administer them," they explained, "the Executive and his immediate subordinates have submitted themselves to the government of the Confederate States. They have thrown off their allegiance to the United States, and are now diligently and laboriously preparing themselves to wage war against the government of the Union . . . but as true and loyal citizens of Virginia, we can and must declare, that in our calm and deliberate judgment, it will be the duty of the people of North Western Virginia, to provide, in the lawful and constitutional mode, for the exercise of those Executive and Legislative functions of our State government, which have been entrusted to those who are faithless and disloyal, and thus save ourselves from that anarchy which so imminently threatens us."[62]

The men who were elected to and in June attended the second convention in Wheeling took action as revolutionary as the action that the convention in Richmond took in April. Carlile once again took the lead. "Let us assemble a Legislature here, of our own," he proposed, "sworn to support, not the Southern Confederacy Constitution, but that which Washington and Madison formed, the constitution of our fathers, under which we have grown and prospered, as never people grew and prospered before. . . . Let us organize a Legislature, swearing allegiance to that government, and let that Legislature be recognized by the United States Government, as *the* Legislature of Virginia."[63] The men in Wheeling re-created the government of the state to restore Virginia to its rightful place as one of the United States. They acted for all of the loyal people of Virginia and declared vacant all Virginia state offices that were then occupied by disloyal men who acted in concert with the Richmond convention. The delegates then elected and installed a new governor, lieutenant governor, and attorney general for Virginia, much as the Convention of 1776 had done when it elected Patrick Henry the state's first governor.

On 20 June 1861 Francis H. Pierpont took office as governor of Virginia under the convention's authority and delivered an inaugural address, the first inaugural address that any governor of Virginia ever delivered.[64] "A new doctrine has been introduced by those who are at the head of the revolution in our Southern States," Pierpont declared, "that the people are *not* the source of all power. Those promulgating this doctrine have tried to divide the people into two classes: one they call the laboring class, the other the capital class. They have for several years been industriously propagating the idea that the capital of the country ought to represent the legislation of the country, and guide it and direct it; maintaining that it is dangerous for the labor of the country to enter into the legislation of the country. This, gentlemen, is the principle that has characterized the revolution that has been inaugurated in the South; they maintaining that those who are to have the privilege of voting ought to be of the educated class, and that the legislation ought not be represented by the laboring class."

Pierpont then declared, "We representing the loyal citizens of Virginia, have been bound to assume the position we have assumed to-day, for the protection of ourselves, our wives, our children, and our property. We, I repeat, have been *driven* to assume this position; and now we are but recurring to the great fundamental principle of our fathers, that to the loyal people of a State belongs the law-making power of that State. The loyal people are entitled to the government and governmental authority of the State. And, fellow-citizens, it is the assumption of this authority upon which we are now about to enter."[65]

On the Fourth of July, the president of the United States informed Congress that he recognized the new government in Wheeling as the legitimate government of Virginia. The disloyal people of Virginia, he announced, had "allowed this great insurrection to make its nest within her borders; and this Government has no choice left but to deal with it where it finds it. And it has the less regret, as the loyal citizens have in due form claimed its protection. These loyal citizens this Government is bound to recognize and protect as being Virginia."[66]

Acting in strict conformity with the Virginia Constitution of 1851, Pierpont's government and the General Assembly that met in Wheeling functioned in the Ohio Valley and some of the mountain counties of western and northwestern Virginia and also from time to time, as contending armies moved back and forth across the landscape of eastern Virginia, in some of the counties and cities in the Potomac River valley, on the Eastern Shore, and in the vicinity of Norfolk and Portsmouth. Voters in those areas elected a General Assembly that met under the authority of the Virginia Constitution of 1851 and on the dates that the constitution specified. The General Assembly of Virginia that met in Wheeling elected two senators who represented the loyal state of Virginia in the United States Senate from the summer of 1861 until the summer of 1863, and voters in two congressional districts elected congressmen who represented loyal Virginians in the United States House of Representatives.

As the men in Wheeling were restoring their part of Virginia to the Union, the convention in Richmond reassembled in June and again in November to prosecute the war. The General Assembly of Virginia that met in Richmond resumed its regular meetings on 2 December 1861, on the same day that the General Assembly of Virginia that met in Wheeling also resumed its regular meetings. The governor and General Assembly in Richmond refused to acknowledge the existence of the governor and assembly of the other Virginia and readily admitted members from western counties that were also represented in the other government of Virginia. Throughout the Civil War the president and Congress of the Confederacy treated the government in Richmond as the legitimate government of Virginia.

Virginia had two state governments between June 1861 and April 1865, one with its capital in Richmond that governed the state that was part of the Confederate States of America and the other with its capital at Wheeling until

June 1863 (when the new state of West Virginia came into being) and after that in Alexandria that governed the state that was part of the United States of America. Yet the residents of each Virginia firmly believed that they, and not the residents of the other Virginia, were the patriotic Virginians who were the true heirs of the American Revolution. In taking their own revolutionary actions—in rescinding Virginia's ratification of the Constitution of the United States and ratifying the Constitution of the Confederate States, for one, and, for the other, in displacing and replacing all of the officers of the state government and remaining loyal to the United States—the people of the two Virginias explained their actions in very similar terms.

Men from both Virginias who marched off to war and the women of both Virginias who sent them into battle defended their actions as consistent with the spirit of their Revolutionary ancestors. The Republican editor of the Wheeling *Daily Intelligencer* printed an editorial to that effect on 4 July 1861. "We hope this day will be celebrated with an enthusiasm about which there will be no mistake," he wrote, "with a spirit which will indicate that our people still remember and appreciate the noble stand taken by our fathers in '76, the glorious freedom thereafter achieved, and the blessings and liberty which we have since enjoyed under the splendid Government then founded, and which is now sought to be distroyed by traitors in arms. Let every man devote the day to his country, that the fires of patriotism may continue to burn even more brightly than ever."[67]

The editor of the *Daily Richmond Enquirer* published a longer editorial on the same theme that same day. He stated that he was "happy to see so many proofs" that "the 4th of July will be generally observed throughout the Southern Confederacy. . . . The deed which this day we celebrate, is a glorious and inspiring endorsement of the present attitude of the Confederate States. We, too, have been wronged and insulted, and we too have exhausted the cup of patience and drawn the sword of self-defence. We too have taken our separate and equal station among the nations of the earth. . . . 'Tis meet that the South, which has been ever faithful to free government, should not forget Liberty's first anniversary while founding a second. Let her make both equally honorable. The second but proves her reverence for the first."[68]

The men who restored loyal government in northwestern Virginia assumed the leadership of the movement for separating their loyal Virginia from the disloyal Virginia. Pierpont even ordered that Daniel Webster's pledge "Liberty and Union" be added to the state seal.[69] A convention that met in Wheeling in the autumn of 1861 wrote a new state constitution that, not without a great deal of contention among the delegates, was a kind of mirror image of the earlier Virginia constitutions about which those westerners and their predecessors had often complained.

What in June 1863 became the first Constitution of West Virginia jettisoned all pretense of state's rights and specifically recognized the supremacy of the Constitution and laws of the United States over the constitutions or laws of any or all of the states. It included a provision to allow for amendments as times changed, which none of the previous Virginia constitutions had permitted. It required that voting be by secret ballot rather than by public voice vote. It provided that seats in the legislature be reapportioned following each federal census in order that legislators as nearly as possible represented their constituents and not regions or other interests. It required that all taxes be assessed on the market value of land and items of personal property. It forbade the state from contracting a permanent debt of the kind that old Virginia had created when constructing internal improvements in eastern Virginia for which all Virginians had paid. It abolished the old county court system that had vested legislative, executive, and judicial powers in one body of men and created a new and more democratic local government structure resembling the New England township, and it severely restricted the tenures and political influence of county sheriffs. It created a free public school system, the first in any state south of the Mason-Dixon Line. The new constitution, which Congress eventually required to be amended to abolish slavery, was much more democratic than any previous Virginia constitution and contained numerous reforms that could never have been adopted in old Virginia. The differences that had evolved between eastern and western Virginians were clearly evident in the changes to their government that the Virginia men who resided in the Ohio Valley made in 1861 when writing the first constitution for themselves, for a state that they nevertheless named West Virginia, not willing even in the naming of the new state to lose all the better resonances and connections with old Virginia.[70]

The admission of West Virginia as one of the United States in June 1863 required that the government of Virginia that had its capital in Wheeling move out of the new state and back into the old. Before moving, it gave its consent as the Constitution of the United States required for the formation of the new state out of an existing state.[71] The new capital of the loyal government of Virginia was Alexandria, across the Potomac River from Washington, D.C. There, the governor and the General Assembly quickly realized that changing circumstances required them, also, to write a new state constitution. So many counties that were part of Virginia when the Constitution of 1851 was adopted were no longer a part of Virginia that the districts defined in the constitution for legislative and judicial elections were obsolete, and the constitution could not be amended to realign them. Moreover, Pierpont soon concluded that his Virginia could not function as a slave state. The Emancipation Proclamation did not apply within his Virginia, meaning that he and the United States Army were under conflicting legal responsibilities concerning the thousands of men and women who escaped from slavery and were within their jurisdictions. Recognizing that the changing nature of the war and the problem of slavery required him and the residents of the Virginia he governed to make radical changes, Pierpont recommended that the General Assembly summon a constitutional convention and that the convention abolish slavery in Virginia.

From 13 February through 11 April 1864, seventeen delegates, some of whom were owners of slaves, wrote a new constitution for Virginia. They voted with only one nay on 10 March for a provision declaring, "Slavery and involuntary servitude (except for crime) is hereby abolished and prohibited in the State forever."[72] Church bells rang throughout the city, and men fired a hundred guns in celebration, events that newspapers throughout the United States reported and often saluted. The new constitution guaranteed the vote to all white men age twenty-one or older who had lived in the state for one year (reduced from three years in the Constitution of 1851) but disfranchised all men who had taken part in the army of "the so-called confederate government, or under any rebellious State government." The new Constitution of Virginia, unlike the new Constitution of West Virginia, included no provision for amending it, but it required that voting be by ballot rather than by voice vote.[73] Except in the abolition of slavery, the new Virginia Constitution of 1864 was much less a reformation of the Constitution of 1851 than the West Virginia Constitution of 1863, but the abolition of slavery in Virginia, even in part of Virginia, was truly revolutionary.

The convention that had first met in Richmond in February 1861 also decided on the day of its adjournment, 1 May 1861, to revise the constitution of the state that was soon to become one of the Confederate States of America.[74] It was obvious that references to the United States of America needed to be changed to the Confederate States of America, but Alexander Hugh Holmes Stuart, of Augusta County, proposed the appointment of a committee to review the entire constitution and recommend other changes.[75] A distinguished former Whig congressman and cabinet officer and until the last minute on 17 April a committed opponent of secession, he had other revisions in mind, too. Stuart chaired the committee that included three other Whigs and three Douglas Democrats, all originally opponents of secession and representing different geographical regions of the state.[76]

The committee introduced a plan of constitutional revision at the second session (also known as the first adjourned session) of the convention on 19 June, but the delegates did not begin debate on the proposal until 16 November, early in the third (or second adjourned) session.[77] Introducing the draft revisions and sounding like James Madison and in his first sentence like the 1860 Republican Party state convention, Stuart reported from the committee, "Governments are instituted for the protection of the rights of persons and property; and any system must be radically defective, which does not give ample security to both." He then laid the groundwork for the changes that his committee proposed. "The great interests of every community may be classed under the heads of labor and capital," he proclaimed, "and it is essential to the well-being of society, that the proper equilibrium should be established between these important elements." Stuart denounced the excessive democracy in the states that remained in the United States and identified three capital defects in its political culture that endangered free men's rights to own and control their own property and therefore preserve their own liberty: "the system of free schools, by which the children of the poor are educated at the expense of the rich"; the abolitionists' "war on property, under the mask of simulated philanthropy"; and "universal suffrage and the election of all officers by the direct vote of the people."

By contrast, Stuart continued on behalf of the committee, which the resignation from the convention of one western Whig reduced to six members, the principles underlying the proposals that his committee submitted were better suited to the "more conservative and rational principles" that "still prevail" in the Confederate States of America. "This is due," he explained, "mainly, to the institution of slavery, which constitutes a partial restriction on the right of suffrage." Probably not even breaking a smile at that heroic understatement, Stuart expressed exactly the opposite opinions from those that Pierpont had advanced in June about the roles of labor and capital in the government. For his committee Stuart condemned the provisions of the Virginia Constitution of 1851 that allowed almost universal white manhood suffrage as "an unfortunate change" that "introduced a large class of irresponsible voters who have but little interest in the Commonwealth, and who do not, in any degree participate in the burthens of taxation, which may be imposed by representatives of their selection. Every consideration of principle and expediency requires that this error should now be corrected." Because many of the recently enfranchised white men paid few or no taxes, Stuart argued, it would not violate the Revolutionary principle of no taxation without representation to deny them the vote. "The tendency of these provisions," Stuart concluded, "is, to the most hateful of all despotisms—the despotism of an unrestrained numerical majority."

"In the judgment of your committee," Stuart said later when changing subjects, "it was a wide departure from the true principles of republican government, to require that ministerial offices, such as sheriffs, clerks, attornies for the Commonwealth, commissioners of revenue, constables, &c., should be elected by the direct vote of the people." The committee's proposal gave the governor power to appoint the state's judges subject to the advice and consent of the state's senate and gave the state's judges the power to appoint necessary local officials, including county sheriffs. A minority (one or two members) of the committee even recommended that the provisions in the Constitutions of

1776 and 1830 be restored and that voters not be allowed to elect justices of the peace and that the General Assembly should once again elect the governor.[78]

The constitutional revision that emerged from the convention in December 1861 was a more modest revision of the Constitution of 1851 than the committee's majority recommended. The convention's proposal retained viva voce voting for all elections. It offered voters an immediate choice that under the Constitution of 1851 they would not have been able to make until 1865, whether to base legislative representation on the number of voters in each district or on a mixed basis of population and payment of taxes, which would preserve an extra measure of legislative power to protect the interests of owners of large numbers of slaves. The proposed revised constitution included the equality of taxation clause that the convention submitted to the May 1861 referendum and that had been ratified then, and it restored to the General Assembly the appointment of all trial judges and appellate court judges and vested in the courts the appointment of sheriffs, clerks, constables, and prosecuting attorneys.[79]

On 5 December the convention submitted the revised constitution to a ratification referendum scheduled for 13 March 1862. The referendum allowed voters to vote separately on whether to restrict the suffrage to adult white men who paid taxes.[80] The public and the press paid little attention to the constitutional revision during the winter, and marching and fighting armies made it difficult for men in many parts of the state to vote in March.[81] On 2 May 1862 the governor announced that 13,233 men had voted for the revised constitution and 13,911 against it and that 16,518 men had voted for and 9,201 men against the proposed restriction of the suffrage.[82]

That little more than 27,000 men voted in the wartime 1862 referendum makes it difficult to ascertain the larger public's opinions (that is, the opinions of the adult white males) on whether it was wise to restrict the number of public officers that the voters could elect, but that almost two-thirds of the men who voted favored restricting the vote to adult taxpaying white men suggests that arguments such as those that Stuart made against unchecked democracy resonated with a substantial portion of the voting population. In any event, the Constitution of 1851 with the amendment added in May 1861 remained in full effect until April 1865 in the Virginia that was part of the Confederate States of America.

The opponents of secession in the first Virginia Convention of 1861 wanted to keep Virginia in the Union and to preserve old Virginia with as little change as possible. They had not prevailed with arguments and votes, but events in South Carolina and in Washington that were beyond their control tipped the course of human events in the opposite direction. The extraordinary military leaders who waged the war for them prolonged the bloody contest for four years during which, even if the political leaders of old Virginia and of the Confederacy did not change their minds or purposes, the political leaders of the United States did. The most important was Abraham Lincoln's decision to wage war against slavery in order to preserve representative government and the free-labor economy. Perceiving that the existence of slavery had created the national divisions that erupted into war and perceiving also that abolishing slavery could energize the military forces of the United States and weaken those of the Confederacy, he issued an emancipation proclamation on 1 January 1863.

For the men who fought for the United States, the meaning and purpose of the war began to change. The war became not merely a war to restore and preserve republican government, free labor, and the United States but a war to end slavery in order to restore and preserve republican government and free labor. Lincoln's proclamation also intensified Confederate determination to win independence from the old Union that by then openly and directly threatened the existence of slavery and the society on which it was based in every Confederate state. The changing nature of the war led some Southern people and some people in old Virginia to think more closely, as Alexander H. H. Stuart had done, about the critical differences between the society and culture in which they lived and the society and culture in which their political and military adversaries lived.

One of those people was Frank Heath Alfriend, a young journalist who was the son of a prominent Richmond insurance executive. He lucked into the editorship of the *Southern Literary Messenger* at the end of December 1863 when a friend purchased the once-prestigious monthly magazine. For the first six months of 1864, Alfriend was the last editor of the journal that Edgar Allan Poe had once edited.[83] In January and May 1863 before he became its editor, the bold and self-confident young man published two articles in the magazine. Their titles were "The Great Danger of the Confederacy" and "A Southern Republic and a Northern Democracy."

In "The Great Danger" Alfriend declared that old Virginia and the Confederacy were fighting to preserve good government by men who knew how to govern and to prevent the spread into Virginia and the Confederacy of dangerous ideas about equality and democracy, ideas that threatened what he called the "benign institution of slavery which is now the pride and glory of the South." He heaped scorn on the North's "spirit of *levelling* agrarianism, which succeeded in degrading everything beneath the heel of an ignorant and vicious democracy, which sought to remove every barrier of distinction between virtue and vice, between enlightenment and ignorance, which sought to *equalize* all by entitling all alike to the fullest enjoyment of the rights of citizenship."[84] Alfriend believed that the white people of the Confederacy and the white residents of the Confederate state of Virginia had to be saved from a politics of democracy and equality.

In "A Southern Republic and a Northern Democracy" Alfriend praised the aristocratic origins of Virginia's colonial statesmen and the republican, not democratic, political structure that they erected. He contrasted the North and the South in order to explain and vindicate the South. Listen to him on Northern democracy: "The North carrying out to its legitimate conclusion, the pernicious doctrine of the Declaration of Independence, that 'all men are born free and equal'"—his quotation was incorrect and more nearly resembled George Mason's first draft for the Virginia Declaration of Rights than Thomas Jefferson's Declaration of Independence—"recognizing no distinction whatever of race, intellect, or character, witnesses in its fullest development, that never-ending conflict of classes, between the rich and the poor, those who have accumulated property, and the breadless pauper, the 'codfish' element, and the idle, starving 'sans culottes.' And this perpetual strife between the conservative elements, property and intelligence, and the revolutionary materials, ignorance and indigence, will continue to agitate Northern society, until the bloody drama of the Parisian massacres shall be re-enacted in the streets of their cities, and a whirlwind of passion and strife shall sweep over their land, with such scenes of bloodshed and desolation, as have never been rivalled, save in the annals of revolutionary France." He wrote that very shortly before an anticonscription riot in New York that he could have pointed to in order to demonstrate the truth of what he wrote.

"The South, on the other hand," Alfriend began his next paragraph, "by a fortunate dispensation of Providence" did not have "that turbulent factious element, known at the North as the 'working class.'" Instead, the Southern states possessed enslaved laborers, "a class of population noted for its want of enterprise, intellect, or any quality which could make it a disturbing element of society, and peculiarly adapted to a condition of absolute subordination, by a characteristic docility, and inability to provide for its own wants when beyond the control of the superior race." That sounded more like Jefferson's *Notes on the State of Virginia* than his first quotation sounded like Jefferson's Declaration of Independence, or more, in fact, like Abel P. Upshur's 1839 essay in the *Southern Literary Messenger* "On Domestic Slavery."[85]

The brassy and opinionated young writer characterized Lincoln's election as "a complete triumph of Democracy. Elected by the foreigners and the working classes, he came into power as an avowed champion of the interests of the poor and labouring classes, which he declared to be in conflict with those of the slave-holding aristocrats of the South. Democracy triumphed, and despotism has followed." In the South, by contrast, Alfriend boasted that civilization and order flourished by "the universal recognition by our people of slavery as the foundation of all their hopes of national prosperity." The word "our" in that sentence certainly referred to the educated property-owning white people, the class to which Alfriend belonged and to and for whom he wrote, the only class that in his social and political economies mattered or was entitled to any benefits.[86] And that placed Alfriend back in the company of James Madison, who during and after the American Revolution believed that because Virginia's economy and society were based on slavery, the state had and required an aristocratic rather than a democratic government.

Frank Heath Alfriend was a politically inexperienced writer of no great influence, but he was an intelligent young man who during his lifetime kept well informed about public events and changing political fashions. In his two *Southern Literary Messenger* articles in the middle of the Civil War, he captured much of the essence of the political outlook and enunciated the bases of the political culture that had flourished in Virginia for generations before the two secession crises of 1861. That outlook animated public life for the largest and most influential portion of the white men and women who lived during the Civil War in the Confederate state of Virginia that had its capital in Richmond.

9

CAUSES
LOST

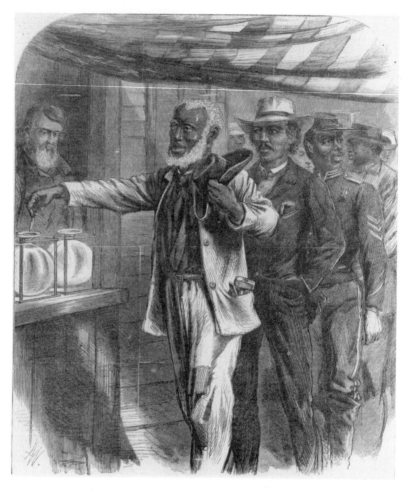

The First Vote *(courtesy of the Library of Virginia)* appeared on the cover of Harper's Weekly *for 16 November 1867, three and a half weeks after the 22 October election for members of a constitutional convention in Virginia. Under orders from Congress and the United States Army, black Virginians voted for the first time that day. The scene set the stage for twenty-five years of contentious politics. Images such as this inspired black Virginians and some white Virginians who sought ways to cooperate in the new political economy of free labor, but they frightened men who resisted changes that the federal government imposed on them. Black men voting became the symbolic as well as the visible reality that drove politics in Virginia for the remainder of the nineteenth century.*

After the confederate armies surrendered in the spring of 1865, a farmer near Winchester plowed up the bones or rotting remains of two Confederate soldiers. Another farmer working nearby did the same thing. What did those farmers then do? They went into town to speak to Mary Dunbar Williams, who four years earlier had organized the ladies of Winchester to provide nursing care for the Confederate men who had been wounded during the first of the many engagements in or near that town. Williams and her sister-in-law and companion in that good work, Eleanor Frances Williams Boyd, organized the ladies of Winchester again. By October of the following year, even though Boyd's husband died during the meantime, they arranged for the bodies of nearly twenty-five hundred Confederate soldiers to be recovered from shallow graves and local battlefields and reinterred with dignity and respect in a new cemetery in Winchester. It was called the Stonewall Cemetery, named not for Stonewall Jackson but for a real stone wall. At the dedication ceremony on 25 October 1866, former Virginia governor and Confederate brigadier Henry A. Wise spoke for two hours about the past and the future and in praise of the men who died in the war that they had lost but for a cause that he denied was, in fact, lost. "If our cause is lost," he declaimed significantly, "it was false; if true its not lost."[1]

Those women and many thousands like them elsewhere in Virginia and in the states that had been part of the Confederacy formed memorial associations to provide honorable burials for fallen soldiers. They also created Confederate Memorial Day, an annual spring occasion for families and survivors to decorate the graves of their war dead and remember their loss and the loss of the cause for which they died. Those women, who were all decorously identified in public by the names of their husbands—such as Mrs. Philip Williams and Mrs. Rev. Andrew H. H. Boyd—created the culture of the Lost Cause that provided the foundation for the civic and political cultures for a large majority of Virginia's and the South's white people for decades.

Those were some of the women of the Confederacy to whom Jefferson Davis in 1881 dedicated his *Rise and Fall of the Confederate Government.* He dedicated it to the women who had cared for wounded soldiers and looked after families and farms when men were off fighting, and he also dedicated it to the women "whose annual tribute expresses their enduring grief, love, and reverence for our sacred dead," women "whose patriotism will teach their children to emulate the deeds of our revolutionary sires."[2] Davis included in his dedicatory sweep more than those thousands of Southern white women who voluntarily cooked, sewed, and nursed for the Confederate army during the four years of war; who ran the farms, plantations, and small businesses when the men went off to fight and after some of them did not come back; who labored for wages and sometimes died in munitions factories; and who raised money for uniforms and to support widows and orphans; more than the few notable women who engaged in espionage or disguised themselves as men and fought on the battlefields; more than those socially prominent Virginia women who raised money to construct a gunboat, the *Lady Davis,* for the Confederate navy. In the concluding phrases of his dedication, Davis slipped into the present tense and looked to the future. He included the women who were memorializing the dead and who were teaching the young people of the next generation about the Confederacy and the war long after the war was lost and there was no longer a Confederacy.

Those were the women *of* the Confederacy to whom Davis dedicated his book, not merely to the women who resided in the Confederacy and who supported it during the war, and certainly not to the white and American Indian women in Virginia who remained loyal to the United States or who quietly sat out the war at home; and not to the millions of African American women who resided in the Confederacy, most of whom were enslaved when the war began and who gained their freedom by its outcome, by the failure and collapse of the Confederacy. None of them was a woman of the Confederacy. Davis left them out of his Confederacy; but by including the women of the Confederacy who after the war tended the graves and memorialized the service of the men who had died in its defense, Davis indicated that he, like Wise, believed that the cause was not lost.

But what was that cause? The phrase "lost cause" emerged into common parlance soon after the end of the Civil War, or, as it was variously called, depending on the political viewpoint of the writers and speakers who referred to it, the Great Rebellion, the War between the States, the War to Save the Union, the War to End Slavery, or the War of Northern Aggression. The men and women who wrote and spoke about the lost cause tried to explain military defeat to themselves and to others and to reconcile themselves to that defeat. They, too, refused to believe that thousands of their brothers, sons, fathers, husbands, cousins, and sweethearts had died in defense of a bad cause. Much as for the Northern opponents of slavery who believed that the spirit of John Brown's martyred body had gone marching off to war along with the army of the United States, the cause for which the Confederate army had fought went marching on after the end of the war.

The phrase "lost cause" quickly gained popularity in the former Confederacy, aided no doubt by the publication in New York in 1867 of Edward A. Pollard's nearly eight-hundred-page pro-Confederate book, *The Lost Cause: A New Southern History of the War of the Confederates; Comprising a Full and*

*Authentic Account of the Rise and Progress of the Late Southern Confederacy—
The Campaigns, Battles, Incidents, and Adventures of the Most Gigantic Struggle of the World's History, Drawn from Official Sources, and Approved by the
Most Distinguished Confederate Leaders.*[3] Pollard had been a fierce secessionist
who in 1861 began to write for the *Richmond Examiner* and along with John
Moncure Daniel, the paper's owner and editor, became a relentless critic of
Jefferson Davis and the conduct of his administration during the war. Pollard's book is full of accusations that Davis was responsible for the military
defeat of the Confederacy. The still-partisan journalist extolled the genius
of the South's military leaders and condemned the amoral incompetence of
the North's political and military leaders, leaving an inept Southern political
leader, Jefferson Davis, to take responsibility for the loss of the war.

Betrayal became a common way of explaining the defeat. Antebellum
Southern civilization, as Pollard and many other writers from the South explained the events of the 1860s, was so obviously superior to Northern culture and the South's military leaders were so much more talented than the
North's that even the North's larger population and greater industrial capacity
could not have permitted it to triumph over the South unless the South had
been betrayed or God had willed that the old South be destroyed. Unwilling
to admit that the South and God were not on the same side, Pollard wrote
that Davis was an inept meddler in military matters of which he knew too
little and consequently made it impossible for Confederate generals to win
the war. Other writers found other men or events to blame: Robert E. Lee's
plans for the 1862 Maryland campaign being carelessly dropped on the road
with a packet of cigars and falling into Northern hands; Stonewall Jackson's
being accidentally killed; General Longstreet's arriving too late on the scene at
Gettysburg. Had any of thousands of other events been managed differently
or better, the outcome of the war would naturally have been different. Finding
scapegoats or plausible excuses allowed men and women to understand the
military defeat of the Confederacy in a way that did not imply that their men
had died in vain or threaten their belief in the righteousness of the cause.

The Confederacy's loss was otherwise almost impossible to believe and
nearly impossible to explain. That event utterly undermined every principle on which their society and belief systems had been based before April
1865. The military defeat and the abolition of slavery that it brought with
it required new thinking as well as new behaviors to allow the people of the
South, both white and black, to find new ways to live. It toppled their old
forms of government, which the triumphant national government replaced,
and it brought about revisions in all of the ways in which white people and
black people interacted with each other, in the relations between people who
owned property and people who did not, and between people who worked
for themselves and people who worked for others. During the years after the

war, the people of Virginia and elsewhere in the South experimented with life in a completely new world.

The new Southern world was unimaginably new. The outcome of the war had ended slavery but left the freed people in Virginia, a circumstance that white Virginians from Thomas Jefferson's day on had always pronounced intolerable. The first full session of the General Assembly that met after the end of the war adopted An Act Providing for the Punishment of Vagrants to manage "a great increase of idle and disorderly persons in some parts of this commonwealth," meaning the freed people, the only population group significantly displaced as a consequence of the war and the only large group who if they left their former owners would be without employment. The law authorized local law enforcement officers to take into custody people who were without work, who went begging door to door, or who "refuse to work for the usual and common wages given to other laborers in the like work in the place where they then are." The law authorized local governments to hire out vagrants, force them to work wearing a ball and chain, jail them, or expel them from the jurisdiction, all with no opportunity for legally challenging the judgments or actions of the law-enforcement officers.[4] What was called the Vagrancy Act of 1866 so severely restricted the personal behavior of black Virginians that a United States Army general pronounced it merely slavery by a different name.[5] It probably never occurred to the white men of that legislature that they should not continue to regulate and restrain the black people in their midst as they had always done, especially considering how much more dangerous their predecessors had sometimes regarded uncontrolled free black people than enslaved and therefore properly controlled black people.

White Southerners had a hard time adjusting their thinking and their actions. Countless anecdotes from the time illustrate the difficulties of adaptation and expose their core beliefs. When Joseph Bryan, who became one of Virginia's wealthiest and most influential industrialists and financiers, began to practice law during those years, he defended a black man in a criminal trial and, after making what he regarded as a very effective speech to the jury, won an acquittal. How Bryan's son told and the family liked to remember and re-tell the story suggests that for several generations they shared the attitudes of the elderly foreman of the jury who told Bryan later in the day, "You done mighty well today, Joe. . . . But don't think you can do it every time, because you can't. When we got back in the jury room I says to the jury, says I: 'Gentlemen,' I says, 'here's old John R. Bryan, ruined by the war, and here's his son, a poor young man, trying to make a living. What's one Nigger more or less to us' Says I: 'Let the d——d black rascal off,' says I,' and help the young man along.' And that's how it come about, Joe!"[6]

White Southerners' responses, such as the Virginia Vagrancy Act, to the emancipation of the slaves coupled with congressional determination to guarantee that emancipation became genuine freedom led Congress to impose military rule in the South. In the spring of 1867, the military officers ordered that new state constitutions be drafted and that black men be allowed to vote and hold political office. On 15 April a remarkable event took place in Richmond where, as elsewhere in Virginia, African American men began eagerly preparing to participate in politics and government. Black and white men organized a meeting in the city's largest theater and invited some experienced local white political leaders to address the soon-to-be-enfranchised black men. The principal speaker was Raleigh Travers Daniel, recently the city's prosecuting attorney and a prominent Whig from before the war. He presumed that the black men attended because they needed to hear the most respectable white men tell them how to vote, so he advised them to eschew radical Northern reformers who wanted their votes only to line their own pockets and who certainly did not, as the white gentlemen of Virginia certainly did, understand black Virginians and have their best interests and the interests of both races at heart. Daniel told his audience of black Virginians that they and white Virginians were dependent on each other and therefore had a common interest that neither shared with any radical Northerners. Daniel said that the past and slavery were gone and should be forgotten. He blamed slavery on the kings of England and New England merchants, absolving white Virginians of responsibility for black Virginians' previous condition of servitude. "We have endeavored to act toward you kindly and justly," Daniel told his audience, "and to deal with you just as we did before your liberation. We have not blamed you for that, for we know that you are not responsible for it at all."[7]

What did the black members of the audience think of that expression of regret at the emancipation of the state's slaves? The newspaper reports of the event did not say, nor did they record whether black men in the audience regarded it as a fearful thing or a laughable thing that a white man promised to treat free black men as he had treated enslaved black men. The reports also did not indicate whether members of the large black audience went away pleased, displeased, puzzled, or angry after Daniel advised them to listen to the voices of experienced men such as himself and to remember that their jobs and the food and clothing that their families needed depended on good relations between white employers and black employees that imprudent conduct of black voters could jeopardize.

The actions of the state's black voters in the October election indicate that they did not take the patronizing advice of white political leaders with prewar ideas about politics and society. On 22 October 1867 several thousand black Virginia men voted in the referendum on holding the constitutional convention and in the election of delegates. More than two dozen won election to the convention. Both events would have been unimaginable to any white Virginians at any previous time. The convention also included several men who had moved to Virginia from Northern states during or after the Civil War and who, with a small number of white Virginia Unionists and the African American members, formed a majority of the convention. White Virginians watched apprehensively as the convention provided for universal manhood suffrage for everybody except Confederate veterans, created the state's first system of free public schools, abolished the undemocratic county courts that the grandees had used for nearly two hundred and fifty years to dominate local government, and created a democratic system of local government resembling the alien New England townships.

In December 1867, while the convention was at work, Daniel helped organize a new political party in Virginia in open opposition to the black and white radicals. The name of the new party was the Conservative Party, the same as a number of other Southern political parties that formed to oppose the radical changes that were taking place in or being imposed on the South. The Conservatives desired in as many ways as possible to preserve as many aspects as possible of prewar society. Daniel served for nearly six years as the state chair of the Virginia Conservative Party and at the end of that time, in the autumn of 1873, was elected attorney general of the state.[8]

The events of 1867 and 1868 prompted journalist Edward A. Pollard to write another book. He had published *The Lost Cause* in 1867, a mere two years after the end of the war, composing a few introductory chapters and some concluding chapters to frame revised accounts of battles and politics that he had published during the war. In 1868 he seized on the new relationships between white people and black people in Virginia for another, though not nearly so long, book, *The Lost Cause Regained.* Reflecting on the new Southern world, Pollard wrote about the inherent biological inferiority of Africans (he described them as a distinct species of separate creation) and mixed-race African Americans (he described them as hybrid mongrels doomed to sterility and extinction). He also wrote about the responsibility of Southern white men to protect the remnants of their prewar culture from the reforming zeal of radical Republicans and their civil rights acts and reconstruction laws. Seeing in the aftermath of the war what he had not seen clearly at the end of the war when he wrote *The Lost Cause,* Pollard declared in *The Lost Cause Regained* that the antislavery attack on Southern civilization that propelled the Republican Party into power in 1861 and caused the Civil War was but the first of two Republican Party attacks on Southern civilization. The second was a renewal of a campaign for what Thomas Jefferson, James Madison, and John Taylor of Caroline had feared, creation of so strong a national government that it could extinguish the rights of people in their separate states to govern themselves as they pleased, including the ability of white people to govern inferior black residents differently than superior white residents. White Southerners should resume the struggle that Jefferson, Madison, and Taylor had begun seventy years earlier, Pollard wrote, which was only in part a defense of slavery and much more a defense of white supremacy and state's rights. Preservation of white supremacy and state's rights, not slavery, was what Pollard declared in his revisionist history in 1868 to be the meaning of the Civil War. It was also his clarion call for the next generation of Southern political leaders.[9]

Shaping the lessons of history and teaching them properly were essential to regain the cause that was not yet lost and to inculcate a proper understanding of the past in the children of the future. Jefferson Davis understood that when he composed the dedication of his book. Pollard's polemics, the oratory of Confederate veterans, writers of histories, and the women who buried and memorialized the dead all drew attention to the social values and political principles of the past and reshaped them into valuable political tools for the future. Confederate cemeteries and memorial ceremonies played an important part in that work, as did the erection later in the century of statues and monuments to Confederate soldiers and heroes on courthouse lawns and in the parks of the state's cities. The landscape of Virginia became a reminder of the losses and sacrifices of white men and women. The landscape thereby became a powerful educational tool that by focusing attention on those themes forced other themes such as the real causes and immediate consequences of the war into the background. The cemeteries and public art interpreted the war in a noble and heroic way that left no place for shame or second thoughts or slavery. The lost cause gained capital letters. The Lost Cause became a lens through which survivors and descendants of the Confederacy reinterpreted the war and its outcome, a lens that perfectly matched the political creed that Pollard enunciated in *The Lost Cause Regained*.[10]

A large proportion of white Virginians appears to have embraced that perspective during the years following the end of the war, perhaps without thinking through all of the intermediate steps between the old facts and their new beliefs. That perspective disclosed itself in the state's new political environment. In 1871 the Conservative Republican governor proposed that payment of an annual poll tax be made a prerequisite for voting, and within five years the Conservatives amended the state constitution to deny the vote to men who had not paid the poll tax or had been convicted of petty crimes. The intent of the two amendments was to make it more difficult for black men to vote. They were rooted in a realistic understanding that many poor black families could not afford to pay the tax and in a racist belief that black men were inherently less honest than white men and also were more likely to commit petty criminal acts or to continue a common practice from slavery times when enslaved people routinely appropriated chickens, swine, and other articles of food from their own owners.[11] The numbers of black voters and officeholders declined for a time during the 1870s.[12]

The new politics and the new economy of what soon came to be called the New South did not immediately settle into a clear radical and conservative polarity or even into a clear black and white division. Some leading members of the Conservative Party, as Raleigh Travers Daniel appears to have hoped would happen after he made his 1867 speech, appealed for support from the newly enfranchised black men and tried to influence their votes in legitimate, traditional ways. Conservatives in the city of Richmond even threw a barbecue for black voters at the end of June 1869 on one of the islands in the James River. During the event a footbridge collapsed, and one of the city's leading white bankers and Conservative Party leaders who hosted the event fell into the river and drowned. A large crowd of black men joined his funeral procession two days later.[13]

Several black Conservatives won election to the General Assembly that year, among them James W. D. Bland, of Prince Edward County, who was elected to the Senate of Virginia. He had been born free and was just as interested as the white Conservatives were to promote and to unite reconciliation and economic recovery. He opposed exclusion of former Confederates from the franchise, and at the poll when he won election, the voters ratified the new constitution and stripped out of it the clauses disfranchising former Confederates. Most of the state's Conservative Party leaders endorsed that course of action and in the process agreed to accept enfranchisement of black men. Bland's promising legislative career was brief. In the spring of 1870 he was killed along with about sixty other white and black people when the floor in the overcrowded Capitol courtroom collapsed. The Senate of Virginia adopted respectful resolutions of condolence, and more than two hundred people, many of them white, attended his funeral in Farmville.[14]

The willingness of a significant portion of Conservative Party members to accept black suffrage and to serve in the General Assembly with black members, many of whom had been enslaved not long before, appeared to signal the possibility of a thorough reconstruction of the state's politics and culture regardless of what Edward A. Pollard wrote and in spite of the centuries of slavery and the racial prejudice that had festered as slavery flourished. Indeed, the new realities of the postwar period no doubt persuaded some white people that black and white men were going to take part in public life together, anyway, and they should reconcile themselves to that reality and devise new means of doing the public's business.

The participation at leadership levels in the Conservative Party of a number of prewar Whigs may account for part of that change in postwar attitudes. Whigs had been less confrontational than Democrats before the war, perhaps to prevent divisions between the Northern and Southern Whigs, who differed in their attitudes about slavery and its introduction into the western territories. Virginia's former Whigs may have been marginally more inclined to adjust to the new conditions, and black voters may have been marginally less inclined to distrust them than the former Democrats. That is not to say that the former Whigs who assumed leadership roles in the new Conservative Party jettisoned their old racism and elitism, merely that they may have been temperamentally somewhat more inclined to adapt themselves to the new realities. Old Whigs engineered the compromise that removed disfranchisement of former Confederates from the constitution in 1869 and allowed black suffrage to remain.

The Conservative Party attracted such a large proportion of white men in Virginia, including many Republicans, that it might have prevailed over the radical Republicans even without the votes of black men. Regardless of their different individual opinions about black men in politics, members of the Conservative Party shared a desire to revive the state's economy. At the legislative session that met during the winter of 1870–71, they passed the law popularly known as the Funding Act of 1871.[15] Conservative Parties in some states of the former Confederacy repudiated some or all of their antebellum state debt after the Fourteenth Amendment to the Constitution of the United States invalidated Southern state debts accumulated during the Civil War, but the Virginia Conservatives pledged the state to pay off the full principal and accrued interest on the antebellum debt that the state had created for promoting the construction of canals, toll roads, and railroads, less about one-third that they calculated was West Virginia's portion. By honoring the remainder of the state's financial obligations, the politicians and businessmen of Virginia hoped to attract Northern and European capital with which to rebuild and expand the transportation network and industrial enterprises.

The Funding Act of 1871 appeared to make good, sound business sense, and nearly all of the African American members of the General Assembly joined a majority of white members in voting for it. In reality, it turned into a disaster. The national financial Panic of 1873 dried up capital resources. The interest rate on the public debt was high, and tax revenue was inadequate to pay the interest and the principal. Unwilling or unable to raise taxes and therefore unable to pay for the new public schools and also pay off the debt, the state government staggered into a terrible financial crisis that destroyed whatever goodwill among the nation's investors the promise to pay the debt had created. A decade of political turmoil and hot debate about the public debt poisoned the politics of Virginia and amplified other differences of opinion among the Conservatives. During the 1870s the underfunding of the public school system cost them whatever goodwill they had earned among black voters.

The new public school system was one of the most remarkable and conspicuous changes that took place in Virginia after the Civil War. The federal government's Bureau of Refugees, Freedmen, and Abandoned Lands (the

Freedmen's Bureau) formed the first statewide system of public schools—for black people—in Virginia during the second half of the 1860s. The constitution that went into effect in 1870 created a new statewide system of free public schools for both black and white students. The eagerness with which black students, including many adults, embraced the first opportunity for education surprised nearly all white people, who probably had never considered that black people knew anything about the value of education or could appreciate its importance. Black children and adults knew, and they eagerly crowded into the new schools, as did white children, but within less than a decade the new schools became overcrowded, dilapidated, and short of money.

Edward A. Pollard was astonished, and in the spring of 1870, even before the state's new school system went into operation, he admitted that he had erred two years earlier in *The Lost Cause Regained* in his assessment of the freed people. "The writer has to confess," Pollard wrote for *Lippincott's Magazine,* a widely read national journal, "that he was educated in that common school of opinion in the South that always insisted on regarding the negro as specifically inferior to the white man—a lower order of human being, who was indebted for what he had of civilization to the tuition of slavery, and who, taken from that tuition, was bound to retrograde and to relapse into barbarism and helplessness." Pollard wrote that he was "prepared to witness with pity what the whole South arranged itself to see—the misfortune and inevitable decline of the negro from the moment his emancipation was declared."

The schools were only part of the reason Pollard changed his mind. "He feels more like exclaiming, 'A discovery!'" Pollard wrote of himself, "than writing in any more deliberate mood of the proofs he has obtained concerning the new condition of the negro. It is that this singularly questionable creature has shown a capacity for education that has astonished none more than his former masters; that he has given proofs of good citizenship which are constantly increasing; that his development since emancipation is a standing surprise to candid observers among the Southern whites themselves; that his condition since then has been on the whole that of progress, and in the face of difficulties that would soon have tested and broken down that progress had it been factitious or dishonest; and that, so far from being a stationary barbarian or a hopeless retrograde, the formerly despised black man promises to become a true follower of the highest civilization, and new object of interest to the world, and an exemplary citizen of the South."[16]

That thousands of formerly enslaved Virginians displayed a sincere interest in education, responsible and productive work habits, and stable family lives completely overthrew all of Pollard's old beliefs. It is likely that some other observant white men of Virginia experienced similar surprise and that some of them therefore declined to accept the whole of the political creed that Pollard had outlined two years earlier in *The Lost Cause Regained.* What further surprises Pollard might have embraced will never be known because he died near the end of 1872 at the early age of forty.

During the 1870s disillusionment among the state's black population (and among its white population, too) about the condition of the schools alienated some men who had voted for the Conservative Party, leading men within the Conservative Party to become disillusioned with one another. They argued about how and what to tax and how much, about how much or how little to appropriate for the public schools, about how to refinance the debt at a lower rate of interest, and what to do about the long-term problem with the state's bonds that allowed owners to clip off the coupons and send them to the state treasury to pay their taxes, which reduced the already inadequate supply of money that entered the treasury annually.

Conservatives also battled each other in the General Assembly when owners and presidents of railroads sought permission to rebuild or expand their lines or to acquire one another's lines. The legislature retained the sole authority to issue or amend charters of incorporation, which meant that corporations had to appeal to the General Assembly for permission to issue additional stock for rebuilding old lines or consolidating short lines into long lines. Rather than cooperate in the interest of a unified system of railroad lines throughout the state, the owners competed for capital investment from the North and Europe, and they sought approval for charter amendments that benefited their own companies and opposed amendments that benefited any others. Just as ownership of land and control of labor and public office had been inextricably intertwined during the previous two and a half centuries, ownership or control of railroads and of legislative power to protect the interests of railroads became one of the choice baubles of post–Civil War politics and finance.[17]

Two railroad executives emerged as important competing Conservative Party leaders, John Strode Barbour and William Mahone. Barbour had been president of the Orange and Alexandria Railroad since 1851 and was eager to extend the line south into North Carolina, ultimately forming what became the Southern Railway, one of the most important in Virginia. Mahone had constructed the line from Norfolk to Petersburg before the Civil War, in which he served ably as a brigadier general in the Confederate army, and sought to acquire the line from Petersburg to Lynchburg and also the Virginia and Tennessee line from Lynchburg to Bristol, ultimately forming what became the Norfolk and Western, also one of the most important in Virginia. The politics of the railroad business presented the Conservative Party with one of its most difficult dilemmas, somewhat comparable in magnitude to the problems of paying off the debt and paying for the schools and complicated by the Panic of 1873, following which Northern syndicates gained control of most of the major Virginia lines, including both Barbour's and Mahone's.

Leaders of all political factions in Virginia were caught up in the late nineteenth-century American industrial development boom, however much they differed about means and competed with one another for capital and advantage. Old Whigs, old Democrats, and new Conservatives, both black and white, looked forward to promoting a new and more prosperous economic order that came to be called the New South. It was to be a South without slavery and that embraced modern industrial and commercial business enterprises, a South that economically resembled the victorious and thriving North.[18]

Newspaper editors of all political factions throughout the state wrote often and enthusiastically about economic progress and change, especially about the importance of railroads, which required large capital investments and corporate structures and were impossible to construct or operate without all of the implements of modern finance capitalism, none of which old John Taylor of Caroline, who died half a century earlier, would have sanctioned. The editor of the evocatively titled *Rockbridge Enterprise,* published in the little college town of Lexington, in Rockbridge County, reported in February 1880 on some recent regional economic progress and some local problems. His language was fairly typical. "WINCHESTER has her glove factories, shoe factories, paper factories, foundaries, sumac mills, and other industrial enterprises," he wrote, "and Staunton, too, is booming up with aspirations to become the Birmingham of the valley. When will the time come for Lexington to shake off the lethargy of inaction, to wake up from the sleep almost equal to that of death? Eh! when she gets a railroad and not before, then will there be some goaheadadiveness, some life, some business vim and, not the least of all, an influx of population to shake up the dry bones of old foggism a result most devoutly to be wished."[19]

Old fogyism was a much-used phrase with which enterprising Virginians of the time condemned less enthusiastic men or people who seemed rooted hopelessly in the agricultural past. The editor's new word, "goaheadadiveness," epitomized the innovative spirit of the times, when it seemed that not even the flexible and capacious English language contained enough vigorous words adequate to the task. Men like the editor of the *Rockbridge Enterprise* who promoted industrialization were trying to build a new Virginia as part of a new South that had its roots in the antebellum internal improvements movement, not in the plantation past, and that would be an integral part of a new American economic order. So, too, the Virginia Conservative Party, which was under the direction of lawyers, railroad officials, bankers, and businessmen. It was a Gilded Age party very like many elsewhere in the United States during the decades after the American Civil War.[20]

No nostalgia for plantation days, notwithstanding a popular new genre of mythmaking literature that portrayed the good old days of the slave South, blinded them to new economic opportunities, and the fever for investment and industrialization on the Northern model became infectious. A young law student at the University of Virginia, Woodrow Wilson, caught the fever and inserted into an 1880 public lecture on English reformer John Bright a typical paean to the promise of a new South. He may have shocked his audience when he stated that "*because* I love the South, I rejoice in the failure of the Confederacy," but he stated common beliefs when he continued, "Suppose that secession had been accomplished? Conceive of this Union as divided into two separate and independent sovereignties! To the seaports of her northern neighbor the Southern Confederacy could have offered no equals; with her industries she could have maintained no rivalry; to her resources she could have supplied no parallel. The perpetuation of slavery would, beyond all question, have wrecked our agricultural and commercial interests, at the same time that it supplied a fruitful source of irritation abroad and agitation within. We cannot conceal from ourselves the fact that slavery was enervating our Southern society and exhausting to Southern energies. We cannot conceal from ourselves the fact that the Northern union would have continued stronger than we, and always ready to use her strength to compass our destruction."[21] Young Wilson was one of many Southerners who simply abandoned or openly disavowed the prewar generation's firm belief that slavery was morally right and essential for white civilization in the South. They rewrote history to allow them to ignore an essential part of their past as they strove to fashion a different future.

The future that those enthusiastic men worked to create kept bumping to a halt against the realities of the 1870s. The public debt and the accruing interest on it drained away resources needed for economic development and endangered the new public school system. During legislative debates on the appropriation of money for the public schools in 1878, John Warwick Daniel, a member of the Senate of Virginia and an attorney who often worked for the railroads, including Barbour's Orange and Alexandria, objected to raising tax rates to pay for public schools. He described the school appropriation bill as a disguised method of avoiding payments on the principal and interest of the debt. "He said," according to a newspaper report, "he would rather see a bonfire made of every free school in the State, and a bonfire then made of his own home, than that this bill and those that are to follow it should pass."[22] When questioned more than a year later about that report, Daniel issued a public letter to explain that he "believed then, and believe now, that stark repudiation lurked behind" the school appropriation bill. "I said," he quoted himself, "'It were better to burn the schools than sustain them on money taken by force from others; for when the children grow up and realize that they were the wards of repudiation they would blush for their pretended patrons. It were better for the State to burn the schools than pass this bill *and the repudia-*

tion measures which, as I believe, were to follow; and I would rather burn my own house and start life again penniless, houseless, and honest than see her do it.'"[23]

The assembly nevertheless passed the bill and sent it to the new governor, Frederick William Mackey Holliday, for whose recent inaugural reception at the governor's mansion the Ku Klux Klan had decorated the parlors and halls "with State and national colors and flowers."[24] He vetoed the bill. Holliday's long veto message echoed what Daniel had said and also disclosed their elitist belief that educating all children in the state was not necessary or even good policy. "Our fathers did not need free schools to make them what they were," Holliday lectured the legislators. "Happy this generation could it rival them in those virtues that go to make up the glory of a commonwealth! They would not have tolerated them on the soil of Virginia had they to be established by the denial of their honest debts. . . . Public free schools are not a necessity. The world, for hundreds of years, grew in wealth, culture, and refinement, without them. They are a luxury, adding when skilfully conducted, it may be, to the beauty and power of a state, but to be paid for, like any other luxury, by the people who wish their benefits."[25]

Holliday's veto message was mired in the values of the privileged grandees of old. He extolled the achievements of "our fathers" who had created modern civilization without public schools, but those prosperous white men had access to private tutors and schools. His evocation of the leaders of the past—white male leaders, all, even if he did not say so—silently dismissed the potential for success of people—both white people and black people, male and female—who did not in his generation have access to public schools. Holliday presumably believed that if poor people wanted schools, they would find ways to afford to pay for schools themselves. He certainly was not going to force white taxpayers to pay for schools for black people, who he believed did not need them. Holliday's veto message would have pleased the opponents of change who in the Constitutional Convention of 1829–30 rejected without any discussion at all a proposal to create a system of public schools in Virginia to educate its citizens for better citizenship. The people who had governed and still governed had always been well-enough educated; their constituents, their inferiors, did not need education. Holliday's veto message was not unlike the political writings of John Taylor of Caroline, for whom civic leadership belonged by right only to the elites, to the privileged white men of the past who were "our fathers" of earlier generations and Holliday's own brothers of "this generation." So much for the hopes of the state's black students and also its poor white students.

Holliday and the preceding Conservative governors vetoed some of the laws designed to refinance the public debt at a lower interest rate and to stop allowing coupons to be used to pay taxes, and the appeals court judges that the Conservative majority in the General Assembly appointed invalidated others. By the time of Holliday's veto of the 1878 school appropriation bill, the split within the Conservative Party was so severe that William Mahone set out to form a new political party to settle the problem of the debt. He called for a convention to meet in Richmond in February 1879 to organize the new party, which even before it was formally created was called the Readjuster Party because it proposed to adjust, or readjust, the payment of the public debt. Mahone's call for the convention invited all men in Virginia, irrespective of race, who agreed with the proposed party's purpose, a clear appeal to the state's black voters, nearly all of whom by then were Republicans.

At that well-attended meeting in Mozart Hall in Richmond, a New Kent County delegate identified in the newspapers as "WM. T. JEFFERSON (COLORED)" announced that he and the other black delegates were delighted to attend "in response to the call which convened the people of Virginia without distinction of color." The newspaper reported that he stated that he was "a Republican—a Radical, if you choose—but no Conservative in the Convention was a more ardent Re-Adjuster than he. All the colored people in his district are Re-Adjusters and ready to shake hands with all other Re-Adjusters upon it." The report of his brief speech continued, "We have been taxed, and taxed almost to death. . . . As to the debt, we don't want to pay a cent of it. We think we paid our share of it, if it ever was justly chargeable upon us, by long years of servitude. And then, as Virginia has been reconstructed in her territory and in her government, we think that her debt should be reconstructed too." After the applause subsided, he concluded, "We are humble citizens— the humblest in the Commonwealth—and we treat white people invariably with a great deal more courtesy than we receive, because we are anxious not to offend you, and to win your good will. We are for peace, and we accept the overture made to us as heartily as it is tendered, for we feel that your interests and our interests are identical," which stimulated another round of applause,[26] and not because he had meant at all what Raleigh Travers Daniel had meant with similar words but in a different context twelve years earlier.

Readjusters won majorities in both houses of the General Assembly that autumn, and the assembly elected Mahone to the United States Senate and passed a debt settlement bill that Holliday vetoed. Readjusters also elected several members of Congress early in the 1880s, outpolling the Funders, as the Conservatives and Democrats called themselves, in several regions of the state. During their brief time of success, Readjusters did well in south-central and southeastern Virginia where the rural population contained the largest proportion of African Americans and in the mountains and southwestern Virginia where the rural population contained the smallest proportion of African Americans. They also did well in several of the state's cities, suggesting that their promise to solve the debt problem and their promise to save the public school system resonated more strongly with the state's electorate than the warnings of their opponents about the potential for economic disaster in readjustment and their fearmongering about the presence of black men in the Readjuster Party.

As the 1881 gubernatorial and legislative elections approached, black members of the Republican Party and the leaders of the Readjuster Party moved toward a merger. Even though the Readjusters had been receptive to black participation in their new party, most black political leaders remained committed to the Republican Party. In March 1881 a convention of about three hundred black Republican men met in Petersburg to consider an alliance with the Readjusters. Mayor William E. Cameron, a white Readjuster whose city government had been notably fair to the city's many black residents, attended the convention and welcomed the delegates. Early in the proceedings the delegates learned that when Congress had recently convened, Mahone caucused with the Senate Republicans. They cheered the news and for the remainder of the convention acted as if the Readjusters had already joined the Republicans rather than as if the Republicans were debating whether to join the Readjusters.[27] Three months later the Readjuster Party state convention adopted a platform that pledged support for the public schools, abolition of the poll tax and the whipping post, and other reforms that the Republican convention had endorsed, and for the time being the two parties had joined each other.[28]

The Readjuster convention nominated Mayor Cameron for governor and waged a campaign that illustrated how far apart Mahone's Readjusters had grown from the residue of Conservative Funders, who nominated John Warwick Daniel for governor. The debt, not the participation of black men in the Readjuster campaign, was the principal issue, and Readjusters appealed openly to both black and white men on the financial problems and the damage that the inability of the state to support the public schools adequately had done to all of the state's children. Funders appealed to voters on the grounds that if the state defaulted on even a part of its debt obligations, as the bills that the Readjusters promised and had passed provided, it would be impossible for Virginians to attract enough capital to revive the economy. The Funders declared that both the honor of the state and the state's economic future were at stake.

The Readjuster candidate for attorney general, Frank S. Blair, appealed to poor voters and parents everywhere, remarking on the campaign trail that the state's honor would not buy anybody a breakfast and that people needed practical relief from the consequences of the treasury deficit. Funders gleefully ridiculed Blair and the Readjusters for placing mundane private concerns above the state's sacred honor to meet its financial obligations.[29] Blair tried in vain to turn the advantage back toward himself, but the Funders refused to acknowledge any legitimacy in his point, leaving him no leverage for engaging in debate with them, and they relentlessly attacked him for stating that a poor man's breakfast was more important to the state than the state's honoring of its financial obligations.

The Funders, however, had nothing to offer but ridicule. For nearly ten years they had conspicuously failed to pay the interest or principal of the debt, and they had allowed appropriations for the public schools to fall to a fraction of what they had been in the beginning. The voters responded to the Readjuster campaign, and the Readjusters won a majority in the House of Delegates and all of the statewide offices, placing Cameron in the governor's office. A prominent Readjuster, John Sergeant Wise, later explained in an autobiographical novel entitled *The Lion's Skin* why the Funder appeal finally failed. "A wag of the period," he wrote, almost certainly referring to himself, "defined a Virginian Debt-payer as one who 'would rather owe you all his life than cheat you out of a cent.'"[30]

The first half of Cameron's four-year administration, which began on New Year's Day 1882, was a whirlwind of change. The Readjusters passed a debt settlement bill that within two years even the Funder Conservatives, who converted themselves into Democrats, accepted. They also overhauled the boards of visitors and curricula of the Medical College of Virginia, the University of Virginia, and the new agricultural and mechanical college that evolved into Virginia Tech. They reduced taxes on farms and small businesses, and they raised taxes on railroads by having tax assessors set the value of railroad property instead of allowing railroad executives to decide how much tax to pay. Even as most taxpayers' bills went down, tax revenue went up; the legislature restored funding to the public schools, the Funder budget deficit disappeared, and a surplus accumulated in the state treasury. The Readjusters also followed through on the political agenda of their black allies and abolished the poll tax as a prerequisite for voting, outlawed humiliating and brutal public whippings for petty offenses, established a mental hospital for African Americans, and created the South's first public college for the preparation of teachers in the state's segregated public schools, the school that evolved into Virginia State University. The radicalism of the changes that the Readjusters put into place rivaled what radical Republicans had proposed at the end of the Civil War.[31]

Listen to how different Cameron's 1883 address to the General Assembly on the public schools was from Holliday's 1878 veto message. "The condition of the public free school system," Cameron reported, "should engage the active interest of every citizen of this commonwealth. There is no individual and no element of our population but should rejoice to know that the state in the past two years has been able almost to double the facilities for free education." The governor declared that "the executive of the commonwealth knows no higher duty than to contribute all in his power to furnish the means for teaching all the people to understand their rights, to know the limits of their privileges, and to feel and perform the full measure of their duties. To those whom we have armed with the powers and responsibilities of citizenship, present or future, a high obligation exists. To call human beings into the front of the battle of life and deny them or obstruct them in the means which are essential to their intelligent use of freedom would be as gross an abuse as to call men into real war and fail to put into their hands the weapons with which to make them soldiers. It is to be hoped that these views will meet with no opposition in Virginia, and that all persons of all classes will agree that our best policy, as our highest duty, dictates the free education of all the children of all classes of our people."[32]

The broad inclusiveness of Cameron's message, embracing white and black Virginians and including the previously spurned poor Virginians, and the reforms that the Readjusters implemented indicated that most of the leading Readjusters had moved a long way from the elite perspective of the colonial and antebellum grandees. Their commitment to reform even in the face of intense opposition from the Funders led them into coalition with black men and many white Republicans that exercised its own alchemy on the thinking of Cameron and Mahone and others like them.

Listen to Mahone, who in 1882 received an invitation to deliver the annual address in Boston to celebrate George Washington's birthday. He did not go, but he sent a long public letter to be read on the occasion, and it was widely reprinted, including in the Virginia press. Mahone commented at length on his state's African Americans and their role in his political movement. "Our people have declared popular education to be among the most sacred duties and trusts of representative government, and are bravely executing that honorable decree," he wrote. "With valuable and beneficient results we are rapidly guaranteeing a priceless ballot to all entitled to it under the American theory. Conspicuous among the achievements of the advanced thought that places Virginia in full alignment with the highest American civilization is the prompt justice with which she deals with an element of population which has been the fruitful source of passionate disputation. Virginia has closed the long strife, which Mr. Jefferson foresaw and dreaded as he would dread 'the fire-bell at night,' over the status of the colored man. His political equality is secured throughout her domain. Never undervaluing the reciprocity of kindness between the races in the South in their peculiar and trying relations in the past, Virginia accepts the 'inexorable logic of facts,' and tenders the colored man the complete justice which his conduct as a citizen challenges and exacts. We are equally gratified with what we are doing for the colored man and what he is doing for himself. He vindicates himself and justifies us in our determined efforts for his moral and intellectual advancement. In Virginia he is at last in the full panoply of acknowledged citizenship. Conscious of the settlement in his favor of the question of his right to pursue the duties and

privileges of citizenship, his conduct commands the approval of even the se-
verest critics. Our treatment of the colored people elevates them as citizens,
and promotes their productive capacity. They are indefinitely with us, and no
substitute for their labor, which is peculiarly fitted to the Southern section of
the Union, has yet been found."[33]

Mahone's personal attitudes toward African Americans evolved to match
his increasingly egalitarian political creed. During the Civil War he had commanded the Confederate brigade that slaughtered waves of United States soldiers who poured into the Crater near Petersburg. Mahone's Brigade became
almost as well known as the Stonewall Brigade or Hood's Texas Brigade. Early
in the years of the Conservative Party, Mahone had been at or near the center in opposing the radical reforms of the Republicans, but by the end of the
1870s and increasingly in the 1880s he adapted and adopted new attitudes.
He treated African Americans with respect and accorded them the dignity
of citizens, in contrast to the open hostility of John Warwick Daniel and the
arrogant condescension of Raleigh Travers Daniel. Mahone's comment on
African American labor suggests that he continued to believe that the state's
black population was better suited to be a laboring class rather than a leading
class, and he did not allow black politicians to rise too high in his party. Later
in the 1880s Mahone opposed the one black Virginian who ran for Congress
as a Republican. Nevertheless, most black Virginians recognized Mahone as
a genuine friend and his Readjuster-Republican coalition as their political
home. He even corresponded with humble black Virginians regularly, perhaps
making him unique among the state's white political leaders of the time. Billy
Mahone was reconstructed.

Preserved among Mahone's surviving papers in the library at Duke University is a manuscript volume that his political adversaries, had they known
about it, might have killed to obtain. It contains a list of African American
clergymen with whom he corresponded and asked for political assistance
during one of his campaigns. Mahone's secretary compiled the list on the back
pages of a bound record book that already contained a list of the surviving
members of Mahone's Confederate brigade. Two lists in one book, one of
influential black political supporters in his new political campaigns, one of
white Confederate soldiers in his old military campaigns, and both lists in a
volume that bore the double-entendre label "Mahone's Brigade."

Mahone's actions and attitudes as well as the actions and public policies
adopted by Cameron and their biracial Readjuster-Republican coalition created a new political culture and a new political agenda in Virginia, an agenda
that was new not just within the old South but also in the United States. The
Readjusters succeeded by appealing openly to black voters, incorporating
their proposals into the party platform, and asserting that black men should
be treated as equal citizens with white men. Black political leaders thrived

during the brief Readjuster ascendancy and carried their talents and industry back into the Republican Party afterward. The Readjuster reforms were the real reconstruction of Virginia's political culture. The Readjuster Party was the most radical reforming party in all of Virginia's history.

It was also the most brittle. Democratic acceptance of the outlines of the Readjuster debt settlement led to defections from the Readjuster ranks by many white men who had agreed with the Readjusters only on the debt question. Mahone's joining with the Republicans delighted the state's black voters because it meant that Mahone could use federal patronage to build a powerful political organization in which they could play important leadership roles, but it drove away most of the old white Conservatives and outraged nearly all of the Democrats who feared that very thing. Mahone's own domineering managerial style also alienated some of his loyal followers, and scarcely two years after the triumphal success of the 1881 general elections, the coalition began to fall apart.

Mahone's opponents seized and thereafter never again released the initiative. They used the issue of race that he had tried to mute in pursuit of larger economic and social objectives that he had come to believe were beneficial to everybody. A great many less-flexible white Virginians could not embrace Mahone's alliance with the Republicans and his stated belief in the rights of black citizens. A few days before the 1883 legislative election, halfway through Cameron's four-year term as governor, a street brawl in Danville, where Readjusters were prominent in the municipal government, helped tip the balance against the Readjusters. It arose from seemingly petty matters of public protocol, whether black men and women were demonstrating proper deference to white men and women on the public streets. That lack of deference, which white people characterized as insolence, was a constant irritating reminder of how much things had changed in less than twenty years and of how degrading it could be for people who regarded themselves as proper white gentlemen and ladies to be inconvenienced or ignored by people most of them probably still regarded as in every way inferior. Those scenes occurred in the streets and other public places all the time and nearly everywhere. They were constant reminders to the white ladies and gentlemen of changes and challenges to their once-dominant position. Each repetition grated on raw nerves.[34]

Wendell Phillips Dabney, who was the son of a man who had been born into slavery and freed himself to become a successful entrepreneur, later recalled one such episode from that time. One day on his way home from school with his books under his arm, he encountered a "tall, thin, cadaverous looking 'rebel.'" The man, "noticing among the school books a history, said, 'Here, boy, let me see that book.' Opening, he began to read a chapter on the war. Then the floodgates of profanity opened to their fullest extent. He cussed every Yankee S—— of a B—— in this world, and hoped every damned rascally dog of them would die in torture and particularly the 'low-life scoundrel' who wrote that damned lie about the South." The man hurled the student's precious book into the street. "I picked it up," Dabney resumed his narration, "and as he did not know me, I made to him and concerning him several remarks which indicated that in slinging billings-gate I was no slouch either. . . . Fleetness of foot saved me from the heavy cane he always carried, though the wind wafted to my flying ears information as to what kind of G—— d—— little nigger S—— of a B—— I was."[35]

The street fight in Danville on the eve of the 1883 legislative elections quickly became, because of effective Democratic Party propagandizing, the tool with which they defeated the Readjusters by appealing to white voters whose racism had not abated or had even intensified since the Civil War. Democrats falsely charged that Danville's city government was under the domination of radical black Readjusters and that race riots, which is how they portrayed the Danville event, were what white Virginians might expect from continuation of Readjuster rule of the state. Democrats swept the 1883 legislative elections and in 1885 elected a full slate of Democrats to statewide office. The Readjusters by then were a dead political party. Some of its most ardent white reformers and most of its black members returned to the Republican Party, but more white men sought refuge in the reformed Democratic Party that Mahone's old railroad rival John Strode Barbour built into a formidable machine devoted to white supremacy. Barbour's Democratic Party deconstructed the Readjuster reconstruction. That cause, too, was lost, the cause of the freed people of Virginia and with it, also, the cause of the poor white people of Virginia.

It was not difficult for Barbour's party to destroy the Readjusters and to prevent the Republicans from picking up enough pieces to be a serious political competitor. Most of the white reformers among the Readjusters had moved much further and faster away from the past than a large proportion of white Virginians were willing to go, further even than many of Mahone's own white allies. Comparatively few white men were willing to go as far as Mahone and Cameron or even as far as Edward A. Pollard appeared willing to go near the end of his short life. The political catechism of Pollard's *Lost Cause Regained,* not Cameron's declarations about public education or Mahone's lecture on citizenship, was the better fit for the white men and women in Virginia who mourned the losses of the past, memorialized the Confederate dead, and erected statues and monuments. John Warwick Daniel believed that he was uttering a common opinion when in the autumn of 1883 he thundered, "I am a Democrat all the way up and all the way down, all through and all around. . . . I am a Democrat because I am a white man and a Virginian."[36] Democrats in the General Assembly elected Daniel to succeed Mahone in the United States Senate when the Republican's term expired in 1887, replacing him with the man who was willing to sacrifice the public schools on a funeral pyre to honor financial obligations.

Humorist and essayist George William Bagby was but one of many writers, orators, journalists, and politicians who also believed what Daniel and many of those white Virginians believed. His writings reinforced those beliefs. In the spring of 1880, about the time that the editor of the *Rockbridge Enterprise* was writing about goaheadadiveness and Woodrow Wilson was making his oration looking forward to the New South, Bagby wrote a more commonly held sentiment about the fate of the Old South. He published a little pamphlet significantly entitled *John Brown and Wm. Mahone: An Historical Parallel, Foreshadowing Civil Trouble.* "Miserable South!" Bagby wrote,

"VICTIM OF ONE PARTY, TOOL OF THE OTHER!

despised by all the world, and for no crime but that you Christianized a race of savages thrust upon you by mercantile greed—how sad is your fate! Miserable South! friendless upon the earth, orphaned and abhorred among the nations, forgotten it would seem of God—what a destiny is yours!"[37]

For decades after Mahone's death in 1895, he remained the most hated man in Virginia. Two years after his death, a little more than a decade following the collapse of the Readjusters, and not long before the Democrats completed their systematic campaign to drive African American men out of polling places and public offices and impose white supremacy, William L. Royall wrote a book. He was one of the attorneys who had represented the bondholders during the protracted political and legal wrangling, and he wrote a short book to defend the Funders and condemn the Readjusters. Whether many people ever read Royall's little book is doubtful, but its thesis, which he epitomized in the title and subtitle, expressed what became, or maybe by then had already become, the lesson that textbook writers, popular historians, journalists, and white political candidates and orators propagated well into the twentieth century. Royall's book was the *History of the Virginia Debt Controversy: The Negro's Vicious Influence in Politics.*[38]

10

AN
ANGLO-SAXON
ELECTORATE

Carter Glass (1858–1946) (courtesy of the Library of Virginia) served in the General Assembly, in the House of Representatives, as secretary of the Treasury, and in the United States Senate. As a member of the Virginia Constitutional Convention of 1901–2 he played a leading role in the disfranchisement of the state's African American men and also of a substantial portion of the state's white men. Like most white Virginians of his time, Glass believed in the innate inferiority of African Americans, and he and most of the other members of the convention sought to restore control of Virginia politics and government to what they regarded as the best class of white men.

I F WOOD BOULDIN WENT INTO ISAAC
Edmondson's barbershop in the town of Halifax, also known as Halifax
Court House and as Houston, between the summer of 1901 and the summer
of 1902, it is intriguing to speculate about the conversation that they might
have had. They were almost the same age: Wood Bouldin was born in the
adjacent county of Charlotte in 1838, and Isaac Edmondson was born in Halifax County about 1840. By 1901 they had lived as near neighbors in the same
little town for more than twenty years, but they were different in many ways.
Bouldin was white. He was a veteran of the Confederate army and the son of a
man who had signed Virginia's Ordinance of Secession in 1861 and served on
the Virginia Supreme Court of Appeals. He was the long-serving commonwealth's attorney for Halifax County and for many years was a member of the
state central committee of the Democratic Party.[1] Edmondson, on the other
hand, was black. He was born into slavery and after working as a farm laborer
in the first years after emancipation established himself in the respectable
profession of barber, for most of the time the only barber in the county seat.
He also worked part time as a janitor in the courthouse, where Bouldin had
his law office. For one two-year term, from 1869 to 1871, Edmondson was a
member of the House of Delegates in the first sessions of the General Assembly of Virginia in which African Americans ever served.[2] What did they talk
about in 1901 or 1902 if Bouldin sat in Edmondson's barber chair while the
black man cut the hair or shaved the whiskers of the white man who was then
serving in the state constitutional convention with ninety-nine other white
men and debating methods to disfranchise and expel from public life as many
as possible of the state's black men? What might Wood Bouldin have said?
What might Isaac Edmondson have said? What might Isaac Edmonson, in
particular, have thought and not said?

The white Democrat and the black Republican lived contemporary but
not parallel lives. If they reflected on their political pasts at the barbershop or
when they encountered each other in the courthouse, they would have realized
that their lives had ups and downs at precisely opposite times. The abolition
of slavery in the mid-1860s, the admission of black men into Virginia's political world when Edmondson was elected to the General Assembly at the end
of the 1860s, and the brief ascendancy of the Republican-Readjuster coalition
early in the 1880s were times of excitement and opportunity for Edmondson
and men like him and times of disappointment and uncertainty for Bouldin
and many other white Virginia men. Conversely, the derailment of the Re-

publicans' plans at the end of the brief Reconstruction of the 1860s and the overthrow of the Readjusters in the mid-1880s would have been times of fresh opportunity and optimism for Bouldin and of disappointment and disillusionment for Edmondson. The two men were entering their seventh decades when the twentieth century began and had lived more than half their lives since the abolition of slavery. Their adult lives spanned the arc between one system of racial domination that slavery and the black codes of the old South created and enforced and another system that the emerging racial segregation known as Jim Crow re-created and reenforced. Men like Isaac Edmondson watched, almost helplessly, as men like Wood Bouldin systematically chipped away at the democratic rights that freedmen had received and sought to exercise. For the Wood Bouldins of Virginia, the Constitutional Convention of 1901–2 was another time for them to be optimistic. For the Isaac Edmondsons, it was to usher in the worst times since slavery.

The Virginia Democratic Party of which Bouldin was an important local leader and one of a considerable number of responsible state leaders had reformed itself in the 1880s to destroy the Readjusters and pursued a white supremacy agenda thereafter, but it was not a united party any more than the Conservative Party before it had been. For more than three decades, the party had a two-headed leadership. Railroad executive John Strode Barbour, a skillful manipulator with ties to national business leaders and access to money, and his sometime rival John Warwick Daniel, one of the most popular Lost Cause orators in Virginia, shared the party leadership during the overthrow of the Readjusters in the 1880s and represented the state in the United States Senate together from 1889 until Barbour's death in 1892. Barbour's skill in organizing and directing party affairs matched William Mahone's abilities, and together with Daniel's popular oratory they formed an uneasy but effective team. Following Barbour's death the Democrats in the General Assembly elected an almost unknown railroad attorney, Thomas Staples Martin, who may very well have purchased his seat with railroad money judiciously distributed to members of the legislature. Martin was at least the equal of the skillful Barbour in the arts of political manipulation and fund-raising, and Martin and Daniel, too, formed an uneasy but effective team during the remainder of the 1890s and the following decade.[3]

Republicans remained a threat to the Democrats but a gradually declining one. For a decade beginning late in the 1880s, another potential threat arose in the form of the Populists. Elsewhere in the South and also in the Great Plains, the People's Party, as it was formally styled, swiftly gained political influence with a program of economic reforms that appealed to farmers and others vulnerable to business cycles, bank foreclosures, and the increased economic and political power of railroads and other large corporations. In several states, including neighboring North Carolina, Populists made common cause with

Republicans and African Americans during the 1890s and won victories in congressional and statewide elections. They even temporarily gained control of the state government of North Carolina.

That did not happen in Virginia. The state's Democratic Party leaders had already suppressed just such a biracial class upheaval in the form of the Readjusters. Gun-shy Republicans did not tie themselves to black voters again, and the Populists essentially gave up after an initial attempt to organize black Populists in some Virginia counties. The state's Populist leaders were, for the most part, white planters engaged in large-scale commercial agriculture, and they made few direct appeals to poorer farmers and consequently developed only a rudimentary and almost entirely ineffective state political organization. Even when they ran candidates for statewide office, they campaigned on issues that only Congress could address, giving them little to offer to voters that Democrats could not match or exceed.[4] Moreover, Daniel and a considerable portion of the state's congressional Democrats and members of the General Assembly supported some of the Populists' most popular proposals, among them currency inflation through an increase in federal coining of silver. Daniel campaigned enthusiastically for such reforming national Democrats as William Jennings Bryan, who in 1896 was the presidential candidate of both the Populists and the Democrats, even as Martin stood steadfastly by his railroad allies in opposition. With many of the state's Democrats supporting important elements of the Populists' national agenda and with the state's Populists having no state agenda of their own and no chance of an alliance with Republicans, the Populists posed no serious threat to Democratic control of the General Assembly.

The divided party leaders contrived to hold the party together in spite of their divisions on important national issues.[5] The rather reclusive Martin valued control more than he insisted on an unobtainable uniformity of opinion, and he concentrated on protecting his supporters and himself. "I remember Senator Martin's saying to me once," an admirer wrote many years later, "that in politics a man should never look for a fight."[6]

One thing all Virginia Democrats appeared to agree on by the 1890s was white supremacy. White politicians, journalists, clergymen, scientists, and writers and speakers from a wide variety of backgrounds propagated ideas of white supremacy and black inferiority during the final decades of the nineteenth century and the first decades of the twentieth. Many of them sounded like Abel P. Upshur, who in the *Southern Literary Messenger* late in the 1830s had defined slaves and free blacks as a separate and inferior caste, or like Edward A. Pollard, who in *The Lost Cause Regained* late in the 1860s had described Africans and people of African extraction as an inferior species. The later writers and speakers adduced evidence from science, statistics, and much subjective common knowledge in support of their opinions. Philip Alexander

Bruce, for instance, a descendant of a wealthy Virginia planter family and an influential writer of Virginia history, published several volumes extolling the virtues of the white Virginia contemporaries of his ancestors and their institutions and beliefs, but his 1889 book, *The Plantation Negro as a Freeman: Observations on His Character, Condition, and Prospects in Virginia,* extolled nobody. Bruce wrote that African Americans in Virginia had deteriorated as a class since emancipation and were incapable of playing any productive part in society other than as menial laborers.[7]

When Bruce was writing his book, a small group of socially prominent white women created the Association for the Preservation of Virginia Antiquities. They contributed to the public's understandings about race and class in Virginia's evolving history by acquiring several historic sites, including the old churchyard on Jamestown Island, where important events took place during the seventeenth and eighteenth centuries. Preserving those sites gave them a public forum for emphasizing the sacrifices and contributions of the elite white men who had founded the colony of Virginia in the seventeenth century. The unease of the leaders of the APVA with American democratic culture was evident in their words and their selection of sites to preserve and in the ways they interpreted the colony's history to the people of the state. For the association's early leaders, Virginia's history was the history of its great white men, and whatever detracted from the glory of those men or competed with them for attention or influence was to be ignored or deprecated, including the extension of the franchise to all white men in 1851 and to black men in the 1860s.[8]

Much the same could be said of the Daughters of the American Revolution and the Daughters of the Confederacy as well as of Mary Tucker Magill and Rose Mortimer Ellzey MacDonald, the authors of some of the most popular histories of Virginia that were used as textbooks in the state's schools during the first decades of the twentieth century. Textbook writers and popular authors celebrated the First Families of Virginia and the heroes of the American Revolution and the Civil War. Organizations such as the Sons of Confederate Veterans created censorship committees that reviewed new books and campaigned against the use in the state's schoolrooms of texts that presented interpretations of American and Virginia history that they believed were politically incorrect for their times.[9]

A popular new genre of literature often referred to as the plantation novel contributed to and popularized that particular interpretation of the past. Those novels and romanticized reminiscences and tales reinforced perceptions that Virginia's glory days were in the past, but they also carried the political message of Pollard's *Lost Cause Regained* to many people who never read his book or even heard of him. The lessons of Letitia M. Burwell's 1895 *A Girl's Life in Virginia before the War* were fairly typical. She wrote about her childhood and visits to plantations in the state where all the white men were cultured gentlemen and all the white women were refined ladies. "The negroes on these estates," she liked to recall, "appeared lively and happy—that is, if singing and laughing indicate happiness; for they went to their work in the fields singing, and returned in the evening singing, after which they often spent the whole night visiting from one plantation to another, or dancing until day to the music of the banjo or 'fiddle.'"[10]

"O Bright-winged peace!" Burwell rhapsodized, "long didst thou rest o'er the homes of old Virginia; while cheerful wood fires blazed on hearth-stones in parlor and cabin, reflecting contented faces with hearts full of peace and good will toward men! No thought entered there of harm to others; no fear of evil to ourselves." Paraphrasing chapter 4, verse 8 of Paul's Epistle to the Philippians, she threw a cloak of Christian approbation over the society of her youth as she remembered or wanted to remember it, writing, "Whatsoever things were honest, whatsoever things were pure, whatsoever things were gentle, whatsoever things were of good report, we were accustomed to hear around those parlor firesides; and often would our grandmother say: 'Children, ours is a blessed country!'"[11]

As in most or all of the memoirs and fictions, the Civil War ended all that was good for masters and for slaves. "And then came the long dark days," Burwell sighed, "the days when the sun seemed to shine no more; when the eyes of wives, mothers, and sisters were heavy with weeping; when men sat up late in the night studying military tactics; when grief-burdened hearts turned to God in prayer.... Only the negro slaves stayed with us, and these were encouraged by our enemies to rise and slay us; but God in his mercy willed otherwise. Although advised to burn our property and incited by the enemy to destroy their former owners, these negro slaves remained faithful, manifesting kindness, and in many instances protecting the white families and plantations during their masters' absence."[12]

Burwell dedicated her reminiscences to her nieces, "who will find in English and American publications such expressions applied to their ancestors as: 'cruel slave-owners'; 'inhuman wretches'; 'southern taskmasters'; 'dealers in human souls,' etc. From these they will naturally recoil with horror. My own life would have been embittered had I believed myself to be descended from such monsters; and that those who come after us may know the truth, I wish to leave a record of plantation life as it was. The truth may thus be preserved among a few, and merited praise may be awarded to noble men and virtuous women who have passed away."[13]

And with those noble men and virtuous women who had passed away, so passed their version of civilization, a civilization that in hindsight lost its hard edges and gained a new luster that contrasted dramatically with postwar realities. By the opening of the twentieth century, many white Southerners and

Virginians remembered or learned about a past that could never have existed for more than a very small minority of Virginians. Their historical literature largely ignored the experiences of small farmers and artisans of both races, and it also ignored most women, professional men, and poor people generally. Readers of histories, reminiscences, and romances about Virginia saw the past through eyes like those of Letitia Burwell, for whom "whatsoever things were honest, whatsoever things were pure, whatsoever things were gentle, whatsoever things were of good report," the things that were almost exclusively the property of the wealthier white planter families, became generalized to belong to the whole population, as if all white and all black people in their little cabins shared equally in the honest, pure, gentle, and good things that plantation slavery had in fact bestowed upon only a very few people like Letitia Burwell and her immediate white family.

Among the most popular Virginia writers at that time was Thomas Nelson Page, who wrote history, fiction, and verse that combined all of the nostalgia for lost glories and virtues with a verisimilitude that further reinforced his readers' politically correct perceptions and in some instances led people into misremembering the past. In *The Negro: The Southerner's Problem,* Page wrote in 1904 that "a bill to abolish slavery in Virginia had failed in her General Assembly" in January 1832 "by only one vote and that vote the casting vote of the speaker."[14] That falsehood, which Page or anyone else could easily have checked by consulting the assembly's published legislative journals, crept into textbooks and historical narratives and persuaded several generations of Virginians that the state's late antebellum political leaders had not approved of slavery and would have abolished it if they could. Page and many other writers elided from their historical narratives two or three decades of increasingly proslavery thought and action leading up to the Civil War, lending support to their companion assertion that Virginia had not seceded from the United States in 1861 and Virginians had not fought against the United States during the Civil War in order to preserve or even because of slavery.

Page and other writers absolved the state's white political leaders of any responsibility for the existence of slavery. They also blamed radical Republicans in Congress for granting black Virginians the right to vote after the war, which they asserted had debased the state's political culture and public life. For decades that literature, those schoolbooks, and those attitudes guided the beliefs of their children and grandchildren. Virginia history textbooks continued to teach the same lessons well into the 1950s and 1960s, informing the political perspectives of men and women who lived into the latter years of the twentieth century and the early years of the twenty-first, confirming them in the political catechism that Edward A. Pollard had propounded in the 1860s.

A belief in the inferiority of men and women of African descent lay at the heart of that political ideology. Dr. Paul Brandon Barringer was typical in his opinions on those subjects but superior in his credentials as an advocate for them. A physician who had studied in Europe as well as in New York, Barringer was dean of the faculty and in charge of the medical school at his alma mater, the University of Virginia, at the turn of the twentieth century and was a founder of its teaching hospital. He was president of the Medical Society of Virginia in 1906 and from 1907 to 1913 was president of the state's principal land-grant college, then known as the Virginia Agricultural and Mechanical College and Polytechnic Institute. In 1900 Barringer delivered several major lectures on the subject of the South's African Americans and had them reprinted as pamphlets for wide distribution.[15]

"The American Negro—His Past and Future," a lecture that Barringer delivered before the Tri-State Medical Association early in 1900 and reprinted at least three times, was his most thorough explanation of the science and sociology of racial differences. He pronounced residents of Africa to be barbarians and savages incapable of serious moral or physical improvement. Their descendants, even under the supervision of white Americans during slavery days, were apt to relapse speedily into the same condition. "I will show from the study of his racial history (phylogeny)," Barringer wrote, "that his late tendency to return to barbarism is as natural as the return of the sow that is washed to her wallowing in the mire. I will show that the ages of degradation under which he was formed and the fifty centuries of historically recorded savagery with which he came to us cannot be permanently influenced by one or two centuries of enforced correction if the correcting force be withdrawn." In short, "if you scratch a negro you will find a savage."

Barringer declared that the South's African Americans who had been born too late to profit from the civilizing influences of enslavement "are absolutely worthless and no industry can be successfully maintained which is entirely dependent upon their labors." Even the public school systems that Southern states, including Virginia, created and paid for did not keep descendants of slaves from deteriorating into a savage and violent criminal class, their natural condition, because the teachers in many of the schools were also black. Barringer predicted that "the temporary elevation produced by this discipline of slavery" could not be sustained and suggested that the only hope for the South's white population to save itself from being irresistibly drawn down into a sink of savagery and brutality was to create "an education of trade or industrial type, given at the hands of well-chosen white teachers, who will teach him to respect, to obey, and to work."[16]

Barringer preached that same message of rudimentary agricultural and industrial education and moral improvement to the prestigious Southern Educational Association at its annual convention in Richmond later the same year.[17] He was not an original thinker, but he was a more than ordinarily respected speaker and writer in Virginia, and his words, like the words of many other modern men of science and influence, represented the best scientific thinking of the time and influenced and reinforced the social and political implications of that thought.

Another University of Virginia professor, historian Richard Heath Dabney, wrote a long letter for publication in the *Richmond Times* in October 1901 to announce his considered opinion that white Virginians had no responsibility for and nothing to gain by paying tax money to educate black Virginians, presumably believing with Frederick William Mackey Holliday more than two decades earlier that people who could profit from education could afford it and people who could not afford it would not likely profit from it. Dabney endorsed the principal purpose of the constitutional convention that had recently begun, which was to drive black Virginians out of politics and to deny black men the right to vote.[18] The editors and publishers of the influential *Richmond Times* needed no persuasion. "God Almighty drew the color line," the newspaper's editor had written early in 1900, "and it cannot be obliterated. The negro must stay on his side of the line and the white man must stay on his side, and the sooner both races recognize this fact and accept it, the better it will be for both."[19]

For fifteen years, by then, the state's Democrats had been pursuing a policy designed to ensure precisely that. During the final years of the nineteenth century, Congress and Northern Republicans largely abandoned their support of African Americans in the South and allowed Southern states to evade the requirements of federal civil rights laws and the Fourteenth and Fifteenth Amendments. In 1884, in the first session of the General Assembly after Democrats won majorities in both houses of the legislature, the members passed over the veto of the Readjuster governor an election law known as the Anderson-McCormick Act.[20] It replaced all officers of election in the state with three-member boards for each county and city and authorized the General Assembly to elect all the board members, effectively giving the Democratic Party a monopoly on voter registration and the conduct of elections.

The Virginia Constitutions of 1864 and 1869 had required that all voting be by ballot rather than voice vote, a reform that advocates believed would relieve men from pressure of landlords, employers, or other overbearing men who could retaliate if voters defied their wishes. Voting by ballot was not voting in secret, though. Candidates printed ballots bearing their names, and political parties printed ballots containing the names of their nominees and distributed them to voters who deposited them in ballot boxes on election day. The different candidates' or parties' ballots were often on paper of different size, shape, or color. Every election officer and most observers could easily see how each voter voted, and they contrived many ways to regulate who voted and to influence the count. Both Democrats and Republicans in late

nineteenth-century Virginia resorted to intimidation, fraud, deceit, vote buying, and manipulation of ballots and the ballot box.

The documents that defeated candidates filed when challenging an election's fairness or legality, along with testimony of witnesses and participants,
disclosed the many ways in which partisans attempted to prevent opponents'
supporters from voting or later to disqualify their votes. Men in charge of con-
ducting the election sometimes set up separate ballot boxes for Republican
and Democratic candidates, made white and black voters stand in separate
lines, or badgered or delayed black voters so relentlessly that some of them
gave up and left the polling place or had to leave in order to go to work and
missed the opportunity to vote.[21]

In one of many such examples, a man testified that at the congressional
election in Petersburg in November 1888, he "was at the 6th Ward polls about
two hours during the morning, and again from soon after 3 o'clock p.m. till
after the polls had closed." He witnessed one of the techniques that Democrats used to prevent black men from voting and Republicans from winning.
"During the progress of the election," he testified, "I noticed some things that
I regarded as peculiar, one of which was that while all the colored voters were
required to approach the polling place on one side of a plank and the white
voters on another, certain colored voters were conducted to the window
where the voting was going on, on the same side with the white voters, and
allowed to vote." Those black men were almost certainly known to be willing to vote for Democrats. "At each time during the day that I was there," the
witness continued, "there was on the side of the plank appointed for colored
voters a long row of voters who complained of the delay of the election. I tried
to vote in the morning, but had to leave before I succeeded. When I returned
in the afternoon, about 3.15 p.m., so great was the crowd of voters on the colored side that I despaired of being able to vote. Finally, I voted by chance; the
long line of voters had moved away from the plank and the short line had
formed between them and the plank. I thought it a chance to get in my vote,
and moved from the long line and took a place in the short line. The judges
ordered the police to arrange the line; they decided to allow the persons in the
short line to vote, and so I voted. If it had not been for this I would have been
among the large number of persons who were in line waiting to deposit their
votes when the polls closed."[22]

The men who perfected and practiced those tactics were not ashamed of
themselves; indeed, some of them and their descendants bragged about their
ingenuity. "There were many methods of stuffing the ballot box," a man who
grew up in King and Queen County in those days reported proudly in his
autobiography many years later. "It was usually placed from ten to twenty feet
from the door, where the voter stood. A judge of the election would take the

Republican ticket in his left hand, from the voter, but put in the box a Democratic ticket, which he had concealed in his right hand. Another common trick was to put a handful of Democratic tickets in the ballot box, when the Republican judge was taking a drink of water or liquor, or had turned his back. Sometimes, when the judge would go to dinner or to the toilet, a duplicate box, filled with Democratic tickets, would be substituted for the original box. Then sometimes the Democrats would have two tickets printed, a large one that most people voted, and which was shown around, and a very small one which the Republicans never saw until the ballot box was opened at night. The old reliables would fold three or four of these small tickets into such a small package that the size was no larger than a regular ticket. When the ballot box was opened, all seemed very much surprised that it contained many more tickets than voters. Of course, this trick was pulled off in the Republican precincts. The officials either had to throw out the whole vote in that precinct or blind-fold a judge and get him to draw out the excessive number of tickets. My Uncle Atwood Walker was always one of the judges of the elections at Stevensville, and was the one that they always blind-folded. It is said that he had such a keen sense of touch that he nearly always drew out a Republican ticket."[23]

Ten years of such flagrant and often embarrassing dishonesty and violence at polling places disgusted many Virginians and left too much to chance. In 1894 the General Assembly passed the Walton Act that required use of the secret, or Australian, ballot. The state provided printed ballots containing all candidates' names and allowed voters to mark them in secret. The act required that each voter draw a line "through three-fourths of the length of the name" of every candidate that the voter voted against.[24] That left local officers of election wide discretion in counting ballots. They could declare that some ballots obviously marked for Republican candidates were nevertheless improperly marked, and they could count others marked for Democrats even if obviously marked improperly.

During the years in which the Anderson-McCormick and Walton Acts were in force, the number of black Virginia men who were able to register, to vote, or to win election to public office declined, and after 1890 the number of Republicans who voted in Virginia also declined in most counties and cities, although in the mountains of western Virginia white Republicans remained numerous, regularly winning local, legislative, and congressional elections and often helping the party win more than 40 percent of the vote in statewide and presidential elections.

Because Republicans continued to present serious challenges to Democrats in some places in spite of the Democrats' domination of the election process, the corruption continued and became so outrageous that some Democrats began agitating for a convention to write a new state constitution that would enable them to win elections without the blatant corruption. If certain men could not register and vote, it would not be necessary to cheat in order to win. They eventually persuaded the General Assembly to authorize a convention to rewrite the state constitution, and the Democratic Party state convention promised that the convention would submit the new constitution to a referendum for ratification. That may have been because Martin and Daniel disagreed about the wisdom of holding a convention. Martin worried that once a convention went to work, it could not be controlled, but Daniel was one of the most energetic proponents of a disfranchisement convention and became chair of the convention's critical committee on the franchise.

In two sessions between the summer of 1901 and the summer of 1902, eighty-eight Democrats and twelve Republicans (all but one of them elected from western and southwestern Virginia, and one of those as an independent candidate) drafted the Constitution of 1902, by far the longest Virginia constitution ever, containing 197 sections, some of them in multiple parts, running to more than 220 paragraphs and filling 65 pages in the official edition published as an appendix to the convention's journal. Like other state constitutions written during the latter decades of the nineteenth century and the first decades of the twentieth, the Virginia Constitution of 1902 contained many detailed provisions concerning courts, local government, and other subjects, insulating the institutional status quo from easy modification.

It was no accident that when the delegates first assembled, they unanimously elected John Goode president,[25] the one member who had served in the Convention of 1861 and had signed the Ordinance of Secession. In his address accepting the presidency, he denounced the Constitution of 1869 that the Convention of 1901–2 was preparing to replace. He proclaimed that the Convention of 1867–68 "was composed of aliens to the Commonwealth, and newly emancipated slaves. Virginians to the manner born, who owned the property and paid the taxes, and who represented the virtue and intelligence of the Commonwealth, were placed under the ban of proscription and excluded from its halls." The other delegates applauded that reading of history, even though it was far from entirely accurate. Moreover, getting to the primary purpose for which the convention was called, Goode declared, "The right of suffrage is not a natural right. It is a social right and must necessarily be regulated by society." Goode then pronounced an anathema on the grant of suffrage to black Virginians during Congressional Reconstruction. "Congress," he charged, "not only committed a stupendous blunder, but a crime against civilization and Christianity, when, against the advice of their wisest leaders, they required the people of Virginia and the South, under the rule of bayonet, to submit to universal negro suffrage." The record of the convention's proceedings indicates that the delegates applauded again.[26]

Breaking as sharply as they could with the spirit and the letter of the Constitution of 1869, the delegates in 1901 and 1902 stripped out of the Declaration of Rights the additions made during the Conventions of 1864 and 1867–68 that recognized the supremacy of the Constitution of the United States, denounced rebellion against the United States, and outlawed slavery by a state constitutional provision. The members of the Convention of 1901–2 retained the clause that the Convention of 1867–68 had added that reserved to the people of Virginia all other rights and liberties not enumerated in the Declaration of Rights, which in that age of white supremacy became once again de facto, even if not de jure, a declaration of the rights of white men.[27] It is more than merely symbolic that the shortest section in the constitution, Section 140, stipulated in full, "White and colored children shall not be taught in the same school."

William A. Anderson, a Confederate veteran from Lexington and one of the authors of the Anderson-McCormick Election Act, made disfranchisement of African Americans the subject of his presidential address to the Virginia State Bar Association in 1900. Denouncing the grant of voting rights to black men as one of the greatest mistakes in American history, he outlined and endorsed the methods by which other Southern states had contrived to circumvent the stipulations of the Fifteenth Amendment that prohibited states from denying men the right to vote based on their race or previous condition of servitude. Anderson was elected president pro tempore of the convention and while serving in that office won election to the first of two consecutive four-year terms as attorney general of the state.[28] Other leading members of the convention also undertook serious and time-consuming research to craft constitutional provisions on the franchise that would stand in the face of the Fifteenth Amendment. Allen Caperton Braxton, an attorney from Staunton, corresponded with judges, lawyers, legislators, and constitutional convention delegates in other Southern states that had already disfranchised African Americans, and he brought his copiously stocked legal arsenal to the convention with him.[29]

Article II of the new constitution, which treated the elective franchise and qualifications for office, consisted of twenty-one substantial paragraphs and was in two main parts. For the elections to be held before the General Assembly could put the restrictions into effect, men could register to vote in one of three ways: as war veterans and their adult sons; as property owners who had paid at least $1.00 in taxes during the previous year; or any man who could give a satisfactory explanation of any portion of the new state constitution. The constitution also deprived men convicted of crimes of the right to vote, continuing the prohibition included in the earlier constitutions and voting laws. The convention assembled a substantial dossier of information relating to payment of taxes and commission of petty crimes in order that the delegates could disfranchise as large a proportion of the black electorate as possible for reasons other than race.[30]

The constitution created an administrative structure and allowed the legislature to pass enabling laws after the first election to make it difficult or impossible for men to register and vote. The constitution required payment of a poll tax of $1.50 for each of three years preceding an election, meaning the effective exclusion from the ballot box of many poor black and white men. The poll tax was the one tax that the state did not make any effort to collect. The law allowed people to pay it voluntarily, but they had to pay it several months in advance of each election, making it less likely that poor white or black men would remember to pay it on time and to save and present the receipt to the voter registrar in order to qualify to register. The constitution and new laws also required each man who wished to vote to seek out a registrar annually and go through a complex process of registration and examination without any guidance from the registrar, vesting in the registrar extraordinary powers of discretion to determine a man's eligibility to vote. It also created new electoral boards to oversee the conduct of elections and the certification of election returns. Local judges, all of whom the General Assembly elected, appointed all officers of election. That gave the Democratic Party a monopoly on the registration process and a majority of election officials at every polling place.[31]

Much of the debate during the convention about details of disfranchisement revolved around whether the various proposals such as literacy tests and understanding clauses would disfranchise poorly educated white men as well as black men and whether the disfranchisement of some white men was a price worth paying in order to disfranchise black men or was, itself, another desirable objective that would raise the tone of public life by restricting voting and office holding to the best-educated and most respectable white men.

Delegate Carter Glass, a Lynchburg journalist and member of the Senate of Virginia, took charge of the drafting and passage of the suffrage article. He explained to the convention that its provisions would "not necessarily deprive a single white man of the ballot, but will inevitably cut from the existing electorate four-fifths of the negro voters." The other delegates applauded before Glass could conclude his thought, "That was the purpose of this Convention." When a delegate then interrupted to ask Glass whether the result would be achieved by fraud or discrimination, he indignantly replied, "By fraud, no: by discrimination, yes. But it will be a discrimination within the letter of the law, and not in violation of the law." Then he suddenly exclaimed, "Discrimination!" as if realizing that the question implied that discrimination was a bad thing. "Why, that is precisely what we propose; that, exactly, is what the Convention was elected for—to discriminate to the very extremity of permissible action under the limitations of the Federal Constitution, with a view to elimination of every negro voter who can be gotten rid of, legally, without materially impairing the numerical strength of the white electorate."[32]

During debate on what was called the understanding clause that permitted registrars to question men about their qualifications or require them to analyze a provision in the state constitution to the registrar's satisfaction, Alfred P. Thom, a corporate lawyer from Norfolk, correctly predicted how the provisions of the new constitution would operate. "I do not expect an understanding clause to be administered with any degree of friendship by the white man to the suffrage of the black man," he explained. "I expect the examination with which the black man will be confronted, to be inspired by the same spirit that inspires every man upon this floor and in this convention. I would not expect an impartial administration of the clause. I would not expect for the white man a rigid examination. The people of Virginia do not stand impartially between the suffrage of the white man and the suffrage of the black man. . . . By purging your electorate and making it, to all intents and purposes, an Anglo-Saxon electorate, you liberate the honest heart of the people of Virginia to demand honesty in elections."[33]

A few minutes after Thom spoke, one of the convention's few opponents of disfranchisement, Republican Albert P. Gillespie, the commonwealth's attorney of Tazewell County in southwestern Virginia, condemned the entire suffrage article. "I have been taught to believe," Gillespie told the other delegates, "that where a man was guilty of a fraud, or of cheating another man, the man who committed the fraud should be punished, that a man who steals a vote should be punished. But what is the remedy suggested here. The remedy suggested here is to punish the man who has been injured . . . in other words, the negro vote of this Commonwealth must be destroyed to prevent the Democratic election officers from stealing their votes, for it seems that, as long as there is a negro vote to be stolen, there will be a Democratic election officer ready to steal it."[34]

Registration and voting dropped precipitately in Virginia as a result of the Constitution of 1902. In the 1900 presidential election 264,357 Virginia men voted; in 1904 a mere 130,842. The Republican vote fell from 43.8 percent to 35.2 percent of the total. The number of white voters declined by about 50 percent, and the number of black votes declined by about 90 percent[35] and remained insignificantly small in all but a few communities until the mid-1960s. In spite of what Carter Glass stated, more white men than black men lost the right to vote as a consequence of the disfranchisement provisions he prepared and pushed through the convention. Most of the white men were Republicans or were poor and could not afford to pay the poll tax or manage to negotiate the complex and protracted voter registration process. The effect of the Constitution of 1902 was to reduce the Virginia electorate to a smaller proportion of the adult male population than at any other time, almost completely reversing the democratic reforms embodied in the Constitutions of 1851, 1864, and 1869 and disfranchising even more Virginia men than the old colonial laws of the grandees first passed in 1670.

The members of the Convention of 1901–2 who spoke in favor of the disfranchisement of African Americans openly disagreed with Thomas Jefferson's revolutionary statement that all men are created equal, just as Abel P. Upshur, Benjamin Watkins Leigh, and the leading opponents of universal white manhood suffrage had argued in the Convention of 1829–30. They made no apologies for depriving black Virginians of the right to vote. Indeed, they were proud of what they did and spoke frequently and plainly about the necessity to reserve the right to vote and to serve in public office to the most respectable and able white men. The leading members of the convention referred back to the politics of antebellum Virginia—in the good old days before the Civil War and before the expansions of the franchise that began half a century earlier—as the political culture that they wished to restore to what Alfred Thom called an Anglo-Saxon purity.

Deeply committed to the ethos of the old Virginia, the delegates gave a standing ovation on one of the last days of the convention to Clarence Jackson Campbell when he resumed his seat after returning home to Amherst County where he presided over a session of the county court. At that session Campbell had been deeply humiliated, something that no white Virginia man who considered himself to be a gentleman could accept, and he reacted much as a Virginia gentlemen of the antebellum period would have reacted and for that received the approbation of the convention's members.

As county judge Campbell had earlier authorized a local pharmacist to sell "medicated" alcohol even though the county did not permit the sale of alcoholic beverages. A national officer of the Anti-Saloon League denounced Campbell's action and sarcastically questioned "which had been doctored most, the whiskey or the judge." Campbell had then pronounced the prohibitionist in contempt of court, but when Campbell presided at his court in June 1902, a formidable phalanx of able attorneys appeared and argued that his contempt of court citation was illegal. Campbell had no choice but to reverse his own ruling and vacate the citation. Thus humiliated, he retrieved his honor as a gentleman of the old school might have. He went out to where he had tied his horse and buggy, retrieved the whip, and soundly thrashed the agent of the Anti-Saloon League, for which action his convention colleagues gave him a standing ovation the next day after he rode the train back to Richmond to take part in the final sessions of the convention. He and they understood the full implications of his whipping of the agent of the Anti-Saloon League, who by virtue of being whipped was publicly branded as the social inferior of the dishonest but honorable Judge Campbell. Several years later the General Assembly removed Campbell from office for multiple counts of misbehavior, including conniving with a relative to sell the medicated alcohol, but it did not list the whipping.[36]

The poll-tax requirement created a new form of political corruption. In direct violation of the spirit, though not of the letter, of the state's new constitution and often in direct violation of both the spirit and the letter of the laws passed to implement it, both political parties raised money, often making assessments against holders of public office to pay the poll taxes of men who would vote for their candidates.[37] A Lynchburg corporation court judge who endorsed disfranchisement from the bench in open court also attempted to immunize officers of election with a judicial opinion in 1911. He ruled that however incompetent or illegal the action of an election official, the registration form, if filled out to the registrar's satisfaction, was valid and could not be challenged even though state law clearly provided for appeals.[38] Registrars were largely free to register or to refuse to register whomever they pleased.

The final and at the time the most controversial act of the Convention of 1901–2 was to refuse to honor the Democratic Party's promise that the convention submit the constitution to a referendum for ratification or rejection. The members feared that men who would likely lose the right to vote under the new constitution would not vote to ratify it. After long and surprisingly learned legal arguments citing the actions of the Virginia Conventions of 1776 and 1864—Wood Bouldin made the longest and one of the most learned speeches in opposition to a referendum—the delegates voted to proclaim the constitution in effect as of 10 July 1902.[39]

Eleven months after the Constitution of 1902 went into effect, the Supreme Court of Appeals took judicial notice that all of the state officials, including members of the General Assembly and the judges of the court themselves, had taken an oath to support and defend the new constitution and were exercising their duties under it. The judges then declared unanimously that the new constitution "having been thus acknowledged and accepted by the officers administering the government and by the people of the State, and being, as a matter of fact, in force throughout the State . . . is the only rightful, valid, and existing Constitution of this State, and that to it all the citizens of Virginia owe their obedience and loyal allegiance."[40] All of "the people of the State" had not approved it, but by then the new constitution with its disfranchisement provisions was a fait accompli. The Supreme Court of the United States in effect agreed in 1904 when it later declined to act on a suit brought to block the 1903 elections scheduled to take place under the new constitution. The judges ruled that "the thing sought to be prohibited has been done and cannot be undone by any order of court." In fact, that statement applied to the promulgation of the Constitution of 1902, also.[41]

One of the convention delegates, future congressman Walter A. Watson, had grumbled that the disfranchisement provisions were too weak and might still allow some black men and too many poor and illiterate white men to register and vote, so on 18 September 1902 when registering in his native Nottoway County, he made a conspicuous point of submitting himself to be examined under the constitution's understanding clause. "I could have registered under property or as the son of a soldier," he noted in his diary, "but thought our people ought to set an example to the more illiterate whites who might be indisposed to submit to an examination." A couple of weeks later, after he had thus tried by example to dissuade poor white men from attempting to register, Watson encountered "an old slave darkey"—a man who had been born into slavery, as Isaac Edmondson had been—"who believed great harm of the new Constitution and told me the negroes held me accountable for what they considered a serious attempt upon their liberty."[42]

The language in which Watson recorded the conversation suggested that he was surprised that a black man could have thought that he had or was entitled to any rights to be deprived of. But black Virginians knew precisely what was happening and that they were losing a priceless right of citizenship. What expression of dismay might Watson have written in his diary had he heard what Charles Wilson Butler said when he attempted to register on 13 September in Warren County, many miles to the north of Nottoway? A blacksmith, Butler had been born in 1853, perhaps into slavery. When the registrar asked him the meaning of Section 4 of the new constitution, Butler replied firmly, "You men have no right to refuse to register me." But the registrar refused and wrote "not admitted" in his official List of Colored Applicants Refused Registration.[43]

William C. Pendleton, a journalist and regional historian in southwestern Virginia, wrote about the initial registration of voters in that area. "It was painful and pitiful," he recalled, "to see the horror and dread visible on the faces of the illiterate poor white men who were waiting to take their turn before the inquisition." Illiteracy was still widespread in Virginia three decades after its first public school system went into operation, reflecting the priorities of the white politicians who had been in charge of state and local governments during almost all of those years. As VIRGINIA FREEWOMAN had written back in 1829, the state's political leaders denied education to people and then denied them the right to vote because of their ignorance or illiteracy. Pendleton continued his commentary, "They had seen some of their neighbors and friends turned away because they were unable to answer satisfactorily the questions put to them by the registrars; and it required much earnest persuasion to induce them to pass through the hateful ordeal. This was horrible to behold, but it was still more horrible to see the marks of humiliation and despair that were stamped upon the faces of honest but poor white men who had been refused registration and who had been robbed of their citizenship without cause. We saw them as they came from the presence of the registrars with bowed heads and agonized faces." "When they spoke," Pendleton concluded sadly, making a mess of his figure of speech, "in many instances, there was a tear in the voice of the humiliated citizen."[44]

On the other hand, in the summer of 1904 the editor of the *Richmond Times-Dispatch* wrote proudly, "We have eliminated the objectionable negro vote and many objectionable white voters have been retired," a very slick way to gloss over the disfranchisement of thousands of white men. "The Virginia electorate is now composed of the best white men in the State, is composed in great degree of Democrats who have the true interests of the State, political and otherwise, at heart, and the party is in position to give the people the best government they have ever had. There is now no occasion and there can be no pretext for dishonest methods of any description whatsoever, nor for any sort of manipulation under the regime of what is regularly called 'machine politics.' The party may safely commit its interests and affairs to popular decision, and it should, therefore, adopt plans by which all questions of party concern may be submitted unreservedly to popular vote by ballot."[45]

Regardless of what Thomas Martin may have apprehended when members of his party succeeded against his wishes in calling the constitutional convention, the constitution that the delegates wrote and put into effect worked very much to the benefit of the Democratic Party leadership. The General Assembly in which his dominant faction held a comfortable majority elected all of the state's judges, who in turn appointed the election officials. The provisions of the new constitution and the revised election laws that the assembly enacted to implement them allowed party officials in the state's cities and counties to manage local governments and local politics more easily and effectively. Party leaders did not always get their way thereafter, and opposition men won election to the assembly from time to time and to Congress from some districts and to the governorship on a few occasions, but even after the assembly enacted the progressive reform to permit primary elections to select candidates for office, Martin was able to continue winning nomination and election to the United States Senate.[46]

Following Daniel's death in 1910, former governor Claude A. Swanson joined Martin in the Senate and succeeded Daniel as the other half of the party's leadership team. For nearly a decade Martin and Swanson directed the party's organization, as its members and opponents called it, with skill and enough subtlety that even though they had talented adversaries who from time to time mounted opposition to their leadership, they did not lose control. The party's machinery and the new constitution actually allowed them to strengthen their hold over the political process and the courthouse rings, the men in the counties and cities who made it work. The organization was friendly to the state's business, banking, railroad, and industrial leaders; it received money from them and from Virginia native and New York financier Thomas Fortune Ryan; and it distributed money to pay poll taxes and to elect the party's candidates to local and legislative offices.

The Democratic Party included men opposed to nearly all changes and also other men who approved of some changes to educational and public health policies that they believed would be beneficial to the state's businesses. Swanson, in fact, was one of the governors who made improvements to the state's poorly funded public school system by increasing appropriations.[47] Such changes as made it through the General Assembly in education, public health, and public welfare during the Martin and Swanson years were rudimentary compared to reforms undertaken in states with fully developed Progressive movements, but they appeared to be significant in Virginia, where people who might have benefited from or desired increased public services from their government had little or no access to the ballot box and therefore no effective means of influencing debate or decisions on public policies.

Such changes as the party's leadership permitted were implemented so as not to require high taxes, impose restrictive regulations on businesses, or disturb the established social boundaries between the better class of white people and the working class of white people. Most importantly, they did not in any way undermine the subordination of all black Virginians to all white Virginians or enable many black Virginians to take part in the political process.[48] The Democratic majorities in the all-white, all-male General Assembly also refused to approve amendments to the state and federal constitutions to allow women to vote, even respectable white women from reliably Democratic families.[49] After ratification of the Nineteenth Amendment to the Constitution of the United States in 1920 forced woman suffrage on the reluctant men of Virginia, Democrats and Republicans sought to retain male domination over the political process, and the dominant Democrats showed no timidity or scruples about harassing white women from Republican families who tried to register or to vote. Republican Party leader Henry W. Anderson, a distinguished attorney, later published a "list of questions asked the wife of one of the most intelligent men in this State in one of the cities in the Western part of the State" in 1920, when women were first eligible to register:

"How many historical flags has the United States?
"Who discovered the Rocky Mountains and when?
"Name the first state to grant suffrage to women and when.
"What State passed the Port bill and when?
"What State had its boundary changed three times by the U.S. Government and what was its number when admitted?

"What State was the last to ratify the woman suffrage amendment?

"How many men between 18 and 45 years of age served in the World War from the United States?

"What State was originally named Albemarle?"

Anderson pointed out that no one could answer the questions "without an extensive reference library." He complained that "these questions are not asked only in those counties in which the negro population is large"—which he agreed was good policy—"but also in those sections of the State where there are few negroes but the Republican vote is large, and they are asked for the express purpose of disqualifying white voters of the State who are opposed to the dominant organizations. They, of course, have that effect."[50]

Democratic and Republican opponents of the Martin organization did not so much disagree with its probusiness, white supremacy policies as they disapproved of the domineering, manipulative, and often-undemocratic methods by which Martin (and to a lesser extent, Swanson) ran the party machinery. The corruption of the political process was pervasive and involved both political parties. In the 1920 congressional campaign in the district that included the Shenandoah Valley and the northern Piedmont and Blue Ridge counties, the badly divided Democratic Party pulled out all the stops to beat back a stiff Republican challenge. Democratic county treasurers paid men's poll taxes and probably the poll taxes of some of the first women who ever voted in Virginia. Democratic county registrars illegally but publicly assisted Democrats to register to vote and later boasted about it. Democratic election judges illegally but publicly assisted Democrats to mark their ballots and later boasted about it. And even though the law required that each voting precinct be overseen by three judges of election representing the two major political parties, in some places, as in Albemarle County, the county judge who appointed all the election officials appointed men who had voted in the Democratic Party primary earlier that year to serve as Republican precinct judges in the general election. In one of those precincts the Democrat who served as the Republican judge testified that there had been no real Republican judge there for at least eight years. The corruption was so widespread that the Republican majority in the House of Representatives, after taking more than 2,000 pages of sworn testimony from officials and voters, disallowed about one-third of all of the votes cast in the district. The House disallowed a few more Democratic than Republican votes, converting a narrow Democratic victory into a narrow Republican victory.[51]

During the prolonged inquiry into party misbehavior in that election, Campbell Bascom Slemp, then the Republican congressman from southwestern Virginia and probably the most influential Republican in the South, somehow acquired and then published in the *Congressional Record* the correspondence of some Democratic Party officials who were raising money and paying poll taxes for the 1922 congressional race in his district. Slemp hoped thereby to buttress the charges that Republicans were making about the illegal and unethical behavior of the state's Democrats.[52] At almost the same time, though, Democrats somehow obtained photostatic copies of some of Slemp's private correspondence with Republican Party workers and men whom he had helped acquire federal jobs and had those letters printed in the *Congressional Record*, too. The letters clearly demonstrated that Slemp financed the state's Republican Party through dunning public officials, and that he awarded the best jobs to the men who contributed the most money. The Democrats believed that publication of the letters would destroy the Republican's political future.[53]

Neither party gained or lost by the publication of the two sets of letters. It was very well known that both parties employed those tactics. The state's election laws virtually required that they do so in order to function. The editor of the Roanoke *Times* headlined his editorial on the publication of the private letters "When the Pot Calls the Kettle Black." The Bristol *Herald-Courier's* articles made it appear that each party's leaders were merely jealous of the other party for occasionally beating them at the same game. The editor of the *Southwest Times* in Pulaski wrote, "Honestly, it is so funny for Mr. Slemp to charge the Democrats of the Ninth District with the use of money to further their cause that no surprize should be elicited if marble and bronze statues throughout the Ninth were to grin.... Since when have the Republican leaders in the Ninth District sprouted wings of political integrity and discovered horns and cloven hoofs on their political adversaries? It is to laugh!"[54]

But it was not funny, nor were other consequences of the undemocratic political structure that the Constitution of 1902 reinforced. The ideology of white supremacy that Paul Brandon Barringer enunciated on the eve of the Convention of 1901–2 fitted hand in glove with the undemocratic elitism of the founders of the Association for the Preservation of Virginia Antiquities and other Virginia organizations and institutions. Most of the state's leading educators, journalists, businessmen, and white clergymen shared in the racism and elitism that in Virginia were closely linked. Faculty members at the University of Virginia joined Barringer to become national leaders in the eugenics movement that sought to protect what they and many other Americans believed was best in Anglo-American culture from threats from inferior people such as Asians, Eastern Europeans, and of course Africans and their descendants.

There were other classes of inferior people, too, many of them poor or poorly educated white Virginians. The medical science of the time to which Brandon and the other University of Virginia researchers contributed identified some diseases as inheritable, and they classified some manifestations of socially undesirable behavior as inheritable diseases. Among them were epilepsy, feeblemindedness, alcoholism, and inability to restrain sexual appetites. In their opinion, improvement of society required that those conditions be eliminated, and the best way to eliminate them was to stop the train of inheritance, to prohibit those undesirable people from breeding.[55]

In Virginia's mental hospitals, as elsewhere in the United States, physicians surgically sterilized men and women who appeared to exhibit evidence of those supposedly inherited diseases or undesirable traits. Legal challenges to the practice in several states threatened to remove from the state's agents the ability to improve the culture by that means. So the Virginia General Assembly enacted a new law to authorize the practice, and hospital administrators, physicians, and attorneys contrived a rigged case to obtain from the Supreme Court of the United States a ruling to legalize involuntary surgical sterilization. They selected a young white unmarried woman, Carrie Elizabeth Buck, then confined to a public mental hospital, to be the plaintiff and entered into the court record a medical determination that she was feebleminded, was the daughter of an unmarried feebleminded mother, and was the mother of an illegitimate feebleminded infant. The evidence for the diagnosis of congenital, inherited social incapacity was that Buck's mother was not married when Carrie Buck was conceived, and that Buck was not married when she gave birth. In fact, Buck's mother was married, Buck had been raped, and Buck's infant baby was not then or thereafter feebleminded. The sexual promiscuity that the two births supposedly demonstrated was the evidence that Buck was incapable of living a moral life in decent society and therefore should not be allowed to have more children.

The contrived case had its intended result, and in 1927 the Supreme Court of the United States in *Buck v. Bell* gave its enthusiastic approval for states to require people to undergo involuntary surgical sterilization if deemed likely to produce children with inherited medical or socially unacceptable conditions. During the following decades about 8,300 institutionalized Virginians were sterilized against their will or without their knowledge, and more than 50,000 other Americans in other states were, too. Medical men and social engineers in Adolf Hitler's Germany openly admired and emulated the Virginia example. The Virginia advocates of eugenic sterilization did not speak or write openly and in exactly the same terms as the Germans did about creating a master race, but they did speak and write about improving the genetic health of Americans and American society, and some of them took pride in the admiration of the Nazis. No doubt, though, many of the Virginians, Americans, and Europeans who were sterilized probably were medically fit, mentally sound, and socially responsible, even though laws, judges, and hospital staffs in Virginia defined them as not socially desirable.[56]

A distinguished Virginia public health pioneer, Dr. Bathurst Browne Bagby, the man who recalled with pride how his uncle had cheated Republican voters in King and Queen County, sharply criticized the performance of Virginia's state and local governments for neglecting the health and safety of powerless Virginians. "In reading the discussions on taxes," he wrote to the Richmond *News Leader* in 1927 when the governor and the General Assembly were reorganizing the administration and revamping the tax laws in order to reduce spending and taxes, "I am carried back to the 'good old days' when taxes were low. . . . I remember the dilapidated one-room school that ran only five months in the year, and was often conducted by a teacher whose chief qualification was that she was a near relative of a school trustee.

"I remember the 'good old days' when we did not have to pay taxes to keep up our normal schools, our insane asylums, our hospitals, our feeble-minded institutions, our tuberculosis sanatoria, our state department of welfare, or our state department of health. If we had such activities at all, they were so inadequately supported that they were of little service to the people of the state.

"I remember the good old days when the county of King and Queen hired an old peg-leg negro man to mind a crazy woman who lived one mile below Stevenville. He tied her hands behind her, hobbled her ankles and led her about with a rope. She was securely tied to her bed at night with rope and chain. Of course, she developed bed sores. Now, after forty years, I can still hear her raving and see the ropes cutting into her flesh. When she was laid to rest in the grave, behind DUDLEY DIGGES' old home, the closing words of the prayer of her preacher, UNCLE KINGSTON ROY, where these: 'LORD, yesterday her mind and her body was diseased, she was full of sores; but we thank Thee, LORD, that now her soul is at rest with Thee.'

"Yes, they were the 'good old days' of low taxes and lower service, of larger ignorance and blacker misery."[57] Bagby feared in the 1920s that the state's political leaders were going to turn back the clock on the modest improvements in education and public health that he had seen during his career.

That was the government that twentieth-century Virginians got after 1902 when what Alfred Thom called "the honest heart" of its "Anglo-Saxon electorate" was let loose, when the ability to control government was once again confined to a small minority of elite white people.

11

THE
BYRDOCRACY

Harry Flood Byrd (1887–1966) (courtesy of the Library of Virginia) was a member of the Senate of Virginia, governor, and from 1933 to 1965 a member of the United States Senate. As the dominant leader of the small group of white men who directed the Democratic Party of Virginia, he was the most influential white man in twentieth-century Virginia. His party organization insisted on maintaining white supremacy and preventing most white and black Virginians from voting. A skillful political manipulator, he pursued government policies and a political agenda that favored business interests at the expense of labor and that resisted expanding public services and improving public education. In the 1950s Byrd mobilized his organization against desegregation of the public schools. His Massive Resistance laws threatened the existence of the state's public school system and contributed to the demise of his organization shortly after his death.

THE EARLIEST SURVIVING TEXT OF A speech in the Papers of Harry Flood Byrd Sr. in the library of the University of Virginia is an undated typescript prepared during his first campaign for a seat in the Senate of Virginia in 1915. It bears revisions in his characteristic scrawl, and phrases from the speech and its key elements appeared in his hometown newspaper, the *Winchester Evening Star,* which he owned, on 23 July, 27 September, and 9 and 29 October 1915. The speech is about public education and public highways. Byrd favored allowing voters to elect superintendents of schools rather than having the state board of education appoint them; he wanted to forbid the state board of education from frequently changing which textbooks could be used in classrooms; and he supported a system of public education that prepared boys and girls for what he called useful work rather than for college. Byrd also criticized engineers of the state's highway department for operating the public highway system inefficiently and without adequate knowledge of local needs. He proposed that local political leaders, not professional engineers alone, determine what roads to build and how to keep them in repair. "We are confronted by the fact," Byrd's text states, "that we must get back to the fundamental principles of representative government, of government of the people, by the people and for the people, and away from government of local affairs by State Bureaus and the centralization of power at the State Capital."[1]

Byrd won the election in 1915 and was reelected twice. He served for ten years in the Senate of Virginia, where he became one of the assembly's strongest critics of the reforming administration of Governor Westmoreland Davis. Byrd charged him with concentrating political power in the office of governor. Byrd's 1915 speech and his criticisms of Davis contained the essence of all of his speeches and public papers for the entire span of fifty years between his first election to the Senate of Virginia in 1915 and his retirement from the Senate of the United States in 1965. In effect, Byrd delivered the same message in every speech for half a century, for one-seventh of the whole history of Virginia. He altered the nouns and the names to suit the occasion of each subsequent version of the speech, and after his term as governor, from 1926 to 1930, he transferred the object of his criticism from the state government to the federal government. After that, except briefly during the administration of Governor James H. Price, from 1938 to 1942, there is almost no complaint in his public or private utterances about concentration of power in the hands of the governor of Virginia or in the Virginia state government in Richmond.

For the rest of his life, Byrd ineffectively fought concentration of power in Washington and simultaneously and very effectively wielded extraordinary political power concentrated in Richmond through the agencies of his political party organization, the substantial majority that his Democratic Party organization always had in the General Assembly, and the power of the office of governor that he had increased.

Harry Byrd was the dominant person in Virginia's politics and government from 1922 when he became chair of the Democratic Party's state central committee until his retirement from the United States Senate in 1965. He was in charge of the majority faction of the Virginia Democratic Party for more than half of the time between the Democrats' overthrow of the Readjusters in the 1880s and his own death in 1966. He was the dominant political personality in Virginia for forty-three years, for about one-eighth of the whole history of Virginia between the arrival of Captain Christopher Newport at Jamestown in 1607 and his own retirement. Byrd's dominant role in the dominant faction of the dominant party in the state lasted longer and was of more consequence to state government and to the people of the state than the political leadership role of any other Virginian ever. It was not only unparalleled in Virginia's history, it may have been without parallel in the South's history and perhaps in the nation's.[2]

Virginia's laws gave Democratic Party officials almost complete control over the political processes long before Byrd rose to political prominence, and the party's leaders at the state and local levels had polished their techniques of management to a high gloss. Unlike the members of many or most durable political organizations, Byrd and his political organization displayed admirable personal honesty. They did not steal money, they did not accept secret bribes, they did not funnel public money into the pockets or bank accounts of their supporters or even of themselves. They set a standard of public probity that earned praise even from some of their political opponents. Byrd had famous twinkling eyes, a handsome, boyish face (during the early years), and a modest public decorum that sometimes diverted attention away from his manipulative manner and the undemocratic conduct and consequences of his political behavior. A man introducing Byrd as the speaker at a gathering of Democrats in the 1920s or early 1930s referred to some of the public criticism of Byrd. Then he turned and pointed toward Harry Byrd and told the audience to look at him, as if to ask, Could that man do those wicked things? They looked, and they just laughed.[3]

Byrd and his organization thrived on praise for the public policies they promoted that saved taxpayer money and also on their reputation for personal honesty as if they deserved special credit with the voters for not being crooks, as if it was their special qualification for public leadership that they possessed the virtues that ordinary people practiced to keep out of hell and the penitentiary.[4] But Byrd's own father was once quoted as saying that although his son was a genius at organizing and running things, "Harry had the face of a angel, but the heart of a pirate."[5]

Harry Byrd and his political allies did worse than steal money. They stole democracy. It is true that he and his closest political supporters did not disfranchise black and poor white Virginians in 1902. The generation that preceded them did that, so in effect Byrd and his fellow party leaders were receivers of stolen goods, but they approved of and politically profited from and also prolonged that sabotage of representative democracy and therefore were fully culpable accomplices after the fact. Many of the senior party officials early in Byrd's career had taken part in the disfranchisement, and most of them supported him later. After 1902 the Virginia electorate was small and therefore easily managed in the hands of skillful political manipulators, than whom none was more skillful than Harry Byrd.

He succeeded in a political system that was less democratic than it had ever been, even during the most restrictive days of the colonial period. He and his organization killed every attempt to expand the electorate, whether by reducing or eliminating the poll tax, making the process of voter registration easier, requiring that tax collectors and registrars treat white people and black people alike, treat Democrats and Republicans alike, or in any other way to make it practicable for people who were not likely to support their political agenda to vote against it or to vote at all. Their deliberate refusal to change anything in the way that the state's politics worked had racist origins and effects, and it also had elitist social and political origins and effects.

In January 1922 following a chain of fortuitous circumstances that had they taken different turns might have altered the course of twentieth-century Virginia history, Harry Byrd became chair of the Democratic Party state central committee. In the autumn of 1919 Senator Thomas Staples Martin had died, and Governor Davis, eager to take over and remodel the party into a more progressive one, named Carter Glass, an old foe of the organization, as Martin's successor in the United States Senate. The other senior party leader, Senator Claude A. Swanson, quickly seduced Glass into joining the organization, and Davis's challenge to Swanson in the 1922 senatorial primary was already going nowhere when two other senior party officials died, Congressman Henry D. Flood and party chair Rorer James. Byrd was a member in good standing of the Martin-Swanson organization and was also Flood's nephew and an increasingly influential member of the Senate of Virginia midway through his second four-year term. The party's remaining leaders helped him obtain the chairmanship, giving him a remarkable opportunity in a critical year to make a statewide name for himself.[6]

In 1922 the Democratic Party organization smashed Davis's challenge to Swanson's renomination, and Byrd helped Democrats defeat Republicans for political control of the mountainous Ninth Congressional District in south-western Virginia. He led a successful referendum campaign the following year to defeat a proposal to issue bonds to finance highway construction. Byrd's success in the referendum literally paved the way for his election as governor in 1925. Construction of roads thereafter was by his pay-as-you-go system of financing from current revenue raised by vehicle licenses and taxes on gaso-line and tires. Byrd became famous for advocating and building good roads, although the state built new roads more slowly under the pay-as-you-go plan than it would have had it raised more money more speedily by issuing bonds.

Byrd acquired a reputation as a progressive governor, progressive by the lean standards of the 1920s. His first executive action as governor was to estab-lish the eight-hour day as the standard for state employees, which might have seemed like a progressive reform had the standard before he became governor not been a seven-hour day.[7] What Byrd called the Program of Progress con-sisted of a reformation of the state's tax structure and a comprehensive admin-istrative overhaul of the state government bureaucracy to increase administra-tive responsibility and efficiency.[8] He promoted it as good for business, and he promoted it as good government and as a means of keeping taxes low, but one of its undoubted consequences was an increase in the concentration of polit-ical power in the office of governor. The reforms reduced from seven to three the number of statewide officeholders the people directly elected. The gover-nor gained additional appointive powers and supervisory and budget powers that in their effects directly contradicted nearly everything that he had said in his 1915 speech and during his opposition to Westmoreland Davis's compara-tively modest reforms of the state budget system. Davis in turn became a per-sistent critic of excessive concentrations of political power in the governor's office and in Richmond when and after Harry Byrd was governor.

Byrd's administrative reorganization was much admired and in some re-spects deserves to be. He hired a nationally known consulting firm to study the state bureaucracy and to recommend changes consistent with the best private-sector business practices. The consulting firm also studied the orga-nization and administration of the state's city and county governments and found them badly overstaffed, chronically inefficient, easily susceptible to cor-ruption, and in need of a drastic reformation in the interest of economy, effi-ciency, and honest public administration, the trinity of administrative goals that Byrd campaigned on when pushing through his reform of the state's bu-reaucracy. "In fact," the consultants' report summarized the findings, "there is nothing to commend the present form of county government in Virginia. In many of the counties it is grossly political, careless, wasteful, and thor-oughly inefficient. It has been that way for years, but still it exists and seems to flourish."[9]

Byrd quietly killed that part of the consultants' report so dead that not even his most strenuous critics realized how well he had deprived them of ammunition with which to attack his overall plan by pointing out how much the operations of the local courthouse rings contradicted the principles on which the state reorganization was based and how cynical it was for Byrd to place the one on the high road to enactment and to steer the other into the ditch. The courthouse rings supplied jobs to the organization's key supporters at the local level and were both the fulcrum and the lever by which the state's party officials commanded loyalty, enforced discipline, and to a very remarkable extent determined who could register to vote and whose votes got counted.[10]

Byrd's reform of the state government and his saving of the courthouse rings from reform worked together to reinforce the power of the party leadership to manage all governments in the state and all Democratic Party affairs with concentrated efficiency when it was in possession of the governorship (which it was for all but four years from 1926 to 1966) and had a majority in both houses of the General Assembly (which it had in every single one of those years). Byrd's advocacy of efficiency and economy earned praise even as it deflected the attention of some journalists and historians away from the operational consequences that clearly augmented the political power concentrated in the small inner circle of the Byrd organization. Political opponents of Byrd's reorganization of the state government were unable to weaken or destroy the power-enhancing, undemocratic political culture that flourished through the linkage of the courthouse rings with the governor's increased appointive powers and the General Assembly's ability to regulate local governments and to appoint all of the judges in the state and through them the state's election officials.

Byrd's Republican opponent in the 1933 senatorial election charged that Byrd and his organization were "substituting Byrdocracy for democracy in Virginia."[11] Some Democratic leaders, too, who began their careers earlier in the century when a very modest progressivism wielded some significant influence in the party, objected to Byrd's administrative reforms as benefiting the wrong people. Former governor and then Congressman Andrew Jackson Montague praised some of the proposals and then lectured Byrd perceptively but condescendingly that "efficiency of government is not the chief end of republican institutions. A satisfied, contented, prosperous, and enlightened people is such an end. . . . The duty of statesmanship is to balance the efficiency of government with popular approval, an equilibrium desirable and essential."[12]

Montague's comment suggests that he feared that Byrd confused ends and means. Byrd himself was almost certainly not confused. He probably foresaw the consequences and made certain that everybody knew that the enlargement of the powers of the governor's office did not take place until after his term concluded. Byrd's reforms were not otherwise progressive. He displayed little or no interest in either changing or expanding the role of the state government in Virginia. He boasted that his was a businessman's administration, and the policies that he advocated throughout his long career were favorable to business interests, hostile toward organized labor, and utterly dismissive of unorganized working people. By the 1920s the domination of public life in Virginia by an elitist minority was deeply entrenched in law and custom and, as Montague hinted, could be injurious to Virginia and to many Virginians. Because such a large proportion of the population was excluded from the political process, there was no effective political constituency left to advocate public policies that the party organization's principal leaders disliked.

The organization, therefore, faced few or no demands that it could not defeat for improved schools, better public health programs, speedier construction of highways, improved police or fire protection, or a decent system of public libraries; and it initiated few innovations or improvements. Back during World War I, for instance, a friend of Byrd who lived near him in Frederick County was looking over the records of the men who were drafted into the army, and he was appalled to observe that one in ten was unable even to sign his own name and half were functionally illiterate. As a consequence of their ignorance of public events, three out of four of them appeared to be entirely lacking in patriotism. He urged Byrd to support better public education in Virginia,[13] but Byrd never did. Nor did Byrd or his organization ever allow voters to elect school superintendents, as he suggested in 1915, or even (with one exception) to elect local school board members.

None of this is to suggest that Byrd sought power for himself merely for the sake of wielding power. Powerful political leaders in the United States have virtually never done that. Political leaders seek political power in order to pursue objectives: to steal money, to hide misfeasance, or more often to promote economic, social, or foreign policy objectives. Harry Byrd and his organization adopted or protected public policies that they regarded as good for the state as a whole or for its politically dominant leaders. That was what John S. Battle meant when he was running for governor in 1949 and blandly dismissed criticism of the organization as unfounded. "This so-called iniquitous machine," he explained, "is nothing more nor less than a very loosely knit group of Virginians—no membership, no roll—but simply the people in Virginia who usually think alike, who are interested in the welfare of Virginia, who are supremely interested in giving Virginia good government and good public servants, and they usually act together."[14]

That sounded good, but it was a very small group of genuine insiders about whom he spoke, the men who actually consulted and made decisions that were almost always consistent with what Harry Byrd wanted. They, and only they, always, or nearly always, thought alike. They, and only they, were

the ones whose thinking counted. Byrd was very adept at letting his many supporters believe that their opinions influenced his decisions more than they
did and that they were part of an organization that listened to and followed
the wishes of the men in the precincts and legislative districts. The files of correspondence with those men that Byrd preserved clearly indicates, though,
that he flattered those men and let them think that they were more important
to policy considerations and management of the organization than they were,
which kept them faithful supporters of him and his policies and candidates.
The organization was not, within itself, a democracy. Observers knew who
the main men were, but even some men, like John Battle, who mistakenly
thought that they were insiders may not have known how few true insiders
there really were at any given time. If Byrd had not saved his huge files of correspondence, for whatever reasons, we still might not know.

Byrd had very few trusted friends and advisers at any time during his career. During the 1920s and 1930s Richmond businessman William T. Reed
was one, Appomattox state senator Samuel L. Ferguson was another, and
Everett Randolph "Ebbie" Combs, from Lebanon, in Russell County, was
the other; and even before Reed and Ferguson died in the mid-1930s, the
silver-haired Combs became and remained until his retirement for health
reasons at the end of the 1940s the grayest and most eminent éminence grise
in all of Virginia's long history.

Byrd and Combs met early in 1922 not long after Byrd became chair of
the party's state central committee and Combs, the clerk of Russell County,
became chair of the party in the Ninth Congressional District, the district
in southwestern Virginia where Republicans remained strong and regularly
elected some local officials and also the district's congressman. Byrd and
Combs engineered what was called the Redemption of the Fighting Ninth and
elected Democrat George C. Peery to Congress.[15] After Byrd became governor in 1926, he installed Combs in the state comptroller's office in Richmond
and later made him chair of the new State Fee Commission, later renamed
the State Compensation Board. It regulated the incomes, budgets, and office
perquisites of a large number of city and county employees, many of whom
received income from fees that they collected in lieu of a salary, a practice
that was an antique relic of the colonial government and that the consultants
who studied local government had condemned. Those courthouse ring officials helped Byrd become governor. "The fee officers had a meeting in Richmond Monday," Combs reported to him in mid-March 1925 a few months
before the nominating primary, "and I find that you are very strong all over
the State."[16] Because Byrd and Combs almost always thought alike and trusted
each other on everything, they formed a perfect team of political managers.
Until Combs's retirement at the end of the 1940s, he was by a narrow margin
the second most powerful man in Virginia and probably the most feared.[17]

The Byrd organization was not only undemocratic in operation, it was also antidemocratic in its policies and actions. The most antidemocratic and the most corrupt and corrupting aspect of the political process was the poll tax. Because everyone who voted had to have paid the poll tax, both political parties and both factions within the Democratic Party had to raise large sums of money to pay the taxes of voters who could not pay for themselves. It was not strictly legal for party workers to pay poll taxes of other men, but it was not a practice that any Democratic public prosecutor would prosecute a Democrat for doing. The consequence was a great deal of illegal and unethical and undemocratic political activity in which Harry Byrd and all of the other party leaders actively and regularly participated. Indeed, they directed it. The surviving correspondence files of Byrd and his allies are filled with details about raising money and paying poll taxes.

In 1922, for example, when Byrd and Combs were working to redeem the Ninth District's congressional seat from the Republicans, the party leaders received a plea for help on behalf of a man who had moved to the area two years earlier but could not vote "because he has not been properly fixed up." They asked how to have his back taxes paid "in order that we may have the proper stunt done for him here."[18] Paying other men's poll taxes (and beginning in 1920 paying some women's poll taxes) required the party to raise money, which during and after Byrd's tenure as chair of the party central committee it did in part by dunning political officeholders and public employees. In 1922 not long after Byrd became chair of the committee, Jacob N. Brenaman, then the secretary of the committee and an employee of the Senate of Virginia, wrote to him about the clerk of the senate, his boss, who he complained was not paying enough of his salary into the party treasury. "I think Joe Button should give $500 as he got a raise of $1500 in salary," Brenaman wrote. "He only gave $50 to the campaign. I agreed to give $500 if he would raise my salary $500. He went up in the air when it was suggested that he raise my salary $500 although he had asked me to see a number of members in the interest of his raise of $1500."[19] Brenaman was contriving to create a direct diversion of $500 of tax money through his own bank account into the state Democratic Party treasury. A few days later, shortly before he died, he sent Byrd a list of state officials and their salaries and the amounts of money they contributed to the most recent campaign.[20] In the autumn of that year, Byrd suggested that the new secretary "write each of the more important employees a circular letter requesting a contribution to the Ninth District campaign. I do not think that I would write to the minor employees, such as stenographers, janitors, etc."[21]

In August 1924 Byrd wrote to Martin A. Hutchinson, who was working in the office of the secretary of the commonwealth. "I am very anxious to secure a list of the Democratic officeholders in Virginia," he explained. "The purpose of this is to solicit contributions." He instructed Hutchinson to erase carefully from the list of local officeholders the names of all Republicans.[22] Byrd reported to the treasurer of the state committee on 29 September, "So far we have collected about $2,000 in this manner."[23] Two weeks before the election, he asked one of the judges of the State Corporation Commission to work on the employees of his agency to reach its goal.[24] After the election the commissioner of the state Bureau of Labor proudly reported that bureau employees had contributed a total of $200 to the 1924 election campaign and that "our boys contributed their time, day and night, also spent their own money in furthering the campaign; in several cases used their own cars," as if it was deserving of special commendation that the public officials used their own cars at their own expense rather than the agency's government-owned automobiles to raise more than their allotted share. "Should it be necessary to make additional contributions," he reported, "we stand ready to help as our means may permit."[25]

Many Democratic public officials at all levels spent part of their time on the job taking care of the party's financial health and political success. The surviving remnant of the State Democratic Central Committee records includes lists of state employees in 1929 with their salaries and records of their contributions to the Democratic Party. Agency heads collected assessments at a rate of 1 percent of the employees' salary.[26] As O. Victor Hanger, who in 1932 was both secretary of the state central committee and clerk of the Senate of Virginia, wrote to his brother, who worked for him in the clerk's office, "the State Democratic Committee has to depend on the different departments in a large measure to raise the fund with which to run the Campaign. They have laid an assessment against the employees of the Senate, your part of which will be five ($5.00) dollars, and I will appreciate it very much if you will mail me your check for that amount so that I can turn over to them the amount assessed against us. Of course if your heart is enlarged and you want to contribute more than that amount it will be greatly appreciated by them."[27]

In 1933 Ellis F. Hargis, clerk of Russell County and nephew and successor of E. R. Combs in that office, paid another man's poll tax[28] and conspired with an officer of the Clinchfield Coal Company and the treasurer of the town of Lebanon to make certain that reliable Democrats at the mines had paid their poll taxes or had their poll taxes paid for them.[29] Hargis instructed the mine manager to collect the money himself and send it to the treasurer or have the men do it. "Trusting that you gentlemen will go after this matter at once," Hargis wrote, "and divide up the voters so that no man will have more than he feels he can do to see them and urge them to pay their own poll tax."[30] Hargis explained that he was "making an effort to have this done all over the county this year, with a view of getting every Democrat to pay his own poll taxes, thus relieving the party of large expenditures, and making better citizens at the same time."[31]

In 1933 Byrd contributed $500 to qualify voters in two legislative districts,[32] and Combs borrowed $1,000 that year to pay poll taxes in Russell County, cautioning Hargis to "be very careful to qualify no one except those upon whom you can absolutely depend, and I would not undertake to qualify voters who are behind more than one year," presumably because paying back taxes made it too expensive.[33] Hargis reported to Combs in the spring that because the new Roosevelt administration had not yet appointed very many Democrats to federal patronage positions, he could not "borrow against our Federal office holders since none of them are in, and there is no immediate sign of getting any large number of them in."[34] The banking crisis in 1933 made it even more difficult than usual for people to get money to pay poll taxes. Still, a party official in Byrd's own Frederick County reported, "We added about 150 names to the tax list," omitting men who might be "hard to control." He could safely say, "We feel sure that the ones we have put on can be counted on."[35]

In the spring of 1922 Byrd learned that in previous years some Republican county treasurers in the Ninth District had been lax in collecting poll taxes from Republicans but in order to enlarge the list of Republicans eligible to register had collected some poll taxes after the deadline for payment.[36] He quietly informed Democratic officials in the Ninth District that he had arranged secretly to have "special auditors sent to some of the counties to audit the poll taxes promptly on May 8th," the day after the deadline. "This is for the purpose of preventing the Republican Treasurers from padding the list after the date for payment has expired," he explained.[37] Early in the following July, a journalist in Richmond finally learned what had happened and reported "that when treasurers of the thirteen counties of the Ninth District, all of whom are Republicans, closed their poll tax lists on May 7, auditors representing the State Auditor of Public Accounts appeared simultaneously at each treasurer's office and secured from him a certified list of all men and women voters who had paid their poll taxes. Only these certified lists will be used for guidance of judges at the November election. It had long been reported that names of many Republican voters had gotten on the lists after the last day for payment of poll taxes."[38] Democratic public officials did not thus police the behavior of other Democrats but continued, for the most part, to act simultaneously as public officials and as members in good standing of the Democratic Party organization.

It was the business of tax officers and election officers to know who in their communities would likely vote for or against the party organization's candidates. Some county officers served for very long periods of time and in some instances passed the offices along to their sons, grandsons, or nephews, institutionalizing a political influence of great importance. Some of them were very diligent and creative men. In November 1929 the clerk of the southeastern county of Elizabeth City described his new long-range plan. "It shall be our endeavor in this County," he explained to the chair of the state committee, "to make a complete census and record of all the Democrats, with their children and their ages, in order that we may see to it that those Democrats and their children, when they reach the necessary age, have their poll taxes paid and are placed upon the registration books. Each lot will be assigned to some active worker, to look after in every respect politically."[39] When in 1938 Byrd learned that African Americans from Richmond were helping register black voters in three lower Rappahannock River counties, enough, one man remarked, "to give them the balance of power in this section," Byrd's correspondence with his loyal supporters indicates that they planned to take action to stop the registrations but not what action they undertook.[40]

The organization's ability to deliver absentee ballots provided the preferred method of filling ballot boxes and winning elections in southwestern Virginia from the 1920s through the 1940s. Organization Democrats could bend or break the laws that they had made and almost always got away with it. In 1927 the careful Combs consulted with the attorney general, who had received queries about absentee ballots from election officials in southwestern Virginia. The attorney general privately advised Combs, who quietly relayed the information to his lieutenants in the Ninth District, that they should collect all the absentee ballots they could, even going over the state border to obtain ballots from men and women who had temporarily or even permanently moved to coal-mining towns in West Virginia or Kentucky. "You cannot refuse to place a ballot in the box," Combs advised his party workers, "simply because some election officer has exceeded his authority in the matter and has failed in any way to comply with the law." "So long as the voter acts in good faith," Combs continued, knowing that it would be virtually impossible for anybody to prove the contrary, "his vote cannot be thrown out because of the failure of some election officer to comply with the law. The judges of elections should all understand this in order that they may know what their duty is in case of a challenge."[41]

When writing to one another, Byrd organization members from the state committee chair down to the local tax collectors and registrars described their work as "qualifying" voters and "voting" them. Their active verbs, qualifying and voting the reliable Democrats, described the actions of political party operatives manipulating the political process, not the actions of responsible citizens taking part in a free and fair election process. That is, they made certain that organization Democrats' votes were in ballot boxes and counted, even if all of the solemnities of the complicated registration and voting laws had not been punctiliously observed or even if the voter had not personally cast a ballot. A county treasurer in southwestern Virginia explained late in the 1940s, "Down here when a man fails to come in to vote we always mark a ballot and deposit it in the ballot box for him."[42] But in the hotly disputed 1945 primary for lieutenant governor, when the vote went against the organization's favorite in southwestern county of Wise, members of the electoral board there simply destroyed several ballot boxes and their contents. The blatant destruction of ballots failed to turn the trick, though, because a brave judge elsewhere in Virginia—the law permitted the suit to be filed in Richmond rather than on site—invalidated all of the county's remaining votes, allowing the other candidate to win the nomination by an extremely narrow statewide vote.[43] That episode was the worst public election scandal in Virginia during Byrd's lifetime and also one of only two statewide elections between 1922 and 1965 in which his preferred candidate did not win.

When the state's constitution or its laws threatened to create difficulties, party officials brought in the state's attorney general to legitimize what they planned to do. They did that immediately after the 1928 presidential election in which anti-Catholicism and strongly held beliefs about Prohibition caused so many Democrats to vote against the party's Catholic nominee, Alfred E. Smith, that Republican Herbert Hoover won Virginia's electoral votes. The following year, when the state's Democrats were to choose a successor to Byrd as governor, one who Byrd insisted would implement his administrative reforms, the party faced a problem. Party rules stipulated that voters who had not supported the party's nominee in the preceding election could not vote in the party primary. The attorney general declared in a strained decision that made definitions in one part of the law override definitions governing other portions of party rules that the presidential candidate of the Democratic Party was not the nominee of the state party but of the national party, only, and therefore Democrats who had voted for Herbert Hoover for president in 1928 could vote in the 1929 primary.[44] Byrd's choice, John Garland Pollard, won.

The legal and questionable and illegal manipulation of elections that both political parties perpetrated in the state was not unique to Virginia, but its chronic and prolonged practice was a much more serious systemic corruption of democratic politics than the occasional, blatant destruction of a ballot box. It was widespread and belied the often-repeated assertions of the honesty and probity of Harry Byrd and his organization. It became routine. On the day in November 1931 when local elections took place in Frederick County where Byrd owned several large apple orchards, he reassured a friend who was a candidate for reelection. "I went over all my orchard force," he wrote, "and sent all the Democrats up to vote for you and others who would vote for you. I succeeded in keeping at the orchard several Republicans."[45]

Byrd was the most skillful behind-the-scenes political manipulator in twentieth-century Virginia. When in 1933 Congress proposed a constitutional amendment to terminate the failed experiment to prohibit the manufacture, sale, and consumption of alcoholic beverages, the sitting governor, a noted Baptist lay leader who did not drink and did not approve of drinking, refused to call the General Assembly into special session. He knew that it would enact enabling legislation for the necessary ratification convention that he also knew would vote to repeal Prohibition. William T. Reed helped Byrd and his legislative allies employ a little-known provision of the state constitution by which the members of the assembly could call themselves into session. In that instance, removing from the political agenda the divisive issue of Prohibition, about which Byrd cared little or nothing personally, worked to the organization's advantage.[46]

Byrd was also one of the most politically inflexible Virginia Democrats of his generation. He tolerated much less dissent within the party, or even independent-mindedness, than Martin and Swanson had, and he was especially intolerant of anyone who even so much as questioned the policies and practices he had put into place when he was governor. After W. Worth Smith campaigned for the gubernatorial nomination in 1933 against Byrd's preferred candidate, George Peery, Smith felt the sting of Byrd's rejection. "Personally I tried to be loyal to Senator Byrd," he grumbled, "but after a few years I found out that in order to be loyal to him I'd have to become a bullfrog and jump every time he said jump, regardless of my personal views on any subject."[47] Byrd's reputation and conduct indicate that he shared the attitude of William T. Reed toward dissidents. In 1932 Reed told Byrd bluntly, "The only way to make them 'good boys' is to whip the hell out of them and let them come back and prove themselves good before they receive any recognition."[48]

Byrd's inflexibility carried over into national politics and eventually drove away some old and trusted friends and supporters. He and Carter Glass, his longtime colleague in the United States Senate, were much more consistently opposed to the New Deal during the 1930s than a large proportion of the state's voting Democrats, as the election results in 1936 and 1940 demonstrated, to say nothing of the poor white men and women who could not vote in Virginia but shared many economic and social problems with poor white men and women in other Southern states who elected dozens of senators and congressmen who actively supported the New Deal. It is a good rough measure of how far apart Byrd and Franklin D. Roosevelt were that Byrd and his loyal followers were disappointed in Congressman Clifton A. Woodrum, of Roanoke, for supporting the New Deal, and Roosevelt and his allies were disappointed in Woodrum for opposing it.[49] Byrd's opposition to Roosevelt and the New Deal created new adversaries for him in Virginia and was one of the major causes of the rise of a new antiorganization wing of the Democratic Party in the middle of the 1930s. Although Woodrum did not go into the active opposition, some men who shared his political opinions did.

Disagreements about the New Deal were real and profound, but old-fashioned politics created divisions within the state party even before Roosevelt became president in March 1933. Following the 1932 Democratic Party National Convention, in which Byrd was a favorite-son candidate and part of the stop-Roosevelt coalition,[50] he feared that the Roosevelt supporters in Virginia were likely to become dangerous if Roosevelt appointed too many of them to office or allowed Byrd's opponents to control federal patronage.

The Ninth Congressional District in southwestern Virginia was the only district in the state that consistently sent a supporter of the New Deal to Congress. Byrd's men repeatedly tried and failed to field a successful candidate in the Democratic Party primary against John W. Flannagan, who regularly won renomination and reelection as a supporter of the New Deal, the only man from Virginia who served more than one term in Congress as a New Dealer.[51] "I believe the time has come in the ninth district," Combs concluded in 1934, agreeing with Reed, "when the democratic organization should let it be known that it expects to control the policies of the party in that district and that a few dissatisfied kickers will have to go along with the policies of the organization if they expect to get any comfort or recognition."[52]

Byrd's insistence on agreement within the party and on loyalty to his policies and candidates drove a good many men into opposition in the 1930s. Martin A. Hutchinson understood what was happening but professed himself in 1936 "unable to understand the attitude of some of our leaders"—meaning Byrd and Glass—"in giving aid and comfort to those who have all the while opposed the President. I do hope that the common folks of the Nation will have the good of the Nation at heart and that they will come out and vote for the only true friend they have ever had as President."[53]

Hutchinson became one of the leaders of the new opposition. He had entered politics working for Byrd and served as secretary of the commonwealth during Byrd's administration, but after they fell out on a number of issues, he understood as a former insider how Byrd's organization treated its adversaries and apostates. "The Byrd organization has no sympathy whatsoever for any man who desires to think for himself," Hutchinson explained to one of his fellow dissidents, "and for that reason you, myself and others no doubt will feel the ruthless hand of political reaction in Virginia."[54] T. Russell Cather had also been a supporter of Byrd and represented Byrd's own district in the Senate of Virginia—he was the man who had commented on the poor education of men drafted during World War I—but he lost his bid for renomination in the 1939 party primary to a more loyal Byrd supporter who was also a firmer opponent of the New Deal. Cather complained that Byrd had misled him about receiving the organization's support and vowed "that the fight must go on and so long as I retain the physical and mental ability to register a protest I expect to lend my support to any effort which may finally free Virginia of the Byrd dictatorship."[55]

Another man with an occasional independent cast of mind was Ashton Dovell, who as Speaker of the House of Delegates tested the waters in 1940 when he thought that he had earned the right to run for governor the following year, but he returned home from a political tour of the state, as Hutchinson described him, with "every appearance of a man who felt and believed that he had been given the once over by some of his old friends with whom he had worked and that they had passed him under orders from Byrd and his organization."[56] One of Dovell's friends agreed. "It is true that the Byrd organization has passed Dovell by," he observed, "but they used him to serve their purposes and do a lot of work that they wanted done; and when that was completed they threw him overboard. But this shows that this element is running true to form. When one has served them faithfully and well for a given season, and their particular services may no longer be needed, he is slaughtered without a tremor or a sigh. This is the history of the whole organization."[57]

Such disaffection contributed to but did not fully explain an embarrassing episode at the end of 1936. In spite of everything that Byrd could do to prevent it, James H. Price, the lieutenant governor, expertly lined up an overwhelming number of organization loyalists behind his campaign for nomination for governor in 1937. Price had supported Byrd as a member of the House of Delegates during the 1920s and been elected lieutenant governor in 1929. He set aside his ambition to run for governor in 1933 and ran for reelection as lieutenant governor. Price had paid his dues, had worked the system properly, had been loyal, and had carefully cultivated friendships and support from local and regional party leaders. Byrd, though, correctly suspected Price of too much sympathy for the New Deal and of having an independent mind, so he strove mightily to prevent Price from winning the nomination. But Price had secured too many early endorsements, and all of Byrd's alternative candidates self-destructed. At the end of December 1936, many months before the primary election, Byrd gave up and with most of the other insiders who had not already pledged their support to Price conceded in what was called the Christmas rush, saying that he had no wish to dictate who should be governor.[58]

Martin Hutchinson's brother wrote to congratulate him on their prevailing over Byrd for the first time, which was also to be the last time. Of course, he wrote of Byrd, "the public knows he has no desire to dictate who shall be Gov.—It seems his desire has changed at the right time namely 'When he no longer has the power' what a happy co-incident indeed!"[59] Byrd himself privately acknowledged the truth of that statement in a short letter to the widow of Sam Ferguson, who had been one of his most trusted assembly colleagues. "It just seemed to be impossible to work out a solution," he reflected sadly. "Everything we could think of doing was done."[60]

Price made a poorly conceived and halfhearted attempt to break the Byrd organization. He dismissed Combs from the Compensation Board and appointed Hutchinson in his place. (Byrd's supporters in the General Assembly elected Combs clerk of the Senate of Virginia.) Price and State Senator Charles Harkrader, a newspaperman from Bristol, in the southwest, persuaded Roosevelt to appoint Floyd Roberts, a state judge who was one of their allies, to a vacant federal judgeship for the western district of Virginia. Byrd and Glass invoked senatorial courtesy and killed the nomination. Roosevelt then gave up his attempt to purge from office or break the power of Democrats who opposed the New Deal, and he abandoned Price.[61] Four years after Byrd for the only time in his career after the 1920s saw a man he did not approve of take office as governor, he had the satisfaction of seeing one of his most respectable and talented allies installed in that office. That governor, Colgate Whitehead Darden, replaced all of Price's appointees. Harkrader began to refer to Harry Byrd as "Harry the Hater,"[62] and many years later J. Lindsay Almond, who rose to the governor's office before Byrd turned on him following a major policy disagreement, predicted that for his destruction of Roberts's promising judicial career, Byrd would "go through Hell crackling like a dry poplar."[63]

The organization's ability to exclude dissidents from influential Democratic Party positions crippled the antiorganization men, and young men of independent minds who wished to establish themselves in politics found it hard to break into the closed circle. As Hutchinson phrased it, "Byrd and his gang have the money and the local office holders." Sometimes, Hutchinson reflected, "I feel like saying with the Prophet of old 'How long Oh Lord, how long will we have to endure the affliction which has come upon us.'"[64]

It was, indeed, a very formidable organization that never lost another statewide contest after Price's election in 1937, except in 1945 when Byrd's second favorite, who was then a reliable organization supporter, won the nomination for lieutenant governor following the scandal of the destroyed Wise County ballot box. The courthouse rings always provided the votes. A very detailed analysis of the organization completed late in the 1940s concluded that "the total number of Democrats holding some type of position in the State, and consequently somewhat duty bound to support the Democratic candidates, would be approximately fifty-five thousand."[65] Another equally careful study completed about the same time calculated, "On the average, over the years 1925–45, only 11.5 per cent of those 21 and over have voted in Virginia Democratic primaries. . . . Turnout at the polls is so small that the Byrd organization has had to win the support of only from five to seven per cent of the adult population to nominate its candidate for governor in the Democratic primary; its candidate usually has more votes than are necessary."[66]

Political scientist V. O. Key, who conducted the second of the studies, commented on how much the Democratic Party in Virginia differed from any other political party in the South. "Virginia stands alone," he wrote, "as a state in which one Democratic faction consistently commands the support of about three-fourths of those who vote—almost a one-party system within a one-party system."[67] Key selected a particularly apt comparison, considering the character of the organization's leadership, to evoke the political culture of Virginia. "The Commonwealth possesses characteristics more akin to those of England at about the time of the Reform Bill of 1832," he wrote, "than to those of any other state of the present-day South. It is a political museum piece."[68] Key concluded with one of the most famous and often-quoted condemnations of the politics of Harry Byrd's Virginia, "By contrast Mississippi is a hotbed of democracy."[69]

Summarizing his analysis of the state's politics, Key wrote, "In essence, Virginia is governed by a well-disciplined and ably managed oligarchy, of not many more than a thousand professional politicians, which enjoys the enthusiastic and almost undivided support of the business community and the well-to-do generally, a goodly number of whom are fugitives from the New York state income tax. Organization spokesmen in Congress look out for the interests of business, and the state government, although well managed, manifests a continuing interest in the well-being of the well-to-do. The quid pro quo for support of the organization is said to be taxation favorable to corporations, an antilabor policy, and restraint in the expansion of services, such as education, public health, and welfare. The organization pursues a negative policy on public services; if there is an apparent demand it will grudgingly yield a bit here and there, but it dedicates its best efforts to the maintenance of low levels of public service. Yet it must be said that the organization gives good government; while the school system is inadequate it is about as good as the money appropriated will buy. The organization, however, has an 'adding machine mentality'; attached to the fetish of a balanced budget, it takes a short-run view that almost invariably militates against the long-run interests of the state. Men with the minds of tradesmen do not become statesmen."[70]

About the Byrd's organization's insular character, Key wrote with pungent insight, "In almost the manner of a churchly order, or the Communist party, the machine tests the loyalties and abilities of its neophytes. Those with unquestioned faith in the organization and belief in its doctrine, are advanced. Those found wanting, either in ability or doctrine, remain in a lowly status."[71] Key also accurately described how the organization usually selected candidates for statewide office: "Generally over a period of more than a year before the primary, sentiment of the organization rank and file crystallizes. Some aspirants see that they cannot win the favor of the organization stalwarts and drop out of the running. The high command of the organization—Senator Byrd and his close associates—listens to the expressions of approval and disapproval flowing up the hierarchy and eventually reaches a decision. 'The nod' is Virginia terminology for the decision of the high command. Once the 'nod' is given, the newspapers begin to carry announcements by lesser leaders in support of the organization designee and the ranks close for the primary."[72] Nodding quietly in the direction of the favored candidate rather than forthrightly anointing him presented the public the appearance of a consensus arrived at through genteel consultations, as John S. Battle had tried to explain, but like Harry Byrd's twinkling smile it concealed the skillful manipulation of men and process.

Key also correctly identified the critical factors linking political and governmental control. "The powers exercised by the central government of Virginia over local officials," he wrote, "makes it difficult to found an opposition faction on control of local governments. The punitive powers of the organization, through its control of the perquisites of local officials"—the Compensation Board—"and its ability to obstruct local bills in the legislature, can discourage competing factions territorially segregated."[73] Assessing the state of the opposition a decade after Price's failed challenge to the organization, Key concluded, "The opposition consists of labor groups, parts of the Negro population, reform groups, those favoring expanded public services, disaffected Byrd followers, and liberals generally. . . . Theirs has been a unity of desperation." Within the Democratic Party of Virginia, Key wrote, setting up a play on Harry Byrd's name, "One wing is strong and well feathered; the other flutters limply."[74]

V. O. Key accurately described the functioning of the Byrd organization, its base of political support, and the public policy consequences of its domination of the state's politics, but he was a poor prophet in suggesting near the end of the 1940s that the opposition was so feeble that it merely fluttered limply. Because of the undemocratic and antidemocratic actions and policies of the Byrd organization, increasing numbers of Virginians after World War II challenged it at the polls and in the General Assembly. Often during those years Byrd was distracted from close management of his organization. In the United States Senate he presided over his famous committee that identified wasteful or inefficient federal government spending, but even though he was one of the best-known members of the Senate, he was probably also one of its most overrated members. He never sponsored or could claim credit for passage of any major piece of legislation, and although he spoke constantly on the Senate floor and to business and professional organizations in opposition to every major reform proposed while he was a member of the Senate, he was seldom able to delay, and he was never able to block, passage of any one of those bills.[75] That preoccupation may have played a small part in his failure to recruit and nurture a new generation of compatible and talented political leaders in Virginia, and that in turn may have contributed to or added to the seriousness of the challenges that his organization faced.[76] Still, Byrd and his organization did not lose.

Hutchinson ran against Byrd and lost in the Democratic senatorial primary in 1946, and antiorganization candidates seriously threatened organization candidates in several statewide primaries, even forcing Byrd once to enlist some Republicans to help his preferred candidate win the nomination for governor.[77] Although the men who won nomination for the most important offices—governor, lieutenant governor, attorney general, and United States senator after Carter Glass died in 1946—and who won election were not always Harry Byrd's first choices, never after James Price in 1937 did the party nominate a man he could not comfortably accept.

Byrd's allies and supporters in the General Assembly beat back nearly all attempts at significant increases in spending for education or other public services. The independently minded legislators who were referred to at the end of the 1940s and early in the 1950s as Young Turks never gained enough members in the two houses of the General Assembly to dislodge the powerful Byrd organization leaders who dominated all of the committees. Speaker E. Blackburn Moore, who was personally and politically very close to Byrd, presided over the House of Delegates from 1950 to 1967 and used his power to keep the few Republicans and all of the Young Turks politically impotent. He refused to appoint Republicans and some of the more annoying Young Turks to committees, or he appointed them to committees that never met. Sometimes he or his friends who presided over the committees refused to notify them of committee meetings or summarily killed their bills in committee.[78] The humiliating degradation of elected legislators was a conspicuous mockery of the parliamentary practices that had evolved in Virginia during the colonial period and that provided the most important model for representative government when the United States came into being. In the Virginia General Assembly, even while Byrd was distracted with his futile attempts to reduce federal spending and even after Combs retired from politics at the end of the 1940s, the organization remained in firm control until after the crisis of Massive Resistance reached its denouement.

The longevity of the Byrd organization and its enduring domination of the state's politics owed much to the political and financial support that Byrd and the organization received from the state's (and the nation's) business leaders, who shared with him a strong suspicious dissatisfaction with the increasingly expensive and intrusive actions of the federal government, beginning in the 1930s and continuing almost unabated throughout the remainder of Byrd's life. He and they distrusted and disliked the activities and consequences of the New Deal and the Fair Deal and their successors of the 1960s. They opposed the higher taxes on businesses and wealthy people that accompanied those policies.[79] They particularly despised the intervention of the federal government into their special field of managing race relations at the state level.

The poll tax that had been instituted in 1902 to preserve political white supremacy served as the symbolic lightning rod that attracted opponents of the chronically corrupted political process. Several times during the final years of the 1930s and during the 1940s, Republicans, Democratic opponents of the organization, and even some organization members in good standing, such as Governor Darden, recommended abolition of the poll tax. Stalwart defenders of white supremacy always rolled out distorted memories of William Mahone's Readjusters or pointed to actions of Eleanor and Franklin Roosevelt that appeared to threaten that most important basis of the Democratic Party's claim to leadership. Supporters of the Byrd organization and of the poll tax defeated all attempts at change.[80]

The fate of a 1941 study of the poll tax that Governor Price requested from the Virginia Advisory Legislative Council is particularly illuminating. Prepared by University of Virginia political scientist Robert K. Gooch, the report branded the poll-tax law as administered in Virginia a source of political corruption and an embarrassment to the state. It also declared bluntly that opposition to repeal was "founded on disbelief in political democracy as the basis of government. . . . Advocacy of retention of the poll-tax and genuine belief in political democracy are basically irreconcilable."[81] Gooch understood that the poll tax operated as the property qualification had functioned before 1851 and that men who believed in retaining the poll tax not only wanted to keep African Americans from voting but also to keep too many white Virginians from voting. Those men did not accept the essential political equality of white people that had gained acceptance in Virginia during the 1830s and 1840s and brought about universal white manhood suffrage in 1851. Instead, they shared the racist and elitist ideas of the men who in 1902 had destroyed universal white manhood suffrage. The Advisory Legislative Council refused to release or publish Gooch's report. Legislative officials loyal to Byrd persisted in that suppression and would not even allow a graduate student to see its copy in the 1960s. Ultimately, Gooch published his own copy nearly thirty years after completing the study.[82]

So powerful was the opposition to any relaxation in the regime of white supremacy that early in 1948 some of Byrd's most stalwart supporters in the General Assembly tried to enact a bill to exclude the name of Harry Truman from the ballot in that autumn's presidential election. But that bill was so indefensible that even a majority of the Democrats in the General Assembly refused to support it. Byrd later issued a statement that he would remain silent—called at the time a golden silence—during the campaign. He had, in fact, not given any genuine support to a Democratic Party presidential candidate since 1932. Byrd's endorsement of Roosevelt in 1936 was grudging, and in 1940 and 1944 he effectively sat out the presidential contests, nominally endorsing but not supporting Roosevelt. Thereafter he placed himself at so great a distance from the national leadership of his party that his silences were golden opportunities for Republicans to lure Virginia Democrats into voting for Republican presidential candidates. In 1948, though, Byrd's silence backfired. Many of his supporters voted for the segregationist governor of South Carolina, J. Strom Thurmond, rather than for the Republican nominee, allowing the still-small number of African American voters in Virginia to swing the state for Harry Truman,[83] the last time since 1872 and the last time but one in the twentieth century that a Democratic presidential candidate carried the state.

The civil rights movement that was then gaining strength in the country eventually undermined the foundations of the Byrd organization's control of state politics and government. After the Supreme Court of the United States ruled in 1954 that mandatory racial segregation in public schools was unconstitutional, Byrd and the General Assembly responded with a program that they called Massive Resistance. The legislature passed a law empowering the governor to close any school that desegregated. Within five years many white Virginians decided that support for the poor public school system was more important than maintaining segregation. Moreover, in 1959 federal and state courts declared the Massive Resistance laws unconstitutional. Massive Resistance was not simply a sad lapse of leadership or merely a crass ploy to prolong the dominance of Byrd's political organization. It may have been both of those things, but it was also the logical consequence of the beliefs and actions of Harry Byrd and his closest allies throughout his long career. The poll tax, the exclusive party organization, the elitist views of its leaders, and the state's enforcement of racial segregation were all of a part, a deliberate and systematic denial of the basic rights of American citizenship and of human rights perpetrated with what criminal lawyers accurately define as malice aforethought.

Men who shared Byrd's perspective on politics and public policy continued for years after his death in 1966 to be a majority of the General Assembly, even though some of them stopped defending their support of Massive Resistance after it had failed. They were the men who prevented Virginia from ratifying the Equal Rights Amendment in the 1970s, using the same kinds of arguments and parliamentary tactics that the organization's leaders had employed to defeat ratification of the woman suffrage amendment in the 1910s and to impose and defend Massive Resistance to desegregation in the 1950s. Some of them recalled, sometimes ruefully and sometimes wistfully, the rough efficiency with which the organization had conducted its political business. At the conclusion of a hectic General Assembly session in 1973, an exasperated member of the Senate of Virginia sighed, "It makes you appreciate Harry Byrd. He really knew how to run things."[84]

What destroyed the organization, just as what had destroyed slavery, were actions of the federal government, some of them at the instigation of Virginians who used the federal courts to invalidate its practices. In no Southern state was the civil rights movement so conspicuously a legal challenge to segregation and Jim Crow and so little a political challenge. The Supreme Court cases that outlawed the poll tax originated in Virginia,[85] forcing open the ballot box to black people and many poor white people who had been excluded during the long reign of the Byrd organization. Congressional passage of the Civil Rights Act of 1964 and the Voting Rights Act of 1965 enabled significant numbers of African Americans in Virginia to register and vote and run for office for the first time since the 1880s and to be elected to city and county offices and the General Assembly.

Harry Byrd died in 1966 just as the actions of Congress and the federal courts were beginning to take effect. If at any time during the 1950s or 1960s anybody knew about or remembered Byrd's campaign speech of 1915, it would have been a delicious irony to point out an inconsistency between that speech and one of the actions of the General Assembly when fighting against desegregation. In 1915 Byrd had advocated public election of local school superintendents, but the assembly never changed the law, and in fact only one jurisdiction in the entire state during his lifetime ever persuaded the legislature to allow its voters to elect members of the school board. (Everywhere else city councils and county boards of supervisors appointed school board members.) Arlington County was the only jurisdiction in which voters gained the right to elect school board members, but after the elected school board there voted in the mid-1950s to allow a token desegregation of the public schools in compliance with the law of the land as the Supreme Court of the United States had enunciated it, the assembly jerked away the right of the voters to elect a school board that might again do something that Byrd and the organization did not approve.[86] Yet another sacrifice of democracy on the altar of white supremacy and political control.

The real and lasting legacy that Harry Byrd left Virginia was not the public policies that he promoted or the defeat of policies he opposed. It was that advocates of alternatives were systematically and deliberately excluded from the political process to such an extent that their voices could not be heard and their alternative proposals never got seriously considered. Advocates for those alternatives had no voice, no opportunity to make their case, no chance to participate in their own government. In 1949 when Francis Pickens Miller was running for governor in the party primary against one of the Byrd organization's loyal members, he made a speech in southwestern Virginia and likened the organization's domination of Virginia public life to the tyranny in the Soviet Union. A member of the audience went up to him afterward and asked, "Tell me, how can I git out of Russia without having to leave Virginia?"[87]

The organization collapsed speedily following Byrd's resignation from the United States Senate in 1965 and his death the following year. Virginians who believed in democratic government and liberty for all had outflanked him in the courts and in Congress and had destroyed his organization's ability to exclude most of the state's residents from the political system, which was the essential basis for his organization's ability to control the state's politics. What Byrd and his organization left behind was an undemocratic legacy of exclusiveness, arrogance, and bitterness. Both his methods and his policies were undemocratic and antidemocratic. His personal financial probity counts for little when weighed in the scales with the effects on his fellow citizens of his public policies and even more so of his political actions. He and his organization killed every political challenge, every proposal for democratic change, and every chance to revive representative democracy in the state. His opponents throughout the one-seventh of Virginia's history in which he dominated its dominant political party and therefore dominated the state criticized and challenged him, but his organization had made it impossible for them to defeat him.

The bitterness of people whom the government under the Byrd organization deprived of their citizenship rights was intense. So was the disappointment of his supporters whom he alienated. What those men said about him was not much different from what his other critics said, but because they had been beneficiaries of the organization before being its victims, their complaints are particularly revealing. Listen to J. Lindsay Almond. He was never an intimate of Byrd or one of the organization's insiders, but he was an able organization man who served in Congress, as attorney general, and as governor. He defended the bad cause of Massive Resistance in court and in the governor's office, but rather than persist and go to jail, as Byrd wanted him to, Almond abandoned Massive Resistance in January 1959 after federal and state courts declared unconstitutional the laws that implemented it. Almond supported John F. Kennedy for president at the Democratic National Convention in 1960, "which did not sit well," he remarked understatedly, "with the mogul of Winchester."[88] He soon suffered Byrd's wrath. After Kennedy later appointed Almond to the Court of Customs and Patent Appeals, Byrd delayed a vote on confirmation for fourteen months. "He never spoke to me again," Almond recalled. "He would turn his back on me in a crowd. He wouldn't even speak to my wife."[89] Having freed himself from the need to conform any longer to Byrd's wishes, Almond wrote, "It is quite a relief to experience absolution from being across the Senatorial barrel with a 'Byrd-noose' around your neck."[90]

Halfway through Byrd's long political career and shortly before the United

States entered World War II, Jonathan Daniels, a crusading Southern reformer, condemned and ridiculed the undemocratic and antidemocratic practices of the Byrd organization. "The Virginia pattern," he wrote in a widely
noted journal article in 1941, "shows that it is easy for the people to lose their
liberties in this American democracy, but even in a democracy it is hard as hell
to get them back. . . . Virginia, it seems to me, has a first-class claim on democracy's cradle and also on democracy's jail." He concluded, "It's a joke, but at
this time in the world's history it isn't so funny in this country as it would be
perhaps in Berlin or Rome. There they could laugh and laugh."[91] Many years
later Mary Aydelotte Marshall, who got into politics in the 1950s attempting
to keep the public schools in Northern Virginia open during Massive Resistance and later served with distinction in the General Assembly, recalled how
in those days people paraphrased Daniels in mock imitation of Colonial Williamsburg advertising slogans. "Come to Virginia and see the birthplace of
American democracy," she said and then paused for effect before concluding,
"and its grave."[92]

12

I WAS
BORN
BLACK

Maggie Lena Walker (1867–1934) (courtesy of the Library of Virginia) was a nationally recognized African American Richmond banker and business leader whose achievements earned praise from white Virginians because she succeeded by the standards that white men valued. They pointed to her success to justify the form of white supremacy that they imposed in Virginia, but she never accepted racial segregation as right. In fact, Walker enjoyed greater success than most white business leaders and like many other professional or economically successful African Americans in Virginia, she used her influence to undermine segregation and racial prejudice.

"I GOT INVOLVED IN THE CIVIL RIGHTS movement on June 18, 1913, in Alexandria," Sam Tucker once said. "I was born black."[1]

By the legal definition then in force in Virginia, Tucker was actually born "colored." Three years, three months, and one day before he was born, the all-white, all-male General Assembly of Virginia changed the legal definition of the word *colored*. Prior to that time, as Thomas Jefferson had explained in 1815 when demonstrating by computations that Virginians could simultaneously be biologically white and legally enslaved, the state's laws defined as "Negro" or "colored" every person with one-quarter or more African ancestry.[2] The act of March 1910 declared, "Every person having one-sixteenth or more of negro blood shall be deemed a colored person, and every person not a colored person having one-fourth or more of Indian blood shall be deemed an Indian."[3] Interestingly, the law did not define a white person; instead, it defined who was not white. It designated who was to be subjected to the operations of the laws that imposed separate and unequal status on people who were not at least fifteen-sixteenths white. The law defined people who were colored. Because uncolored people needed no definition, they were, by implication, normal.

The definition of race was of considerable importance to the state's political leaders early in the twentieth century, perhaps of more importance than at any previous time. Eleven years before Tucker's birth and eight years before the passage of the new law, white supremacists in Virginia, like others elsewhere in the southeastern states, promulgated a new constitution openly designed to exclude from public life and from the suffrage as many as possible of Virginia's African Americans. Nearly three centuries of sexual relations between people of African, American Indian, and European ancestry and between their descendants made it increasingly difficult with the aid of the human eye alone to determine whether or how much African or American Indian "blood," to employ the legal language of the time, some Virginians possessed.

The difficulty of definition predated even Jefferson's snarled discussion of biology and law; indeed, it was the occasion for his computations and explanation because some people slipped unnoticed from one defined category into another. Some of Sally Hemings's children and grandchildren, who may also have been Thomas Jefferson's, were so light-skinned that they successfully passed into white society unobserved, in the process shedding and denying their African ancestry and all that it meant and also shedding and denying their cultural, familial, and social connections with residents of Monticello.

The race to which people with a geographical multiplicity of family heritages belonged was sometimes a function of a person's own self-definition (men and women who passed from colored into uncolored communities) and sometimes of a community's agreed-upon understandings based on how and with whom people lived and associated. Later, for instance, Barack Obama was almost universally regarded as black because his father was black but not white because his mother was white. He defined himself as black by how and with whom he lived, and other people defined him as black for the same reasons and also because he was not entirely white.

The uncertainties of clear classifications had always posed difficulties for the white people in Virginia who were charged with administering the laws relating to racial definitions that for more than three centuries white Virginians believed were necessary. In 1853, for instance, John Ferguson, a Richmond barber and successful real estate investor, went into the city's hustings court with his family and demonstrated that he and his wife and therefore all of their children were of less than one-fourth African ancestry, whereupon the court granted them a certificate that they were "not negros." Nevertheless, five years later when one of his sons appeared in the Richmond mayor's court charged with assault, the mayor ruled that even though legally Ferguson's son was not "a negro," he was not therefore white. Black witnesses could therefore legally testify against him, which they could not do had Ferguson been legally white. The Fergusons were both legally colored and legally uncolored, but even though they were legally uncolored, they were not therefore legally white.[4]

Such confusion deeply disturbed some twentieth-century white Virginians. Ten years after Sam Tucker's birth, classical pianist and composer John Powell published a long article in the *Richmond Times-Dispatch* announcing that he was worried about the possibility that people who possessed undetectable African ancestry might legally marry white people and secretly pollute the gene pool of the superior white race. Citing the genetic laws that Gregor Mendel had discovered, Powell wrote that it was "undeniable that the Negro as a whole is becoming whiter," and he provided what he believed was an ominous illustration. "I recently stood for forty-five minutes on the northeast corner of Second and Broad Streets in Richmond," he related, identifying one of the clear boundaries between the city's white and black business districts. "During this time I counted among the passers-by over 200 Negroes, of whom only five were black. In addition, I counted over thirty individuals of whom I could not with any degree of certainty state whether they were white or colored." Accompanying Powell's article in the newspaper was another by Earnest Sevier Cox, who gave himself credentials as a scientific ethnologist and who was a prolific author of books and articles on the subject of race.[5] In his companion piece to Powell's article, Cox wrote, "Civilization issues from the white race and in preserving the white race we preserve civilization. . . . There is no doubt but that the blood of the negro is prepotent when mixed with the blood of any other race. Negro race traits and predispositions revert in mixbreeds far removed from the pure negro. This is but the expression of a well-known biologic law, and arises from the fact that the negro is the most primitive and generalized type of man."[6]

None of what Cox wrote was scientifically valid, even by the standards of the time, but it was persuasive to people who wanted to believe it. The page-wide headline that embraced the Powell and Cox articles in the *Richmond Times-Dispatch* was, "Is White America to Become a Negroid Nation? Yes, Unless Anglo-Saxons Wake To Danger, Declares World Noted Ethnologist." Powell and Cox created the Anglo-Saxon Clubs of America to require complete separation of pure white people from all nonwhite people in order to prevent the ruination of the white race. The following year, in 1924, the General Assembly passed An Act to Preserve Racial Integrity that defined all Virginians as "white" or "colored" and required all "colored" Virginians to register their status, pay a fee to be registered, and pay a fine if they failed to do so.[7]

In 1925 Powell and Cox received powerful assistance from Walter Scott Copeland, editor of the Newport News *Daily Press*.[8] After Copeland's wife was affronted when she attended a dance recital at Hampton Institute and, because she arrived late, had to sit next to some African Americans, he published two editorials charging that the white men who supported and operated the black college were undermining white supremacy and the purity of the white race.[9] The Copelands joined forces with the Anglo-Saxon Clubs of America, and together they persuaded the General Assembly to pass one of the strongest laws in the country requiring separation of the races in public meetings.[10]

In 1928 the assembly considered but did not pass another racial purity bill to redefine the races even more clearly. The debates revealed serious differences of opinion about the issue of race in Virginia. Not only did the obvious range of skin colors from quite black to quite white demonstrate that people of European and African ancestries had produced children together, Virginia Indians had also married or had children with white Virginians and black Virginians, too. Were those men and women and children white or colored or Indian? In 1925 Pamunkey Chief George Major Cook had published a strong denunciation of the 1924 law for its impact on the state's Indians and in the process aligned himself, perhaps inadvertently, with Powell and Cox in their condemnation of African Americans. When the new bill was before the Senate of Virginia early in 1928, Cook opposed it but in his testimony made it plain that he would rather die than be black or be regarded as black.[11] He desired to preserve his Indian identity and heritage in the face of white prejudice against black Americans, but in his wish to be not white, he had to condemn being identified as colored, placing him and other Virginians in a conundrum that white Virginians' persistent desire to classify people by race trapped the state's Indian populations for much of the twentieth century.[12]

The 1930 General Assembly passed a revised version of the 1928 bill and decreed, "Every person in whom there is ascertainable any negro blood shall be deemed and taken to be a colored person, and every person not a colored person having one-fourth or more of American Indian blood shall be deemed an American Indian; except that members of Indian tribes living on reservations allotted them by the Commonwealth of Virginia having one-fourth or more of Indian blood and less than one-sixteenth of negro blood shall be deemed tribal Indians so long as they are domiciled on said reservations."[13] The 1924 law had effectively abolished the legal status of Indian in Virginia, but the wording of the 1930 law carefully allowed proud white descendants of Pocahontas (who certainly had no "negro blood" when she married John Rolfe in 1614) and descendants of several other colonial families to be legally white and therefore superior.

The 1930 law created what became known as the one-drop rule. Anyone having so much as one drop of "negro blood" running through his or her veins became legally "colored." But, as Powell had observed, it was not always possible to perceive whether a person possessed that drop, leaving the field open for a medical statistician, Walter Ashby Plecker, director of the state Department of Health's bureau of vital records, to begin his own campaign to document the racial histories of people and families he believed were secretly not white.[14] He worked tirelessly and remorselessly to index and collate vital statistics records. He persecuted and prosecuted people whom he believed were illegally passing as white, and he challenged their legal right to marry white people or to send their children to public schools intended for white pupils. Plecker also altered birth and marriage records to conform them to his belief that all Indians in Virginia had more than the legal minimum of African "blood" in their family histories and were therefore not Indians, thereby once again defining Virginia's Indians out of legal existence.

Insofar as Plecker was concerned, all Virginia Indians were also born black. In 1943 he published a circular for the instruction of local officials who kept birth and marriage records to prevent the state's Indians, whom he called "these mongrels," from evading the law as he interpreted it and defining themselves differently than he and his prejudiced and incomplete genealogical research defined them. "All certificates of these people showing 'Indian' or 'white' are now being rejected," Plecker wrote categorically, "and returned to the physician or midwife, but local registrars hereafter must not permit them to pass their hands uncorrected or unchallenged and without a note of warning to us. One hundred and fifty thousand other mulattoes in Virginia are watching eagerly the attempt of their pseudo-Indian brethren, ready to follow in a rush when the first have made a break in the dike."[15] He also distributed a printed list of surnames for each of the counties to alert county officials about which families he believed were illegally evading the law.[16] For decades thereafter members of the state's Indian tribes remembered and resented the harassment to which "old Plecker" subjected them and their families.[17]

The confrontational tactics and sometimes coarse arguments of Powell and Cox and the abusive behavior of Plecker affronted the sensibilities of an important and influential population of white Virginians who firmly believed, quite mistakenly as it turned out, that they had already contrived a peaceful way to manage relations between white people and black people that was entirely acceptable to both white and black Virginians. Those white leaders timidly refrained from effectively opposing the objectives and projects of the radical racial separatists even though they feared that the radicalism would disturb what they believed were amicable and admirable relations between the races in Virginia. And, as usual, they virtually ignored the state's Indians.

Those socially prominent and prosperous members of the white Virginia elite held generally low opinions of all working people as a class and of all black people as a race, but they were comfortable enough in their own status that they could condescend to be outwardly polite to some of the vast majority of individual men and women whom they regarded as their inferiors. The perspective of those elite white Virginians was not necessarily less racist than that of the Anglo-Saxon Clubbers, but it was infused with a greater degree of class consciousness and has been accurately described as less brutal but also less honest than the racism that underlay the open hostility and contempt that many white Southerners routinely displayed toward African Americans.[18] Not often overtly rude to their household servants and often self-consciously polite to the few professional black men and women of their acquaintance, those elite white Virginians believed that they had found a means for the different races to dwell together harmoniously. In that, white Virginia men and women who tried to set the tone of public discourse and behavior, in spite of yielding to Powell and Cox and allowing Plecker to run riot, deluded themselves about their own attitudes and also deluded themselves into believing that the few respectable black professional men and women of their acquaintance (and therefore also most or all other black people) shared their beliefs.[19]

African American men and women whom those elite white Virginians regarded as respectable were often fairly conspicuous in the state's cities and could be found in many small towns. They included physicians, educators, insurance executives, building contractors, attorneys, members of the clergy, and a few bankers. Within the restrictions of segregation, black men and women pursued their own personal agendas and created their own cultural and economic institutions. In the Jim Crow economy of the twentieth-century South, black people often patronized black-owned businesses rather than shop in

white-owned places that did not welcome them, and every Virginia community had its black business district with its own commercial and community
leaders.

Elite white Virginians could be comfortable with elite blacks because they
shared some of the same fundamentally important bourgeois values. To a remarkable extent white and black Virginians who were fortunate enough to
obtain some education shared many cultural values and aspirations with other
middle-class and bourgeois Americans. Both prized education, economic success, participation in fraternal and service organizations, and membership in
mainline Protestant churches. They attired themselves with stylish but modest
dress, and they carried themselves in public with dignity and self-restraint.[20]

No black Virginian more conspicuously exemplified the bourgeois values
and earned the respect of both black and white Virginians (and Americans
elsewhere) than Maggie Lena Walker. She became a teacher before taking over
a small Richmond social service organization and its savings bank, which she
nourished into one of the largest African American business enterprises in the
South. It spun off other businesses and also published a newspaper. Her St.
Luke Penny Savings Bank eventually merged with other black-owned banks in
Richmond and as Consolidated Bank and Trust Company survived the banking crisis of the 1930s that destroyed many white-controlled banks. Walker
was the first black woman in the United States to serve as a bank president.
She was also a nationally respected business woman and advocate of education; and she was a member of women's clubs and national organizations that
worked for improvements in the lives of women and children and chipped
away at racial segregation and discrimination. Walker succeeded in American
capitalism by the most demanding standards that white men valued. Indeed,
she exceeded the achievements of most of them. Governors and other white
men in the state spoke proudly of her accomplishments and regarded her success as vindicating their own personal values and their brand of separate but
equal race relations, but she never accepted segregation as a natural or proper
social system and worked hard within it to create cracks in it and to further
the interests of people trapped in it.[21]

The 1907 celebration of the three-hundredth anniversary of the founding
of Virginia furnished an opportunity for elite white Virginians and elite black
Virginians to show themselves off to the nation and the world as they desired
to be seen and exhibited how many important values they shared. At a lavish,
months-long commemorative fair near Norfolk, the white leaders celebrated
Virginia's contributions to the nation, including its military successes during
the Civil War, engrafting onto the national narrative of American history the
Lost Cause interpretation of that war as one in a series of struggles for individual freedom and state's rights, in effect inviting the victorious United States
to reconcile itself with the defeated South rather than requiring the defeated

South to reconcile itself with the victorious North. By then, even though the
Confederacy had certainly lost the Civil War, its white Southern interpreters
and their sympathizers had nevertheless won the history, and with that victory
the right to regulate race relations as they pleased. The exhibition was more a
celebration of early twentieth-century Virginia as part of a modern, industrial
America than it was a commemoration of the founding of the colony.[22]

Black Virginians under the leadership of Richmond attorney and businessman Giles B. Jackson obtained a grant of money from the federal government (not from the state sponsors of the celebration) to erect a large building
on the fairgrounds where they highlighted the achievements of the nation's
African Americans (and especially of Virginia's African Americans) since the
abolition of slavery. Their Negro Building included a series of moving and innovative tableaux that celebrated artist Meta Warrick staged to document the
history of slavery as well as of freedom for Virginia's African Americans. The
exhibitions in the large building most conspicuously trumpeted the economic
success of freed slaves and their descendants.[23]

Jackson and Daniel Webster Davis, an educator and poet of note, published a book to accompany the 1907 celebration of Virginia's founding and
progress. Their *Industrial History of the Negro Race of the United States* contained photographs of Warrick's tableaux, but it most strongly emphasized
the economic successes of the state's black population. The word *Industrial* in
the title may have been a deliberate choice on the parts of Jackson and Davis
to soothe white sensibilities by evoking Booker T. Washington's apparently
accommodationist approach to racial segregation that eschewed overt opposition to white-imposed segregation and emphasized economic independence for African Americans through industrial (often interpreted as menial
or manual) education. The product of Davis's facile pen, the book's prose
praised black achievement in a manner intended to inspire admiration and
ambition in young black men and women but also in a way that could prevent white readers (if any) from perceiving black economic achievements as
a threat. With frequent references to the degraded condition from which in-
dustrious black men and women had raised themselves to attain success by
the same measures of economic achievement that white men and women valued, the book was both celebratory and obsequious. *The Industrial History of
the Negro Race* successfully walked a narrow line between the expectations of
white and black Virginians in part by adopting or focusing on values that were
of great interest to white Virginians, too.[24]

Like many other white leaders in the state, Governor Henry Carter Stuart
approved of the economic goals that Jackson and Davis celebrated, and like
most other white men in the state, he approved of placing limits on them. In
a lecture to a large black audience in Richmond's Fifth Street Baptist Church
in the spring of 1914, he said, "I am in favor of your people having all of your

rights, with the understanding that you have no part in the government of this country.... The white people do not propose that you shall participate with them in the governing of the people of this country. This is the view of the South"—by which, of course, he meant the white political leaders of the South—"and if you will accept this view and consider this question settled, all other questions can be left to the people North of the Potomac for settlement." Stuart washed his hands of any responsibility for black Virginians who, without any share in government, would have little or no influence over the economic and social conditions that could ease or impede their opportunities to live decent lives. "I have always said," the governor continued, "that there would never be any trouble if the questions be left to the best class of white people and the best class of Negroes. I am in favor of your advancing as far and as rapidly as you can if you do not jostle us on our side of the line.... While I am Governor, I assure you that you shall have a square deal. The statement which I have made is the decree of the Ages, the two races must live apart. You need us and we need you in accordance with the plans that I have outlined."[25]

A member of the audience that day was John Mitchell Jr., editor since the 1880s of the *Richmond Planet* and a fearless crusader against lynching and racial prejudice and also (up to that time) a successful businessman and a bank president. He did not for an instant accept what the governor said. Mitchell complained in a sharp editorial in his newspaper that listening to Stuart was like "listening to the fatherly advice of an ex-slave-owner, who had in mind the 'Old Antebellum Negro' rather than the 'New Post-bellum Negro.'" The governor's tearful references to his old mammy and fond recollections of enslaved childhood playmates did not persuade Mitchell or the other black members of the audience that he had any genuine sympathy for them. Stuart's speech as a whole and particularly his stated belief in the full exclusion of African Virginians from voting and holding office fell flat.[26]

As in the past Mitchell minced no words and pointed out the hypocrisy that he saw and heard. He regularly exposed the inequalities and insulting subordinations that white supremacy imposed on black members of society. In 1928 when the General Assembly was first debating the one-drop bill, Mitchell wrote sarcastically, "The bill provides a protection to the white person against the intermarriage with a Negro, but makes no provision for the protection of a Negro against intermarriage with a person not a Negro." Then he stuck in the knife and gave it a wicked twist. "Let us see," he continued, "To equalize the situation, the bill should be so amended as to define a Negro as being any person who may have no perceptible trace of white blood in his or her veins."[27] That would have made a large proportion of "colored" Virginians (the people John Powell observed were not black but still clearly colored) into white Virginians on grounds equally defensible or spurious as the definition that the General Assembly enacted in 1930.

When Samuel Wilbur Tucker, who was "born black" in 1913, was a young-ster in northern Virginia, he was very likely aware of discussions that white and black Virginians were having about each other (he may not then have been aware of the discussions that Indian Virginians were also having). He and all other children learned from their parents, ministers, and teachers and from behavior that they observed and from the language that they heard what people of different colors and classes regarded as proper or as improper under different circumstances. Henry C. Stuart and John Mitchell Jr. were very nearly contemporaries, but they grew up with different understand-ings of their separate worlds and their places in the world that they shared. Stuart remembered his childhood during the final years of slavery times and immediately afterward in very different ways than Mitchell remembered his childhood during the same decades.[28] Stuart and white Southerners of his and the following generations learned that white people possessed the skills, talents, intelligence, and the accumulated experience of their ancestors that entitled them alone to govern. That was what he meant by "the decree of the Ages." Young black children like Sam Tucker, who grew up to become a distin-guished civil rights lawyer, learned very different lessons about white people. Tucker's later law partner, Oliver White Hill, recalled that during his child-hood he learned that white people "had their stereotypes about Negroes," that they "were supposedly lazy, untrustworthy, stupid." On the other hand, Hill admitted, "we had stereotypes about them, too. For example, some Negroes said the white man was so crooked that he would steal the pennies off his dead mother's eyes. Another stereotype was that two kinds of white folks existed: good ones and bad ones. You could always tell the good ones because they were buried at least six feet deep."[29]

All people of whatever race grew up with their own personal experiences and understandings gained through their own unique personal histories and based also on when and where they were born and lived or went to school and what behaviors they observed and learned. As in slavery times and afterward, twentieth-century Virginians lived in a wide variety of communities, and consequently in some places African Americans enjoyed more leeway than in others. In the state's cities and larger towns, patterns of residential racial segregation evolved, in some cases enforced by law, that facilitated the devel-opment of black entrepreneurship but also may have reduced the frequency of routine interactions between white and black Virginians. The residential and economic segregation may have promoted rather than damped down be-liefs about racial differences and increased suspicion, but at the same time it allowed elite black and white men and women to interact with stiff politeness.

In rural areas and perhaps in small towns, white and black people often lived and worked in less clearly segregated areas, bringing them into more fre-quent personal contact and creating different community dynamics and standards than developed in urban centers. For example, about 1887 a small-time African American merchant named Leonard R. Flemings was elected a justice of the peace in the lower Northern Neck county of Lancaster.[30] By then justices of the peace no longer presided over courts of record, and original documents concerning his service are scarce, but items that he signed were copied into the county's official records often enough to demonstrate that he served continuously—was reelected every fourth year—for about thirty-two years.[31] Flemings was a delegate to the Republican Party state convention in 1896,[32] and in spite of the provisions of the Constitution of 1902 and the revised election laws adopted during the ensuing session of the General Assembly that were explicitly designed to deprive African Americans of the vote and to keep them out of public office, he continued to be reelected a justice of the peace as late as 1915.[33] His name disappears from rosters of magistrates published between 1919 and 1927,[34] but in 1927 he was elected again and was reelected two more times and was still in office when he died in 1937.[35]

Flemings was undoubtedly one of the longest-serving black public officials in Virginia's history, certainly the man with the longest service during the first half of the twentieth century. His unusual career, the exception that proves the rule, may be explained by circumstances particular to the locality. Rural Lancaster County had a black majority when he entered politics, and in spite of a large migration of African Americans out of racially segregated Virginia during the early decades of the twentieth century, it remained a majority-black county well into the 1920s. Illiteracy among African American adults in the county was very high, which made voter registration more difficult after 1902, but numerous black men (and after 1920 a few black women) in the county nevertheless managed to register and to vote. In 1927 almost one-third of the registered voters in Flemings's White Chapel Magisterial District were black, more than in any other district in the county.[36] The state did not compile or publish voter registration figures giving racial identifications, but that figure seems remarkably high, and black people registered in Lancaster and two neighboring counties in larger numbers than elsewhere in the region during the 1930s.[37] Elections for justices of the peace may have been regarded as nonpartisan, and in a district with a large black population and a significant number of black voters, local white political leaders may have deemed it in their interest to have a respectable property-owning black man serve as one of the petty magistrates.

The region's weekly newspapers did not report or comment on the relatively unnewsworthy campaigns for justice of the peace, nor did they report on what might have been regarded as shocking news elsewhere in Virginia, that an African American man repeatedly won election. Flemings was not identified as African American in the occasional newspaper reports of his being elected or in the state's published lists of magistrates. That suggests that locally his elections were not regarded as remarkable, but it concealed from white Virginians elsewhere and from historians later that a black man was repeatedly winning elections in the state during a time when all black men were believed to have been effectively excluded from public office.

In a rural portion of Essex County, not far from where Leonard Flemings lived, people who resided in a community with almost every possible admixture of ancestral heritages sent their children to a public school without any apparent regard for their skin colors or the skin colors of their ancestors and without much conspicuous racial prejudice.[38] In Caroline County not far away from Essex County in the other direction from Lancaster County, residents of another rural community with a similar disregard for racial classifications and differences took little disapproving notice when Richard Perry Loving married Mildred Delores Jeter. They had to marry in Washington, D.C., because he was legally white and she was legally colored, which made their marriage illegal in Virginia; but their legal classifications and the personal relations between men and women and boys and girls in their community disposed their neighbors not to care very much about whether the marriage was legal or to regard it as improper.[39] Variations in skin color were commonplace and often of little importance in African American communities but never tolerated in white communities.

If Maggie Walker might be seen as an exemplary African American, Virginius Dabney might be regarded as an exemplar of elite white Virginians. He was the son of University of Virginia historian Richard Heath Dabney who had argued in 1901 that white Virginians should not have to pay for schools for black Virginians because white Virginians could not benefit in any way from the education of black Virginians. From 1928 to 1936, V. Dabney, as he was known, was a columnist for the *Richmond Times-Dispatch,* and from 1936 until he retired in 1969, he was the newspaper's editor. Unlike his father, he gained a reputation as a Southern progressive and in 1932 published a book entitled *Liberalism in the South,* in which he made the case for the state's version of a civil, almost genteel, separate but equal society. His chapters on the colonial and antebellum South (and especially his discussions of colonial and antebellum Virginia) portrayed the state's political leaders as wise and tolerant and its planters as humane masters of slaves they had inherited and could not decently dispose of. In his chapters on the Civil War and Reconstruction, Dabney blamed Northerners for disrupting the high-toned republicanism of political life in Virginia and forcing the state to accept participation in politics by freedmen not equipped morally or intellectually to take on that responsibility. As a consequence of the political reaction and upheavals of the 1870s and 1880s, by the beginning of the twentieth century the influence of lower-class white politicians was ascendant in Virginia, and they enacted demeaning segregation statutes. Reflecting a viewpoint repeatedly expressed by people of his class, Dabney wrote in 1932 that the "respectable Negro" should be allowed to vote, but he excused the mass disfranchisement of the sort his father had advocated in 1901 (the year of his own birth) as permissible at that time because "the great majority of blacks were unclean in person and slovenly in attire" and "the ubiquitous saloon and its readily purchased fire water were conducive to clashes between the lower orders of both races."[40]

Dabney later wrote editorials in favor of removing some of the humiliating attributes of racial segregation such as laws requiring segregated seating on city buses, but like most other white men and women in Virginia during the first half of the twentieth century who believed that they were more tolerant than their white inferiors and more decent in their behavior than the lower South rabble-rousers, he and they almost always qualified their willingness to see black men and women treated fairly by stating that they did not desire social equality and that they also believed that respectable black men and women did not, either. The phrase "social equality" encompassed many facets of life in the twentieth-century segregated South, including mixed-race seating in public venues, private mixed-race socializing, and, in particular, interracial sex. So often did the equivocations associated with social equality in their writings and speeches segue into references to black-on-white rape and the degradation of Southern white ladies that explicit mental images of black men having sexual relations with white women must have lurked ubiquitously in their minds and informed their concept of social equality.[41]

Men like Dabney could interact with reserved civility with their domestic servants and with African American men and women of what they regarded as the better classes, the men and women who were educated, dressed well, and conducted themselves with proper decorum. The V. Dabneys of Virginia were comfortable addressing professional black men and women with appropriate courtesy titles like Doctor and Professor and Reverend if they had earned those titles, but white men and women of Dabney's class and time almost never accorded courtesy titles of Mr. or Mrs. or Miss to black men or women of any social rank, including educators, bankers, or attorneys. Conversely, the racial etiquette that white people created for the segregated South required that black people of every class address white people of any class with courtesy titles appropriate to their status. That etiquette was part of what every child who grew up in the segregated South learned. The practice of white people addressing all but a few African Americans by their first names and expecting that all black people accord all white people a courtesy title appeared to the white people to allow for respectful and peaceful interpersonal relations between members of the races. (Those white people also exhibited similar attitudes toward and expected a similar deference from white men and women who were beneath them in social status.) Black people found themselves unable to object effectively or to escape from the daily and hourly humiliations associated with that etiquette of white supremacy.[42] Consequently, black participants in a meeting in the governor's office one day regarded it as a signal achievement, perhaps a unique triumph, that Maggie Walker was able by force of her personality and the example of her business success to cow the governor's secretary into addressing her as "Mrs. Walker."[43]

Dabney and other white men and women like him found comfort in and support for their opinions from a substantial and respectable body of scientific and historical literature, from the medical theorizing of Paul Brandon Barringer to William Graham Sumner's pioneering 1910 sociological study, *Folkways,* to studies of slavery and Reconstruction by respected scholarly historians Ulrich B. Phillips and William A. Dunning. More rigorous and respected than the numerous fulminations of Earnest Sevier Cox, that literature reinforced the beliefs that the white elite already held, and it often portrayed African Americans as having an almost childlike simplicity of mind that allowed them to assimilate white attitudes and to behave as if they had a natural puppy-dog-like disposition to please white people.[44] Even the discredited science of Robert Bennett Bean could find welcome refuge in their Virginia. A native Virginian, he conducted studies of human brains early in the twentieth century and either fudged his evidence or found what he expected and wanted to find. His three 1906 publications, one in a reputable national medical journal and two in a widely read popular journal, appeared to prove the innate inferiority of people of African origin or descent to people of European origin and descent.[45] Bean's own mentor demonstrated that his work was entirely unsound, but that did not prevent the medical school at the University of Virginia from hiring him in 1916 and keeping him on the faculty until he retired in 1942.[46]

So deeply internalized were the attitudes of genteel white supremacy in the elite white population that when those white men and women unexpectedly encountered black people who clearly did not fit into their preconceptions, they either did not know how to react or they erupted in anger or vented their uncomprehending frustrations in rude and insulting ways. Early in the 1930s, for example, at a ceremony in one of Richmond's posh hotels, the governor presented awards to the city's new crop of Eagle Scouts. The last scout in line was James Jackson, a young black man who had struggled to create a Boy Scout troop for African Americans and who was almost certainly the first black Virginian to earn the prized rank of Eagle Scout. But when Governor John Garland Pollard reached the end of the line and was about to present the award to Jackson, he realized that Jackson was African American. Pollard froze with indecision, then he stepped back, scowled, and with an expression of disgust tossed the award to Jackson, who let it fall to the floor. Jackson then clicked his heels and saluted the governor. The governor looked in vain at the other scouts for sympathy at the awkward position in which he found himself, then he brusquely turned away and stalked out. Jackson resigned from the Boy Scouts.[47]

Largely unconscious of how their actions appeared to black Virginians, white Virginians of the class to which Pollard and Dabney belonged persisted in believing that they had fashioned amicable relations between the races under their own good management and that black Virginians also approved of the arrangement. As a beneficiary rather than a victim of that system, Dabney was willing to accept some change but felt no urgency in the matter. He once told an interviewer, "Within a century or so" the African American laboring class might be able to improve its condition.[48] Only a few unusually perceptive white Virginians demonstrated that they could see through the self-delusions that allowed Dabney to be so patient about deplorable and humiliating aspects of other people's lives that he would not have accepted for an instant in his own.

One white man who did see through it all was Louis I. Jaffé, editor of the Norfolk *Virginian-Pilot,* the best and one of the most distinguished white journalists in twentieth-century Virginia and the recipient of a Pulitzer Prize for his 1928 editorials condemning lynching. Jaffé was born into an immigrant Jewish family and was more than ordinarily sensitive to how people perceived unfair treatment. Writing in the 1920s about an attempt by councilmen in another city to force an old black janitor out of his job at the public library in order to install a white man in his place at a larger salary, Jaffé exploded in exasperation, "What exhibition of rapaciousness, race prejudice and political spoliation could be cheaper, commoner or meaner? These are the little tyrannies and petty skulduggeries that make bitter the relations between the races and mock the strivings of the more enlightened Southern elements for a better and fairer racial adjustment."[49]

Cheap. Common. Mean. Jaffé selected his adjectives deliberately to brand the actions of those white men as beneath the proper standards that decent white men prized. Outrageous tyrannies such as lynching and the many petty humiliations and skulduggeries associated with segregated seating on city buses, unfair treatment of an old janitor in a public library, contemptuous refusal to treat black Virginians with respect, and blatant exclusion of them from the political process meant that white supremacy was unacceptable to the state's African Americans, even though Dabney and most other prominent white Virginians believed otherwise.

As a result of white people's blindness to the consequences of their beliefs, the essential causes of some serious and pervasive problems simultaneously became as invisible to them as the protagonist in Ralph Ellison's 1952 novel, *The Invisible Man,* became to the white people in his midst. For example, a study that the Richmond Council of Social Agencies conducted in 1929 identified numerous gross insufficiencies in the city's African American neighborhoods. It contained statistical and anecdotal evidence of uniformly inferior standards of social services, schools, recreational facilities, housing, streets, and water and sanitation, and it itemized deplorable standards of public health, low life expectancy, a high rate of stillbirths, and an appalling rate of infant mortality in the Jim Crow sections of the city. The report failed, however, in spite of the presence of a few black members on the study commission, openly to acknowledge the relationship between those conditions and the city's and state's laws requiring racial segregation and providing less money for schools and all public services for black Virginians than for white Virginians. As with a similar report that the mayor had issued in 1914, the 1929 report consequently made few fundamental recommendations for improvements,[50] leaving the impression that white people believed that life for black Virginians was naturally like that; that it was naturally nasty, poor, and short, that white people could do nothing about it, and that black people acknowledged and accepted it.

"It is incredible how ignorant most white people are of the life Negroes have to live in this democracy," reminisced Thomas Calhoun Walker late in life. Walker was born into slavery in Gloucester County and from the late 1880s through the 1930s was one of the few black attorneys in rural southeastern Virginia. He worked constantly for improved public services, better schools, and decent treatment of the state's African Americans but continuously marveled at "how little even those in authoritative positions realize the extent to which race maladjustments are in their keeping."[51] He included an entire chapter titled "Getting On with Folks" in his mid-twentieth-century autobiography to explain how he worked within the expectations and prejudices of white Virginians to wring some concessions from them without affronting or frightening them and thereby dooming his efforts. In doing so, his behavior necessarily comforted white leaders and confirmed them in their opinions, but doing so also simultaneously allowed Walker and other men and women like him, who had to work within a system of segregation that they could not fundamentally change, to undermine it in many small ways and in some larger ways that during the early decades of the twentieth century also remained virtually invisible to elite white people.

Gordon Blaine Hancock was two generations younger than T. C. Walker and Leonard Flemings and also a much more conspicuous advocate for Virginians and Americans who had been born black or colored or not-white. He earned a doctorate in sociology and taught at Virginia Union University, in Richmond, and therefore might be addressed as Dr. Hancock or Professor Hancock; and he was a Baptist minister and could also be addressed as Reverend Hancock. Between 1929 and 1968 he wrote more than two thousand articles for the Associated Negro Press that criticized segregation and advocated economic independence, education, and racial pride.[52] In one of his regular 1930s columns for the Norfolk *Journal and Guide,* the largest-circulation black newspaper in Virginia and at that time the most influential, Hancock reminded his readers of what men like him and Walker believed and why they acted as they did. "No sensible Negro wants to be segregated," Hancock wrote, "except under circumstances where it has become necessary to accept segregation in particular to combat segregation in general. . . . Our practice is more eloquent than our theory. We know that segregation is a bad thing; but we know that the consequences of not accepting it may be worse. Herein lies the pity!"[53]

Plummer Bernard Young agreed. Editor and publisher of the Norfolk *Journal and Guide* and eventually the successor to Mitchell as the most respected and influential black journalist in Virginia, Young had a reputation among white Virginians as nonconfrontational, but he was usually so in his tactics, not in his beliefs.[54] At the time that Walter Scott Copeland was damning Hampton Institute in 1925 and laying the political groundwork for strengthened laws on racial segregation, Young condemned Copeland's ideas and acts. "We may be injured in our lawful privileges and immunities," Young wrote in his newspaper, "segregated in our living and jim-crowed in our travels and personally insulted in our homes and business places by low white persons who have some sort of business to transact with us or our wives, but we are not to accept any such treatment and conduct as the measure of our just deserts. It is for us to make our own measurements of ourselves, and that by the highest and not by the lowest standards, and by sticking to it compel others to appreciate the fact that we know we are unjustly treated and protest against it."[55]

Young's phrase "low white persons" was typical of the language that he and men like him often inserted into their complaints about Jim Crow's injustices and indignities. By placing blame on "low white persons," they excluded and thereby appeared to excuse men and women of V. Dabney's class from responsibility and sought to enlist them in righting some minor wrongs rather than drive them into defense of the greater wrongs of segregation and its written laws and unwritten etiquette.

Dabney, Hancock, and Young served together on interracial committees that produced some hopes and little else during the 1930s and 1940s. They were mismatched and unlikely ever to agree on fundamental changes because their different perspectives were essentially incompatible.[56] Dabney sometimes wrote and acted as if he believed that white society had a responsibility to make the "equal" part of "separate but equal" a reality in order to justify and preserve the "separate" part, but because separate was never equal, men and women who shared the beliefs and values of Hancock and Young and Mitchell frightened Dabney and most other white Virginians when they did challenge the essential inequality and injustice of white supremacy.

Black challenges to elite white values and practices came through the courts, a direction that white Virginians probably never anticipated. The challenges came not through insurrection or race riot, as some white people feared, or through elections and the political process, which white people had made virtually impossible. Ever since the 1880s when the biracial Readjuster coalition fell apart, white supremacists in Virginia had constructed a political system that made it virtually impossible for enough black Virginians to vote that they could have any serious influence on public policy or elect legislators or county or municipal officers. Even though some black Virginians in some places voted during the first decades of the twentieth century, they had no political leverage with which to make a significant difference in the operations of the state's politics or in its public policies.

The state's feeble Republican Party, after largely abandoning its few remaining black allies at the end of the nineteenth century, rudely cast them aside in 1921. The state convention that year excluded most of the black members elected to it and adopted a platform that Democrats who promulgated the Constitution of 1902 could have written. It declared that "the white people of Virginia, constituting over two-thirds of its population, holding ninety-five per cent of its property, with centuries of discipline and training in self-government, are charged with the solemn duty to all the people of this State to see that the State and local governments of this Commonwealth are conducted and administered in accordance with these self-evident principles," meaning the exclusion of black men and women from public life. The Republican platform also declared that "the solution of these delicate human problems"—meaning relations between the races and the required subordination of black people to white people—"must be found in the application of moral principles, not in political agitation; in practical justice founded upon facts; in a spirit of open-mindedness, sympathy and understanding by those immediately concerned of both races, having in view the higher interests of the State and the happiness and prosperity of all its people." In his long acceptance speech to the convention, the party's nominee for governor, Henry W. Anderson, repeated those platitudes that endorsed the status quo,[57] leaving no room for black Republicans to hope for favors from their old political party and consequently dooming them to wait for the "century or so" that Dabney and other excessively patient white Virginians were prepared to wait before welcoming any substantial improvements in the lives of the black people of Virginia.

In the Norfolk *Journal and Guide,* P. B. Young denounced the Republicans' actions in language as strong as he could muster. "That Afro-Americans should be eliminated altogether, from any participation whatever in the political affairs of the state," he wrote, "is a proposition so revolutionary in itself and so contrary to the spirit of democracy, and so inconsistent with the duties and responsibilities of citizenship placed upon all Americans, that it is hard to believe that the leaders of either party expect it to be accomplished."[58] But leaders of both parties obviously did.

In the *Richmond Planet* editor John Mitchell Jr. headlined his attack on the Republican convention's platform "Outlawing the Negro."[59] In retaliation against the Republicans for what almost immediately became known as their lily-white ticket, Mitchell persuaded some of the state's African American leaders to nominate an all-black ticket of Republican candidates for statewide office. The so-called lily-black ticket included Mitchell as the candidate for governor and Maggie Walker as the candidate for state superintendent of public instruction. The lily-black Republicans had no hope of winning, Mitchell did not even campaign much, and the ticket fared poorly on general election day; but the lily-white Republicans had no hope of winning, either, and that ticket also fared poorly on general election day.[60]

In part as a consequence of Young's more cautious approach to protecting powerless black Virginians from powerful white Virginians (and his general dislike of Mitchell), he openly denounced Mitchell's ineffectual foray into confrontational politics. That two of the state's most influential black leaders fundamentally disagreed on political tactics early in the 1920s when the state's two political parties essentially shunned black Virginians contributed to widespread black apathy and indifference toward the political process from which they were largely excluded.

A decade later, to the puzzlement of oblivious white Democrats and Republicans alike, black voters in Virginia began a slow abandonment of the Republican Party's presidential and congressional candidates and embraced national Democratic leaders such as Franklin D. Roosevelt in spite of the hostility that the principal leaders of Virginia's Democratic Party displayed toward the New Deal of the 1930s and to the participation of black men and women in politics at all. In some of the state's cities, black men and women consequently found it somewhat easier to register and vote, but their participation worked no change in the state's Democratic Party or in the commitment of its leadership to white supremacy. When in 1936 Portsmouth newspaper editor Norman R. Hamilton defeated anti–New Deal Democratic congressman Colgate Whitehead Darden, a rising star in the Byrd organization, he received some support from the congressional district's black voters. When Hamilton ran for reelection against Darden in 1938 and opened an office for black campaign workers, Darden's supporters openly denounced him for soliciting black votes and circulated campaign literature with captions such as "Look, Hamilton's a nigger lover!" and "See, the niggers are set up better than your own people by him," and "If you vote for Hamilton, niggers will be teaching your children soon." Darden defeated Hamilton, for which Hamilton blamed the racist political attacks.[61]

Having no powerful political muscle, the state's black people, chiefly its schoolteachers and the parents of schoolchildren, pushed their own agenda of change that required no political muscle. Unable to persuade city and county school boards to provide decent school buildings, adequate books, laboratories, and libraries, or even buses to transport students to school in rural areas, they raised money to improve the schools and to purchase and operate buses, even though they paid taxes that provided schools and buses for white children. The state's black schoolteachers organized and energized the Virginia State Teachers Association, which helped coordinate that work and also conducted voter registration and civic education campaigns to help African Americans make changes in their communities that unsympathetic Democratic local officeholders failed to provide.

Among the many leaders who took part in that movement, Luther Porter Jackson, a professor of history at Virginia State College, worked tirelessly to compile data, educate people, and stimulate them to action. During the 1940s he wrote a monthly column for the Norfolk *Journal and Guide* that sometimes urged collective community action, sometimes advocated voter registration, and frequently documented African American contributions to American life and extolled the economic and political achievements of black Virginians during the decades after the Civil War. Jackson's advocacy worked as a statewide stimulant for local activism, and it resulted in the publication of a significant body of scholarship, including three books, that advanced the understanding of African American life in Virginia.[62] A man of the younger generation, Jackson inserted into his articles and books no deferential tropes of the kind that D. Webster Davis or P. B. Young employed to avoid annoying white readers, and he energetically promoted black participation in politics and public life. Like Mitchell before him, Jackson probably knew that few or no white people read his newspaper columns and books, and therefore he was free to be forthright in writing directly to and for black readers and in advocating political and legal action that attacked racial segregation and discrimination.

Black teachers, students, and parents created the civil rights movement in Virginia before World War II. They filed lawsuits to force school districts to provide transportation, to equalize school facilities, and to pay black and white teachers on the same wage scale, thereby bringing men like Sam Tucker and Oliver Hill into courtrooms where they made the most formidable challenges to Jim Crow in Virginia and to Harry Byrd's undemocratic and antidemocratic political organization. Even though the political process did not work democratically in Virginia, the American legal process eventually worked justly. A remarkable company of black civil rights attorneys used the legal institutions and principles that many generations of white Virginia men had created to attack the undemocratic segregated society and political culture that those same generations of white Virginia men had also created.

The essential power of the ideas of freedom and equality and justice that had been abroad in Virginia since the American Revolution began to work for black Virginians again for the first time since Billy Mahone's Readjuster Party. In a revealing passage in his autobiography, attorney Thomas Calhoun Walker recalled a speech that he once had to make when pleading for the right to represent a man in a county court after the local commonwealth's attorney objected to his taking part in the trial. "I have qualified in the courts of Gloucester County," Walker quoted himself as having said. "I have read and studied the same books that the commonwealth attorney has studied, not one of which I wrote. These books were all written by eminent judges and lawyers of the white race and it is their conception of the dignity and righteousness of the law which, presumably, we all wish to see prevail in the state of Virginia." The judge granted Walker the right to represent his client in court in spite of the objections of the commonwealth's attorney.[63]

Walker won one of many such minor victories that day and took one of many early and small steps toward holding white Virginians to account for violating their own values by appealing directly to those values. As the Swedish sociologist Gunnar Myrdal predicted during World War II in his insightful and influential *An American Dilemma: The Negro Problem and Modern Democracy,* the country's democratic ideals of liberty, equality, and justice provided the most powerful weapons for African Americans who were fighting against racial discrimination and for admission for the first time into the mainstream of American life.[64]

World War II energized black Americans to attack discrimination and segregation. African American servicemen had been largely relegated to segregated units, usually under the command of white officers, and were discriminated against in many ways even as they contributed much toward winning a war that was supposedly being waged to make the world safe for democracy and freedom. The racial ideology of the Nazis and the brutal treatment that some Japanese army units displayed toward members of races that they deemed inferior made the inequalities that burdened African Americans starkly evident and even more morally indefensible. Black men and women who served in the war or came of age at that time challenged Jim Crow in ways their parents and grandparents had not. Just as there had been a generational difference between John Mitchell Jr. and P. B. Young, members of the generation who came of age during and after World War II were much bolder. Walker, Young, and Hancock gave place to Jackson, Tucker, and Hill.

The civil rights movement in Virginia became largely a courtroom drama, not a street drama or a political movement. The white men who had founded and by then had directed public affairs in Virginia for three and a half centuries had developed a judicial system and a conception of the rule of law that, in spite of their many breaches of its canons and failures to enforce its terms, nev-

ertheless provided black men and women in mid-twentieth-century Virginia
the tools with which to fight the failures and to right some of the wrongs. The
political and legal cultures of Virginia that had developed during the centuries
were responsible, at least in part, for the largely peaceful and overwhelmingly
legalistic form that the civil rights movement took in Virginia, in contrast to
what happened in some other states where the fight against racial segregation
took place primarily in the streets, and where the opposition to the struggle
was more often violent.

It is true that Virginia's state courts, filled entirely by judges that the Byrd
organization's majorities in the General Assembly selected, remained unre-
ceptive and usually hostile to lawsuits requiring equality within the separate
but equal doctrine, to say nothing of direct challenges to segregation per se,
but the catalog of major civil rights lawsuits that Virginians filed and that
Virginia attorneys successfully pursued through the federal courts is very impressive. The federal courts and the United States Congress imposed many
changes on Virginia's political and legal cultures, which white Virginians resistant to change bitterly denounced as unacceptable outside interference with
the state's domestic affairs, but in truth it was not outside interference but a
peaceful domestic insurrection. Many of the most important of those changes
came about because black Virginians directly challenged American apartheid
as it was practiced in their state and with the aid of Sam Tucker, Oliver Hill,
Spottswood Robinson, Victor Ashe, Roland Ealey, Ruth Harvey Charity,
Martin Martin, Henry Marsh, and other brave and able attorneys pursued
them through the federal courts to successful conclusion.

The lawsuits began when Virginia citizens went to court, and the next
generations of attorneys after T. C. Walker were much more eager to press for
change however they could. In 1939 Sam Tucker organized a sit-in at the Alexandria public library after he was refused service there. The peaceful symbolic
protest called attention to the inequalities and indignities that pervaded the
Jim Crow South, where everything was always separate and unequal, never
separate but equal.[65] The action predated by nearly two decades a technique
that civil rights activists effectively employed elsewhere in Virginia and the
South. For the most part, even though African American attorneys represented
clients challenging aspects of segregation in Virginia, it was students, parents,
and teachers who originated the cases and called in the attorneys to represent
them. The Virginia lawyers were often members of the National Association
for the Advancement of Colored People and had convenient and ready allies
in the NAACP's legal defense division with its headquarters in nearby Washington, D.C.; but it was the Virginia clients and the Virginia attorneys who
led the way, often pushing further and faster than some of the association's
cautious legal strategists desired.[66]

In 1939 Aline Black volunteered to file a lawsuit on behalf of herself and the other African American teachers in Norfolk to require the city's public school system to pay black and white teachers on the same pay scale, for which boldness she lost her job. Another teacher, Melvin O. Alston, then stepped in as plaintiff. Attorney Oliver Hill and his former Howard University law school classmate Thurgood Marshall, of the NAACP, took the case to the Supreme Court of the United States, which in 1940 sustained a federal court ruling against the Norfolk school board and required that white and black teachers be paid on the same salary schedule. Black later reclaimed her job, but the case did not establish a precedent that school officials in other jurisdictions in the state or the South thought that they had to follow.[67]

Thereafter, community leaders and activists pursued local, case-by-case challenges to the inequities and iniquities of legalized racial discrimination. Percy Casino Corbin, in the western county of Pulaski, filed suit in federal court on behalf of his children charging that the county's segregated school system provided his children facilities that were manifestly inferior to those provided for white children and also required that his children endure long daily bus rides to and from the inferior schools. A federal district court agreed and in 1949 ordered remedial action to reduce inequality in the educational facilities that the school system provided for the county's white and black pupils.[68]

In 1944 Irene Morgan filed suit in federal court after she was arrested for refusing to sit in the back of a bus as she returned home to Baltimore after visiting her mother in Gloucester County. Her black civil rights attorneys carried her case all the way to the Supreme Court, too, and in 1946 it ruled that state laws requiring segregated seating in common carriers operating in interstate commerce were an unconstitutional state burden on commerce and an encroachment on the federal government's constitutional power to regulate interstate commerce.[69]

By 1951 the high school that Prince Edward County had constructed for black students was so dilapidated, inadequate, and grossly overcrowded that the students went on strike. One of them, Barbara Johns, persuaded Oliver Hill and Spottswood Robinson, then partners in the most important black law firm in Virginia, to challenge separate but equal head-on and no longer pursue a seemingly endless series of local equalization suits like the ones that Black and Corbin had filed. The suit, styled *Davis v. Board of Education of Prince Edward County* for the leading plaintiff, Dorothy Davis, got lumped in with other such suits from Kansas, South Carolina, Delaware, and the District of Columbia and was twice argued before the Supreme Court of the United States, with Thurgood Marshall making the principal argument for the students. In 1954 the Supreme Court unanimously ruled in the combined cases styled *Brown v. Board of Education of Topeka, Kansas,* that mandatory racial segregation in public schools was unconstitutional throughout the United

States. One of the most important civil rights cases in the country's history, its Virginia component began when black high school students got fed up with how the white-run county school board and administration had treated them.[70]

In the 1960s community activists Evelyn Thomas Butts, of Norfolk, and Annie E. Harper, of Fairfax County, separately challenged the state's imposition of the poll tax as a prerequisite for voter registration. Rejected as they no doubt expected to be in the state's courts, they, too, appealed to the federal courts, and in its 1966 ruling the Supreme Court of the United States declared that imposition of a poll tax was an unconstitutional burden on the right of suffrage. That case together with a 1964 constitutional amendment outlawing imposition of a poll tax for voting in federal elections and the provisions of the 1965 Voting Rights Act finally removed the most important of the barriers that for more than half a century had prevented most black Virginians and many poor white Virginians from registering and voting.[71]

Because Virginia resident Richard P. Loving, a white man, had married Virginia resident Mildred Jeter, a black woman who also identified herself sometimes as Pamunkey, in Washington, D.C., the sheriff of Caroline County arrested them in their bed in 1958. Marriage between people of different races was legal in Washington but illegal in Virginia, where the state's law also made it illegal for people of different races to return to Virginia after being married elsewhere. The judge recited and endorsed the law and the state's history of prohibiting interracial marriages. He also went well beyond the statute and cited a higher law. "Almighty God created the races white, black, yellow, malay and red," he announced, "and he placed them on separate continents. And but for the interference with his arrangement there would be no cause for such marriages. The fact that he separated the races shows that he did not intend for the races to mix."[72] Their case, *Loving v. Virginia,* reached the Supreme Court of the United States, which in 1967 overruled a unanimous holding of the Virginia Supreme Court of Appeals and declared that all state laws forbidding interracial marriage were unconstitutional.[73]

Those were but a few of the most important of the civil rights cases that arose in Virginia. Together they profoundly influenced the course of American law and race relations and began a slow transformation of the ways in which black people lived in their home state. The civil rights movement in Virginia was both a democratic and a democratizing event. It was democratic in that the students, teachers, and other community activists initiated the first lawsuits and organized demonstrations and boycotts. They campaigned to mobilize public opinion, organized local protest marches, and conducted sit-ins to gain access to places of business and public facilities such as libraries that had denied them service. In the beginning some of them pushed further and faster against racial segregation than the state's principal civil rights organization, the NAACP, wished to move. The civil rights movement was also democratizing in that it brought into the political process many people who had been disfranchised or excluded from participation in public life.

In addition to the many people who moved civil rights to the center of the political stage, a number of leaders emerged whose talents and achievements made them, together, some of the most successful revolutionaries in Virginia's history. W. Lester Banks, for example, executive secretary of the state's NAACP from 1947 to 1976, challenged racial segregation in public transportation and public education and bravely drove about the state pursuing justice with the letters NAACP, like a bull's-eye, conspicuous on the rear window of his automobile.[74] He and his fellow leaders deserve to be classed with the earlier revolutionaries like Thomas Jefferson, Patrick Henry, and George Washington who created a new nation and with the eighteenth-century Baptists whose campaign for religious liberty prompted the General Assembly to pass the Act for Establishing Religious Freedom.

Those civil rights activists faced formidable and tenacious resistance, and their successes were always accompanied by disappointments. After the apparent triumph of *Davis v. Prince Edward County* in which the Supreme Court of the United States required states to desegregate public schools with "all deliberate speed," Virginia's school officials and most of its political leaders chose to disobey and adopted what they called a policy of Massive Resistance. The Prince Edward County government simply abolished the public school system rather than desegregate it, and the county board of supervisors then appropriated taxpayers' money (raised from both white and black taxpayers) to support private, white-only academies. Even after additional court action and reluctant intervention from the governor forced the county to re-create a public school system, an overwhelming majority of the county's white parents continued to send their children to the private academies, leaving the county's African American children, nearly all of whom had lost several years of education at critical stages in their development, stuck with decidedly inferior schools and no ability to recover what they had lost. It was a hollow victory for many of the black people of Prince Edward County.[75] Parents in New Kent County also had to file a suit and carry it all the way to the Supreme Court, too, which then, finally, required school districts throughout the South to demonstrate actual desegregation.[76]

A large proportion of Virginia's leading white politicians, journalists, educators, and members of the clergy initially stood with the Virginius Dabneys of the state in recommending moderation when the frontal assault on segregation began early in the 1950s, but most of them later gave overt support, or by their silence gave tacit support, to Massive Resistance, by which Harry Byrd's political organization attempted to block desegregation of the public schools and prevent further desegregation of the society.

A particularly rich and condensed statement of the beliefs about racial differences that animated the political leaders of Virginia during that time is in the defiant radio and television address that Governor J. Lindsay Almond made on 20 January 1959 when he sought to rally all Virginians, by which he meant all white Virginians, behind his closings of the public schools that the federal courts had been ordered to desegregate. "To those of faint heart," Almond began his most corrosive run-on sentence; "to those whose purpose and design is to blend and amalgamate the white and Negro race and destroy the integrity of both races; to those who disclaim that they are integrationists but are working day and night to integrate the schools; to those who don't care what happens to the children of Virginia; to those false prophets of a 'little or token integration'; to those in high places and elsewhere who advocate integration for *your* children and send their *own* to private or public segregated schools; to those who defend or close their eyes to the livid stench of sadism, sex immorality and juvenile pregnancy infesting the mixed schools of the District of Columbia and elsewhere; to those who would overthrow the customs, mores and traditions of a way of life which has endured in honor and decency for centuries and embrace a new moral code prepared by nine men in Washington whose moral concepts they know nothing about; to those who would substitute strife, bitterness, turmoil and chaos for the tranquility and happiness of an orderly society; to those who would destroy our way of life because of their pretended concern over what Soviet Russia may think of us; to all of these and their confederates, comrades and allies let me make it abundantly clear for the record now and hereafter, as Governor of this state, *I will not yield* to that which I know to be wrong and will destroy every rational semblance of education for thousands of the children of Virginia."

Almond then called on "the people of Virginia to stand firmly with me in this struggle. . . . The people of Virginia through their elected representatives and by registering their convictions in the exercise of their franchise have repeatedly made it crystal clear that they cannot and will not support a system of public education on a racially integrated basis."[77] Almond appealed to Virginia's system of representative government as validating the laws and social customs he sought to preserve and also his authority for upholding them. But in his Virginia the whole people had no political voice. What Almond really said was that a majority of the minority of white people who voted had supported the system of mandatory segregation of public schools and of the society in general. They had elected him to two terms as attorney general of the state and to one term as governor when the most important issue that he had to deal with in both offices was the challenge to the state's Jim Crow laws that residents of Virginia had begun. He shamelessly disclosed what he and many of them believed.

Their attitudes about race were of the utmost importance to them, and they fought with every political weapon they had against change. The appeals to American democratic values and principles that Gunnar Myrdal had suggested eventually would dismantle racial segregation and dissipate racial prejudice had less effect on Virginia's white political leaders (who seldom gave more than lip service to democratic ideals and principles, anyway) than Myrdal had foreseen.

Every Virginian who was "born black" like Sam Tucker or was born Indian like Chief Cook necessarily had a different kind of life than any Virginian who was born legally uncolored. The state's laws and social and cultural histories placed Virginians of different races and different classes in categories that were difficult to escape, even though brave men, women, and children made valiant and often successful attempts during the twentieth century. Oliver Hill, who lived into the twenty-first century and became known as the dean of the state's civil rights attorneys, later reflected on his mixed feelings after decades of distinguished civil rights advocacy. "I believe that most white folks thought that segregation was right and proper," he wrote with sadness in his autobiography at the end of the twentieth century, "and apparently saw nothing wrong with unequal treatment of Negroes. However, the few whites who would discuss the situation talked as if the only reason that segregation existed was because the law required it. This type of talk led some Negroes to believe that if the segregation laws did not exist, segregation would vanish. In a backhanded way, this led many Negroes to believe that white folks had greater respect for the law than they in fact did. However, when the Supreme Court ruled the segregation laws unconstitutional, many Negroes experienced a rude awakening as white folks' reputed great respect for the law disappeared. Like many other people, segregationists only respect the law when they perceive it is favorable to them. Many white folks sought every conceivable means to circumvent the change that the law mandated."[78]

It was not the laws that made distinctions between men and women who were born white and men and women who were not. White people, most of them men, made those laws, and the laws that they made reflected common and persistent attitudes that white people in Virginia and elsewhere in the United States held about black people. The attitudes, as Hill knew, both predated and long outlasted the laws.

13

THE
SPIRIT OF
VIRGINIA

Douglas Southall Freeman (1886–1953) and Virginius Dabney (1901–1995) (both cour-
tesy of the Library of Virginia) were influential Richmond journalists and historians
who publicized a version of Virginia's history and a definition of its culture that authors
of textbooks and popular literature on Virginia repeated in numerous venues through-
out the twentieth century. Even though both men were at times privately critical of the
undemocratic politics of Harry Byrd's Democratic Party organization, their writings
romanticized the past and diverted attention away from many of the undemocratic
aspects of the state's political culture that supported that organization.

If THE GENERAL ASSEMBLY AT ANY time during the twentieth century had emulated the House of Representatives and created an Un-Virginian Activities Committee, the members would surely have turned their suspicious eyes toward southwestern Virginia. Ever since the Civil War the inhabitants of the large region of mountains and valleys west of the Blue Ridge and south of the latitude of Roanoke had been well aware of how the political culture of their region differed from that of eastern Virginia. Easterners were also well aware of the differences, much as they had been aware before the Civil War of the large differences that existed between the residents of eastern Virginia and the Virginians of the Ohio Valley. Indeed, after the Civil War southwestern Virginia presented to the keen observer very much the same set of alternative political values and behaviors that the northwestern inhabitants had exhibited before they created their own separate state. So distinctive did the politics of the southwestern region become that by the early years of the twentieth century, it was the only geographical region in the United States popularly known by its congressional district number, as the Ninth District, or the Fighting Ninth.

The first English-speaking men and women who in the middle of the eighteenth century settled in the valleys of the upper Tennessee River watershed formed small communities or lived on their farms scattered up and down the river and creek valleys. The landscape did not permit large-scale tobacco farming or much in the way of extended commercial agriculture other than grazing and hog raising. As a consequence few men became truly wealthy, and those who were more wealthy than the norm were not so much more wealthy or socially exalted as in the east. The society and politics that evolved were much less stratified than in the old tobacco-growing regions of Virginia. Local political institutions were structurally the same as in the east, but in the west the justices of the peace, militia officers, and other local leaders resembled the men they governed and commanded more than the grandees in the east resembled their neighbors. Westerners, whether small farmers or the relatively more prosperous elites, comfortably shared a commitment to political liberty and equality in the eighteenth century long before those values gained currency among the voting men and political leaders of eastern Virginia.[1]

Living separated from one another as they did permitted men in the mountains to be their own complete masters, on a smaller scale but much like the colonial planters. They prided themselves on their self-reliance and personal independence so much that militia officers often had to persuade their men to take to the field because ordering them did not always work. One officer grumbled in 1774 that he could not order his men about as required for the public safety because "Every Dog Doeth acording to freedoms of his own Will."[2] In southwestern Virginia, as elsewhere in the state's mountains, men came to associate their independence and personal liberty with the mountains themselves. "Mountains has always been friendly to liberty," wrote a local man who in 1781 drafted a plan for mobilizing southwestern volunteers to defend Virginia from British invaders.[3] The phrase "Mountains has" appears at first glance to be a grammatical infelicity uncharacteristic of the writer, but perhaps it was not. "Mountains" might not be a plural noun in that context but a singular noun describing the region.

The recognition that residents of the area shared more with one another than they shared with residents east of the mountains contributed to a plan concocted in the mid-1780s to create a new state of Franklin from portions of Virginia and North Carolina. In their missives to Congress, the residents of Washington County who supported the separation described themselves as "inhabiting valleys, intermixed with and environed by vast wilds of barren and inaccessible mountains." They asked Congress to approve boundaries that followed the contours of the landscape and to create "a convenient terri-tory, not too small for the support of authority, nor too large for the security of freedom" in order to "prevent the encroachments of arbitrary power on the Asylums of freedom." Ignoring the Indians with whom they often found themselves in conflict, the white men described themselves as the "first occu-pants and Aborigines of this Country; freemen claiming natural rights and the privileges of American Citizens."[4] There were local political rivalries that fed into that failed separatist attempt,[5] but the movement probably reinforced rather than diluted regional self-consciousness.

By the time that the first historians wrote about southwestern Virginia in the mid-nineteenth century, they perceived or repeated what had become commonplace there, that residents in Virginia's mountains resided in a com-paratively democratic society and practiced politics in a more democratic man-ner than in the east. The writers gave credit to the mountains. Robert R. How-ison, for example, in the second volume of his *History of Virginia* published in 1848, and Henry Howe, who published *Historical Collections of Virginia* in 1849, wrote romantically about the first settlers and their hardy independence, which manifested itself in their political behavior. Howe in fact began his account by declaring, "The inhabitants of the mountain counties are almost perfectly independent" as a direct consequence of where and therefore how they lived.[6]

Soon thereafter George Washington Lafayette Bickley published a history of Tazewell County. It was the first book-length history of any southwestern county, and he promised that it was to be the first in a set of county histories in which he would present a "complete history of south-western Virginia," including the counties that later formed the heart of the Ninth District and a few in what became southern West Virginia. Bickley never completed his shelf of southwestern Virginia books, but in his volume on Tazewell County he clearly expressed a strong regional awareness. "If nature may be said to have been partial to any county, it was to this," he wrote about Tazewell. "Here is one of the most salubrious climates in the world—water of the purest quality, and a soil naturally productive, and capable of being swelled, in its productive agency, to almost any extent. . . . When geological surveys shall have been made by the state government, and the mineral wealth of this region be made known, the rush by our eastern brethren will not be for the western states, but the western part of their own. For the eastern Virginian, in leaving his plains for a new home in the mountains of Virginia, will not regard his steps as so many taken toward his grave, for he will know that here, *care insures health.*"[7]

Southwestern Virginia gained its unique political identity in 1872 when the General Assembly drew new congressional district lines for the first time since the creation of West Virginia deprived the state of many of its mountain counties. That was when the area became the Ninth District.[8] The boundaries have since fluctuated, reaching sometime farther east and north than at other times, but its heart has remained the same, in the mountains and valleys of the southwestern tip of Virginia. And as with the men of the Ohio Valley counties of Virginia before the Civil War, the people in the Ninth District have nearly always diverged in political interests and conduct from the other regions of what remained Virginia.

Between the end of the Civil War and the end of the nineteenth century, the district's voters elected Democrats to the House of Representatives nine times and Republicans twice. One of the Democrats supported the Readjusters in the beginning but turned his back on them later, but another man won election to Congress from the Ninth District running as a Readjuster, not as a Democrat or a Republican. In 1916 Louis I. Jaffé, then on the verge of becoming one of the state's premier journalists, wrote with only some exaggeration that "of all the districts in Virginia, the Ninth is the most truly Democratic. It was the Ninth in the chaotic years which followed Appomattox, that sent to Richmond solid delegations of white Democrats when the populous eastern districts packed the General Assembly with a motley crew of radical Republicans and negroes."[9]

By the time Jaffé wrote, enterprising businessmen from Pennsylvania and elsewhere had taken the lead and opened mines to extract the coal in southwestern Virginia. The region shifted its political alignment and became more Republican. The competitiveness of political campaigns that had always characterized the district became more intense and gave it the well-known nickname of the Fighting Ninth. During the twentieth century the district continued its independent trend. Republicans Campbell Slemp and his son Campbell Bascom Slemp won the district's congressional seat every year from 1903 through 1920 when Republicans almost never won a congressional election anywhere else in the state, and another Republican won the district in 1928 and served for one two-year term. The defeat of Republicans in the Ninth District that Harry Flood Byrd helped engineer in 1922 was an event of signal importance in the state's political history and as much as any other one thing propelled him into the dominant position in the state for the next four decades.[10]

Mines eventually brought labor unions. In no other large area of the state did unions successfully recruit so many men as in southwestern Virginia during the first decades of the twentieth century. That may have worked to separate the interests of traditional Democratic political leaders in the area from a substantial number of Ninth District voters during the 1930s, when they repeatedly elected a New Dealer to Congress. Democrat John W. Flannagan represented the district in Congress from 1931 to 1949 and was one of only two congressman from Virginia who supported the New Deal and the only one who served more than one term.[11]

The district remained out of step with the state for the remainder of the twentieth century. When Democrats were ascendant elsewhere, Ninth District voters elected Republicans to Congress and the General Assembly. When Republicans began to supplant Democrats in eastern congressional districts, Ninth District voters sent Democrats to Congress. That trend continued through 2010, when Republicans after several attempts finally defeated progressive Democrat Frederick C. Boucher, who had represented the district since 1983, during hard times for the Democratic Party in most other parts of Virginia.

It may be no accident that some of the most formidable opponents of Harry Byrd's Democratic Party came from southwestern Virginia. Martin A. Hutchinson, originally from Giles County, led the antiorganization faction of the Democratic Party for more than a decade beginning late in the 1930s. Republican Theodore Roosevelt "Ted" Dalton, from Radford, posed the most serious threat in the 1950s to the Democrats' long hold on the governor's office,[12] and A. Linwood Holton, from Wise County and Roanoke, began to break the Democratic Party's control of state government when he won election in 1969 as the first Republican governor of the state in a century.[13]

The Ninth District had another regional historian after Bickley, and he tried to explain why and how the area differed so much from the rest of Virginia. In 1927 William C. Pendleton, a Republican newspaper editor who was born not long after Bickley wrote about Tazewell County, published *Political History of Appalachian Virginia, 1776–1927*. It was an account of how the political culture of southwestern Virginia, not of the whole Appalachian region, had followed a different trajectory from the rest of the state. Pendleton wrote that in the beginning "the people of Appalachian Virginia, almost *en masse,* aligned themselves behind Thomas Jefferson.... Furthermore, the people of Appalachian Virginia have, from that period up to the present time, faithfully adhered to the principle of popular government, except on occasions when diverted therefrom by artful politicians, or when prevented from exercising their political faith by the operation of unfair suffrage and election laws."[14]

Voting men in the region had been badly divided about the wisdom of secession early in 1861 and remained divided during the Civil War, when both armies crisscrossed the mountains to gain control of the railroads and mountain passes as well as the important salt deposits at Saltville.[15] By the 1920s, though, as Pendleton explained in words very unlike what white Virginians elsewhere in the state employed, "most of us have realized that instead of being our enemy, Lincoln was our true-hearted friend. Today his memory is cherished quite as cordially at the South as it is at the North and the West; and we recognize him as one of the greatest and purest men America, or even the world, has ever produced. And we have an abiding conviction that if he had lived to fill out his second term, the people of the South would have been saved from the despised period of Reconstruction days, and would not now be enthralled by the racial problem which threatens our social and political life." Pendleton concluded, "It may safely be said that the most woeful event of the Civil War, and the most serious calamity inflicted upon the people of the South, was the horrible assassination of Abraham Lincoln on the night of April 14th, 1865."[16] For Pendleton and doubtless for many other southwestern Virginia Republicans, their natural democratic political lineage ran from Thomas Jefferson through Abraham Lincoln to the twentieth-century Republican Party.

Pendleton published his history of southwestern Virginia during the gubernatorial administration of Harry Flood Byrd and on the final two pages condemned what he saw Byrd doing. Pendleton interpreted Byrd's reorganization of the state bureaucracy and his consolidation of control over the Democratic Party as the latest in a long line of undemocratic acts. "This reform scheme is proclaimed by the Governor and his associates a 'progressive movement,'" Pendleton wrote. "Is it not likely that they are moving in the wrong direction? They ought to realize that going forward to wrong principles of government is really going backward and that going backward to right principles is going forward. Have the people of Virginia become so degenerate and the electorate so corrupted that they are no longer fit to govern themselves? If so, the Goddess of Liberty should be removed from the Great Seal of the Commonwealth and the Dollar ($) Mark placed thereon as an appropriate symbol of the sordid spirit that now controls political thought in Virginia.... In passing upon these so-called reform measures, the Virginia electorate—or rather the remnant that now composes the electorate—will have to make choice between Jeffersonian popular government and bureaucratic—oligarchic—machine government. God save the Commonwealth!"[17]

Pendleton's irreverent attitude toward and criticisms of the state's political leaders for failing to live up to the promise of Thomas Jefferson's Revolutionary words about political liberty and equality, to which he believed southwestern Virginians remained committed, would have attracted the attention of any Un-Virginian Activities Committee. Members of any such committee could literally have thrown many books at Pendleton to prove that he did not understand the true essence of Virginia and failed to appreciate its political leaders.

In an introduction entitled "The Spirit of Virginia" that journalist and historian Douglas Southall Freeman composed for publication in 1940 in the Virginia Writers' Project's *Guide to the Old Dominion,* he described what he believed was the dominant ethos of Virginia. "In the cultured circles of the larger eastern cities of the Commonwealth," Freeman wrote, "there is a curious commingling of yesterday and today. . . . There is a deliberate cult of the past along with typically American business activity. All eastern Virginians are Shintoists under the skin. Genealogy makes history personal to them in terms of family. Kinship to the eighth degree usually is recognized. There are classes within castes. Alumni of the various colleges have different affiliations. A pleasant society it is, one that does not adventure rashly into new acquaintanceship but welcomes with a certain stateliness of manner those who come with letters from friends. If conversation rarely is brilliant, it is friendly and humorous and delightsome to the alien except when it passes to genealogical abstrusities."[18]

The "cultured circles" of white people became in that passage on the very first pages of his introduction Freeman's way of focusing attention on the core values of the state's social and governing elite, but his doing so also served to eliminate everybody else and their beliefs from his discussion of the population of Virginia, as if the populations he eliminated were not worth writing about. Freeman's descriptions of what the people of that privileged and self-satisfied population believed about themselves and about Virginia subtly transformed their beliefs into a blanket characterization of the beliefs and attitudes of the whole population. "The Spirit of Virginia" thereby became a kind of ethnic cleansing of the history and culture of the state.

Freeman did admit, almost sheepishly, "Politically, the ominous conditions in Virginia are the gradual atrophy of local self-government, the failure of well-educated, unselfish men and women to participate actively in the public service, and the abstention of tens of thousands from the exercise of the franchise."[19] He wrote those words as if he regarded those failings as minor imperfections in an admirable commonwealth, and he did not reflect then or elsewhere or at other times on the consequences for the disfranchised or on the undemocratic or antidemocratic spirit that animated—or, perhaps better, inanimated—the minds of the blasé cultured elites. Even as the elite white men and women had deliberately made it difficult or impossible for those many other Virginians to take part in public life and change anything, they also readily relinquished their own independence and ideas about politics to another even smaller group of people—the political leaders—as if those other people, alone, were somehow specially qualified or entitled to think and to act politically, and as if that was the unremarkable natural order of things.

Freeman's "Spirit of Virginia" was not an aberration, and it did not inadvertently generalize from a part to the whole. He wrote often in editorials and in his books on Virginia subjects that the state's culture was unique and especially admirable because of the values that its white elites nurtured. He idealized the values in the 1930s in his four-volume biography of Robert E. Lee that won a Pulitzer Prize and again in the 1940s and early 1950s in an even longer biography of George Washington that won him a posthumous second Pulitzer Prize. Freeman wrote on that same theme for decades.[20]

In 1924 in a little essay in the *Nation* entitled "Virginia: A Gentle Dominion," Freeman singled out for special commendation the reputation that he stated Virginians had as being kindly. "That quality is consideration for the feelings of other people," he explained. "A man may be fairly sure in Virginia of a courteous answer to his inquiries and of a friendly reply to his greeting. Whether a mountaineer on the side of a wretched little clearing or the inheritor of a great name chatting over his first editions, the average Virginian displays an inherited thoughtfulness for the sensibilities of another. He dislikes to say unpleasant things or to touch a sore spot, and he is equally anxious not to have his own bruises handled or his own feelings hurt. All this sounds very much like boasting that lacks the very quality it describes; yet there is no understanding Virginia, and her people's courtesy, their reserve, and their sense of values unless one realizes that an atmosphere of goodwill and friendliness is prized above industrial advance or agricultural progress."[21] Freeman disclosed some of his own social prejudices when he referred disparagingly to Virginians who might live beside a "wretched little clearing" in the mountains and then singled out wealthy Virginians from venerable old families as the ones who possessed precious books.

At the time Freeman wrote about gentle and genteel Virginia, labor unions were successfully appealing to the country's working men and women who thought that they were underpaid or mistreated. He looked for and found a different story in Virginia. "Consideration is certainly one of several explanations of the comparative amity between employer and employee in Virginia," he wrote. "Their relationship rests on the first law of the South—that a white man is a white man and must be treated as such regardless of his station."[22]

In that sentence Freeman tacitly admitted that white people normally treated black people differently than they treated white people, meaning that white people treated black people worse than they treated white people. It is doubtful that many of Freeman's readers would have not known that variations on the phrase "like a white man" meant good, fair treatment. What that meant about treatment of black people therefore did not need explanation.

Freeman backhandedly commended the state's white people and their treatment of the state's black people by writing approvingly of how much some of the state's black people acted like respectable white people, even suggesting that they shared the Shintoism that he referred to in "The Spirit of Virginia" later. "The Virginia Negro is the blue-blood of his race," wrote Freeman, as he characterized the state's black population in 1924 with both pride and condescension but not much accuracy, "and has behind him nearly a century more of life on the continent than have most colored people of the cotton belt. Many Virginia Negroes are the descendants of seventeenth-century slaves; perhaps the majority date their American 'line' from around 1750.... They have their social strata, their clubs, their fraternal organizations, their vigorous churches, their stores, their doctors and dentists, and even their banks, though these last, it must be admitted sorrowfully, are entirely too prone to fail."[23] Whether black banks failed more often than white banks may perhaps be doubted, but it is revealing that Freeman did not resist the temptation thus to cast doubt on the abilities and practices of black people who owned businesses.

Freeman wrote with strained politeness in 1924 about the Democratic Party apparatus that Thomas Martin and Claude Swanson had run for years and that was beginning to fall into the hands of Harry Byrd. Freeman sometimes criticized the undemocratic workings of the organization privately, but he seldom did so publicly. Praising the honesty and gentility of the organization's leaders, he lamented in passing that too few Virginians could vote, noting "that a State of 2,300,000 does not poll in the average Democratic primary more than 150,000 votes. In the general election the number will not exceed from 200,000 to 230,000." But he refrained from drawing the obvious conclusions from the dismal facts that he recited. "It is all a political curiosity," he concluded. Freeman blamed the nonvoters for being "a people too considerate of office-holders" rather than blaming the constitution and laws that made it too difficult or impossible for them to vote. "Indifference is a killing obstacle in the way," he wrote, and then again he blamed the victims for embracing his own historical outlook, for their and his "belief that a State which has been well governed heretofore will be governed equally well in the future."[24]

The past was always very much alive for Douglas Southall Freeman and frequently skewed how he viewed the present and looked toward the future. His influential personal example and his numerous books, articles, speeches, and editorials reinforced the similar beliefs of many other white Virginians.

He was neither the first nor the last to write about Virginia that way. Many twentieth-century white men and women wrote about the small population of Virginians that he wrote about as if it was the only population of Virginia, as if its values were the values of everybody or the only values that mattered. Those writers often quoted or cited one another as authorities for their characterizations, so that a circular repetition evolved that appeared to prove their point again and again by reference to other writers but in fact merely repeated the same assertions. That body of literature had an insular quality about it that was curiously congruent with the insular quality of their culture.

They liked to cite or quote from Arnold Toynbee's *A Study of History,* which examined the whole of human history and was based in large part on published historical literature and cultural commentary. In volume four Toynbee included a very long section entitled "The Cause of the Breakdowns of Civilizations" and within it a long subsection called "Failure of Self-Determination" and within that a shorter sub-subsection on "The Nemesis of Creativity" and within that a still shorter sub-sub-section on "The Idolization of an Ephemeral Self." There, in a few pages on South Carolina, Toynbee coupled that singular Southern American state with Virginia. "A foreign observer who visited 'the Old South' in the seventy-third year after General Lee's capitulation at Appomattox Court House," he wrote late in the 1930s, would find that "the memory of the catastrophe of 1861–5 is as green in our generation as if the blow had fallen only yesterday; and 'the War' still means the Civil War on many Virginian and South Carolinian lips." For most of the rest of the world by then a reference to "the War" meant the World War of 1914–18. "Again," Toynbee continued, "if there is talk of local politics or family affairs, the stranger will often discover, to his surprise, that the persons and events which are the topics of conversation are a century or a century and a half old. In fact, twentieth-century Virginia or South Carolina makes the painful and uncanny impression of a country living under a spell, in which Time has been made to stand still." And several pages later Toynbee wrote, "The former exaltation of Virginia and South Carolina is the veritable cause of their abasement now. They have failed to rise again from the prostration in the Civil War because they have never succeeded in forgetting the height from which that fearful catastrophe once hurled them."[25] He condemned them for living too much in the past, but they prided themselves on living contentedly in its afterglow.

Other writers nearly always ignored Toynbee's message, and the titles of his sections, and his comment about abasement, but they nevertheless cited him as an eminent authority on Virginia's cultural values for paraphrasing the essence of what other commentators had previously published. For instance, citing Toynbee and Freeman in 1955, the French cultural geographer Jean Gottmann wrote, "It is usually agreed that Virginians are a fairly homogeneous population, descended mainly from the early settlers of pre-Revolutionary times and predominantly of Anglo-Saxon blood."[26] His commissioned analysis entitled *Virginia at Mid-Century* included some valuable information about African Americans and nonelite white people in the state, but its overall characterization of the people and the spirit of the state referred back to and very closely resembled what Freeman and Toynbee wrote, and it took prosperous, cultured white Virginians and their values as the norm. "Virginia stands out as a highly individual state in the nation," Gottmann wrote, "not only because of her past, but also because of her present; not only because of a set of economic features all her own, not duplicated elsewhere, but also because of a way of doing things that is Virginian and different from what can be expected from the neighbors."[27] He relied on and repeated what elite white Virginians wrote and said about themselves, and his book thereby became another commentary that subsequent writers relied on as having independently verified the essence of the Virginia spirit.

Themes of exceptionalism and essential greatness appeared irresistible to most white men and women in the state who wrote about Virginia during the first two-thirds of the twentieth century, and those writings influenced what other people thought and wrote. "Virginia is, of course, a sovereign entity with its own ecology and a host of special attributes," popular national journalist Cabell Phillips wrote in the same year that Gottmann published his scholarly analysis. "But more than any of its forty-seven sister states, it is also a state of mind—a very special state of mind. To say, 'I am a Virginian,' or 'My family, of course, came from Virginia,' is to impute a certain modest elegance to one's genes and chromosomes, to suggest a superior quality of character, breeding and gentility, as well as to fix the physical boundaries of a routine biological fact. The remarkable thing is that this assumption is so rarely challenged. Texas, for example, is a state of mind, too, but when a Texan tells you where he is from he instinctively puts up his guard and throws in an unspoken dare to 'make something of it.' Virginians aren't defensive about being Virginians. Their attitude is a sort of regal humility that gently compels acceptance of the Virginian on his own terms."[28]

"The upper-class world," agreed Virginian Marshall Fishwick in a 1959 book devoted to Virginia's culture, "was and still is family-centered and perpetuated. Masculinity, class consciousness, conformity of dress, ancestor reverence, and scorn of competition are also stressed. To be properly molded, Virginians are usually sent to such preparatory schools as Woodberry Forest, Virginia Episcopal School, or the Episcopal High School, founded in 1839 on a hill outside Alexandria." The schools he mentioned were all exclusively for the sons of Freeman's cultured elites. Fishwick was a keen commentator on social and cultural phenomena and wrote some trenchant criticism of the cultural elites of Virginia. He also wrote about the African American population of the state and about the majority of its white residents who were not among the elites, but when he concluded his analysis of the state's political and cultural leaders, he slipped into the litany of Freeman, Toynbee, and the others and wrote as if a small masculine minority was or represented everybody. "The state is close-knit," Fishwick wrote, setting up one of the most pungent sentences in his book, "because the families are self-contained and clannish. These are parochial land-rooted people of a continuous social character composed of the same kind of families and attitudes. Virginia is a vast cousindom. Second and third cousins are known, visited, and accepted as a necessary part of life. Large families have always been the rule. A state-wide interlocking kinship does more to foster Virginia-centeredness than any other factor. Mass media notwithstanding, the favorite indoor sport in Virginia is still climbing about on the family tree."[29]

Early in the 1970s Francis Pickens Miller told two stories in one paragraph of his autobiography that delighted men and women who had never become personally invested in that version of Virginia culture or those assumptions about the state's unique greatness. Miller sought to expose what he believed were some of the deleterious long-term consequences to the minds and spirits of Virginians who lived comfortably in the culture that Freeman and the other commentators had described and under the Byrd organization's long regime. "I have lately been told," Miller wrote, "that when a corporation wants to test a new product in the U.S.A. it selects two cities for tryouts: one that will try anything, the other that will not try anything much. Richmond is usually chosen as the city that will not try anything much." He let the reported unwillingness of Richmond residents even to consider change stand in for his condemnation of the state's political and cultural leaders for supinely accepting the stagnant status quo.[30]

On a trip to Richmond during his campaigning days, Miller related in the same paragraph of his autobiography, "I was received with great courtesy and spent hours in delightful conversation with the most charming people. But I found no concern about the nation or the world deep enough or serious enough to cause anyone to feel responsible for discussing national policy and recommending the development of new lines of policy. The general reaction was a whimsical look, followed by, 'Why, Francis, you don't suppose anything we said would make any difference, do you?' and my silent reflection was, 'No, I don't suppose it would, because I don't think you would have anything to say!' The upper classes in Richmond were well satisfied with things as they were in the Old Dominion and saw no reason to bestir themselves."[31]

At the time that Miller was butting his head against the Byrd organization and what he believed was a deplorable public apathy that the organization's long dominance of the state had fostered, the General Assembly established a seven-member state commission composed of politicians and educators to oversee the publication of three new textbooks on Virginia's history and government. Early in the 1950s the commission members selected three respected professors, each with a doctorate in history and each to be principal author of one of the three textbooks. One of them taught at Madison College, and two taught at Longwood College, two of the state's oldest teachers colleges. The commissioners also appointed one or more public school teachers to work with each historian and commissioned one team to write a history of the state for use in the fourth grade, one a textbook on the state's history and geography for use in the seventh grade, and one a textbook on history and government for use in high school.[32]

Even if some of the commissioners may never have read any of the literature or poetry or historical narratives of Thomas Nelson Page, they appear to have held the same beliefs about Virginia and the lessons of its history that Page propagated in the many volumes of his writings late in the nineteenth century and early in the twentieth. When Page wrote about the responsibilities of historians of Virginia late in the nineteenth century (when Letitia Burwell was rhapsodizing about the good old slavery days), he asked rhetorically, "What nobler task can he set himself than this—to preserve from oblivion, or worse, from misrepresentation, a civilization which produced as its natural fruit Washington and Lee!"[33] That the culture produced Washington and Lee meant to Page that it was so excellent that its failings could be excused or overlooked or forgotten. The historian of Virginia should strive to pass on to his or her readers only the best parts of the old civilization, which is precisely what Douglas Southall Freeman tried to do.

The textbook project hit many potholes in the road to publication because the professional historians did not understand and present Virginia's history that way, the way the commissioners wanted it understood and presented. The writers submitted drafts that alarmed the commissioners, who made deletions or rewrote passages of which they disapproved, seeking to incorporate into the prose a proper appreciation for what they called the "Virginia spirit."[34] The changes that the commissioners made to the seventh-grade textbook particularly annoyed its principal authors, Dr. Francis Butler Simkins, of Longwood College, a distinguished historian of the South, and his wife, Margaret Robinson Simkins, a public school teacher in Farmville. She later recalled, "We had a good chapter on Negro disfranchisement under the Constitution of 1902. The commission said the Negro children were going to use the book also, and there was enough hard feeling already, so they took it out." The problem was not simply that the commissioners did not want to create more hard feelings among black children, they also wanted the narrative of Virginia's history to emphasize its heroic and virtuous side and to ignore its undemocratic acts and not remind the excluded people of their exclusion from public life.[35]

During the preparation of their manuscript, Francis and Margaret Simkins met with one of the commission members, whom Francis B. Simkins characterized as "a real Virginia aristocrat." The commission member told them that he wanted all of the writers "to emphasize the greatness of Virginia and take out any reference to poor people living in Virginia." The commission member also told them, "What you ought to do is make every seventh grader aspire to the colonnaded mansion; and if he can't get there, make him happy in the cabin."[36] What the commission member told them, in effect, was to let the plantation culture of the previous century and the exclusion of a majority of the state's adults from public life appear to be part of the natural order of things that was not to be changed. Most Virginians had dwelled in cabins or small houses and not in mansions both before the Civil War and afterward, but the commission member's comment clearly exposed what he and perhaps others believed was still the ideal. All of the other people who did not live in mansions would have to learn quietly to accept that ideal as if it was the only possible reality or aspiration.

As published, the fourth-grade history and the seventh-grade history and geography textbooks portrayed Virginia's white leaders in unfailingly flattering lights, its enslaved residents as happy and contented beneficiaries of benign masters who civilized and Christianized them, and its Indians as savage barbarians in some contexts or as primitive simpletons in others. The books included very little about the final decades of the nineteenth century or the first half of the twentieth century, as if the excellent old culture that had produced Washington and Lee was gone forever and there was little else worth writing about afterward.

Dr. Marvin W. Schlegel, also a history professor at Longwood College, submitted the manuscript on history and government for high school use. The commissioners decided that it was entirely unacceptable. Acting through a representative of the New York publishing house that had the contract for printing the high school text, the commissioners entrusted the manuscript to historian and archivist W. Edwin Hemphill, the founding editor of *Virginia Cavalcade* magazine at the Virginia State Library, and instructed him to alter its tone and substance to conform to the proper Virginia spirit. When the commissioners hired Schlegel to write the book, they had identified and dignified him as Dr. Schlegel, but when they passed his work on to Hemphill for revisions to conform it to their version of a proper Virginia textbook, they demoted Schlegel to a mere "native of Pennsylvania."[37]

"Although the commission itself did not write the books," Schlegel later groused, "it kept full control over them by refusing to approve anything which did not accord with its views. . . . In other words, the purpose of the Virginia histories was to inculcate in the student a pride in Virginia's past and a desire to keep that past unchanged in the future—the beliefs which were held, by no coincidence, by the then dominant conservative political organization."[38]

Shortly after the books were published, Schlegel addressed a symposium at Longwood College on the subject of interpreting Virginia history. He made some wry comments. "This delicate balance between praise and criticism" that historians practiced, he told the audience, "is a fairly simple task for a native Virginian, who knows instinctively the difference between good and bad in our past. If the historian, however, should have arrived in Virginia too late in life to acquire a complete understanding of the values of our Commonwealth's culture, he should not attempt to write a Virginia history textbook at all; if he does get involved in such a project anyhow, the safest rule for him to follow is that, in case of doubt, always lean toward the idealist side. In so doing he is more likely to arrive at the truth as Virginians see it." He did not have to specify which Virginians. Having had the humiliating experience of seeing a book of which he disapproved published with his name on the title page, he closed his lecture sarcastically, "To avoid any possible confusion, it may be wise to conclude with the conventional disclaimer and point out that the opinions expressed in this paper are not necessarily those of the speaker."[39]

At the same symposium at which Schlegel poked his thumb in the eyes of the textbook commissioners, Lawrence Burnette Jr., an editor at the New York publishing house Charles Scribner's Sons, which published two of the three textbooks, spoke at length about the problems he had encountered during his firm's publication of scholarly and popular works on Virginia as well as textbooks for the state's public schools. Virginia, as he personified the state and its culture when perhaps unknowingly echoing Arnold Toynbee, "derives vicarious pleasure from its tragedy. It preaches a broad ideological tolerance but practices a close intellectual communion. Its intelligentsia are intelligent but anti-intellectual. . . . No other state makes such a concerted effort to indoctrinate its young in its history, and there is no question that the effort accomplishes its end."[40]

"The saga of Virginia," Burnette went on to explain at greater length, "has taken on so many of the qualities of folklore that it is now largely academic to attempt the separation of fact from lore. Any attempt to challenge popular misconceptions is simply dismissed as 'revisionistic.' A scholar accustomed to basing his work on documents, authority, and expert opinion is rudely shocked when he learns that the ultimate authority in Virginia history is *vox populi*." He also did not have to specify which *vox* spoke loudest and most authoritatively. By way of example, he remarked, "Some popular heroes are clung to despite the gnawing fear that they do not fit the Virginia ideal. Thomas Jefferson and Patrick Henry have had enough of their objectionable radicalism canonized out of them to make them respectable, orthodox saints."[41]

Burnette continued, "Perhaps the most sacrosanct of all Virginia institutions is our visible government—as distinct from the more powerful 'invisible' government," by which he meant the Byrd organization. "Virginians are highly sensitive to this conflict between governmental ideals and practices. . . . To one uninitiated in the Virginia historical tradition, its rites, sacraments, rituals, and taboo suggest a religion of narcissism. It seeks the perpetuation of its own past glory, the suppression of all forms of heresy and schism, and a philosophical isolation from its adversaries—that the faith may be kept pure and unspotted. The writers and editors of its missals, prayer books, and chronicles would do well to remember that sycophancy is a sin but apostasy is a mortal sin."[42]

Burnette was correct in pointing out the "concerted effort" that the state government took to propagate a particular version of Virginia's history. As a part of its campaign begun in the 1920s and continued beyond the end of the century to attract tourists to Virginia and to entice them to spend money in the state, the General Assembly created the Commission on Conservation and Development that, among other things, began placing markers along the state's highways to commemorate historic events, places, and people. The highway marker program was innovative, the first of its kind in the country. Together with the many monuments and statues throughout Virginia that honored Confederate soldiers, those highway markers made the landscape itself a powerful educational text. The lesson of Virginia's history that the landscape was made to teach during the middle third of the twentieth century was of the accomplishments of white men who achieved their greatest nobility in times of crisis: in the founding of the colony early in the seventeenth century, in winning independence during the latter part of the eighteenth century, and in fighting for the Confederacy during the middle of the nineteenth century. In its first decades the highway marker program erected more signs to glorify Virginia's Civil War military history than any other topic, almost more than all other topics combined. As with the textbooks of the 1950s, the historic markers largely ignored African Americans and their history and in some instances described the state's Indians as primitive savages and their acts of resistance to inevitable and admirable Anglo-American westward expansion as outrages.[43]

One or two academic historians wrote textbooks on Virginia's history during the early years of the twentieth century, but, surprisingly, no professional historian undertook to write a full history of Virginia at any time during the entire century. In 1971 Virginius Dabney published a long narrative history of the colony and state soon after he retired as editor of the *Richmond Times-Dispatch,* in the same year that Francis Pickens Miller published his memoirs. In *Virginia, the New Dominion,* Dabney attempted to sum up the insights of the existing historical literature at a time when he believed that the state was at a major turning point in history, hence his subtitle. "It is not the commonwealth that George Washington and Thomas Jefferson knew," Dabney wrote at the conclusion of his foreword, "nor yet that of Woodrow Wilson and Carter Glass. It retains many of the qualities that endeared it to those notable men, but it also is imbued with characteristics nowhere evident in the Virginia of their time. Some Virginians are nostalgic at this hour for the *Old* Dominion, and all of us must cherish and revere its virtues. But let us today salute the *New* Dominion, with its challenges and its promise."[44]

In most respects Dabney remained a man of the old dominion, and his treatment of some of the episodes of the Virginia of his own time reveals his ambivalence about and insecurity with the new. For example, in the foreword he wrote correctly but a bit condescendingly, "Our Negro citizens are among those who have not received their due. Their achievements have too often been ignored, and they have suffered from a one-sided presentation of the facts." Dabney then revealed that the roots of his own beliefs and perceptions were in the past. "Race relations in the commonwealth have been transformed," he wrote, "and many of the manifest injustices from which black citizens suffered have been ended, albeit not without certain traumatic effects, accompanied by swings of the pendulum that have gone too far in the opposite direction."[45] At the beginning of the 1970s, when advocates of changes in the old and un-equal racial status quo were still demanding many more changes, they had al-ready changed more than Dabney could comfortably accept.

When researching and writing his historical narratives, which also in-cluded a history of the city of Richmond and histories of the University of Virginia in the twentieth century and of Virginia Commonwealth Univer-sity, Dabney read and summarized the historical literature available to him. Some of it was good, but much of it was superficial or celebratory.[46] He was not a scholar at heart or an original or insightful thinker, and his narratives consequently reflected to a large degree his own early education and beliefs together with the perspectives and purposes of the writers on whom he relied. All historians necessarily rely on the work of the men and women who went before them, but Dabney did little original archival work or critical think-ing that might have stretched his attitudes and conclusions beyond what he found readily available on the bookshelves of the Virginia Historical Society and the Virginia State Library or in the library that housed the old reference works and clipping files of the *Richmond Times-Dispatch* and the *Richmond News Leader.*

Dabney's sources and his own early education and predispositions shaped his understandings and his narrative. Like many another writer on the rela-tionship between Virginia's Indians and its first English settlers, he incon-sistently—and without exhibiting that he was aware of the inconsistency—described the Indians both as hostile or savage adversaries and as the colonists' friendly assistants.[47] He wrote that slave owners in Virginia treated their en-slaved property well, certainly better than slave owners elsewhere, but that enslaved people sometimes revolted, nevertheless, to him a puzzling contradiction.[48] When Dabney discussed proposals for emancipation, he stressed the many obstacles that white Virginians faced and adduced as a way of explaining why only a few of them took serious steps to abolish slavery.[49] His chapter on nineteenth-century slavery bore the remarkable title "The Sable Cloud," as if black people or enslaved black people were the problem, not the institution of slavery or white peoples' enslavement of black people. When Dabney wrote that chapter, he had access to little scholarship to help him see that the Revolutionary period debate about the morality of slavery collapsed into a proslavery ideology during the final decades prior to the Civil War. As he frequently did elsewhere in the book, Dabney easily found ways or excuses to exonerate white men and women who employed violence and oppression to control enslaved and free black people. About the slave code and the laws imposing restrictions on the lives of free blacks he wrote, "The legislation was indeed extremely bad, but it was leniently enforced, for the most part, as was frequently the case with such laws in Virginia during the antebellum era."[50] Dabney prevaricated or equivocated and often wrote as if he believed that assertions that elite white Virginians did not behave as badly as they might have or as badly as white people behaved elsewhere excused them from responsibility for engaging in what was still undeniably bad behavior.

Reflecting the state of scholarship at the time, Dabney's treatment of such subjects as nineteenth-century industrialization and the rapid construction of railroads, in which Virginians were every bit as energetic and optimistic as other Americans, was deeply flawed. Ignoring or merely ignorant of the way of life of most of the state's hardworking small farmers, who were the majority of the whole population, and also ignoring the state's large enslaved population, he generalized romantically and perhaps reflexively about the "simple, rural, pastoral life of most Virginians in the years before the Civil War."[51]

Dabney's treatment of the four years of the Civil War is, not surprisingly, the longest chapter in the book and led directly into a chapter on postwar changes that reflected the perspectives of the historians who during the first decades of the twentieth century wrote academic and polemical treatments of Reconstruction and its aftermath. Dabney's inability to think far outside the intellectual parameters of his own privileged, educated, white class and time caused him to frame his section on Reconstruction and its aftermath as a morality play. His 1971 book repeated the essence of his 1932 *Liberalism in the South*. The federal government had spoiled the naturally decent relations between good Virginia white people and good Virginia black people that had obtained during slavery times when it forced onto those good white Virginians the participation in public life of inexperienced black people, bringing out the worst in the state's poorly educated white men. The behavior of bad white Virginians led to bad behavior of black Virginians. Dabney's interpretation shifted the responsibility for disfranchisement, mandatory racial segregation, lynching, and much other inexcusable behavior off the shoulders of the class of good white Virginians to which he belonged and onto the shoulders of inferior white men, the federal government, and the victims themselves.[52]

Dabney was the first person to write at length about the twentieth century in the context of the state's entire history. His perceptions of the twentieth century were entirely consistent with his perceptions of the nineteenth. Dabney remained comfortably in step with the state's political leadership in his attitudes about race and also about organized labor. Repeating what Byrd organization politicians had said during the Great Depression about Virginians being less badly off than other Southerners, Dabney wrote, "The year 1937 was marred, however, by fifty strikes in various parts of Virginia, brought on by increased industrialization, enactment of the Wagner labor relations act, interunion rivalries, and improved business conditions. There was little violence."[53] To Dabney, a labor strike, even a nonviolent one, was a blemish on the state's reputation, and he conspicuously omitted to mention (perhaps even to consider?) the possibility that any actions of employers could have been a cause for a strike.

Dabney disclosed a deep ambivalence about Harry Byrd. Early in his career Dabney had privately criticized the undemocratic politics of Byrd's organization, but by the 1940s and 1950s he readily accepted the social and political consequences of the organization's public policies. As Dabney often did, so as not to offend anybody by taking a firm stand that might reflect poorly on any of the state's leaders or leading families, he took the hard edges off Byrd's reputation by writing with a certain amount of inexactitude. "Numerous persons who disagreed with Senator Byrd in Washington admired, respected and liked him," Dabney wrote. Byrd was a "gracious host," he continued, "charming companion and courteous foe—although capable of occasional demagoguery—he was almost worshipped by many. Yet large numbers of working-class citizens, especially Negroes, detested him." Then, in one of the greatest understatements ever made about Harry Byrd, Dabney wrote blandly, "They felt that he did not have their interests at heart."[54]

In *Virginia, the New Dominion* the timidity of Freeman's gentle dominion led Dabney into many obfuscations and misleading or incorrect statements. In fact, the old dominion stood quietly behind Dabney and peered over his shoulder so far as to block his view and cast shadows on parts of the state's history and allow other parts a disproportionate share of the light. Toward the end of his treatment of the state's twentieth-century political leaders, Dabney lapsed, almost inevitably, back into the traditional explanation of how and why those political leaders acted as they did, excusing them and minimizing the consequences of their actions by giving them venerable precedents for their many undemocratic practices and policies. Like Freeman, Dabney omitted a large proportion of the state's population when he wrote, "The state's

preponderantly Anglo-Saxon background goes far to explain the conservatism of Virginians and their adherence to British principles of liberty and democracy, handed down over the centuries from the time of Magna Carta,"[55] as
if that made all that they did OK, as if Magna Carta and centuries of English
political and legal history transformed the slavery regime and the Byrd organization into agencies of liberty and democracy.

Virginius Dabney's long historical narrative stood alone on the state's bookshelves for the remainder of the twentieth century. It was the only extended
history of the state available for teachers preparing their classes, for college
students studying the state's history, for newspaper editors composing editorials, for political speech writers, and for people who wished to place their own
lives and experiences into the historical context of the state's history. Dabney's
interpretive narrative was consistent in detail and tone with much of what
was in the elementary and secondary textbooks used in Virginia's public and
private schools. Most people who grew to adulthood and entered public life
at any time in the twentieth century learned the same general history of the
state and nation. That history was also consistent, for the most part, with the
popular literature of Freeman and the others and also with the underlying beliefs of the state's political leaders. Indian Virginians and African American
Virginians found the books deeply offensive, but white Virginians living in
their comfortable mansions found them reassuring, and other white Virginians in their cabins may have found that the books legitimated the sway over
the state's public life of a social and political culture to which they did not
personally belong or may have silently learned from the books that they were
not good enough to share in the state's governance.

What the textbooks and the popular literature on Virginia taught was a
privileged white man's version of Virginia's past. What they taught left out a
majority of the Virginians and their histories: black men, nearly all women,
and working and poor white people. What they taught could lead people in
Virginia to view their history in exclusively political terms, and politics in Virginia had traditionally been the domain of prosperous white men. It could
lead those white men, in turn, to believe that they represented everybody or
to forget that they did not represent everybody. Those white political leaders and an overwhelming majority of the state's newspaper editors and popular writers almost always talked and wrote about Virginia as if there were no
other Virginians and as if they were the sole, true custodians of the spirit of
Virginia.

People who grew up in Virginia during most of the twentieth century got
taught a history of their state and nation that prepared them to perceive that
the federal government had been a threatening presence in the lives of all Virginians ever since James Madison and Thomas Jefferson wrote the Virginia
and Kentucky Resolutions of 1798; a federal government that had twisted the

plain language of the Constitution into a shapeless excuse for erecting a national banking system that drew wealth and independence away from Southern planters; that threatened or destroyed the rights of Virginians to manage or dispose of their enslaved property as they pleased; that during the Civil War destroyed the excellent civilization that had flourished there; that debased Virginia's political system at the end of that war by allowing in former slaves and poor white trash; that imposed heavy taxes on businesses and farmers; that gave dangerous powers to national labor organizations; that told business owners whom they could and could not serve and hire and how much to pay and also made them pay for health insurance and retirement accounts for their employees; that during the second half of the twentieth century destroyed the legal right of white people in their states to maintain relations between the races as they pleased, to treat African Americans as less than second-class citizens; and that there was nothing essentially wrong in state governments denying the elemental American right of white and black men and women to vote.

The historical literature available to most people presented those interpretations as if they were incontestable and inevitable facts of history. The books also ignored or selectively elided out unpleasant aspects of Virginia's history, such as the development of a proslavery ideology and a companion proslavery theology before the Civil War and also the contradictions between what Virginia's political leaders said that they believed and what they in fact did. As in Virginius Dabney's book, the literature extolled representative democracy, individual liberty, and theories of limited government in spite of abundant evidence that those were ideals of political life rather than reality for Virginia's residents.

14

PUBLIC
GOOD
AND
PRIVATE
INTEREST

Mills Edwin Godwin Jr. (1914–1999) (courtesy of the Library of Virginia) served as a Democrat in the House of Delegates and the Senate of Virginia and was elected lieutenant governor in 1961 and governor in 1965. A committed supporter of Massive Resistance to court-ordered desegregation of the public schools in the 1950s, he proposed a large and important program of political and educational reform while governor in the 1960s. Switching to the Republican Party, he won election as governor a second time in 1973 and presided over an administration that did not propose any major reforms. Godwin's change of party and his career exemplified the changes and the continuities of twentieth-century Virginia politics.

MARION G. ROBERTSON MADE A speech to the Democratic Party state convention in Williamsburg on 11 June 1978 to urge the nomination of Conley Phillips, a Norfolk city councilman, for the United States Senate. After Phillips lost the nomination, Robertson promised that he and the thousands of people he had inspired and organized to take part in the local mass meetings and in the state convention would be back in the future. Two years after a former governor of Georgia, Democrat Jimmy Carter, won election to the presidency as an openly born-again Christian, Robertson led the campaign to nominate a born-again Democratic Christian to the United States Senate from Virginia, and he promised to assist the party win future elections and in particular to elect evangelical Christian candidates. Robertson was the only person who was not a candidate for the nomination or a prominent officeholder who addressed the convention, a recognition of the importance of the role that he played in the party that year. He was also the only person who talked about the party's future.[1]

Pat Robertson, as he was better known, reintroduced organized evangelical Protestant Christianity back into party politics in Virginia. He was a new figure at the party's convention in Williamsburg, but his name was not new to the party. From the 1910s to the 1960s, his father, A. Willis Robertson, had been a reliable member of the Democratic Party organization that Harry Flood Byrd directed from 1922 until 1966. Willis Robertson and Harry Byrd were seatmates in the Senate of Virginia in the 1910s and together represented the state in the United States Senate from 1946 until Byrd's retirement in 1965. Pat Robertson's appearance at the head of a large group of recently energized evangelical Protestants at the 1978 state convention symbolized important changes that were taking place in the political culture in the state, changes that nevertheless reflected long and durable continuities.

Other events of the Democratic convention and of the Republican Party state convention that year also symbolized the changes and continuities in the politics of post–Harry Byrd Virginia. The man who received the Democratic Party's nomination for the Senate was former state attorney general Andrew Pickens Miller, the son of Francis Pickens Miller, who during the 1940s and 1950s was one of the party's leading opponents of the Byrd organization. Francis Pickens Miller appeared in the gallery during the convention and when introduced received a hearty ovation from the delegates. H. Lester Hooker also appeared at a different hour and on the opposite side of the gallery. When introduced he received only a smattering of polite applause because almost nobody knew who he was. Hooker had managed Claude A. Swanson's primary and general election campaigns for the United States Senate in 1922 and served on the influential State Corporation Commission from 1924 until 1972. He was the last surviving relic of the Byrd organization's antecedent, the Martin-Swanson organization. His appearance at the 1978 convention was also symbolic and signified the continuing relevance of the party's past even as it strove to create a new future.

The convention's presiding officer, John Warren Cooke, was a symbol of the party's more recent past. He was the last son of a Confederate veteran to hold high public office in Virginia and had broken into politics early in the 1940s as a young supporter of the Byrd organization. During the critical struggle over Massive Resistance to the federal courts' orders to desegregate the state's public schools, he was majority leader of the House of Delegates; his predecessors had been called floor leaders, so as not even to acknowledge the presence of the small minority of Republicans. Cooke served as Speaker of the House from 1968 to 1980 and was the first to appoint Republicans and dissident Democrats to influential committees and to treat them as the representatives of Virginia's voters rather than as mere cannon fodder in the legislative battles or like bastards at the family picnic. In January 1977 he defended that innovation when members of the House Democratic Caucus complained about his actions. Cooke told them that if Virginia voters, for whatever incomprehensible reasons, elected Republicans to represent them in the General Assembly, those Virginians deserved for their representatives to have a chance to represent them.[2] He returned a measure of democracy to one of the key institutions of republican government in Virginia. During his long career John Warren Cooke, a product of the old politics, had gradually accommodated himself to changed and changing circumstances.

At the 1978 Democratic Party state convention, Cooke presided over a body that was quite unlike any that had ever assembled before that decade. The delegates included many old Byrd organization regulars and unrepentant Massive Resisters, like James Thompson, who succeeded Cooke as majority leader of the House of Delegates. It included young reformers intent on destroying the last remnants of the Byrd organization and re-creating the state's Democratic Party in the inclusive, progressive image of the national party. It included union members, who had been despised and excluded from the inner councils during Byrd's years. It also included many women, as party conventions had since the 1920s, but in the early years women had been tolerated, not welcomed; in 1978 one even campaigned for the party's senatorial nomination. And it included scores of African Americans, among them the mayor of the capital, Richmond, men and women who never had a chance for effective political action while the Byrd organization was still thriving but who, following the Voting Rights Act of 1965 and the other changes that the civil rights movement had forced on the state's politics, stepped up and eagerly took part in Democratic Party politics.

In accepting the party's nomination, Andrew Miller promised to conduct a spirited campaign for the seat that Willis Robertson had once held, and many of the convention's Democrats hoped that he would run in his father's footsteps, but he did not. He ran a cautious campaign that disappointed and dismayed those Democrats. Miller praised the party's traditions and some of its old leaders in order not to alienate the thousands of Democrats who had been Byrd organization supporters for years and who remained a considerable portion of the party's electoral base. It might have been a good thing that Francis Pickens Miller died not long after the convention adjourned. Hearing his son's appeals to old Harry Byrd's old followers might have killed him.

Miller lost the race to a Republican. It was not the first time in the decade that a Republican defeated a Democrat in a Senate race, but it symbolized the passing of the Democratic Party's nearly century-long dominance and the emergence of the Republican Party of Virginia as a formidable political force.

The events of the 1978 Republican Party state convention also reflected significant signs of the transformations taking place in Virginia politics. Richard Obenshain, the man who won the Republican nomination for the United States Senate that year, was a superior political organizer, not unlike Harry Byrd had been. Obenshain created a grassroots Republican Party organization in Virginia during the 1970s that allowed the party to thrive on the deepening disagreements within the national and state Democratic Parties that alienated many Virginia Democrats. Alienation intensified during that decade and afterward as the state's Democratic Party, including an influx of ardent white reformers and black activists, began to try to move the party away from its Byrd organization past.

At the contentious Republican Party state convention early that summer, Obenshain narrowly defeated former governor Linwood Holton, who had battled the Byrd Democrats during the previous decades in hopes of creating a competitive, two-party politics and restoring political democracy to Virginia. Building on the work that Theodore Roosevelt Dalton had done during the 1940s and 1950s, Holton won election as governor in 1969 and then struggled against the Democrats who controlled the General Assembly to change state government and politics. But even as Holton made a national name for himself as the first Republican governor of Harry Byrd's Virginia, Obenshain and people with a different political agenda began seizing control of the Republican Party. Holton had symbolized a progressive, reforming alternative to the old politics in Virginia, but Obenshain symbolized something else, a determined and well-organized activism dedicated to transforming the Virginia Republican Party into a powerful unit within the national party that was itself becoming more unified as a national opposition to the Democrats. For several decades, by then, Democrats had been stretching elastic interpretation of the Constitution of the United States and enlarging the powers of the national government far beyond anything that Alexander Hamilton or Henry Clay or John Marshall had ever imagined. Obenshain's Virginia Republicans appealed to Harry Byrd's Democrats on issues of national politics on which they largely agreed, luring away Democrats who had already become accustomed to voting for Republicans for president even as they continued to vote for Byrd organization Democrats for local, legislative, and state offices.[3]

Obenshain and the new Republicans, whom he recruited every bit as energetically as Pat Robertson had recruited born-again Christians, treated Holton rudely. A few weeks later Obenshain was killed in an airplane crash on the way to a campaign rally. The party's central committee then spurned Holton again and nominated an outsider, the second runner-up, rather than the former governor, almost literally driving him out of politics.[4] The new nominee, John Warner, defeated Miller in the general election.

After the events of the civil rights movement removed some of the principal props that held up the Byrd organization, some men, like John Warren Cooke, quietly accommodated themselves to the changes and became leaders in the post-Byrd Democratic Party. Others staked out more independent political careers. Harry Flood Byrd Jr., namesake eldest son of the old party leader and an influential member of the Senate of Virginia during the Massive Resistance controversies, succeeded his father in the United States Senate in 1965. In 1971 he declared himself an independent and no longer a Democrat, although he continued to caucus with the Democrats in order to retain his committee seniority, having and eating his political cakes simultaneously. By that act, Harry Byrd Jr.—Little Harry as he was sometimes known—went one step beyond what his father had done since the 1940s in refusing to support the presidential nominees of his own party; but young Harry Byrd did not, as some other old Byrd organization Democrats did in the 1970s and afterward, go all the way over into the Republican Party.

Mills Edwin Godwin Jr. did go all the way. He more than any other one Virginia politician most clearly symbolized both the practical changes and the ideological continuities in Virginia politics during the final decades of the Byrd organization and in the years after old Harry Byrd died.

Godwin entered politics by defeating a Byrd organization stalwart in 1947 for the seat in the House of Delegates representing the rural southeastern counties of Isle of Wight and Nansemond and the little city of Suffolk. During the final years of the 1940s and first years of the 1950s, a small contingent of young assembly members, known at the time as the Young Turks, attempted to moderate some of the rigid policies that the organization had pursued for decades, most notably by increasing appropriations for public schools and abolishing the poll tax as a prerequisite for voting. Most of them gave covert or overt support to leaders of the antiorganization faction that challenged Byrd when he ran for renomination in 1946 and 1952 or to Byrd's chosen candidates for governor in 1949 and 1953. Godwin kept a discreet distance from the Young Turks but also from the organization's inside leaders. Winning election to the Senate of Virginia in 1952, he emerged during the middle years of the decade as one of the most able and determined advocates of Massive Resistance.

A handsome and imposing man of intelligence and natural ability, Godwin was a forceful speaker, even though he was not eloquent or inspiring. He had a reserved dignity that allowed him to present himself as a man of gravitas and as a natural leader. As a result of his obvious talents and hard work on behalf of Massive Resistance, Godwin won the Democratic Party's nomination and then the general election in 1961 to become lieutenant governor. Shrewdly perceiving that racial segregation was no longer to be a firm political foundation on which to build, he antagonized many of his fellow Massive Resisters in 1964 when he campaigned for the election of President Lyndon B. Johnson.[5]

The following year Godwin won election as governor of Virginia. During his term that began in January 1966, he proposed and successfully moved through the General Assembly a budget of reform legislation that shifted some key public policies away from the central agenda of the Byrd organization. The General Assembly passed a sales tax, the first significant new tax in decades; it established a statewide system of community colleges that provided inexpensive higher education and occupational training; it issued bonds to raise money quickly for education and other projects; and it produced a wholesale overhaul of the state's constitution at the end of the 1960s that abolished the laws and political practices that had restricted the electorate and given Democratic Party operatives the ability to control who could vote and who could not. Those changes in election laws merely accommodated the state's constitution to a new political reality, for those old laws and practices had fallen into the dustbin following congressional passage of the Voting Rights Act of 1965 and federal court decisions and a constitutional amendment that abolished the poll tax as a prerequisite for voting. With the other changes during Godwin's term as governor, however, he and the General Assembly achieved some of the principal objectives of the Young Turks and even some of the goals of such old Republicans as Ted Dalton and Linwood Holton.[6]

By the time Godwin's term concluded in January 1970, Harry Byrd and his organization were no longer the prime issues in Virginia politics. Racial prejudice continued to lurk just beneath the surface and broke out conspicuously from time to time as continuing resistance to desegregation of the public schools led to court-ordered busing of pupils within school districts to create desegregated schools in communities that were residentially segregated. By the 1970s and 1980s, though, the political climate in Virginia had changed enough and the threat that Massive Resistance had posed to public education had become unpopular enough that Godwin and most of the supporters of Massive Resistance who were still active in public life changed their explanations of their 1950s actions. They began to claim credit for the largely peaceful desegregation that they had tried to prevent by stating that their resistance had bought time for the change to take place without excessive disruption. But, like the post–Civil War revisionist memoirs and polemics that erased defense of slavery from the political history of late antebellum Virginia and as a cause of the Civil War, the post–Massive Resistance revisionist explanation ignored the realities of the past. The apt name itself continued to remind people that Godwin and the others had created a program of Massive Resistance, not Massive Wait a Minute.

Linwood Holton succeeded Godwin as governor in 1970, and by the time his term was coming to a close four years later, a new generation of Virginia Democrats that made the Young Turks look tame by comparison was on the verge of taking over the party. Their principal champion was Henry Howell, of Norfolk, a man who had supported the civil rights movement early on when very few white men, much less white Democrats, did. Howell was also one of the few Democrats in Virginia who had a reforming economic agenda. He attacked the policies of banks, corporations, and public utilities, on the boards of which many prominent political leaders then sat, that he believed were treating Virginia residents unfairly. With his coarse voice and willingness—even eagerness—to denounce his adversaries in plain and forthright language, Howell tapped into some of the resentment at the status quo that many Virginians had harbored for decades. In 1971 following the death of the state's lieutenant governor, Howell won the office in a three-way special election against a Democrat and a Republican. Characteristically, he delighted in calling his opponents, George Rawlings and George Saffron, George I and George II.

Howell appeared radical in the context of Virginia's political past, although it was often remarked that elsewhere he would have been unremarkable. His brash oratorical style and his direct appeals to poor white voters and African Americans were startling breaks with traditions in twentieth-century Virginia. Howell's style and his proposals alarmed old Byrd organization Democrats and men like Godwin who regarded political leadership, however much wire-pulling was necessary for success, as an honorable calling reserved for cultivated gentlemen, not for the democratic likes of Henry Howell. Nothing so much separated their public images than Godwin's grave reserve and Howell's delight in pledging to "keep the big boys honest."[7]

Howell's conduct deeply offended Godwin, and the behavior of his supporters insulted him, so when Howell began his campaign for governor, Godwin let it be known that he would accept the Republican Party's nomination in order to keep Howell out of the governor's office. The Virginia Republicans, already beginning to be divided among themselves about what the future of their party should be, eagerly accepted Godwin's offer and helped him defeat Howell by a narrow margin in November 1973. Godwin's election to a second term as governor, and as a Republican this time, eased the transition of many former Byrd organization Democrats into the Republican Party. The issues and the ideas were also making that move possible. The Democratic Party became less like the party of old Harry Byrd, and the Republican Party became more like Byrd's old Democratic Party.

The distinguishing feature of Godwin's second administration was not change but conservation of the new status quo. The modifications in the politics and policies of the state that Godwin had presided over during the 1960s were important, but they were also limited. They were not first steps away from the traditions and practices of twentieth-century Virginia politics, they were the only steps. The changes in the political culture of Virginia that Godwin and Obenshain symbolized took place slowly during the course of three decades and had many confluent causes. People in Virginia may have perceived the changes as glacial, and people outside Virginia may have noticed only the high points: Holton's election as the state's first Republican governor in 1969, Godwin's reelection as a Republican in 1973, and most spectacularly the election to statewide office of L. Douglas Wilder, an African American. In 1985 the voters of the state elected him lieutenant governor, and in 1989 they elected him governor.

In 1971 Wilder became the first black member of the Senate of Virginia in the twentieth century. He was the odd man out, but he was a charming and intelligent man who possessed good senses of timing and of the dramatic. He used persistence and pressure in just the right mixture to achieve several of his legislative objectives. In 1985 Wilder astonished nearly everybody except himself by winning the Democratic Party's nomination for lieutenant governor and then astonished them again by winning the general election. When he set out to run for governor in 1989, most Democrats cringed at the thought, not necessarily because they believed that he was unqualified but because they believed that the state's voters would not possibly elect him. But by an extremely narrow margin, they did. The campaign that Wilder ran was another revealing symbol of how even such a radical change as the election of an African American governor in the state where American slavery was created took place within the context of continuity. Wilder campaigned for governor as an old-fashioned Virginia gentleman, soft-spoken, well tailored, dignified, and nonthreatening. Consciously or unconsciously he imitated Godwin's public demeanor. In the most inspired and perhaps most effective act of the campaign, Wilder had himself shown in statewide television advertisements walking down a shaded street of what appeared to be a small town in Southside Virginia talking with the white sheriff who in a vintage Southern accent endorsed the election of a black governor.

A national economic slowdown forced Wilder at the beginning of his term to cut the state budget significantly, winning praise from some of the state's leading newspaper editors, who by then had not endorsed any Democratic candidate for state office for many years. Wilder, in fact, often aligned himself then and thereafter with the state's Republican journalists and middle-of-the-road politicians rather than take the leadership of the progressive Democrats. During the decades following Harry Byrd's death and the collapse of his political organization, the state's political landscape shifted and changed, and the old divisions became blurred. Slowly, the new Republican Party of Virginia gained the upper hand at the expense of the old Democratic Party, which never re-created itself into a cohesive or persuasive alternative to the Republican Party that Obenshain built. Republicans had already succeeded in winning presidential elections in the state: after 1948 they won every presidential election but one (in 1964) for the next sixty years. They won a majority of the state's congressional delegation at nearly every election after the 1960s, elected Republicans to the United States Senate and to statewide offices in addition to the governorship beginning in the 1970s, and finally, in 1999, won control of both Houses of the General Assembly for the first time ever.

In spite of what Pat Robertson said in his speech to the Democratic Party convention in June 1978, he did not come back. Like many other Virginia Democrats, he and his evangelical political allies transferred their allegiance during the ensuing years to the Republican Party. His change of political coat did not escape notice then, but he did not mention his experiment with Democratic Party politics in either edition of his autobiography. When he moved from one party to the other, Robertson was one of the two best-known Virginians in the nation. The other was Jerry Falwell, a Lynchburg Baptist minister who, like Robertson, was an effective pioneer in using television to expand the range of his ministry. Robertson and Falwell also used that medium for political purposes. Though very unlike in many ways and with differing religious perspectives, they shared social, moral, and political values. Together during the same decade that Obenshain's Republicans took charge of the state Republican Party they led many thousands of Virginians toward a new or renewed political commitment to social values that were then gaining importance nationally and that, at the national level, the Republican Party most successfully advocated and exemplified.[8]

Robertson had returned to his native Virginia from New York in the 1950s and established a television ministry in Portsmouth, later moved to Virginia Beach, that evolved into a national network of Christian broadcasting outlets. After becoming a born-again evangelical Christian rather than a mere Baptist, he relied on faith and prayer to provide the financial resources and partnerships for his ministerial work. Robertson often related the divine interventions that assisted his ministry and on his live television broadcasts asserted the importance of faith, prayer, and divine intervention by reciting episodes of faith healing. Like many Christians of an earlier time, Sir William Berkeley in seventeenth-century Virginia, for one, Robertson firmly believed that God worked miracles on earth every day and that the Devil worked mischief on earth every day, too.[9]

Robertson believed that there was no strict boundary line between religion and politics. He described the Bible as "not an impractical book of theology, but rather a practical book of life containing a system of thought and conduct that will guarantee success. And it will be true success, true happiness, true prosperity, not the fleeting, flashy, inconsistent success the world usually settles for. The Bible, quite bluntly, is a workable guidebook for politics, government, business, families, and all the affairs of mankind."[10] When he ventured into partisan politics late in the 1970s, it was to apply the commandments of the Bible to the salvation of the nation.

"From its founding until about 1960," Robertson wrote in his autobiography, "Americans were united by at least a common ethic. Essentially, the country had been founded as a Christian nation, adopting biblical principles and governing itself pretty much under biblical countenance. There was a work ethic and a moral restraint based on an underlying philosophical system of honor and decency that prevailed even in the face of frequent and flagrant violations. Today, the United States struggles under a social philosophy of pluralism. There is no unified reality. Many disparate, frequently cacophonous voices echo from one shore to another. Confusion is triumphant." Robertson blamed Satan.[11]

In 1986 Robertson published a book on American history, *America's Dates with Destiny*. "During the past twenty-five years," he complained, "early American history has been rewritten. This generation of public school students can go through twelve years of elementary and high school and another four years of college without one lesson featuring the central role of America's Judeo-Christian heritage in the founding and later history of the nation.... And the central role of Christian faith and biblical truth in shaping the charters of our original colonies, the curriculum of our original schools and universities, even the Declaration of Independence and the Constitution, has been censored from the historic record."[12]

Blaming intellectuals, judges, politicians, and federal bureaucrats whom Satan had sent to destroy the American nation and to undermine true religion, Robertson denounced separation of church and state as a perversion of the beliefs of the nation's founders and called for a return to earlier fundamental values and biblical precepts.[13] His history book contained separate chapters that condemned moral relativism and the Supreme Court's decision legalizing abortion, and it essentially endorsed the administration of President Ronald Reagan.

Robertson turned the final sections of *America's Dates with Destiny* into a political platform for the 1988 presidential election campaign. "Great segments of the American electorate are awaking to a new sense of patriotism and political concern," he declared. "Led by evangelical Christians determined to bring about a new era of spiritual and political renewal, more people will vote and vote wisely than in any other presidential election in the nation's history." Robertson then asked his readers, "Can we endure if we forsake the God of our fathers and strip from our national consciousness the teachings of the Holy Bible? Can we endure if we continue such profligate waste in government, the accumulation of such an unsupportable debt, and the amassing of power in the central government with the resulting loss of freedom and individual initiative by the people? . . . Can we endure if we refuse to declare acts of our citizens either right or wrong and if we accept as part of our lifestyle blatant immorality, adultery, drunkenness, and drug abuse?"[14]

Robertson's answer, of course, was no, and in 1988 he sought the Republican Party's presidential nomination to restore what he and many other people believed was a correct Christian approach to public policy and to cast Satan out of American public life. His campaign relied on reviving a belief that the people of the United States from the very beginning had been God's chosen people. That placed them in his own time directly in Satan's crosshairs. Robertson's campaign appeal was nothing new in American history. It had deep resonances in the language of the founders of Virginia and the Pilgrim separatists of the seventeenth century, in the language of the American Revolution, in Abraham Lincoln's patriotic state papers during the American Civil War, and in the messianic visions of Woodrow Wilson and Franklin D. Roosevelt, who in the twentieth century hoped that the League of Nations and the United Nations would enable the wholesome example of the United States to save the world.

Pat Robertson did not receive the Republican Party nomination in 1988, but his waging of simultaneous religious and political campaigns was not the sole reason. Other political and religious leaders by then were preaching the same political messages. In 1979, one year after Robertson's appearance at the Democratic Party state convention, Jerry Falwell founded the Moral Majority, a national organization that, although not officially affiliated with the Republican Party, became closely identified with that party because of Falwell's support in 1980 of its presidential nominee, Ronald Reagan. The minister and the president shared many values. Leaving the old issues of racial segregation aside or hiding them behind the curtain, Falwell, Reagan, and many other Virginians and Americans emphasized other shared ideas and ideals.

Falwell reluctantly and only temporarily entered the political arena, which

Baptists traditionally had avoided as violating their belief in separation of church and state. In sermons, speeches, articles written for the religious press, and radio and television addresses, Falwell laid out an internally consistent political agenda that he summarized in detail in 1980 in a book-length political manifesto entitled *Listen, America!* Echoing other writers and ministers stretching all the way back to the early years of the seventeenth century, he preached, as Robertson did, that the United States was a chosen nation and Americans were a chosen people. "I believe that God promoted America to a greatness no other nation has ever enjoyed," Falwell wrote, "because her heritage is one of a republic governed by laws predicated on the Bible."[15] Basing his political views on the spiritual and moral principles that he had always emphasized in his ministry, Falwell rooted his politics in the Bible, which he interpreted literally. His political theology was also (and, he said, therefore) fiercely anti-Communist. "The free-enterprise system is clearly outlined in the Book of Proverbs in the Bible," he wrote. "Jesus Christ made it clear that the work ethic was a part of His plan for man. Ownership of property is biblical. Competition in business is biblical. Ambitious and successful business management is clearly outlined as a part of God's plan for His people. Our Founding Fathers warned against centralized government power, concluding that the concentration of government corrupts and sooner or later leads to abuse and tyranny."[16] The almost seamless transition in that paragraph from biblical precept to capitalist theory to disapproval of the powerful federal government was typical of Falwell's political addresses and sermons. He spoke less about Satan than Robertson and more about Communism and how the federal government failed to combat the evils that had plunged the country into moral decay. Otherwise, though, their political sermons delivered essentially the same message of personal morality and national salvation.

Certain passages in the Bible forbid many practices that Falwell and Robertson believed were dangerously undermining the country and its values. In *Listen, America!* Falwell included a full chapter on the fundamental importance of the family as the basic, traditional unit of society. He condemned the feminist movement and the proposed Equal Rights Amendment to the United States Constitution as direct threats to the family unit. So, too, were homosexuality, abortion, drug use, alcohol abuse, and rock music, as were federal court rulings limiting or eliminating from public schools all religious exercises and Bible reading. Falwell included a chapter on each in *Listen, America!* "Communists seek to discredit the authority of the Word of God," he wrote. "Today in America we find the Bible being questioned by many of our people,"[17] suggesting there as he often did elsewhere that skeptics as well as atheists were inadvertently or secretly supporting a godless Communism and its objectives. "Families in search of freedom to educate their children according to religious principles originally settled this land," he explained. "There is a vicious assault upon the American family. More television programs depict homes of divorced or of single parents than depict the traditional family. Nearly every major family-theme TV program openly justifies divorce, homosexuality, and adultery."[18]

Falwell frequently ascribed subversive motivations to advocates of practices he abhorred. For instance, "Homosexuals cannot reproduce themselves, so they must recruit. One has only to read an American newspaper to find sordid instances of homosexual exploitation of young boys and girls. Why must they prey upon our young?" Closely related to homosexuality in his fears was the feminist movement, which he described bluntly as "unisexual." Feminists, he preached, "desire to eliminate God-given differences that exist between the sexes; that is why they are prohomosexual and lesbian." He concluded, without citing any names, numbers, or evidence, "In fact, it is shocking, how many feminists are lesbians."[19] Falwell also denounced un-Christian dangers that he perceived lurking in social reform proposals. "I am against federally funded day-care centers," he announced in Listen, America! "that would bring the age of mandatory school attendance down to two years old. This would get children away from their parents and under the early influence of public education. . . . Communists believe in taking children away from the family and raising them separately so they can indoctrinate them with government loyalty. How I fear this will happen to our own children."[20]

Analysts pointed out soon after the Moral Majority made its debut in American politics and others confirmed later that it engaged the loyalties of only a small proportion of the population. Some of Falwell's provocative remarks offended people who did not share his fundamentalist, literal reading of the Bible or left him open to ridicule, but the importance of the moral values that he and Robertson sought to preserve resonated strongly with the American public then and thereafter.[21] It was those beliefs, those ideas, that increasingly separated many Virginia Democrats from their old party and allied them with the Republican Party because it was, by and large, the national Democratic Party that promoted or sanctioned modification of fundamentally important traditional relationships between races, genders, and generations as well as the allotment of responsibilities between the federal and state governments. After the specter of Harry Byrd and his powerful political organization faded into the past, it was those beliefs, those ideas that in large measure drove the changing politics of Virginia.

The social and moral messages of Robertson and Falwell had broad appeal among Virginians who may have been uncomfortable with clergymen taking such active roles in partisan politics. Their political message was broadly consistent in many ways with the beliefs that the traditional political leaders of Virginia had long promoted and that Ronald Reagan often stressed during the 1970s and 1980s. The televangelists, as Robertson and Falwell were sometimes called, did not have to march in the van of a large following to help tip the state's political allegiance from the Democratic Party to the Republican. It was tipping that way already, because the ideas, the political issues, the secular parts of their messages were gaining ground nationally and within the state. The radical changes that the sexual revolution and the counterculture of the 1960s and 1970s brought with them provoked strong opposition in Virginia. Obenshain, Reagan, Robertson, and Falwell campaigned and preached against those changes much more effectively than any of the Virginia advocates or defenders of the changes ever tried.

The social values and political messages—the Spirit of Virginia—that schoolbooks and popular literature on Virginia taught provided many Virginians a firm foundation of beliefs that produced a strong inertial force resistant to those changes and directed resentment toward the federal government for its role in permitting or promoting the changes. Most of the state's cultural arbiters, shapers of public opinion, and political leaders were fully invested in that culture, and they, too, as evangelists for social and political continuity, propagated their beliefs industriously and effectively. At its most fundamental level, their message was that what was good and wholesome for individual Virginians was also good and wholesome for all Virginians and all Americans.

In ways that may be difficult to document or calculate but the results of which were easy to perceive at the time, the rise to prominence of Virginia's Republicans late in the twentieth century was tied to national political debates that involved both moral and social issues and the intimate relationship between social values and political decisions regarding taxes and spending, which in a different way linked individual self-interest with public policy considerations.

Taxes and social issues dominated the political life of late twentieth-century and early twenty-first-century Virginia. Some issues of public policy, such as education, brought the two together. The state had a long tradition of good private and parochial schools, going far back into the nineteenth century when there were few or no public schools. Those private and parochial schools continued to thrive in many parts of the state during the twentieth century as attractive but expensive alternatives to less excellent and poorly funded public schools. Parents who could afford to send their children to the better private schools may have spent more of their money to educate their children than they would have spent had they paid higher taxes to bring the public schools up to their standards. The number of private schools increased during the third quarter of the twentieth century following federal court orders to desegregate the state's public schools. Many thousands of white parents created new racially segregated private schools and paid even more of their own money to educate their children there. Moreover, in Virginia, as elsewhere in the United States during the final years of the twentieth century and the early years of the twenty-first, an increasing number of parents chose to send their children to private or parochial schools or to educate them at home because of the perceived inferiority of the public schools or because they wanted moral and religious instruction for their children that the public schools could not or did not provide.

As a consequence of the widespread availability of good private schools for people who could afford them, for whatever complex of reasons, an influential constituency for providing resources to improve public schools had little or no immediate personal or family stake in spending additional tax money for that purpose. It was not just about money, only, or a revival of the elitist hostility to public education that Frederick William Mackey Holliday disclosed in his lecture to the General Assembly in 1878. It was chiefly about the value that those parents placed on education and about the kind of education that they wanted their children to receive. Parents who could afford good education for their children had expensive, attractive options to the public schools, but parents who could not afford to take advantage of those options had no other choice than to send their children to public schools that were often of inferior quality. The private choices that some Virginians made for their children had political consequences that may have limited the choices that other Virginians had in obtaining a good education for theirs and therefore directly and probably adversely affected the public good.

Political disagreements about what government should spend money doing and whether each proposal was worth the cost and who should pay what proportion of the cost had figured in political debates throughout history. The people with the most powerful political influence usually, but not always, made the most consequential decisions, and in some instances the consequences were long-lasting grievances. The social service state, for example, that arose beginning in the 1930s and continued to increase in size and importance until the 1990s had the effect of transferring money from some people to other people, some of whom could not or did not work. It was natural that the recipients of that largesse opposed attempts to reduce or eliminate what they believed they were legally entitled to receive. At the same time some people who paid taxes that supported the programs resented having their wealth transferred against their wishes to people who in some or many instances they may have regarded as undeserving.

Virginia's political leaders and voters relied on their private personal beliefs when they made choices about public policies, but they also often protected the interests of themselves and the social class to which they belonged. As was evident all the way back to the General Assembly session in the summer of 1619, decisions about public policy that officeholders made revealed what was most important to them. The history of politics in Virginia, as well as in the United States, exhibits continuing debates about choices between or among alternatives that reveal the tensions that naturally exist in any society. People in American society were and are individuals with rights and responsibilities that they believe government should protect, but the government sometimes limited their freedoms in order to protect the rights or advance the interests of other persons, groups, or the whole community. In pursuing their own interests, people sometimes individually or by employing the power of government produced results that were injurious to other people or to the community. That was what Lionel Gatford referred to back in 1657 when he juxtaposed "Publick Good" and "Private Interest" in the title of his book recommending changes in the colony's governance that required greater attention to the first and less of a free rein to the second. The conflict between private interests and the public interest, however defined, is visible in nearly every major political event in Virginia's history.

At the midpoint of the twentieth century, political scientist V. O. Key inserted into his analysis of Virginia's political culture an important commentary about public opinion and public policy. He wrote that one of the most important tools with which Harry Byrd's Democratic Party organization was able to maintain its long dominance was its "allying with itself the business and financial interests of the state. It has in effect brought into camp most of the people who might furnish opposition leadership. In the counties usually the local banks and other businesses, such as retailing, are allied with the local organization, while larger enterprises have their connections with organization leaders higher in the hierarchy. Virginia, like many another commonwealth, presents an example of the extraordinary success of the corporations and of the wealthy in persuading the upper middle class that their interests are identical." The community leaders throughout the state—"the banker, the preacher, the lawyer, the doctor, the merchants, and often the newspaper owners"—not only supported the Byrd organization but individually "surrender their self-interest" and their political independence to support the organization's probusiness agenda and its opposition to reformers, organized labor, and a big and active national government.[22] What for the first two centuries of Virginia's history had been government of, by, and for tobacco planters became during the third and fourth centuries government largely of, by, and for businessmen.

Opposition to organized labor was one of the centerpieces in the Byrd organization's political agenda. It surfaced in state politics many times, and not only when Congress or Democratic presidents at various times between the 1930s and 1960s sought to protect or to advance the economic and political agendas of national labor unions. Events in Virginia brought that opposition to the fore, too. The only time that the state's governor invoked the 1928 antilynching law that the General Assembly passed when Byrd was governor was during a sit-down strike in the city of Covington in 1937, one of the labor disputes that in Virginius Dabney's remembrance "marred" that year in the state's history. The law prohibited gatherings of people to commit illegal acts, and Governor George C. Peery declared that union strikers by forming a picket line and keeping nonunion workers from entering a nylon plant illegally prevented nonunion workers from using the public roads to go to work. That broke the strike.[23]

Early in 1946 Governor William M. Tuck responded to a strike at the Virginia Electric Power Company, the state's largest public utility, by employing a wartime law that declared all of the state's adult men to be members of the State Guard. Tuck called the strikers into active duty and with the force of martial law behind him ordered them back to work, which broke the strike. The General Assembly then took advantage as soon as it could of a provision in the new Taft-Hartley Act that allowed states to outlaw a favorite practice of labor unions, which was to negotiate contracts with business and industrial firms that required the firms to hire only union members.[24] The closed shop, it was called, had enhanced the economic and ultimately the political power of labor unions and provoked an antiunion reaction and the passage in Virginia and several other states of what business and antiunion political leaders shrewdly called right-to-work laws.

Throughout the 1950s and 1960s and into the 1970s when Democrats running for national office promised to repeal the provision of the Taft-Hartley Act that permitted state right-to-work laws, most of Virginia's political leaders condemned the political actions of unions as posing a radical danger to the freedom of the state's working men and women. In fact, in spite of their name, those laws were much more beneficial to the state's business leaders than to the state's working men and women. Even though labor unions never exercised much influence in Virginia's politics, the presence and activities of unions continued well into the twenty-first century to provoke intense reactions from some politicians. In 2006 the General Assembly refused to confirm the governor's nomination of an officer of the state's largest labor organization to be secretary of the commonwealth for the sole reason that he was a union official.[25]

Twelve days before the 1977 general election, the editor of the influential *Richmond News Leader* filled the entire editorial page with a list of contributions that labor unions had made as of that date to the primary and general election campaigns of Henry Howell, the Democratic Party nominee for governor that year. The editor described the list as "of staggering import." Total union contributions to Howell constituted almost one-fourth of all of the reported contributions to his campaign. The editor pointed out that the Republican nominee, John Nichols Dalton, "has reported from organized labor not one cent." The editor's short explanation accompanying the list concluded, "Labor contributes to Howell, because labor can count on him to perform dutifully in labor's behalf. As the accompanying list amply attests, Henry Howell is labor's boy."[26]

The editor published denunciations of Howell every day from then until the election and on the eve of the election filled nearly half of the editorial page with a list of union contributions to Howell reported since the previous publication, separating contributions from unions in Virginia and those from national organizations. The editor pointed out that union contributions from outside the state exceeded those from unions inside the state by almost two to one and predicted confidently that if Howell was elected, he would be the willing agent of labor leaders outside of Virginia whose purposes were different from and therefore hostile to the true spirit of Virginia's culture and interests.[27]

What neither editorial about union contributions to Howell's campaign mentioned was that Howell also received large campaign contributions from Virginia corporations and owners of Virginia business firms, probably more than from unions, and that Dalton received a great deal more money from business owners, corporations, and trade associations with headquarters in the state and also from corporations and trade associations with headquarters elsewhere.[28] The editor selectively deployed evidence to damn Howell because he received campaign contributions from organized working people and to praise Dalton, who received even larger campaign contributions from organized business people. The editor did not question whether Dalton, by accepting those contributions, might therefore be regarded as an agent of those businessmen. As was and is often the case, what was not said was as important and silently persuasive as what was. The newspaper's editorials clearly reflected the underlying rationale of the state's long-standing public policies. Whatever businessmen believed was good for Virginia; whatever working people, organized or unorganized, believed could not be good for Virginia.

The responses of Virginia politicians to the existence and proposals of labor unions were consistent with the beliefs that several generations of Virginia's most influential political leaders held about economic and social issues and about the relationship between people who worked and their employers. Those episodes all fitted a pattern that is readily apparent in Virginia's laws and practices since at least as early as the laws and orders of the first General Assembly in the summer of 1619 that regulated the lives of working people (the majority of all Virginians) for the advantage of owners and employers (the wealthiest minority).

Since long before Bacon's Rebellion, economic issues, usually exhibited in taxing and spending practices, had provoked public disagreements that exposed some of the most important beliefs of those leaders and how the beliefs of other people on some occasions were significantly different. Taxes and debates about public policies were at the center of much of Virginia's twentieth-century political history, beginning with the 1923 statewide referendum on issuing bonds for the construction of highways. The memory of the crippling effects that the public debt created for constructing the antebellum internal improvements projects had imposed on the state's postbellum economy worked to the advantage of Harry Flood Byrd and the men who successfully opposed the issuance of bonds. The alternative pay-as-you-go proposals that Byrd advocated resulted in a lower long-term cost but slower short-term construction of highways. That slower pace, however, did not prevent him and his supporters from giving him the reputation as the man whose policies got Virginia's transportation network out of the mud.[29]

A desire to keep state and local taxes low featured in nearly every defense of the reform of the state bureaucracy that Byrd undertook later in the 1920s and in the opposition of his organization then and thereafter to expansion of state and local government services and enlargement of the role of the federal government in people's lives. Opposition to taxation appeals to an immediate private interest in ways that a proposal to increase taxes for some future general benefit seldom does. That political reality served the organization long and well. That was one reason why the assembly's enactment of a sales tax and the issuance of bonds to improve education and for other purposes forty years later made Mills Godwin appear to be a major reformer during his first administration as governor. Those measures obscured, though, how much else remained relatively unchanged then and thereafter in the political beliefs and practices of Godwin and most other Virginia politicians. The sales tax of the 1960s, like the county taxes on tithables in the seventeenth century and the state's tax on land during the American Revolution that had both come in for serious criticism, was a regressive tax; that is, people with smaller incomes paid a larger proportion of their wealth in taxes than people with larger incomes paid. In that regard, the imposition of the tax was an innovation, but the nature of the tax was not.

The political history of Virginia following Godwin is almost as much a continuing debate about public services, public policies, and taxes as it is about the moral issues that Robertson and Falwell discussed. Republicans succeeded in gaining the upper hand in the state in part by their opposition to increased taxes. When combined with the moral and social issues about which Robertson and Falwell preached, taxation provided Virginia Republicans with increasingly impressive electoral victories. Republicans won all three statewide offices simultaneously in 1997 and two years later for the first time in history won control of both houses of the General Assembly. The overriding issue in the 1997 and 1999 campaigns was taxes. Candidates who opposed programs that required raising taxes or who supported reducing or eliminating taxes were the most successful.

James S. Gilmore won election as governor in 1997 in part as a consequence of his promise to eliminate the ad valorem personal property tax on automobiles. Since Byrd's days, all revenue from taxes on personal property and real estate had gone into the treasuries of counties and cities. Gradual elimination of the tax therefore required that the General Assembly compensate the localities from the state's general revenue. As it happened, the cost to the state of reducing or eliminating the tax was much greater than anticipated (or admitted), and a brief but deep recession that hit the national economy during Gilmore's term made it impossible for the governor and the assembly to complete the plan to eliminate the tax. They had to reduce state services to find the money to compensate the localities, and that had two unanticipated (or undisclosed) consequences. Jurisdictions with wealthier inhabitants who owned more and more-expensive automobiles received more compensation than jurisdictions with poorer inhabitants who owned fewer and less-expensive automobiles, in effect, another regressive tax change. The need to reimburse cities and counties from the state's treasury also increased the dependence of all local governments on the assembly. That in effect reduced the ability of local governments and their constituents to determine for themselves how much or how little to spend on schools or other local projects because they could not know from year to year, or even from month to month, how much money the assembly would dole out to them.[30]

During the final years of the twentieth century and the early years of the twenty-first, as the Byrd organization faded further into the past and as racial segregation ceased to be such an important issue in public discourse, Virginia's political leaders and voters concentrated on other public policy issues that exposed their private interests and affected the public interest. In that changed political atmosphere, candidates of the Republican Party were usually more imaginative, energetic, and successful than candidates of the Democratic Party in appealing to Virginia's voters and their private interests on issues of morality, economics, and the role of the federal government that they believed or said were for the public good.

15

VIRGINIA
ABSTRACTIONS

VIRGINIA
MAY 2 1 1956
STATE LIBRARY

the Defenders' NEWS and VIEWS

Published by Defenders of State Sovereignty and Individual Liberties
1210 Traveler's Building   Richmond, Virginia

Vol. I, No. 1   August 1955

"We, in Prince Edward County, want the Defenders to know that we appreciate their help in informing other areas of our problem. It has proved that we are not standing alone in this fight to maintain segregation, and at the same time provide education for our children. Perhaps we know better than anyone else that it is necessary for all of us to band together if we are to preserve our way of life."

August 5, 1955

(signed) JACK BRUCE, *Member*
Board of Supervisors

In recent months our membership has grown to such proportions that we are having difficulty keeping in touch with each other. We are proud of our membership growth and chapter expansion. It means progress. We feel that you naturally want to know what is happening in various parts of our Commonwealth through the efforts of our members. We know you have ideas which should be shared with all who have joined our ranks. Our NEWS AND VIEWS publication can disseminate the facts to serve such a purpose. You will hear from us often. Drop a line to our State Office, let us know what you are doing and thinking in your community, and what you would like to hear from us.

* * * * * * *

The following, Section 3, from the CERTIFICATE OF INCORPORATION OF DEFENDERS OF STATE SOVEREIGNTY AND INDIVIDUAL LIBERTIES, outlines the purposes of the organization. The will of the people in the various localities, acting in unity, can make the purposes effective.

SECTION III

"The purposes for which this association is formed are: to disseminate amid the people information concerning the fundamental principles and concepts of our federal government and a due regard for that federal system; to teach and proclaim the necessity of the Federal Government restricting itself to its proper sphere and of preserving the sovereignty of the states; to instill a recognition of the worth to each individual of the historic liberties the citizens of the United States have enjoyed, and to increase the determination to defend those liberties by all honorable and lawful means against all efforts to encroach thereon; to seek by all honorable and lawful means the retention by each state of its full right and power to regulate within its borders, in the manner it believes to be most conducive to the happiness and good of its citizens, its own domestic arrangements, and within the limits of the law at any time existing, to study, investigate, plan and advocate means and methods by which the people of each state may enjoy to the full this right and power in any of its

The August 1955 first issue of the newsletter of the Defenders of State Sovereignty and Individual Liberties (courtesy of the Library of Virginia) announced the growth in membership of the year-old organization founded to mobilize public opinion in opposition to the Supreme Court's orders to desegregate the state's public schools. The organization's title drew on the state's-rights rhetoric and language of individual liberty that several generations of Virginians had employed to oppose actions of the federal government of which they disapproved. The liberty that the Defenders extolled was the liberty of white Virginians through their political process to require mandatory racial segregation and to be free from federal interference with laws and social customs that denied basic liberties of American citizenship to a large portion of Virginia's population.

LATE IN APRIL 1861 THE MEMBERS of the Virginia convention that met in Richmond adopted a state flag. The delegates had just voted to sever the political connection between Virginia and the United States and taken the first steps toward creating a new political connection between Virginia and the Confederate States. Former governor Henry A. Wise and former president John Tyler wanted the convention to adopt a new design for the state flag. Tyler informed the delegates that in fact Virginia had no official state flag. Since the 1830s and without any legal authorization, the state had been using a blue flag with the state's 1776 seal in the center. Tyler asked, "What made it the flag of Virginia?" Thomas Jefferson's grandson George Wythe Randolph replied so persuasively that the delegates adopted an ordinance declaring that the design already in use would be the official flag of Virginia. To Tyler's query, Randolph had replied, "Usage, sir."[1]

Early in December of that year during the Virginia convention that met in Wheeling, a delegate grumbled that "Virginia abstractions are the most abstract of all abstractions."[2] William Erskine Stephenson was frustrated that other delegates were impeding the work of democratizing the government of the new West Virginia by making abstract orations about political theory rather than discussing practical operations of state and local government. The debate that day was about whether to require that all voting be by ballot rather than by public voice vote, which had been the practice since the earliest days of the colony. Delegates who wanted the change told of episodes at recent polls when advocates of secession intimidated or attacked voters or threatened to cut off their credit if they voted against secession. Political democracy, the reformers argued, required that all voters be free to vote as they desired. The men who opposed the change complained that requiring secrecy was insulting to honorable and independent gentlemen who were not afraid to announce their choices openly. They dismissed the fears as frivolous or failed to understand the vulnerability of men without substantial property and the social standing that went with it, men who could not always afford to proclaim their choices publicly. The defenders of the old way that gentlemen had engaged in politics appealed to tradition and invoked timeless values. In the process their speeches raveled off into generalities and political abstractions.[3]

Randolph's pithy rely to Tyler and Stephenson's exasperated comment point to the central importance of continuity and ideas in Virginia's political culture, even though individual Virginians did not always revere the past or understand the ideas in the same way. Words and phrases such as "freedom," "liberty," "republican government," "representation," "state's rights," "limited government," and "the people" appeared in nearly every public discussion and in private letters and conversations about politics during the dramatic year 1861. Nineteenth-century political oratory in its Virginia setting seemed to require those familiar abstractions much as a basket requires a bottom. Indeed, the fifteenth clause in the Virginia Declaration of Rights of 1776 that Patrick Henry proposed in committee stated, "That no free Government or the Blessing of Liberty can be preserved to any People but by a firm adherence to Justice Moderation Temperance Frugality and Virtue and by frequent recurrence to fundamental Principles."[4]

The language of fundamental principles—state's rights, limited government, and individual liberty—gained powerful currency during the decades between the American Revolution and the American Civil War. Mid-nineteenth-century Virginia men and women did not even think that they needed to explain to each other the meaning of phrases that seemed to embody their fundamental beliefs. They should have explained, though, because the abstract phrases meant different things to different people in differing circumstances. It was easy to miss the imprecision with which they used the language and the contradictions and inconsistencies evident in the statements and actions of people who spoke and wrote those words. Like philosophical propositions and religious creeds, those terms carried important but different meanings for each person. With independent existences of their own and detached from the changing daily details of governance and politics, the phrases and associated articles of belief became vitally important. They became self-evident, dominating terms of political discourse. When Stephenson complained about the abstractness of Virginia abstractions in 1861, he meant that by a kind of perverse variation on Gresham's law about bad money driving out good, the very utterance of the often-repeated phrases drove out facts and reasoned arguments.

The phrase "state's rights" was the most abstract and imprecise of all. In some contexts it clearly meant the right of a state government to do some specific thing, but in most other contexts it meant the right of the people of a state to be free from some other specific thing that the United States government might do. Ever since the debates in 1787 and 1788 about ratification of the Constitution of the United States, Virginians and other Southern politicians, lawyers, judges, and editors had deployed the words to condemn actions or anticipated actions of the federal government of which they disapproved. They extolled individual liberty and the benefits of limited government, even though when legislating in Richmond they often ignored what they said that they believed and governed vigorously and restricted individual freedoms or abridged people's rights, especially when it was necessary to protect slavery or to control enslaved people.

Both sides in most major political controversies in Virginia used the same venerable and often abstract language. During the civil rights struggles of the twentieth century, advocates of abolishing racial segregation used the Revolution's language of individual freedom and equality. Opponents of change tried to deflect argument away from how human beings treated one another and toward a doctrine of long usage that ignored what it was that the state asserted a right to do. The men and women who argued for state's rights during the civil rights period actually argued for the right of the state government to treat some Virginians unfairly and as inferior to others.

As part of its defense of segregation, the General Assembly created a Commission on Constitutional Government that published pamphlets and circulated draft editorials and speech texts that linked state's rights and individual liberty all the way back through American and English history to Magna Carta. The commission's members and publications praised the state's-rights writings of the nineteenth century and denounced actions of the federal government during the twentieth century for violating what it asserted were fundamental liberties that in fact belonged to white people only. They portrayed the federal government as a threat to the rights of the people and the states.[5]

Other defenders of racial segregation followed a closely parallel course. They formed private organizations such as the Defenders of State Sovereignty and Individual Liberties, which was the Virginia counterpart of the White Citizens Councils of the lower South. For the most part the Defenders of State Sovereignty eschewed the violence and intimidation that White Citizens Councils sometimes employed and, like the Commission on Constitutional Government, relied on repetition of carefully selected venerable political verities.[6] State sovereignty and state's rights were political shibboleths of long usage that diverted attention from the fact that the individual liberties the Defenders sought to protect included the individual liberty of some white Virginians to deny to all African Americans the liberty that they sought to acquire.

James J. Kilpatrick led the state's-rights charge to preserve racial segregation in the 1950s. Editor of the influential *Richmond News Leader* during Massive Resistance, he worked behind the scenes with Harry Flood Byrd and members of the state commissions that tried to prevent implementation of federal court orders to desegregate the public schools. Kilpatrick resurrected John C. Calhoun's nineteenth-century doctrine of interposition—interposing, or placing, the power of the state government between its people and the federal government—as the constitutional foundation and historical precedent for Massive Resistance.[7] In spite of his confident and vigorous prose, Kilpatrick was no expert on what he wrote about and was learning his history as he wrote about it. David John Mays, a respected attorney and Pulitzer Prize–winning historian who fully supported the state's attempts to prevent desegregation, privately observed that Kilpatrick was "more eloquent than sound in some of his ideas on the Constitution, and during his long series of editorials on the subject was often only a little ahead of his reading, and John Taylor, Calhoun, etc., were until then only names to him."[8]

Kilpatrick imperfectly understood during his most intense period of propagandizing that interposition was a discredited and moribund constitutional doctrine that could not work as he hoped even if he could bring it back to life. However much he and the legislators believed in state's rights and interposition, those were not the objectives for which they fought. They defended state's rights in order to defend the demeaning and undemocratic laws of white supremacy and racial segregation, a fact that Kilpatrick let out of the transparent bag with his later and extremely unsubtle book, *The Southern Case for School Segregation*.[9] Massive Resisters clothed their campaign to maintain a racially segregated society in an abstract set of formidable and enduring theories of state's rights and limited government that gave urgency and persuasiveness to the opposition that they made to the federal government in order to protect and to preserve Virginia's right to enforce racial segregation and white supremacy.[10] As advocates of civil rights could have pointed out, no ideal theory of limited government and no complementary theory of individual liberties were visible in the state's laws dictating racial segregation and enforcing white supremacy.

Virginia's politicians and legal establishment argued on behalf of limited government when they denounced actions of the federal government of which they disapproved, but they continued to govern the state with few limitations. The inconsistency discloses that the powerful abstract doctrines such as state's rights and limited government were useful ideas and even respectable subjects of intellectual debate, but it was ideas about public policy that propelled or retarded changes and guided political agendas in Virginia, even on occasions when those ideas or agendas conflicted with those old Virginia abstractions. Virginia politicians were not unique among American politicians in often failing to notice the differences between what they said they believed and how they acted. In truth, the experience in Virginia mirrors to a greater or lesser degree the experience in other states and in the United States itself.

As political scientist V. O. Key observed in the twentieth century, Virginia's political and business leaders and the opinion leaders often walked hand in hand.[11] Theories of limited government and enlightened self-interest yielded to state activism when businessmen and political leaders perceived it to be in the interest of the public or of themselves. From the General Assembly's creation of the Board of Public Works in 1816 to the beginning of the American Civil War, the state government played a very active role in assisting corporations to improve the state's transportation networks. Through the board the state provided public money to private corporations to finance construction of bridges, toll roads, canals, and railroads. Between the war and the beginning of the twentieth century, the General Assembly continued to play an influential economic role by the way it exercised its power to grant or to amend charters of incorporation and by the ways political factions sought to solve the problem of the public debt.

An innovative provision in the Constitution of 1902 empowered the state government to assume a new economic function. In addition to disfranchising African Americans, the Convention of 1901–2 also came into being to reduce the political influence of railroads and other large corporations, to prevent practices such as the railroads' charging more per ton-mile for short-haul than for long-haul freight, and to rationalize the state's laws relating to corporations generally and remove politics from the process of creating corporations. Allen Caperton Braxton took the lead on that subject and did even more elaborate surveying of judges, corporate-law experts, and state regulatory officers than he had done on the subject of disfranchisement.

Against much determined opposition from some of the corporate attorneys in the convention, Braxton succeeded in including in the constitution a new article on corporations. Almost fifteen pages long, it created a new constitutional entity, the State Corporation Commission, and vested in it so many independent executive, legislative, and judicial functions that it soon ranked with the executive branch, the legislature, and the courts as the fourth main branch of state government. Widely hailed early in the twentieth century as an innovative solution to some of the problems that accompanied an explosion in the number and size of corporations, the commission earned Braxton a brief national notoriety and even speculation that he might be the 1904 Democratic Party vice presidential nominee.

Braxton, however, was no radical reformer. In answer to critics who viewed the commission as an infringement of the ability of businessmen to conduct their businesses as they pleased, he stated that the purpose of the commission was to make it impossible for real radical reformers to produce just that kind of interference and to shield business from the dangers of socialism. What Braxton did after the convention adjourned spoke eloquently to his purposes. He left his small general-law practice in Staunton and moved to Richmond where he became general counsel of the Richmond, Fredericksburg, and Potomac Railroad.[12] The dangers of socialism in Virginia were slight, indeed, and the commission seldom acted against corporate interests. Later in the century Henry Howell attacked decisions of the State Corporation Commission on the grounds that they protected corporations rather than the public.

Some important features of Virginia's legal system and political culture arose without much thought or debate about the consequences, became embedded in constitutional law or practice, and institutionalized undemocratic practices and governmental structures. Local government offers a prime example. By multiple incremental individual steps that the General Assembly took beginning late in the eighteenth century and continuing into the twentieth to solve specific local problems, incorporated municipalities in Virginia became legally independent of neighboring counties. In addition to a council and mayor, each incorporated city had the same set of local officials as each county—clerk, commissioner of revenue, treasurer, voter registrar, prosecuting attorney, judges, clerk of court, and a city sheriff or city sergeant with comparable responsibilities to the county sheriffs—and all with equal authority. Each city had its own sources of revenue, its own school system, its own courts of record, its own law-enforcement officers, its own deed books and land records, and every authority and responsibility that each of the counties had. Even though a city might be completely surrounded by a county, it was not for any legal purpose a part of that county, and county officers had no jurisdiction for any purpose within a city.[13] Native Virginians accepted that separation as natural; immigrants to Virginia had difficulty understanding the bizarre and unique structuring of local government.

Article VIII of the Constitution of 1902 gave implicit constitutional sanction and protection to the unique Virginia system of independent cities that had developed without plan or rationale during the nineteenth century. For the twentieth century it prescribed in detail uniform systems of government for incorporated towns and cities of different sizes, specifying how they were to be structured and what their powers and responsibilities were and were not to be. That was a subtle but significant modification of the state's constitution, which also specified that every city charter change required legislative approval before it went into effect. Requiring legislative authorization for changes to local government structures, though, was not an innovation in constitutional practice. At the basic level of their own municipal charters, residents of Virginia's cities lacked full legal authority to govern themselves as they wished, and that affected their lives in numerous ways.

The population of Virginia became much more densely concentrated during the twentieth century than it had been, and the state for the most part skipped speedily during the middle half of that century from a rural and small-town culture to a suburban culture. During that time, rather than reconsider and significantly change governmental structures or modify their functions to meet radically changed circumstances, the assembly made numerous piecemeal minor adjustments in response to particular needs in individual localities. When facing unprecedented conditions assembly members developed no comprehensive plan or long-range vision and created a hodgepodge of diverse local governments that silently gained acceptance as if it had to be that way or there were some rational or prudential reasons for it.

As suburban populations increased, the councils of many Virginia cities and towns sought to annex residential neighborhoods in adjacent counties.

Constitutional conventions and General Assemblies had never authorized cities on their own or in cooperation with counties to permit the residents to decide for themselves in which jurisdiction they would live and consequently where city and county boundaries should be. Annexation was a judicial process conducted without a referendum. Judges whom the majority party in the General Assembly selected decided whether a city or town could annex part or all of a county in a judicial process that closely resembled a condemnation proceeding when a government condemned a dangerous and dilapidated structure or seized a property for unpaid taxes.[14]

Late in the 1960s when the growth of the African American population of Richmond and the departure of many white residents to neighboring counties threatened to produce a black majority in the city, some white members of the city council secretly planned to annex white neighborhoods in either Henrico or Chesterfield County to increase the number of white voters in the increasingly black city. They eventually succeeded in acquiring a suburban neighborhood in Chesterfield County because the court ruled that the increased tax base of the neighborhood entitled the city to the property. African Americans in the city sued in federal court charging that the annexation was racially motivated and therefore violated the Voting Rights Act of 1965. During the hearing of the court case, a federal judge suspended all municipal elections in the city from 1970 to 1979, so not only did the citizens of both jurisdictions have no say in which jurisdiction they lived, for almost a decade they had no say in who governed the city, either.[15]

As a result of that event and other proposed annexations that might have incorporated large numbers of county residents into their neighboring cities, some wide disparities developed within the state. During the 1970s and 1980s Virginia legislators prohibited some cities from even considering annexation of adjacent densely populated suburbs, freezing the cities in place with little or no taxing capacity to pay for increasingly expensive responsibilities that citizens demanded and that federal and state laws imposed.[16] Responsibilities that residents of highly suburbanized counties placed on their governments prompted the assembly to grant some of them authority comparable to that which cities exercised, and the state of Virginia became a peculiar patchwork of urban cities and rural counties and of rural cities and urban counties. The most populous jurisdiction in Virginia at the beginning of the twenty-first century was the suburban Northern Virginia county of Fairfax.

Legal and constitutional restrictions of that sort probably imposed limits on the imaginations of legislators and politicians. Throughout the nineteenth century the General Assembly had continued, as it had during the seventeenth and eighteenth centuries, to be very stingy in sharing political responsibility with or granting authority to county and city governments. The state's Supreme Court of Appeals recognized and endorsed the long-standing practices that treated local units of government as creatures and agents of the state. In 1896 when repeating and reaffirming that interpretation of the constitutional law and practice of Virginia, the judges for the first time cited a new non-Virginia authority, the Dillon Rule, indicating that Virginia's practices were in keeping with the fundamental principles of local government that obtained in other states.[17]

The rule was named for a nineteenth-century state and federal judge who from the bench and in a treatise on municipal government stated the reality that all institutions of local government in the United States derived their powers from state constitutions and state laws. Unlike state governments, which had their own constitutions, each local government relied on state statutes or constitutional authorization for its existence and the definition of its authority. The subordinate, agency status of city and county governments nationwide was, according to Judge Dillon, precisely what the Supreme Court of Appeals stated it to be in Virginia. That had given and continued to give to the General Assembly a capacity to legislate on virtually all local matters if it chose. The state's twentieth-century courts usually construed and enforced the Dillon Rule strictly, and twentieth-century legislators generally doled out grants of authority to city and county governments with a very small spoon. The assembly authorized some significant innovations, such as the country's first city-manager form of municipal government in 1908 in Staunton and in the 1930s the first of what became a statewide system of juvenile and domestic relations courts; but in every instance the final decision on important matters of municipal government (and on many minor matters, too) rested with the legislators in Richmond, not with the citizens or voters in their cities and towns. Local government in the state remained a very limited form of democracy.[18]

A dozen years after Harry Byrd restructured the state government bureaucracy to increase efficiency and refused to do the same for local governments in order to preserve the institutions and courthouse rings that supported his political organization, the Virginia Commission on County Government issued a report sharply critical of the institutional structures of county government and the manner in which the General Assembly determined what local government officers could do and not do. "If local government perishes," the commissioners wrote in 1940, "democratic self-government is in danger. The Commission is convinced that unless rapid progress is made in the reorganization and rehabilitation of Virginia county government the last vestiges of 'home rule' in Virginia counties will shortly be lost." The report was a direct challenge to the Byrd organization's employment of the state's constitution and laws and the manner in which it ran the state, but it also unknowingly echoed the essence of Byrd's 1915 campaign speech that denounced concentration of government power in Richmond. "If the present rapid trends toward 'state centralization' continue," the commissioners predicted, "within ten years, and assuredly within this generation, the Virginia county as we know it will remain only a name and its officers will perform 'state functions' in the 'provinces' which were once self-governing counties."[19] Virginia's county governments continued to exist, but the General Assembly did nothing to invigorate democracy in local government.

Even while Virginia politicians used the language of limited government to denounce a strong and active federal government, they made certain that the state government remained strong and active. The constitutional amendments that Byrd pushed through in the 1920s included two new and powerful sentences that explicitly clothed the General Assembly with extremely broad and unspecified authority. Section 63, ratified in 1928, read, "The authority of the General Assembly shall extend to all rightful subjects of legislation, and a specific grant of authority in this Constitution upon a subject shall not work a restriction of its authority upon the same or any other subject. The omission in this Constitution of specific grants of authority heretofore conferred shall not be construed to deprive the General Assembly of such authority, or to indicate a change of policy in reference thereto, unless such purpose plainly appear."[20]

What had always been implicit in Virginia's constitutional practice became explicit in its constitutional law. Byrd did not mention the amendment in the pamphlet that he prepared to guide his ratification campaign,[21] as if he wished not to call attention to it or as if it actually made little practical difference but merely immunized the legislature against legal challenges to its broad exercise of power. More than forty years later when a constitutional revision commission prepared a new draft constitution for the General Assembly to consider, it made one reinforcing stylistic change—"all rightful subjects of legislation" became "all subjects of legislation not herein forbidden or restricted"—and recommended incorporating the language into the new state constitution, which the members of the assembly readily did as Section 14 of Article IV of the Constitution of 1970.[22]

In many respects the constitution ratified in 1970 was innovative. It was certainly a significant improvement on the Constitution of 1902, but in some essentials it was the logical successor of the state's earlier constitutions, and not only because it included the 1928 amendment that removed any doubts about whether the General Assembly's undefined powers were unlimited. In 1969 the assembly created an advisory commission to make recommendations for revising the state constitution, and it then acted as a constitutional revision council itself. The legislators debated and rewrote parts of the commission's draft before submitting to the voters for ratification a new constitution that in reality was an amendment in the form of a substitute. The members of the General Assembly did not allow a popularly elected constituent assembly that they could not control to reform the state's fundamental law. The legislators reserved to themselves complete control over the contents of the new constitution, subject only to the voters' taking it or leaving it in the ratification referendum.

The 1969 report of the constitutional revision commission included a long section on city and county government structures and responsibilities. The legislators who debated the commission's proposals accepted many of its recommendations, but they rejected the commission's suggestion that the new constitution modify the relationship between the state government and the localities by abolishing or significantly reducing reliance on the Dillon Rule. Virginia was one of the states that most strictly applied the rule. In most other states constitutions or laws specified broad parameters within which local governments could individually act, significantly called Home Rule. The members of the constitutional revision commission believed that strict application of the Dillon Rule inhibited local initiative and thwarted democracy at the community level. In spite of that, or perhaps because of that, the legislators rejected the commission members' recommendation,[23] and thereafter the General Assembly and the state's judges continued to apply the Dillon Rule strictly. Towns, cities, and counties all routinely requested special acts of assembly to allow them to govern themselves, even in some very minor matters.[24] In an admittedly extreme example that nevertheless illustrates the sweep of the legislature's dominance, the General Assembly passed a state law in 2003 granting permission requested by some school districts to display on their school buses decals of American flags "no larger than 100 square inches."[25]

In other cases government officials deliberately shaped public policies so as to prevent change, especially democratic or egalitarian change. A new clause in the Bill of Rights of the Constitution of 1970 prohibited the state government from discriminating on the basis of race or sex. It was different in language but appeared to be similar in meaning to the Equal Rights Amendment that Congress submitted to the states a few years later but that failed to be ratified. Both houses of the Virginia General Assembly refused to approve the amendment, as the mostly male legislators declined for a variety of reasons to grant women equal rights with men. The seven white male judges of the Supreme Court of Virginia interpreted the new clause in the state's Bill of Rights so as to limit the rights of women. They stated that the meaning of the new clause in the Constitution of Virginia was "no broader than the equal protection clause of the Fourteenth Amendment to the Constitution of the United States."[26] That meant that no state court could interpret the state's Bill of Rights so as to permit women more legal rights in Virginia than were permitted to all American women by the Constitution of the United States, which had no clause guaranteeing women equal rights with men. By construing the meaning of the different language in the Virginia and United States Constitutions as the same, the state judges allowed federal judges' interpretation of the federal constitution to limit the meaning of a clause in the state constitution and denied, or in order to deny, Virginia's women full legal equality with Virginia's men.

The General Assembly's insistence on preserving the essence of the Dillon Rule and the Supreme Court's obiter dictum limiting the scope of a portion of the state's Bill of Rights were both in keeping with previous generations of law and politics in the state and represented but two, though two very important, continuations of government and politics as usual in Virginia. Those decisions conformed to the long-prevailing practices of the state's political and social leaders, indicating that even though the politics of the state changed following the death of Harry Byrd and the collapse of his organization in the 1960s, many of the core values and political practices that the organization had inherited in the nineteenth century and that sustained it during much of the twentieth century continued in force, even into the twenty-first century. Governmental institutions and practices in Virginia had long since become structurally undemocratic, and that pulled its political culture, which had a long history of inhospitality to democracy, along in a continuing evasion or denial of some cardinal tenets of American democracy.

The influence of Virginia's political leaders in shaping its political culture has always been powerful, but they could not always control everything. Prosperous white Virginia men at the beginning of the twentieth century enjoyed such political power that they could enforce their devotion to white supremacy, but they could not permanently enforce their devotion to male supremacy. Support for woman suffrage was gaining ground nationally during the two decades prior to ratification of the Nineteenth Amendment in 1920, but the men in the Virginia General Assembly defeated all proposals to amend the state constitution to grant the vote to Virginia women and refused to ratify the Nineteenth Amendment that granted the vote to American women. One of the strongest arguments, and one that elite white Virginia women opposed to woman suffrage also used, was that allowing any women to vote might jeopardize the recent denial of the vote to African American men.[27]

Many supporters of woman suffrage in the United States believed that if the wholesome values of the nation's mothers and wives could have effective political power, it would improve the tone of politics and the quality of government and family life in the country. But many of the Virginia men who opposed woman suffrage argued that women should not take part in the unclean business of politics, a politics that the male political leaders, themselves, had made unclean. The somewhat romanticized characterizations of the roles and responsibilities of elite white women that opponents of woman suffrage employed was also somewhat demeaning or condescending, however much they couched it in the gentle and genteel tones that Douglas Southall Freeman used in his 1924 essay, "Virginia: A Gentle Dominion."[28]

The place in society that the state's leading men believed women should occupy provided many other examples of conflicts between stated beliefs and actual practices. Faculty members and male students at the University of Virginia during the decades before women could attend as undergraduates treated the few women who enrolled in graduate programs rudely. They sometimes refused to talk to the women, segregated them in classrooms, or stamped their feet or made other noise when the women tried to speak or ask questions in class. Opposition to women having equal access to higher education with men was not a unique Virginia phenomenon, but women did not gain admission to the University of Virginia's undergraduate programs until 1970, which made it one of the last state universities in the country to admit women.[29] The crude and chauvinistic behavior of the young Virginia gentlemen, and of some of the faculty members, too, exhibited the same dismissive attitudes about women that the legislators displayed. It should not have surprised anybody in a society that had always been under the control of elite white men that they continued to act, as VIRGINIA FREEWOMAN had written back in 1829, as if they were the "Lords of the Creation."[30]

The few women who served in the General Assembly in the 1920s reported that their male colleagues treated them politely, but that was not always the case. In February 1958 Kathryn Stone, of Arlington, the first woman to serve in the House of Delegates in more than twenty years, offered an amendment to limit the scope of a bill designed to harass members of the National Association for the Advancement of Colored People, one of several measures the legislators enacted to punish supporters of civil rights. Frank P. Moncure, of Stafford County, subjected her to a withering series of demeaning insults in an obvious attempt to frighten or subdue her into giving up, to make her cry and thereby expose her contemptible weakness and kill her amendment. Most of the other Virginia gentlemen in the chamber sat quietly and did not come to her defense or attempt to restrain Moncure's bullying behavior.[31] In February 1980 the *Washington Post* published a long article documenting the chronic low-grade discrimination and sexual harassment that men in the General Assembly continued to impose on women legislators and lobbyists. "The legislators treat you much nicer when you go visit their homes or home district offices," a woman lobbyist stated. "But boy, you get them in Richmond, and it's like one big fraternity party or locker room. . . . They are *SO* immature."[32]

The moral issues that Pat Robertson, Jerry Falwell, and other Virginians brought to the fore in the 1970s and 1980s shifted attention away from race and brought gender relations to the fore. In the process an issue like abortion, which was the most intensely divisive issue in state politics beginning in the

1980s, brought forth from both sides the language of individual rights and limited government. Opponents of abortion denounced the federal government on moral grounds for tolerating or protecting abortion and also for violating state's rights and making the federal government too powerful. At the same time they deployed the formidable power of the state government to protect human lives while those lives were still within the womb. Men and women on the opposite side of the question also employed the language of limited government to demand that the state government not interfere with what they regarded as a natural human right of a woman to have control over her own body and its reproductive functions. "Right to Life" versus "Right to Choose" presented a classic confrontation between competing moral beliefs fought out in the political and legal arenas. Some of those moral issues were not susceptible of compromise or easy settlement, and public debate as well as legislative tactics got played out as in a nasty zero-sum game in which there could be only a winner and a loser. In such circumstances democracy and effective representative government were often the losers, as were the abstract abstractions.

The language of individual liberty and equality and the language of state's rights and limited government have served many different purposes, including the disfranchisement of African Americans in 1902 and the decades-long regime of involuntary surgical sterilization of people whom state officials deemed morally or socially unfit. The social and economic policies that political leaders pursued often required positive state government action that did not always comport with the abstract theories about limited government. The complexity of society and the many competing interests persuaded twentieth-century legislators to introduce and to enact more rather than fewer laws as time went on, which was not what their campaign speeches suggested that they would do. Indeed, in order to handle all of their proposals to regulate human behavior, the assembly began meeting annually in the 1960s rather than every other year. Statistics published in the volumes of laws adopted at each session of the General Assembly demonstrate that the number of bills that legislators introduced and the number of laws that they passed increased during the final decades of the twentieth century and scarcely tapered off during the first decade of the twenty-first.

	Bills introduced	Laws passed
1960	1,079	619
1970	1,624	809
1980	1,566	795
1990	1,637	981
2000	2,333	1,070
2010	2,135	871

People who dislike restrictions on their personal behavior have a long and distinguished history on which to rely. The American Revolution stands at the head of the line of formidable precedents. Dislike and suspicion of strong and intrusive government have almost always been distinguishing and animating features of American politics because of the potential for restricting individual liberty. Few Virginia politicians, though, have been consistent in the application of their political theories. Colonial tobacco planters, nineteenth-century railroad executives, and twentieth-century business and industrial leaders deployed government power to stimulate and to guide economic growth and also to insulate themselves from the influence of organized labor. In the twentieth and twenty-first centuries, they offered tax exemptions and other financial incentives to businesses to move their headquarters or factories to Virginia, which meant in practice that state and local governments starved their public treasuries in the hope that in the long run the economic benefits to themselves, to the community, and to the state would be worth the cost. Public officials engaged in those economic development policies for decades, apparently without ever calculating the short- and long-term gains and losses to city, county, and state treasuries or to the economic welfare of Virginia and Virginians.[33]

Virginia's political culture has almost always exhibited an inhospitality to change because the people in charge contrived and protected institutions and practices that worked to their advantage. As a result the state's constitutions and laws have created undemocratic institutions and practices that are also resistant to change. An unexamined reverence for the Spirit of Virginia that Douglas Southall Freeman, Virginius Dabney, and others propagated in the twentieth century allowed a mythic version of the past to constrict the range of options that the state's political leaders contemplated. That reverence, more importantly, either blinded them and the larger public to the undemocratic features of their government or allowed them to ignore or to accept those features as if they were part of the inevitable natural order of things.

Two public discussions in the anniversary year 2007 demonstrated that the appeal of the ideas remained strong but that the meanings of the ideas remained unclear. Early in the General Assembly session that year, the members debated whether to make a formal apology for the role that Virginia's government had taken in creating and preserving slavery and the subsequent discrimination and humiliation imposed on African Americans during the Jim Crow period. A member of the House of Delegates appeared to dismiss the significance of slavery with an apparently offhand remark that "our black citizens should get over it."[34]

That seriously offended the assembly's African American members, and what had begun as a proposal to make amends and to acknowledge past injustices generated new hard feelings. Members of both parties and both races in the General Assembly eventually crafted and adopted a long resolution apologizing to African Americans for what previous generations of white men and women did to their ancestors and also to Virginia's Indians for what those generations of white men and women did to theirs.[35] Of symbolic but no practical importance, the resolutions lost some of their value as a consequence of the arguments that preceded their adoption.

"Virginia is commemorating the 400th anniversary of the settlement of Jamestown," wrote Michael Paul Williams, a columnist for the *Richmond Times-Dispatch,* following adoption of the resolution, "an event viewed with ambivalence by some black and American Indian residents. For them, Jamestown was the beginning of an enslavement, displacement and decimation— it's more cause for lament than celebration." Williams was African American, unlike any regular columnist for that newspaper before the final decades of the twentieth century. Some things had certainly changed, but others had not. "This commemoration," he then predicted, "will be the next installment of Virginia history—a history that has been soft on the villains and tended to wallpaper over atrocities. The state has only recently sought to redress some of these wrongs, such as the attempt to reclassify American Indians into extinction and the closing of Prince Edwards County's public schools in defiance of desegregation."

"Every time I glimpse my byline," Williams wrote, "I see the name of a former slave owner. My ancestry is largely a blank slate, my ancestral home a mystery. Dotting Richmond's most prominent boulevard are granite monuments to the defenders of slavery. I'm weary of explaining what should be obvious— why our state and nation's unapologetic stance regarding the enslavement of my ancestors is a source of pain."[36] The monuments are bronze, not granite, but they all memorialize Confederates except one. Getting the newest monument, of Arthur Ashe, erected took great effort. Williams had good reason not to just "get over it."

The other public discussion during the anniversary year followed a remark that the Speaker of the House of Delegates made early in September, that immigration had brought so many people to Virginia from elsewhere in the United States and the world that a significant portion of the state's population did not share the "values we have in Virginia."[37] His comment suggested to some people that he was intolerant of immigrants and to others that he was worried only about the consequences of the arrival of illegal immigrants. One of the most interesting things about the ensuing brief and inconclusive public discussion was that even though people talked with reverence about Virginia's cardinal values, nobody defined them. Nobody defined "the values we have in Virginia," just as nobody defined the Virginia abstractions that had annoyed William Erskine Stephenson late in 1861.

Something similar to that discussion took place the following year after a campaign official commented on how different the voters in Loudoun County, northwest of Washington, D.C., were from the people of "real Virginia."[38] Immigration of people to the suburbs of the national capital had accelerated rapidly after the 1940s and filled much of the region with people who grew up elsewhere and did not learn their American and Virginia history from the same textbooks or assimilate the Spirit of Virginia in the same way as people who grew up in most other parts of the state. Northern Virginia by then was a region with its own capitalized regional identity. In the first decades of the twenty-first century, it had the most ethnically, culturally, religiously, and economically diverse population that any part of Virginia had ever had. It differed significantly in many ways from the rest of Virginia, from the "real Virginia."

The densely suburbanized portions of Northern Virginia could become in the twenty-first century the conspicuous alternative to the rest of Virginia that the Ohio Valley counties had been during the nineteenth or the Fighting Ninth during the twentieth. It perhaps might lead the way in changing the political culture of the entire state in fundamentally important ways. That is probably what worried the Speaker of the House and the campaign official.

Whether anything of the kind takes place remains to be seen. In spite of many changes that took place in Virginia's political culture and institutions during the centuries after the settlement of Jamestown in 1607, it is the continuities that attract the eye of the observer of the long term. Human history is constant change, but it is the continuities that constitute the context in which change took place in Virginia. To a certain extent every group of people or organization develops a corporate culture that constantly renews itself. The personalities and policies, the rules and regulations, the habits and practices of a group of people are rooted in and in turn create and reinforce a common set of assumptions, beliefs, and behavior patterns. Unless some dramatic change suddenly occurs, such as a speedy mass turnover of the population, gradual change in the composition of the organization's membership works but slow change in its corporate personality. New individuals merge into the group and are more likely than not to adapt to its prevailing corporate ethos, else they do not last long or they become conspicuous nonconformists and therefore marginal participants. The political culture of Virginia is a particularly good example of how that holds true at the large scale of a political community and the long period of time in which historians observe changes and continuities.

It is a cultural and institutional manifestation of part of Sir Isaac Newton's first law of motion, that an object at rest tends to remain at rest. The other part of Newton's law is that an object in motion tends to remain in motion. The inertial force of stability has generally characterized Virginia's political culture and institutions more than the inertial force for change. The restoration of traditional white elite domination of government in the 1880s led directly to the reversal by 1902 of almost all of the democratic reforms of the

1850s and 1860s and thence to the decades-long undemocratic rule of the Byrd organization. The laws, practices, institutions, and beliefs that supported the machine's domination could not be swept away and replaced all at once or even rapidly after Byrd's death and the abolition of the poll tax in the 1960s. Indeed, in many respects, although certainly not in all, the Republican Party's displacement of the Democratic Party late in the twentieth century represented continuity more than change. Party labels changed, but politics did not. The Democrats' inability to form themselves into effective challengers to the Republicans with an appealing alternative political agenda allowed the Republicans to set the terms of public debate and to preserve rather than to change many essential elements of the state's political culture.

The two parties nevertheless remained competitive during the final decade of the twentieth century and the first decade of the twenty-first. That may indicate how similar they were rather than how closely divided the state was between different competing sets of ideas—or that party leaders gravitated toward the extremes, leaving voters leaderless in the moderate center. Without the benefit of hindsight, that can be difficult to determine. Still, so obviously radical an event as the election of L. Douglas Wilder, an African American, to the governorship in 1989 did not signal a major turning point in state politics, nor did any other single event other than the replacement of the Democratic Party with the Republican Party indicate that a transformational event had taken place.

Many variable circumstances contributed to the two-party competitiveness of early twenty-first-century Virginia politics, but a principal defining characteristic may remain a resistance to fundamental change. The inertial power of the demographic and cultural changes taking place in Virginia early in the twenty-first century—most obviously in Northern Virginia where in the early years of the twenty-first century about one-third of all residents of Virginia lived without having learned about the Spirit of Virginia at a young age—could lead to a significant reformation of the state's political culture, but perhaps the impetus for change will shatter against the inertial power of institutional and political continuity. Political scientists and historians of the future will watch and analyze what the peoples of the state do about democracy in Virginia.

NOTES

Abbreviations and Short Titles

DVB   John T. Kneebone et al., eds., *Dictionary of Virginia Biography* (Richmond, 1988–)

JSH   *Journal of Southern History*

LVA   Library of Virginia

PRO   Public Record Office Series, National Archives of Great Britain

PRO CO   Public Record Office, Colonial Office series, National Archives of Great Britain

RG   Record Group

Statutes at Large   William Waller Hening, ed., *The Statutes at Large: Being a Collection of All the Laws of Virginia, from the First Session of the Legislature, in the Year 1619 . . .* (Richmond, etc., 1809–23)

UVA   University of Virginia

VHS   Virginia Historical Society

VMHB   *Virginia Magazine of History and Biography*

WMQ   *William and Mary Quarterly*

Prologue

1. Thomas Yong to Worthy Sir, 13 July 1634, LVA, quotations on unnumbered pp. 4, 5, 8; also printed in Plowden Charles Jennett Weston, ed., *Documents Connected with the History of South Carolina* (London, 1856), 29–44, *Collections of the Massachusetts Historical Society*, 4th ser., 9 (1871): 81–115, and in part in Clayton Colman Hall, ed., *Original Narratives of Early American History: Narratives of Early Maryland, 1633–1684* (New York, 1910), 53–61.

2. J. Mills Thornton III, "The Thrusting Out of Governor Harvey: A Seventeenth-Century Rebellion," *VMHB* 76 (1968): 11–26.

3. George Donne, "Virginia Reviewed" (n.d., ca. 1638), quotation on fol. 13, Harleian MSS, 7021, British Library; also printed in part in T. H. Breen, ed., "George Donne's 'Virginia Reviewed': A 1638 Plan to Reform Colonial Society," *WMQ*, 3d ser., 30 (1973): 449–66.

4. L.G. [Lionel Gatford], *Publick Good Without Private Interest. Or, a Compendious Remonstrance of the Present Sad State and Condition of the English Colonie in Virginea. With a Modest Declaration of the Several Causes Why it Hath not Prospered Better*

Hitherto; as also, a Submissive Suggestion to the Most Prudentiall Probable Wayes, and Means, Both Divine and Civill for its Happyer Improvement (London, 1657), 10, 11, 16.

5. Morgan Godwyn, *The Negro's & Indians Advocate, Suing for Their Admission into the Church: or, A Persuasive to the Instructing and Baptizing of the Negro's and Indians in our Plantations. Shewing That as the Compliance Therewith Can Prejudice no Mans Just Interest; So the Wilful Neglecting and Opposing of it, is no Less than a Manifest Apostacy from the Christian Faith. To Which is Added, A Brief Account of Religion in Virginia* (London, 1680), 76 (quotation), 167–74.

6. Gilbert Chinard, trans. and ed., *A Huguenot Exile in Virginia: or Voyages of a French-man Exiled for His Religion with a Description of Virginia and Maryland* (New York, 1934), 142, translating Durand Dauphiné, *Voyages d'un Francois, Exilé pour la Religion, avec Une Description de la Virgine & Marilan dans L'Amerique* (The Hague, 1687), 96, "arrivant chez lui, jecreus d'aborder dans un aflez grand Bourg, & je sceus ensuite que rout lui apartenoit."

7. Hunter Dickinson Farish, ed., *Journal and Letters of Philip Vickers Fithian, 1773–1774: A Plantation Tutor of the Old Dominion* (Williamsburg, 1943), 211.

8. Anthony S. Parent Jr., *Foul Means: The Formation of a Slave Society in Virginia, 1660–1740* (Chapel Hill, 2003).

9. John Hammond, *Leah and Rachel: Or, The Two Fruitfull Sisters Virginia and Maryland: Their Present Condition, Impartially Stated and Related* (London, 1656).

1   For the Glory of God and the Good of the Plantation

1. Jon Kukla, *Speakers and Clerks of the Virginia House of Burgesses, 1619–1776* (Richmond, 1981), 3–10, 31–34; Warren M. Billings, *A Little Parliament: The Virginia General Assembly in the Seventeenth Century* (Richmond, 2004), 5–10.

2. Ralph Hamor, *A True Discourse of the Present Estate of Virginia, and the Successe of the Affaires There Till the 18 of June, 1614. Together, with a Relation of the Severall English Townes and Forts, the Assured Hopes of That Countrie and the Peace Concluded with the Indians. The Christening of Powhatans Daughter and her Mariage with an English-man. Written by Raphe Hamor the yonger, Late Secretarie in that Colony* (London, 1615), 33.

3. Quotations from the Book of Common Prayer taken from an 1844 London facsimile of Richard Grafton's 1559 London first edition.

4. Quotations from the Bible taken from a 1969 University of Wisconsin Press facsimile of Roland Hall's 1560 Geneva first edition.

5. *DVB* 2:377–78.

6. William J. Van Schreeven and George H. Reese, eds., *Proceedings of the General Assembly of Virginia, July 30–August 4, 1619* (Jamestown, 1969) (including on even-numbered pages a facsimile of the original in the National Archives of Great Britain, PRO CO 1/1, and on odd-numbered pages a transcription), 14.

7. Ibid., 34.

8. Susan Myra Kingsbury, ed., *Records of the Virginia Company of London* (Washington, DC, 1906–35), 3:483–84.

9. *Proceedings of the General Assembly,* 12, 68.

10. Kukla, *Speakers and Clerks of the Virginia House of Burgesses,* 8–9, 33; *Proceedings of the General Assembly,* 68.

11. *Proceedings of the General Assembly,* 12.

12. Ibid., 16.   13. Ibid., 16, 18.   14. Ibid., 20.

15. Ibid., 18, 20, 22, 24, 34, 36, 38.

16. Ibid., 20, 22, 36.   17. Ibid., 24, 26.   18. Ibid.

19. Ibid., 28.   20. Ibid.   21. Ibid., 30.

22. Virginia Company Records, 16 July 1621, Ferrar Papers, Magdalene College, Cambridge Univ.

23. *Proceedings of the General Assembly,* 30.

24. *Statutes at Large* 1:301–2.

25. *Proceedings of the General Assembly,* 68.

26. Ibid., 30.   27. Ibid.   28. Ibid., 32.

29. Ibid., 34.   30. Ibid., 38.   31. Ibid.

32. Ibid., 42.   33. Ibid.   34. Ibid., 40.

35. Ibid.   36. Ibid.   37. Ibid.

38. Ibid., 42.   39. Ibid., 44.   40. Ibid., 44, 46.

41. Ibid., 46.   42. Ibid., 46, 48, 50.   43. Ibid., 50.

44. Ibid., 50, 52.   45. Ibid., 50, 52.   46. Ibid., 52.

47. Ibid.   48. Ibid., 52, 54.   49. Ibid., 54.

50. Ibid., 60.   51. Ibid., 56.   52. Ibid.

53. Ibid.   54. Ibid., 56, 58.   55. Ibid., 58.

56. Ibid.   57. Ibid., 58, 60.   58. Ibid., 60.

59. Ibid., 62.   60. Ibid.   61. Ibid.

62. Ibid., 62, 64, 66.   63. Ibid., 66, 68.   64. Ibid., 68.

65. Ibid., 68, 70.   66. Ibid., 70.   67. Ibid.

68. John Rolfe to Sir Edwyn Sandys, Jan. 1619/20, Farrar Papers, Magdalen College, Oxford Univ.

69. It is possible that a few Africans were already in Virginia, depending on whether a census of white and black residents of Virginia was taken before or after August 1619. Cf. William Thorndale, "A Passenger List of the 1619 *Bona Nova*," *Magazine of Virginia Genealogy* 33 (1995): 3–11, and Martha W. McCartney, "An Early Virginia Census Reprised," *Quarterly Bulletin of the Archaeological Society of Virginia* 54 (1999): 178–96. For what is known about that ship and its human cargo, see Engel Sluiter, "New Light on the '20. and Odd Negroes' Arriving in Virginia, August, 1619," *WMQ,* 3d ser., 54 (1997): 395–98, and John Thornton, "The African Experience of the '20. and Odd Negroes' Arriving in Virginia in 1619," ibid., 55 (1998): 421–34.

70. William Capps to John Farrar, 31 Mar. 1623, Manchester Papers, PRO 30/15/2, no. 322.

2   True Religion and a Civil Course of Life

1. Philip L. Barbour et al., eds., *The Complete Works of Captain John Smith (1580–1631)* (Chapel Hill, 1986), 3:295.

2. Edward L. Bond, *Damned Souls in a Tobacco Colony: Religion in Seventeenth-Century Virginia* (Atlanta, 2000), 1–3; Edward L. Bond, ed., *Spreading the Gospel in Colonial Virginia: Sermons and Devotional Writings* (Lanham, MD, 2004), 1–64.

3. Douglas Bradburn, "The Eschatological Origins of the English Empire," in *Early Modern Virginia: Reconsidering the Old Dominion,* ed. Douglas Bradburn and John C. Coombs (Charlottesville, 2011), 15–56; Rebecca Anne Goetz, *The Baptism of Early Virginia: How Christianity Created Race* (Baltimore, 2012), esp. 1–12, 22–60, 72–85.

4. George Percy, "Trewe Relacyon of the proceedings and ocurrents of momente wch have hapned in Virginia from the tyme Sr. Thomas Gates was shippwrackte upon the Bermudes Ano: 1609 untill my departure outt of the country wch was in Ano: Dmi 1612," 17–18, Americana MS 106, Elkins Collection, Free Library of Philadelphia.

5. William Strachey, comp., *For the Colony in Virginea Britannia, Lawes Divine, Morall and Martiall, &c.* (London, 1612), 1.

6. Ibid., 2–4.

7. Ibid., unnumbered pages following p. 89, which is misnumbered 41.

8. William J. Van Schreeven and George H. Reese, eds., *Proceedings of the General Assembly of Virginia, July 30–August 4, 1619* (Jamestown, 1969) (including on even-numbered pages a facsimile of the original in the National Archives of Great Britain, PRO CO 1/1, and on odd-numbered pages a transcription), 42.

9. Edward L. Bond and Joan R. Gundersen, "The Episcopal Church in Virginia, 1607–2007," *VMHB* 115 (2007): 174.

10. *Statutes at Large* 1:240–43.

11. Ibid., 241–42.

12. Warren M. Billings, ed., "Some Acts Not in Hening's *Statutes*: The Acts of Assembly, April 1652, November 1652, and July 1653," *VMHB* 83 (1975): 31.

13. By the end of the seventeenth century, vestrymen began filling vacancies among their number, as did justices of the peace, creating self-sustaining institutions that under ordinary conditions answered to no one else. During the eighteenth century rapid population growth and circumstances peculiar to some localities required divisions of parishes and elections of vestry members, and clergymen gained some measure of job security and could not be summarily dismissed at the whim of the vestrymen (Joan Rezner Gundersen, "The Myth of the Independent Virginia Vestry," *Historical Magazine of the Protestant Episcopal Church* 44 [1975]: 133–41).

14. Bond and Gundersen, "Episcopal Church in Virginia," 175–83.

15. John Ruston Pagan, *Anne Orthwood's Bastard: Sex and Law in Early Virginia* (Oxford, 2003), 120–22.

16. *Statutes at Large* 1:421, 520–21.

17. Ibid., 400.

18. Ibid., 399–400.

19. Ibid., 418, 424.

20. John Clayton, *The Defence of a Sermon, Preach'd upon the Receiving into the Communion of the Church of England, the Honourable Sir Terence Mac-Mahom, Baronet, and Christopher Dunn: Converts from the Church of Rome* (Dublin, 1701), preface, unnumbered.

21. Babette M. Levy, "Early Puritanism in the Southern and Island Colonies," *Proceedings of the American Antiquarian Society*, n.s., 70, pt. 1 (1960), esp. 92–122.

22. John Yong to Dear Sir, 13 July 1634, Acc. 20966, LVA.

23. Jon Butler, ed., "Two 1642 Letters from Virginia Puritans," *Proceedings of the Massachusetts Historical Society* 84 (1972): 99–109.

24. *DVB* 1:445–47.

25. Steven D. Crow, "'Your Majesty's Good Subjects': A Reconsideration of Royalism in Virginia, 1642–1652," *VMHB* 87 (1979): 158–73.

26. Kevin Butterfield, "Puritans and Religious Strife in the Early Chesapeake," ibid., 109 (2001): 5–36, which argues that Puritans and Prayer Book churchmen in Virginia were less compatible.

27. Warren M. Billings, *A Little Parliament: The Virginia General Assembly in the Seventeenth Century* (Richmond, 2004), 76–78.

28. Records of the operations of seventeenth-century Virginia parishes and parishioners are not adequate for attempting such close study as New England townships have received. In studying the eighteenth century, Clive Raymond Hallman, "The Vestry as a Unit of Local Government in Colonial Virginia" (PhD, Univ. of Georgia, 1987), and John K. Nelson, *Blessed Company: Parishes, Parsons, and Parishioners in Anglican Virginia, 1690–1776* (Chapel Hill, 2001), 13–16, placed the parish and the county on a parity, and Joan R. Gundersen, "The Non-Institutional Church: The Religious Role of Women in Eighteenth-Century Virginia," *Historical Magazine of the Protestant Episcopal Church* 51 (1982): 347–57, examined an eighteenth-century parish as a social unit of importance.

29. *Statutes at Large* 2:101–2.

30. Ibid., 3:82, 325–28, 530–34, 5:245–46, 426–30.

31. Ibid., 3:326, 327.

32. William H. Seiler, "Land Processioning in Colonial Virginia," *WMQ*, 3d ser., 6 (1949): 416–36, which also contains evidence that after the disestablishment of the Church of England in 1786, local boards of overseers of the poor (who inherited one of the social responsibilities of the parishes) continued the practice. In King and Queen County the court ordered that the property lines be processioned in 1867 and 1868 after the destruction of the local land records during the American Civil War (King and Queen Co. Processioners Report Book, 1867–68, King and Queen Co. Courthouse).

33. David D. Hall, "The Chesapeake in the Seventeenth Century," in *A History of the Book in America*, vol. 1, *The Colonial Book in the Atlantic World*, ed. Hugh Amory and David D. Hall (Cambridge, 2000), 57–65.

34. *Statues at Large* 2:102.

35. Accomack Co. Wills, Deeds, Orders (1672–82), 159–68 (quotation on 160), 172, 183.

36. Princess Anne Co. Order Book 1 (1691–1709), 444–45.

37. Perry Miller, "Religion and Society in the Early Literature of Virginia," in *Errand into the Wilderness* (Cambridge, MA, 1956), 99–140; Darrett B. Rutman, "The Evolution of Religious Life in Early Virginia," *Lex et Scientia: Journal of the American Academy of Law* 14 (1978): 190–214; James Horn, *Adapting to a New World: English Society in the Seventeenth-Century Chesapeake* (Chapel Hill, 1994), 381–418; Edward L. Bond,

"Source of Knowledge, Source of Power: The Supernatural World of English Virginia, 1607–24," *VMHB* 108 (2000): 105–38.

38. Warren M. Billings, with the assistance of Maria Kimberly, ed., *The Papers of Sir William Berkeley, 1605–1677* (Richmond, 2007), 116.

39. Ibid., 309.

40. Ibid., 506.

41. Ibid., 531.

42. Ibid., 609–10.

43. On public display in 2007 in the archaeological museum on Jamestown Island.

44. Neville Williams, "The Tribulations of John Bland, Merchant: London, Seville, Jamestown, Tangier, 1643–1680," *VMHB* 72 (1964): 19–41; *DVB* 2:5, 7–8, 14.

45. Bruce E. Steiner, "The Catholic Brents of Colonial Virginia: An Instance of Practical Toleration," *VMHB* 70 (1962): 387–409; *DVB* 2:215–16.

46. Bond, *Damned Souls,* 160–74.

47. *Statutes at Large* 1:532–33.

48. Jon Kukla, "Order and Chaos in Early Virginia: Political and Social Stability in Pre-Restoration Virginia," *American Historical Review* 90 (1985): 275–98; Brent Tarter, "Reflections on the Church of England in Colonial Virginia," *VMHB* 112 (2004): 346–59; Alexander B. Haskell, "'The Affections of the People': Ideology and the Politics of State Building in Colonial Virginia, 1607–1754" (PhD diss., Johns Hopkins Univ., 2004).

49. *DVB* 3:285–86.

50. Ibid., 1:539–43; P. G. Scott, "James Blair and the Scottish Church: A New Source," *WMQ,* 3d ser., 33 (1976): 300–308.

51. Kukla, "Order and Chaos in Early Virginia," 297–98.

52. Ibid.; Edward L. Bond, "Anglican Theology and Devotion in James Blair's Virginia, 1685–1743: Private Piety in the Public Church," *VMHB* 104 (1996): 313–40.

53. Hugh Jones, *The Present State of Virginia. Giving A Particular and Short Account of the Indian, English, and Negroe Inhabitants of that Colony. Shewing Their Religion, Manners, Government, Trade, Way of Living, &c. with a Description of the Country. From Whence is Inferred a Short View of Maryland and North Carolina. To which are Added, Schemes and Propositions for the Better Promotion of Learning, Religion, Inventions, Manufactures, and Trade in Virginia, and the Other Plantations. For the Information of the Curious, and for the Service of Such as are Engaged in the Propagation of the Gospel and Advancement of Learning, and for the use of all Persons Concerned in the Virginia Trade and Plantation* (London, 1724), 48.

3   The Grievances of the People

1. Warren M. Billings, *Sir William Berkeley and the Forging of Colonial Virginia* (Baton Rouge, 2004), 210–11, 232–55.

2. Warren M. Billings, with the assistance of Maria Kimberly, ed., *The Papers of Sir William Berkeley, 1605–1677* (Richmond, 2007), 568–73.

3. Ibid., 575–76.

4. *Statutes at Large* 2:101–2.

5. Ibid., 280.

6. William J. Van Schreeven and George H. Reese, eds., *Proceedings of the General Assembly of Virginia, July 30–August 4, 1619* (Jamestown, 1969) (including on even-numbered pages a facsimile of the original in the National Archives of Great Britain, PRO CO 1/1, and on odd-numbered pages a transcription), 70.

7. Jon Kukla, *Political Institutions in Virginia, 1619–1660* (New York, 1989), 88, 98–99, 113–14, 117–18, 162–64, 170–71; Warren M. Billings, *A Little Parliament: The Virginia General Assembly in the Seventeenth Century* (Richmond, 2004), 22, 28, 31, 35, 45–46, 95, 126, 177, 211; Robert Brenner, *Merchants and Revolution: Commercial Change, Political Conflict, and London's Overseas Traders, 1550–1653* (Princeton, 1993); John R. Pagan, "Dutch Maritime and Commercial Activity in Mid-Seventeenth-Century Virginia," *VMHB* 90 (1982): 485–501; Victor Enthoven and Wim Klooster, "The Rise and Fall of the Virginia-Dutch Connection in the Seventeenth Century," in *Early Modern Virginia: Reconsidering the Old Dominion,* ed. Douglas Bradburn and John C. Coombs (Charlottesville, 2011), 90–127.

8. Kukla, *Political Institutions in Virginia,* and Billings, *A Little Parliament,* provide a convincing alternative to a sturdy interpretation of seventeenth-century Virginia, Bernard Bailyn's "Politics and Social Structure in Virginia," in *Seventeenth-Century America: Essays in Colonial History,* ed. James Morton Smith (Chapel Hill, 1959), 90–115, which depicted Virginia's social and political structures as less stable and effective, an interpretation that also informs Edmund S. Morgan's *American Slavery, American Freedom: The Ordeal of Colonial Virginia* (New York, 1975). See also Brent Tarter, "Bacon's Rebellion, the Grievances of the People, and the Political Culture of Seventeenth-Century Virginia," *VMHB* 119 (2011): 3–41, and John C. Coombs, "Beyond the 'Origins Debate': Rethinking the Rise of Virginia Slavery," in Bradburn and Coombs, *Early Modern Virginia,* 239–78.

9. Thomas Mathew, "The Beginning, Progress, and Conclusion of Bacons Rebellion in Virginia in the Years 1675 & 1676" (1705), 1–3, Thomas Jefferson Papers, ser. 8, vol. 1, Library of Congress.

10. C. S. Everett, "'They shalbe slaves for their lives': Indian Slavery in Colonial Virginia," in *Indian Slavery in Colonial America,* ed. Alan Galley (Lincoln, NE, 2009), 67–108.

11. Wilcomb E. Washburn, *The Governor and the Rebel: A History of Bacon's Rebellion in Virginia* (Chapel Hill, 1957), 20–26; Michael Leroy Oberg, ed., *Samuel Wiseman's Book of Record: The Official Account of Bacon's Rebellion in Virginia* (Lanham, MD, 2005), 144.

12. Everett, "'They shalbe slaves for their lives,'" 78–90.

13. Washburn, *The Governor and the Rebel,* 40–48.

14. Nathaniel Bacon to Sir William Berkeley, 25 May 1676, *Papers of Sir William Berkeley,* 523.

15. *Statutes at Large* 2:326–33; *Papers of Sir William Berkeley,* 504–10.

16. *Statutes at Large* 2:341–51; *Papers of Sir William Berkeley,* 534–38.

17. *Papers of Sir William Berkeley,* 537.

18. "Declaration of the People against Sir William Berkeley," n.d. (ca. 30 July 1676), two copies in Egerton MSS 2395, British Library.

19. John Harold Sprinkle Jr., "Loyalists and Baconians: The Participants in Bacon's Rebellion in Virginia, 1676–1677" (PhD diss., College of William and Mary, 1992), is the most thorough analysis of the men who are known to have exercised leadership roles during the rebellion, but there is no comparable study of Bacon's followers and probably no other resources than the county grievances and close analysis of the events of the rebellion for retrieving their motivations.

20. Wiseman's copies of most of the essential documents that the commissioners collected are in PRO CO 5/1371, but the full final report is in the Pepsyian Library, Magdalene College, Cambridge Univ. It was published with an index that the printer unfortunately muddled in *Samuel Wiseman's Book of Record.*

21. Herbert Jeffreys, Sir John Berry, and Francis Moryson to Thomas Watkins, 27 Mar. 1677, *Samuel Wiseman's Book of Record,* 106.

22. Ibid., 104–5.

23. Ibid., 60, 90–92, 93, 130.

24. Ibid., 90–91.

25. *Papers of Sir William Berkeley,* 520–21. The Long Assembly was a subject of remark only in the grievances of Stafford County (PRO CO 1/39, fol. 203) and Surry County (ibid., fol. 207).

26. PRO CO 1/39, fols. 194–255, CO 1/40, fols. 140–47; nineteenth-century transcriptions of some of them were printed in *VMHB* 2 (1894): 166–73, 2 (1895): 289–92, 380–92, 3 (1895): 35–42, 132–47, and in H. R. McIlwaine, ed., *Journals of the House of Burgesses of Virginia, 1659/60–1693* (Richmond, 1914), 99–113.

27. PRO CO 1/39, fol. 240.

28. Ibid., fol. 217.

29. Ibid., fol. 228.

30. *Samuel Wiseman's Book of Record,* 250–56; PRO CO 1/39, fols. 246–49, 250–51, 255.

31. PRO CO 1/39, fol. 216.

32. Ibid., fol. 225.   33. Ibid., fol. 194.   34. Ibid., fols. 223–27.

35. Ibid., fol. 233.   36. Ibid., fols. 207–9.   37. Ibid., fol. 209.

38. Ibid., fol. 214.

39. The most thorough analyses of Virginia society and politics in relation to Bacon's Rebellion found conspicuous class cleavages and conflicts throughout the colony and time period: Warren M. Billings, "'Virginia's Deploured Condition,' 1660–1676: The Coming of Bacon's Rebellion," (PhD diss., Northern Illinois Univ., 1968), Morgan, *American Slavery, American Freedom,* 215–49, and Alexander B. Haskell, "Deference, Defiance, and the Language of Office in Seventeenth-Century Virginia," in Bradburn and Coombs, *Early Modern Virginia,* 158–84.

40. Lancaster Co. Orders, etc. (1655–66), 87.

41. Surry Co. Deeds, Wills, etc., no. 1 (1652–72), 166.

42. Lancaster Co. Order Book 1 (1666–80), 206; H. R. McIlwaine, ed., *Minutes of the Council and General Court of Colonial Virginia,* 2d ed., rev. (Richmond, 1979), 299.

43. Surry Co. Deeds, Wills, etc., no. 2 (1671–84), 103.

44. Westmoreland Co. Deeds, Patents, etc. (1665–77), 17–18a.

45. Peter Thompson, "The Thief, the Householder, and the Commons: Languages of Class in Seventeenth-Century Virginia," *WMQ*, 3d ser., 63 (2006): 253–80.

46. Henrico Co. (PRO CO 1/39, fol. 233), Isle of Wight Co. (ibid., fol. 225), Rappahannock Co. (ibid., fol. 197), York Co. (ibid., fol. 240), and the first set from Nansemond Co. (ibid., fol. 246); Bacon's declarations (PRO CO 1/37, fols. 128–29, 130–31, 133, 178–79); and the brief news sheet, *Strange News from Virginia; Being a Full and True Account of the Life and Death of Nathanael Bacon Esquire* (London, 1677), 5.

47. Surry Co. Deeds, Wills, etc., no. 2, fols. 40–44.

48. Ibid., fol. 40.

49. *Minutes of the Council and General Court*, 367; Surry Co. Deeds, Wills, etc., no. 2, fol. 69.

50. *Papers of Sir William Berkeley*, 459.

51. Billings, *Sir William Berkeley*, 227–28; Alexander B. Haskell, "'The Affections of the People': Ideology and the Politics of State Building in Colonial Virginia, 1607–1754" (PhD diss., Johns Hopkins Univ., 2004), esp. 177–215.

52. *Papers of Sir William Berkeley*, 507.

53. *Minutes of the Council and General Court*, 252, 288.

54. PRO CO 1/39, fols. 246–47.

55. *Papers of Sir William Berkeley*, 520–21 (quotation on 520), 537.

56. Sir William Berkeley to Thomas Ludwell, 1 July 1767, ibid., 537.

57. PRO CO 1/36, fols. 113–14.

58. Copies in PRO CO 1/37, fols. 29–30, and in Egerton MSS, 2395, fols. 601–2, British Library.

59. Sir William Berkeley to Henry Coventry, 2 Feb. 1676/77, *Papers of Sir William Berkeley*, 570.

60. *Statutes at Large* 2:352–60.

61. Philip Ludwell to Right Honorable, 28 June 1676, PRO CO 1/37, fol. 38.

62. David D. Hall, "The Chesapeake in the Seventeenth Century," in *A History of the Book in America*, vol. 1, *The Colonial Book in the Atlantic World*, ed. Hugh Amory and David D. Hall (Cambridge, 2000), 57–65.

63. "Declaration of the People against Sir William Berkeley," n.d. (ca. 30 July 1676), two copies in Egerton MSS 2395, British Library.

64. PRO CO 1/37, fols. 243–44.

65. PRO CO 1/40, fols. 140–47 (quotation on 140).

66. *Samuel Wiseman's Book of Record*, 32–33; *Papers of Sir William Berkeley*, 550; *Statutes at Large* 2:380–81.

67. *Journals of the House of Burgesses, 1659/60–1693*, 66.

68. Moreover, when those laws were published early in the nineteenth century in *Statutes at Large*, William Waller Hening erroneously believed the same thing and incorrectly identified the laws of that session as "Bacon's Laws," perpetuating a misinterpretation that has misled some historians; see Washburn, *The Governor and the Rebel*, 13–14, 60, 67, and Brent Tarter, "Long before the NHPRC: Documentary Editing in Nineteenth-Century Virginia," *Documentary Editing* 30 (2008): 37–38.

69. PRO CO 1/39, fol. 243.

70. Ibid., fol. 247.

71. *Samuel Wiseman's Book of Record,* 250.

72. William Sherwood to Right Honorable, 1, 28 June 1676, PRO CO 1/37, fols. 1, 39–40.

73. Nicholas Spencer to My Lord, 6 Aug. 1676, Coventry Papers, 77, fol. 170, Longleat, Warminster, UK.

74. PRO CO 1/40, fols. 148–61 (quotations on 148 and 155).

75. Philip Ludwell to Right Honorable, 28 June 1676, PRO CO 1/37, fols. 35–38.

76. William Sherwood, "Virginias deploured Condition Or an Impartiall Narrative of the Murders comitted by the Indians there, and of the Sufering of his Mat^ies Loyall Subiects under the Rebellious outrages of Mr Nathaniell Bacon Junr to the tenth day of August A° dom 1676," 9, George Chalmers Collection, New York Public Library; Mathew, "Beginning, Progress, and Conclusion," 41; freeholders of Gloucester County to Sir William Berkeley, n.d., ca. 28 June 1676, *Papers of Sir William Berkeley,* 540; *Samuel Wiseman's Book of Record,* 151.

77. *Papers of Sir William Berkeley,* 572–73.

78. Ibid., 537.

79. Billings, *Sir William Berkeley,* 265–66; *Papers of Sir William Berkeley,* 608–9, 633; Herbert Jeffreys, Sir John Berry, and Francis Moryson to Thomas Watkins, 4 May 1677, PRO CO 1/40, 130–31 (quotation).

80. Washburn, *Governor and Rebel,* 60–63.

81. Excellent analyses of the status and roles of white women in the families of late seventeenth-century tobacco planters, esp. Kathleen M. Brown, *Good Wives, Nasty Wenches, and Anxious Patriarchs: Gender, Race, and Power in Colonial Virginia* (Chapel Hill, 1996), Terri L. Snyder, *Brabbling Women: Disorderly Speech and the Law in Early Virginia* (Ithaca, NY, 2003), and Snyder, "'To Seek for Justice': Gender, Servitude, and Household Governance in the Early Modern Chesapeake," in Bradburn and Coombs, *Early Modern Virginia,* 128–57, demonstrate that the men of those families restricted the social and political independence that some women had displayed before and during Bacon's Rebellion.

82. Credit where credit is due: Jon Kukla in a review in the *North Carolina Historical Review* 54 (1977): 321–22, characterized Morgan's *American Slavery, American Freedom* as a study in the origins of the Old South.

4 The Grandees of Government

1. Thomas Jefferson, *Reports of Cases Determined in the General Court of Virginia, from 1730, to 1740; and from 1768, to 1772,* ed. Thomas Jefferson Randolph (Charlottesville, 1829), 118.

2. Roger Atkinson to Samuel Pleasants, 1 Oct. 1774, Roger Atkinson Letterbook, UVA.

3. William Byrd to Charles Boyle, earl of Orrery, 5 July 1726, in Marion Tinling, ed., *The Correspondence of the Three William Byrds of Westover, Virginia, 1684–1776* (Charlottesville, 1977), 1:355. Extended commentaries on the values of the plantation elite are T. H. Breen, *Tobacco Culture: The Mentality of the Great Tidewater Planters on the*

Eve of Revolution (Princeton, 1985), and Michal J. Rozbicki, *The Complete Colonial Gentleman: Cultural Legitimacy in Plantation America* (Charlottesville, 1998).

4. James Laverne Anderson, "The Virginia Councillors and the American Revolution: The Demise of an Aristocratic Clique," *VMHB* 82 (1974): 56–74; Emory G. Evans, *A "Topping People": The Rise and Decline of Virginia's Old Political Elite, 1680–1790* (Charlottesville, 2009).

5. Alexander Spotswood to the Board of Trade, 9 Mar. 1713/14, PRO CO 5/1316, fol. 505.

6. Kevin R. Hardwick, "Narratives of Villainy and Virtue: Governor Francis Nicholson and the Character of the Good Ruler in Early Virginia," *JSH* 72 (2006): 39–74; Leonidas Dodson, *Alexander Spotswood, Governor of Colonial Virginia, 1710–1722* (Philadelphia, 1932), 157–88, 270–73.

7. William Byrd to Francis Otway, 10 Feb. 1741, *Correspondence of the Three William Byrds* 2:577–78.

8. Jon Kukla, *Speakers and Clerks of the Virginia House of Burgesses, 1643–1776* (Richmond, 1981), 20–24, 123–28.

9. Jack P. Greene, "The Attempt to Separate the Offices of Speaker and Treasurer in Virginia, 1758–1766," *VMHB* 71 (1963): 11–18.

10. John Kirkpatrick to George Washington, 14 Aug. 1756, in W. W. Abbot et al., eds., *The Papers of George Washington: Colonial Series* (Charlottesville, 1983–95), 3:352.

11. David John Mays, *Edmund Pendleton, 1721–1803: A Biography* (Cambridge, MA, 1952), 1:174–208; Joseph Albert Ernst, "The Robinson Scandal Redivivus: Money, Debts, and Politics in Revolutionary Virginia," *VMHB* 77 (1969): 146–73.

12. John Gilman Kolp, *Gentlemen and Freeholders: Electoral Politics in Colonial Virginia* (Baltimore, 1998), 36–58, significantly revising downward the estimates in Robert E. Brown and B. Katherine Brown, *Virginia, 1705–1786: Democracy or Aristocracy?* (East Lansing, MI, 1964), 125–50.

13. Kolp, *Gentlemen and Freeholders,* 59–80.

14. Charles S. Sydnor, *Gentlemen Freeholders: Political Practices in Washington's Virginia* (Chapel Hill, 1952), as substantially revised in Jack P. Greene, "Society, Ideology, and Politics: An Analysis of the Political Culture of Mid-Eighteenth-Century Virginia," in *Society, Freedom, and Conscience: The American Revolution in Virginia, Massachusetts, and New York,* ed. Richard M. Jellison (New York, 1976), 14–76, and Kolp, *Gentlemen and Freeholders.*

15. Charles Campbell, ed., *The Bland Papers; Being a Selection from the Manuscripts of Colonel Theodorick Bland, Jr., of Prince George County, Virginia* (Petersburg, 1840–43), 1:27.

16. Robert Beverley, *The History and Present State of Virginia* (London, 1705), preface.

17. Jack P. Greene, *The Constitutional Origins of the American Revolution* (Cambridge, 2010), 19–66.

18. [Richard Bland], "A Modest and true State of the Case," n.d., 4, Thomas Jefferson Papers, ser. 1, Library of Congress; the printed text is Richard Bland, *A Fragment on the Pistole Fee, Claimed by the Governor of Virginia, 1753,* ed. Worthington Chauncey Ford (Brooklyn, 1891), quotations on 37–39.

19. Jack P. Greene, ed., "The Case of the Pistole Fee: The Report of a Hearing on the Pis-

tole Fee Dispute before the Privy Council, June 18, 1754," *VMHB* 66 (1958): 399–422 (quotations on 408–9, 411).

20. William Stith to bishop of London, 21 Apr. 1753, 13:43 (in the old classification of the papers), Fulham Palace Papers, Lambeth Palace Library, London, UK, and John Blair to bishop of London, 15 Aug. 1754, 15:238 (in the old classification of the papers), ibid.

21. Richard Bland, *A Letter to the Clergy of Virginia, in Which the Conduct of the General-Assembly is Vindicated, Against the Reflexions Contained in a Letter to the Lords of Trade and Plantations, From the Lord-Bishop of London* (Williamsburg, 1760), 9.

22. Ibid., 18.

23. Richard Bland, *Colonel Dismounted: or the Rector Vindicated. In a Letter Addressed to His Reverence: Containing A Dissertation upon the Constitution of the Colony. By Common Sense* (Williamsburg, 1764), 20–21.

24. Ibid., 21–22.

25. Ibid., 23.

26. Ibid., 25.

27. Ibid., 27.

28. William J. Van Schreeven, Robert L. Scribner, and Brent Tarter, eds., *Revolutionary Virginia, the Road to Independence: A Documentary Record* (Charlottesville, 1973–83), 1:19, 20–21, 7:722–27. Bland's fellow burgess in the Two-Penny Act pamphleteering, Landon Carter, wrote and published several articles during the Stamp Act debates that endorsed exactly the interpretation that Bland advanced. See Jack P. Greene, ed., "'Not to be Governed or Taxed, but by . . . Our Representatives': Four Essays in Opposition to the Stamp Act by Landon Carter," *VMHB* 76 (1968): 259–300.

29. Richard Bland, *An Inquiry into the Rights of the British Colonies, Intended as an Answer to The Regulations Lately Made Concerning the Colonies, and the Taxes Imposed upon them Considered. In a Letter Addressed to the author of that Pamphlet* (Williamsburg, 1766), 13.

30. Ibid., 20; Beverley, *History and Present State of Virginia*, 65.

31. Bland, *Inquiry into the Rights of the British Colonies*, 30.

32. [Thomas Jefferson], *A Summary View of the Rights of British America: Set Forth in Some Resolutions Intended for the Inspection of the Present Delegates of the People of Virginia, Now in Convention, by a native, and Member of the House of Burgesses* (Williamsburg, 1774).

33. Alexander Purdie and John Dixon's Williamsburg *Virginia Gazette*, 1 Aug. 1766.

34. Thomas Jefferson to William Wirt, 5 Aug. 1815, in J. Jefferson Looney et al., eds., *The Papers of Thomas Jefferson, Retirement Series* (Princeton, 2004–), 8:643.

35. Botetourt to earl of Hillsborough, 23 May 1769, PRO CO 5/1347, fol. 81.

36. Richard Bland's *To the Clergy of Virginia* (Williamsburg, n.d.) was published between Aug. 1773 and Sept. 1774 when Clementina Rind conducted one of the printing houses in Williamsburg.

37. Ibid., 2.

38. Richard Bland to Thomas Adams, 1 Aug. 1771, Adams Papers, VHS, also printed in *VMHB* 6 (1898): 127–34 (quotation on 132).

39. John K. Nelson, *A Blessed Company: Parishes, Parsons, and the Parishioners in Anglican*

Virginia, 1690–1776 (Chapel Hill, 2001), esp. 43–47 on taxation; Edward L. Bond, ed., *Spreading the Gospel in Colonial Virginia: Sermons and Devotional Writings* (Lanham, MD, 2004), 1–4; and Jacob M. Blosser, "Pursuing Happiness in Colonial Virginia: Sacred Words, Cheap Print, and Popular Religion in the Eighteenth Century," *VMHB* 118 (2010): 210–45.

40. Thad W. Tate, "The Coming of the Revolution in Virginia: Britain's Challenge to Virginia's Ruling Class, 1763–1776," *WMQ*, 3d ser., 19 (1962): 323–43; Woody Holton, *Forced Founders: Indians, Debtors, Slaves, and the Making of the American Revolution in Virginia* (Chapel Hill, 1999).

41. Lyman H. Butterfield, Leonard C. Faber, and Wendell D. Garrett, eds., *Diary and Autobiography of John Adams* (Cambridge, MA, 1961), 2:119–20.

42. [John Adams], *Thoughts on Government: Applicable to the Present State of the American Colonies. In a Letter from a Gentleman to His Friend* (Philadelphia, 1776).

43. [Carter Braxton], *An Address to the Convention of the Colony and Ancient Dominion of Virginia; on the Subject of Government in General, and Recommending a Particular Form to Their Consideration. By a Native of that Colony* (Philadelphia, 1776), quotations on 15, 17; Michal Jan Rozbicki, *Culture and Liberty in the Age of the American Revolution* (Charlottesville, 2011), esp. 78–162.

44. *Revolutionary Virginia, the Road to Independence* 7:449–50.

45. Ibid., 449.

46. Ibid., 651.

47. Edmund Randolph, *History of Virginia*, ed. Arthur H. Shaffer (Charlottesville, 1970), 256.

48. Richard Henry Lee to Charles Lee, 29 June 1776, in James Curtis Ballagh, ed., *The Letters of Richard Henry Lee* (New York, 1911), 1:203.

49. Patrick Henry to John Adams, 20 May 1776, in Robert J. Taylor et al., eds., *Papers of John Adams* (Cambridge, MA, 1977–), 4:200–202.

50. Julian P. Boyd et al., eds., *The Papers of Thomas Jefferson* (Princeton, 1950–), 1:356–65 (quotation on 362).

51. Ibid., 476–77.

5 All Men Are Not Created Equal

1. Robert A. Rutland, ed., *The Papers of George Mason, 1725–1792* (Chapel Hill, 1970), 1:277.

2. Julian P. Boyd et al., eds., *The Papers of Thomas Jefferson* (Princeton, 1950–), 1:429.

3. Brent Tarter, "The Virginia Declaration of Rights," in *To Secure the Blessings of Liberty: Rights in American History,* ed. Josephine F. Pacheco (Fairfax, VA, 1993), 37–54.

4. Thomas Ludwell Lee to Richard Henry Lee, 1 June 1776, Lee Family Papers, UVA.

5. Ibid.

6. Edmund Randolph, *History of Virginia*, ed. Arthur H. Shaffer (Charlottesville, 1970), 253; William J. Van Schreeven, Robert L. Scribner, and Brent Tarter, eds., *Revolutionary Virginia, the Road to Independence: A Documentary Record* (Charlottesville, 1973–83), 7:302, 454.

7. *Papers of George Mason* 1:278.

8. William T. Hutchinson et al., eds., *The Papers of James Madison,* Congressional Series (Chicago and Charlottesville, 1962–91), 1:173–74.

9. Ibid., 174–75; *Revolutionary Virginia, the Road to Independence* 7:450, 456–58.

10. Tarter, "Virginia Declaration of Rights," 47–48.

11. John Page to Thomas Jefferson, 26 Apr. 1776, *Papers of Thomas Jefferson* 1:288.

12. *Revolutionary Virginia, the Road to Independence* 7:654; Randolph, *History of Virginia,* 260.

13. *Revolutionary Virginia, the Road to Independence* 7:708.

14. Paul K. Longmore, "'All Matters and Things Relating to Religion and Morality': The Virginia Burgesses' Committee for Religion, 1769 to 1775," *Journal of Church and State* 38 (1996): 775–97.

15. Attorney General John Randolph has been identified as author of the response (Lewis Peyton Little, *Imprisoned Preachers and Religious Liberty in Virginia* [Lynchburg, 1938], 255), but internal evidence strongly suggests a member of the county court or perhaps the county clerk.

16. "An Address to the Anabaptists imprisoned in Caroline County, August 8, 1771," Alexander Purdie and John Dixon's Williamsburg *Virginia Gazette,* 20 Feb. 1772.

17. *Revolutionary Virginia, the Road to Independence* 3:441–42, 450–51.

18. Ibid., 451, 453.

19. Ibid., 7:188–89, missing portions replaced from the recitation of the petition's substance in the convention's journal (ibid., 557) and from the text as printed when less badly deteriorated in *VMHB* 18 (1910): 38–39.

20. Petition of 160 inhabitants of Prince Edward Co., 24 Sept. 1776, presented to the House of Delegates on 11 Oct. 1776, Legislative Petitions, Prince Edward Co., RG 78, LVA.

21. Raymond C. Bailey, *Popular Influence upon Public Policy: Petitioning in Eighteenth-Century Virginia* (Westport, CT, 1979), very accurately described the petitioning process but failed to notice how it changed during and after the American Revolution, a process described for the states generally in Ruth Bogin, "Petitioning and the New Moral Economy of Post-Revolutionary America," *WMQ,* 3d ser., 45 (1988): 391–425.

22. [James Madison], *To the Honorable the General Assembly of the Commonwealth of Virginia. A Memorial and Remonstrance* (Richmond, 1785). Thomas E. Buckley, SJ, *Church and State in Revolutionary Virginia, 1776–1787* (Charlottesville, 1977), and John A. Ragosta, "Fighting for Freedom: Virginia Dissenters' Struggle for Religious Liberty during the American Revolution," *VMHB* 116 (2008): 226–61, thoroughly and clearly described the political history of the enactment of Jefferson's statute; Jewel L. Spangler, *Virginians Reborn: Anglican Monopoly, Evangelical Dissent, and the Rise of Baptists in the Late Eighteenth Century* (Charlottesville, 2008) more thoroughly than any previous writers on the subject placed religious beliefs and practices at the center of the Baptist challenge to Anglican Virginia, significantly revising and in effect reversing the emphases of Rhys Isaac, *The Transformation of Virginia, 1740–1790* (Chapel Hill, 1982), which treated the transformation of Virginia as a social one played out in a religious context.

23. John A. Ragosta, *Wellspring of Liberty: How Virginia's Religious Dissenters Helped Win the American Revolution and Secured Religious Liberty* (New York, 2010).

24. *Acts Passed at a General Assembly of the Commonwealth of Virginia . . .* (Richmond, 1786), 26–27.

25. *Revolutionary Virginia, the Road to Independence* 3:59, 161, 191–95 (quotation on 192), 202, 350–51.

26. Her letter does not survive, but a copy of the text of her brother's response clearly indicates the nature of her request. Richard Henry Lee to Hannah Corbin, 17 Mar. 1778, in James Curtis Ballagh, ed., *The Letters of Richard Henry Lee* (New York, 1911–14), 1:392–94.

27. Louise Belote Dawe and Sandra Gioia Treadway, "Hannah Lee Corbin: The Forgotten Lee," *Virginia Cavalcade* 29 (1979): 70–77.

28. Accomack Co. Deed Book 6:448–50.

29. *Statutes at Large* 9:57.

30. George Mason to unidentified recipient, 2 Oct. 1778, *Papers of Mason* 1:434.

31. *Revolutionary Virginia, the Road to Independence* 3:54–55, 63–67, 70–71.

32. Ibid., 77–78, 80–82, 87–88, 100–101, 110–13, 117–19.

33. *Statutes at Large* 9:9–35.

34. Ibid., 14.

35. James Cleveland quoted in Lund Washington to George Washington, 29 Feb. 1776, in Philander D. Chase et al., eds., *The Papers of George Washington: Revolutionary War Series* (Charlottesville, 1985–), 3:396.

36. *Revolutionary Virginia, the Road to Independence* 6:474–77.

37. Legislative Petitions, Kentucky Counties, n.d., received 28 Oct. 1785, RG 78, LVA.

38. Michael A. McDonnell, *The Politics of War: Race, Class, and Conflict in Revolutionary Virginia* (Chapel Hill, 2007).

39. L. Scott Philyaw, "A Slave for Every Soldier: The Strange History of Virginia's Forgotten Recruitment Act of 1 January 1781," *VMHB* 109 (2001): 367–86.

40. Legislative Petitions, Berkeley Co., n.d., received 18 Nov. 1780, RG 78, LVA.

41. Legislative Petitions, Amherst Co., n.d., received 9 Nov. 1780, ibid.

42. Harrison M. Ethridge, "Governor Patrick Henry and the Reorganization of the Virginia Militia, 1784–1786," *VMHB* 85 (1977): 427–39.

43. *Statutes at Large* 9:65–66.

44. Legislative Petitions, Orange Co., n.d., received 3 Nov. 1777, RG 78, LVA.

45. Legislative Petitions, Culpeper Co., n.d., received 4 Nov. 1777, ibid.

46. Legislative Petitions, Charlotte Co., n.d., received 26 May 1780, ibid.

47. Robert A. Becker, *Revolution, Reform, and the Politics of American Taxation, 1763–1783* (Baton Rouge, 1980), esp. 82–89, 194–206; G. Melvin Herndon, *Financing the Revolution in Virginia: Taxes, Trade, and Tobacco* (Jamestown, 1981), esp. 41–51.

48. *Statutes at Large* 10:501–17 (quotation on 504).

49. Ibid., 11:140–45.

50. George Mason to unidentified recipient, 2 Oct. 1778, *Papers of Mason* 1:435.

51. Roger Atkinson to Sammy (Samuel Pleasants), 20 Nov. 1776, Roger Atkinson Letterbook, UVA.

52. *Revolutionary Virginia, the Road to Independence* 6:287–90.

53. The first recorded roll-call vote took place on 2 Nov. 1779, *Journal of the House of Delegates of Virginia, Anno Domini, 1779* (Williamsburg, 1779 [1780]), 43. During the 1790s the practice became more common.

54. *Papers of Thomas Jefferson* 6:284–94.

55. Holly Brewer, "Entailing Aristocracy in Colonial Virginia: 'Ancient Feudal Restraints' and Revolutionary Reform," *WMQ*, 3d ser., 54 (1997): 307–46.

56. *Papers of Thomas Jefferson* 6:294–308 (quotation on 298).

57. *Revolutionary Virginia, the Road to Independence* 7:709.

58. [Samuel Johnson, attrib.], *Taxation No Tyranny, An Answer to the Resolutions and Addresses of the American Congress* (London, 1775), 89; Michal Jan Rozbicki, *Culture and Liberty in the Age of the American Revolution* (Charlottesville, 2011).

59. *Statutes at Large* 9:471–72.

60. Ibid., 11:39–40.

61. Randolph, *History of Virginia*, 193.

62. Fredrika Teute Schmidt and Barbara Ripel Wilhelm, "Early Proslavery Petitions in Virginia," *WMQ*, 3d ser., 30 (1973): 133–46.

63. Legislative Petition, Halifax Co., n.d., received 10 Nov. 1785, RG 78, LVA.

64. Cf. Sylvia R. Frey, "Between Slavery and Freedom: Virginia Blacks in the American Revolution," *JSH* 49 (1983): 375–98, accepting an estimate by Thomas Jefferson that 30,000 or more black Virginians may have joined the British; Cassandra Pybus, "Jefferson's Faulty Math: The Question of Slave Defections in the American Revolution," *WMQ*, 3d ser., 62 (2005): 243–64, arguing that the total was probably smaller.

65. *Statutes at Large* 11:308–9.

66. Luther Porter Jackson, "Virginia Negro Soldiers and Seamen in the American Revolution," *Journal of Negro History* 27 (1942): 247–87.

67. Edward C. Carter II et al., eds., *The Virginia Journals of Benjamin Henry Latrobe, 1795–1798* (New Haven, 1977), 1:83.

6   On Domestic Slavery

1. Trial record of Gabriel, 6 Oct. 1800, testimony of Ben Woolfolk, Executive Papers of Governor James Monroe, RG 3, LVA; Michael L. Nicholls, *Whispers of Rebellion: Narrating Gabriel's Conspiracy* (Charlottesville, 2012), 51.

2. Robert Sutcliff, *Travels in Some Parts of North America, in the Years 1804, 1805, & 1806* (York, UK, 1811), 50.

3. Lacy K. Ford, *Deliver Us from Evil: The Slavery Question in the Old South* (New York, 2009), 17–77.

4. Will of Richard Randolph, dated 18 Feb. 1796, proved 18 Apr. 1797, Prince Edward District Court Will Book 2: 4.

5. Henry Stephens Randall, *The Life of Thomas Jefferson* (New York, 1858), 1:11; Lucia Stanton, *"Those Who Labor for My Happiness": Slavery at Thomas Jefferson's Monticello* (Charlottesville, 2012); Henry Wiencek, *Master of the Mountain: Thomas Jefferson and His Slaves* (New York, 2012).

6. Thomas Jefferson, *Notes on the State of Virginia,* ed. William Peden (Chapel Hill, copyright © 1955 by the University of North Carolina Press, renewed 1982 by William Peden; used by permission of the publisher), 163.

7. Ibid., 162.

8. Thomas Jefferson to James Monroe, 20 Sept. 1800, Julian P. Boyd et al., eds., *Papers of Thomas Jefferson* (Princeton, 1950–), 32:160.

9. Ibid., 6:298.

10. Jefferson, *Notes on the State of Virginia,* 137–38.

11. Peter S. Onuf, *Jefferson's Empire: The Language of American Nationhood* (Charlottesville, 2000), 142–88.

12. Jefferson, *Notes on the State of Virginia,* 138.

13. Ibid.   14. Ibid., 138–39.   15. Ibid., 139.

16. Ibid.   17. Ibid., 139–40.   18. Ibid., 140.

19. Cf. Annette Gordon-Reed, *Thomas Jefferson and Sally Hemings: An American Controversy* (Charlottesville, 1997), and *The Hemingses of Monticello: An American Family* (New York, 2008), with Eyler Robert Coates, ed., *The Jefferson-Hemings Myth: An American Travesty* (Charlottesville, 2001).

20. Thomas Jefferson to Francis C. Gray, 4 Mar. 1815, in J. Jefferson Looney et al., eds., *The Papers of Thomas Jefferson, Retirement Series* (Princeton, 2004–), 8:310–11 (quotations on 311).

21. Thomas Jefferson to Edward Coles, 25 Aug. 1814, ibid., 7:603. The episode was sometimes misunderstood later to be a motion that Bland made to abolish slavery in Virginia.

22. John Pendleton Kennedy, ed., *Journals of the House of Burgesses of Virginia, 1766–1769* (Richmond, 1906), 259; *Statutes at Large* 6:104–12, 8:358–61.

23. Thomas Jefferson to Edward Coles, 25 Aug. 1814, *Papers of Thomas Jefferson, Retirement Series* 7:603–5.

24. *Acts Passed at General Assembly of the Commonwealth of Virginia* (Richmond, n.d. [1805]), 35–36; Eva Sheppard Wolf, *Race and Liberty in the New Nation: Emancipation in Virginia from the Revolution to Nat Turner's Rebellion* (Baton Rouge, 2006).

25. Steven Deyle, *Carry Me Back: The Domestic Slave Trade in American Life* (Oxford, 2005). If the number of Virginia slaves that Edward Bancroft estimated were purchased in southeastern slave markets during those decades was correct (Frederic Bancroft, *Slave-Trading in the Old South* [Baltimore, 1931], 384–87), and if the value of those enslaved laborers that Ulrich B. Phillips calculated was also correct (Ulrich Bonnell Phillips, *American Negro Slavery: A Survey of the Supply, Deployment, and Control of Negro Labor as Determined by the Plantation Régime* [New York, 1929], 359–95, esp. chart following 370), the monetary value of the Virginia slave export business was almost certainly greater than any other commodity exported from Virginia by the end of the 1850s.

26. Ford, *Delivery Us from Evil,* esp. 302–28, 375–84, 388–89.

27. Thomas C. Parramore, *Southampton County, Virginia* (Charlottesville, 1978), 98–104.

28. Philip J. Schwarz, *Twice Condemned: Slaves and the Criminal Laws of Virginia, 1705–1865* (Baton Rouge, 1988); James M. Campbell, *Slavery on Trial: Race, Class, and Criminal Justice in Antebellum Richmond, Virginia* (Gainesville, FL, 2007).

29. *Acts Passed at a General Assembly of the Commonwealth of Virginia* (Richmond, 1831), 107.

30. *Acts Passed at a General Assembly of the Commonwealth of Virginia* (Richmond, 1832), 22.

31. Ibid., 20.

32. *Acts Passed at a General Assembly of the Commonwealth of Virginia* (Richmond, 1833), 14–15.

33. Marie Tyler-McGraw, *An African Republic: Black and White Virginians in the Making of Liberia* (Chapel Hill, 2007), esp. 23–61.

34. *The Confessions of Nat Turner, The Leader of the Late Insurrection in Southampton, Va. As Fully and Voluntarily Made to Thomas R. Gray* (Baltimore, 1831), 11; Anthony Santoro, "The Prophet in His Own Words: Nat Turner's Biblical Construction," *VMHB* 116 (2008): 114–49.

35. Scot French, *The Rebellious Slave: Nat Turner in American Memory* (Boston, 2004), esp. 49–51; Randolph Ferguson Scully, *Religion and the Making of Nat Turner's Virginia: Baptist Community and Conflict, 1740–1840* (Charlottesville, 2008).

36. The debates are summarized in Joseph C. Robert, *The Road from Monticello: A Study of the Virginia Slavery Debate of 1832* (Durham, NC, 1941), with excerpts from the most consequential speeches; in Alison Goodyear Freehling, *Drift toward Dissolution: The Virginia Slavery Debate of 1831–1832* (Baton Rouge, 1982); and in Ford, *Deliver Us from Evil*, 361–84. A modern edition of the orations is Erik S. Root, ed., *Sons of the Fathers: The Virginia Slavery Debates of 1831–1832* (Lanham, MD, 2010). Thomas Nelson Page inaccurately wrote in his influential *The Negro: The Southerners' Problem* (New York, 1904), 235, that "a bill to abolish slavery in Virginia had failed in her General Assembly" in January 1832 "by only one vote and that vote the casting vote of the speaker."

37. Legislative Petitions, Lancaster Co., n.d., received 23 Jan. 1838, RG 78, LVA.

38. Fredrika Bremer, *The Homes of the New World; Impressions of America,* trans. Mary Howitt (New York, 1853), 2:536.

39. Thomas R. Dew, *Review of the Debate in the Virginia Legislature of 1831 and 1832* (Richmond, 1832).

40. Erik S. Root, *All Honor to Jefferson? The Virginia Slavery Debates and the Positive Good Thesis* (Lanham, MD, 2008), suggests a more sudden transformation of opinion following the 1832 legislative debates and the publication of Dew's *Review.*

41. Martha Haines Butt, *Antifanaticism: A Tale of the South* (Philadelphia, 1853); Mary Henderson Eastman, *Aunt Phillis's Cabin, or, Southern Life as It Is* (Philadelphia, 1852).

42. George Fitzhugh, *Sociology for the South: Or, The Failure of Free Society* (Richmond, 1854) and *Cannibals All! Or, Slaves Without Masters* (Richmond, 1857).

43. Jewel L. Spangler, *Virginians Reborn: Anglican Monopoly, Evangelical Dissent, and the Rise of the Baptists in the Late Eighteenth Century* (Charlottesville, 2008); Charles F. Irons, *The Origins of Proslavery Christianity: White and Black Evangelicals in Colonial and Antebellum Virginia* (Chapel Hill, 2008). See also Michael O'Brien, *Conjectures of Order: Intellectual Life and the American South, 1810–1860* (Chapel Hill, 2004),

2:938–92, and Elizabeth Fox-Genovese and Eugene D. Genovese, *The Mind of the Master Class: History and Faith in the Southern Slaveholders' Worldview* (New York, 2005), 473–527; Ford, *Deliver Us from Evil,* 481–534.

44. Stephen Jay Gould, *The Mismeasure of Man* (New York, 1981).

45. *Proceedings and Debates of the Virginia State Convention, of 1829–30* (Richmond, 1830), esp. 65–79.

46. Abel Parker Upshur, "On Domestic Slavery," *Southern Literary Messenger* 5 (1839): 678.

47. Ibid., 685–86.

48. Ibid., 687.

49. Ibid., 679.

50. *Acts of the General Assembly of Virginia* (Richmond, 1848), 117–21.

51. E.g., Thomas E. Buckley, SJ, "Unfixing Race: Class, Power, and Identity in an Interracial Family," *VMHB* 102 (1994): 349–80; Joshua D. Rothman, *Notorious in the Neighborhood: Sex and Families across the Color Line in Virginia, 1787–1861* (Chapel Hill, 2003); Melvin Patrick Ely, *Israel on the Appomattox: A Southern Experiment in Black Freedom from the 1790s through the Civil War* (New York, 2004).

52. *New Constitution of the Commonwealth of Virginia, Adopted by the State Convention, Sitting in the City of Richmond, on the 31st Day of July, 1851* (Richmond, 1851), 19–20 (Sections 19–21), printed with *Journal, Acts and Proceedings of a General Convention of the State of Virginia* (Richmond, 1851).

53. George H. Reese, ed., *Proceedings of the Virginia State Convention of 1861* (Richmond, 1865), 2:184–85.

54. John Letcher to editor, 25 June 1858, in *Daily Richmond Enquirer,* 30 June 1858.

55. *Proceedings of the Virginia State Convention of 1861* 1:468.

7   Constitutions Construed

1. William T. Hutchinson et al., eds., *The Papers of James Madison,* Congressional Series (Chicago and Charlottesville, 1962–91), 14:163–64.

2. William Wirt, *The Letters of the British Spy* (Richmond, 1803), 6.

3. *McCulloch v. Maryland,* in Henry Wheaton, ed., *Reports of Cases Argued and Adjudged in the Supreme Court of the United States, February Term, 1819* (New York, 1819), 400–437 (vol. 17 of *United States Reports*), quotations on 415, 421.

4. Carter Goodrich, "The Virginia System of Mixed Enterprise: A Study of State Planning of Internal Improvements," *Political Science Quarterly* 44 (1940): 355–86.

5. The Richmond Junto was famous in its time and was believed to be very influential, but scholarly investigators have disagreed about its membership and the extent of its influence: Harry Ammon, "The Richmond Junto, 1800–1824" *VMHB* 61 (1953): 395–418; Joseph H. Harrison Jr., "Oligarchs and Democrats: The Richmond Junto," ibid., 78 (1970): 184–98; F. Thornton Miller, "The Richmond Junto: The Secret All-Powerful Club—or Myth," ibid., 99 (1991): 63–80.

6. Goodrich, "The Virginia System"; John D. Majewski, *A House Dividing: Economic Development in Pennsylvania and Virginia before the Civil War* (New York, 2000);

Sean Patrick Adams, *Old Dominion, Industrial Commonwealth: Coal, Politics, and Economy in Antebellum America* (Baltimore, 2004).

7. Arthur Singleton (pseud. of Henry Cogswell Knight), *Letters from the South and West* (Boston, 1824), 57.

8. William G. Shade, *Democratizing the Old Dominion: Virginia and the Second Party System, 1824–1861* (Charlottesville, 1996), esp. 114–57, 178–79.

9. Thomas Jefferson, *Notes on the State of Virginia,* ed. William Peden (Chapel Hill, 1955), 118–20.

10. F. Thornton Miller, *Juries and Judges versus the Law: Virginia's Provincial Legal Culture, 1783–1828* (Charlottesville, 1994), 34–46, 90–102.

11. Ibid., 12–33, 109–12.

12. *Alexandria Herald,* 3 June 1816.

13. *Richmond Enquirer,* 31 Aug. 1816; *Niles' Weekly Register* 3 (14 Sept. 1816): 37–40 (quotation on 38).

14. *Richmond Enquirer,* 9, 11 Aug. 1825.

15. Trenton E. Hizer, "'Virginia is Now Divided': Politics in the Old Dominion, 1820–1833" (PhD diss., Univ. of South Carolina, 1997), 211–13. The convention's work is described in Dickson D. Bruce Jr., *The Rhetoric of Conservatism: The Virginia Convention of 1829–30 and the Conservative Tradition in the South* (San Marino, CA, 1982); Alison Goodyear Freehling, *Drift toward Dissolution: The Virginia Slavery Debate of 1831–1832* (Baton Rouge, 1982), 36–81; Robert P. Sutton, *Revolution to Secession: Constitution Making in the Old Dominion* (Charlottesville, 1989), 72–102; Hizer, "'Virginia is Now Divided,'" 221–68; Kevin R. C. Gutzman, *Virginia's American Revolution: From Dominion to Republic, 1776–1840* (Lanham, MD, 2007), 135–205.

16. *Proceedings and Debates of the Virginia State Convention, of 1829–30* (Richmond, 1830), 100.

17. Ibid., 750, 786–87.

18. *The Memorial of Sundry Citizens of the County of Halifax, to the Virginia Legislature, Praying for the Establishment of Free Schools in the State* (Richmond, 1854), 3, 4.

19. *Proceedings and Debates,* 25–31. At the request of the memorialists, the state's attorney general, John Robertson, drafted the document (*Daily Richmond Whig,* 15 Oct. 1829).

20. *Proceedings and Debates,* 31, 32.

21. Ibid., 371–74.

22. Ibid., 223–24, 234–35.

23. Most notably Abel P. Upshur, of Northampton Co. (ibid., 68), Philip Pendleton Barbour, of Orange Co. (ibid., 92–93, 97–98), and Littleton Waller Tazewell, of Norfolk (ibid., 331).

24. William J. Van Schreeven, Robert L. Scribner, and Brent Tarter, eds., *Revolutionary Virginia, the Road to Independence: A Documentary Record* (Charlottesville, 1973–83), 7:449.

25. *Proceedings and Debates,* esp. 65–79.

26. Ibid., 160.

27. Especially Benjamin Watkins Leigh, of Chesterfield Co. (ibid., 322), and Philip Norborne Nicholas, of Richmond (ibid., 322–24).

28. Ibid., 150.

29. *Papers of James Madison,* Cong. Ser., 11:280–93.

30. William Cabell Rives, ed., *Letters and Other Writings of James Madison* (1865), 4:28–30.

31. *Proceedings and Debates,* 537–39, 573–74; Drew R. McCoy, *The Last of the Fathers: James Madison and the Republican Legacy* (Cambridge, 1989), esp. 240–52.

32. The statewide totals were 26,055 for ratification, 15,567 against, but the numbers of eligible voters in the east and west differed significantly, leaving the western advocates of reform at a distinct disadvantage, which is clear in the referendum results from the western and eastern regions (*Proceedings and Debates,* 903; Hizer, "'Virginia is Now Divided,'" 264–65).

33. *Proceedings and Debates,* 897–98.

34. Ibid., 898.

35. Ibid., 898–99.

36. Ibid., 900; Christopher M. Curtis, "Reconsidering Suffrage Reform in the 1829–1830 Virginia Constitutional Convention," *JSH* 74 (2008): 89–124.

37. *Proceedings and Debates,* 895–96, 897.

38. Ibid., 899–900.   39. Ibid., 899.   40. Ibid.

41. Ibid., 900–901.   42. Ibid., 901–2.   43. Ibid., 902.

44. James Madison to Lafayette, 1 Feb. 1830, draft, James Madison Papers, Library of Congress; printed with stylistic modifications in Rives, *Letters and Other Writings of James Madison* 4:58–61.

45. *Proceedings and Debates,* 790.

46. *New Constitution of the Commonwealth of Virginia, Adopted by the State Convention, Sitting in the City of Richmond, on the 31st Day of July, 1851* (Richmond, 1851), 3–36, printed with *Journal, Acts and Proceedings of a General Convention of the State of Virginia, Assembled at Richmond, on Monday, the Fourteenth Day of October, Eighteen Hundred and Fifty* (Richmond, 1850 [1851]).

47. Shade, *Democratizing the Old Dominion,* esp. 174–78, 262–73; Sutton, *Revolution to Secession,* 107–15.

48. John Herbert Claiborne, *Seventy-Five Years in the Old Dominion* (New York and Washington, DC, 1904), 131.

49. *New Constitution of the Commonwealth of Virginia,* 5; the debates are summarized in Shade, *Democratizing the Old Dominion,* 274–83, and Sutton, *Revolution to Secession,* 122–36.

50. G. Alan Tarr, *Understanding State Constitutions* (Princeton, 1998), esp. 99–103, 105–6, 118–19, 121–23, 125, 128–30.

51. *New Constitution of the Commonwealth of Virginia,* 24, 26, 27, 34.

52. Ibid., 30, 31, 33, 34, 35.

53. Ibid., 8–9.

54. Ibid., 18.

55. *Acts of the General Assembly of Virginia Passed at the Extra and Regular Sessions in 1849 & 1850* (Richmond, 1850), 10–11; *Statement Shewing the Data Upon Which Apportionments of Representation, in the Bill Concerning a Convention, Are Based,* House Doc.

40 (1850); Francis Pendleton Gaines Jr., "The Virginia Constitutional Convention of 1850–1851: A Study in Sectionalism" (PhD diss., Univ. of Virginia, 1950), 89–90.

56. Craig M. Simpson, *A Good Southerner: The Life of Henry A. Wise of Virginia* (Chapel Hill, 1985).

57. *New Constitution of the Commonwealth of Virginia*, 19–20.

58. Robin L. Einhorn, *American Taxation, American Slavery* (Chicago, 2006).

59. *New Constitution of the Commonwealth of Virginia*, 7–8, 9–12.

60. Ibid., 13–14.

61. *Journal, Acts and Proceedings*, 419; Schedule, Section 3, printed with *New Constitution of the Commonwealth of Virginia*, 37.

62. Gaines, "Virginia Constitutional Convention of 1850–1851," 286–87.

8 House Divided

1. *Portions of Journal of Secret Session of the Convention, Withheld From Publication At Its Session Ending May 1, 1861*, published as an appendix to *Journal of the Acts and Proceedings of a General Convention of the State of Virginia, Assembled at Richmond, on Wednesday, the Thirteenth Day of February, Eighteen Hundred and Sixty-One* (Richmond, 1861), 10–11, printed also in vol. 1 of George H. Reese, ed., *Journals and Papers of the Virginia State Convention of 1861* (Richmond, 1966).

2. *Abingdon Democrat*, 8 Feb. 1861.

3. Granville Davisson Hall, *The Rending of Virginia, a History*, ed. John Edmund Stealey III (Knoxville, 2002), 142–43.

4. The most thorough account of the convention up to its second vote on secession is Thomas Webster Richey, "The Virginia State Convention of 1861 and Virginia Secession" (PhD diss., Univ. of Georgia, 1990).

5. The tabulations are: in the *Richmond Daily Whig*, 3 Dec. 1860, which reported the highest vote total for electors pledged to three of the candidates, Bell, 74,681; Breckinridge, 74,323; Douglas, 16,375; in the *Daily Richmond Enquirer*, 30 Nov. 1860, which reported on only two candidates, Bell, 74,304; Breckinridge, 74,180; in the Washington *National Intelligencer*, 3 Dec. 1860 (excluding the return from Wyoming County, which was received too late to be counted), Lincoln, 1,929; Bell, 74,584; Breckinridge, 74,335; Douglas, 16,296; in the *Daily Richmond Enquirer*, 24 Dec. 1860 (excluding Wyoming County, the tabulation for which arrived too late to be counted), Lincoln, 1,929; Bell, 74,701; Breckinridge, 74,379; Douglas, 16,292; and in *The Tribune Almanac for 1861* (New York, 1861), Lincoln, 1,929; Bell, 74,681; Breckinridge, 74,323; Douglas, 16,290.

6. Secretary of the Commonwealth, Election Records, no. 279, RG 13, LVA.

7. MS Journal of the Secretary of the Commonwealth for 29 Nov. 1860, 273–74, RG 13, LVA, and Executive Papers of Governor John Letcher, 30 Nov. 1860, RG 3, LVA. Both contain the names of the candidates for presidential elector that the secretary certified to the governor and that the governor by proclamation announced were elected, but neither record contains vote totals.

8. Wheeling *Daily Intelligencer*, 10, 15 Nov. 1860.

9. Constitution of Virginia (1851), Article III, Section 4; *Acts of the General Assembly of Virginia, Passed at the Session Commencing 4th December 1843, and Ending 15th February 1844* (Richmond, 1844), 26–32; *Acts of the General Assembly of Virginia, Passed in 1852–3* (Richmond, 1953), 3–7; *Acts of the General Assembly of Virginia, Passed in 1857–8* (Richmond, 1858), 17–32; Attorney General John Randolph Tucker to Governor John Letcher, 27 Nov. 1860, printed in Richmond *Daily Dispatch,* 1 Dec. 1860, and in many other state newspapers.

10. *Alexandria Gazette and Virginia Advertiser,* 26–28, 30 July 1860.

11. John M. Smith to John Letcher, 23 Sept. 1860, Executive Papers of Governor John Letcher, Letters Received, RG 3, LVA.

12. Attorney General John Randolph Tucker to John Letcher, 27 Nov. 1860, printed in Richmond *Daily Dispatch,* 1 Dec. 1860, and in many other state newspapers; *Daily Richmond Enquirer,* 30 Nov. 1860; Washington *National Intelligencer,* 3 Dec. 1860.

13. Richmond *Daily Dispatch,* 6 Dec. 1860, and printed in many other state newspapers.

14. Henry T. Shanks, *The Secession Movement in Virginia, 1847–1861* (Richmond, 1934), 115–19; William A. Link, *Roots of Secession: Slavery and Politics in Antebellum Virginia* (Chapel Hill, 2003), 199–211.

15. Elizabeth R. Varon, *Disunion! The Coming of the American Civil War, 1789–1859* (Chapel Hill, 2008).

16. Frances W. Saunders, "Equestrian Washington: From Rome to Richmond," *Virginia Cavalcade* 25 (1975): 4–13; Elizabeth R. Varon, "'The Ladies Are Whigs': Lucy Barbour, Henry Clay, and Nineteenth-Century Virginia Politics," *Virginia Cavalcade* 42 (1992): 72–83.

17. Incomplete file of MS election returns, Papers of the Virginia Convention of 1861, RG 93, LVA, and printed in George H. Reese, ed., *Proceedings of the Virginia State Convention of 1861* (Richmond, 1965), 1:792–96.

18. Shanks, *Secession Movement in Virginia,* 148–57; Daniel W. Crofts, *Reluctant Confederates: Upper South Unionists in the Secession Crisis* (Chapel Hill, 1989), 174–75, 361–63, 367–73; Link, *Roots of Secession,* 224. For a detailed analysis of 1860 and 1861 votes in the southeastern county of Southampton, see Daniel W. Crofts, *Old Southampton: Politics and Society in a Virginia County, 1834–1869* (Charlottesville, 1992), 170–92.

19. William H. Gaines Jr., *Biographical Register of Members of the Virginia State Convention of 1861, First Session* (Richmond, 1969).

20. An approach suggested by Virgil A. Lewis, *West Virginia. Its History, Natural Resources, Industrial Enterprises and Institutions* (n.p., n.d. [Charleston, WV, 1904]), 1–28; Richard Orr Curry, *A House Divided: A Study of Statehood Politics and the Copperhead Movement in West Virginia* (Pittsburgh, 1964), 13–27; John Alexander Williams, "The New Dominion and the Old: Ante-bellum and Statehood Politics as the Background of West Virginia's 'Bourbon Democracy,'" *West Virginia History* 33 (1972): esp. 323–29; and Daniel W. Crofts, "Late Antebellum Virginia Reconsidered," *VMHB* 107 (1999): 253–86.

21. Robert Johnston to John Letcher, 9 May 1861, Executive Papers of Governor John Letcher, RG 3, LVA.

22. Kenneth W. Noe, *Southwest Virginia's Railroad: Modernization and the Sectional Crisis* (Urbana, IL, 1994), 67–84.

23. Accomack Co. Order Book (1860–62), 488.

24. Joseph C. G. Kennedy, comp., *Population of the United States in 1860; Compiled from the Original Returns of the Eighth Census* (Washington, DC, 1864), 516–20.

25. Crofts, "Late Antebellum Virginia Reconsidered," 281–82; William W. Freehling, "Virginia's Reluctant Secession," *North and South* 5 (May 2002): 80–89; William W. Freehling and Craig M. Simpson, eds., *Showdown in Virginia: The 1861 Convention and the Fate of the Union* (Charlottesville, 2010), ix–xx.

26. *Proceedings of the Virginia State Convention of 1861* 1:636–54, 660–81.

27. Ibid., 2:233–37.

28. Ibid., 1:750–51; John Majewski, *Modernizing a Slave Economy: The Economic Vision of the Confederate Nation* (Chapel Hill, 2009), 125–30.

29. *Proceedings of the Virginia State Convention of 1861* 3:725–26, 729.

30. Ibid., 139, 474.

31. Ibid., 92.

32. Ibid., 1:505.

33. Ibid., 3:162–63, gives the vote as 88 to 45 but lists the names of only 40, not 45, men who voted for the resolution, and it mistakenly included the name of James B. Mallory among the nays rather than the yeas (ibid., 370). The twentieth-century edition of the *Proceedings* took its text from the debates as reported in the semiweekly *Richmond Enquirer,* which on 8 Apr. 1861 got the numbers wrong, put Mallory's name in the wrong list, and also omitted the names of four men (among them former president John Tyler) who voted for secession. The report of the 4 Apr. 1861 vote printed in the *Richmond Daily Whig* on 5 Apr. 1861 got the numbers and names correct. The official 1861 printed text of the convention's journal (there is no surviving clerical manuscript record) is also imperfect. It records the number of favorable votes as 45 and contains the names of those 45 men, and it records the names of the 90 men who voted against the resolution but records the number as 89 on one page and as 90 on another (*Appendix to the Journal, Commencing with a Journalized Record of the Proceedings in the Committee of the Whole upon Federal Relations,* 31–33, published with the 1861 *Journal of the Acts and Proceedings of a General Convention of the State of Virginia* and reprinted in facsimile in vol. 1 of the 1966 *Journals and Papers of the Virginia State Convention of 1861*).

34. William W. Freehling, *The Road to Disunion: Secessionists Triumphant, 1854–1861* (New York, 2007).

35. Charles B. Dew, *Apostles of Disunion: Southern Secession Commissioners and the Causes of the Civil War* (Charlottesville, 2001).

36. Craig M. Simpson, *A Good Southerner: The Life of Henry A. Wise of Virginia* (Chapel Hill, 1985), 248–50; Edward L. Ayers, *In the Presence of Mine Enemies: War in the Heart of America, 1859–1863* (New York, 2003), 135–36, 138.

37. Simon Cameron to John Letcher, 15 Apr. 1861, *Proceedings of the Virginia State Convention of 1861* 4:26–27.

38. *Lynchburg Daily Virginian,* 2 May 1861.

39. Freehling, "Virginia's Reluctant Secession."

40. Bell Irvin Wiley, *The Life of Johnny Reb: The Common Soldier of the Confederacy* (Indianapolis, 1943); James M. McPherson, *What They Fought For, 1861–1865* (Baton Rouge, 1994); Aaron Charles Sheehan-Dean, *Why Confederates Fought: Family and Nation in Civil War Virginia* (Chapel Hill, 2007); Chandra Manning, *What This Cruel War Was Over: Soldiers, Slavery, and the Civil War* (New York, 2007).

41. *Alexandria Gazette,* 20 May 1861.

42. The texts are most closely analyzed in Douglas Southall Freeman, *R. E. Lee: A Biography* (New York, 1934–35), 1:431–47, Elizabeth Brown Pryor, *Reading the Man: A Portrait of Robert E. Lee through His Private Letters* (New York, 2007), 276–97, and Pryor, "'Thou Knowest Not the Time of Thy Visitation': A Newly Discovered Letter Reveals Robert E. Lee's Lonely Struggle with Disunion," *VMHB* 119 (2011): 277–96.

43. Papers of the Virginia Convention of 1861, RG 83, LVA.

44. Curry, *House Divided,* 46–54; Charles H. Ambler, Frances Haney Atwood, and William B. Mathews, eds., *Debates and Proceedings of the First Constitutional Convention of West Virginia (1861–1863)* (Hunting, WV, 1939), esp. 1:188–89, 193–94.

45. Curry, *House Divided,* 46–54, 141–47.

46. Secretary of the Commonwealth Executive Journal (1861), 233–34; also printed in *Daily Richmond Enquirer,* 18 June 1861, and several other state newspapers.

47. Williams, "The New Dominion and the Old," esp. 317–48; Ken Fones-Wolf, "'Traitors in Wheeling': Secessionism in an Appalachian Unionist City," *Journal of Appalachian Studies* 13 (2007): 75–95.

48. *DVB* 2:553–54.

49. *Traitors in Wheeling* (Wheeling, n.d. [1861]), copies in Alexander Campbell Papers, West Virginia Collection, West Virginia Univ., and in UVA.

50. Charles H. Ambler, ed., "Diary of John Floyd," *John P. Branch Historical Papers of Randolph-Macon College* 5 (1918): 173.

51. Charles Henry Ambler, *Sectionalism in Virginia from 1776 to 1861* (Chicago, 1910); Shanks, *Secession Movement in Virginia,* 1–65.

52. Robin L. Einhorn, *American Taxation, American Slavery* (Chicago, 2006).

53. *Cooper's Clarksburg Register,* 5 Nov. 1858.

54. Wheeling *Daily Intelligencer,* 3 May 1860.

55. *Proceedings of the Virginia State Convention of 1861* 4:228.

56. Ibid., 405.

57. Ibid., 563–65.

58. Papers of the Virginia Convention of 1861, RG 93, LVA; Secretary of the Commonwealth Executive Journal (1861), 234; also printed in *Daily Richmond Enquirer,* 18 June 1861, and several other state newspapers.

59. *Proceedings of the Virginia State Convention of 1861* 4:147–48, 158–78 (quotations on 172–73).

60. Virgil A. Lewis, ed., *How West Virginia Was Made: Proceedings of the First Convention of the People of Northwestern Virginia at Wheeling May 13, 14, and 15 1861, and the Journal of the Second Convention of the People of Northwestern Virginia at Wheeling . . .* (Charleston, WV, 1909), 37–38.

61. John S. Carlile, James S. Wheat, C. D. Hubbard, F. H. Pierpont, Campbell Tarr, G. R. Latham, Andrew Wilson, S. H. Woodward, and James W. Paxton, "To the People of North Western Virginia," n.d., Wheeling *Daily Intelligencer,* 21 May 1861.

62. John S. Carlile, James S. Wheat, C. D. Hubbard, F. H. Pierpont, Campbell Tarr, G. R. Latham, Andrew Wilson, S. H. Woodward, and James W. Paxton, "To the People of North Western Virginia," 22 May 1861, Wheeling *Daily Intelligencer,* 27 May 1861.

63. *How West Virginia Was Made,* 107–10 (quotation on 108).

64. Cf. Brent Tarter, "'If the ritual doesn't change, the times do': Swearing in Virginia's Governors," *Virginia Cavalcade* 50 (2001): 168–77.

65. Wheeling *Daily Intelligencer,* 21 June 1861.

66. Abraham Lincoln to the Senate and House of Representatives, 4 July 1861, *Congressional Globe,* 37th Cong., 1st sess., appendix, 2.

67. Wheeling *Daily Intelligencer,* 4 July 1861.

68. *Daily Richmond Enquirer,* 4 July 1861.

69. Edward S. Evans, *The Seals of Virginia* (Richmond, 1911), 39–40, and illustration 17; also published as a part of the official *Report of the Virginia State Library for the Year 1909–1910* (Richmond, 1911).

70. John E. Stealey III, "Western Virginia's Constitutional Critique of Virginia: The Revolution of 1861–1863," *Civil War History* 57 (2011): 9–47; *Debates and Proceedings of the First Constitutional Convention of West Virginia,* with text of constitution and implementation schedule at 3:859–88.

71. *Journal of the House of Delegates, of the Commonwealth of Virginia, Extra Session, Held in the City of Wheeling, on Thursday, December 4th, 1862* (Wheeling, 1862), 29–30; *Journal of the Senate, of the Commonwealth of Virginia, Extra Session, Held in the City of Wheeling, on Thursday, December the 4th, 1862* (Wheeling, 1862), 24–25.

72. *Journal of the Constitutional Convention Which Convened at Alexandria on the 13th Day of February, 1864* (Alexandria, VA, 1864), 17–18.

73. Sara B. Bearss, "Restored and Vindicated: The Virginia Constitutional Convention of 1864" (paper presented at the Virginia Forum, Longwood University, 24 Apr. 2009); *Constitution of the State of Virginia, and the Ordinances Adopted by the Convention Which Assembled at Alexandria, on the 13th Day of February, 1864* (Alexandria, VA, 1864), quotations on 14, 8.

74. Henry Thomas Shanks, "Conservative Constitutional Tendencies of the Virginia Secession Convention," in *Essays in Southern History,* ed. Fletcher Melvin Green (Chapel Hill, 1949), 28–48.

75. *Proceedings of the Virginia State Convention of 1861* 4:773–74.

76. Ibid., 794.

77. *Journals and Papers of the Virginia State Convention of 1861* 1:252, 327.

78. *Daily Richmond Enquirer,* 20–21 Nov. 1861, and also printed as doc. 33 in vol. 3 of *Journals and Papers of the Virginia State Convention of 1861,* quotations on 4, 5, 6, 7–8, 9, 14.

79. Text of proposed constitution printed as final document in vol. 2 of *Journals and Papers of the Virginia State Convention of 1861.*

80. Ibid., 1:441–42.

81. Shanks, "Conservative Constitutional Tendencies," 43–46.

82. Secretary of the Commonwealth Executive Journal (1862), 120.

83. *DVB* 1:65–67.

84. Frank H. Alfriend, "The Great Danger of the Confederacy," *Southern Literary Messenger* 35 (1863): 39–42 (quotations on 40, 41).

85. Abel Parker Upshur, "On Domestic Slavery," ibid., 5 (1839): 677–87.

86. Frank H. Alfriend, "A Southern Republic and a Northern Democracy," ibid., 37 (1863): 283–90 (quotations on 286, 287).

9 Causes Lost

1. Confederated Southern Memorial Association, *History of the Confederated Memorial Associations of the South* (New Orleans, 1904), 314–18; *New-York Times,* 26 Oct. 1866, and Richmond *Daily Dispatch,* 29 Oct. 1866 (reprinting from the *New-York Tribune* and inadvertently omitting the essential word *not*). The excerpt from the speech (misdated Jan. 1867) printed in Barton H. Wise, *The Life of Henry A. Wise of Virginia, 1806–1876* (New York, 1899), 398–401, stresses the forward-looking aspects of Wise's postwar thinking and omits this passage.

2. Jefferson Davis, *The Rise and Fall of the Confederate Government* (New York, 1881), unnumbered dedication page in front matter of vol. 1.

3. Edward A. Pollard, *The Lost Cause: A New Southern History of the War of the Confederates; Comprising a Full and Authentic Account of the Rise and Progress of the Late Southern Confederacy—The Campaigns, Battles, Incidents, and Adventures of the Most Gigantic Struggle of the World's History, Drawn from Official Sources, and Approved by the Most Distinguished Confederate Leaders* (New York, 1867).

4. *Acts of the General Assembly of the State of Virginia, Passed in 1865–66* (Richmond, 1866), 91–93.

5. General Alfred H. Terry in *Daily Richmond Whig,* 26 Jan. 1866.

6. John Stewart Bryan, *Joseph Bryan: His Times, His Family, His Friends* (Richmond, 1935), 160–61.

7. *Daily Richmond Whig,* 16 Apr. 1867.

8. *DVB* 3:689–91.

9. Edward A. Pollard, *The Lost Cause Regained* (New York, 1868), esp. the chapter on "The Inferiourity of the Negro," 118–53.

10. Caroline E. Janney, *Burying the Dead but Not the Past: Ladies' Memorial Associations and the Lost Cause* (Chapel Hill, 2008); Jane Turner Censer, *The Reconstruction of White Southern Womanhood, 1865–1895* (Baton Rouge, 2003); William Alan Blair, *Cities of the Dead: Contesting the Memory of the Civil War in the South, 1865–1914* (Chapel Hill, 2004); W. Fitzhugh Brundage, *The Southern Past: A Clash of Race and Memory* (Cambridge, MA, 2005); Gaines M. Foster, *Ghosts of the Confederacy: Defeat, the Lost Cause, and the Emergence of the New South, 1865 to 1913* (New York, 1987).

11. Pippa Holloway, "'A Chicken-Stealer Shall Lose His Vote': Disfranchisement for Larceny in the South, 1874–1890," *JSH* 75 (2009): 931–62.

12. *Acts and Joint Resolutions Passed by the General Assembly of the State of Virginia during the Session of 1876–77* (Richmond, 1877), 280–82; Tipton Ray Snavely, *The Taxation of Negroes in Virginia* (Charlottesville, 1917), 18–20; Richard L. Morton, *The Negro in Virginia Politics, 1865–1902* (Charlottesville, 1919), 90–96; Robert E. Martin, "Negro Disfranchisement in Virginia" (MA thesis, Howard Univ., 1938), 85–86.

13. *DVB* 2:190–91; *Richmond Daily Enquirer and Examiner, Richmond Dispatch,* and *Richmond Whig,* all 3, 5, 6 July 1869.

14. *DVB* 2:8–10; *Richmond Daily Dispatch,* 2 May 1870; *Petersburg Daily Index,* 3, 4 May 1870.

15. *Acts and Joint Resolutions Passed by the General Assembly of the State of Virginia, at its Session of 1870–'71* (Richmond, 1871), 378–81.

16. Edward A. Pollard, "The Negro in the South," *Lippincott's Magazine* 5 (1870): 383–91 (quotation on 383).

17. Allen W. Moger, "Railroad Practices and Policies in Virginia after the Civil War," *VMHB* 59 (1951): 423–57.

18. Paul M. Gaston, *The New South Creed: A Study in Southern Mythmaking* (New York, 1970).

19. Lexington *Rockbridge Enterprise,* 19 Feb. 1880.

20. The extent to which the political and economic policies that drove politics in Virginia and the other Southern states after the Civil War differed from the political and economic interests that predominated before the war figures importantly in the scholarship on the Conservative Party and the problems it faced. Cf. Jack P. Maddex Jr., *The Virginia Conservatives, 1867–1879* (Chapel Hill, 1970), and James Tice Moore, *Two Paths to the New South: The Virginia Debt Controversy, 1870–1883* (Lexington, KY, 1974), and also James Tice Moore, "Redeemers Reconsidered: Change and Continuity in the Democratic South, 1870–1900," *JSH* 44 (1978): 357–78.

21. Woodrow Wilson, "John Bright," 6 Mar. 1880, in Arthur S. Link et al., eds., *The Papers of Woodrow Wilson* (Princeton, 1966–94), 1:608–21 (quotation on 618–19).

22. *Richmond Daily Whig,* 30 Jan. 1878.

23. John W. Daniel to W. T. Taliaferro, 19 Sept. 1879, in Richmond *Daily Dispatch,* 24 Sept. 1879.

24. *Richmond Daily Dispatch,* 2 Jan. 1878.

25. *Journal of the House of Delegates of the State of Virginia, for the Session of 1877–8* (Richmond, 1877 [1878]), 428–29.

26. *Richmond Daily Whig,* 26, 27 (quotation) Feb. 1879.

27. Ibid., 15, 16, 18 Mar. 1881.

28. Ibid., 3, 4 June 1881.

29. Willie Walker Caldwell, *Stonewall Jim: A Biography of General James A. Walker, C.S.A.* (Elliston, VA, 1990), 172.

30. John S. Wise, *The Lion's Skin: A Historical Novel and a Novel History* (New York, 1905), 303.

31. Carl N. Degler, *The Other South: Southern Dissenters in the Nineteenth Century* (New York, 1974), 264–315; Moore, *Two Paths to the New South,* 83–92; Jane Dailey, *Before Jim Crow: The Politics of Race in Postemancipation Virginia* (Chapel Hill, 2000),

48–102; Steven Hahn, *A Nation under Our Feet: Black Political Struggles in the Rural South, from Slavery to the Great Migration* (Cambridge, MA, 2003), 367–84, 400–411.

32. *Journal of the House of Delegates of the State of Virginia for the Session of 1883–4* (Richmond, 1883 [1884]), 20.

33. William Mahone to John D. Long, 11 Feb. 1882, reprinted in *Richmond Daily Whig*, 15 Mar. 1882.

34. Dailey, *Before Jim Crow*, 103–54.

35. "Autobiography of Wendell Phillips Dabney," undated typescript, 27–28, Wendell Phillips Dabney Collection, Cincinnati Historical Society Library, Cincinnati Museum Center, Cincinnati.

36. John Warwick Daniel address at Fincastle, VA, 23 Oct. 1883, Richmond *Daily Dispatch*, 26 Oct. 1883.

37. George William Bagby, *John Brown and Wm. Mahone: An Historical Parallel, Foreshadowing Civil Trouble* (Richmond, 1880), 21.

38. William L. Royall, *History of the Virginia Debt Controversy: The Negro's Vicious Influence in Politics* (Richmond, 1897).

10   An Anglo-Saxon Electorate

1. *DVB* 2:124.

2. Forthcoming biography, online *Encyclopedia Virginia*.

3. Allen W. Moger, "The Origin of the Democratic Machine in Virginia," *JSH* 8 (1942): 183–209.

4. William Du Bose Sheldon, *Populism in the Old Dominion: Virginia Farm Politics, 1885–1900* (Princeton, 1935); Robert Saunders, "Southern Populists and the Negro, 1893–1905," *Journal of Negro History* 54 (1969): 240–61, esp. 240–41.

5. Allen W. Moger, "The Rift in Virginia Democracy in 1896," *JSH* 4 (1938): 295–317.

6. Wythe W. Holt, "The Senator from Virginia and the Democratic Floor Leadership: Thomas S. Martin and Conservatism in the Progressive Era," *VMHB* 83 (1975): 3–21; Martin quoted in Walter Edward Harris to Harry F. Byrd, 2 Feb. 1933, Harry Flood Byrd Sr. Papers, UVA.

7. Philip Alexander Bruce, *The Plantation Negro as a Freeman: Observations on His Character, Condition, and Prospects in Virginia* (New York, 1889).

8. James Michael Lindgren, *Preserving the Old Dominion; Historic Preservation and Virginia Traditionalism* (Charlottesville, 1993).

9. Fred Arthur Bailey, "Free Speech and the Lost Cause in the Old Dominion," *VMHB* 103 (1995): 237–66.

10. Letitia M. Burwell, *A Girl's Life in Virginia Before the War* (New York, 1895), 130–31.

11. Ibid., 177.

12. Ibid., 180–82.

13. Ibid., unnumbered dedication page.

14. Thomas Nelson Page, *The Negro: The Southerners' Problem* (New York, 1904), 235.

15. *DVB* 1:364–65.

16. Paul B. Barringer, "The American Negro—His Past and Future," *Transactions of the*

Second Annual Session of the Tri-State Medical Association (1900): 41–69 (quotations on 44, 55, 57, 69).

17. Paul Brandon Barringer, "Negro Education in the South," *Educational Review* 21 (1901): 233–43.

18. *Richmond Times,* 6 Oct. 1901.

19. Ibid., 12 Jan. 1900.

20. *Acts and Joint Resolutions Passed by the General Assembly of the State of Virginia during the Extra Session of 1884* (Richmond, 1884), 146–51.

21. Ronald E. Shibley, "Election Laws and Electoral Practices in Virginia, 1867–1902: An Administrative and Political History" (PhD diss., Univ. of Virginia, 1972), esp. 60–214; Wythe Holt, *Virginia's Constitutional Convention of 1901–1902* (New York, 1990), 59–74.

22. Testimony of A. J. Smith, *John M. Langston v. E. C. Venable,* 16 June 1890, 51st Cong., 1st sess., House Report no. 2462, 26.

23. Bathurst Browne Bagby, *Recollections* (West Point, VA, 1950), 64–65.

24. *Acts and Joint Resolutions Passed by the General Assembly of the State of Virginia during the Session of 1893–'94* (Richmond, 1894), 862–67 (quotation on 865).

25. *Report of the Proceedings and Debates of the Constitutional Convention State of Virginia Held in the City of Richmond June 12, 1901, to June 26, 1902* (Richmond, 1906), 1:18.

26. Ibid., 19, 20.

27. Printed and bound with *Journal of the Constitutional Convention of Virginia* (Richmond, 1901 [1902]), 1–65; Allen W. Moger, *Virginia: Bourbonism to Byrd, 1870–1925* (Charlottesville, 1968); Raymond H. Pulley, *Old Virginia Restored: An Interpretation of the Progressive Impulse, 1870–1930* (Charlottesville, 1968), 1–91; Holt, *Virginia's Constitutional Convention.*

28. William A. Anderson, "Virginia Constitutions," *Virginia State Bar Association Proceedings* (1900), 145–78; *DVB* 1:161–63.

29. *DVB* 2:198–200; Allen Caperton Braxton Papers, UVA.

30. *Acts and Joint Resolutions Passed by the General Assembly of the State of Virginia during the Extra Session of 1902–3–4* (Richmond, 1902 [1902–4]), 561–67.

31. Docs. 1, 2, 7, 8, 9, 12, 14, 17, printed and bound with *Journal of the Constitutional Convention of Virginia.*

32. *Report of the Proceedings and Debates* 2:3076–77.

33. Ibid., 2972, 2975.

34. Ibid., 3014.

35. Herman L. Horn, "The Growth and Development of the Democratic Party in Virginia since 1890" (PhD diss., Duke Univ., 1949), 102–13.

36. *DVB* 2:559–60.

37. Tipton Ray Snavely, *The Taxation of Negroes in Virginia* (Charlottesville, 1917), 18–20; Richard L. Morton, *The Negro in Virginia Politics, 1865–1902* (Charlottesville, 1919), 90–96; Robert E. Martin, "Negro Disfranchisement in Virginia" (MA thesis, Howard Univ., 1938).

38. *Anderson v. Craddock,* reported in *Virginia Law Register* 17 (1911): 359–69.

39. *Journal of the Constitutional Convention of Virginia* (Richmond, 1901 [1902]), 504–5.

40. *Taylor v. Commonwealth,* reported in *Virginia Reports* 101 (1903): 829–32.

41. *Jones v. Montague,* reported in *United States Reports* 194 (1904): 147–53 (quotation on 153), and *Selden v. Montague* decided the same day, reported ibid., 153.

42. Walter A. Watson, *Notes on Southside Virginia,* ed. Mrs. Walter A. Watson and Wilmer L. Hall (Richmond, 1925), 219, 220.

43. Warren Co. List of Colored Applicants Refused Registration, 1902–3, LVA.

44. William C. Pendleton, *Political History of Appalachian Virginia, 1776–1927* (Dayton, VA, 1927), 459.

45. *Richmond Times-Dispatch,* 8 June 1904.

46. Larry Sabato, *The Democratic Party Primary in Virginia, Tantamount to Election No Longer* (Charlottesville, 1977), 26–39, 112–13.

47. Henry C. Ferrell, *Claude A. Swanson of Virginia: A Political Biography* (Lexington, KY, 1985), esp. 70–85.

48. Pulley, *Old Virginia Restored,* 92–170; Ronald L. Heinemann, *Depression and New Deal in Virginia: The Enduring Dominion* (Charlottesville, 1983); William A. Link, *A Hard Country and a Lonely Place: Schooling, Society, and Reform in Rural Virginia, 1870–1920* (Chapel Hill, 1986); J. Douglas Smith, *Managing White Supremacy: Race, Politics, and Citizenship in Jim Crow Virginia* (Chapel Hill, 2002); Elna C. Green, *This Business of Relief: Confronting Poverty in a Southern City, 1740–1940* (Athens, GA, 2003); Pippa Holloway, *Sexuality, Politics, and Social Control in Virginia, 1920–1945* (Chapel Hill, 2006); Clayton McClure Brooks, "Conversations across the Color Line: Interracial Cooperation and the Making of Segregation in Virginia, 1900–1930" (PhD diss., Univ. of Virginia, 2006), 175–230.

49. Suzanne Lebsock, "Woman Suffrage and White Supremacy: A Virginia Case Study," in *Visible Women: New Essays on American Activism,* ed. Nancy A. Hewitt and Suzanne Lebsock (Urbana, IL, 1993), 62–100; Elna C. Green, *Southern Strategies: Southern Women and the Woman Suffrage Question* (Chapel Hill, 1997), esp. 151–77.

50. Henry W. Anderson, "Popular Government in Virginia," *University of Virginia Record, Extension Series* 11 (June 1927): 66–68.

51. *Contested-Election Case of Paul v. Harrison,* 67th Cong., 2d sess., House Report 1101; *Congressional Record,* 67th Cong., 4th sess., 545–47.

52. *Congressional Record,* 67th Cong., 2d sess., 13,095–98.

53. Harry F. Byrd to George C. Peery, 27 Nov. 1922, Byrd Papers, UVA; *Congressional Record,* 67th Cong., 4th sess., 537–38; Guy B. Hathorn, "The Political Career of C. Bascom Slemp" (PhD diss., Duke Univ., 1950), 165–91.

54. Roanoke *Times,* 4 Oct. 1922; Bristol *Herald-Courier,* 7 Oct. 1922; Pulaski *Southwest Times,* 4 Oct. 1922.

55. Gregory Michael Dorr, *Segregation's Science: Eugenics and Society in Virginia* (Charlottesville, 2008); J. Douglas Smith, "The Campaign for Racial Purity and the Erosion of Paternalism in Virginia, 1922–1930," *JSH* 68 (2002): 65–106.

56. Paul A. Lombardo, *Three Generations, No Imbeciles: Eugenics, the Supreme Court, and Buck v. Bell* (Baltimore, 2008); *DVB* 1:437–38, 2:372–73.

57. *DVB* 1:275–76; Richmond *News Leader,* 28 Apr. 1927.

11   The Byrdocracy

1. Undated typescript in box 65 with other documents and records from the 1910s rather than in the Speech Files, Papers of Harry Flood Byrd Sr., UVA.

2. The best-informed accounts of Byrd's career and legacy are James R. Sweeney, "Harry Byrd: Vanished Policies and Enduring Principles," *Virginia Quarterly Review* 52 (1976): 596–612; Robert T. Hawkes Jr., "Harry F. Byrd: Leadership and Reform," in *The Governors of Virginia, 1860–1978,* ed. Edward E. Younger and James Tice Moore (Charlottesville, 1982), 233–46; and Ronald L. Heinemann, *Harry Byrd of Virginia* (Charlottesville, 1996). Excellent accounts of the operations of his political organization are V. O. Key, *Southern Politics in State and Nation* (New York, 1949), 19–35; Herman L. Horn, "The Growth and Development of the Democratic Party in Virginia since 1890" (PhD diss., Duke Univ., 1950); Edward T. Folliard's ten-part series in the *Washington Post,* 9–14, 16–19 June 1957; and J. Harvie Wilkinson III, *Harry Byrd and the Changing Face of Virginia Politics, 1945–1966* (Charlottesville, 1968).

3. Frank Guerrant to Byrd, 20 Dec. 1933, Byrd Papers.

4. Credit where credit is due: Finley Peter Dunne put expressions similar to this into the voice of his alter ego, fictional Chicago barkeeper Mr. Dooley. Finley Peter Dunne, *Observations by Mr. Dooley* (New York, 1902), 170, and *Dissertations by Mr. Dooley* (New York, 1906), 201.

5. Richard Evelyn Byrd quoted in G. H. Branaman to Jay W. Johns, 24 Sept. 1940, copy, Byrd Papers.

6. Henry C. Ferrell, "The Role of Virginia Democratic Party Factionalism in the Rise of Harry Flood Byrd, 1917–1923," *East Carolina College Publications in History* 2 (1965): 146–66.

7. *Richmond Times-Dispatch,* 2 Feb. 1926.

8. George B. Tindall, "Business Progressivism: Southern Politics in the Twenties," *South Atlantic Quarterly* 62 (1963): 92–106.

9. New York Bureau of Municipal Research, *County Government in Virginia: Report on a Survey Made for the Governor and His Committee on Consolidation and Simplification* (Richmond, 1928), 6.

10. Joseph A. Fry, "Senior Advisor to the Democratic 'Organization': William Thomas Reed and Virginia Politics, 1925–1935," *VMHB* 85 (1977): 453–59; Heinemann, *Harry Byrd,* 80–81.

11. *Richmond Times-Dispatch,* 29 Oct. 1933.

12. Andrew Jackson Montague to Byrd, 12 Mar. 1927, Executive Papers of Governor Harry Flood Byrd, RG 3, LVA.

13. T. Russell Cather to Byrd, 14 Jan. 1918, Byrd Papers.

14. *Richmond Times Dispatch,* 24 May 1949.

15. Joseph A. Fry and Brent Tarter, "The Redemption of the Fighting Ninth: The 1922 Congressional Election in the Ninth District of Virginia and the Origins of the Byrd Organization," *South Atlantic Quarterly* 77 (1978): 352–70.

16. E. R. Combs to Byrd, 13 Mar. 1925, Everett Randolph Combs Papers, UVA.

17. *DVB* 3:395–97.

18. C. B. Neel to E. R. Combs, 18 Apr. 1922, Combs Papers.

19. Jacob N. Brenaman to Byrd, n.d. (probably shortly after 19 Apr. 1922), Byrd Papers.

20. Brenaman to Byrd, 25 Apr. 1922, and an undated typescript list initialed "J.N.B." and labeled in Byrd's scrawl "State Committee," ibid.

21. Byrd to James M. Hayes Jr., 9 Oct. 1922,ibid.

22. Byrd to Martin A. Hutchinson, 23 Aug. 1924, and 26 Aug. 1924 circular letter, ibid.

23. Byrd to William H. Schwarzschild, 29 Sept. 1924, ibid.

24. Byrd to Berkeley D. Adams, 18 Oct. 1924, ibid.

25. John Hopkins Hall to Byrd, 8 Nov. 1924, ibid.

26. State Democratic Central Committee Records, LVA.

27. O. Victor Hanger to Harry B. Hanger, 14 Sept. 1932, State Democratic Central Committee Records.

28. Ellis F. Hargis to G. A. Ferguson, 13 Mar. 1933, Combs Papers.

29. R. W. Ervin to C. A. Fuller, 6 Mar. 1933, ibid.

30. Hargis to Ervin, 8 Mar. 1933, ibid.

31. Hargis to J. G. Albert, 9 Mar. 1933, ibid.

32. E. R. Combs to Hargis, 28 Apr. 1933, ibid.

33. Combs to Hargis, 25 Apr. 1933, ibid.

34. Combs to Hargis, 18 Apr. 1933, ibid.

35. Burr Harrison to Byrd, 8 May 1933, Byrd Papers.

36. A. K. Morrison to Byrd, 25 Apr. 1922, ibid.

37. Byrd to C. M. Shannon, 6 May 1922, ibid.

38. *Richmond Times-Dispatch,* 9 July 1922.

39. H. H. Holt to J. Murray Hooker, 22 Nov. 1929, State Democratic Central Committee Records.

40. C S. Towles to Byrd, 3 May (quotation), 2 June 1938, and Byrd to Towles, 28 May 1938, Byrd Papers.

41. E. R. Combs to Ellis F. Hargis, 12 Oct. 1927, Combs Papers.

42. Quoted in Horn, "Democratic Party," 257.

43. Court decision printed in full in *Richmond Times-Dispatch,* 30 Sept. 1945.

44. John R. Saunders to State Democratic Executive Committee, 31 Jan. 1929, printed in *Report of the Attorney General to the Governor of Virginia, from July 1, 1928, to June 30, 1929* (Richmond, 1929), 96–97; Alvin L. Hall, "Virginia Back in the Fold: The Gubernatorial Campaign and Election of 1929," *VMHB* 73 (1965): 280–302; Larry Sabato, *The Democratic Party Primary in Virginia, Tantamount to Election No Longer* (Charlottesville, 1977), 40–45.

45. Byrd to Phillip Williams, 3 Nov. 1931, Byrd Papers.

46. Fry, "Senior Advisor to the Democratic Organization," 467.

47. *Richmond Times-Dispatch,* 16 July 1936.

48. Byrd to William T. Reed, 7 July 1932, 29 July 1932, Reed to Byrd, 30 July 1932 (quotation), Byrd Papers.

49. Martin A. Hutchinson to Clifton A. Woodrum, 30 Aug. 1934, Martin A. Hutchinson Papers, UVA; Greensboro *Daily News,* 19 July 1936, clipping in Executive Papers of Governor George C. Peery, RG 3, LVA; Harold L. Ickes, *The Secret Diary of Harold L.*

Ickes (New York, 1953–54), 3:332; James E. Sargent, "Clifton A. Woodrum of Virginia: A Southern Progressive in Congress, 1923–1945," *VMHB* 89 (1981): 341–64.

50. Brent Tarter, "A Flier on the National Scene: Harry F. Byrd's Favorite-Son Presidential Candidacy of 1932," *VMHB* 82 (1974): 282–305; cf. Ronald L. Heinemann, "'Harry Byrd for President': The 1932 Campaign," *Virginia Cavalcade* 25 (1975): 28–37.

51. James M. Ollinger Jr., "The Congressional Career of John W. Flannagan, Jr." (MA thesis, East Tennessee State Univ., 1954).

52. E. R. Combs to C. S. Carter, 1 Oct. 1934, Combs Papers.

53. Martin A. Hutchinson to Ivy B. Morgan, 3 Aug. 1936, Hutchinson Papers.

54. Hutchinson to Lloyd M. Robinette, 24 Mar. 1941, ibid.

55. Charles J. Harkrader to Hutchinson, 7 Jan. 1939, T. Russell Cather to Hutchinson, 5 Aug. 1939 (quotation), ibid.

56. Hutchinson to Robinette, 9 June 1941, ibid.

57. Robinette to Hutchinson, 21 Mar. 1941, ibid.

58. Alvin L. Hall, "James Hubert Price: New Dealer in the Old Dominion," in Younger and Moore, *Governors of Virginia*, 277–90; John Syrett, "Ambiguous Politics: James H. Price's First Months as Governor of Virginia," *VMHB* 94 (1986): 453–76.

59. Martin A. Hutchinson to Curry P. Hutchinson, 28 Dec. 1936, and Curry P. Hutchinson to Martin A. Hutchinson, 28 Dec. 1936, Hutchinson Papers.

60. Byrd to Mrs. Sam L. Ferguson, 26 Dec. 1936, Byrd Papers.

61. Alvin L. Hall, "Politics and Patronage: Virginia's Senators and the Roosevelt Purges of 1938," *VMHB* 82 (1974): 331–50; A. Cash Koeniger, "The New Deal and the States: Roosevelt versus the Byrd Organization in Virginia," *Journal of American History* 68 (1982): 876–96.

62. Charles J. Harkrader to Martin A. Hutchinson, 7 Jan. 1939, Hutchinson Papers.

63. J. Lindsay Almond to Harkrader, 18 July 1963, photocopy, Charles J. Harkrader Papers, UVA.

64. Hutchinson to Lloyd M. Robinette, 9 June 1941, Hutchinson Papers.

65. Horn, "Democratic Party," 330.

66. Key, *Southern Politics in State and Nation,* 17.

67. Ibid.   68. Ibid. 19.   69. Ibid., 20.

70. Ibid., 26–27.   71. Ibid., 26.   72. Ibid., 411–12.

73. Ibid., 33.   74. Ibid., 412.

75. Heinemann, *Harry Byrd of Virginia,* esp. 418–19.

76. Wilkinson, *Harry Byrd and the Changing Face of Virginia Politics.*

77. Peter R. Henriques, "The Organization Challenged: John S. Battle, Francis P. Miller, and Horace Edwards Run for Governor in 1949," *VMHB* 82 (1974): 372–406.

78. James Robert Sweeney, "Byrd and Anti-Byrd: The Struggle for Political Supremacy in Virginia, 1945–1954" (PhD diss., Univ. of Notre Dame, 1973), 230–62.

79. Key, *Southern Politics in State and Nation,* 26–27.

80. Conley L. Edwards, "A Political History of the Poll Tax in Virginia, 1900–1950" (MA thesis, Univ. of Richmond, 1973); Robert K. Gooch, *The Poll Tax in Virginia Suffrage History: A Premature Proposal for Reform* (Charlottesville, 1969).

81. Gooch, *Poll Tax in Virginia Suffrage History,* quotations on 21, 22.

82. Ronald Edward Shibley, "Election Laws and Electoral Practices in Virginia, 1867–1902: An Administrative and Political History" (PhD diss., Univ. of Virginia, 1972), 247, recounting how in the 1960s he had been denied permission to see surviving copies in the council's possession.

83. James R. Sweeney, "The Golden Silence: The Virginia Democratic Party and the Presidential Election of 1948," *VMHB* 82 (1974): 351–71.

84. *Washington Post,* 25 Feb. 1973.

85. *Harper et al. v. Virginia State Board of Elections et al., United States Reports* 383 (1966): 663–86.

86. *Acts and Joint Resolutions of the General Assembly of the Commonwealth of Virginia* (Richmond, 1956), 949–50.

87. Francis Pickens Miller, *Man from the Valley: Memoirs of a 20th-Century Virginian* (Chapel Hill, 1971), 182–83.

88. J. Lindsay Almond to Charles J. Harkrader, 18 July 1963, photocopy, Harkrader Papers.

89. *Washington Post,* 12 May 1974.

90. J. Lindsay Almond to Carleton A. Harkrader, 6 Aug. 1963, photocopy, Harkrader Papers.

91. Jonathan Daniels, "Virginia Democracy," *Nation* 153 (26 July 1941): 74.

92. Conversation with Mary Aydelotte Marshall, 22 Feb. 1979, Richmond.

12   I Was Born Black

1. *Richmond Times-Dispatch,* 10 Feb. 1986; see also S. J. Ackerman, "The Trials of S. W. Tucker," *Washington Post Magazine,* 11 June 2000, 14–18, 24–25, 28–29, reprinted as "Samuel Wilbert Tucker: The Unsung Hero of the School Desegregation Movement," *Journal of Blacks in Higher Education* 28 (2000): 98–103.

2. Thomas Jefferson to Francis C. Gray, 4 Mar. 1815, in J. Jefferson Looney et al., eds., *The Papers of Thomas Jefferson, Retirement Series* (Princeton, 2004–), 8:310–11 (quotations on 311).

3. *Acts and Joint Resolutions (Amending the Constitution) of the General Assembly of the State of Virginia* (Richmond, 1910), 581.

4. Richmond City Hustings Court Minutes 20 (1853): 401; Richmond *Daily Dispatch,* 25 Aug., 1 Sept. 1858; Christopher J. Tucker, biographical research on John E. Ferguson, *DVB* files, LVA; James M. Campbell, *Slavery on Trial: Race, Class, and Criminal Justice in Antebellum Richmond, Virginia* (Gainesville, FL, 2007), 165–66.

5. *DVB* 3:500–502.

6. *Richmond Times-Dispatch,* 22 July 1923.

7. *Acts and Joint Resolutions (Amending the Constitution) of the General Assembly of the State of Virginia* (Richmond, 1924), 534–35.

8. *DVB* 3:456–57.

9. Newport News *Daily Press,* 15, 20 Mar. 1925.

10. *Acts and Joint Resolutions (Amending the Constitution) of the General Assembly of the State of Virginia* (Richmond, 1926), 945–46.

11. *Richmond News Leader,* 8 July 1925, 30 Jan. 1928; *Richmond Times-Dispatch,* 4 Feb. 1928; *Richmond Planet,* 11 Feb. 1928; *DVB* 3:422–23.

12. See, e.g., Helen C. Rountree, *Pocahontas's People: The Powhatan Indians of Virginia through Four Centuries* (Norman, Okla., 1990), 219–42; Paul T. Murray, "Who Is an Indian? Who Is a Negro? Virginia Indians in the World War II Draft," *VMHB* 95 (1987): 215–31.

13. *Acts of the General Assembly of the State of Virginia* (Richmond, 1930), 96–97; Richard B. Sherman, "The 'Teachings at Hampton Institute': Social Equality, Racial Integrity, and the Virginia Public Assemblage Act of 1926," *VMHB* 95 (1987): 275–300, and "'The Last Stand': The Fight for Racial Integrity in Virginia in the 1920s," *JSH* 54 (1988): 69–92; J. Douglas Smith, *Managing White Supremacy: Race, Politics, and Citizenship in Jim Crow Virginia* (Chapel Hill, 2002), 76–106.

14. Extra No. 1 and Extra No. 2, both dated Mar. 1924, issued with *Virginia Health Bulletin* 16 (1924).

15. Walter Ashby Plecker, circular letter, Jan. 1943, Acc. 10972, UVA.

16. Walter Ashby Plecker, circular letter, Dec. 1943, Rockbridge Co. Clerk's Correspondence, 1912–43, Rockbridge Co. Records, LVA.

17. E.g., Alaine Adkins and Ray Adkins, *Chickahominy Indians–Eastern Division: A Brief Ethnohistory* (Philadelphia, 2007), 106–27, and Rosemary Clark Whitlock, *The Monacan Indian Nation of Virginia: The Drums of Life* (Tuscaloosa, 2008).

18. Smith, *Managing White Supremacy,* esp. 197, 201.

19. Ibid., 3–5, 10–11, 12–13, 33–39, 67–76.

20. Clayton McClure Brooks, "Conversations across the Color Line: Interracial Cooperation and the Making of Segregation in Virginia, 1900–1930" (PhD diss., Univ. of Virginia, 2006), 10–89.

21. Gertrude Woodruff Marlowe, *A Right Worthy Grand Mission: Maggie Lena Walker and the Quest for Black Economic Empowerment* (Washington, DC, 2003).

22. *The Official Blue Book of the Jamestown Ter-Centennial Exposition, A.D. 1907. The Only Authorized History of the Celebration* (Norfolk, 1909); Carl Abbott, "Norfolk in the New Century: The Jamestown Exposition and Urban Boosterism," *VMHB* 85 (1977): 86–96; Brent Tarter, "Making History in Virginia," ibid., 115 (2007): esp. 21–23.

23. W. Fitzhugh Brundage, "Meta Warrick's 1907 'Negro Tableaux' and (Re)Presenting African American Historical Memory," *Journal of American History* 89 (2003): 1368–1400.

24. Giles B. Jackson and D. Webster Davis, *The Industrial History of the Negro Race of the United States* (Richmond, 1908).

25. *Richmond Planet,* 9 May 1914.

26. Ibid.

27. Ibid., 11 Feb. 1928.

28. Jennifer Lynn Ritterhouse, *Growing Up Jim Crow: How Black and White Southern Children Learned Race* (Chapel Hill, 2006).

29. Oliver White Hill, *The Big Bang:* Brown v. Board of Education *and Beyond: The Autobiography of Oliver W. Hill, Sr.,* ed. Jonathan K. Stubbs (Winter Park, FL, 2000), 2.

30. Brent Tarter, biographical research on Leonard R. Flemings, *DVB* files, LVA.

31. Flemings's name appears as a justice of the peace in documents recorded several times each year in the county deed books beginning in July 1887 through the end of the cen-

tury and in all of the secretary of the commonwealth's *Annual Report* lists from 1904 through 1917.

32. *Washington Post,* 2 Apr. 1896.

33. *Virginia Business Directory and Gazetteer, 1906* (Richmond, 1906), 666; *Virginia Business Directory and Gazetteer, 1917* (Richmond, 1917), 579; Secretary of the Commonwealth *Annual Report*s for 1905–17. The *Report* for 1918, perhaps because of a wartime restriction on use of paper, omitted lists of justices of the peace, and his name does not appear in the election year of 1919, suggesting that if he were in office in 1917, he probably continued until 1919.

34. Secretary of the Commonwealth *Annual Report*s for 1917–26 do not include his name in the list of the county's magistrates.

35. Kilmarnock *Rappahannock Record,* 10 Nov. 1927, 5 Nov. 1931, 7 Nov. 1935; Secretary of the Commonwealth *Annual Report*s for 1927–37.

36. Kilmarnock *Rappahannock Record,* 16, 23 June 1927.

37. C. S. Towles to Harry F. Byrd, 3 May, 2 June 1938, Harry Flood Byrd Papers, UVA.

38. Smith, *Managing White Supremacy,* 224–26.

39. Robert A. Pratt, "Crossing the Color Line: A Historical Assessment and Personal Narrative of *Loving v. Virginia,*" *Howard Law Journal* 41 (1998): 229–44.

40. Virginius Dabney, *Liberalism in the South* (Chapel Hill, 1932), quotations on 253–54.

41. See the treatment of Dabney in John T. Kneebone, *Southern Liberal Journalists and the Issue of Race, 1920–1944* (Chapel Hill, 1985), and in Maria Morris Nitschke, "Virginius Dabney of Virginia: Portrait of a Southern Journalist in the Twentieth Century" (PhD diss., Emory Univ., 1987).

42. Bertram Wilbur Doyle, *The Etiquette of Race Relations in the South: A Study in Social Control* (Chicago, 1937), 142–46; Ritterhouse, *Growing Up Jim Crow,* 29–32, 55–56, 80–81.

43. Marlowe, *Right Worthy Grand Mission,* 171–72.

44. See, e.g., Doyle, *Etiquette of Race Relations.*

45. Robert Bennett Bean, "Some Racial Peculiarities of the Negro Brain," *American Journal of Anatomy* 5 (1906): 353–432, and "The Negro Brain" and "The Training of the Negro," *Century Magazine* 72 (1906): 778–84, 947–53.

46. *DVB* 1:420–22; Stephen Jay Gould, *The Mismeasure of Man* (New York, 1981), 77–82.

47. Larissa M. Smith, "Where the South Begins: Black Politics and Civil Rights Activism in Virginia, 1930–1951" (PhD diss., Emory Univ., 2001), 75–76.

48. Ralph J. Bunche, *The Political Status of the Negro in the Age of FDR,* ed. Dewey W. Grantham (Chicago, 1973), 210–13 (quotation on 211).

49. Alexander Leidholdt, *Editor for Justice: The Life of Louis I. Jaffé* (Baton Rouge, 2002); Norfolk *Virginian-Pilot,* 22 July 1927.

50. *The Negro in Richmond: The Report of the Negro Welfare Survey Committee* (Richmond, 1929). Cf. *Annual Message and Accompanying Documents of the Mayor of Richmond to the City Council for the Year Ending December 31, 1912* (Richmond, 1913), and editorial in *Richmond Planet,* 7 June 1913. See also Bunche, *Political Status of the Negro,* 568–69, Pippa Holloway, *Sexuality, Politics, and Social Control in Virginia, 1920–1945* (Chapel Hill, 2006), and Brooks, "Conversations across the Color Line," 175–230.

51. Thomas Calhoun Walker, *The Honey-Pod Tree: The Life Story of Thomas Calhoun Walker* (New York, 1958), 201.

52. Raymond Gavins, *The Perils and Prospects of Southern Black Leadership: Gordon Blaine Hancock, 1884–1970* (Durham, NC, 1977).

53. Gordon B. Hancock, "Between the Lines," Norfolk *Journal and Guide,* 21 July 1934.

54. Smith, "Where the South Begins," 156–63.

55. Norfolk *Journal and Guide,* 28 Mar. 1925.

56. Gavins, *Perils and Prospects of Southern Black Leadership,* esp. 51–99, 118–57; Smith, *Managing White Supremacy,* 14–15, 46–47, 63, 285–88.

57. Norfolk *Virginian-Pilot,* 15 July 1921; *The Republican Party in Virginia Platform Adopted by the State Convention Held at Norfolk, Va., July 14, 1921* (n.p., n.d.), 5; *Freedom in Virginia: An Address by Henry W. Anderson, Esq., Nominee of the Republican Party for Governor for Virginia, Delivered Before the Republican State Convention at Norfolk, July 14, 1921* (n.p., n.d), esp. 18–25.

58. Norfolk *Journal and Guide,* 23 July 1924.

59. *Richmond Planet,* 23 July 1924.

60. Andrew Buni, *The Negro in Virginia Politics, 1902–1965* (Charlottesville, 1967), 50–89; Henry Lewis Suggs, *P. B. Young, Newspaperman: Race, Politics, and Journalism in the New South, 1910–1962* (Charlottesville, 1988), 50–52; Ann Field Alexander, *Race Man: The Rise and Fall of the "Fighting Editor," John Mitchell Jr.* (Charlottesville, 2002), 186–89; Smith, *Managing White Supremacy,* 64–67; Brooks, "Conversations across the Color Line," 231–316.

61. Buni, *Negro in Virginia Politics,* 106–23; Bunche, *Political Status of the Negro,* 205 (quotations), 323–26, 440, 442–43, 438–46, 552, 553–54.

62. Michael Dennis, *Luther P. Jackson and a Life for Civil Rights* (Gainesville, FL, 2004).

63. Walker, *Honey-Pod Tree,* 160.

64. Gunnar Myrdal, *An American Dilemma: The Negro Problem and Modern Democracy* (New York, 1944), esp. 2:1021–24.

65. Smith, *Managing White Supremacy,* 260–70.

66. Smith, "Where the South Begins," 81–94, 137–68, 281–86, 297–99; Peter Wallenstein, *Blue Laws and Black Codes: Conflict, Courts, and Change in Twentieth-Century Virginia* (Charlottesville, 2004), esp. 82–141.

67. Hill, *Big Bang,* 122–36; Smith, "Where the South Begins," 137–66; *Alston v. Board of Education of the City of Norfolk,* reported in *United States Reports* 311 (1940): 693.

68. *DVB* 3:465–66; *Corbin et al. v. County School Board of Pulaski County, Virginia, et al.,* reported in *Federal Reporter,* 2d ser., 177 (1949): 924–28.

69. Hill, *Big Bang,* 138–43; Smith, "Where the South Begins," 208–17; *Morgan v. Virginia,* reported in *United States Reports* 328 (1946): 373–94.

70. Hill, *Big Bang,* 148–51, 162–67; *Brown v. Board of Education of Topeka, Kansas,* reported in *United States Reports* 347 (1954): 483–96.

71. *DVB* 2:449–50; *Harper et al. v. Virginia Board of Elections,* reported in *United States Reports* 383 (1966): 663–86.

72. Judge Leon Bazile quoted in *Loving et ux v. Virginia,* reported in *United States Reports* 388 (1967): 1–13, at 3.

73. Peter Wallenstein, *Tell the Court I Love My Wife: Race, Marriage, and Law: An American History* (New York, 2002); *Loving v. Virginia*, reported in *United States Reports* 388 (1967): 1–13.

74. *DVB* 1:321–23.

75. Hill, *Big Bang*, 174–80, 183; Jill Ogline Titus, *Brown's Battleground: Students, Segregationists, and the Struggle for Justice in Prince Edward County, Virginia* (Chapel Hill, 2011), based on her more detailed work Jill L. Ogline, "A Mission to a Mad County: Black Determination, White Resistance, and Educational Crisis in Prince Edward County, Virginia" (PhD diss., Univ. of Massachusetts, Amherst, 2007).

76. *Griffin et al. v. County School Board of Prince Edward County*, reported in *United States Reports* 377 (1964): 218–34; *Green et al. v. County School Board of New Kent County*, reported ibid., 391 (1968): 430–42.

77. Address of Governor J. Lindsay Almond Jr., 20 Jan. 1959, audio recording, WRVA 386, Radio Station WRVA Collection, LVA (punctuation and capitalization as printed in *Richmond Times-Dispatch*, 21 Jan. 1959).

78. Hill, *Big Bang*, 73.

13   The Spirit of Virginia

1. Albert H. Tillson Jr., *Gentry and Common Folks: Political Culture on a Virginia Frontier, 1740–1789* (Lexington, KY, 1991).

2. William Doak to William Preston, 22 Sept. 1774, Lyman C. Draper MSS, 3QQ101, State Historical Society of Wisconsin, Madison.

3. Proposals for Raising Men, 1781, Defense of Southwestern Virginia, Colonel William Preston Papers, Auditor of Public Accounts, RG 48, LVA.

4. Copy of "The Memorial of the Freemen inhabiting the Country Westward of the Alligany or Apalachian Mountain, and Southward of the Ouasioto," n.d. (ca. 1785) (quotations), and Charles Cummings to His Excellency the President of Congress, 7 Apr. 1785, both in item 48, Papers of the Continental Congress, RG 360, National Archives and Records Administration.

5. Peter J. Kastor, "'Equitable Rights and Privileges': The Divided Loyalties in Washington County, Virginia, during the Franklin Separatist Crisis," *VMHB* 105 (1997): 193–226.

6. Robert R. Howison, *History of Virginia, from the Discovery and Settlement by Europeans to the Present Time* (Philadelphia and Richmond, 1846–48), 2:233–38; Henry Howe, *Historical Collections of Virginia* (Charleston, SC, 1849), 152–60 (quotation on 152).

7. George Washington Lafayette Bickley, *History of the Settlement and Indian Wars of Tazewell County, Virginia; With a Map, Statistical Tables, and Illustrations* (Cincinnati, 1852), quotations on 264, 266.

8. *Acts and Joint Resolutions Passed by the General Assembly of the State of Virginia at the Session of 1871–'72* (Richmond, 1872), 258–59.

9. Louis I. Jaffé, "Winning the 'Fighting Ninth' for Trinkle," *Richmond Times-Dispatch*, 8 Oct. 1916.

10. Joseph A. Fry and Brent Tarter, "The Redemption of the Fighting Ninth: The 1922 Congressional Election in the Ninth District of Virginia and the Origins of the Byrd Organization," *South Atlantic Quarterly* 77 (1978): 352–70.

11. James M. Ollinger Jr., "The Congressional Career of John W. Flannagan, Jr." (MA thesis, East Tennessee State Univ., 1954).

12. *DVB* 3:669–71.

13. Edward Younger and James Tice Moore, eds., *The Governors of Virginia, 1860–1978* (Charlottesville, 1982), 393–408; Linwood Holton, *Opportunity Time* (Charlottesville, 2008).

14. William C. Pendleton, *Political History of Appalachian Virginia, 1776–1927* (Dayton, VA, 1927), 97–98.

15. Kenneth W. Noe, *Southwest Virginia's Railroad: Modernization and the Sectional Crisis* (Urbana, IL, 1994), 85–138; Brian Dallas McKnight, *Contested Borderland: The Civil War in Appalachian Kentucky and Virginia* (Lexington, KY, 2006).

16. Pendleton, *Political History of Appalachian Virginia*, 269–70.

17. Ibid., 602–3.

18. Douglas Southall Freeman, "The Spirit of Virginia," introduction to *Virginia: A Guide to the Old Dominion, Compiled by Workers of the Writers' Program of the Work Projects Administration in the State of Virginia* (New York, 1940), 3–4.

19. Ibid., 7.

20. Keith D. Dickson, *Sustaining Southern Identity: Douglas Southall Freeman and Memory in the Modern South* (Baton Rouge, 2011).

21. Douglas Southall Freeman, "Virginia: A Gentle Dominion," *Nation* 119 (16 July 1924): 69.

22. Ibid.

23. Ibid., 70.

24. Ibid., 71.

25. Arnold J. Toynbee, *A Study of History* (London, 1935–61), 4:289, 291.

26. Jean Gottmann, *Virginia at Mid-Century* (New York, 1955), 45.

27. Ibid., 557.

28. Cabell Phillips, "Virginia—The State and the State of Mind," *New York Times Magazine,* 28 July 1957, 18–19, 41, 51 (quotation on 18).

29. Marshall W. Fishwick, *Virginia: A New Look at the Old Dominion* (New York, 1959), 198, 267.

30. Francis Pickens Miller, *Man from the Valley: Memoirs of a 20th-Century Virginian* (Chapel Hill, 1971), 80.

31. Ibid.

32. *Textbooks for Teaching Virginia History, Government, and Geography: Report of the Virginia History and Government Textbook Commission to the Governor and the General Assembly of Virginia* (Richmond, 1951; also issued as Senate Doc. no. 14). The three textbooks were Raymond C. Dingledine Jr., Lena Barksdale, and Marion Belt Nesbitt, *Virginia's History* (New York, 1956), for elementary school; Francis Butler Simkins, Spotswood Hunnicutt, Sidman P. Poole, [and Margaret Robinson Simkins], *Virginia:*

History, Government, Geography (New York, 1957), for the seventh grade; and William Edwin Hemphill, Marvin W. Schlegel, and Sadie Ethel Engleberg, *Cavalier Commonwealth: History and Government of Virginia* (New York, 1957), for high school.

33. Thomas Nelson Page, "The Old South," ca. 1887, printed in *The Old South, Essays Social and Political* (New York, 1892), 51.

34. Fred R. Eichelman, "A Study of the Virginia History and Government Textbook Controversy, 1948–1972" (PhD diss., Virginia Polytechnic Institute and State Univ., 1975); Adam Wesley Dean, "'Who Controls the Past Controls the Future': The Virginia History Textbook Controversy," *VMHB* 117 (2009): 318–55; Carol Sheriff, "Virginia's Embattled Textbook: Lessons (Learned and Not) from the Centennial Era," *Civil War History* 58 (2012): 37–74.

35. Francis B. Simkins and Margaret Robertson Simkins quoted in William K. Stevens, "Textbook Authors' Aim: A Conservative Rural Audience," Norfolk *Virginian-Pilot*, 28 Oct. 1965.

36. Ibid.

37. W. Edwin Hemphill quoted ibid.

38. Marvin W. Schlegel, "What's Wrong with Virginia History Textbooks," *Virginia Journal of Education* 64 (Sept. 1970): 10–11 (quotations on 11), and "What a Good Virginia History Textbook Should Be," ibid., Oct. 1970, 7.

39. Marvin W. Schlegel, "How to Write a Virginia History Textbook," in *Virginia in History and Tradition: Institute for Southern Culture Lectures at Longwood College, 1957*, ed. R. C. Simonini Jr. (Farmville, 1958), 106–13 (quotations on 109–10, 113).

40. Lawrence Burnette Jr., "Editorial Problems in Virginia History," ibid., 115–16.

41. Ibid., 119.

42. Ibid., 119, 120.

43. Brent Tarter, "Making History in Virginia," *VMHB* 115 (2007): 30–31; Caroline E. Janney, "War over a Shrine of Peace: The Appomattox Peace Monument and the Retreat from Reconciliation," *JSH* 77 (2011): 91–120.

44. Virginius Dabney, *Virginia, the New Dominion* (Garden City, NY, 1971), xv.

45. Ibid., xiii–xiv, xv.

46. Tarter, "Making History in Virginia," 3–44.

47. Dabney, *Virginia, the New Dominion*, cf. 11–12, 35–38, 44–45, 67, and 13.

48. Ibid., 53–54, 84–85, 190–91, 224–25, 241–44.

49. Ibid., 186–88.   50. Ibid., 235.   51. Ibid., 254.

52. Ibid., 355–56, 362–63.   53. Ibid., 502.   54. Ibid., 554.

55. Ibid., 574.

14   Public Good and Private Interest

1. None of the state's major daily newspapers that covered the convention quoted at large from Robertson's speech: Norfolk *Virginian-Pilot*, 9–11 June 1978; Richmond *News Leader*, 8–12 June 1978; *Richmond Times-Dispatch*, 9–11 June 1978; *Washington Post*, 9–11 June 1978.

2. Personal recollection from attending the House of Delegates Democratic Caucus, 11 Jan. 1977. As I recall, Cooke began, "If for whatever incomprehensible reasons Virginia voters elect Republicans to the House of Delegates . . ."

3. James R. Sweeney noted some of the critical issues in an important and insightful essay, "Harry Byrd: Vanished Policies and Enduring Principles," *Virginia Quarterly Review* 52 (1976): 596–612.

4. The convention required six ballots to make a choice: Richmond *News Leader,* 2–5 June 1978; *Richmond Times-Dispatch,* 2–6 June 1978; *Washington Post,* 2–4 June 1978. Later reminiscences of the convention muted the conspicuous hostility toward Holton, e.g., Frank B. Atkinson, *The Dynamic Dominion: Realignment and the Rise of Two-Party Competition in Virginia, 1945–1980,* 2d ed., rev. (Lanham, MD, 2006), 393–434, and Linwood Holton, *Opportunity Time* (Charlottesville, 2008), 185–87.

5. James R. Sweeney, "A New Day in the Old Dominion: The 1964 Presidential Election," *VMHB* 102 (1994): 307–48.

6. Edward Younger and James Tice Moore, eds., *The Governors of Virginia, 1860–1978* (Charlottesville, 1982), 373–91; James Tice Moore, "Three Who Dared: Virginia's Outstanding Governors of the Twentieth Century," *Virginia Cavalcade* 32 (1983): 101–13.

7. There is, unfortunately, no good published scholarship yet on Henry Howell, but his early career has been treated in two fine papers, Joseph Wayne Grimsley Jr., "The Rise of 'Howling Henry': Henry Howell's Entry into Virginia Politics, 1948–1953," oral presentation at the third annual Virginia Forum, 12 Apr. 2008, University of Mary Washington, and "Defeating the Defenders: Henry Howell Jr. and the Backlash against Massive Resistance for Norfolk Public Schools in 1959," oral presentation at the fourth annual Virginia Forum, 24 Apr. 2009, Longwood University.

8. Steven M. Teles, *The Rise of the Conservative Legal Movement: The Battle for Control of the Law* (Princeton, 2008); J. Brooks Flippin, *Jimmy Carter, the Politics of Family, and the Rise of the Religious Right* (Athens, GA, 2011); Daniel T. Rodgers, *Age of Fracture* (Cambridge, MA, 2011).

9. Pat Robertson with Jamie Buckingham, *The Autobiography of Pat Robertson: Shout It from the Housetops!,* 2d ed., rev. (South Plainfield, NJ, 1995), 266, 284–86, 293–94; Pat Robertson with Bob Slosser, *The Secret Kingdom* (Nashville, 1982), 194.

10. Robertson, *Secret Kingdom,* 44.

11. Ibid., 177.

12. Pat Robertson, *America's Dates with Destiny* (Nashville, 1986), 15.

13. Ibid., 84–85.

14. Ibid., 296–97.

15. Jerry Falwell, *Listen, America!* (Garden City, NY, 1980), 16.

16. Ibid., 13.

17. Ibid., 95.

18. Ibid., 121.

19. Ibid., 185.

20. Ibid., 132.

21. E.g., John H. Simpson, "Support for the Moral Majority and Its Sociomoral Platform," and J. Milton Yinger and Stephen J. Cutler, "The Moral Majority Viewed Sociologi-

cally," both in *New Christian Politics,* ed. David G. Bromley and Anson Shupe (Macon, GA, 1984), 65–68, 69–90; and Frank Lambert, *Religion in American Politics: A Short History* (Princeton, 2008), 184–217.

22. V. O. Key, *Southern Politics in State and Nation* (New York, 1949), 33–34.

23. Joseph A. Fry, "Rayon, Riot, and Repression: The Covington Sit-Down Strike of 1937," *VMHB* 84 (1976): 3–18.

24. William Bryan Crawley Jr., *Bill Tuck: A Political Life in Harry Byrd's Virginia* (Charlottesville, 1978), 89–134.

25. *Richmond Times-Dispatch,* esp. 8, 11–13 Feb., 8 Mar. 2006.

26. *Richmond News Leader,* 27 Oct. 1977.

27. Ibid., 7 Nov. 1977.

28. Untabulated lists filed in Campaign Contributions and Expenditure Records, 1977, State Board of Elections, RG 14, LVA.

29. Ronald L. Heinemann, *Harry Byrd of Virginia* (Charlottesville, 1996), 32–37.

30. E.g., Thomas R. Morris and Robert S. Hodder Jr., "Fixing Virginia's Tax Structure," *Virginia News Letter* 77 (Jan. 2001), and Neal Menkes, "A Review of the State-Local Fiscal Relationship in Virginia: Not So Good Now and It Could Get Worse," *Virginia News Letter* 86 (Nov. 2010).

15   Virginia Abstractions

1. George H. Reese, ed., *Proceedings of the Virginia State Convention of 1861* (Richmond, 1965), 4:551, 677–78.

2. William Erskine Stephenson, of Wood County, 5 Dec. 1861, in Charles H. Ambler, Frances Haney Atwood, and William B. Mathews, eds., *Debates and Proceedings of the First Constitutional Convention of West Virginia (1861–1863)* (Huntington, WV, 1939), 1:190.

3. Ibid., 178–97.

4. William J. Van Schreeven, Robert L. Scribner, and Brent Tarter, eds., *Revolutionary Virginia, The Road to Independence: A Documentary Record* (Charlottesville, 1973–83), 7:450.

5. James R. Sweeney, ed., *Race, Reason, and Massive Resistance: The Diary of David J. Mays, 1954–1959* (Athens, GA, 2008), esp. 215–29.

6. *DVB* 3:542–44.

7. He published two collections of his editorials: James Jackson Kilpatrick, *Interposition: Editorials and Editorial Page Presentations, 1955–1956* (Richmond, 1956), and *The Sovereign States: Notes of a Citizen of Virginia* (Chicago, 1957).

8. Mays, *Race, Reason, and Massive Resistance,* 83–84, 133, 220 (quotation), 234–35, 267.

9. James Jackson Kilpatrick, *The Southern Case for School Segregation* (New York, 1962).

10. William P. Hustwit, "From Caste to Color Blindness: James J. Kilpatrick's Segregationist Semantics," *JSH* 77 (2011): 639–70.

11. V. O. Key, *Southern Politics in State and Nation* (New York, 1949), 33–34.

12. *DVB* 2:198–200; Allen Caperton Braxton, "The Virginia State Corporation Commission," *Virginia Law Register* 10 (1904): 1–18; Thomas Edwin Gay Jr., "Creating the

Virginia State Corporation Commission," *VMHB* 78 (1970): 464–80; George Harrison Gilliam, "Making Virginia Progressive: Courts and Parties, Railroads and Regulators, 1890–1910," ibid., 107 (1999): 189–222.

13. The antecedents of the legal separation of city and county governments reach back at least as far as the American Revolution: Chester W. Bain, *"A Body Incorporate": The Evolution of City-County Separation in Virginia* (Charlottesville, 1967); E. Lee Shepard, "Courts in Conflict: Town-County Relations in Post-Revolutionary Virginia," *VMHB* 85 (1977): 184–99; Brent Tarter, ed., *The Order Book and Related Papers of the Common Hall of the Borough of Norfolk, Virginia, 1736–1798* (Richmond, 1979), 22–23; see also David K. Roberts, "Separate, but Equal? Virginia's 'Independent' Cities and the Purported Virtues of Voluntary Interlocal Agreements," *Virginia Law Review* 95 (2009): 1441–1597.

14. Chester W. Bain, *Annexation in Virginia* (Charlottesville, 1966).

15. John V. Moeser and Rutledge M. Dennis, *The Politics of Annexation: Oligarchic Power in a Southern City* (Cambridge, MA, 1982).

16. Andrew V. Sorrell and Bruce A. Vlk, "Virginia's Never-ending Moratorium on City-County Annexations," *Virginia News Letter* 88 (Jan. 2012).

17. *City of Winchester v. Redmond*, reported in *Virginia Reports* 93 (1896): 711–18.

18. *The Constitution of Virginia: Report of the Commission on Constitutional Revision to His Excellency, Mills E. Godwin, Jr., Governor of Virginia, the General Assembly of Virginia, and the People of Virginia, January 1, 1969* (Charlottesville, 1969), 228–30.

19. *Report of the Virginia Commission on County Government to the Governor and the General Assembly, January, 1940* (Richmond, 1940), quotations on 13, 16.

20. *Report of Drafting Committee of the Commission to Suggest Amendments to the Constitution of Virginia* (Richmond, 1927), 30, 33.

21. Harry Flood Byrd, *The Constitution of Virginia: A Discussion of the Amendments Proposed to the Constitution of Virginia* (Richmond, 1928).

22. *Report of the Commission on Constitutional Revision*, 150–53; A. E. Dick Howard, *Commentaries on the Constitution of Virginia* (Charlottesville, 1974), 1:534–39.

23. Research Memoranda 70, 72, 79, Commission on Constitutional Revision, RG 87, LVA; *Report of the Commission on Constitutional Revision*, 216–29; *Proceedings and Debates of the Senate of Virginia Pertaining to Amending of the Constitution* (Richmond, 1971), 312–13, 338–39; *Proceedings and Debates of the Virginia House of Delegates Pertaining to Amendment of the Constitution* (Richmond, 1971), 504–6; Carolyn J. Moss and Deborah D. Roberts, "A New Forum for State-Local Dialogue," *University of Virginia News Letter*, Feb. 1989.

24. Dick Hall-Sizemore and M. H. Wilkinson, "Home Rule in Virginia: Perception and Reality," *University of Virginia News Letter* 66 (Mar./Apr. 1990); Robert M. DeVoursney, "The Dillon Rule in Virginia: What's Broken? What Needs to Be Fixed?" ibid., 68 (July/Aug. 1992); Stan Livengood, "Intergovernmental Relations in Virginia: The Dillon Rule in Action," in *Government and Politics in Virginia: The Old Dominion at the 21st Century*, ed. Quentin Kidd (New York, 1999), 111–22.

25. *Acts of the General Assembly of the Commonwealth of Virginia, 2003 Regular Session* (Richmond, 2003), 1:181–82; *Fairfax Times*, 28 Mar. 2007.

26. *Archer and Johnson v. Mayes et al.*, reported in *Virginia Reports* 213 (1973): 633–41 (quotation on 638).

27. Suzanne Lebsock, "Woman Suffrage and White Supremacy: A Virginia Case Study," in *Visible Women: New Essays on American Activism,* ed. Nancy A. Hewitt and Suzanne Lebsock (Urbana, IL, 1993), 62–100; Elna C. Green, *Southern Strategies: Southern Women and the Woman Suffrage Question* (Chapel Hill, 1997), esp. 151–77.

28. Douglas Southall Freeman, "Virginia: A Gentle Dominion," *Nation* 119 (16 July 1924): 69–71.

29. Phyllis Leffler, "Mr. Jefferson's University: Women in the Village!" *VMHB* 115 (2007): 56–107.

30. *Richmond Enquirer,* 20 Oct. 1829.

31. *Richmond Times-Dispatch,* 21, 22 Feb. 1958; *Washington Post,* 22, 23, 26, 28 Feb., 2 Mar. 1958.

32. *Washington Post,* 24 Feb. 1980.

33. Michael Dennis, *The New Economy and the Modern South* (Gainesville, FL, 2009).

34. Charlottesville *Daily Progress,* 16 Jan. 2007 (quotation); *Richmond Times-Dispatch,* 17 Jan. 2007.

35. House Joint Resolution no. 728, "Acknowledging with profound regret the involuntary servitude of Africans and the exploitation of Native Americans, and calling for reconciliation among all Virginians," in *Acts of the General Assembly* (Richmond, 2007), 3:2706–7.

36. Michael Paul Williams, "Apology Tiff Is a Sorry Spectacle," *Richmond Times-Dispatch,* 26 Jan. 2007.

37. Ibid., 11 Sept. 2007.

38. Ibid., 19 Oct. 2008.

INDEX

Italicized page numbers refer to illustrations.